Self and Sovereignty

Self and Sovereignty examines the shifts in Muslim thought and politics in response to colonial rule in India through to the period of decolonization and partition.

Commencing in colonial times, this book explores and interprets the historical processes through which the perception of the Muslim individual and the community of Islam has been reconfigured over time. *Self and Sovereignty* examines the relationship between Islam and nationalism and the individual, regional, class and cultural differences that have shaped the discourse and politics of Muslim identity.

As well as fascinating discussion of political and religious movements, culture and art, this book includes analysis of:

- press, poetry and politics in late nineteenth-century India
- the politics of language and identity - Hindi, Urdu and Punjabi
- Muslim identity, cultural difference and nationalism
- the Punjab and the politics of union and disunion
- the creation of Pakistan

Covering a period of immense upheaval and sometimes devastating violence, this work is an important and enlightening insight into the history of Muslims in South Asia.

Ayesha Jalal is a MacArthur Fellow and Professor of History at Tufts University, USA. Her books include *The Sole Spokesman: Jinnah, the Muslim League and the Demand for Pakistan* (CUP, 1985/94) and, with Sugata Bose, *Modern South Asia* (Routledge, 1988).

SOAS LIBRARY
WITHDRAWN

SOAS
18 05494 3

Self and Sovereignty

Individual and Community in South Asian Islam Since 1850

AYESHA JALAL

London and New York

First Published in Great Britain 2000
by Routledge
2 Park Square, Milton Park, Abingdon, Oxon, OX14 4RN

Simultaneously published in the USA and Canada
by Routledge
270 Madison Ave, New York NY 10016

Routledge is an imprint of the Taylor & Francis Group

Transferred to Digital Printing 2005

The right of Ayesha Jalal to be identified as the author of this work
has been asserted by her in accordance with the Copyright Designs and
Parents Act 1988

© 2000 Ayesha Jalal

Typeset in Giovanni Book by Eleven Arts, Keshav Puram, Delhi-110035

All rights reserved. No part of this publication may be reproduced,
stored in a retrieval system, or transmitted, in any form or by any means,
electronic, mechanical, photocopying, recording, or otherwise,
without the prior permission of the publishers.

British Library Cataloguing in Publication Data
A catalogue record for this book is available from the British Library

Library of Congress Cataloging in Publication Data
Jalal, Ayesha
Self and Sovereignty: individual and community in South Asian Islam
since 1850/Ayesha Jalal

p.cm
Includes bibliographical references and index
1. Muslims—India—History. 2. Islam and politics—India.
3. India—History—British occupation, 1765–1947. 4. Pakistan—History. I. Title

DS432.M84 J35 2000
954.03—dc21
99-049757

ISBN 0-415-22077-7 (hbk)
ISBN 0-415-22078-5 (pbk)

SOAS LIBRARY

Contents

List of Maps

Preface

I n his final testament on Islam and nationalism in March 1938, the poet and philosopher Muhammad Iqbal (1877–1938) compared the upholders of nationalism with those who, he had come to believe, had rejected the finality of the Prophet Muhammad. Between these political and theological concepts, Iqbal wrote, 'there exists a deep inner relationship which can be clearly demonstrated only when a Muslim historian gifted with acute insight, compiles a history of Indian Muslims with particular reference to the religious thought of their apparently energetic sects'.[1] As an individual Muslim historian writing about my community, I am offering whatever insights I have been able to garner through research on the relationship between Islam and nationalism as well as the individual, sectarian, regional and class differentiations that shaped the discourse and politics of Muslim identity. I have been emboldened to do so by Iqbal's conception of the Muslim community, put forth in his 1910 address at Aligarh University, which in his view was structured by the religious ideal though not by its 'theological centralization' that would 'unnecessarily limit the liberty of the individual'.[2] Offering a keen insight into the dilemma of the Muslim individual caught between the internal strictures of the community and an externally imparted identity, Iqbal once wrote:

[1]Muhammad Iqbal's essay on Islam and nationalism in response to a statement by Maulana Husain Ahmad Madani published in *Ehsan*, 9 March 1938 in Latif Ahmed Sherwani (ed.), *Speeches and Statements of Iqbal*, Lahore: Iqbal Academy, 1977, p. 263.

[2]Muhammad Iqbal, *The Muslim Community—A Sociological Study*, Muzaffar Abbas (ed.), Lahore: Maktab-e-aliye, 1983, pp. 16–17.

The religious bigot considers me an infidel
And the infidel deems me to be a Muslim![3]

The idea of the individual in Muslim thought has often been obscured in historical scholarship by an all-too-easy elision of religious difference with an essentialized Indian Muslim community. Unlike the duality between the individual and the community in most variants of western liberal thought, the search for a balance between the will of the individual and a collective ethos has animated the intellectual history of Islam. Drawing upon the doctrine of submission only to Allah's sovereignty, a strand of resistance to religious orthodoxy has ensured the resilience of individual autonomy in relation to the collective will of the community. The role of the individual and the crafting of communitarian discourses of Muslim identity in South Asia must therefore be placed in their proper historical context.

In effacing the individual and privileging the telos of partition, South Asian historiography has succumbed to a communitarian mode of analysis in trying to describe and interpret the complex and historically shifting configurations of social relations in South Asia. Informed by the categories of the British colonial state, this discourse has confused the role of religion in the articulation of cultural differences and, in the process, obscured the variegated motivations and aspirations underlying the subcontinent's embattled politics of identity and contested sovereignty. This book explores and interprets the historical processes through which the relationship between the Muslim individual and the community of Islam was reconfigured in colonial South Asia. By unravelling the myriad threads and twists in the Muslim sense of identity, their ideas of sovereignty and the ways in which they adjusted to the concept of citizenship in the modern nation–state, it aims at reconceptualizing the formation of religiously informed identities. While exploring the nexus of culture and political power, the analysis avoids presuppositions which unproblematically link a religiously informed cultural identity with the politics of cultural nationalism. Rather than assuming the prior existence of a community of Muslims, the purpose is to investigate how perceptions of cultural difference, despite class, regional and sectarian variations, led to the articulation of a discourse based on the colonial state's privileging of religious distinctions in Indian society.

The historical spotlight of this work is on the Muslim conceptions of *khudi* or self, and the related concept of self-determination or *khudikhtiyari*, in collective assertions of sovereignty. But it is not exclusively focused on the Muslims. It questions the arbitrary computations of the colonial state, subjecting the categories of 'Muslim', 'Hindu' and 'Sikh' to rigorous historical scrutiny. A study of self and sovereignty, it aims at contributing to a broader understanding of the processes informing conceptions of community and 'nation' in both anti-colonial thought and politics. From the multiple and conflicting Indian Muslim

[3]Cited in Khalifa Abdul Hakim, *Fiqr-i-Iqbal*, Lahore: Bazm-i-Iqbal, 1988, p. 121.

responses to the onset of colonialism and 'modernity' emerged one of the more important critiques of the European model of the nation–state and its concomitant, territorial nationalism.

In the revised edition of his *Imagined Communities*, Benedict Anderson decided to shift the locus of the formation of nationalist discourse from local dynasties to the colonial state. Contrary to Anderson's claims, strenuous attempts by the votaries of colonial modernity to shape national imaginings through their key institutions of power—the census, map and museum[4] were never wholly successful in shrinking the mental horizons of the colonized peoples of Asia and Africa. It is a cardinal historiographical error to presume that identities as well as ideas about sovereignty were confined within the territorial framework established by the imperial powers, even if colonial frontiers continue to define the borders of most post-colonial nation–states. This is to unduly privilege what has been called official nationalism of post-colonial states at the cost of the multiple alternative strands of popular nationalism as well as communitarianism and universalism that may have lost out in the final battle for state power.

Anderson's general theory on the nation as an imagined community does not sufficiently problematize the relationship between colonialism and assertions of cultural difference in contexts where there were competing definitions of identity and multiple claims to nationhood. *Self and Sovereignty* is about the contestations of colonial definitions of sovereignty and modernity in South Asian normative thought and political practice with special, but by no means only, reference to the Muslim individual and the community of Islam. It also examines the relationship of this contestation with anti-colonial nationalism. The ground for such an investigation had to be cleared by dismantling the spurious opposition between 'communalism' and 'nationalism'. One of the key analytical conventions used by scholars of South Asia to deal with the problem of cultural difference, this binary blurs the overlaps between the material and spiritual realms as well as the colonial public and the indigenous private. Worse still, the pejorative connotation of 'communalism' implies that all assertions of cultural difference in the face of a rational and inclusionary nationalism are bigoted and therefore illegitimate.

Revisiting the history of the making of the nation puts to rest many of the false assumptions of retrospectively constructed nationalist narratives, whether of the Indian or the Pakistani varieties. Once this is done, the historic processes of inclusion and exclusion in any particular community imagined as a nation fall into sharp relief with all their facets of generosity and bigotry. Such an approach immediately calls into question the widely held notion of Muslim 'separatism' at a time when the idea of an Indian nation was itself in the process of being forged, negotiated and contested. Assessing the interplay

[4]Benedict Anderson, *Imagined Communities: Reflections on the Origins and Spread of Nationalism*, London: Verso 1991, pp. 163–86.

between class, region and community helps in exploring the territorial and extra-territorial allegiances of India's Muslims in both their restrictive and expansive dimensions. There were many competing narratives drawing on affiliations of linguistic and religious community that tried contributing to the discourse on the Indian nation. Far from reflecting a neat Hindu–Muslim divide, the nationalist narratives authored by Hindus and Muslims of different regions and classes displayed considerable variety and evoked multiple visions of nationhood. Muslim voices sought location within that emerging discourse on the Indian nation while trying to find accommodation for their sense of cultural difference. What has been branded 'separatism' may well have been something more akin to exclusion on the part of that variant of the Indian nationalist discourse which rose to a position of dominance.

South Asian historiography has tended to underplay the exclusionary aspect of this nationalism which only succeeded in eliciting a stronger reaction from its sceptics and critics. Indian Muslims in certain regions displayed a healthy scepticism of an inclusionary nationalism unable to shed the premises of its religious majoritarianism. Instead of dismissing Muslim contestations of the Congress as 'communal', this study highlights and re-examines those facets in Muslim discourse and politics which apparently could not be accommodated within the broader framework of an all-India nationalism. These according to conventional arguments stem from the pervasiveness of communitarian idioms in Muslim self-projections of identity and history. On this ahistorical view, Muslim discourse, standing outside liberal democratic theory, could not palpably reconcile itself to a mainstream Indian nationalism fashioning itself on notions borrowed from the European model of the nation–state.

There is something curious about this proposition. After all, the very discourse and politics which supposedly rejected the idea of the modern nation–state ended up creating one after a bitter and hard-fought process of negotiations. Moreover, the seeming obsession of Muslims with the community as opposed to the individual is based on a particular reading of Islamic normative theory which cannot be taken as an adequate gauge for the actual practice of their politics. Apart from discrepancies between normative theory and political practice, the Muslims of South Asia have not been any less individualistic for projecting a communitarian vision of their religiously informed cultural differences. By outlining the context and the concepts which moulded constructions of Muslim identity from the late nineteenth century, the analysis aims at uncovering the elements of an alternative view of South Asian history, one which instead of excluding and misunderstanding cultural differences might be amenable to accommodating them in more creative ways.

If keeping a balance between the individual and the community steers the analysis away from an essentialization of Muslim identity and politics, the emphasis on the region is intended as a corrective to an uncritical and historically ungrounded privileging of the 'nation' in the singular or inclusionary sense of the word. By locating the problem of cultural difference and matching assertions of sovereignty in the dialectic of region and centre in late colonial India, this work engages not only with the dominant concerns in South Asian historiography but also with the larger theoretical literature on identity formation, contested sovereignties, competing nationalisms and the normative issue of balancing communitarian and individual citizenship rights.

The study begins with a broad but historically and culturally nuanced exploration of the interplay between the individual and the community in the period before the great mutiny revolt and formal loss of sovereignty in 1857. It assesses how a regionally variegated cultural milieu that was both Muslim and Indian informed the identities of the faithful, individually as well as collectively. The substantive chapters engage in a thorough historical investigation of Muslim identity and politics from c.1857 to 1947 in both the majority and minority provinces of colonial India with special reference to the Punjab as the locus of historical initiative in moulding communitarian discourse and politics shifts to that region in the 1920s. The epilogue offers an analysis of the implications of the post-colonial transition for Muslims scattered across separate sovereign states. The objective of conceptualizing and historicizing the twin issues of Muslim cultural differences and Muslim politics, is to completely rethink and renegotiate the problem of difference and identity in the South Asian context.

After outlining the backdrop of the imbrication between the individual and the community before 1857 in the opening chapter, the following one considers how the print and publication media was deployed by the votaries of a Muslim and a Hindu 'community' during the late nineteenth century to gain a hearing from their own co-religionists as well as the colonial state. Weaving in the poetic dimension with the outpourings of an expanding press, chapter two takes account of the political context as well as the specific concerns that found ashraf (literally the respectable classes) Muslims couching their class interests in a communitarian mode. The critical role of language in the processes of differential identity formation in north India and the Punjab are delineated in chapter three. Using the counterpoint between language and religion, it shows how the identities of Urdu, Hindi and Punjabi were transformed to claim language as a basis of identity for communities bounded by religion. These alterations at the level of discourse were linked to the contradictions arising from the efforts to give a legal definition to the Indian Muslim in the British judicial system. This is the theme of chapter four which also places the construction of the political category of Muslims in 1909 within the context of the emerging narratives on the Indian nation, nationality and citizenship. Defined as an abstract legal and political category, Muslims could evolve a common sense of nationality only by consciously reconfiguring their individual self-identification with the religious community. This was initially sought to be achieved at the level of ideas until the outbreak of the First

World War dramatically altered the context of Indian politics, forcing Muslims, jointly and severally, to redefine their notions of identity as well as sovereignty.

Indian Muslim reactions to the defeat of Ottoman Turkey in the First World War and the possible dismantling of the *khilafat* are subjected to a detailed examination in chapter five. An investigation of Indian Muslim notions of nationalism and universalism at key defining moments like the *khilafat* movement is designed to be of comparative and general relevance to the community of scholars and students working on different parts of Asia and the Islamic world. Unravelling the diverse strands in the imaginings of 'community' and 'nation' helps untangle the knots into which South Asian historiography has tied itself in studying the nexus between identity, sovereignty and citizenship. A careful analysis of the discourse on the rights of religiously enumerated communities during the *khilafat* and non-cooperation agitations of the early 1920s helps connect the realms of ideas and political practice. The chapter underscores how the presence of at least three different notions of sovereignty—divine, spiritual and temporal—in Islamic thought created space for individual Muslims wanting to situate the community of Islam on the drawing board of the Indian nation. Muslim discourses were now orchestrated in a broad public arena with the mass mobilization of Indians in the name of Islamic universalism and Indian nationalism. Pointing to the significance and frailty of the rare blending of Islamic and Indian nationalist symbols in the early 1920s, the chapter serves as a link to understanding the nature of contested sovereignties in the late-colonial period.

The next two chapters focus on the key interaction between region and religion in the formulation of a discourse on the Muslim 'nation'. Chapter six explores the interplay of the formal and informal arenas of politics, especially in the Punjab and also Kashmir, in the late 1920s and early 1930s and the ways in which this contributed to Hindu–Muslim conflicts in the subcontinent as a whole. By focusing on the close intermeshing of communitarian and nationalist discourses and politics of Muslims and Hindus alike outside the formal institutional mechanisms of the colonial state, the chapter highlights some of the enduring intellectual and political trends in late-colonial and post-colonial South Asia. Chapter seven underlines the dilemma of what is defined as the 'missing centre' in the tussle between the Congress's brand of inclusionary nationalism and the varied forms of Muslim resistance to it. It dwells in detail on the problems cultural difference posed in the quest for citizenship rights in late-colonial India. Chapter eight traces the move from the Muslim discourse of communitarian difference to that of national distinctiveness. This represented not only an explicit revolt against minority status but also an implicit coup against the dominant binary mode which extolled secular nationalism as legitimate and denigrated the politics of Muslim difference as illegitimate religious communalism. Contesting teleological readings of the history of South Asian nationalisms, the analysis shows why the orchestration of separate nationhood cannot be seen as an inevitable overture to exclusive statehood.

The graphic and often grim story of the failure to preserve the unity of Punjab and of India, and the violence that accompanied partition, is told in chapter nine. Through a close study of hitherto unused historical evidence, it advances the notion of 'banded individuals' as perpetrators of what has generally been described as collective violence. The chapter also offers a new angle of vision on the gender dimension in the partition holocaust. In fast-moving events during 1946–7, there were options other than partition which have more often than not been lost sight of in the historical literature. The creation of Pakistan in 1947 saddled the new entity with an ideology of Muslim nationhood which could not plausibly be squared with the territorial contours of its truncated statehood.

The epilogue analyses the post-colonial transition which splintered the imagined political community of Indian Islam into citizens of two, and after 1971 three, different sovereign juridical states. It examines the extent to which discomfort with difference was a product of inclusionary nationalism and, consequently, equal citizenship—the key defining features of modern nation–states. The paradox of inclusionary nationalisms, whether of the secular or Islamic sort, ending up as narrative constructions of exclusionary majoritarian identity provides the warp and woof of the arguments about identity, sovereignty and citizenship in the history of Muslims in South Asia.

* * *

It is only the grace of Allah that has given me the strength and fortitude to complete a work of this magnitude. *Iman*, faith, sustained me during the difficult years of writing this book which coincided with my lengthy battle against the forces of religious and national bigotry entrenched in the upper echelons of the American academy. This study is the culmination of two decades of research and study of the problems of identity, sovereignty and citizenship with particular reference to the Muslims of South Asia. I have sought to go far beyond my earlier publications in terms of both the range of sources and argument. While concentrating on the Muslim individual and the community of Islam, the analysis hopes to contribute as much to an understanding of Hindu and Sikh discourses on identity, nationalism and citizenship rights, not to mention the welter of regional and subregional identities in the subcontinent.

During 1994–5 my research was supported by a grant from the Social Science Research Council. While most of the book was written between mid-1995 and 1998, I greatly benefited from the privilege of being a Fellow of the John D. and Catherine T. MacArthur Foundation while making the final revisions and refinements to the manuscript at Harvard University during the academic year 1998–9. I am honoured by the trust the MacArthur

Foundation has reposed in me and hope that this work will justify its investment in my future career.

The bulk of the research is based on relatively unknown Urdu and Punjabi sources as well as a fascinating collection of hitherto unused official papers of the late-colonial state that I was able to locate in archives and libraries in Pakistan. All translations and romanizations of Urdu and Punjabi are mine except when these are available in the cited work. I would like to thank the National Commission on Historical and Cultural Research in Islamabad for letting me use some of the primary materials housed in its library. The *Secret Police Abstracts of Intelligence* provided rare insights into district-level politics and social relations in the Punjab and shed useful comparative light on Sind and the NWFP. A similar acknowledgement is due to the National Documentation Centre in Islamabad. I was able to use important materials in its possession as well as its published set of documents relating to the partition of the Punjab.[5] The representations made before the boundary commission headed by Sir Cyril Radcliffe give the lie to arguments about religion being the only basis for the partition of the Punjab and, by extension, India. Over the years many individuals in Lahore and Islamabad have assisted my research endeavours. I am grateful to them for their enduring support.

I am indebted to the staff of the India Office Library in London for bringing me any number of requested documents. Salim al-Din Quraishi's deep knowledge of this great archival collection's Urdu sources was immensely helpful. I also want to convey my appreciation to all those student research assistants, notably David Bernstein and Cindy Posma, who facilitated my negotiations with the Columbia Library and also Harvard's Widener Library. The diligence with which I was furnished with books, articles as well as slides was a much-needed reassurance. I would like to thank my colleagues at the Columbia History Department, especially David Cannadine, Carol Gluck and William Harris, for their strong and consistent support. A word of appreciation is also due to Barbara Locurto and Kirsten Olsen who went far beyond their duties as departmental secretaries to make my years at Columbia as pleasant as possible. Among my doctoral students at Columbia, Ritu Birla, Farina Mir, Elizabeth Kolsky, Mridu Rai and Nerina Rustomji have throughout provided me with intellectual nourishment and moral support. I particularly enjoyed my long conversations with Mridu Rai on various aspects of the history of Islam and nationalism in the subcontinent. In addition, Judith Vladeck and Debra Raskin need to be applauded for their professionalism and public conscience.

I have presented portions of this work at seminars and conferences at many institutions, including the University of Cambridge, Harvard University, Tufts University, Amherst Five College Consortium, Yale University, Dartmouth

[5]*The Partition of the Punjab: A Compilation of Official Documents*, 4 vols., Lahore: Sang-e-Meel Publications, 1993.

College, Cornell University, Columbia University, University of Pennsylvania, University of Texas at Austin, Oberlin College, University of Michigan at Ann Arbor, University of California at Berkeley and Stanford University. Papers based on this research were also given at conferences in Tashkent and Berlin. I have lectured on this subject before lively audiences of specialists and non-specialists alike in Pakistan, India, Sri Lanka, the United States and Canada. Some of the questions raised at these meetings have helped me sharpen my arguments. Very special thanks are due to a number of individuals. Chris Bayly read the entire manuscript in its penultimate version and offered valuable comments and encouragement. I have also gained from the fine historical insights of Susan Bayly, Leonard Gordon, David Ludden and David Washbrook. The anonymous reader for Oxford University Press, New Delhi, provided very helpful comments. I am lucky to have two superb academic publishers and editors in Rukun Advani of OUP and Heather McCallum of Routledge; their competence and enthusiasm have made my task of bringing this book before the public eye a smooth and pleasurable experience. Amartya Sen and Emma Rothschild have given generously of their wisdom, friendship and support throughout the long years that this book has been in the making.

My warmest and deepest thanks are to my family, specially my mother whose faith in me is an abiding source of strength. If God's blessedness is a good mother than I have been extremely fortunate. It is only as a small token of my debt to her that this book is dedicated to my mother and my late father, the two individuals without whom none of this would have been possible. My siblings and their families have been as wonderful as ever in understanding and accommodating me. Among friends, Durre Ahmed in Lahore, Manana Freyre in New York and Nita Nazir in London have done much to sustain and uplift me through trying times. Scaling the distance from Lahore to London, Naazish Ataullah was present at the birth of the theory of the else. Yet when it has come to giving emotional and intellectual support, Sugata Bose surpassed all others. Not only did he play the part of comrade in my battle against injustice, but was an understanding and caring friend who, even at seemingly hopeless moments, never faltered in his belief in my capacity to triumph over adversity. He has seen this book through each and every stage of its conception and creation. I value his comments, to say nothing of our many discussions on the issues emerging from my research and writing. This book is as much a tribute to his faith in me and my work, as it is a statement of my own long and revealing journey through archives and libraries, probing the historical relationship between Islam and nationalism in general and *Khuda, khudi,* and *khudikhtiyari* in particular. I can only hope that readers of this work will forgive any blemishes and relish whatever it might have to offer by way of illumination.

Ayesha Jalal
May 1999

List of Abbreviations

AICC	All-India Congress Committee
AIML	All-India Muslim League
EPW	Economic and Political Weekly
IESHR	The Indian Economic and Social History Review
IOL	India Office Library
INA	Indian National Army
MAS	Modern Asian Studies
MLA	Member of the Legislative Assembly
MLNG	Muslim League National Guard
NDC	National Documentation Centre
NCHCR	National Commission on Historical and Cultural Research
NPP	Note on the Punjab Press
NWFP	North West Frontier Province
NWP	North Western Provinces
PMSF	Punjab Muslim Students Federation
PNNR	Punjab Native Newspaper Reports
QAP	Quaid-i-Azam Papers
RNPP	Report on Newspapers and Periodicals in the Punjab
RSS	Rashtriya Swayamsewak Sangh
SGPC	Shiromani Gurdwara Prabandhak Committee
SNPAI	Secret North West Frontier Province Abstract of Intelligence
SPPAI	Secret Punjab Police Abstract of Intelligence
SSPAI	Secret Sind Police Abstract of Intelligence
TP	Transfer of Power Documents
UP	United Provinces

Chapter 1

The Muslim Self and
the Loss of Sovereignty:
Individual and Community Before 1858

'I have none of the hallmarks of a Muslim; why is it that every humiliation that the Muslims suffer pains and grieves me so much?', the great Persian and Urdu poet Mirza Asadullah Khan Ghalib (1797–1869) once mused.[1] For a non-conformist who spurned the orthodox view of Islam, though not the basic tenets of the faith, Ghalib's pathos for the Muslims is as touching as it is revealing. It offers an insight into the self-identification of one of the leading literary figures of nineteenth-century northern India. Associated with the court of the last Mughal emperor, Bahadur Shah Zafar, Ghalib was personally affected by the erosion of Muslim power which culminated in the dramatic loss of sovereignty in 1857. Yet his poetry and prose, imbued with idioms and motifs drawn from a cultural milieu that was both Muslim and Indian, tended to be more individualistic than communitarian in expression.[2] This was in keeping with literary conventions prior to 1857 in contrast to the dominant trend from the late-nineteenth-

[1] Cited in Ralph Russell and Khurshidul Islam (eds), *Ghalib 1797–1869: Life and Letters*, Delhi: Oxford University Press, 1994, p. 38 [henceforth *Ghalib Life*].

[2] This is not to deny that the search for a Muslim identity in India has a prior history, extending back at least a hundred years. The instability which characterized Mughal rule following the death of Aurangzeb in 1707 had stirred a variety of Muslim reform movements aimed at internal purification of the faith, most notably that of Shah Waliullah (1703–62) and Sayyid Ahmad of Rai Bareilly (1786–1831). For an overview, see Annemarie Schimmel, *Islam in the Indian Subcontinent*, Leiden: E.J. Brill, 1980, chapter five. Also see Peter Hardy, *The Muslims of British India*, Cambridge: Cambridge University Press, 1972, chapter two and Aziz Ahmad, *Studies in Islamic Culture in the Indian Environment*, Oxford: Clarendon Press, 1964.

century when a more self-conscious attempt was made to project the collective identity of the Muslims.

The shift from the individual to the collective in the poetry and prose of Muslims need not be overdrawn to appreciate the differences in the historical contexts of Ghalib and his contemporaries, and their successors in late nineteenth century British India. To some extent the individual and the collective remained imbricated in Muslim poetry and prose even after the formal loss of sovereignty and the onset of 'modernity' in the mid-nineteenth century appeared to encourage the privileging of collective themes through a rapidly expanding print media. But it is the oft-cited absence of the individual in what has come to be regarded as an overwhelmingly collective Islamic ethos which makes the poetry of Ghalib and other outstanding literary figures of the time, Mir Taqi Mir (1722–1810) and Hakim Momin Khan Momin (1801–52) for instance, an excellent source to tap the individual consciousness of a Muslim.

THE MUSLIM AS INDIVIDUAL

When asked if he was a Muslim, Ghalib is known to have said that he was only half Muslim: he drank wine but did not eat pork. Mir Taqi Mir who dominated the literary scene in northern India prior to Ghalib was given to even greater impudence in matters to do with religion. 'Do not ask of my sect or faith,' Mir once said; he had long ago abjured Islam and with a sacred mark on the brow now kneeled in the temple.[3] Displaying a visceral aversion for religious leaders, Muslim and Hindu alike, and cherishing his own individuality, Mir declared that instead of joining with the Sheikh and Brahman, he would make his *kaaba* separately.[4] Such irreverence towards established religious norms did not vitiate Ghalib's and Mir's sense of belonging to the community of Muslims. Nor did being a Muslim inhibit them from interacting closely with members of other communities. Ghalib went to the extent of saying that even a Brahman

---

[3] *Mir ke deen-o-mazhab ka ab puchhte kya ho, unne to*
Qashqa kheincha, der mein baitha, kab ka tarak islaam kiya.

بیر کے دین و مذہب کا اب پوچھتے کیا ہو ان نے تو

تِنقہ کھینچا دیر میں بیٹھا کب کا ترک اسلام کیا۔

(K.C. Kanda, *Masterpieces of Urdu Ghazal: From 17th to 20th Century*, [second edition] New Delhi: Sterling Publishers Ltd, 1994, pp. 80–1).

[4] *Shirkat-i-Sheikh wo Brahman say Mir*
Apna kaaba juda banaenge.

شرکتِ شیخ و برہمن سے میر

اپنا کعبہ جدا بناۓگے۔

true to his faith could die in the idol house and qualify for burial in the *kaaba*.[5] His rejection of social closure on the basis of religion is underscored in a couplet where he asserts that as a *muwahid*, or a believer in the unity of God, he had abandoned cultural rituals which set one community apart from another. When there are no rituals to separate communities, all would believe in the unity of God and true faith could be established.[6]

So how significant was being a Muslim in the self-definition of the personal identity of these poets? It was clearly not insignificant given the frequency with which the duality between a *kafir* (non-believer) and a Muslim is invoked in the poetry of both Mir and Ghalib. In Muslim mystical poetry, from which the two poets drew their inspiration, the unresponsive beloved is often likened to a *kafir* or an idol. Mir considered the religion of love to be the hallmark of a *kafir*[7] while Ghalib asserted: 'Why should my life be dearer than the idol? Isn't faith dear to me?'[8] And then again: 'Why did I give my heart deeming her faithful Asad? I erred thinking the *kafir* was a Muslim.'[9] The imagery of a

---

[5] *Wafadari, bashrat-i-astwari, asal iman hai*
Maray buth khana main toh kaaba main gharo Brahman ko.

وفاداری، بشرطِ استواری، اصل ایمان ہے

مرے بت خانے میں تو کعبہ میں گاڑو برہمن کو۔

(In Ghulam Rasul Mehr [comp.], *Nawa-i-Saroosh*, Lahore: Sheikh Ghulam Ali and Sons Pvt. Ltd Publishers (no date), [henceforth *Ghalib, Nawn-i-Saroosh*] p. 412.)

[6] *Hum muwahid hain, hamara kaish hai tarq-i-rasoom*
Millaten jab mitt gain, ajza-i iman ho gein.

ہم موحد ہیں، ہمارا کیش ہے ترکِ رسوم

ملتیں جب مٹ گئیں، اجزائے ایمان ہو گئیں۔

(Ibid., p. 369)

[7] *Sakht kafir tha jin nay phela Mir*
Mazhab-i-ishq akhtiyar kiya.

سخت کافر تھا جن نے پہلے میر

مذہبِ عشق اختیار کیا۔

(Imtiaz Ali [comp.], *Mir, Ghalib, Dagh, Momin Ki Mashoor 100 Ghazhlain*, Lahore: Maktaba Imtiaz [no date], p. 11.)

[8] *Kiun kar use buth say rakhoon jan aziz*
Kiya nahin hai mujhe iman aziz?

کیوں کر اس بت سے رکھوں جان عزیز

کیا نہیں ہے مجھے ایمان عزیز؟

(Ghalib, *Nawa-i-Saroosh*, p. 245)

[9] *Dil diya jaan ke kiun useko wafadar Asad*
Ghalti ki kay jo kafir ko Musalman samjha.

دل دیا جان کے کیوں اس کو وفادار اسد

غلطی کی جو کافر کو مسلمان سمجھا۔

(Ibid., p.131)

kafir and an idol is sustained in the more self-consciously Muslim poetry of
Hakim Momin Khan Momin, an avid follower of Sayyid Ahmad of Rai
Bareilly even though he did not directly participate in the so-called Wahabi
movement.[10] Momin's name literally means a practising Muslim. In one
verse Momin complained that the idol had always been his enemy; this is
what his name had done to him.[11]

The distinction between a non-believer and a believer in the poetry of
Mir, Ghalib and Momin might suggest the all-pervasiveness of Muslim identity
which many observers of Islam are wont to detect in the self-perceptions of
the faithful. Yet Muslimness, however defined, cannot be seen in isolation
from the myriad other social relationships informing the worldview of the
individual Muslim. There is nothing particularly unusual about the attachment
of Muslims to the symbols of their collective religious identity. It has nevertheless
fuelled the misconception that the notion of the individual in Islam is either
non-existent or at best weakly articulated. It is true that Muslims identify
strongly and passionately with the Quran, their Holy Prophet and a range of
other Islamic symbols. Yet identification with a common set of symbols and
beliefs cannot be seen as grounds for the erasure of the individual in Muslim
consciousness. Unlike other great religious traditions Islam does not
acknowledge any mediation between the individual and God, whose unity is
complete and absolute.[12]

The *shahada* or confessional statement *la illah illa Allah*—there is no God
but God—is the foundational principle of Islam. It is the intermeshing of the
Arabic letters ‏ا‎ *alif* for Allah and ‏ل‎ *lam* that have inspired some of the greatest
Muslim thought and art in the Islamic world. India has been no exception.

---

[10]Yet Momin's sense of self is even more poignant given the communitarian flavour
of Shah Waliullah and Sayyid Ahmad's movement which moved him deeply. Already
by the first half of the nineteenth century the reformers were no longer targeting
'some individuals at the top' but concentrating attention 'on the reform of the
community as a whole'. (Qeyamuddin Ahmad, *The Wahabi Movement in India*, Calcutta:
Firma K.L. Mukhopadhyay, 1966, p.14)

[11]*Dushman-i-Momin hi rahe buth sada*
Mujh say mera nam nai ye kyah kiya.

‏دشمن مومن ہی رہے بُت سدا‎

‏بُھ سے میرے نام نے یہ کیا کیا۔‎

(Ali [comp.], *Mir, Ghalib, Dagh, Momin ki Mashoor 100 Ghazlain*, p. 89.)

[12]Here I am making a distinction between Islamic metaphysics and Muslim social
practices. Many Muslims have of course revered and been guided by spiritual mediators.
Even the intercession of the Prophet of Islam as the ultimate bearer of the divine
message is a form of mediation. Historically, the overlapping of normative and mystical
Islam has left a more indelible mark on Muslim thought than the volatile politics of
mosque and shrine in certain regions of the subcontinent might seem to suggest.

Admiring their calligraphic uses in minor arts and architectural inscriptions, Annemarie Schimmel notes that 'these weighty words have been ornated with so intricate and bewildering interlacing ornaments that an uninitiated would scarcely imagine that the essence of Muslim faith is concealed behind them'.[13] According to an old Islamic saying, calligraphy is the geometry of the spirit; it is through writing and reciting the letters, words and verses of the Quran that the Muslim strives for unity with the one and only Allah.[14] It is a quest which is meaningless without the initial negation followed by absolute affirmation. Removing the *alif* from the *la* leaves the *lam* with the vertical stem dropping into the circular ں *nun* without the diacritical point or the *nokta*, invoking the visual image of the sword of negation. Since the letter *nun* resembles an ink-pot, the calligraphic *lam* as sword symbolizes the pen. The missing *nokta* signifies the individual seeking inner spiritual union with the mysterious and original diacritical point of *ba* ب in the *bismillah*, in the name of Allah, which opens the first chapter of the Quran, and by implication with all the lines and circles of divine creation.[15] Not only are the proportions of calligraphy a key to the apportioning of space in Islamic art and architecture,[16] but the constitutive elements linking the Quranic revelation with Muslim spirituality, the moving force in both intellectual and artistic creativity.

Defying formal laws of composition, the Quran emerges like a formless ocean, a central motif in Persian–Urdu poetry:

Joyful is the drop dissolving in the ocean
An excess of pain itself becomes the remedy.[17]

This was how Ghalib evoked the idea of *fana* or annihilation which together with that of *baqa* or salvation gives expression to the believer's longing for union with divine creation. It is not the form of the Quranic revelation but its *haqiqah* or formless essence and the concept of *tauhid* or the unity of creation which has informed the artistic creations of Muslims the world over.

Untranslatable into any material form, the Quran as the word of Allah

---

[13]Annemarie Schimmel, *Gabriel's Wing: A Study Into the Religious Ideals of Sir Muhammad Iqbal*, Leiden: E.J. Brill, 1963, p. 89.

[14]Seyyed Hossein Nasr, *Islamic Art and Spirituality*, Albany: State University of New York, 1987, pp.18–19.

[15]Ibid., pp. 24–6 and Seyyed Hossein Nasr, *Ideals and Realities of Islam*, Lahore: Suhail Academy, 1994, pp. 60–1.

[16]Nasr, *Islamic Art and Spirituality*, p. 26.

[17]*Ishrat-i-katra hae darya main fana ho jana*
Dard ka hadd saay guzarna hae dawwa ho jana.

عشرتِ قطرہ ہے دریا میں فنا ہو جانا

درد کا حد سے گزرنا ہے دوا ہو جانا۔

(Ghalib, *Nawa-i-Saroosh*, p. 174)

has been the main source of inspiration for Muslim arts—not only calligraphy and architecture but also poetry. In Titus Burckhardt's astute estimation, the 'Quran does not satisfy'; 'it expands the soul by lending it wings, then lays it low and leaves it naked; for the believer, it is both comforting and gratifying, like a rainstorm'. As the radiation of the divine sun on the human desert, its spirit is invoked in the fluid rhythms of an arabesque and, in the abstract and crystalline nature of the architecture.[18]

Calligraphy is considered the noblest of Islamic arts.[19] According to an early Sufi saying, there is no letter in any language which does not worship God. The calligrapher with the calamus, symbolizing the letter *alif* for Allah, knows something of the complex mythology of writing the sacred script. As is the wont of an *abd* or slave of Allah, the calligrapher invariably pleads forgiveness for daring to imitate the word of God. Every letter of the Arabic language signifies multiple meanings to Muslims, especially those of the mystical bent. As a great Sufi poet put it:

This *alif* was first one in origin;
Then is produced the numbers of connection

. . .

When the *alif* is bent like a reed
Then its both ends become crooked, and it is a *ba*
When *alif* becomes a horseshoe, it is a *nun*.[20]

But the *nun* can just as well be an inkpot into which the calligrapher dips the *alif* of the unity of creation, presenting immense possibilities for the artistic expression of the divine idea. The imagery of the pen and the tablet is widespread in mystical poetry whose regional variations have been the more powerful influences in shaping a sense of Muslimness than the pontifications of the theologians of Islam in their different settings.

If Arabic is the language of God, Persian it is said is the language of paradise. Yet it was in Urdu that Ghalib made his most profound statement on his idea of the self: 'When there was nothing, there was God; if there had been nothing, there would have been God. Being drowned me; if I had not been what would there have been?'[21] This daring couplet is explicable only in terms of

---

[18]Titus Burckhardt, *Art of Islam: Language and Meaning*, London: Islamic Festival Trust Ltd, 1976, p. 45.

[19]For an evocative and sensitive analysis, see Annemarie Schimmel, *Calligraphy and Islamic Culture*, New York: New York University Press, 1984.

[20]Ibid., pp. 94–5.

[21]Na tha kuch toh khuda tha, kuch na hota toh khuda hota
Doboyah mujh ko honay nai, na hota main toh kya hota.

نہ تھا کچھ تو خدا تھا، کچھ نہ ہوتا تو خدا ہوتا

ڈبویا مجھ کو ہونے نے، نہ ہوتا میں تو کیا ہوتا۔

(Ghalib, *Nawa-i-Saroosh*, p.125)

the Islamic notion of the individual believer's relationship with God. In delineating a direct and unmediated relationship between the individual and the Creator—based on outright negation, followed by an absolute affirmation—Islam allows maximum autonomy to the Muslim self which is subject only to the will of Allah, the one and only sovereign of the world. Mir acknowledged the dangers of reposing such autonomy in the individual even as he noted the responsibility it entailed:

By naming him the crown of things,
God in His grace has honoured man.

But strange is man in word and deed,
Self-willed, self-loving, full of self-conceit.

Fitting it was in gratitude,
Obeisance to Him he should make.

But man's defiant nature,
Will not let him bow.

Mir! a handful of dust, my God!
How did he attain such heights? [22]

Since a Muslim is answerable only to God, the responsibility for deeds, good

[22] *Usko tarjih sab ke upar de,*
Lutf-i-Haq ne ki izzat afzai.
Hairat aati hai uski baaten dekh,
Khud sari, khud sataai, khud raai,
Shukr ke sijdon mein yeh wajib tha,
Yeh bhi karta sada jabin sai.
So to uski tabiat-e-sarkash,
Sar na laai faro ke tuk laai.
Mir naa chiz musht-e-khaak Allah,
Un ne yeh kibriya kahaan paai.

اس کو ترجیح سب کے اوپر دے

لطفِ حق نے کی عزت افزائی

حیرت آتی ہے اس کی باتیں دیکھ

خد سری، خد ستائی، خودرائی

شکر کے سجدوں میں یہ واجب تھا

یہ بھی کرتا سدا جبیں سائی

سو تو اس کی طبیعتِ سرکش

سر نا لائی فرد، کہ تک لائی

میر نا چیز، مشتِ خاک، اللہ

اُن نے یہ کبریا کہاں پائی

(Kanda, *Masterpieces of Urdu Ghazal*, pp.106–9)

and bad, falls entirely on the individual. There is no provision for the atonement of individual sins by the collectivity as in the Christian tradition.

This in part explains the problems many western scholars have faced while grappling with the idea of the Muslim self, far less that of the individual.[23] Annemarie Schimmel attributes this to the apparent absence of a notion of the individual in Islam as 'a normative being ... whose rights are central in interhuman relations and who works freely in the spirit of realization of the "human values"' which are intrinsic to the European conception of 'humanism'. The Muslim self appears either as *abd*—an absolute slave of God—or the *insan al-kamal*, the inflated perfect being who is Allah's viceregent on earth.[24] A demand for total submission to God and the accent on responsibility to the community has been interpreted as the lack of an adequate conception of individual rights in Islam. Yet it is the fact of the individual's right to an unmediated relationship with Allah that explains the series of Islamic injunctions on personal responsibility to the community. The temporal side of existence is more than adequately balanced with the spiritual. It is the personal relationship of the individual with God, conveyed by the term *iman* or faith, that informs a Muslim's submission to Allah. Islam is submission and a Muslim is one who submits. Allah for the Muslim is a personal God. If *la illaha illa Allah* constitutes a Muslim's faith, then the uniqueness of the Creator expressed by the concept of *tauhid* or the unity of creation, in both its absolute and eternal attributes, is the soul of Islam. Rejecting the pantheistic notion of God's immanence, Muslims believe that Allah is unlike any created being. He is not a person but transcendental. This does not foreclose the possibility of a Muslim's personal relationship with Khuda, Rabb, Allah, Parwardigar, Malik-ul-mulk, to give just some of the many names used to refer to God.[25]

[23]*Khudi* or the self in Muslim thought and poetry is the inner disposition of the believer which in Persian also means the ego. Muhammad Iqbal the leading Indian Muslim poet and philosopher of the twentieth century used the term to refer to the self-affirming and dynamic individual—the *insan-ul-kamal* (see chapter four below). While the self is more personal and has embedded in it an intrinsic autonomy from society at large, the *fard* or the individual is an entity whose autonomy has to be measured in its balance with other individuals and a community, however defined. The concepts of self and individual and the subtle analytical distinction between them is of crucial significance for this study. The way in which the Muslim idea of the *fard* (individual) and *infaradaiyat* (individuality) differs from the individualism of western humanist thought is discussed in the text here. The related notion of *shakhsiyat* or personality is of less direct relevance to the discussion but can be seen as epitomizing certain attributes of the individual, including the sense of self felt by an individual.

[24]Annemarie Schimmel, *Deciphering the Signs of God: A Phenomenological Approach to Islam*, Albany: State University of New York Press, 1994, pp. 179–80.

[25]For an insightful discussion of this, see R.A. Nicholson, *The Idea of Personality in Sufism*, (reprint), Lahore: Sheikh Muhammad Ashraf, 1970.

The *miraj sharif* or ascension of the Holy Prophet to the heavens and his almost breathtakingly close proximity to God's presence is a leitmotif in Muslim consciousness. Asked whether he wanted direct communion with God or His presence among his *ummat* or community, Muhammad is said to have opted for the latter. Man chose to remain separated from God. So fate too is not without choices. The Prophet was moved to the core of his soul when he heard the Lord say: 'Call unto Me and I will answer you.' In prayer a Muslim comes closest to God. While the Prophet was overcome by fear at the prospect of coming face to face with God, for the Muslim, Allah is reality, *al-Haq*, the loving one, *al-Wadud*, who is the only true Beloved. Love of Allah, the central theme of Sufi poetry, resonates through a vast corpus of Muslim thought, both oral and written, and enlivens genres as far apart as the *ghazal* and the *kafi*. Sufi poetry and philosophy the world over is ample testimony that Islam as a historical force, which cannot be confined to the view of its theologians alone, allows space for personal religion.[26]

Yet the Muslim individual is not simply a spiritual but also a temporal being. The Quran stresses the importance of maintaining a balance between the individual and the community. After all, no one could assert *la illaha illa Allah* without *Muhammad-ur Rasul Allah*. Belief in the uniqueness of Allah is meaningful only in the context of the Prophet's community. This is why far from treating them as oppositional, the individual and the community in Islam are seen to balance each other. The emphasis is on the community which forms the network of social relationships and the context conditioning the individual. Balance is the essence of the Quranic message to the Muslims. It is a balance in which responsibility to the community justifies the individual's right to an autonomy which is circumscribed only by complete submission to the will of Allah. And it is the Quranic injunctions on how to maintain that balance which appear to give the community an edge over the individual.[27]

Rejecting as it does any duality of individual and community, and instead stressing the imperative of balance between the two, the Islamic worldview has been open to multiple appropriations at different times in Muslim societies. A purely doctrinal approach to Islam might seem to highlight the communitarian aspects of the religion to all but the most discerning analyst. An examination of the historical experiences of Muslims in their specific geographical contexts reveals a rather more complex and nuanced picture. The subjectivity of the Muslim as individual finds ample voice in poetry and prose, whatever the spatial or temporal nature of the historical context. It is a subjectivity which borrows heavily from Islamic idioms, but one whose expression is interspersed with a welter of other demarcators of identity such as territory and language.

[26]Ibid., p. 20.
[27]See Ernest G. McClain, *Meditations Through the Quran: Tonal Images in an Oral Culture*, Maine: Nicholas Hays, 1981, p. 65 and chapter four below.

THE CITY AS IDENTIFIER

Like a Persian or an early Mughal miniature where the apportioning of non-homogeneous space invokes multiple levels of consciousness, interpreting the territorial aspects of Muslim identity is like contemplating a two-dimensional landscape without letting the roving eye fall into a purely three-dimensional perspective. A depiction of reality beyond mundane materiality, the Persian miniature in portraying discontinuous space in an imaginal world is at once expansive in its evocation of the transcendental and restricted in its detailing of forms, objects as well as events within the human soul.[28] The spiritual bond with the *ummah* or the worldwide community of Islam meshes with associations to family and the larger kinship group. A Muslim's identification with a non-territorial community of Islam and the sense of belonging to a territorially located community means that space is both infinite and finite at the same time. It is this dialectic inherent in their religiously informed cultural identity that has lent historical complexity and depth to the Muslims' relationship with the *watan* or homeland.

An affinity to territory is typically decried in normative Muslim thought as detracting from identification with a non-territorially defined *ummah*. But the ideological conception of the community has not been matched by any lack of attachment with territory on the part of Muslims. Even the Prophet of Islam felt compelled to enjoin his followers to free the Arabian peninsula of non-Muslims and keep it as an exclusive preserve of the Muslims. Stated at a time when Islam had not attained the geographical spread that it did in subsequent centuries, the Prophet Mohammad's advice to the *ummah* underlines the importance of the territory where the holy places were situated. To this day, Mecca and Medina occupy a special place in Muslim consciousness the world over.[29]

A specific geographical location like Arabia has been a powerful religious symbol for Muslims over the centuries. But the sense of belonging to a given territory has provided a more immediate point of reference for their sense of identity. Mir Taqi Mir took the point to its mystical heights when he declared:

Why talk of Mecca or Kaaba, who cares for pilgrimage?
Dwellers of the street of love, greet these places from afar.[30]

This is an allusion to a Muslim's spiritual relationship with the *kaaba*, the ubiquitous centre or the *qiblah*, the direction in which prayers are said, which

[28]See Nasr, *Islamic Art and Spirituality*, pp. 177–84.

[29]For the cosmological and theosophical significance of the *kaaba* in Muslim thought, see Henry Corbin, *Temple and Contemplation*, trs. Philip Sherrard, London KPI and Islamic Publications, 1986, chapter four.

[30]*Kis ka kibla, kaisa Kaaba, kaun haram hai, kiya ahraam,*
Kuche ke uske baashindon ne sab ko yehin se salaam kiya.

is everywhere and yet a specific space sanctified by the Holy Prophet's prostration before Allah. As the material and spiritual centre of Islam, which in mystical belief is thought to be situated exactly opposite the heavenly throne, praying in the direction of the *kaaba* is not only the spatialization of the Muslim belief in one God but also of membership in the *ummah*.[31] The architectural geometry and sacred space of the *kaaba* has been reproduced by Muslims everywhere in the world, from the mosque as the place of collective worship to the home as private abode. In facing towards it in ritualistic prayer, Muslims approximate the Prophet's first prayer at the *arsh* or the divine throne and the second on the *farsh* or earthly ground of the *kaaba*. The symbolism of reversing the separation of *arsh* from *farsh*, of the divine from the human, of the transcendental from the phenomenological through prayer reverberates in Muslim arts, architecture and poetry in equally vigorous measure. By sanctifying the interior of the home as well as the mosque with prayer, Muslims create their own sacred space, separate from but never disjoined from the *kaaba*, the centre of all peripheries to which all points return.[32]

The idea of space as universal and specific, conveyed by the rich symbolism of the *kaaba*, has allowed the articulation of territorial identity in the Muslim psyche to take a variety of forms. In India it found expression in a genre of Urdu poetry known as *shahr-i-ashoob* or *ashoobia shairi*, lament for the city, which encapsulates the socio-cultural turbulence of cities in the late Mughal period. Unlike the love poetry where the individual yearns for the beloved, whether human or divine, in the *shahr-i-ashoob* the poet locates his existential self through an attachment to a *watan*, or homeland. Yet it would be erroneous to regard this genre of poetry as proto-nationalist, pure and simple. There are certainly references to *qaum* or a social collectivity which does not translate easily into the English term 'nation'. The connotations of the word 'nation' in popular discourse militates against its straightforward equation with the Urdu word *qaum* which is used rather loosely and can refer to a clan, religious community, or a sect. Without contextualizing the use of words like *qaum* and *watan*, Urdu poetry can become a hunting ground for many imagined 'nations' and 'nationalisms'. Such an exercise amounts to thwarting any effort at disentangling the individual identity of the Muslim from the discourse on the Muslim community and nation.

Until 1857 there was no obvious invocation of the national idea in the

<hr>

کس کا قبلہ کیا کعبہ کون حرم ہے کیا احرام

کوچہ کے اُس کے باشندوں نے سب کو یہیں سے سلام کیا۔

(Kanda, *Masterpieces of Urdu Ghazal*, p. 79)

[31]See Annemarie Schimmel, 'Sacred Geography in Islam', in Jamie Scott and Paul Simpson-Housley (eds), *Sacred Places and Profane Spaces: Essays in the Geographics of Judaism, Christianity, and Islam*, New York: Greenwood Press, 1991.

[32]For an illuminating discussion, see Nasr, *Islamic Art and Spirituality*, chapter three.

form it has come to assume in the post-colonial Indian state's secular nationalism and Pakistan's two-nation theory. The city or place of abode appears central to the sentiments of the poet as part of a given social setting. Ghalib felt passionately about the city of his birth, Agra, and considered his move to Delhi as an exile. For him Agra was the 'playground' of his 'love-distracted heart' where the 'drunken breeze of morning ranged through her gardens to lift up and to bear away men's hearts so that the drunkard longed no longer for his morning draught, so that the pious heart bent his mind no more to prayer'. He longed for the 'grain of dust of that land', for 'every leaf in those fair gardens' and for the ripples of its rivers.[33]

Even as early as the late seventeenth century, Wali Muhammad Wali (1667–1707) of the Deccan, considered by many to be the father of Urdu poetry, had evoked the notion of the Muslim *qaum* as well as the *watan* or territorial homeland while celebrating his attachment to a city like Surat on the one hand and Hindustan on the other. The themes of the *shahr-i-ashoob* spawn a rich social commentary on the vibrancy of life as well as the historical causes of degeneration and civil strife in various urban centres of the subcontinent. Those excelling in this genre included Shafiq Aurangabadi, Shakir Naji, Shah Hatim, Mir Taqi Mir and Mirza Rafi Sauda. Mir noted that the wilds of today had been bustling towns of yesterday and spoke patriotically of the spirit of martyrdom stirring his heart to put the oppressor's might to the test.[34] There was also an element of satire and humour in this poetry before 1857. After the suppression of the revolt the *shahr-i-ashoob* began taking the form of *marsiyas*, or dirges, drenched in blood and tragedy.

Much the same sort of trend had attended Aurangzeb's overrunning of the city-states of Bijapur and Golconda. The Bijapuri poet Ansari compared the situation in his conquered homeland to the advent of *kufar* (infidelity) and found little pleasing about the new circumstances. A Muslim conqueror being billed a *kafir* in a poetic lament about the destruction of a style of life is a warning against any facile equation of an individual's religiously informed identity with an undifferentiated community of Islam. In this instance Ansari's identity, Muslim and Bijapuri, leads him to dub the new political dispensation *kufar*. An allusion to the loss of spirituality resulting from conquest and a remapping of physical space, this was a sentiment shared by other poets of Bijapur. Many wrote long *masnavis* (poems in rhyming couplets) on the devastation of their beloved city and the ensuing displacement. Despite the

[33]Russell and Islam (eds), *Ghalib Life*, p. 29.
[34]*Mir jangal paray hain aaj yahan*
Log kiya kiya yahin kal thay bastay.

میر جنگل پڑے ہیں آج یہاں

لوگ کیا کیا یہیں کل تھے بستے۔

(Kanda, *Masterpieces of Urdu Ghazal*, p. 8)

common bond of Islam, the poets responded to the Muslim invasion with chagrin. As far as they were concerned, the Mughals were marauders who had destroyed the peace of Bijapur and snuffed out the lights of its cultural efflorescence under the Adil Shahis. The local poets of Golconda felt much the same when Aurangzeb's troops marched victoriously into their city. Writing *ashoobia shairi* they carped and complained about the new administration's sins of omission and commission and invoked the lost historical glory of Golconda.[35]

In the heartland of Muslim power in northern India, Mirza Rafi Sauda in his *Qasida Shahr-i-Ashoob* wrote movingly about the anarchy, unemployment, corruption and incompetence of the nobility and the service gentry, and the hunger of the poor which accompanied the collapse of the Mughals. He observed that there was no respectable profession left to pursue. In a potent comment on the invasion of sacred space, Sauda recorded that the mosques were desolate with only donkeys roped up there.[36] Khwajah Mir Dard (1720–84), otherwise given to mystical contemplation, also spoke feelingly about the dismal state of politics at the twilight of Mughal supremacy. In one of his poems, suffused with nostalgia for the past glory of the Mughals, Dard compared the changed circumstances to a storm preceding death and yearned to return to his original home which for him could no longer be Hindustan:

Do you know, O Dard, all these folks,
Whence they came, whither they go?[37]

The uprootedness and lack of direction among the Muslims following the attenuation of centralized Mughal power is a theme which pervades the *ashoobia* poetry of this period. But it is by no means restricted to this genre. It is communitarian to the extent that it bemoans the fate of the Muslims as a whole, but the expression remains that of the individual poet paying homage to the city of his birth or subsequent abode.

The importance of territorial location as a signifier of identity is further underscored by the linking of city names to the surnames of key figures like Akbar Allahabadi, Nazir Akbarabadi, Ismail Meeruti, Mirza Khan Dagh Dehlavi to name a few. Clearly, then, the religious identity of individual Muslims was closely intermeshed with the territorial contours of the cities in

[35] Muzaffar Abbas, *Urdu Main Qaumi Shairi* (in Urdu), Lahore: Maktabah-yi 'Aliyah, 1978, p. 52.

[36] Ibid., p. 65.

[37] *Dard kuchh malum hai yeh log sab,*
Kis taraf sa aae the kidhar chale.

درد کچھ معلوم ہے یہ لوگ سب

کس طرف آۓ تھے کیدھر م چلے۔

(Kanda, *Masterpieces of Urdu Ghazal*, p. 67.)

which they lived. So great was the attachment that many resisted taking up jobs which entailed being footloose and moving to another city. Altaf Husain Hali (1837–1914) complained bitterly of his brief stint in Lahore where he was bereft of friends, physically unwell, and utterly miserable. Later, another import to the Punjab from the North West Provinces, Muhammad Husain Azad (1830–1910), castigated Muslim youth for this unenterprising resistance to mobility and extolled the virtues of *hubb-i-watani* or patriotism.[38] The passion for one's city, encompassing as it did a range of cultural experiences and social relationships, was not one that could be easily submerged in the largely imagined identifications of the Muslims with India and Islam. And this despite the fact that the extra-territorial loyalties of Muslims, especially those belonging to the *ashraf* or professional classes, often led them to nostalgically identify with places and countries of their ancestral origin.

The city's role as one of the primary signifiers of identity axes any notion of the absence of territorial loyalties in the consciousness of Muslims living in the different regions of the subcontinent. Not only was territorial attachment a common feature of the Muslim psyche, irrespective of class, but together with language paved the way for an expansion in the spatial scales of loyalty, be it to a region or India as a whole. But with the commodification of physical space and individual talent under colonial rule, the new landscape of territorial identities was unlike an Islamic miniature. A colonized subject was not free to organize space, moving from detail to detail without needing to arrange it into a single unifying visual order.[39] The introduction of the three-dimensional perspective into the miniature had already rearranged the canvas around a single vanishing point against which all other forms and objects in the composition are subordinated. This was distinct from the miniature of old with its own unique sense of space, time, movement, colour and form. Before the European influences on colour and perspective were transmitted by the Jesuits to Akbar's royal studios in the sixteenth century through gifts of Flemish tapestries,[40] the miniature was the repository of the transcendental and inner spiritual space based on the *alam al-khiyal*, or imaginal world. Here events occurred in real but not necessarily physical fashion. The viewer is guided through several stages of consciousness beyond the phenomenological, or the physical world (*mulk*), to the intermediary world (*malukat*) of cognitive intellect and the divine world (*jabarut*) of intuition.[41] It was the injection of the Cartesian logic of duality between the spiritual and the temporal domains which made certain that the reconfiguring of Muslim identity under colonialism would be as much about the recovery of the spiritual self as about

[38]See chapter two below.
[39] J.M. Rogers, *Mughal Miniatures*, New York: Thames & Hudson, 1993, p. 70.
[40]Ibid., pp. 70–3.
[41]Nasr, *Art and Islamic Spirituality*, p. 181.

the renegotiation of physical and material space. This makes it all the more important to explore the spiritual dimensions in the regional and local landscapes of Muslim consciousness prior to the onset of British colonialism.

REGION AND LANGUAGE IN MUSLIM CONSCIOUSNESS

Region and language for the most part have always cut across religiously defined communitarian and ideologically informed national identities in the subcontinental context. As illustrated by the *ashoobia* poetry, the city was the primary source of identity for many using Urdu as the medium of their expression. Yet Urdu was mainly, though by no means exclusively, the language of the *shurfa* or the respectable classes concentrated around urban centres like Delhi and Lucknow in the north and Hyderabad in the Deccan. The themes treated in the poetry, to say nothing of its stylistic formalizations, owed a great deal to the prevailing tastes of the *umara* or nobility which also held the purse strings sustaining many poetic livelihoods. Ghalib's profoundly stoical posture in much of his *ashiqana* or love poetry takes a mighty fall when the giant of Urdu literature takes to pleading for pecuniary help from his patrons.

Competition for royal patronage among poets incited bitter rivalries and jealousies. This found poetic expression in a profusion of lampoons and satires.[42] Ghalib's ire focused on Mirza Zauq, designated as poet laureate by Akbar Shah and employed as tutor by Bahadar Shah II. Younger than Zauq but vastly superior to the royal favourite, Ghalib had to pay the price for writing a *qasida* praising the emperor's key rival to the throne. It was only after Zauq's death that Bahadur Shah Zafar appointed Ghalib as poet laureate.[43] Dependence on patrons whose tastes dictated poetic expression could breed some of the worst forms of sycophancy. Yet much depended on the individual patron and poet. After all, some of the best-known Urdu poetry of mid-nineteenth-century northern India was patronized by royal courts at Delhi and Lucknow.[44]

The Urdu of the common people, less liable to being encumbered by the whimsical fancies of the aristocracy, found expression in a thriving folklore heavily coloured and textured by the local north-Indian environment. Much of the folklore was a result of collective creativity and passed on orally from one generation to the next. Covering every aspect of life, Urdu folklore displays its debt to Islam and its Indian context in equal measure. Frequently borrowing

[42]Muhammad Sadiq, *A History of Urdu Literature*, Delhi: Oxford University Press, 1995 (second edition), p.10.

[43]S.M. Burke and Salim al-Din Quraishi, *Bahadur Shah: The Last Mogul Emperor of India*, Lahore: Sang-e-Meel Publications, 1996, p. 211.

[44]Sadiq, *A History of Urdu Literature*, pp.11–12.

from local dialects, whether *Brajbhasha* or *Awadhi* in the north or *Deccani* in the south, Urdu folklore has maintained stronger ties with the soil than the idiomatically more structured products of elite poetry. Songs sung at marriages, seasonal festivals, the birth of a child, or even a mother's lullaby convey the easy coexistence of local and regional flavours with religious idioms. In so far as all folklore leans towards the celebration of collective activity, it may not seem to offer the most fertile ground for exploring the consciousness of the Muslim as individual. What it does provide, however, is an indication of how individuals related to a social collectivity, locally and regionally based, without being overwhelmed by religious differentiations.

Few well-known poets of Urdu dabbled with folklore, deeming it too unsophisticated or loose an expression of their literary prowess. There were exceptions like Nazir Akbarabadi (1740–1830), who as his name suggests was a resident of Agra, the city built by the Mughal emperor Akbar. Preferring the lifestyle of a mystic, Akbarabadi shunned the company of poets associated with the Mughal court and made a conscious attempt to relate to the poor and lowly. In what is a measure of the arrogance and elitism of the Urdu literary tradition, Akbarabadi's poetry was for long dismissed as sensationalist and dropped from the purview of respectable and high-class poetry. Yet here was a man thoroughly at home with the physical geography and socio-cultural ambience of Agra and its environs. Although a Muslim, Akbarabadi found much cause for exhilaration in the religious festivals of Hindus, in seasons and lives of ordinary folk, in animals, etc., in short all those spheres of cultural life which were marginalized in the highbrow poetry designed to cater to aristocratic and upper class tastes.[45]

If class distinctions accounted for the variations in its written and oral traditions, Urdu was a further touch removed from other regional languages. Despite the common Persian and Arabic influences, Urdu remained primarily the language of the north Indian heartland, extending to the urban centres of the Punjab where the elite, Muslim and Hindu, embraced it with alacrity under the auspices of the colonial state. Narratives of identity in other regional languages reveal the colourful collage of Muslim India in its manifold complexities and subtleties. While sharing the Islamic imprimatur in varying measures, especially in their Sufi mystical forms, the regional language poetry and prose of the north-western Muslim-majority provinces of Punjab, Sind, and the North West Frontier Province have borne the marks of the different geographical and social settings. This is truer still of Bengali Muslim literature, to say nothing of the Deccan and further south, which despite many common Islamic nuances has been tinged with regional symbols and idioms unlike those of the north-western areas.

[45]See ibid., chapter eight and Ali Ahmad Fatmi, 'Nazeer Akbarabadi ki Awami Shairi', in Qamar Rais (ed.), *Urdu Mein Lok Adab,* New Delhi: Simant Parkashan, 1990.

A thorough exploration of the multifaceted regional threads informing the literature of Muslims living in different parts of the subcontinent is beyond the scope of this enquiry. Here it will suffice to note two main strands of Islamic influence on the regional cultural formations in the subcontinent. The first bases itself on a history of commercial links between Arab traders and the south-western regions of undivided India while the second with its Persian imprint affected the present concentrations of Muslim populations in north-western India as well as Bengal. These two distinct cultural influences overlapped and reshaped one another as they came into contact with a predominantly non-Muslim setting. Sufi mystics before and during the period of the Delhi Sultanate (1206–1526) played a major part in accommodating Islam to different regional contexts in India. This more than the fact of Muslim conquest and establishment of sovereignty gave impetus to a slow but steady process of conversion to Islam. The intermingling of Sufi mystical thought with popular Hindu *bhakti* practices gave rise to a vast repertoire of poetry in regional languages, allowing for the greater accessibility of Islamic beliefs and rituals to a predominantly non-Muslim population. A direct relationship between the individual and God came to be substituted in the Indo-Islamic mystical tradition by the devotee seeking intercession from a revered local Sufi master to reach the Supreme Being.

The shrine of the holy man as a place of devotion may be deemed contrary to the strict precepts of Islam. Yet *maqbaras* or tombs of Sufi saints, both men and women, have been the focal points of religious devotion in South Asian history, often cutting across the communitarian divide. Unlike the *masjid* or mosque, which is a space of collective worship, the tomb with its striking paradisiacal imagery conveys an individual Muslim's belief in spiritual salvation after corporeal death. The mosque and the tomb are distinct but closely interconnected expressions of the same idea. If the act of worship in the mosque symbolizes the meeting of heaven and earth, the *arsh* and the *farsh*, the octagonal tomb with or without the *char bagh* or four-part garden represents paradise on earth. As the final resting place of the believer, the tomb evokes the organic unity of being, covering the spiritual and secular realms. This facilitated borrowings from regional traditions, not in some syncretic weave obliterating the religiously informed cultural identities of Muslims but permitting the emergence of what has been variously described as Indo-Persian or the Indo-Islamic style of the arts.

Not all Muslim tombs are sacred. But even secular mausoleums are deeply spiritual in conception. The popularity of shrine-based worship in the subcontinent can be attributed to the parallel between the idea of the Hindu temple as a sacred mountain covering the cavern concealing the spark of divine light and the tomb sheltering a crypt that conceals the seed of eternity.[46] Such

---

[46]Burckhardt, *Art of Islam*, pp.174–5.

spiritual compatibility made it relatively easier to adopt Hindu architectural techniques in constructing Muslim tombs. Variations in the style of tombs in the different regions reflect an individual Muslim patron's taste and the availability of building materials and artistic skills. It was in multilayered accretions that Islam made its impact on distinct regional cultural formations, shaping them as well as being reshaped by them. While it is possible to discern certain similar patterns in the Indianization of Islam, there can be no denying the distinctiveness lent by the various regional contexts to its actual practice.

Bengali Muslim literature, for instance, is a blend of a script derived from Sanskrit and Hindu Vaishnavite idioms interlaced with Persian and Arabic vocabulary as well as motifs. Unlike the regional language literature of the North Western Provinces, which flourished in the main as an oral tradition, in Bengal the Muslims both contributed to and benefited from a well-developed literate tradition. A succession of autonomous Muslim kingdoms during the Sultanate period actively patronized the Bengali language which in turn encouraged Muslim poets to use Islamic religious imagery and rework Persian and Arabic folk-tales into the vernacular. This process of indigenization gave creative impetus to a rich regional literature in which Bengali Muslims can be seen comfortably relating to their Islamic identity in a language and literary tradition shot through with Hindu religious symbolisms.[47] If religion separated the Hindu from the Muslim in Bengal, language was a powerful cement with potentially far-reaching effects. It was only in the second half of the nineteenth century that Bengali Muslims, in reaction to a growing trend of Sanskritization of the vernacular, self-consciously expunged idioms and motifs more obviously associated with Hindu Vaishnavism and opted for Persian and Arabic vocabulary to give fuller expression to their literary uses of Islamic imagery.[48] A kind of cultural self-defence on the part of literate Bengali Muslims, it did not erode the power of language as a vital signifier of their regional identity.

What distinguishes the poetry of Bengali Muslims from that of their co-religionists in other regions is that, instead of remaining steeped for the most part in an oral tradition, a much greater proportion of it was written and recorded. Even where the autonomous regional kingdoms promoted the vernacular language, as in Sind under the Kalhoras and Talpurs, the oral tradition remained by far the more dominant in the north-western concentrations of Muslim populations. Without implying the complete absence of a literate tradition in these regions, it is nevertheless important to

---

[47]See Inam-ul Haq, *Muslim Bengal Adab*, Urdu translation from the Bengali *Muslim Bangla Sahitya*, Karachi: Government of Pakistan Press, 1957, Asim Roy, *The Islamic Syncretic Tradition in Bengal*, Princeton: Princeton University Press, 1983 and Sukumar Sen, *Islami Bangla Sahitya* (Bengali), Burdwan: Barddhaman Sahityasabha, 1951.

[48]Rafiuddin Ahmed, *The Bengal Muslims, 1871–1906: A Quest for Identity*, Delhi: Oxford University Press, 1981, chapter four.

note the relatively greater development of a recorded literature in the vernacular by Muslims in Bengal than in Sind, Punjab, the North West Frontier Province and Baluchistan. Yet the fact of a mainly oral tradition did not undermine the affinity to the regional language or, for that matter, curtail the productivity of Sindhi, Punjabi, Pathan and Baluchi poets. As in the case of Bengal, the Muslims of these areas related strongly to their spoken language which they used in creative ways to evoke their regional as well as Islamic identity.

During the thirteenth century, Muslim mystics fleeing the Mongol hordes settled in the Indus valley region and the Punjab which share a common mystical folklore. Baba Fariduddin Ganj-i-Shakar (1175–1265) used the local Punjabi dialect of Pak Pattan for his mystical songs. By the fifteenth century there was a thriving tradition of mystical verses in Punjabi and Sindhi, both excellent mediums for the expression of spiritual feeling. These were sung in the form of *dhoras, kafis* and *way* based on indigenous musical modes and not in the quantitative meters of the Persian *ghazal*. The dominant motif of the longing soul as a woman seeking union with the ultimate beloved in Muslim mystical poetry was borrowed from the popular religious traditions of Hinduism. Intermeshed with romantic *qissas* or local folk-tales, the lover's quest for union with the beloved was readily understood by the peasantry and the illiterate, not least because of its evocation of everyday life in all its rhythms, tastes and essences.[49]

In Sind, the land of many distinguished Sufi mystics, the vernacular poetry hums in unison with the local environment, unconstrained by the proximity to political power or the narrowness of a purely communitarian worldview. The poetry of Shah Abdul Latif of Bhit Sharif (1689–1752) conveys his deep attachment to Sindhi soil and recounts the lives of ordinary rural folk weighed under by exploitative landlords and moneylenders. An iconoclast who acknowledged no authority which encumbered his thought, abjured religious orthodoxy and lashed out at what he regarded as social injustices, Shah Abdul Latif Bhitai is among the finest exponents of resistance poetry in a region with a long and rich history of the genre. Bhitai firmly believed in the doctrine of *wahdat-ul-wujud*, or the unity of existence. This made him a renegade for those subscribing to the orthodox, transcendentalist point of view. Yet Bhitai's poetry, compiled from what has been related by a chain of local bards in his magnum opus *Shah-jo-Rissalo* or the book of Shah, is not the less Muslim for its rejection of social conventions devoid of aesthetic qualities. It is divided into a number of chapters called *surs*, or melodies, each of which represents Sindhi culture in its different locales. The message covers a wide spectrum, a moralism and a code of ethics based on the poet's own interpretations of the

[49]For an excellent discussion, see Annemarie Schimmel, *Mystical Dimensions of Islam*, Chapel Hill: University of North Carolina Press, 1975, pp. 383–402.

Quran, the self-pride of the folk heroine Marvi and a sense of fellowship with humanity. According to folk belief, Bhitai as a young lad refused to learn beyond the letter | *alif*, the ultimate symbol of the unity of God.

It was an early display of a passion that was to seize him for the rest of his life. Immersed in the Sufi concept of *tasawuff*, or contemplation of God, Bhitai's poetry is deeply spiritual, articulating a philosophy of love which places him in the same league as many other Muslim mystics removed both in space and time. This commonality, however, is punctuated by local nuances in which Bhitai is as much a Muslim as he is a Sindhi. Yet at the same time, the poetry displays a wide-ranging humanism based on its principal inspiration, the idea of Divine Love. All these features combined in one make Bhitai the leading cultural protagonist of Sind in ways which only those versed in the vernacular can truly appreciate. Yet, it is still possible to salute Bhitai, a Muslim mystic whose poetic chantings, while situated in his regional setting, had the broad-mindedness of vision to trek the heights of a humanism in which no social demarcator matters, only the spirit and the soul take flight. As he puts it:

Oh my lord! Bring prosperity on Sind
My beloved Allah, render everyone
comfortable in this world.[50]

And then at his sublime best, Bhitai honours the unity of God and his creation:

From one, many to being came;
'many' but One-ness is;
Don't get confounded, Reality
is One, this truth don't miss
Commotions vast display—all this
I vow, of loved—one is.[51]

Free of any bigotry, Bhitai like the great *bhakti* poet Kabir propagated the message of the pacifist:

Let them say; but don't return vile words
Syed says, with all make your 'self' mild
Patience is great force, jealousy pays nothing.[52]

A similar worldview was enunciated by earlier and subsequent Sindhi Sufi poets such as Sachal Sarmast (1739–1826).[53] It is a worldview or, perhaps

---

[50]Muhammad Bachal Tonyo, *Legacy of Bhitai Shah Abdul Latif*, Karachi: Muhammad Bachal Tonyo, 1992, p. 35.

[51]Ibid., p. 68.

[52]Ibid., p. 72.

[53]See Schimmel, *Mystical Dimensions of Islam*, pp. 393–6.

more aptly, a way of looking at things which brings out the relative harmony with which the Muslim as individual related simultaneously to the local environment, a living culture and Islamic doctrines.

Sindhi mystical poetry with its gentle-mannered touches had never been without its echoes in neighbouring Punjab, not a region generally associated with temperamental mildness. Yet the Sufi mystical and folk tradition in Punjabi poetry vibrates with many of the same sentiments as can be found in its counterpart in Sind. Equally influenced by the Islamic impact, in its Persian and Arabic variants, the mainly oral literature of this region was disseminated by itinerant local bards and subsequently recorded. There are few aspects of the cultural life of the land of the five rivers which have not been evoked by the Sufi mystical poets of the Punjab, beginning with Baba Farid Ganj-i-Shakar and continuing with Shah Hussain (1539–93), Sultan Bahu (1631–91) and Baba Bulleh Shah (1680–1758) during the Mughal period.[54] Scaling the breadth and depths of this rich and often deceptively simple poetry is a subject worthy of a separate study. What is of relevance here is the extent to which the autonomy of the individual found voice in the Sufi poetry of the Punjab. It is an exercise in autonomy which finds a poet like Baba Bulleh Shah composing a seemingly profane couplet: 'Drench yourself in wine and feast on roasted flesh, roasting on the fires flaming out of the bones. O Bullah, break into the house of God and swindle this cheat of cheats'.[55] The sheer joy in the ordinary delights of life and the familiarity with which Bulleh Shah addresses God is just one example of the type of poetry which has over the centuries imbued subjectivity into the consciousness of the common folk of the Punjab. It is a subjectivity which resists submitting to the religious authority of the local mullah and claims complete freedom in matters to do with the worship of God. Bulleh Shah is a particularly fiery protagonist of the individual Muslim's sense of identity. In one of his much loved *kafis* or poems entitled 'Bullah how do I know who I am', he asserts that he was not a mullah, a *kafir* or even Pharoah; not an inhabitant of Arabia or of Lahore; he knew of no religion and was neither Muslim nor Hindu.[56] In another *kafi*, 'Leave

---

[54]See Lajwanti Rama Krishna, *Panjabi Sufi Poets: AD 1460–1900*, Oxford, 1938 (reprint) Lahore: Panjabi Adabi Laihr, 1992.

[55]*Pee sharab tey kha kebab, hait bal hadiyan de aag*
Bullehya bhan ghar rab da, ise thugan day thug noon thug.

پی شراب تے کھا کباب، میٹھ بال ہڈاں دی اگ
لمیا بھن گھر ربڈا، ایس ٹھگاں دے ٹھگ نوں ٹھگ۔

(Najm Hosain Syed, *Recurrent Patterns in Punjabi Poetry* [second edition], Lahore: Panjabi Adbi Markaz, 1986, p. 28.)

[56]*Bulleha! Kiwe jahnan main koon?*
Na main Momin wich maseytan
Na main wich kufar di reet ahn
Na main pakaan wich peleast ahn

knowledge alone my friend', the poet declaims on bookish knowledge and exclaims that he is neither a Sunni nor a sage, but one inspired who needed only the Arabic letters ا *alif* and م *meem* (which roughly correspond to the English alphabets 'A' and 'M') to understand the meaning of life from his spiritual leader, Shah Inayat.

Yet this denial of any limiting identity, spatial or religious, should not be misread to mean a rejection of this mystical bard's very real sense of himself as an individual. As he goes on to say: 'I regard myself as the first, no second do I acknowledge, nor consider wiser than myself.'[57] There cannot be a more emphatic assertion of the individual than in this simple utterance. It is communicated in a language of such marvellous lyrical quality that it is a crying shame that oral Punjabi has never made the transition into the more formalized and structured syntax accessible to its speakers.[58] So one must take a moment to honour the memory of all those bards of the Punjab to whom one owes a historical debt for transmitting the gems of wisdom, love and spirituality which stud the mystical poetry of this region. More to the point, Bulleh Shah's assertion of his individuality in all its multifaceted dimensions was not without a sense of balance. His primary human attachment was formed by his love and devotion for his *murshid*, or spiritual leader, Shah Inayat, in search of whom he left Kasur to come to Lahore, a city he did not identify with. Released from all external signifiers of identity other

---

Na main Musa, na Fhiron
Bulleha kiwe jahnan main koon?

. . .

Na main bheet mazhab da paya
Na main Adam Huwa jahya
Na kuj apana nam durhiya
Na wich baithaan, na wich bhoon
Bulleha kiwe jahnan main koon?

بُلھا! سیہ جاناں میں کون؟

نہ میں مومن وچ مسیتاں   نہ میں وچ کفر دی ریت آں

نہ میں پاکاں وچ، پلیت آں   نہ میں موسٰے، نہ فرعون

بُلھا سیہ جاناں میں کون؟

. . . . .

نہ میں بھیت مذہب دَلیا   نہ میں آدم حَوا لھایا

نہ کجھ اپنا نام دَھریا   نہ وچ بیٹھس، نہ وچ بھَون

بُلھا سیہ جاناں میں کون؟

Taufiq Rafat (trs.), *Bulleh Shah: A Selection*, Lahore: Vanguard Publications, 1982, pp. 68–71.

[57]Abdul Majid Bhatti, *Kafian Bulleh Shah*, Islamabad: Lok Virsa, 1975, p. 63.

[58]This is a theme developed more fully in chapter three.

than the spiritual bond he had forged with Shah Inayat, Bulleh Shah in his usual disarming and endearing manner could declare:

Neither Hindu nor Muslim
I sit with all on a whim.
Having no caste, sect, or creed,
I am different indeed.
. . .
I am not sinner or saint
knowing no sin nor restraint.
Bulleh tries hard to shirk
the embrace of Hindu and Turk.[59]

The discovery of a statement of individuality in Punjabi Sufi poetry is no ordinary one. It points to the presence of this notion in Muslim consciousness which was moulded by Islam as much as by local and regional cultures in all their myriad tastes and textures. Yet the idea of the individual did not efface relationships with other individuals or the larger community, be they of Islam or the linguistic region. There is no absence of Islamic influences, whether based on Sufi thought or culled from the *sharia*. Written in the form of questions and answers dealing with religious issues, these were known as *pakki rotis*, which literally means cooked bread. In addition, Punjabi literature has borrowed much from the *bhakti* tradition and imparted strands of romanticism into the poetry as well as the *qisas*. At the same time there is a sense of active involvement with a social setting which is largely though not exclusively rural. The combined effect of this is a reservoir of insights into a cultural tradition which, sadly enough, still awaits a wide-ranging and systematic scholarly analysis. Much has been written on Waris Shah's late-eighteenth-century popular folk love tale *Heer Ranjha*, in which the heroine Heer and the hero Ranjha appear as the archetypes of common Punjabi consciousness. But the veritable inversion of gender relations in this widely read *qissa*, a product of an apparently male-dominated society, has not received the consideration it deserves in charting the role of women's autonomy and their resistance against societal bondage. Heer assumes the power of choice and rejection, preferring the socially condemned cowherd Ranjha to the material security offered by marriage into the Khera clan. As she tells her relatively timid beloved: 'Dear Ranjha ... I refuse to accept Khaira as my husband and if he dares to come to me I will, with the help of Punj Peer [five saints], beat him up.'[60] A woman's revolt and subsequent union with her beloved, who always disguises his real self and remains a mystery, symbolizes the reality of temporal appearances as perceived in much of Punjabi Sufi and folk literature.

[59]Rafat (trs.), *Bulleh Shah*, pp. 176–7.
[60]Cited in Shafqat Tanveer Mirza, *Resistance Themes in Punjabi Literature*, Lahore: Sang-e-Meel Publications, 1992, p.16.

The defiance of authority, societal and political, is a theme which finds adequate amplification in all the regional literatures of the northwest. A corollary of the individual derived from the Islamic idea of an unmediated relationship between God and the believer, it has historically provided legitimacy to stolid regionally based resistance against would-be overlords irrespective of religious denomination. Portrayals of the folk heroes and heroines of Sind and the Punjab, even when permeated with Islamic idioms, are replete with dauntless acts of resistance against the political authority of a succession of Muslim dynasties centred around Delhi. This, more than any other single feature highlights the role of the region and, by implication, language in the self-definitions of identity on the part of variously situated Muslims.

Nowhere is this borne out more strikingly than in the North West Frontier region where Pathan tribesmen, jointly and severally, have historically resisted outside attempts at their subjugation. The poetry of Khushal Khan Khattak (1613–89) powerfully relates a Pathan's sense of self-pride and dogged attachment to unfettered autonomy. Composed at the time of Aurangzeb's incursions into the region, Khushal Khan's poetry soars freely against the backdrop of the lofty and indomitable mountainous peaks of the North West Frontier region:

Black is the Moghul's heart towards all us Pathans,
Well am I acquainted with each one of their designs.
. . .
Enough for a Pathan his rug and blanket;
No care is mine for couches or for cushions.
Freedom is mine, though plain and coarse my clothes;
Relieved now am I of velvet and of brocade;
A rass-built hut is now so dear to me,
I had rather be seated there than in Palaces of stone.

What though my food is only soup and curd?
With the wealth of the Moguls my chests are full.[61]

This rejection of Mughal grandeur and preference for the simple life of a Pathan was based on Khushal Khan's personal discomfiture at Aurangzeb's deception, a sovereign whose methods he wholeheartedly deplored and one whom he considered an unacceptable blot on the name of Islam.

Demonstrating the close nexus between a regional and linguistic identity, the poet laureate of the Pathans pays homage to his own language with more than a surfeit of hubris:

[61]C.E. Biddulph (ed.), *Afghan Poetry of the Seventeenth Century: Being Selections From the Poems of Khush Hal Khan Khatak*, Peshawar: Saeed Book Bank & Subscription Agency, 1983, pp. 63–4.

Persian poetry have I learnt, I have the taste for all;
Pushtoo poetry I prefer, each one thinks his own the best.
In measure, in meaning, in nicety, in metaphor,
Have I the Pushtoo language made to rival with the Persian.
The Pushtoo tongue is difficult, its measures hard to find;
. . .
Pearls of speech are they which I, Khush-hal have strung together;
Liars are all who say that such as I have written in Pushtoo,
There are any other such verses, or ever have been before.[62]

Yet Khushal Khan was perfectly comfortable with his other identities as a
Muslim of the Sunni Hanafi sect, a member of the Khattak tribe, and a Pathan
who unlike the Afridis, Mohmunds and Shinwaris had refused to be
browbeaten by the tyrannical Aurangzeb. He accepted the supremacy only of
the Creator and upheld all the basic tenets of Islam. In his later life he was
tormented by his lack of true religiosity and confessed:

No Jew or Infidel is there whose behaviour is so vile
As I know myself to have been in word and deed.
The Hindoo even rises at midnight for adoration,
Yet feebler am I than he in the practice of devotion.
With a thousand other thoughts in my heart I bend my knee in prayer:
All through my life it is thus my devotions have been said.
. . .
I have never cared for right or wrong so that it pleased me.
When have I had concern for the lawfulness of my food?
. . .
My nature is as that of the seventy-two heresies from the Faith,
Though in my professions I am of the band of the True Believers.
. . .
If in observance of rites consist true Muhammadanism,
Happy for me, for then perchance I am a good Mussulman.[63]

Like his counterparts in other regional narratives of identity, Khushal Khan
Khattak prized his own self-understanding and showed little patience for the
Islam preached by illiterate local mullahs:

I am a drinker of wine, why does the Priest quarrel with me?
Our natures are made by Fate, would that I could make his like mine![64]

A veritable icon in popular Pathan consciousness over the centuries, Khushal
Khan's lilting verses resound with a trenchant commentary on the ills besetting

[62]Ibid., pp. 76–7.
[63]Ibid., p. 72.
[64]Ibid., p. 81.

the tribal social order. He bemoans the infighting and betrayals which had enabled Aurangzeb to spread discord among the Pathans, who he believed were better than the Mughals in every respect except for the lack of the most elementary concord among them. This feeling of pre-eminence over others, including fellow Muslims, has always been part and parcel of the Pathan sense of identity. As the following *tappa*, one of the oldest forms of expression in Pathan society with the first line shorter than the second, puts it: 'Who will gain victory over us? We are Pukhtuns [Pathans] and we shall die in the love for Pukhto.'[65] A manifestation of the self-pride and honour, which along with the notions of protection and hospitality towards guests and revenge for all insults are among the principles of *Pukhtunwali* or the code of conduct underpinning Pathan tribal society, this exuberant assertion conveys the cultural ethos of a people who have defied external pressures more effectively than their own internal fissures. So strong is the competitive spirit among the Pathans that even the next of kin is deemed to be untrustworthy. Pukhtun women can be heard admonishing their sons not to lag behind their cousins. Together with proverbs like 'Every Pukhtun is a complete mound and there is no half a mound amongst the Pukhtuns', this attitude has bred an intense form of individual identity.[66] Yet it is one that coexists with a binding communitarian code, which, when it conflicts with Islamic strictures, invariably prevails.[67]

To furnish additional evidence based on other regions would be stretching the point without actually advancing the argument. Regional and linguistic identities have absorbed the Islamic impact to such an extent that they cannot simply be submerged in the dominant narrative of an inclusionary nationalism, whether of the Indian or the Muslim assortment. It is this remarkable capacity to influence as well as blend into multifarious regional settings which in large part explains Islam's appeal for Muslims of various class, regional, linguistic and sectarian denominations in the subcontinent quite as much as anywhere else in the world. But without denying the Islamic impact, it is necessary to give historical voice to these narratives which are frequently lost sight of in the historiography of the dominant discourse on Indian and Muslim nationalisms. The historical interactions of these narratives with the broader conceptions of an Indian and a Muslim 'nation' produced an array of weaves, each with its own specificity and subjectivity. An exploration of the relationship between Indian and Muslim nationalisms can be far more meaningful if one remains alert to the innumerable class, regional and linguistic sensibilities underlying them.

[65]Inamullah Jan, 'Pukhtunwali in Historical Perspective', unpublished doctoral dissertation, Quaid-i-Azam University, Islamabad, 1979, p.18.

[66]Ibid., p.79.

[67]For an anthropological study of the concept of *Pukhtunwali*, see Akbar S.Ahmad, *Millennium and Charisma Among Pathans: A Critical Essay in Social Anthropology*, London: Routledge, 1976.

MUSLIMS, THE IDEA OF INDIA AND THE REVOLT OF 1857

The idea of India or, more aptly, of Hind or Hindustan had an amorphous presence even in a period when references to one's *qaum* and *watan* did not fit neatly into the overarching mould of either a Muslim or an Indian nationalism. These were latter-day products of the creative imaginings which contributed to the construction of the dominant narrative discourses of both Muslim and Indian nationalism. Yet references to Hind or Hindustan in the poetry of Muslims in the first half of the nineteenth century cannot be dismissed merely on account of the teleological problems arising from treating poetic invocations of the *qaum* or the *watan* as the overture to Muslim or Indian nationalism. A careful location of the context in both spatial and temporal terms precludes the more unpardonable pitfalls of historical teleology.

There was as yet no obvious tension in an affinity with one's city, a region, Hind and a religiously informed cultural identity. This might seem surprising only if one mistakes the later politicization of identity, a result of the introduction of the electoral principle in India and the ensuing battle of communitarian-based popular discourses, for the projection of identity as a lived cultural experience. Even after the suppression of the 1857 revolt snuffed out the last remnants of Muslim sovereignty, it was more the loss of an established way of life than the political fact of foreign rule per se which seems to find expression in the poetic angst of a Ghalib.

For someone who both witnessed and recorded that watershed event in the history of Muslims in India, Ghalib's less-than-enthusiastic support for a Mughal empire reeling under mounting financial and political crises continues to rankle the nationalist mindset on both sides of the 1947 divide. A tribute to the unsurpassed niche Ghalib occupies in the literary heritage of the subcontinent, this urge to own and appropriate has been the wont of nationalist discourses, Indian and Muslim. While the former seeks to portray the rebellion of 1857 as the first war of Indian independence or a protonationalist uprising, the proponents of the latter have been no less impassioned about interpreting it as a *jihad* on the same lines as the so-called 'Wahabi' movement organized by Shah Abdul Aziz (1746–1824) and Sayyid Ahmad of Rai Bareilly.[68] One needs to step out of the nationalist moulds to gain a truer appreciation of how

[68]See K.M.Ashraf, 'Ahiya-i-Islam kai Hami aur 1857 ka Inqilab', in Ahmad Salim (ed.), *1857: Adab, Siyasat aur Muashira*, Lahore: Nigarshat, 1991. Those categorized as 'Wahabis' included the great Muslim reformer Sayyid Ahmad Khan and the poet Hakim Momin Khan Momin, not exactly men of the same ideological ilk. Indeed, the followers of Shah Waliullah, Shah Abdul Aziz and Sayyid Ahmad of Rai Bareilly after the 'Wahabi' trials made a submission to the colonial government pleading that they be referred to as the 'Ahl-i-Hadith'. A response to the official policy of weeding out Wahabis, this is reason enough not to use the term unthinkingly.

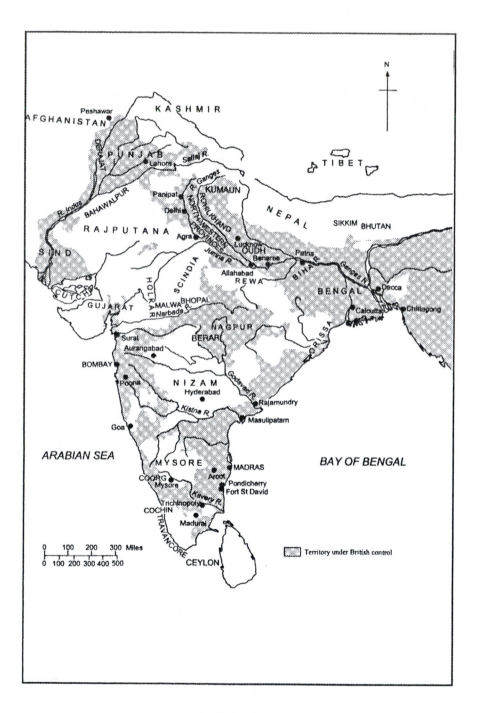

India in 1857

individuals as part of larger collectivities reacted to the outbreak of the military revolt. Discussions on the issue of rebellion and collaboration in 1857 have not allowed sufficient room for individual pragmatism when it has fallen short of the grander ideals of the 'nation'. Thus the discomfort with Ghalib's failure to support the rebels. But one has only to consider the attitude of Bahadur Shah Zafar, the last Mughal emperor who was more a poet than a statesman, to locate Ghalib in his proper context. It is an exercise that has to be undertaken in order to sift out the individual consciousness of a Muslim from the collective narratives of Indian or Islamic nationalism.

The supremo of Urdu lyrical poetry at its lilting best was no less pragmatic than countless others who saw no reason to perpetuate the puerile myth of Mughal sovereignty. As many found cause to rebel as chose not to. Among those who were reluctant supporters of the revolt was no less a person than the decrepit Bahadur Shah Zafar who was often scoffed at in his own palace and, even if loved, commanded more respect as a poet than a king of Hindustan.[69] As he himself acknowledged:

I am the light of no one's eye, nor the balm of anyone's heart,
One who couldn't come to anyone's aid, I am a mere handful of dust.[70]

In his first address to the rebels, the last remnant of the Mughal dynasty denied that he was a king. This was matched by a self-statement in which the emperor described himself as a *faqir*, a beggar unconcerned with fighting; a recluse who simply wanted to be left alone.[71] Sovereignty in any case had been lost a hundred years ago. Bahadur Shah Zafar recounted the circumstances which had led the Mughal court to hand over the administration of his empire to the English East India Company. Even while retaining its autonomy under the Maratha protectorate, the Mughal court found it impossible to run the royal kitchen, much less concern itself with the administration of an empire that was by now more a figment of the imagination.[72]

The English kept up the symbols and rituals of the ceremonial sovereignty of the Mughals. But this psychological trope did not prevent the governed from realising that the Mughal emperor was incapable of addressing, much less redressing, the causes of growing social turmoil and economic hardship in the country. Forced to live on a modest pension from the Company, the

[69]Burke and Quraishi, *Bahadur Shah*, p. 90.
[70]*Na kisi ki ankh ka noor hoon, na kisi kai dil ka karrar hoon*
Jo kisi kai kaam naa aa saakee, main wou aik mushtai qubaar hoon

نہ کسی کے آنکھ کا نور ہوں، نہ کسی کے دل کا قرار ہوں

جو کسی کے کام نہ آ سکے، میں وہ ایک مشتِ غبار ہوں۔

[71]*Taqazah*, Fortnightly Lahore, 1986, annual number on the 1857 revolt, pp. 25–6. The entire journal is authored by the editor, Payam Shahjahanpuri.
[72]Ibid., p. 26.

Mirza Asadullah Khan Ghalib
Courtesy: Nehru Memorial Museum and Library

last Mughal emperor had neither a fighting force at his disposal nor the political clout to command the allegiance of a restive populace. Ghalib had his hand on the popular pulse when he asserted that if this was the condition of kingly authority then why should every non-entity in Delhi not lord it over like a nawab.[73] After the outbreak of the revolt people in the street could be heard saying that the man whose head they put their shoes on would be king. The contempt for Bahadur Shah Zafar was powerfully articulated by Muhammad Bakht Khan, the Rohilla Afghan commander of the rebels from Awadh, who walked straight into the emperor's private chambers and declared: 'Old man, we have made you king'.[74] Ghalib conveyed the feeling more elegantly when he compared sovereignty to a cup of wine which constantly changed hands. It was not like the one reserved exclusively for Jamshaid, the Persian king who could look into his chalice and find out what was happening in the world.[75]

Yet while reflecting on the fleeting nature of sovereignty, Ghalib had no illusions about the definite changes which had come to beset his adopted city, Delhi, after the outbreak of the 1857 revolt. Likening its vanquished landscape to the lifeless void of the displaced soul, Ghalib in response to a letter enquiring about conditions in the city wrote:

Delhi's character was based on activities—the qila (fort), Chandni Chawk, the gathering of crowds every day at the Jamia Masjid, every week a trip to the Jamna bridge, every year the festival of flowers—these five things are no longer there. Then you tell me where is Delhi. Yes, there was a city of this name in Hind.[76]

Nor was Ghalib oblivious to the fate that had befallen Muslims in Delhi after the suppression of the revolt:

Now every English soldier that bears arms
Is sovereign, and free to work his will ....

[73] Badshahi ka jahan ye haal ho Ghalib! Toh phir
Kiun na Delhi main haar aik naa cheez nawabi karai

بادشاہی کا جہاں یہ حال ہو غالبؔ! تو پھر

کیوں نہ دِلّی میں ہر اک تا چِز قوابی کرے۔۔

(Ghalib, Nawa-i-Saroosh, p.1090.)
[74] Shahjahanpuri, Taqazah, p. 28 and Burke and Quraishi, Bahadur Shah, pp.149–50.
[75] Sultanate dast bey dast aiye hai
Jam-i-maih; khatm-i-Jamshaid nahin.

سلطنت دست بہ دست آئی ہے

جامؔ ہے، خاتم جمشید نہیں۔

(Ghalib, Nawa-i-Saroosh, p. 308.)
[76] Abbas, Urdu Main Qaumi Shairi, p. 89.

The city is athirst for Muslim blood
And every grain of dust must drink its fill ....[77]

Ghalib had been equally resentful of the Company's intrusive policies, especially the annexation of Awadh in 1856. Yet he could not bring himself to support the rebels. He instead inveighed against their excesses, deploring the spilling of innocent blood and the widespread loot and destruction. Part of the reason for Ghalib's ambivalence towards the revolt was based on his realization of the inherent weaknesses of the Mughals and the relative strengths of the English. As he rued in one of his Persian verses:

The Muslim never became a true ruler at any time—
when the magian went away from the wine house, the Christian grabbed it.[78]

After the revolt had been crushed, pragmatism demanded that he keep his fences mended with the new rulers. Yet the lure of official favours alone does not explain Ghalib's apparent complicity with the Company's administration during and after the revolt. The new cultural influences, especially the introduction of western science and technology undoubtedly excited his imagination. As he put it:

Faith holds me back while infidelity attracts me
The kaaba is behind me and the church ahead beckons me.[79]

From a man who proclaimed himself free of all religions and conventions, this was not an admission of his attraction to the Christain faith but a sign of his open-mindedness to what was new and as yet unknown. This did not ease the pain he felt at Delhi's predicament, and that of Muslims in particular, in the aftermath of the revolt. He was bewildered by the tactics of the new British administration:

Everyday in this city a new law is proclaimed
One just cannot understand what happens here.[80]

[77]Russell and Islam (eds), *Ghalib Life*, p.149.
[78]Cited in Annemarie Schimmel, *A Two-Colored Brocade: The Imagery of Persian Poetry*, Chapel Hill: University of North Carolina Press,1992, p. 119.
[79] *Iman mujhe roke hai joh kheenche hai mujhe kufr;*
Ka'ba mere peeche hai, kaleesa mere aage.

ايما ﺛے ﻟﮯ ﻋﮯ ﺣﮯ ٢ ٤ ﺣﮯ ﻋﮯ ٤ ﻙ
ﻙ ﻟﮯ ٤ ﻋﮯ ﻛﻴﺎ ﻟﮯ ٤ ﻟﮯ ﺁﮮ.

(Ghalib, *Nawa-i-Saroosh*, p. 662.)
[80]*Roz ise shahir main aik hukaam niya hota hai*
Kuch samajh main nahin atta hai kai kiya hota hai.

Unable to comprehend or condone many aspects of the new dispensation, Ghalib at the tail end of his life cuts a sorry figure given to woeful statements like:

He who lives on because he hopes to die
His hopelessness is something to be seen.[81]

The sense of hopelessness was to become a recurrent theme in much of the Urdu poetry and prose written by Muslims after the formal loss of sovereignty. There were Muslims voices other than Ghalib's who were given to perceiving the turn of events from a more communitarian point of view. Momin Khan Momin for instance responded to the 1857 revolt by urging Muslims to wage a *jihad* against the British as a religious duty. In the words of Maulvi Liaquat Ali Khan of Allahabad, one of the key players in the revolt who had rallied Muslim weavers in northern India against the English East India Company:

Fill Hind with Islam in such a way O Shah
That there be no voice other than 'Allah' 'Allah'.[82]

Yet the explicit use of religion in the Muslim call to arms was not without its limitations. Muslims were not alone in revolting against the Company. The importance of non-Muslim participation in the success of the rebellion militated against any attempt to couch the appeal in exclusively Muslim terms. Indeed, the famous Azimgarh proclamation of August 1857, which raised the standard of revolt, was addressed to both Muslims and Hindus. Moreover, the prospect of the restoration of the Shia state in Awadh put the idea of a religious *jihad* at a serious discount for many *maulvis* of the Sunni ilk.

In any case, the Muslim *ulema* of both the Sunni and Shia varieties were unable to agree whether the revolt was a *jihad*. A declaration of *jihad* would make it mandatory for all Muslims to participate in it as a religious duty. Pragmatism in many instances proved to be the better part of the Islamic valour of India's Muslims. The *fatwas* issued are a colourful medley of quite different points of views. In the opinion of some *ulema* there were no grounds for *jihad* so long as Muslims enjoyed religious freedom under Company raj. The leading Shia *alim* of Lucknow, Syed Muhammad, ruled out a *jihad* since nobody qualified as *imam* and went so far as to instruct his followers not to support the rebels. This earned him a pension from the British administration and is another illustration of the practical considerations which influenced

---

روز اس شہر میں اک حکم نیا ہوتا ہے

کچھ سمجھ میں نہیں آتا کہ کیا ہوتا ہے۔

(Ibid., p.1019.)
[81] Russell and Islam (eds), *Ghalib Life*, p. 223.
[82] Abbas, *Urdu Main Qaumi Shairi*, p. 87.

the posture of many Muslims during the course of the revolt. His counterparts among the Sunni *ulema* quibbled over the issue of whether there could be an *imam* who was not of the Quraish tribe. These issues were never resolved and must await fuller treatment in a subsequent chapter.

While Islamic sensibilities undoubtedly prompted some Muslims to join the rebellion, religious motivation alone cannot explain their response to the events of 1857. Depending on personal, local and regional circumstances, many joined to assist in what they saw as the final attempt to be rid of the *farangis* or foreigners whose presence had either eroded their social status or was steadily altering a familiar style of life. The confiscation of *jagirs* by the Company on a large scale in northern India and the subsequent tempering of this policy in the Punjab goes some way in explaining the different responses to the revolt in the two regions. A combination of material concerns and the appeal of Shah Abdul Aziz and Sayyid Ahmad of Rai Bareilly's 'Wahabi' teachings of Islam as well as the organizational networks created by their followers allowed for large-scale participation on the part of dispossessed Muslim *jagirdars* in the North Western Provinces and Bihar. The Muslims in the newly conquered territory of the Punjab had cause to welcome the revival of some of their religious practices proscribed by Ranjit Singh, to say nothing of the colonial state's relatively more moderate approach towards the landed gentry.

The uneven spread of the 1857 revolt, which for the most part was confined to northern and central India, is another reason to avoid a purely communitarian or nationalistic explanation for the motivation behind the events. A reading of the nascent Urdu press of the period, which played a vital part in disseminating the fires of discontent, certainly points to the portrayal of the uprising as an act of divine vengeance against the English:

He it is who gives greatness to the rulers of the world;
He truly is the Giver of royalty to emperors.

He can endow royal power on beggars,
He can give strength and power to the weak.

Strength can He confer on weaklings,
And the mighty He brings to utter ruin. [83]

While giving expression to the Muslim belief in the sovereignty of Allah and summoning divine will to the rebel's cause, care was taken not to play upon the internal divisions of India. Even the seemingly communitarian minded proprietor of the *Delhi Urdu Akhbar*, Maulvi Muhammad Baqar, the father of Muhammad Husain Azad who subsequently did much to promote the Urdu

[83]*Sadik-al-Akhbar*, Delhi, cited in Nadar Ali Khan, *A History of Urdu Journalism: 1822–1857*, Delhi: Idarah-i-Adabiyat-i-Delhi, 1991, p.129.

language, attacked the Christian infidels who were imposing their social customs on Indians. He was particularly concerned to counter the Company's manoeuvres to create splits along religious lines:

Now, brother countrymen and especially those who serve in the army, let us beware of these attempts to divide us—we are united as parts of a body are united. Let us exterminate these people who think we are not united. Let us wholeheartedly put ourselves to this endeavour, and let us sacrifice all our comforts in the task of liberating ourselves from fears (that we will be hurt by our own compatriots).

O brother Hindus and Muslims, we tell you again and again that all the worldly losses you suffer in your attempt to bring about the downfall of the enemies of the Faith is in fact your gain.

Worldly loss is nothing as this world is nothing. It is obligatory on the part of all Hindus and Muslims to regard divine favours as more important than human.[84]

These pious utterances in the name of a single country failed to stem the tide of betrayals which deflected the course of the revolt from its very inception. If the Company's strategy of exploiting religious divisions proved less than successful, propaganda on behalf of the rebels fared no better in piecing together a coherent patriotic front. In an atmosphere of anarchy, Indians fleeced and killed Indians, as they tried pressing home the advantage of the lawlessness created by the breakdown of English control and corresponding lack of organization on the part of the rebels. The *Delhi Urdu Akhbar* noted that not only outsiders but residents of the city themselves were indulging in plunder and violence. Far from demonstrating a communitarian, much less a patriotic or 'nationalistic' spirit, members of the upper classes expended their energies in intrigues and counter-intrigues while the lower castes and classes joined the fray with aplomb, looting arms and ammunition as well as items of daily necessity, with disastrous social consequences.[85]

All this does not lead to the conclusion that the experience of the rebellion was, everything said and done, an atomistic one or that it lacked unity and a measure of coordination among its diverse component units. But the disunities tendencies in the revolt against Company raj, and the petering out of the defiance of authority within the course of a year, suggests that specific acts of defiance and heroism cannot be attributed to religious or national zeal alone. The fact of a common enemy did not paper over the cracks in Indian society. As many Muslims and Hindus revolted against the company as collaborated with it. It was the specific local and regional social and political configurations which ferreted out the rebels from the collaborators.

This was consistent with the overall trend in subcontinental history in which the conflation of a multiple set of identities—class, religious, linguistic,

[84]Ibid., p.105.
[85]Ibid., p. 95.

regional or sectarian—in any given context did not add up in uncluttered fashion at an all-India level. Just as there were upper-and middle-class Hindus and Muslims in Bengal and Punjab who chose not to join hands with the rebels, there were their opposite numbers in northern and central India who reckoned otherwise. But even in regions not generally thought to have participated actively on the side of the rebels, the Punjab for one, there were men like Ahmad Khan Kharal of Jhamhara in the district of Toba Tek Singh who took up cudgels against colonial intrusions.[86] Hence, there can be no denying the multifaceted ways in which Indian society responded to the expansion of the Company's power through subsidiary alliances, wars and outright annexations. Since the process affected the regions and the individuals and the local communities forming them in different ways, the responses to the revolt of 1857 were far too specific, if not discordant, to justify harmonizing them into the dominant melodies of either an Indian or Muslim nationalism.

To be sure, the pro-rebel Urdu press sought to give a semblance of uniformity to the outrage felt by Hindustani sepoys and the localized patriotisms of the inhabitants of Delhi and Lucknow; but the limited circulation of these papers together with the gagging of the vernacular press by the English authorities neutralized the efforts to stretch the spatial scales of loyalty on the part of a heterogeneous populace to encompass the whole of Hindustan or a religious community, whether Muslim or Hindu. According to one estimate the total circulation of vernacular newspapers in the North Western Provinces and Bengal at the time of the revolt was in the order of 5166 while in the Punjab it was no more than 500. With the total publication of vernacular newspapers falling below the 6000 mark, it is reasonably safe to conclude that their influence was at best restricted to a populace of about a hundred thousand or so. Many Urdu newspapers in north-western India were forced to close down during the revolt. In 1853 there had been thirty-five Urdu papers with a publication of 2216. By 1858 there were a dozen Urdu newspapers, half of which had gone into business in the aftermath of the revolt, with a total circulation of only 3223.[87] These statistics suggest that the power of the printed word, though by no means non-existent, had yet to be deployed effectively on the side of a disparate population to square individual, local or regional affiliations with more broadly based communitarian or national ones in order to counter the alien presence.

Such associations as linked an individual's specific circumstances with the larger interests of a 'nation', Muslim or Indian, had not yet found that clear articulation which could vindicate approaches to the revolt of 1857 in most retrospectively constructed nationalist histories. The collapse of the rebellion

[86]Mirza, *Resistance Themes in Punjabi Literature*, pp.102–5.
[87]Abdul Salam Khurshid, *Sahafat: Pakistan wa Hind mein*, Lahore: Shaiq Press, 1963, pp. 157,178.

saw a heightened expression of precisely those communitarian or national characteristics that it has been the purpose here to dissect and reassess. It is necessary to consider why an otherwise divergent, though by no means indifferent, response to the last puff of resistance put up by a perishing Mughal empire inspired such distinct and competing narratives of nationalism, Muslim and Indian.[88]

THE LOSS OF SOVEREIGNTY AND THE REFORMULATION OF IDENTITY

The role of the colonial state in giving impetus to the construction of collective discourses, whether Hindu, Muslim or Indian, is an undeniable one. Queen Victoria's proclamation of August 1858 promising benevolent rule and non-interference in the domain of religion and, by implication, culture was a major landmark in the architecture ushering in new strategies of political survival by dispossessed ruling elites and an army of retainers, both Muslim and Hindu. Along with the stringent curbs on political activity following the quashing of the rebellion, the proclamation was a sleight of hand by which the colonial masters chose to tolerate some debate and dissent as long as these related to the religious and cultural concerns of Indians. This apparent attempt at denuding religion and culture of politics was fraught with consequences for an Indian society experiencing unprecedented changes.

In delimiting a formal sphere of politics the British colonial state aimed at reconsolidating its authority and placing the networks of social collaboration and control on a firmer footing. The thinking which guided the policy marking the transition from Company to Crown raj amounted to creating a wholly artificial separation between a 'political' public and a 'religious' and 'culturally' informed private sphere. In practice this did not preclude the colonial state from adopting policies which indirectly, if not always directly, affected the cultural lifestyles and religious practices of a subject population. Nor did it prevent the overlapping of the two spheres in so far as the expression of religious and cultural concerns was deemed permissible in an otherwise carefully monitored public arena.

The expressed disinterest of the colonial state in the domain of religion had less to do with the 'secular' ideal than with the imperatives of rule. Needing to consolidate authority, the early colonial state selectively appropriated available symbols of cultural legitimacy. The purported separation of a religiously informed domestic sphere and a 'secular' colonial public domain

[88]There were other nationalisms in the making as well, Sikh for instance. See Richard G. Fox, *Lions of the Punjab: Culture in the Making*, Berkeley: University of California Press, 1985 and Harjot Oberoi, *The Construction of Religious Boundaries: Culture, Identity and Diversity in the Sikh Tradition*, Delhi: Oxford University Press, 1994.

was more fictional than real. There was constant involvement of the colonial state in precisely those religious and cultural spheres towards which its 'secular' creed purportedly demanded a studied non-interference. Far from eliminating politics from the realms of religion and culture, the colonial state did much to bring these spheres closer than ever and reshape them in the process. Its own official discourse was tainted by the influence of missionary elements, many of whom had links with like-minded Englishmen occupying positions within the colonial state.[89] The nexus between supposedly autonomous missionary activities and colonial policy came to the fore with decisive effects in the later part of the nineteenth century.

Some of the strands of missionary thinking that influenced colonial perceptions and discourse on Indian society were visible in the Anglo-Indian press even before the suppression of the revolt. The Muslims were identified as the principal instigators of the rebellion in a feeble attempt at reigniting the lost glory of the Mughal empire. For a province which contributed precious little to the revolt, the Punjab was the site of a volley of inflammatory writings against Muslims by the *Lahore Chronicle*.[90] At the height of the rebellion the paper proposed razing Delhi to the ground as retribution for the wrongs perpetrated by rebel forces against European women and children. On 8 July 1857 it alleged that the Muslims were the main culprits and should be treated mercilessly until they changed their ways. In its opinion, Muslims were bound by the teachings of the Quran to be rebellious and the paper hinted that Islam should not be tolerated by the authorities. On 26 September 1857 an editorial declared the policy of religious toleration to be a failure and argued that the 'natives' were perfectly aware that as Christians the English could not separate their institutions, culture, education and literature from religion. The only policy to adopt in India was a 'Christian policy' under the purview of a Christian army which should impose a tax of Rs 20 to Rs 50 on all Bengali and north-western Muslims between the ages of 18 and 60.[91]

Along with its sister paper *The Punjabi*,[92] the *Lahore Chronicle* blamed Muslims for inducing Hindus to rebel. The most prudent policy now was to debar Muslims from government service and suspend expenditure on their education. These views from the Punjab were shared by Anglo-Indian newspapers in other regions. An article in the *Bengal Harkaru* demanded the

[89]See Emmett Davis, *Press and Politics in British Western Punjab, 1836–1947*, Delhi: Academic Publications, 1983.

[90]The paper was started by Munshi Mohammad Azeem, the father of Syed Mohammad Latif, the famous colonial historian of Lahore and the Punjab. By the time of the rebellion, however, the management of the paper was in the hands of an English editorial board.

[91]Khurshid, *Sahafat: Pakistan wa Hind mein*, pp.161–4.

[92]This too had been started by Munshi Mohammad Azeem but was under the control of an English editor.

death of one thousand rebels for each dead Englishman, woman and child while the *Bombay Times* called for the spilling of blood to avenge their deaths.[93] The Delhi-based Anglo-Indian press was no less impassioned in questioning the capacity of Muslims to be loyal to a non-Muslim government. Bahadur Shah Zafar's trial merely accentuated the belief in a Muslim conspiracy to set alight the torches of insurrection. The government prosecutor maintained that the Mughal court had intrigued with the Urdu press to stir up the revolt and made much of the extra-territorial sympathies of certain rebel leaders with the Iranian monarch.[94]

Sayyid Ahmad Khan's essay in 1859, on *The Causes of the Indian Revolt*,[95] aimed at dispelling the notion of Muslim culpability in the insurgency and the rash of allegations against the Muslims' inherent disloyalty to the raj. An employee of the colonial state stationed in Bijnore during the revolt, Sayyid Ahmad had demonstrated his loyalty to the raj by going out of his way to save the lives of a number of English women and children. This did not deter him from blaming the defunct Company's administration for inciting Indians to revolt. In Sayyid Ahmad's view it was the insularity of the rulers from the ruled, and the resultant insensitivity of government policy towards the cultural mores and temperament of Indians, that precipitated the rebellion. A general perception of the government's intention to interfere in the religious and cultural rituals of Indians had brought matters to a head. He made special mention of a letter circulated by a missionary from Calcutta to Indian personnel of government urging them to convert to Christianity. The company's policy of seizing *jagirs* was cited as another major factor prompting the revolt.

Sayyid Ahmad's defence of the Muslim role in the uprising merits special attention. It made few concessions to the heterogeneities of Muslims in India and went so far as to define 'Muslims' as those who had adopted India as their motherland. Giving short shrift to the historical spread of Islam in India, Sayyid Ahmad's thesis on the Muslim *qaum* was to become one of the dominant idioms of the narratives of Muslim identity after the loss of formal sovereignty. It was encouraged and disseminated by a rapidly expanding English and vernacular press and publications market where the initial battles of identity were fought out between those who in the colonial vocabulary happened to belong to any one of India's major religious denominations.

In making religion the primary factor in the definition of 'community', the British laid the basis for a discourse that claimed to represent the interests of the loosely conceived social categories identified by the colonial state. While

[93]In this instance the editor was dismissed by the board of editors.
[94]Khurshid, *Sahafat: Pakistan wa Hind mein*, p.169.
[95]In Hafeez Malik (ed.), *Political Profile of Sir Sayyid Ahmad Khan: A Documentary Record*, Islamabad: Institute of Islamic History, Culture and Civilization, 1982.

finding its most acute manifestation in the print media, the process would not have gained quite the momentum it did were it not for a decision taken in 1853 at the time of the first-ever census in the North Western Provinces. In a complete departure from the policy adopted in the home country to explicitly play down the religious factor, the Company's census enumerators simply did a head count of 'Hindus' and 'Muslims' without actually bothering to spell out what these categories in fact constituted. Although the decennial censuses did not begin until 1871, the provincial censuses in the North Western Provinces, followed by the Punjab in 1855 and elsewhere during the 1860s, cast the die making religion the central factor superceding all forms of social relationships. The census reports reformalized the meaning of religion to mean a community comprising individuals bound by a formal definition and accorded characteristics based on the data garnered by enumerators working on questionable assumptions. They 'created a sense of community more detailed and more exact than any existing prior to the creation of the census'.[96] This set many would-be representatives of these largely theoretical communities at one anothers' throats. For instance, the introduction of caste and occupation in 1872 was not intended to supply information on social and economic realities but to throw the religious dimension into fuller relief. It did so by giving powerful stimulus to the propagation of a discourse in the name of Hindus, some of whom understandably saw this as designed to weaken their numerical strength.

The decision to use religion as the basis for not only enumerating but also governing a complex and highly differentiated society like India was a negation of the strategy of steering politics away from the domains of religion and culture. While religion as social demarcator was intrinsic to the ordering of the colonial public, religion as faith was presumed to be a private matter subject to certain community-defined laws. Consequently, despite the colonial state's proclaimed policy of non-interference in matters to do with the religion and culture of its subjects, these were precisely the concerns which instead of being relegated to the private sphere had to be bandied about in the public arena for political reasons by various social groupings in order to compete more effectively for government patronage. The Indian response, as exemplified in Sayyid Ahmad's exposition on the causes of the revolt, was to try and extract maximum mileage from the colonial perception of religion as the primary factor dominating all aspects of indigenous society. His notion of Muslims as 'foreign' was to dovetail neatly with the view promoted in the Hindu press by an array of individuals otherwise holding different opinions. It was the dialectic between the construction of 'Muslims' by the British as well as the Hindu press and their own self-projections which accounted for

[96]Kenneth W. Jones, 'Religious Identity and the Indian Census', in N. Gerald Barrier (ed.), *The Census in British India: New Perspectives*, New Delhi: Manohar, 1991, pp. 78–84.

the cut and thrust of a selectively and consciously constructed communitarian discourse on Muslim identity in the late nineteenth century.

Like all mothers of invention, the changing colonial context has to serve as the primary backdrop in any study of the discourse on Muslim identity in the late-nineteenth-century. It was the British construction of 'community' out of religious groupings shot through with class, regional, linguistic and sectarian, to say nothing of individual, differentiations which explains the motivation behind the construction of mainly communitarian-based narratives in the late-nineteenth-century. This does not amount to handing over all the levers of the public debate between Indians to the colonial state. A measure of autonomy has to be conceded to many public spirited men, Muslim and Hindu, who in their different ways tried to put stuffing into the legal carcasses of the religious communities with which colonialism had chosen to hallow India's social landscape. Yet the collective impulse guiding the contribution of an individual Muslim like Sayyid Ahmad Khan did not always manage to obfuscate the continuing role of personal circumstance and self-interest. Spatial and temporal location in the colonial context is quite as important for the communitarian strains of the discourse on Muslim identity as for its individual mutations. The Muslim as individual even behind the veil of a communitarian narrative is never completely out of sight. Nor is there a complete absence of references to the individual in the collective discourse of the Muslims after 1858. It was the way in which the balance between the individual and the community came to be struck that had the more profound impact on the reformulations of Muslim identity after the formal loss of sovereignty.

The individual in the singular could not expect rich pickings in a colonial system geared to dishing out rewards, and by the way also punishments, to collectivities aggregated on the basis of religious definition. By the same token, internal differentiations within a community identified by the bond of religion had to be underplayed, if not altogether ignored, in the hope of influencing colonial policy. Whatever the significance of religion as faith for the colonial subjects, it was religion as social demarcator which was most relevant in petitioning on behalf of the community. So the apparent denial of autonomy to the individual in the communitarian discourse of a religious collectivity such as the Muslims was a product of tactical and strategic choices rather than an accurate reflection of the realities on the ground. The wide currency gained by the colonial state's main policy idioms essentialized the religiously informed identities of a highly differentiated subject population now called upon to conceive of itself as members of communities bound by doctrinal creeds. While demarcating the main lines of divisions between 'Muslims' and 'Hindus', the colonial state's social engineering paid little heed to the internal differentiations of class, regional, linguistic or sectarian factors. Effectively stripped of other signifiers of social relationships, individuals were left to give voice to their subjectivity through the medium of collective discourses which in order to achieve their objectives had to be fashioned in a manner that made few concessions to diversities within the community.

It was the privileging of the religious factor in the definition of identity which had the most decisive bearing on the projection of consciousness by individuals variously situated within the colonial system. It was a projection in which religiously informed cultural differences were deployed for political purposes even when they did not add up neatly and unproblematically to inject substance into the formal categories of communities designated by the colonial masters as distinctive social entities. The effacing of the distinction between religion and culture on the one hand and politics on the other followed naturally. This strategic essentializing of the religiously informed cultural identities of Muslims, or for that matter Hindus, as promoted in their respective communitarian discourses, however, did not vitiate the internal differences at the level of practical politics. The 'inevitability' of a Muslim identity with the 'impossibility' of a supra-regional and specifically Muslim politics at the subcontinental level captures the paradox of essentialized categories made to function as existential realities. It is a paradox more amenable to perusal through an exploration of Muslim identity both as a discursive formation and a lived social and political experience beginning in the late nineteenth century.

Chapter 2

Forging a Muslim Community:
Press, Poetry and Politics in the
Late Nineteenth Century

A communitarian Muslim identity was coming to acquire some of
its main idioms during the transition from Company to Crown
raj. There had been a sense of religiously informed cultural differences
in the subcontinent long before the encounter with western colonialism. This
had found expression in literature as well as architecture and inspired a genre
of magnificent miniature paintings. Even in their social and political
performances, differences along lines of religion were negotiable and
amenable to accommodations. C.A. Bayly in his pioneering study on colonial
adaptations of the communication networks of late-eighteenth and
nineteenth-century northern India notes that pre-colonial 'social enquiry and
representation were never communal in the sense that they saw India as a
field of conflict of two irreconcilable faiths'. Indo-Muslim 'governing principles
were not "secular" in the sense that religion was seen as a matter of political
indifference'.[1] The colonial state's avowed policy of neutrality based on
political indifference towards religion was easier to proclaim than translate
into practice. Needing to appropriate the existing symbols of cultural
legitimacy, religion could never be a matter of political indifference for the
British. Intrinsic to the search for collaborators and the organization of social
control, religion in the service of the colonial state's political purposes had
qualitatively different consequences than those in the preceding centuries.

British perceptions of Indian society as an aggregation of religious communities gave impetus to representations of identity in idioms emphasizing
differences, not commonalities, between those who among other things

[1]C.A. Bayly, *Empire and Information: Intelligence Gathering and Social Communication
in India, 1780–1870*, Cambridge: Cambridge University Press, 1996, p. 27.

happened to be Muslim, Hindu or Sikh.[2] British social engineering on its own cannot explain the intensity of the process marking Indian attempts to deploy the categories of the colonial state to Indian social and political advantage. Indian subjectivity, whether interpreted in its individual or communitarian colours, constituted an important dimension in the discourse on identity in the late nineteenth century.

Frequently accorded the pejorative label of 'communalism' in an attempt to distinguish it from the lauded sentiment of 'nationalism', this was a subjectivity which drew upon religion as a signifier of cultural difference. If religion as faith was a matter of individual disposition, religion in the service of communitarian culture was as yet a stretch removed from its subsequent uses as political ideology. The erroneous conflation of the two in most nationalist reconstructions, Indian and Pakistani, has obfuscated the analytical distinction between identity as culture and identity as politics in the history of Muslims in the subcontinent. It is significant that the politically loaded term 'communalism' did not command the centrestage of the public discourse on Muslim identity until after the formal introduction in 1909 of separate or 'communal' electorates at all levels of representation. The process by which the designation of a mode of representation was transformed into an overarching concept will unfold in subsequent chapters. For now it is necessary to probe the narrative inflections and substantive meanings of the discourse on communitarian identities among Indians without the teleological and essentializing tendencies retrospectively conferred upon them by the twentieth-century concept of 'communalism' . Freed of the totalizing power of 'communalism', one can better assess how assertions of Muslim identity, both as an expression of cultural difference and a strategy of politics, were articulated in the second half of the nineteenth-century. This in turn allows for more sensitivity to the emotive nuances underlying the dialogue between the votaries of the 'Muslim' and the 'Hindu' communities than permitted by the practitioners of 'communal' and 'national' histories tracing the mythic genealogy of nation–states.

It has required a curious inversion of logic to examine processes of social differentiation set in motion by the policies of the colonial state through the dichotomy of 'communalism' and 'nationalism'. British principles of enumerating Indian society created notions of 'majority' and 'minority'

[2]British misperceptions of Indian society as demarcated by distinctive communities rather than as a compound of individuals has been the subject of considerable scholarly comment. (See, for instance, Hardy, *The Muslims of British India* and David Lelyveld, *Aligarh's First Generation: Muslim Solidarity in British India*, Princeton: Princeton University Press, 1977, reprint 1991, Lahore: Book Traders.) Looking to identify and, therefore, better control its subjects, a modernizing colonial state constructed categories which, as its own officials were the first to admit, far from accurately reflected social realities in the different regions.

communities drawing equally upon a privileging of the religious distinction. Those who found themselves lumped into the category of 'majority' were no less determined to push the claims of the 'Hindu community' than the advocates of the 'minority Muslim community'. The dialogue between the self-styled representatives of these two communities, though carried out in a regulated colonial public arena, had a greater bearing on the dynamics of differential identity formation than has been acknowledged by the paragons of composite culture and assimilation.

The loss of spiritual meanings and perceived threats to sacred space after the imposition of colonial rule meant that cultural values had to be considerably redefined. Nowhere was the process of the dislocated self seeking to recover lost ground through narratives of religiously defined cultural identities more intense than with respect to the women's question. In a mirror image of the Bengali *bhadralok* formulation of the 'Indian nation',[3] women as a central component in the construction of a new identity for Muslim professional classes bore the brunt of the recasting of the private domain. It was precisely because the public and the private domains had not been rent in twain by the separation of personal laws of religious communities from the civil and the criminal codes of the colonial state that their constant overlapping in the nineteenth century so deeply affected the women's question. More a vanishing point than the subject of an *ashraf* discourse on *qaum*, women in the new miniatures were ornamental objects of domestic space while the residential architecture and the colonial city constituted the landscape of the discourse and politics of these men. The sense of loss to the spiritual self, following the commodification of physical space, made women a key object in the construction of a communitarian identity. It was a quest so thoroughly imbricated in the project of negotiating physical space under colonial modernity that the spiritual or feminine dimensions of Islam rarely if ever managed to triumph. It was the middle- and upper-class women who provided the material for the stereoscopic perspectives.[4] *Ajlaf* or lower class women formed no part of *ashraf* conceptions of Muslim interest.

In a gendered reading of the Muslim communitarian narrative, one scholar has likened *ashraf* representations of their identity as a *qaum* to the vanquished and seduced woman.[5] But the image of the vanquished woman bewailing

[3]Partha Chatterjee, *The Nation and Its Fragments: Colonial and Postcolonial Histories*, Princeton: Princeton University Press and Delhi: Oxford University Press, 1993, chapters six and seven.

[4]An allusion to the shift in perspective in Mughal miniature painting in the sixteenth century due to European influences in which all the objects were hierarchically organized and subordinated to a single vanishing point. (See Rogers, *Mughal Miniatures*, p. 70.)

[5]Faisal Devji, 'Muslim Nationalism: Founding Identity in Colonial India', unpublished doctoral dissertation, University of Chicago, 1993, chapter one. An

her way into seducing the colonial authorities has to be placed in its proper perspective. Not all men from the *ashraf* classes could situate themselves in relation to the colonial state quite as effectively as Sayyid Ahmad Khan. But an English education and western dress did not mean shedding the patriarchal moorings of Muslim society. The perceived ease with which certain *sharif* Muslims had adopted English mannerisms generated ferocious attacks on the Aligarh school. Vilified as *necheris* or naturalists, and often as materialists, these profane men who had accepted alien lifestyles symbolized the loss of cultural and spiritual space in the wake of colonial rule. It followed that their ideas should not be allowed to affect the domestic space of the family. So if the *qaum* was indeed in the image of the woman, that relationship was an inherently problematic one.

It was the reversal of fortunes with the loss of Mughal sovereignty that most agitated the salaried and professional Muslims in north India and their counterparts among the Hindu *bhadralok* in Bengal. What for one became an endless *marsiya* or lament,[6] though for some also the *bang-i-dara* or the call of a moving Muslim caravan, was an opportunity for the other to situate itself pivotally vis-a-vis the British. In so far as the colonial state was one of the primary points of reference for communitarian discourses, Muslim or Hindu, an expanding print and publications market served as the main fount of its construction and dissemination. It was the dialectic between colonialism and the self-perceptions of Indians seeking to project their religious identity for political purposes through print technology which injected a potent layer of ideological differentiations into subcontinental psyches. In the late nineteenth century the notion of Muslims as a distinct community with identifiable interests was propagated vigorously by the Urdu vernacular press and a matching publications market concentrated mainly, but not exclusively, in the North Western Provinces and the Punjab. An active as well as a reactive process, the public debate on 'Muslim interests' was shaped by the twin imperatives of influencing colonial policy and combating the claims put forward on behalf of the 'Hindu' community.

The discourse on 'Muslim interests' was for the most part the handiwork of members of the north-Indian *ashraf* classes smarting under the loss of sovereignty on the one hand, and the onset of western colonialism and 'modernity' on the other. Written in the same accessible 'new' Urdu–Persian script used by substantial sections of the Hindu press in these provinces, the dissemination of the discourse was facilitated by an exponential growth of the print market after the relaxation of government controls and the spread of the colonial

---

engaging theme, it echoes Ashis Nandy's arguments in *The Intimate Enemy: The Loss and Recovery of Self Under Colonialism*, Delhi: Oxford University Press, 1983.

[6]For an analysis of the changes in the genre of the *marsiya* with the onset of colonialism, see Devji, 'Muslim Nationalism', chapter one.

educational system. What gave the discourse on identity a powerful inspirational quality and also a much wider audience was the recourse made to Urdu poetry, by far the most popular form of expression in northern India and also the Punjab. Oral recitations of Urdu poetry at *mushairas*, attended by people in thousands, symbolizing the interaction between private and public space, was a facet of everyday life in northern India and, to a lesser extent, in the Punjab.[7] Both entertaining and evocative, Urdu poetry's capacity to influence a predominantly unlettered population cannot be overemphasized. Not all of the poetry had to be published to reach a receptive audience, more steeped in the oral than the literate tradition represented by the press. Once heard, the favourite poems were recorded in memory, frequently quoted and even rendered as songs. A conscious recasting of poetry for communitarian purposes in the late nineteenth century had an electrifying effect on psyches—be it the literate or the illiterate, the aristocratic or the lowly, in urban or rural areas.

By comparison, the high Islamic arts of calligraphy and miniature painting were slower to respond to the communitarian spirit, dependent as they were on the economies of patronage. The suspension of royal patronage hit the architectural landscape even more decisively. Despite sponsoring Indo-Saracenic styles of architecture, colonial officials mostly deprecated Indian forms, preferring English styles. A desire to emulate the masters among the moneyed classes, landlords in particular, squeezed out many artisans, forcing others to reconfigure their styles to fit the patron's bill. Only the trading and moneylending classes retained a preference for indigenous forms and styles.[8] These were reflected in the residential quarters and bazaars of colonial cities and towns, which were contested spaces in the conflicting narratives of identity. The eclectic though painstakingly decorative motifs and styles on the facades of some of these buildings, capturing the visual dimensions of indigenous space, is the contribution of those urban craftsmen who responded to the invasion of physical space and modernity by giving fantastical release to traditional skills while experimenting with new forms. A changing architectural landscape gave spatial and visual expression to an inner upheaval that found its most potent voice in poetry and prose as a direct result of the new print technologies.

In contrast to Anderson's focus on the newspaper and the novel in the formation of national identity,[9] the historical and cultural context of colonial north India calls for a close examination of the press and poetry in illuminating

---

[7] Despite the colonial disdain for the regional vernacular, the spiritually rich and evocative Punjabi *kafis*, and *bhajans* and *qawalis* were more popular than Urdu poetry among members of all religious communities.

[8] J.L. Kipling, 'Indian Architecture of Today', *Journal of Indian Art*, vol.1, no. 3, p. 1; cited in Kamal Khan Mumtaz, *Architecture in Pakistan*, London: Butterworth Architecture (second edition), 1989, pp. 109–10.

[9] Benedict Anderson, *Imagined Communities: Reflections on the Origin and Spread of Nationalim*, London: Verso, 1991. The novel's role in imagining the nation recurs in a

the dynamics of identity construction. The poetic dimension interwoven with the outpourings of a burgeoning press lends both special texture and greater social depth to the stirrings that animated notions of a distinctive Muslim identity. Together with the contents of the vernacular press in the North Western Provinces and the Punjab, Urdu poetry is an excellent source from where to begin exploring the early narratives on Muslimness. Its ability to transcend the barriers of class and illiteracy enables a more balanced analysis of identity formation than one exclusively focusing on the role of the press. The creative urge of poetry gave it relatively more autonomy from colonial manipulations than the public arena of the press ruled and regulated by governmental strictures. Both mediums shaped and in turn were reshaped by a range of contentious issues. These had far-reaching political implications for relations between the two main religious communities in India.

COLONIALISM AND PRINT IN NORTH-WESTERN INDIA

Prior to the arrival of new print technologies and the modern press, gathering information in the different parts of the empire had required an elaborate system of reporting. Once collected, the reports were despatched through *harkaras* or runners, stationed at suitable distances. *Waqia nagari* or the recording of events became a refined art under Mughal patronage.[10] A *waqia navis*, or the teller of the event, also known as *akhbar navis*, was a trusted employee of the imperial state.[11] Privately owned newspapers were relatively unknown, although a few had appeared by the time of the revolt of 1857. But there had been a transformation around 1830, as Bayly has shown, from an embodied knowledge of an earlier era to the institutionalized information order of the late Company state. Quite apart from the qualitative change in the nature of the state's information-gathering system, an Indian critical 'ecumene' is seen to have flourished in north India before the advent of a colonial public sphere and prefigured public debates which were given a further impetus by print capitalism only in the mid-nineteenth century. In what is a critique of the technological determinism in Anderson's emphasis

---

number of works on South Asian history and literature. (See for example Homi Bhabha [ed.], *Nation and Narration*, London and New York: Routledge, 1990; Partha Chatterjee, *Nationalist Thought in the Colonial World: A Derivative Discourse*, London: Zed Press, 1986 and 1993, especially chapter three, and Sara Suleri, *The Rhetoric of English India*, Chicago: Chicago University Press, 1992.)

[10]See Abd al-Salam Khurshid, *Newsletters in the Orient, With Special Reference to the Indo-Pakistan Sub-continent*, Assen: Van Gorcum, 1956.

[11]A *waqia nigar* was primarily concerned with revenue matters while a *waqia navis* dealt with other issues. Secret agents, *swanih nigars* or *khufia navis*, also wrote reports. (Bayly, *Empire and Information*, p. 15.)

on print, Bayly emphasizes the social formations and linkages of knowledge communities instead of the technical aspects of transmission.[12]

While there certainly existed a vibrant pre-colonial public sphere in which ideas about good governance were eagerly debated, the growth of a print and publications market from the mid-nineteenth century did herald a measure of qualitative change.[13] The single most significant effect of the technologies of print in conjunction with the new idioms of colonial modernity was the shift from *waqia navisi*, depicting human actions in discontinuous space, to *majmua hessiyat* or representations of the collective quality of events based on an artificial perspective of homogeneity and connectedness.[14] This changing form of reporting and information dissemination, personalized and yet depersonalized in its posturing, gave the press and publications market an altogether different role in identity construction during the second half of the nineteenth century. Together with the imperatives of the colonial state, these provided the setting for feverish narratives of identity where individual intent was couched in the language of collective purpose.

Over the years the press in India has attracted considerable scholarly attention. Some of the earlier works focused on the ways in which western print technology helped introduce modern ideas to the different regions of the subcontinent.[15] Recently there has been increasing interest in print journalism as a vital two-way channel for the exchange of information between the colonial state and Indian society. Anderson's espousal of the centrality of print in the formation of nationalisms has generated renewed concern with the role of local and regional presses in fashioning the public discourse in colonial India. The general theory about print capitalism, however, often misses the historical specificities and contingencies that influenced discourses on identity. In particular, it does not sufficiently problematize the relationship between colonialism and assertions of cultural difference in contexts where there were conflicting definitions of national identity.

This section investigates the extent of the colonial role in constructing the public arena of print in two regions of north India. It starts with the premise that the character of the vernacular press in the North Western Provinces and the Punjab had much to do with the location of these regions in the British colonial system. Unlike Bengal which came within the ambit of the Company as early as 1757, the North Western Provinces went through a much slower

[12]Ibid., pp. 341–2.

[13]For an analysis of the impact of print on the fashioning of Muslim identity, see Francis Robinson, 'Technology and Religious Change: Islam and the Impact of Print', *Modern Asian Studies*, 27, 1 (1993), pp. 229–51 (henceforth *MAS*).

[14]Devji, 'Muslim Nationalism', p. 22.

[15]For instance, Davis, *Press and Politics in British Western Punjab, 1836–1947* and Uma Dasgupta, *Rise of an Indian Public: The Impact of Official Policy, 1870–1880*, Calcutta: Rddhi, 1977.

process of absorption, completed only in 1849 with the conquest of the Punjab. The heartland of a fading Mughal imperial system, the experience of the Company state in administering the territories of the North Western Provinces served as the more immediate point of reference than Bengal for many of the subsequent policies adopted in the Punjab. Some broad commonalities in the colonial administration of these two regions notwithstanding, the Punjab occupied a distinctive position in the British scheme for the containment of India. On balance the advantages enjoyed by the Punjab as the last feather to adorn the imperial cap, and the region which displayed least resistance during the revolt of 1857, were vitiated by the sterner measures adopted for its governance. Evident in several spheres of colonial policy, the relative differences between the North Western Provinces and the Punjab were apparent even in the status of the vernacular press.

The quality and the spread of the vernacular press in both regions owed much to the levels of patronage extended by the colonial government. Despite the existence of Urdu newspapers in the Punjab since the 1850s, the provincial press suffered from overregulation and lack of governmental support for over a decade after the suppression of the revolt. During the late 1860s and early 1870s the Punjab government's policy towards the vernacular press was criticised for its 'want of liberality', compared with the one regulating the publication and circulation of newspapers in the North Western Provinces.[16] This was attributed to the Punjab government's direct involvement in the publication of some of the newspapers. The government of the North Western Provinces purchased privately owned papers which in its estimation were of better quality. Of the papers published in the Punjab independently of government patronage several were considered to be equal in quality to those subsidized in the North Western Provinces. The main difference was that government patronage in the form of direct purchases of newspaper stocks in the North Western Provinces had helped create a taste for light literature and the development of a much larger distribution network. Consequently, 'instead of useless talk ... newspapers may now be seen read in village *chaupals* and eagerly devoured by the rustics, who crowd to hear them and often undertake a journey of three or four *kos* for the purpose'.[17]

Another reason why less success attended the journalistic efforts of vernacular newspapers in the Punjab was the more restricted use of Urdu in that province. The switch from Persian to Urdu as the official language of the courts and the medium of instruction in schools was too new to create a receptive audience for Urdu newspapers among a predominantly Punjabi-speaking populace. With literacy rates in 1881 at a paltry 6 per cent for men and a miserable 0.1 per cent

[16]*Nujm-ul-Akhbar*, Meerut, 31 March 1869, *Selections from Vernacular Newspapers Published in Punjab, North Western Provinces, Awadh and the Central Provinces* (henceforth *Selections* followed by IOL serial number and page), L/R/5/46, IOL, p. 156.
[17]*Delhi Society Journal*, May 1872, *Selections*, L/R/5/49, IOL, p. 421.

for women, the Punjab was not the most propitious ground for the advent of a print revolution in Urdu. Together with the stringency of government controls on the Punjab press, these social impediments account for the initially smaller newspaper market in the province.

In the early 1850s the vernacular press in the North Western Provinces had been seen to be 'utterly valueless' as a medium of communication between the rulers and the ruled and in no way representative of public opinion. This was attributed to the 'extreme caution' exercised by editors when dealing with issues of a political nature. With few exceptions, newspapers were devoted to occult science, religion, 'bazaar gossip of the day', news extracted from English journals and the occasional juicy news item on 'the birth of some monstrosity in human form, or the sanctity of some fuqeer'.[18] The situation in the Punjab was even less hopeful. Before 1857 most papers were started by men from outside the province who had been associated in one way or the other with the colonial administration. The only vernacular paper considered of merit was the Lahore-based Urdu bi-weekly *Kohinoor* established in 1850 by Munshi Harsukh Rai with the aid of the Punjab board of administration. As in the case of the North Western Provinces, it was the publication of books by the Kohinoor press which kept the paper financially afloat even after it had outpaced others with a circulation of 227. Urdu print journalism in the Punjab at the time was also hampered by the high operational costs incurred in procuring the services of efficient pressmen and writers from other regions, the North Western Provinces and Bengal in particular.[19]

Contempt for the vernacular newspaper media only strengthened the colonial resolve to direct and control it more closely. In the aftermath of the 1857 revolt, officials acknowledged the greater difficulties involved in controlling the publications market than print journalism. The 'thinking Indian public' was 'a potent minority' largely 'hostile to European Science and Literature, as well as to Europeans and their Government'. There was every reason to fear the political effects on such minds of 'treasonable or foolish publications'; a mere 'falsehood or suggestion ... instilled into the minds of a few individuals' could 'raise a storm or an uneasiness throughout the length and breadth of the land'. This was a clarion call for a more interventionary role by the colonial state in controlling information passing into the print and publications market. But matters could not be allowed to rest there; the content of literary publications was desperately in need of reform. The official mind revealed its true missionary shades when it scorned the 'immoral ... legends, traditions and doctrines' of Hinduism and the 'sensual

---

[18]Notes on Native Presses in the North Western Provinces for the years 1850 and 1851, *Selections From the Records of the Government, North Western Provinces*, V/23/118, IOL, pp. 263, 274, 292 (henceforth *Records* followed by place of publication, IOL serial number and page).

[19]Report on the Native Presses for the year 1853, *Records*, V/23/126, IOL, p. 145.

aspirations which Mahomedanism delights in cherishing'. It was indeed a matter of deep 'sorrow that Native Indian social life, even after 100 years of British efforts to establish decency, is about as prolific in wantonly degrading every-day circumstances, as the most prurient imagination could put in print'.[20]

It followed that Indian society needed more active instruction in not just how to think but also in what to think about. The coincidence of the official mind echoing the views of missionary establishments, already in the business of translating the New Testament into regional languages to hasten processes of conversion, had significant non-coincidental results. In a major administrative decision the press was placed under the foster care of the education department. By influencing the course of indigenous education and actively monitoring the print media the colonial state could try and inculcate western ideas into Indian minds and guide them away from indisciplined fantasies bordering on the sinful. More creditable was the hope of encouraging 'the free and energetic spirit of inquiry' which made the English press such an 'honoured institution'.[21] No less impressive was the desire to nurture Indian authors, recognized as being in frightfully short supply, through the formation of literary societies which 'might encourage both originality and refinement of language'.[22]

These declarations of intent were matched by the mushrooming of literary associations along the lines of the Royal Asiatic Society. Most of these included colonial officials among their members, underlining the active support and patronage of the government. Among the purposes of these associations was to assist the government's education policy by carrying out the translation of western works into Indian vernaculars. Some of the initial debates on the question of language between Indians and Englishmen took place in such associations. There were frequent differences of opinion with some preferring the transmission of western knowledge through translation and others advocating a more direct policy aimed at extending education in English. But even the issue of translation was mired in controversy over the appropriate language to adopt. Sayyid Ahmad Khan, who set up a translation society in Ghazipur, favoured the inclusion of Arabic as one of the languages of translation since Muslim scholars and doctors well versed in it 'sternly hate[d], to read a subject in "Urdu"'. This was contrary to the colonial state's education policy of promoting Urdu as the language of communication between the rulers and the ruled. The director of public instruction in the North Western Provinces roundly attacked the suggestion, seeing it as evidence of Sayyid

[20]Note on the Native Periodicals and Presses for the year 1858, *Records*, V/23/120, IOL, p. 43.

[21]Ibid., p. 44 and Report on the Native Presses for the year 1862, *Records*, V/23/121, IOL, p. 2.

[22]Report on the Native Presses for the year 1862, *Records*, V/23/121, IOL, p. 8.

Ahmad's own class interests and not those of the community he claimed to represent.[23]

Similar debates and disagreements marked the activities of literary societies in the Punjab where between 1849 and 1884 a number of cultural associations were set up. Initially Muslim and Hindu members of the Anjuman-i-Punjab joined hands in opposing the policy of government schools of imparting English education alone. But unity among members of the Punjabi elite soon fell to pieces over issues of representation in educational institutions and government service. By the 1870s Muslims and Hindus preferred forming their own cultural associations to advance the respective interests of their communities in a clear imitation of their opposite numbers in the North Western Provinces. The Anjuman-i-Himayat-i-Islam founded in 1866 by middle-class Muslims and the more socially conservative Anjuman-i-Islami established in 1869 to protect religious endowments were closely linked to the activities of Sayyid Ahmad Khan in the North Western Provinces. These *anjumans* publicized their educational preferences through literary journals, underscoring how well they were aware of the power of literacy and the press.[24]

These developments had received considerable fillip from the Punjab government's policy in the 1860s of employing men from the North Western Provinces like Muhammad Husain Azad and Altaf Hussain Hali as a part of the effort to systematize the print industry and the related spheres of education and literature. Azad and Hali did much to promote the Urdu language in the Punjab through the press and publications market while at the same time selectively introducing English literary conventions into their own literature. Exposed to the English language late in life, both Azad and Hali remained faithful to the classical traditions of Urdu literature in their prose and poetry. The result was the construction and dissemination of a simpler form of Urdu which considerably aided the subsequent popularity of vernacular journalism and poetry in the Punjab. This would have been impossible without the support of the Punjab government, and the personal interest of individuals like Colonel W.R.M. Holroyd and Dr G.W. Leitner, in making translations of western works available in Urdu. The provision of Urdu translations ensured easier access to and incorporation of western literary ideas and styles into the vernacular.

Between 1857 and 1885, newspapers in the Urdu–Persian script maintained a clear lead over those in Devanagari in both the North Western Provinces and the Punjab. About thirty Urdu papers were started in Delhi, seventeen from Lucknow, a smaller number in Agra, Moradabad and Meerut while

[23]Report on the Native Presses for the year 1863, ibid., p. 14.

[24]Khurshid lists nearly two dozen newspapers started by different *anjumans* all over India during the nineteenth century. See his *Sahafat: Pakistan wa Hind mein*, pp. 267–9.

Lahore became home to seven. In 1870 there were thirty-three vernacular newspapers in the North Western Provinces with a total circulation of 7509; some 2109 copies were bought by the government and 360 by European officials in their individual capacity. A preponderance of these were in Urdu, indicating that the readers of newspapers consisted mainly of officials or inhabitants of large towns. Yet the almost equal number of Urdu and Hindi language publications pointed to the growing popularity of the Devanagari character in the North Western Provinces where it was taught in the vernacular schools.[25] There were fewer facilities for the teaching of Hindi in the Punjab, and none at all for instruction in the regional vernacular. The print and publications market here was dominated by Urdu which remained the preferred language of newspapers, though they lagged well behind their counterparts in the North Western Provinces both in numbers and circulation.

By the late 1870s the colonial state had managed to create and systematize the infrastructure for communication through the print media in both the North Western Provinces and the Punjab. Its championing of Urdu had triggered a free flow of journalists and men of letters between the two regions with visible effects not only on the style but also the content of the writings appearing in the press. These similarities cannot be seen to have effaced the differences which continued to distinguish one newspaper from another, far less override the regional variations in the character of the two vernacular presses. So there is reason to pause and consider before interpreting the existence of an infrastructure for communication in print as the precursor to the propagation of internally coherent communitarian discourses on the part of either Muslims or Hindus.

Press and Poetry as Markers of Identity

The conceptual dichotomy between 'communalism' and 'nationalism' has given licence to approaches which teleologically link spatially and temporally specific evidence to these all-encompassing notions. Gyanendra Pandey has stressed the shared genealogy of the ideologies of 'nationalism' and 'communalism' in the context of late-nineteenth and early-twentieth-century colonial India.[26] However, his single-minded determination to portray 'communalism' as a 'construction' of colonial discourse entails missing out much of the context and texture of the communitarian narratives of this period. These were no doubt fashioned in complex interaction with colonial initiatives but retained subjectivity and autonomy, not to mention regional specificity.

[25]Report on the Native Presses for the year 1870, *Records*, V/23/129, IOL, pp. 237, 315.

[26]Gyanendra Pandey, *The Construction of Communalism in Colonial North India*, Delhi: Oxford University Press, 1990.

A scrutiny of the contents of the vernacular press interspersed with popular Urdu poetry composed in the late nineteenth century makes plain their very vital contribution in the construction of narratives of identity. They also expose the misplaced assumptions of 'communal' and 'national' histories once they are stripped of their sweeping concepts to accommodate the historical specificities of subcontinental societies in their various regional settings.

A study of the vernacular press and Urdu poetry in the construction of narratives on Muslim identity focusing on the North Western Provinces, including Awadh, and the Punjab, rather than Bengal or even Hyderabad Deccan can be justified on many grounds. It was areas constituting the North Western Provinces and Awadh, later designated as the United Provinces, which have laid the most convincing claims to fathering the 'two-nation' theory. The Punjab has its own counter-claims. After all, it was the Punjab whose complex religio-political map ultimately shaped the territorial expression of the Muslim 'nation' in the form of truncated statehood. The contents of the press in both regions and also Urdu poetry, with certain qualifications with respect to the Punjab where its popularity was confined to urban centres, are of the essence in weighing the relative merits of these competing claims. Heightening tensions along lines of religious community in the North Western Provinces and the Punjab during the period under review constitute another reason for considering the contribution of these two mediums in the construction of a Muslim identity.

The approach is predicated on the view that differential or assimilative processes of identity formation discovered by those charting the antecedents of 'communalism' or 'nationalism' have not paid sufficient heed to human agency, whether in its individual or collective manifestations, or for that matter to historical indeterminacy in presuming a linear path in the development of narratives on communitarian interests. Instead of simply linking the narratives on identity in a linear and teleological manner, this analysis aims at teasing out the dominant idioms of a spatially and temporally located dialogue between members of different religious communities on the one hand, and the colonial state on the other. In contrast to the imaginative sweeps of Urdu poetry, the vernacular press in the North Western Provinces and the Punjab gave ample voice to individual, class and regional biases even while articulating the interests of communities that were conceptually envisaged on an all-India scale.

British officials observed that Urdu papers edited by Muslims in the North Western Provinces generally 'exhibit[ed] more freedom of expression than others'. This had less to do with Muslim interests as such but was a product of stiff competition in a profession which by Indian standards at best promised an unstable career. Most of the individuals, Muslim and Hindu, who went into the newspaper business did so with a 'view of gaining personal importance and influence, rather than as political or party organs'. Newspapers operated as 'vehicles of personal abuse and threatening expressions' to browbeat their targets into 'becoming subscribers by way of saving their reputation'.[27] This was why colonial officials saw no reason to treat the vernacular press as 'a guide to public opinion, supposing public opinion to exist at all'. It was apparent that the traits of any particular newspaper depended 'entirely on the character of the Editor' and 'the necessities of circumstance and position which shape[d] his interest'.[28]

Even discounting the supercilious arrogance in the colonial view, there is ample evidence that personal ambitions and rivalries continued to scar the face of Urdu journalism in the North Western Provinces throughout the final decades of the nineteenth century. Yet it was the Punjab which took pride of place in the sheer ferocity of personal and business rivalries in the newspaper industry. In some instances newspapers in the Punjab went into business solely for the purpose of doing down a rival. For instance, the proprietor of the *Kohinoor*, Harsukh Rai, expended most of his energies in the 1850s outwitting his business rival Diwan Chand Lal, the owner of the Sialkot paper *Chasma-i-Faiz*.[29] The *Awadh Punch* started in 1877 by Munshi Muhammad Sajjad Husain brought men like Sayyid Akbar Husain Allahabadi (1846–1921) to notoriety and did much to imbue wit and humour into Urdu journalism. But it also did considerable damage to the standards of decency in the vernacular press. As many as forty different papers were started to reproduce and market the entertaining style of the *Awadh Punch*. Following its example with lesser literary prowess in their hands, editors of Punch-style papers engaged in the indecent art of running down opponents in a crass and vulgar manner. The names of the papers speak for themselves. *Sheikh Chili*, invoking the name of the dreamer whose dreams came to nought, made its debut from Sialkot while Riaz Khairabadi's *Fitna* appeared from Delhi. In Lahore, *Tees Maar Khan*, a reference to a paper tiger pretending to be a killer of thirty men, and *Shareer*, which literally means naughty, appeared in 1886 and 1887 respectively. *Chalta Purza*, meaning a busybody, from Delhi was not a bad competitor as far as ingenuity of names is concerned. These were joined in 1886 by the colourfully named Lahore paper *Mullah Dopiaza*, a reference to a popular folk-tale. Started by Muharram Ali Chishti, the influential editor of *Rafiq-i-Hind*, this was intended as a personal organ for blistering attacks on his widening range of opponents.

The continued salience of the individual in the medium which did most to propagate the discourse on identity in its communitarian vein is worth underlining. Indeed, it is impossible to explore the narrative of Muslim identity in the late nineteenth century without reference to a Sayyid Ahmad Khan,

[27] Report on the Native Presses for the year 1862, *Records*, V/23/121, IOL, p. 4.
[28] Report on the Native Presses for the year1863, ibid., pp. 12–13.
[29] Khurshid, *Sahafat: Pakistan wa Hind mein*, pp. 114, 122.

an Akbar Allahabadi, a Shibli Numani (1857–1914) and many more of their stature. So the appearance of a communitarian narrative in itself cannot be seen to have occasioned the erasure of the Muslim as individual. The role of individuals, holding widely different opinions, in the construction of the collective narrative of Muslim identity gave it far greater variety, and also choice, than has been recognized in the ongoing tussle between the inclusionary claims of the proponents of a Muslim cultural nationalism and the exclusionary rejections of secular Indian nationalism. There was much scope for disagreement and a willingness on the part of Muslims to question and resist rather than comply and conform with the consensus of the community, or the *ijma* as it is known in Islamic parlance.

By an unfortunate confluence of logically questionable assumptions, the legitimizing ideals of Islamic solidarity and the normative requirement of subordinating individual will to the *ijma* have been seen as sufficient to transform a Muslim's sense of distinctiveness from non-believers into an affiliation with an essentialized religious community of all-India proportions. On this flawed reading 'communal consciousness' forms an intrinsic part of the Muslim socio-religious and political worldview.[30] Based on a rationalization of normative Islamic discourse, such an interpretation fails to make an analytical distinction between a cultural identity informed by religion and the actual politics of Muslim identity in the subcontinent. One has only to scan the pages of the Urdu press in the late nineteenth century to see that there was no agreement among Muslims as to who could represent, far less arrive at, the consensus of the community. Sectarian divisions splitting the ranks of Indian Muslims made it impossible for any one religious point of view to gain ascendancy in the community. Class was another factor militating against any attempt to give a singular voice to the Muslims of India. Muslims of various classes and sects interpreted the tenets of Islam differently at the level of ideas as well as of practice. It is extraordinary, but revealing, that a decidedly elitist discourse has come to be seen as not only representative of the sentiments of all Indian Muslims but also their 'communal consciousness'. Open to wide and conflicting interpretations along sectarian, class and ideological lines, the normative discourse of Islam was never the only guide to Muslim perceptions of identity or, for that matter, the practice of their politics. This can be made light of only if the strategic essentializing of religious community is deemed more important than its utility as a point of reference for the assertion of cultural difference. Concentrating on the Islamic dimensions of the discourse on Muslim identity, as if these are unproblematically singular in meaning, ignores the spatial and temporal aspects of historical change that shaped the emerging contradictions and contestations within the community of Islam in India.

[30]See Farzana Sheikh, *Community and Consensus in Islam: Muslim Representation in Colonial India, 1860–1947*, Cambridge: Cambridge University Press, 1989.

The historical focus has to be on the context of late-nineteenth-century colonial India, not the presumption of a consensus derived from the normative discourse of Islam, if one is to unravel the many contending threads in the narrative of Muslim identity. Whatever their own opinions on the matter, and they were neither coherent nor unified, colonial policy together with the perceptions of the 'majority' community advanced in the public arena through newsprint as well as religious and literary publications bundled Muslims into an undifferentiated and essentialized category defined by the criterion of religion alone. For Muslim *ashraf* classes just discovering the value of numbers in the contest to safeguard special interests, it made sense to let external constructions of their identity subsume the manifold divisions within the community of Islam in India. Yet, instead of remaining passive recipients of outside stimuli, the architects of the discourse on Muslim identity, severally and jointly, sought to outdo one another in laying claim to the leadership of the community whose existence had been acknowledged both by the colonial state and members of other religious denominations.

Muslim as Rebel, Muslim as Category

The broad contours of the dialogue between the north-Indian Muslim elite and the colonial state on the one hand, and the Hindu press on the other, were outlined soon after the formal cessation of hostilities in 1858. Muslims were by no means alone in facing the brunt of British wrath in the first flush of victory over the rebels. Many were blown off with cannon in a ruthless demonstration of the imperial will to rule. But the depiction of Muslims as the instigators of the rebellion and the selective action against those living in Delhi created a powerful impression of the uneasy coexistence of Indian Islam with British colonialism. Altaf Hussain Hali, who was to become the leading poet of a Muslim communitarian identity, spoke more as a patriot of Delhi than as a member of a religious community when he rued the destruction of his beloved city by yet another set of invaders:

Sometimes Turanis looted homes
At others Duranis stole the wealth
Sometimes Nadar slaughtered the people
At others Mahmud made them slaves
Finally the game was won
By a refined nation of the west.[31]

[31] *Kabhi Turanioon ne ghar luta*
Kabhi Duranioon ne zar luta
Kabhi Nadar ne qatal-i-am kiya
Kabhi Mahmud ne ghulam kiya
Sab se akhir me lai ghi bazi
Aik shaista qaum maghrib ki.

Muhammad Husain Azad, who like Hali also went on to find employment in the colonial administration, contrasted the darkness of an enslaved Hindustan with the refulgence of a victorious England.

Such innocuous sentimentality was quite in contrast to the vitriolic writings of the Anglo-Indian press, determined to show up the Muslims as irremediably disloyal to the Crown. This prompted the governor-general Mayo to depute W.W. Hunter to conduct an enquiry into whether Indian Muslims were bound by their religion to rebel against the Queen. Published in 1871, Hunter's *The Indian Musalmans*, using Bengal as the point of reference, examined evidence presented to the courts set up in the 1860s to try some of the principal actors in the so-called Wahabi insurgency. While denying that Islamic doctrine propelled Muslims to rebel against a non-Muslim ruler, Hunter believed the community in India contained 'fanatical' elements who unless checked could stoke the fires of discontent among their ignorant co-religionists to launch a religious crusade. More weighty for the future course of colonial policy was Hunter's opinion that Muslims, a 'race ruined under British rule', harboured 'intense feelings of nationality' and were prone to giving periodic expression of this in 'warlike enterprise'.[32]

Hunter made clear that his arguments applied only to Bengal and 'not ... all the Muhammadans of India'.[33] Yet his portrayal of the dismal condition of Bengali Muslims gave Muslim elites of northern India a pretext to promote their own specific class and regional interests. Reactions to Hunter's book among the north-Indian Muslim *ashraf* classes were spearheaded by Sayyid Ahmad Khan who published a long essay in response. It was addressed as much to a section of the Hindu press as to the colonial authorities. Mayo's assassination in 1872 by Sher Ali, who claimed he had acted on God's order, was seized upon to target the entire community. The *Benares Akhbar*, started by Raja Shiva Prasad in the Nagari script, saw the incident as proof that Muslims were 'wicked and ill-natured' and would requite leniency and kindness with 'evil'. It was the Muslims who had instigated the disturbances of 1857. 'If Hindus at all took part with them in the affray, it was only as applauders or actors in a theatre'. This was because Hinduism, unlike Islam, did not permit murder and bloodshed of any sort.[34]

کبھی تورانیوں نے گھر لوٹا، کبھی دُرانیوں نے زر لوٹا

کبھی نادر نے قتلِ عام کیا، کبھی محمود نے غلام کیا

سب سے آخر میں لے گئی بازی

ایک شائستہ قومِ مغرب کی۔

(Abbas, *Urdu Main Qaumi Shairi*, p. 134.)

[32]W.W. Hunter, *The Indian Musalmans*, first published in 1871 (new edition), Delhi: Indological Book House, 1969, pp. 143–4.

[33]Ibid., p. 149.

[34]*Benares Akhbar*, 15 February 1872, *Selections*, L/R/5/49, IOL, pp. 123–4.

The *Lawrence Gazette* imputed the assassination to a custom among Afghans who in ill-health or difficulty vowed to 'sacrifice the life of a *kafir*' upon recovery. While it admitted that with the exception of the Afghans no other inter-denominational sects in Islam engaged in the custom, this was just the sort of argument which ended up tarring the entire community with the stray act of an individual by speciously equating specific cultural practices with Islamic religious doctrine.[35]

A strident medley of charges portrayed Muslims as bigots who were temperamentally incapable of receiving new ideas, steeped as they were in 'superstition and prejudice ... from their very boyhood'.[36] The *Benares Akhbar* regretted that 'a residence of 2,000 years in India [sic]' had not succeeded in 'divest[ing] Mahomedans of that prejudice and unkindness' which were 'a bar to all fellowship between the two races'.[37] A common reference to the extra-territorial loyalties of India's Muslims, this evoked anger as well as awe among the Hindu press. The *Almora Akhbar* marvelled at the fact that Muslims from all walks of life, including misers, were generously donating to the relief fund set up for Turkey which was at war with Russia. It observed that the 'identity of religion' was the 'only conceivable cause of the sympathy' between the Muslims of India and Turkey and regretted that no such commonality of feeling existed among Hindus due to internal religious differences.[38]

A few years later the relatively temperate Lahore-based Urdu bi-weekly *Akhbar-i-Am*, edited by Mukhund Ram, disapprovingly cited a pamphlet published by Babu Harish Chandra of Benares accusing Muslims of deliberately wounding Hindu sentiments by publicly slaughtering kine. This outrageous practice had been going on ever since Muslims 'set their thorny foot on this holy land'. Even the British were partial towards Muslims on this matter due to the fear of adverse reactions in the Islamic world. Unlike Muslims who could go to Turkey, Persia, Arabia or Afghanistan, Hindus had 'no other country' in which they could 'seek shelter'. Centuries of 'slavery' had made the Hindus 'docile', 'idle' and disunited while Muslims were 'unruly', warlike and 'united'.[39]

The Vexed Question of Loyalty

The perception of Muslims as more united than the Hindus is a clue of the highest importance in decoding the motivations governing the construction of the discourse on majoritarianism, both in its communitarian and nationalist dimensions. But it was the neat dovetailing of this view with colonial perceptions which lent substance to the idea of Muslims as a

[35]*Lawrence Gazette*, Meerut, 8 March 1872, ibid., p. 152.
[36]*Majma-ul-Bahrain*, Ludhiana, 14 October 1871, *Selections*, L/R/5/48, IOL, p. 626.
[37]*Benares Akhbar*, 30 April 1874, *Selections*, L/R/5/51, IOL, p. 179.
[38]*Almora Akhbar*, 15 July 1877, *Selections*, L/R/5/54, IOL, p. 495.
[39]*Akhbar-i-Am*, 17 December 1881, *Selections*, L/R/5/58, IOL, pp. 747–8.

community with a common set of interests. External depictions of Muslims as a community united by religion offered an opening to those hoping to represent the special interests which the British believed existed and sections of the Hindu press, for purposes of their own, saw no reason to deny. That the opportunity nevertheless produced an internally discordant discourse on Muslim identity underscores the gap between epistemological certitudes and the existential fluidities relating to the community of Islam in India.

Among the many claimants to the leadership of India's heterogeneous Muslims was Sayyid Ahmad Khan who took it upon himself to shepherd a straying flock of co-religionists into greener pastures within the colonial system. While the domain of education concentrated most of his energies, he did not fail to manipulate the print media to articulate a conception of Muslimness consistent with the colonial state's epistemology of communitarianism. The *Aligarh Institute Gazette* which he had started in 1866 became the mainspring for the dissemination of ideas about a Muslim community that was both Islamic and Indian. By 1876 the paper was jubilantly reporting the changing spirit of the times. Prejudices and superstitions were giving way to 'national patriotism and friendly feelings'. Sunnis and Shias had buried their differences and were at one in their support for Turkey. Muslims had every reason to 'congratulate themselves' as the 'feeling of unity of nation and religion now animates the two great divisions of Islam in matters which concern their common interests'.[40] It may have been easier for Muslims to rise above their internal differences on matters concerning co-religionists in Turkey or Persia than to practice unity in religion within India. Remarking on the implications of a declaration of *jihad* by the Sheikhul Islam of Constantinople a few months later, the *Aligarh Institute Gazette* thought it unlikely that Indian Muslims would rush to do battle with infidels. At most they would spread their prayer mats and earnestly urge Allah to come to the assistance of Islam. After all, even the most bigoted Muslim could not deny that 'peace and security ... under British rule' though not 'free from faults' was 'not to be found in any Muhammadan kingdom on earth'.[41]

An enunciation of universal Muslim brotherhood qualified by the boons bestowed by British rule in India gives a measure of the problems in equating epistemological suppositions with existential realities. While Muslims identified with their co-religionists the world over, they were firmly situated in India where it was British rule and not the temporal and spiritual authority of the Ottoman Khilafat which was the salient reality. Sayyid Ahmad Khan, along with poets like Hali and Azad, repeatedly had to take up cudgels against any attempt to confuse the identity of religion with the identity of country. The two were different but not mutually irreconcilable.

In 1874 Hali in his poem 'Hubb-i-Watan', or love of the homeland, wrote

[40] *Aligarh Institute Gazette*, 1 December 1876, *Selections*, L/R/5/53, IOL, p. 706.
[41] *Aligarh Institute Gazette*, 19 June 1877, *Selections*, L/R/5/54, IOL, p. 424.

Sayyid Ahmad Khan
Courtesy: Nehru Memorial Museum and Library

feelingly about the need for a patriotism that was more substantive than a mere attachment to country. Devoid of any sympathy for one's compatriots, such love for the country was nothing short of selfishness. A true patriot was one who regarded all the inhabitants of India, whether Muslim, Hindu, Buddhist, Brahmo Samaj, Shia, Sunni or any other inter-denominational sect as one:

If you want your country's well being
Don't look upon any compatriot as a stranger.[42]

And yet in India there were rifts among scholars, Hindu *pandits* and doctors of medicine; each and everyone had a separate agenda.[43] In a poem also entitled 'Hubb-i-Watan', Muhammad Husain Azad berated his fellow countrymen for paying lip service to a patriotism that was narrow-minded in the extreme. He was troubled by the refusal of many north-Indian Muslim youth to leave the cities of their birth to take up employment in other parts of India. Azad could find no true patriot willing to work towards extricating the *watan* from foreign rule. Indians would do well to take a leaf out of the notebook of the English doctor who upon saving the life of one of the last scions of the Mughal empire asked for no personal reward except the grant of trading facilities for the English.[44]

In 1878 Sayyid Ahmad Khan objected strongly to Lord Northbrook's suggestion that Muslims were 'disloyal subjects of the Crown'. If Indian Muslims disliked British rule, 'a very vague expression' with 'no distinct meaning', neither did they like the rule of other western powers, any Muslim country or even of their erstwhile sovereigns. Dissatisfaction with British rule undoubtedly existed among 'a class of persons', not all of whom were Muslims. But it had nothing to do with 'religious prejudices' and could be 'ascribed to our own incapacity' as well as 'the carelessness of European officers'. Northbrook would have been 'nearer the mark' if he had said that 'no nation on the face of the earth likes subjection to ... foreign rule'. Muslims knew from their religious canons that there was virtue in loyalty and obedience to the government of the time; they could always perform *hijrat* or migrate if life under any political dispensation became unpalatable.[45]

---

[42]*Tum aghar chahtay ho mulk ki kher*
Na kise hum watan ko samjho ghyr.

تم اگر چاہتے ہو ملک کی خیر
نہ کسی ہم وطن کو سمجھو غیر۔

(Altaf Hussain Hali, 'Hubb-i-Watan' in *Jawahar-i-Hali*, Lahore: Karavan Adab, 1989, compiled by Iftikhar Ahmed Siddiqui, p. 204.)

[43]Ibid., p. 205.

[44]Abbas, *Urdu Main Qaumi Shairi*, pp. 124–6.

[45]*Aligarh Institute Gazette*, 31 August 1878, *Selections*, L/R/5/55, IOL, pp. 769–74.

The notion of Muslim disloyalty to the Crown remained a favourite punching bag for Hindu and Christian missionary newspapers alike. Quite as much as Sayyid Ahmad Khan, many Hindu editors in the North Western Provinces and the Punjab were past masters in protestations of loyalty to the raj. In the opinion of the Aligarh paper *Bharat Bandhu*, the Hindu community had taken a turn for the better with the change in political sovereignty. In the previous regime *'our* property and lives were not safe'; 'Hindus were made Musalmans by force'; but now *'we* enjoy perfect security of life and property' as well as 'full religious liberty'.[46] Hailing the arrival of British raj in India as freedom from tyrannical Muslim rule was a powerful idiom in the construction of the early narratives of Hindu identity. The attractions of declaring Muslims disloyal subjects of the British for those authoring the narrative of Hindu identity were, for the most part, more material than cultural or religious in nature.

Intended by sections of the Hindu owned and managed press to tarnish the standing of the Muslim community in British eyes, the charge of disloyalty was used by missionary newspapers like the American Presbyterian Mission's Ludhiana-based *Nur-i-Afshan* to assert the superiority of Christianity over Islam. Equally keen to lock horns with the followers of Hinduism, this Punjab-based paper infused a good deal of bitterness into the vernacular press comment on religion. In 1879 it smugly reported that Muslims neither made 'good rulers nor good citizens' since the Quran did not teach them 'humility, but pride, self-conceit, and love of lust'. There was no code of morality in the Muslim scripture comparable to the ten commandments. Instead the Quran enjoined Muslims to 'carry on religious wars against infidels, to rob and kill them' and, most shockingly, to 'seize their wives'. Their only hope for atonement lay in adopting the Bible whose doctrines would make them 'good administrators and rulers'.[47] Such writings provoked furious rebuttals from the Muslim press, embittering the dialogue between the crusaders of Christianity and Islam. The triangular debate of Christian missionaries with the stalwarts of Islam, and also Hinduism, imparted an acerbic tone to the press in the Punjab, seriously upsetting the delicate matrix of social and political accommodations in the province.

Attributing a religious impulse to a range of postures adopted by Muslims of diverse ideological leanings eroded the distinction between assertions of cultural difference and the politics of communitarianism. An essentializing tendency impatient of nuance, this was deployed in its hackneyed constructions by the missionary and the Hindu press for quite different reasons. For the Muslims, it affixed an externally conceived dimension to

[46]*Bharat Bandhu*, Aligarh Hindi–English weekly, 9 June 1879, *Selections*, L/R/5/56, IOL, p. 460 (my emphasis).
[47]*Nur-i-Afshan*, Ludhiana, 1 May 1879, ibid., p. 350.

their identity which, while seemingly consistent with the normative ideals of Islam, was in contrast to the differential dynamics within the community. Even the most explicitly communitarian narratives of Muslim identity could not deny the multifarious divisions that prevented the faithful from unitedly shouldering the burdens imposed by the ignominy of servitude under foreign rule.

The appearance of Hali's magnum opus, *Musaddas-i-Hali* in 1879, was on the face of it a crowning achievement of Sayyid Ahmad Khan's school in deploying the poetic medium to proclaim a distinctive Muslim cultural identity. A rousing message to his co-religionists to shake off the slumber into which they had fallen, the poem was a stinging critique of an Indian Muslim community that had lost its moorings due to educational backwardness, internal jealousies, religious bigotry, aristocratic avarice and cultural decadence. Having lost sovereignty, wealth, intellect and self-respect, Muslims existed by virtue of their religion alone.[48] Like many of the north-Indian *ashraf* classes, Hali too considered Muslims to be the descendants of foreign conquerors. But the solution he proposed for the Muslims was not to sever ties with India. As he made clear in the majestically crafted *Shikwa-i-Hind*, or complaint to India composed in 1888, the problem of Muslims was precisely the loss of the distinctiveness that had once given them a measure of dignity and humanity. 'We were fire O Hind', he exclaimed, 'you've turned us into ash.'[49] None of this was the fault of India which had not only welcomed the Muslims but bestowed dominion and a plethora of gifts upon them. Hali instead blamed *qismat* or fate which had brought Islam to the subcontinent and made certain that unlike the Greeks the Muslim armies did not turn away from its frontiers in failure.[50] As the metaphor of fire to ashes indicates, Hali recognized the indelible imprint of India on the Muslims. Intended to invigorate his dejected co-religionists, not erect walls of antipathy against non-Muslims, these self-projections of a member of the north-Indian *ashraf* classes were susceptible to serious misinterpretation by those who had always questioned the loyalty of the Muslim to their adopted homeland.

And indeed, Britain's repeated alarms and excursions in the Islamic world were invariably reflected in an ongoing and bitter public debate about the exact connotations of a non-territorially based religious bond for the

[48]Altaf Hussain Hali, *Musaddas-i-Hali*, first published in 1879; my references are to the reprint by Ferozesons, Lahore, (no date).
[49]*Haal apna sakht ibratnak tu ne kar diya*
Aag they ah Hind, hum ko khak tu ney kar diya.

حال اپنا سخت عبرت ناک تو نے کو دیا

آگ تھے اے ہند ہم کو خاک تو نے کر دیا۔

(Hali, 'Shikwa-i-Hind', *Jawahar-i-Hali*, p. 323.)
[50]Ibid., pp. 314–30.

Indian Muslims. With the loss of political sovereignty and the emphasis on communities of religion, the fact of Muslim populations outside India provided a psychological reinforcement for those consigned to the category of a minority. This rather than an alleged religiously determined disloyalty to India or the British raj explains Muslim *ashraf* class attitudes towards co-religionists beyond the territorial confines of the subcontinent. Yet they were careful to stress the difference between an attachment to Ottoman Turkey and other Muslim countries such as Afghanistan. Support for Turkey emanated from a sense of religious duty towards the Sultan who was regarded by some as the spiritual and temporal symbol of authority for all Muslims. The same could not be said of Muslim sentiments towards Afghanistan. In late 1878, worsening relations between the government of India and the Amir of Afghanistan prompted a Muslim to argue in the *Delhi Gazette* that his co-religionists were secretly hoping for an Afghan victory as a precursor to the establishment of Islamic supremacy in India. This was promptly refuted by Munshi Nawal Kishore's *Awadh Akhbar*. Indian Muslims were 'loyal and faithful subjects' and preferred the 'just and peaceful British rule to a barbarous and tyrannical Muhammadan government'.[51] Two years later another paper asserted that while Indian Muslims looked upon 'Afghans as robbers ... and treacherous people', they had the greatest respect for the Turkish Sultan. A declaration of war by Britain on Ottoman Turkey would not incite Muslims to revolt but it would be inadvisable for the government to ignore their feelings on the matter.[52] The *Aligarh Institute Gazette* thought it was pure anachronism for Indian Muslims to look upon the Turkish Sultan as their *khalifa* even in the religious sense. Shias did not recognize any *khalifas* and regarded the twelve *imams* as their religious leaders. Sunnis acknowledged only the five successors to the Prophet as *khalifa*. All claims to *khilafat* were false and it was absurd to recite the name of any Muslim sovereign in the Friday *khutba*.[53]

There was much subtlety and pragmatism in Muslim attitudes towards co-religionists in the Islamic world. Seeing extra-territorial loyalties as proof of the 'Pan-Islamic' sentiments of Muslims ignores the myriad other connections that intersected with their religiously informed cultural identity. In so far as the term 'Pan-Islamism' refers to the idea of Islamic universalism, there can be no denying its significance in Muslim consciousness. But like the term 'Wahabi' and the more recent construction, 'fundamentalism', the term 'Pan-Islamism' was deployed primarily to pinpoint the inherently fanatical and disloyal nature of Britain's Muslim subjects and cannot be used unquestioningly. The *Mihiri Darkhshan* reacted ferociously to an article by Sayyid Ahmad Khan attacking the Khedive of Egypt in which he argued that Muslims could

[51]*Awadh Akhbar*, 20 December 1878, *Selections*, L/R/5/55, IOL, p. 1049.
[52]*Ahsan-ul-Akhbar*, Moradabad, 8 July 1880, *Selections*, L/R/5/57, IOL, pp. 473-4.
[53]*Aligarh Institute Gazette*, 10 July 1880, ibid., pp. 475-6.

make for rebellious subjects and were generally oppressive as rulers. But it demonstrated the ability to distinguish between the convictions of a community and the views of an individual by rejecting the pronouncements as no more than a hypocritical attempt to win favour with the British. If Sayyid Ahmad had been 'poor and expressed such sentiments', his loyalty might be 'free from suspicion'.[54]

Muslims and 'Modernity'

If the debate on their much touted extra-territorial loyalties did not generate agreement among the *ashraf* classes, there were still fewer grounds for unanimity on a range of matters closer to home. By far the most emotive was the multifaceted question of how Muslims could go about accommodating western cultural influences without contravening the religious precepts of Islam. Here was an issue loaded with nuances, owing more to individual preferences than a communitarian consensus, not all of which have been captured by the insistence on consigning it to the suffocating confines of the 'modernity' versus 'tradition' dichotomy. There were hues and layers of grey in exchanges between Muslims of different leanings on the appropriate Islamic response to the western encounter. 'Modernity' itself was a contested idea, open to many varied interpretations. One will have to slip out of the facile and rigid distinctions between so-called Muslim 'modernists' and 'anti-modernists' or 'liberals' and 'traditionalists' to appreciate the subtleties and ambiguities underlying the ideas of those whom these categories have sought to classify.[55]

The vernacular press in the North Western Provinces and the Punjab, backed by an effluence of poetic and prose compositions, was the channel through which educated Muslims aired their views on the extent to which a cultural framework informed by Islam could comfortably receive the influx of western ideas and technology. In 1870 the appearance of Sayyid Ahmad Khan's *Tahzib-ul-Ikhlaq* exhorting Muslims to reform their religious worldview had a catalytic effect on the newspaper business. Threatened by Sayyid Ahmad's bold forays into the domain of Islam, many of his co-religionists ventilated their outrage by resorting to the print medium, colonial modernity's most attractive gift for instantaneous self-promotion. As a leading poetic wit put it, if one could not become a political leader, the next best thing was to become a journalist and edit a newspaper. Such was the power of the press, he sneered, that the rule of thumb was: 'Faced with a gun, bring out a newspapr'.[56] The response to Sayyid Ahmad's arguments

[54]*Mihiri Darkhshan*, 1 June 1879, *Selections*, L/R/5/56, IOL, p. 443.

[55]See W.C. Smith, *Modern Islam in India: A Social Analysis*, London: V. Gollancz, 1946, for an example of the uses made of these categories.

[56]Akbar Allahabadi cited in Ralph Russell, *The Pursuit of Urdu Literature: A Select History*, Delhi: Oxford University Press, 1992, pp. 158–9.

on the compatibility of Islamic teachings and modern ideas was equally sharp in the North Western Provinces and the Punjab. While in the North Western Provinces many new names emerged on the map of Urdu journalism as critics of the Aligarh school, Sayyid Ahmad's religious ideas were given a severe dressing down in the Punjab by the Ahl-i-Hadith's *Ishaat ul Sunnat*.

Not a religious scholar by training, Sayyid Ahmad's approach to Islamic theology and jurisprudence earned him the lacerating abuse of orthodox Muslim *ulema* who were either based at or products of the theological seminary at Deoband, less vociferously, Farangi Mahal in Lucknow and also Barelvi. His promotion of *ijtihad* or independent reasoning and disapproval of *taqlid* or adherence to the four authoritative schools of Islamic jurisprudence set him at loggerheads with the *ulema* who correctly saw in it a barely disguised assault on their pre-eminent status as the religious guardians of the Muslim community. While sharing an *ashraf* culture, an ardour for Urdu and a core of Islamic values with Sayyid Ahmad's associates at Aligarh, the *ulema* preferred to keep these *la-dini* or irreligious Muslims at an arm's length.

The theologians were not alone in opposing Sayyid Ahmad's new-fangled ideas. His support of western knowledge and culture as well as loyalty to the raj drew acerbic comment from Muslims attached to their societal moorings and the ideal of a universal Muslim *ummah*. Among Sayyid Ahmad's fiercest critics was the Persian scholar Jamaluddin al-Afghani who lived in India between 1879 and 1882 and called for Hindu–Muslim unity as the first step to dislodging British colonialism.[57] Afghani's strident anti-colonialism and belief in Islamic universalism found a receptive audience among Muslims put off by Sayyid Ahmad's calculated political subservience to the raj. The froth and fury of the *ulema* and also those moved by the ideal of a universal community of Islam gave hard-pressed Muslim editors the ammunition they needed to advance the sales of their papers in the noble cause of defending the religiously informed cultural sensibilities of Indian Muslims.

While much of the debate focused squarely on the balance between religion and politics, it contained a categorical cultural rejection of the 'Angreziat' or Englishness represented by Sayyid Ahmad Khan and a growing circle of his Muslim admirers. The Urdu weekly *Agra Akhbar*, published by Khwajah Asif Ali, denounced the Muslim Anglo-Oriental University scheme at Aligarh as 'whimsical and chimerical'. Orthodox Muslims regarded its 'projector ... as an apostate from Islam' due to his fascination with 'European notions and sentiments of civilization and reform'. The proposal would never be accepted by 'the bulk' of the Muslims unless Sayyid Ahmad 'yields to their prejudices, and reconciles himself to their sentiments and ways of thinking'.[58]

[57] For Afghani's scathing attacks on Sayyid Ahmad Khan's brand of politics, see Nikki R. Keddie, *An Islamic Response to Imperialism: Political and Religious Writings of Sayyid Jamal ad-Din 'al-Afghani'*, Berkeley: University of California Press, 1968 and 1983.
[58] *Agra Akhbar*, 20 June 1873, *Selections*, L/R/5/50, IOL, pp. 453–4.

Woman as Ornament, Woman as Prostitute

Nothing could upset the already precarious balance between the Aligarh group and their opponents more than the women's question. The patriarchal spirit of the *ashraf* discourse on cultural identity made certain that with the exception of a few skirmishes, the antagonists on both sides of the debate on Muslim modernity avoided coming to blows on gender relations. Women in the eyes of these men were not only unequal but, depending on their class status, dispensable in the construction of a Muslim communitarian identity. Concerned with projecting and preserving their distinctive religiously informed cultural identity, salaried and professional Muslim men were anxious to protect their women from the 'evil' influences of colonial modernity. Women may have been central to the redefinition of a Muslim middle- and upper-class identity, but more as silenced partners than active agents.

Muslim thinkers in theological seminaries like Deoband, ambivalent in their attitude towards European influences, may have been more open-minded when it came to conceiving of equal education for both men and women.[59] But the *ulema* were even more determined to strictly consign women to the sacred geography of the Muslim household. The elaborate detail with which Ashraf Ali Thanawi outlines the ideal Muslim woman in his classic *Bihishti Zevar,* or heavenly ornaments, is more than a male fantasy. Yet it has remained an agenda for perfection, impossible for Muslim women to attain. Ornaments of their homes, not of the heavens, women in the *ashraf* conception were inhabitants of the *zenana*. On the rare occasions when they did go out of the confines of their four walls, they were expected to don the *burqa*—that portable statement of *purdah* or physical seclusion and the cultural marker of the status of whole families as well as individual men.

Education for women, most Muslim men agreed, had to take place within the home. Sayyid Ahmad Khan had cited as one of the causes of the revolt the fear that government intended to force girls to attend schools and 'leave off the habit of sitting veiled'. There was nothing 'more obnoxious than this to the feelings of the Hindustanis'.[60] After visiting Britain and France, Sayyid Ahmad became a strong proponent of women's education. He did not 'know the condition of Hindoo women' but 'kn[e]w that with the Mahomedans female education [wa]s daily on the decline'. During his youth there was 'no house ... without its governess, who taught girls'; sadly, this was now 'the exception, and not the rule'.[61] The *Aligarh Institute Gazette* warned reformers

[59]See Ashraf Ali Thanawi, *Perfecting Women: Maulana Ashraf Ali Thanawi's Bihishti Zevar,* tr. and ed. Barbara Metcalf, Berkeley: University of California Press, 1982. Also see Barbara Metcalf, 'Reading and Writing About Muslim Women in British India', in Zoya Hasan (ed.), *Forging Identities: Gender, Communities and the State in India,* Boulder: Westview Press, 1994.

[60]Malik (ed.), *Political Profile of Sir Sayyid Ahmad Khan,* p. 148.

[61]*Aligarh Institute Gazette,* 25 February 1870, *Selections,* L/R/5/47, IOL, p. 92.

not to 'set down to prejudice and folly all the restraints and regulations which the wisdom of their ancestors ha[d] provided for the *security of the honour of their families*'. Rejecting women's education in government schools, it declared: 'We wish our women to be educated. But if education means letting them loose to mix with whom they please; if it means that as they increase in learning, they shall deteriorate in morals, if it means the loss of our honour and the invasion of the privacy of our homes—we prefer our honour to the education of our women, even though we may be called obstinate, prejudiced, and wrong-headed.'[62]

A protest against missionary excesses, it did not mean keeping women ignorant and susceptible to superstitions and customary practices. A running theme in *ashraf* writings on women was the need for their moral uplift and separation from *ajlaf* women, the demons who brought the *mardana* or male public into the *zenana* while also satisfying the lust of some of the more unpardonable offenders of the prohibition on adultery in Islam. Exploiting weak and vulnerable women for pleasure and condemning them as prostitutes was a perfectly reasonable response to the commodification of social space. Gone were the days of refined culture when the courtesan was the prized jewel of the *nawabzadas*. She was not just a sexual object but the *kafir sanam*, the temporal beloved who inspired the vision of ultimate love with the divine. As such she was often the *saqi*, or bearer of the wine cup, and equally frequently a temporal evocation of the transcendental majesty and beauty of Allah signified by the Arabic words *jalal* and *jamil*. But like the transcendental Being she was often an unattainable beloved given the apportioning of space between the home and the world to sustain the social institution of marriage. It was the struggle to retain a measure of cultural autonomy in the face of alien encroachments that generated the momentum for the education of *ashraf* women. Central to the construction of an *ashraf* identity, women from the middle and upper classes were cast in an image that was the obverse of the unprotected and rejected woman as prostitute.

Despite variations, protagonists of women's education made certain that their proposed reforms were strictly consistent with the emerging *ashraf* code of morality.[63] The redefinition of social space under conditions of colonial modernity saw indigenous patriarchy glorifying women as wives and, above all, mothers. Muslim newspapers, poets and novelists alike poured scorn upon the depravity of lower-class women and their pernicious influence on their middle-to-upper-class sisters. Contaminated by exposure to the irremediably immoral public sphere, they were seen as transmitting the plague of immorality from the world into the home. In 1871 the *Kohinoor* blamed the

[62]*Aligarh Institute Gazette*, 8 July 1870, ibid., pp. 268–71 (my emphasis).
[63]Gail Minault has written extensively on the subject. See her *Secluded Scholars: Women's Education and Muslim Social Reform in Colonial India*, Delhi: Oxford University Press, 1998.

increasing depravity of women on the leniency of colonial laws on adultery as well as better rail facilities and communications which were bringing an ever larger number of men from other provinces to the Punjab in search of jobs. Those of the 'soldier class, both civil and military' were 'instrumental in the spread of the crime'. Cities near the Grand Trunk Road were the worst affected. In Lahore and Amritsar 'scarcely a mohalla ... [could] be found in which ten per cent at least of the women [we]re not of a profligate character'. This in turn was attributed to the discontinuation of the moral and religious training of women. The net result was that women were disgracing themselves in public. They 'bathe naked at rivers in the presence of large assemblies of persons of both sexes, and sing obscene songs in public on [the] occasion of marriage'.[64]

Novels like *Mirat-ul-Arus* or The Bride's Mirror by Nazir Ahmad, published in 1869, set the standard for ideal Muslim womanhood in the character of Asghari.[65] Observing *purdah* and educated in the *zenana*, she was the *ashraf* model of a modern educated woman. What has made her character memorable, quite as much as of Zubaida Khatun's in Hali's acclaimed poem 'Majalis-un-Nisa' (1874), is the almost insufferable capacity to be the perfect domesticated heavenly ornaments of Thanawi's dreams.[66]

The word for woman in Urdu is *aurat*, which literally means the sexual organ. Both as ornament and prostitute, she finds her place in novels and poetry, reflecting the social ambience of late-nineteenth-century northern India that informed the discourse on Muslim identity. Following Nazir Ahmed, a trail of novels including those by Sarshar and Rashid-ul-Khairi abound in portrayals of lower-class women domestic servants fanning familial discord.[67] The only corrective was to educate *ashraf* women so that they might keep a social distance from ill-bred plebeians and perform their roles as wives, mothers, daughters and sisters in conformity with the norms of respectability in polite society. However much they might differ on the content of the education to be imparted, men from *sharif* households considered their women to be the ultimate symbols of a distinctive Islamic cultural identity. The model of womanhood cherished by middle-to-upper-class Muslim men in the late nineteenth and early twentieth centuries was that of the literate but domesticated, wise but chaste, intelligent but submissive wife.

This was in contrast to the other dominant image of woman as prostitute who lured respectable men through temptation and ruined them, financially,

[64]*Kohinoor*, Lahore, 15 July 1871, *Selections*, L/R/5/48, IOL, pp. 393–4.

[65]Deputy Nazir Ahmad, *Mirat-ul-Arus*, reprint, Lahore: Ferozesons (no date).

[66]For a discussion of these two works, see Gail Minault (trs.), *Voices of Silence: English Translation of Khwaja Altaf Hussain Hali's* 'Majalis-un-Nisa' *and* 'Chup ki Dad', Delhi: Chanakya Publications, 1986.

[67]See Fahmida Kabir, *Urdu Novel mein Aurat ka Tasawar: Nazir Ahmad saay Prem Chand tak*, New Delhi: Maktab-i-Jamia, 1992.

morally and psychologically. If Islam had been marginalized by the colonial state, then that marginality could be made palatable if Muslim men could reconfigure the domestic sphere to suit their needs, making a visitation to the public whorehouse a less attractive proposition. In 1879 the *Panjabi Akhbar* regretted that 'prostitutes generally belong[ed] to the Muhammadan religion' and were 'a standing blot to the Muhammadan community [sic]'. It was imperative that the 'respectable classes of Musalmans should ask the Government to adopt some strict measures to check their increase'.[68]

So while the state had to be kept from invading the morality of the community at home, it was expected to play a role in cleaning up the immorality of the community in the neighbourhood.[69] There were evidently multiple ways of conflating and confusing the distinction between the public and the private and, by extension, between politics and religion. Since the restraining of the woman as public commodity was the responsibility of the colonial state, the Muslim communitarian discourse on rights could concentrate on the respectable woman at home. To the extent that it existed, reformist fervour focused on women's rights in marriage, divorce and inheritance. In other words, the Muslim conception of Islamic law was confined to the parameters laid down for it by colonial imperatives. The Muslim woman as individual was simply not an inhabitant of a civil society which if it at all existed in British India was badly squeezed between a colonial 'public' and a communitarian 'private'.

Colonial Modernity and Male Rationality

So *aurat*, whether jealously protected at home and lauded as wife and mother or solicited in the whorehouse and denigrated as prostitute, was intrinsic to the perspective Muslim men brought to bear on their sense of location within colonial space. But it was one thing to write reformist tracts aimed at achieving domestic harmony and quite another to keep peace among a fractured community of Muslims. The limitations of Sayyid Ahmad Khan's representative credentials are illustrated by the refusal of many Muslims to follow his lead. Together with the silencing and elimination of women, the inability of Muslims to accept anyone's authority is underscored in the desperate stands taken by Muslim men, each applying his own reasoning to read the signs of colonial modernity in the light of patriarchal conditions.

Sayyid Ahmad Khan was by far the most eminent in the league. In an article in the *Tahzib-ul-Ikhlaq*, he viewed the Islamic conception of women's rights in far better light than that of the English. Everyone spoke about equality

[68]*Panjabi Akhbar*, Lahore, 14 June 1879, *Selections*, L/R/5/56, IOL, p. 475.

[69]For an insightful account of the implications of the narrowing of domestic space in relation to the state and the market under colonialism, see Radhika Singha, 'Making the Domestic More Domestic: Criminal Law and the "Head of the Household", 1772–1843', *The Indian Economic and Social History Review*, (33: 3, 1996) - (henceforth *IESHR*).

between women and men in the 'civilised countries', presuming it to be inconceivable in Islam. Yet women in England were 'treated as irrational and negative beings'. There, a woman had to be represented by her husband, could not enter into contracts of her own, and all her property upon marriage became the property of her spouse. Deemed too irrational to enjoy legal rights, an English woman could neither bring a claim against anyone, nor could anyone make a claim against her. She could neither buy nor sell goods without her husband's permission. By contrast, Islam granted rights of property and profit to a woman as individual. As a holder of property, a woman could freely enter any contract with a man. Her concurrence was a precondition for the legitimacy of a marriage. In normative Islam, if not necessarily in Muslim practice, a woman could be an independent economic agent. She was not only free to do what she pleased with her business profits, but could do what she liked with the property. A Muslim woman could inherit the property of her relations, sell it, bequeath it to anyone or give it away as *waqf*, and thus acquiring religious virtues equal to a man.[70]

To his credit, Sayyid Ahmad admitted that the charge of women's oppression in Islam was not without an element of truth. With the notable exception of the rules of seclusion, women of civilized countries had 'a decided preference above Hindoostane women in all respects'. Despite 'the superior advantages' conferred upon them by Islam, Muslim women were living in a 'degraded condition', completely 'surpassed by women of the civilised countries' whose laws did not give 'a tenth of the rights and privileges which the Musalman law allows to women'. Blowing the bugle of civilization defined by colonial modernity, Sayyid Ahmad drew a distinction between the 'uncivilization of the Musalmans, and the superior enlightenment of the Western nations'.[71]

His intention was not to pander to all Muslim prejudices; it was to weed out the more obsolete ones. Left at that, it may have been conceivable to gradually muster support for the Aligarh movement. But the policy of active collaboration with the raj insulted the sensibilities of many of Sayyid Ahmad's co-religionists. Opposition to colonialism and westernism, if not rationalism and modernism, fused together in various permutations. The *Awadh Punch* led the charge with its attacks on those who mimicked the English and meekly submitted to their rule. One of its foremost contributors was Sayyid Akbar Husain, better known as Akbar Allahabadi, who in his bitingly humorous and brilliant satirical verses ridiculed Sayyid Ahmad Khan and his Aligarh associates for their shallow imitation of western culture. He did not oppose the new education so much as question the downgrading of religious values in an attempt to serve colonial interests:

[70]*Tahzib-ul-Ikhlaq*, Aligarh, 3 August 1871, *Selections*, L/R/5/48, IOL, pp. 451–3.
[71]Ibid., p. 453.

What our respected Sayyid says is good
Akbar agrees that it is sound and fair
But most of those who head his modern school
Neither believe in God, nor yet in prayer
They *say* they do, but it is plain to see
What *they* believe in is the powers that be.[72]

Akbar was merciless in his contempt for those pioneering the course of future Muslim advance:

In mourning for their nation's plight they dine with the authorities
Our leaders suffer deeply for us, but they suffer at ease.[73]

Nothing annoyed him more than the self-righteousness of men who, while pretending to be anguished by the plight of the poor and lowly, sought publicity through newspapers and sold their conscience for a pittance of material benefits from the colonial state:

I'm actually a nightingale, but since I want to eat
I pretend to be a parrot and accept a council seat.[74]

Such men were misleading ordinary people by denigrating all that was worthwhile in their own culture and tradition. Without a firm basis in religious learning, Muslims were doomed:

Nothing is prohibited, read everyone's writings
But also read the Quranic commentary
When the glory of the world subdues the heart
Think of the Creator and recite his praises.[75]

Scathing and relentless in his criticism of a modernity wanting in spirituality, Allahabadi neither fits the bill of a diehard anti-modernist enamoured of

[72]Cited in Russell, *The Pursuit of Urdu Literature*, p. 147.
[73]Ibid., p. 158.
[74]Ibid., p. 157.
[75]*Kuch mana nahin, har aik ki tahrir parho*
Laikan Quran ki bhi tafseer parho
Azmat duniya ki jab dabai dil ko
Khaliq ka karo khiyal, taqbir parho.

کچھ منع نہیں ہر اک کی تحریر پڑھو
لیکن قرآن کی بھی تفسیر پڑھو
عظمت دنیا کی جب دبائے دل کو
خالق کا کرو خیال تکبیر پڑھو۔

(Akbar Allahabadi, *Kulliyat-i-Akbar Allahabadi*, vol. i, Delhi (no date), p. 120.)

obscurantist *maulvis* nor of a religious bigot. In one of his most-quoted couplets, Akbar asserted that he took no part in religious discussions; he did not have the intelligence to spare. 'Away with pandits and with maulvis too,' he declared, 'I do not want religion, I want faith'.[76] Here was an eloquent statement of an important distinction that was being blurred by the colonial state's presumed separation of the spiritual and material domains. Allahabadi recalled that as a child a *maulvi* tried teaching him knowledge and he in turn tried teaching the *maulvi* reason; the enterprise ended in tears, neither the *maulvi* learned reason, nor Akbar knowledge.[77] He was not opposed to reason and modern science as such but questioned the overconfidence of its protagonists. 'God is beyond the range of telescopes', he exclaimed; the proof of God's existence or non-existence required more than a careful study of maps drawn up by geographers.[78]

Despite a firm commitment to Islam, Akbar Allahabadi refused to shed tears at the loss of Muslim political sovereignty. It was the degenerate state of his co-religionists, not external threats to their existence, which led him to argue that religion was the only basis for the distinctive identity of Muslims.[79] But the assertion of Muslim difference was a far cry from denying any commonality of interests with Hindus. Both Muslims and Hindus should remain true to their own faiths: 'Clash like the waves, but still remain one sea.'[80] After all, India was neither an Islamic country nor of Lakshman and Ram. Every Indian was the pliant well-wisher of the English and Hind simply the warehouse of Europe.[81]

[76]Russell, *The Pursuit of Urdu Literature*, p. 162.

[77]Akbar Allahabadi, *Akbar Allahabadi ke Latife*, compiled by Nadeem Sitapuri, Lucknow, 1955, pp. 20–1.

[78]Russell, *The Pursuit of Urdu Literature*, pp. 144,152.

[79]*Harghiz nahin hum ko sultanate ka afsos*
Hai abtari muhasharat ka afsoos.

ہر گز نہیں ہم کو سلطنت کا افسوس

ہے ابتری معاشرت کا افسوس۔

(Akbar Allahabadi, *Intikhab-i-Kalam-i-Akbar*, compiled by Ghulam Husain Zulfikar, Lahore, 1996, p. 112.)

[80]Russell, *The Pursuit of Urdu Literature*, p. 164.

[81]*Ye baat ghalt hai ke mulk-i-Islam hai Hind*
Ye jhoot hai ke mulk Lakshman wa Ram hai Hind
Ham sab hain matiya-o-kher khwa-i-English
Europe ke leya bas aik godam hai Hind.

یہ بات غلط ہے کہ ملک اسلام ہے ہند

یہ جھوٹ ہے کہ ملک لچھمن ورام ہے ہند

ہم سب ہیں مطیع و خیر خواہ انگلش

یورپ کے لیے بس ایک گودام ہے ہند۔

(Zulfikar (comp.), *Intikhab-i-Kalam-i-Akbar*, p. 112.)

It is a comment on the self-imposed limitations of 'communal' and 'national' historians that Allahabadi, while enormously popular in Urdu literary circles on both sides of the 1947 divide, forms no part of either the Indian or the Pakistani nationalist pantheon.

Maulana Shibli Numani also eludes categorization as a 'liberal modernist' or an 'anti-modern traditionalist'.[82] An associate of Sayyid Ahmad Khan, he adopted the idioms of modernity without disavowing the basic grammar of Islamic learning. The author of a varied corpus of writings on Islamic history, theology, law as well as literary criticism and poetry, Shibli was primarily interested in demonstrating Islam's capacity to absorb modern science. He endorsed Sayyid Ahmad Khan's line that Indian Muslims were legal subjects of the British Crown and not bound either by their religion or history to submit to the authority of the Turkish Sultan. On matters closer to home, by the 1890s Shibli had begun taking a political path different from the one charted by Sayyid Ahmad Khan. His professed discomfort with the ultra-modernism of the Aligarh school in later years might appear to justify classifying him as a 'traditionalist'. But during his sojourn at the Nadwat-al Ulema at Lucknow, which he helped set up with a group of *ulema* in 1894, Shibli was more concerned with bridging the gulf separating the so-called 'modernists' of Aligarh and 'traditionalists' of Deoband and Farangi Mahal than in unequivocally endorsing one or the other point of view. This was an attitude he shared with a succession of Muslim thinkers of widely different ideological and political leanings.

Elements of both tendencies overlapped to a far greater extent in the thought of individuals like Allahabadi and Shibli, and even Sayyid Ahmad Khan, than has been permitted by the oversimplifications implicit in these largely heuristic categories. Sayyid Ahmad Khan's vehicle for articulating 'modernist' ideas, the *Aligarh Institute Gazette*, exhorted Muslims to 'distinguish laws and social customs and institutions from religion in its strict sense'. For instance, the Islamic prohibition on interest was explained away as a product of certain historical circumstances that were no longer applicable. Purely Islamic precepts such as the unity of God, the immortality of the soul and the inspiration of the Holy Prophet had to be 'separated' from matters relating to 'social and political economy, to laws, and institutions'.[83] This was a clear enunciation of a separation of religion and politics in a temporal as opposed

---

[82]There is considerable disagreement on whether Shibli was a 'modernist' or a 'traditionalist'. See Mehr Afroz Murad, *Intellectual Modernism of Shibli Nu'mani: An Exposition of his Religious and Political Ideas*, Lahore: Institute of Islamic Culture, 1976 and Muhammad Aslam Syed, *Muslim Response to the West: Muslim Historiography in India, 1857–1914*, Islamabad: National Institute of Historical and Cultural Research [henceforth NCHCR], 1988, who regards Shibli to be firmly on the side of the 'traditionalists'.

[83]*Aligarh Institute Gazette*, December 1877, *Selections*, L/R/5/54, IOL, pp. 864–5.

to a spiritual sense. Here was pragmatism triumphing over obscurantism, not a denial of religion as the basis of cultural existence. It had accompanied a valiant attempt by Sayyid Ahmad Khan to push the Muhammadan Family Endowment Bill through the legislative council. Intended to prevent the fragmentation of Muslim property through automatic division among the heirs, it gave owners the option of bestowing it on descendants according to preference.

There were howls of protest against the draft bill in the Muslim press. Many newspaper editors charged Sayyid Ahmad Khan of personal bias, class interests and religious deviation. Contesting Sayyid Ahmad Khan's claim to represent the Muslim community, the *Agra Akhbar* declared, 'We do not recognize him as our head, nor has the Government any business to consider him as such.' The 'wants of one class cannot be considered as those of the whole nation'.[84] Others saw the bill as inequitable and, therefore, unIslamic. Maulvi Hasan Ali thought the bill would prevent Muslims from improving their material condition. No one could engage in trade without some inherited money. The bill was calculated to arouse intra-familial hatred and enmity.[85] Sayyid Ahmad's dabbling in the sphere of Islamic legal reform had badly misfired. Yet it was the perceived threat to their culture from Anglicized Muslims of Sayyid Ahmad's ilk that most ruffled his opponents. One paper ruefully commented that Anglicized Muslims wearing western clothes and the Turkish *fez* were to be seen everywhere. If they substituted the Turkish headgear for a European hat they would 'become perfect gentlemen' and could go about kicking and abusing their countrymen and calling them 'damned fools'.[86] The *Delhi Punch* of Lahore published Persian verses ridiculing Sayyid Ahmad Khan and cursing him for being a 'Satan, an apostate, a bastard, a betrayer of mankind, and a ringleader of thieves'.[87] Given the adverse Muslim reaction to his activities, the *Kohinoor* regretted that little good had come of the British decision in 1878 to give Sayyid Ahmad Khan a place in the imperial legislative council.[88]

The leadership of the Muslim community was patently not a settled issue. It was Sayyid Ahmad Khan's proximity to colonial state power which appeared to give a distinctive edge to his version of the elite discourse on Muslim interests. The Aligarh movement which he fathered was to be seen as the purveyor of modernist and rational thinking among the Muslim elite and, ironically enough, also the harbinger of latter-day Muslim political 'separatism' and 'communalism'. By contrast, his more culturally exclusive Muslim opponents, harbouring anti-colonial feelings and sentiments of Islamic universalism, steeped

[84]*Agra Akhbar*, 21 February 1880, *Selections*, L/R/5/57, IOL, pp. 143–4.
[85]*Awadh Akhbar*, 23 February 1880, ibid.
[86]*Jalwah Tur*, Meerut, 16 March 1880, ibid., p. 199.
[87]*Delhi Punch*, Lahore, 13 December 1880, ibid., p. 838.
[88]*Kohinoor*, Lahore, 13 March 1880, ibid., p. 194.

themselves in religious strictures at *madrasas* and *maktabs* only to end up squarely on the side of an inclusionary and 'secular' Indian nationalism. Interpreting this as the product of a straightforward 'modernity' versus 'tradition' dichotomy in Muslim thought is to risk illogicality. It was the perceived absence of religiosity among the 'modernists' and a presumed surfeit of it among the 'traditionalists' which had justified drawing the distinction in the first place. Instead of perpetuating the contradictions implicit in the 'modernity–tradition' opposition, a recognition of its inherent ambiguities may be a more useful way to approach the contending strands of thought that have passed for Muslim minority 'communalism' in subcontinental history.

Community and Class: Conversion, Cow and Conflict

The discourse on Muslim identity, whether propounded by Sayyid Ahmad Khan or his opponents, was unabashedly elitist both in letter and spirit. Notwithstanding the significance of numbers in packaging communitarian demands, there was as yet no visible interest in the fate of the downtrodden Muslim *ajlaf* classes, far less in their mobilization. In so far as Sayyid Ahmad and his contemporaries were concerned with Muslim advancement in the spheres of education and government employment, it was the future of the *ashraf* classes which their representations to the colonial state aimed at securing. But the construction of a distinctive narrative on Muslim identity was not restricted to pleas and petitions by the upper classes or even their internal debates on the quantum of modernity permissible within an Islamic cultural framework. The vast majority of illiterate and semi-literate Muslims may not have had direct recourse to the press and publications market, but their historical experience under colonialism constituted an equally, if not more, powerful thread in the evolving narrative of identity.

At a time when Christian missionary zealots were disturbing the equilibrium of bazaars and fairs with their religious preachings and publishing literature attacking Islam and Hinduism, the sense of danger to one's cultural identity was not the preserve of the upper classes alone. This is yet another reason why the Muslim response to western cultural influences cannot be confined to the 'modernity–tradition' paradigm. Muslims belonging to different economic strata, quite as much as their Hindu counterparts, were agitated by the barbed slights at their respective religions by the crusaders of Christendom. The hustle-bustle of the bazaars and annual festivities during Muharram, Dussehra, Diwali and Baqra Id, as the Id-ul-Azha was known in north-western India and the Punjab, provided the locational venues for exchanges or *munazaras* between the defenders of faiths, Christian, Muslim and Hindu.[89] The press and publications market formed the transmission belt

[89]See Barbara Daly Metcalf, *Islamic Revival in British India: Deoband, 1860–1900*, Princeton: Princeton University Press, 1982, chapter five and Kenneth W. Jones (ed.),

for conveying these ideas to larger segments of the population. The dialectic between the vernacular press and spatially located tensions in the *mofussil* towns and *qasbas* of north-western India, including the Punjab, was indispensable for the construction of that other major pillar of 'communalism'— conflict along communitarian lines in areas where Muslims and Hindus had lived cheek by jowl for centuries.

If one is to disturb the confident assumptions of the elite discourse which for all too long has claimed a monopoly over the 'communal consciousness' of Indian Muslims, the spotlight has to shift towards the attitudes and motives of local actors who influenced the delicate weave of relations at the social base. Scholars who have sought to unveil the 'consciousness' of subaltern agents seem to be a little too confident about the implications of their enterprise. Since recovering the subjectivity of subordinated individuals and social groups constitutes one of the most elusive elements in the historian's craft, an assessment of the vernacular press comment on inter-communitarian relations in the different locales of the North Western Provinces and the Punjab has to be a part of any enquiry into the construction of differential identities. In an incisive comment on the changing character of communitarian relations, the Lucknow-based *Anjuman-i-Hind* admitted that formerly Muslims came to India from 'a feeling of covetousness and desire for wealth', plundered Hindu temples, smashed idols and departed. But now that 'generation ha[d] passed away'; 'all Mahomedans have become as one'; 'children have been born to them; their dear ones lie buried here; and here the survivors reside'. These Muslims were more closely tied to Hindustan than to any of the remaining princely rulers with whom they shared a common religion. Even in the event of a civil war, the Muslims of Hindustan would 'not look upon those of Persia and Arabia as their kinsmen'. The 'two castes', Muslim and Hindu, had adopted each other's customs, not because they regarded the opposite creed as 'superior to their own' but because 'religion, like most other things, is guided by custom'. If only the leaders could 'lay aside their prejudices' and concentrate on matters of common education instead of religion, the face of India would be changed for the better.[90]

Other newspapers concurred that the onus of the responsibility for maintaining a semblance of cordiality between Hindus and Muslims rested with local men of power and pelf. Recanting on an earlier observation that disturbances in Bareilly during Muharram were the result of Muslim aggression, the *Awadh Akhbar* declared that the main culprits were 'the dregs of the Mahomedan community' who had incited similar troubles in the past. They had been encouraged in their nefarious tactics by the Muslim gentry of

---

Religious Controversy in British India: Dialogues in South Asian Languages, Albany: State University of New York Press, 1992.

[90]*Anjuman-i-Hind*, Lucknow, 27 June 1868, *Selections*, L/R/5/45, IOL, pp. 336–7.

rank which instead of 'edifying and reclaiming the mob' had 'the folly secretly to aid their designs' since they were 'nominally of the same religion'.[91] If religion could provide a loose basis for a convergence of interests between the upper and lower classes in a particular town or city, the colonial policy of inflicting a punitive fine on the entire population to pay for the deployment of additional police gave incidents of local conflict a crude veneer of communitarianism. As one paper complained, the measure could be justified only if all the inhabitants of the city were guilty of participating in the fracas. In most instances, the local thugs responsible for the troubles got off scot free while the innocent were forced to pay up.[92]

Implicating the entire population of a city or a rural locality in the acts of a few individuals imbued local tensions and conflicts with communitarian overtones. Aggressive conversion and propagation activities by Christian missionaries lent added weight to the religious dimension. The Moradabad weekly *Lauh-i-Mahfuz* was infuriated with the high-handed practices of the missionaries who considered themselves more powerful than district magistrates. Instead of mission funds being spent on supporting the poor, the money was being wasted on the 'publication of books written with no other object than to expose to ridicule and contempt the Hindu and Musalman religions'.[93]

Even the *Hindu Prakash* took strong exception to the publication of a book on the history of Islam by Reverend Imaduddin of Amritsar, a *maulvi* and religious scholar who had recently converted to Christianity. The book was 'full of contempt and enmity' towards Islam and was written with no purpose other than to 'excite' Muslims to carry out acts for which 'they may be arrested and punished as seditious people'.[94] Various newspapers voiced the intense resentment of Indians towards the missionaries by calling into question the colonial government's proclaimed policy of impartiality in the domain of religion. The British might flatter themselves with the idea of having conferred the gift of religious liberty and toleration on Indian society. But in practice the policy was nothing less than 'a positive evil' since it 'allow[ed] men of various creeds to play fast and loose with religion'. The virus of conversion was infecting social peace and the government had to take steps to prohibit street preaching by men of religion.[95] According to the *Rahbar-i-Hind*, the missionaries under the mistaken impression that the future of British rule in India was contingent upon the spread of Christianity were endeavouring to induce Indians 'by means of threats to become converts'. Spotting the blot in

[91]*Awadh Akhbar*, 18 April 1871, *Selections*, L/R/5/48, IOL, p. 186.
[92]*Rohilkhund Akhbar*, Moradabad, 11 May 1872, *Selections*, L/R/5/49, IOL, p. 277.
[93]*Lauh-i-Mahfuz*, Moradabad, 14 September 1874, *Selections*, L/R/5/52, IOL, p. 484.
[94]*Hindu Prakash*, ibid., p. 552.
[95]*Nizam-ul-Akhbar*, 27 August 1876, *Selections*, L/R/5/53, IOL, p. 471.

the colonial state's purported indifference towards religion, it noted that bishops and chaplains were paid salaries from public revenues. Such 'show of partiality' by government was 'encourag[ing] missionaries to commit objectionable acts'.[96]

Government claims that the subsidy only sought to meet the spiritual needs of British troops was laughed out of court since no such provision existed for Hindus, Muslims or Sikhs serving in the army. The government-sponsored *Anjuman-i-Punjab* calculated that nearly fifty lakh rupees from Indian revenues were being spent on church establishments. It would be more equitable if the government also 'pa[id] the Brahmins and Mullas who administer to the spiritual wants of Hindus and Musalmans'. Otherwise Christians should be made to foot the bill for their own spiritual regeneration and leave Indian money for the welfare of its people.[97]

Irritation with the colonial state's complicity with missionary activities may have remained a debating point, on par with issues like the drain of wealth and military expenditure, if not for the genuine outrage at reports of Hindu and Muslim conversions to Christianity. Anathema to Hindus and Muslims alike, each conversion led to a heightening of religiously based activity aimed at steeling local communities against Christian preachers. Among the first to direct attention to a welter of everyday problems in the localities were cultural associations which in addition to raising issues of social reform also engaged in a variety of welfare-related activities neglected by a colonial state preoccupied with revenue extraction and the preservation of law and order. Apart from opening schools, libraries and orphanages and preaching in public places, the involvement of local Muslim *anjumans* as well as Hindu and Arya *sabhas* in providing social support services strengthened communitarian bonds in no uncertain way. In a context where colonial subjecthood did not extend the basic rights of citizenship, the local community remained the only source of sustenance for large segments of a destitute populace.

The injection of religion, albeit as a symbol of the cultural self-defence of communities, did much to polarize social relations in the North Western Provinces and the Punjab. Hindu revivalist activities, especially vociferous calls to ban cow-slaughter and perennial irritation over the playing of music before mosques, exalated the battles for social space as never before. The reaction of the vernacular press to local troubles dotting the terrain of both regions added fuel to the simmering fires. Sensationalist in the extreme, press comment hiked newspaper sales though not quite in the same proportion as it did communitarian enmities.

Vernacular press coverage of tensions between Hindus and Muslims was

[96]*Rahbar-i-Hind*, Lahore, 27 April 1880, *Selections*, L/R/5/57, IOL, p. 300.
[97]*Anjuman-i-Punjab*, 15 March 1882, *Selections*, L/R/5/59, IOL, p. 175.

laced with charges of partiality by local and district officials. Hindu newspapers censured the British for their weak-kneed handling of Muslims. In instances where the presiding officer happened to be a Muslim, the uproar bordered on hysteria. Islamic rule may be a thing of the past, one paper argued, but Muslim *tehsildars, kotwals* and *thanedars* continued to 'hinder' and 'harass' Hindus celebrating their festivals or performing their religious rites. In the past such acts 'brought the Islamic administration of justice and the courts of law into disrepute' but now Muslims in public offices could 'practice oppression and tyranny upon the Hindus' and let the British government take the blame.[98] Muslim newspapers for their part accused Hindus of slandering Islam and expecting nothing by way of reprisal.

The controversy over the case of Munshi Indarman who set up a press in Moradabad and published a series of books attacking Islam illustrates how the spread of print was sharpening existing religious cleavages and throwing up new kinds of social tensions. For several years, Indarman had been writing anti-Islamic tracts to counter insulting works by Muslims on Hinduism. After becoming a camp follower of the Arya Samaj leader Dayanand Saraswati, Indarman revitalized his campaign with a vengeance. The *Loh-i-Mahfuz* urged the district administration to ban the publications to prevent the eruption of 'a quarrel between the *two sects* of the community'.[99] Another local Muslim paper, *Jam-i-Jamshed*, warned that unless government burnt the books and closed down his press, Indarman was bound to be 'killed someday by some Musalman'.[100]

Evidence furnished by a Muslim deputy collector led the magistrate of Moradabad to fine Indarman and order the destruction of all copies of two objectionable books. This sent the Hindu press into convulsions with reverberations far beyond its epicentre. The Lahore Hindi weekly *Mittra Vilas* regretted that a 'distinguished disciple' of Dayanand Saraswati should be treated so severely when many offensive Christian missionary publications went unpunished.[101] By far the most astute comment was proffered by the *Akhbar-i-Am*, then the largest circulating Urdu paper in the Punjab, which maintained that the failure to ban missionary works had created a false impression among Hindus and Muslims that the government did not want to interfere in such matters. Beginning with attacks on Christianity, Hindus and Muslims in due course started fulminating against each other's religion. Since they were both internally divided, 'one sect denounced the tenets of the other sect'. A book published by the Faruqi press in Delhi, whose title translated into English as *The Beggar's Sword on the Wicked Man's Neck*,

[98]*Samaya Vindo*, 1 November 1876, *Selections*, L/R/5/53, IOL, p. 627.
[99]*Loh-i-Mahfuz*, Moradabad, 29 August 1879, *Selections*, L/R/5/56, IOL, p. 698 (my emphasis).
[100]*Jam-i-Jamshed*, Moradabad, 16 May 1880, *Selections*, L/R/5/57, IOL, p. 366.
[101]*Mittra Vilas*, Lahore, 2 August 1880, ibid., p. 536.

abounded in obscene and abusive statements 'calculated to create more excitement in the minds of the Hindus than the famous greased cartridges of 1858'. Instead of singling Indarman out for punishment, the government was urged to ban all publications intended to inflame religious passions.[102]

The Muslim editor of the *Anjuman-i-Punjab* thought the matter should have been settled amicably. Cases involving 'some great Pandit or Maulvi' required special handling since 'they have thousands of disciples' who could run amok and destroy the calm of the land.[103] There was an upsurge in Arya Samaj activities in the Punjab and the North Western Provinces following Indarman's indictment. Many Hindu papers portrayed Hindus as 'patient and merciful people' whose religion enjoined loyalty while 'cruel and prejudiced' Muslims were bent upon spreading Islam with the sword.[104] Some taunted the Hindus for their slavish mentality.[105] Others let slip their deep-seated resentment of Dayanand Saraswati who abused Hindu gods as well as the *shastras* and the *puranas*. This was why Hindus 'hate[d] him and his followers more than they d[id] the Musalmans'.[106] Like their Muslim counterparts, the narratives of Hindu identity were most revealing when targeting 'others' within.

Whatever else the Arya Samaj might have wanted to achieve by flying Indarman's flag, there was a distinct rise in the curve of social violence in different parts of India. Caused by any number of little local nuisances, these were cloaked in the language of communitarianism. The Hindu edited Urdu tri-monthly *Nasim-i-Agra* remarked that instances of 'misconduct' by 'ignorant Musalmans towards the Hindus' were becoming more frequent. In Mathura, for instance, some Muslims allegedly killed monkeys and forcibly drew water from Hindu wells.[107] Not all transgressions of established rules of behaviour in local society were novel. But there was something plainly unique about the way in which the news reached and affected relatively harmonious segments of the populace. One did not have to be literate to be aware of a scuffle involving Hindus and Muslims in a remote or not-so-remote locality. Despite the continued limitation of the circulation of newspapers in both the North Western Provinces and the Punjab, their content was disseminated through word of mouth at bazaars and local fairs to rouse communitarian emotions.

Against such a backdrop, the age-old issue of cow-slaughter was more conducive to being crafted into a symbol of Hindu–Muslim differences cutting across locality and region. Hindi newspapers wrote melodramatic stories of cunning Muslim officials using the excuse of non-interference in

[102]*Akhbar-i-Am*, Lahore, 11 August 1880, ibid., p. 567.
[103]*Anjuman-i-Punjab*, Lahore, 20 August 1880, ibid., p. 586.
[104]*Mittra Vilas*, Lahore, 6 September 1880, ibid., p. 617.
[105]*Mohan Chandrika*, no.6, ibid., p. 662.
[106]*Mittra Vilas*, Lahore, 15 November 1880, ibid., p. 786.
[107]*Nasim-i-Agra*, 20 November 1880, ibid., p. 787.

religious matters to cover the tracks of co-religionists guilty of indiscretions against this most sacred of animals. Since they had no religious obligation to slaughter cows, the Muslim penchant for doing so was perceived as a premeditated attempt 'to annoy the poor Hindus'.[108] The *Kohinoor* reported how a dispute over the height of the Prahladouri temple adjacent to the shrine of Bahawal Haq in Multan had sparked off a trade war between Muslims and Hindus in the city. District officials had granted permission to Hindus to raise the height of the temple to over forty feet.[109] After keeping mum for three months, some Muslim notables filed a petition with the district administration which decided that if the Hindus raised the temple they could no longer have use of the courtyard and well situated near it and the mosque. Encouraged by the directive, Muslim butchers took to selling beef openly in the market. In retaliation Hindus stopped purchasing mutton from them while Muslims boycotted all Hindu shops. Even Muslim washermen, barbers and sweepers ceased working for Hindus. Alluding to the material dimensions feeding an ostensibly communitarian divide in Multan, the paper observed that 'almost all the ringleaders of the Musalmans owe debts to the Hindus'; one was a secretary to the municipal committee while another was an honorary magistrate. Exercising circumspection, Hindu creditors had refrained from demanding repayment from Muslim debtors. Thousands of Muslims employed by Hindus had also escaped dismissal. Yet the anti-Hindu prejudices of district officials were evident in their decision to permit Muslims to sell beef. By contrast, Hindus were prohibited from opening mutton shops which was tantamount to 'making them Musalmans by force'.[110]

For the remainder of the nineteenth century, the pattern of Hindu–Muslim tensions in the North Western Provinces and the Punjab changed less in substance than in scope. In 1885, the formation of the Indian National Congress added new twists and turns to what by the early 1880s had become fairly predictable narratives of competing identities as articulated by the vernacular press. From an analytical viewpoint, the most important feature of these narratives in relation to conflicts at the social base was the extent to which social flare ups, encapsulated by the term 'riots', were attributed to the 'want of administrative ability on the part of the district officers'. Hindus and Muslims were demanding 'new privileges', not just for the sake of convenience but with 'the object of using them as a means of teasing each other'.[111] More than one newspaper held administrative negligence, or 'more indulgence to

[108]*Kavivachan Sudha*, Benares, 3 January 1881, *Selections*, L/R/5/58, IOL, p. 6.
[109]For a detailed account of the dispute, see J. Royal Roseberry, III, *Imperial Rule in Punjab: 1818–1881*, Lahore: Vanguard, 1988, chapter thirteen.
[110]*Kohinoor*, Lahore, 27 April 1881, *Selections*, L/R/5/58,IOL, pp. 247–8.
[111]*Kohinoor*, Lahore, 28 September 1881, ibid., pp. 563–5.

one class than to another', responsible for ensuring that 'an ordinary case became a religious case'.[112]

Yet Hindu–Muslim tensions erupted as suddenly as they petered out. Most major conflagrations were followed by efforts to rework social accommodations, even if these tended to skirt around the root of the problem and proved to be of a temporary duration. For instance, there were Muslim *ulema* and publicists who periodically vowed not to kill kine as a way of mollifying their Hindu fellow countrymen. *Fatwas* were issued against cow-slaughter, only to be rejected by another Muslim divine or propagandist. Akbar Allahabadi for one showed his impatience with the issue when he wrote:

Better to turn your eyes away from the cow
Whats the use of this daily hue and cry.[113]

Internal divisions among Muslims and Hindus gave rise to a multiplicity of ideas on how to manage relations with those belonging to other creeds. This is why trailing the blaze of social conflicts involving Muslims and Hindus in a doggedly linear manner ends up obfuscating more than it reveals.

The most significant lesson to emerge from the vernacular press coverage of local troubles in the North Western Provinces and the Punjab is that it remained singularly immune to the concept of 'communalism' while describing the outbreaks of violence between Hindus and Muslims. There is no equivalent term in either Urdu or Hindi. The word *qaum* continued to be used interchangeably for a religious, linguistic, regional or a sectarian community. Even colonial officials in late-nineteenth-century India referred to the two religious denominations, Muslim and Hindu, as the 'two castes', the 'two sects' or the 'two classes' of the community rather than 'two communities'. And the causes of local disturbances were ascribed to religious prejudices, intolerance, bigotry or materially based social and political rivalries, not to anything even remotely resembling the twentieth-century idea of 'communalism'.

[112]*Reformer,* Lahore, 4 September 1882, *Selections,* L/R/5/59, IOL, p. 578 and *Akhbar-i-Am,* 24 September 1881, *Selections,* L/R/5/58, IOL, pp. 550–1. For further substantiation of the role of the administrative apparatus in instances of communitarian-based violence, see Sandria B. Freitag, *Collective Action and Community: Public Arenas and the Emergence of Communalism in North India,* Berkeley: University of California Press, 1989. But like Pandey in *The Construction of Communalism in Colonial North India,* she errs in attributing Hindu–Muslim conflicts in local 'public arenas' to the rise of an all-India-based 'communalism'.

[113]*Behtar yehi hai pher lain ankhon ko gaai say*
Kya faida hai roz ki hai hai say.

بہتر یہی ہے پھر لیں آنکھوں کو گائے سے

کیا فائدہ ہے روز کی ہائے ہائے سے۔

(Akbar Allahabadi, *Kulliyat-i-Akbar,* vol. ii, Delhi (no date), p. 121.)

Examining the role of the vernacular press and poetry in the forging of a communitarian identity shows how epistemological certainties can lead to the erasure of distinctions between an elite discourse and the complex, and often ambiguous, existential dynamics at the social base. The discourse of the elite, in any event, was more internally divided than united. Moreover, there appears to be a fine discrepancy between the communitarian claims of the elite discourse, invoking as it does the larger religious community spilling over spatial limitations, and vernacular newspaper accounts of specific local tensions and conflicts. While referring to 'Muslims' and 'Hindus' with broad strokes of the pen as generalizable categories, the press coverage of local troubles in the late nineteenth century is sufficiently laden with multiple meanings as to cast doubt on the sanguine suppositions of historical approaches overwrought by the conceptual dichotomy of 'communalism' and 'nationalism'. The elision of cultural difference with an essentialized community of all-India proportions inherent in the notion of 'communalism' becomes even more untenable when an analytical distinction is made between the different arenas of politics. So it is worth considering how, and with what effect, internal contestations and ambiguities among Muslims at the local and regional levels were sought to be papered over by an elite discourse claiming to represent their interests in all-India terms.

THE PRIVATE AS PUBLIC AND THE POLITICS OF DIFFERENCE

In creating a formal arena of politics, the colonial state was veritably uninterested in extending representation beyond a select strata of Indian society. The exclusionary character of the British Indian political system aimed at consolidating the networks of internal collaboration and keeping them immune from pressures imposed by broader social dynamics. But in proclaiming a relative degree of autonomy for Indians in matters to do with religion and culture, the colonial state erected no more than a notional, indeed hollow, wall of separation between a politically defined 'public' and a religiously informed 'private' sphere. Clashing communitarian narratives in the late nineteenth century, ostensibly emanating from the 'private' domain, flowed in unrestrained torrents into a public arena of informal politics. A rising tide of bigotry within this arena did not fail to affect the nominally representative political institutions set up by the colonial state.

Yet there was no easy congruence between assertions of cultural differences and the politics of a coherent communitarian identity. Colonial schemes of political representation along with its preferred modes of social enumeration had underlined the need for supra-local linkages between members of the same religious denomination. But if there was an array of Indian responses to colonial political and social engineering at the level of discourse, far greater contestation and contradiction marked the arena of actual politics—'Muslim' and 'Hindu'.

Clashes between communitarian-based demands and class, local, regional and sectarian differences intensified with the gradual extension of the elective principle in colonial India. Intended to serve colonial purposes of control and manipulation, not the demands of popular representation, giving a restricted say to a handful of Indians in local and provincial bodies occasioned new strategies to balance the interests of the individual and the community.

That the balance, if at all struck, proved to be a precarious one is not surprising given the specific class and regional circumstances of individuals purporting to represent the general interests of internally differentiated communities. Even in cases of public appointments by the colonial government, considerable disagreement attended the choice of the individual. Instead of being interpreted as rewarding merit, the colonial selection of an individual for public office was attributed to the policy of balancing the interests of communities. Just as Sayyid Ahmad Khan's selection in 1878 to the viceroy's legislative council had agitated several of his co-religionists, the appointment of his son Sayyid Mahmud as chief judge of the Awadh high court drew opposition from European members who questioned his credentials as a representative of the Muslim community.

Confusing government appointments with representation for religious communities in municipalities or legislative bodies could set an unfortunate precedent for the future. As the *Awadh Akhbar* realized, given the sectarian divisions in Islam, as indeed 'among the followers of every other religion ... no Musalman can be considered as their leader by all the sects'.[114] In 1882 the elevation of Raja Shiva Prasad to the viceroy's legislative council also elicited adverse comment from a section of the Hindu press, angry at his lukewarm support for a Sanskritized rather than a Persianized form of Hindi. According to the *Hindi Pradip*, both Prasad and Sayyid Ahmad were unacceptably 'obsequious' to the colonial masters. The difference was that while Prasad was utterly selfish, Sayyid Ahmad 'not only looks to his own interests, but also does good to his co-religionists'.[115] In later years Prasad became a leading proponent of Hindi in the Nagari script in the North Western Provinces, indicating how individuals with access to the colonial state were vulnerable to pressures from newspapers claiming to voice the opinion of a community in the larger public arena.

Yet if the balance between the individual and the community was being shaped by the expanding power of print, the diversity of viewpoints articulated through this medium ensured that it would forever remain an unstable one. Positions taken by individuals cannot be equated with those of the entire community. Just as there was much variety in the sorts of influences to which an individual was subjected at any given moment, there were constant shifts

[114]*Awadh Akhbar*, 23 April 1879, *Selections*, L/R/5/56, IOL, p. 327.
[115]*Hindi Pradip*, Allahabad, January 1882, *Selections*, L/R/5/59, IOL, p. 73.

in the conception of communitarian interests depending on a range of temporal and spatial factors.

Education and Employment

Focusing on the closely intertwined issues of education and government employment prior to analysing more explicitly political questions like electoral representation helps in charting the changing tenor of the social dynamics informing the discourse on communitarian interests during the late nineteenth century. Ever since the publication of Hunter's *The Indian Musalmans* in 1871, Muslim elites in northern India and Bengal had been agitating to improve their proportionate share of the educational and employment resources of the colonial state. A special enquiry by the government of India in the early 1870s noted that Muslims in the North Western Provinces and the Punjab were taking advantage of the educational facilities at the lower levels over and above their respective population proportions. It was in the higher educational institutions that they lagged behind other communities owing to material difficulties and occupational preferences. The situation was dramatically different in Bengal where Hindus had left Muslims well behind in the educational field. In most of western India, parts of Madras as well as the Central Provinces and Berar where Muslims were scattered, hopelessly outnumbered, and spoke a language different from the rest of the population, there were serious obstacles to their educational advance.[116]

The regional diversities in the circumstances of Muslims in the domain of education and, by implication, government employment thwarted attempts to pitch a claim on their behalf in all-India terms. This did not dissuade aspirants to the leadership of India's Muslims from transforming regionally specific concerns into 'national' ones. Syed Ameer Ali shared many of Sayyid Ahmad's ideas on reforming Muslim society and the imperative of loyalty to the raj. But his society of Muslims was centred in Calcutta where the educationally more advanced Bengali Hindus were seizing plum jobs in the colonial government. Ameer Ali's regional and class interests led him to reject Sayyid Ahmad's policy of keeping Muslims strictly aloof from politics. In 1878 he established the first avowedly political organization for middle-class Bengali Muslims, the National Muhammadan Association, which after 1883 was renamed the Central Muhammadan Association.

The words 'National' and later 'Central' in the designation of this Bengali Muslim organization openly challenged Aligarh's pretensions to represent

[116]Extract from the Proceedings of GOI, Home Department (Education), Simla, 13 June 1873, *Selections From the Records of the Government of India, Home Department*, no. cvv. Home Department serial no.2, 'The Education of the Muhammadan Community in British India and their Employment in the Public Service Generally', Calcutta 1886, V/23/46, IOL, p. 227 (henceforth 'The Education of the Muhammadan Community', in *Records*, followed by IOL serial number and page).

the 'nation' of Islam in India. Seeing sense in calling a spade a spade, the vernacular press in north-western India referred to Ameer Ali's organization as the Calcutta Muhammadan Association. In February 1882 the association submitted a memorial to the colonial government, hoping to influence the recently established educational commission of which Sayyid Ahmad Khan was a member. The memorialists slammed the decision requiring candidates seeking employment as pleaders and *munsifs* to pass examinations in English. Previously the exam could be taken in either English or Urdu. Statistics and arguments drawn from Bengal were used to show how the 'well-to-do middle class—the section which forms the backbone of a nation—has become totally extinct among the Muhammadans'. Lacking capital for trade and commerce, Muslims needed government employment to survive. Yet even the best Muslim candidates were victims of 'intrigues' by Hindu officials, jealously guarding the doors to government employment.[117]

These pleadings might have secured a more sympathetic hearing from government if they had been restricted to Bengal. Colonial officials in the different regions of India were averse to being dictated to by a handful of middle-class Bengali Muslims. A judge in Bombay recorded that he had:

no means of knowing what right a body of persons styling themselves the 'National Muhammadan Association', whose headquarters are apparently in Calcutta, have to profess to represent the Muhammadans in British India, who number upwards of 40 million of persons, if, indeed, they have any right to do so at all.[118]

Muslims elsewhere in India were equally sceptical. According to the secretary of the Anjuman-i-Islami in Lahore, the 'memorial might be true ... [for] Bengal Muhammadans' but it 'cannot hold good ... [for] Muhammadans of this Province'. Punjabi Muslims were doing well under British rule. While agreeing with some aspects of their submissions, he regretted that the Bengali memorialists had exonerated their co-religionists who were 'to blame to some extent for their present wretched condition'.[119] Dismissing the case of Muslim 'backwardness', the educational commission concluded that 'a candid Muhammadan would probably admit that the most powerful factors are to be found in pride of race, a memory of bygone superiority, religious fears, and a not unnatural attachment to the learning of Islam'.[120]

The *Mashir-i-Qaisar* disliked the insinuation by the 'Calcutta Muhammadan Association' that Muslims were averse to an English education. Bengali Muslims,

[117]Memorial of the National Muhammadan Association to Lord Ripon, 6 February 1882, ibid., pp. 238–43.

[118]Minute by Justice Bayley, 24 April 1882, ibid., p. 270.

[119]Muhammad Barkat Ali Khan to under-secretary of the government of Punjab, Lahore, 5 August 1882, ibid.

[120]Extract from the education commission's report, chapter ix, section 2, ibid., p. 355.

including women, used the English language with felicity. It was the pro-Hindu policy of the colonial state which was the greatest barrier to Muslim employment in the administrative services. Muslims had 'better claims to State patronage than the Hindus'. What was more, it claimed, Hindus 'eat articles that produce flatulence'; therefore 'their heads are not so strong' and they were 'not fit to manage the affairs of the country'.[121] Such bigotry was matched by the *Hindi Pradip* asserting that improving the condition of the Muslims was akin to 'feed[ing] a serpent'. More to the point, if all Muslims were to be educated 'where will Europeans get bearers, cooks, tailors, sweepers ... and where will we get weavers, cotton-carders, washermen, butchers ...'. Hindus undoubtedly outnumbered Muslims in the public services in Bengal. But then 'Musalmans of Bengal are not such a bigoted and wicked people as those of Upper India'. The Calcutta memorialists should have compared the numbers of Muslims and Hindus in the public services of the Punjab and the North Western Provinces. The proportion of Hindu government servants to Muslims in the North Western Provinces based on population ought to have been in the order of seven to one. Instead, there were twenty Muslim subordinate judges against fourteen Hindu; fifty-four Muslim *munsifs* compared to forty-two Hindus; two Muslim assistant commissioners to one Hindu and 124 Muslim *tehsildars* against 113 Hindus. Sayyid Mahmud was the judge of the Allahabad high court and Muslims predominated in the police.[122]

In 1885 Lord Dufferin's refusal to waive educational qualifications for Muslims seeking admission into government service sounded the death knell of the Calcutta Muhammadan Association's memorial. The *Rafiq-i-Hind* thought the time had come for Muslims to put their 'shoulders to the wheel' and recall 'the maxim that God helps those who help themselves'.[123] Commenting on the time the government had taken to arrive at its decision, Lahore's *Shafiq-i-Hind* jested, 'a mountain laboured and a mouse is born'.[124] A Benares Urdu weekly was sorry that the viceroy had coldly dismissed the demand to reinstate Urdu as the language of Bihar as prompted by religious feeling.[125]

The reactions of regional Muslim elites to the formation of the Indian National Congress in 1885 were governed by the twin issues of education and employment. Although thirty-three Muslims attended the Calcutta Congress in 1886, Anglo-Indian newspapers like the *Pioneer* of Allahabad made much of their apathy and aloofness towards the first self-proclaimed national political organization of Indians. This was ascribed to the strong opposition of Bengali Hindu newspapers to the memorial of the Calcutta Muhammadan Association. Another reason was a recent decision by the

---

[121]*Mashir-i-Qaisar*, Lucknow, 14 March 1882, *Selections*, L/R/5/59, IOL, pp. 161–2.
[122]*Hindi Pradip*, ibid., pp. 236, 672.
[123]*Rafiq-i-Hind*, Lahore, 1 August 1885, *Selections*, L/R/5/62, IOL, p. 521.
[124]*Shafiq-i-Hind*, Lahore, 25 July 1885, ibid., p. 522,
[125]*Rafi-ul-Akhbar*, Benares, 27 July 1885, ibid., p. 523.

colonial government to undertake steps to better balance the proportion of Bengali Muslims in the provincial services and grant some fellowships to them in higher educational institutions. These government concessions explained why Ameer Ali's Central Muhammadan Association and Nawab Abdul Latif Khan's Calcutta Muhammadan Literary Society flatly refused to have any truck with the Congress. Muslims elsewhere viewed the new organization from their own equally limited regional perspectives.

The *Azad* of Lucknow admonished the *Pioneer* for spreading seeds of discord among Indians. Muslims were 'embarked in the same boat with Hindus' and 'equally desirous' to see the progress they made in education reflected in their share of the administration.[126] Signifying its proprietor's continuing support for Sayyid Ahmad Khan, the *Rafiq-i-Hind* noted that Muslims had 'discovered that their interests ... [were] quite distinct from those of Hindus'. Only a sprinkling of Muslims from Awadh had attended the Congress at Calcutta.[127] Most Muslim papers in north India saw the Congress as the vehicle of young Bengal, an opinion that found its clearest expression in the ideas of Sayyid Ahmad Khan. Interpreting his promotion of separate electorates for Muslims and unbending resistance to their participation in the Congress as 'communalism' underestimates the subtle and not-so-subtle religious and cultural influences on those advocating the virtues of 'nationalism'. It was precisely because the religious and cultural concerns of Indians had never remained confined to a so-called 'private' sphere that their discourse and politics in the public arena became so easily tinged with interests which were more narrowly communitarian than broadly 'national' in character. In the absence of a neat separation between the 'public' and the 'private' in colonial India, if such a conceptual distinction can be seen to have an empirical basis at all, religious and cultural considerations paraded as politics in the narratives of 'minority' and 'majority' interests with equal flair.

Yet the intermeshing of religion and culture with politics did not mean that all Indians were inherently bigoted, albeit in varying measures. Religiously informed cultural identities emphasized a sense of difference without foreclosing the possibility of Indians sharing common sentiments and coming together when circumstances were propitious for united action. There were to be sure disagreements on when unity outweighed all other considerations. But these were not simply due to the inexorable nature of religious distinctions in Indian society. Hindus were pitted against Hindus no less than Muslims against Muslims on how and when to bury their internal differences and forge a common front against the raj. Individual preferences based on class and regional location, and not just membership in a religious community, moulded Indian responses in their various permutations and

[126]*Azad*, Lucknow, 11 May 1886, *Selections*, L/R/5/63, IOL, pp. 359–60.
[127]*Rafiq-i-Hind*, Lahore, 25 December 1886, *Selections*, L/R/5/64, IOL, p. 3.

combinations. Consequently, a term like 'communalism' falls hopelessly short of explaining why Indian Muslims, taking their cues from a Sayyid Ahmad Khan or an Ameer Ali, opted to stay away from the Congress.

Representing Communities and Nations

Despite his resolute stance against the Congress, Sayyid Ahmad had always tried dissuading his fellow Muslims from cultural exclusivism and religious bigotry. Not unlike his disciple Hali and critic Akbar Allahabadi, Sayyid Ahmad's Muslimness was consistent with his Indianness. Being Hindu or Muslim was a matter of 'internal faith' and had 'nothing to do with mutual friendship and external conditions'. Quite as much as the Hindus, Muslims too 'consider[ed] India as ... [their] homeland'. For a man who did so much to shape the idea of a distinctive Muslim cultural identity, Sayyid Ahmad confessed that by living together with Hindus in India 'the blood of both have changed, the colour of both have become similar .... We mixed with each other so much that we produced a new language—Urdu, which was neither our language nor theirs'.[128]

Sayyid Ahmad's opposition to the Congress had less to do with the threats it might come to pose to the religious identity of Muslims than with the cultural pretensions and differential claims of the north Indian *ashraf* classes. He saw the Congress as a creation of the more advanced Bengali 'nation' and not of Hindus as such. Ignoring the uneven impact of colonial economic and educational policies in the different regions of India, 'the Bengalis ha[d] made a most unfair and unwarrantable interference with my nation'. He called upon Hindus of the North Western Provinces to 'cultivate friendship' with upper-class Muslims and 'let those who live in Bengal eat up their own heads'. Speaking as a regionalist, he stressed the temperamental and material differences between Bengalis and the 'people of *this country*'. And then displaying his religious biases, he warned that even in Bengal the Congress would sow enmity between Hindus and Muslims who constituted half the population of the province.[129]

Giving full play to his aristocratic airs, Sayyid Ahmad Khan recommended that members of the viceroy's council be chosen from among those of a 'high social position' and 'good breeding' as no one wanted to be placed under the authority of a man of lesser origin even if he possessed the requisite educational credentials. The Congress's demand for competitive examinations to the civil service would prove disastrous for Muslims who were educationally handicapped. This was a sure recipe for placing the whole of India under the rule of Bengalis, 'who at the sight of a table knife would crawl under ... [a]

[128]Speech at Patna on 27 January 1883 in Shan Mohammad (ed.), *Writing and Speeches of Sir Sayyid Ahmad Khan*, Bombay: Nachiketa Publications, 1972, pp. 159–60.
[129]Speech in Lucknow on 28 December 1887, ibid., pp. 180–5 (my emphasis).

chair'; the Rajputs and the 'brave Pathans' would have none of this.[130] He deemed Ripon's introduction of the principle of election to local and municipal bodies in 1882 inimical to 'Muslim interests'. Equating Muslim with *ashraf* interests, he argued that this would be 'like a game of dice, in which one man had four dice and the other only one'. No Muslim would get elected and the 'whole Council will consist of Babu So-and-So Chuckerbutty'. The same would be true of Hindus in 'our Province' although they were relatively better off than the Muslims.[131]

In urging Muslims to reject politics and make humble submissions to the colonial authorities, Sayyid Ahmad was angling for continued government support for the Muslim Anglo-Oriental College. This was the line of an educationist, not a wily political operator with a hidden agenda for a religiously informed cultural nationalism. Frequent references to the Muslim *qaum* in his speeches has given rise to the notion that Sayyid Ahmad Khan fathered the 'two-nation' theory. But he used the term interchangeably to refer to the Indian 'nation' and the Muslim 'community'. Once Sayyid Ahmad explained that by *qaum* he meant the inhabitants of a country even though they might have distinctive characteristics. A year before the formation of the Congress, he had said that 'Hindus and Mussalmans are words of religious significance otherwise Hindus, Mussalmans and Christians who live in this country constitute one nation'. In his 'opinion all men are one'; he did 'not like religion, community or group to be identified with a nation'.[132] That a call for Muslim non-participation in the early Congress should have qualified Sayyid Ahmad for the role of a 'separatist' and anti-nationalist underscores the political nature of the distinction between a 'communalist' and 'non-communalist' posture in retrospectively constructed nationalist pasts.

Although the most prominent spokesman of a north Indian regionally based Muslim elite, Sayyid Ahmad Khan's leadership had never gone unchallenged by the very Muslim *ashraf* classes on whose behalf he made his loudest appeals. Already by the late 1880s Britain's imperial policies in India and new colonial conquests in the Islamic world were leading more and more Muslims to shun Sayyid Ahmad's policy of non-participation in the Congress and stolid loyalty to the raj. Muslims from the North Western Provinces had taken to attending the annual sessions of the Congress in increasing numbers.[133] Encouraged by the trends, Badruddin Tyabji, a Bombay-based lawyer from the Bohra community who in 1887 became the first Muslim president of the Congress, tried parrying Sayyid Ahmad's objections to Congress's 'national' claims. Tyabji was 'not aware of anyone regarding the whole of India as one Nation'. India

[130]Ibid., pp. 204, 209.
[131]Ibid., pp. 180, 184, 210.
[132]Speech at Gurdaspur on 27 January 1884, ibid., pp. 266–7.
[133]Hardy, *The Muslims of British India*, pp. 131–2.

consisted of 'numerous communities or nationals' which had 'peculiar problems' of their own. The Congress had been established to discuss only those issues which affected all communities.[134] Far more significant was Tyabji's readiness to accept that if Muslims were indeed opposed to the Congress then it could not be regarded as 'a general or a National Congress' and it should suspend its annual meetings until the matter had been resolved.[135]

Muslims like Mahboob Alam, the owner of the influential Lahore paper *Paisa Akhbar* whose circulation in 1896 stood at a booming 10,000, thought many educated Muslims supported the Congress in principle but were unable to express this openly since they were in government service. Syed Ameer Ali was an employee of the colonial state and Sayyid Mahmud, who privately sympathized with the aims and objects of the Congress, did not publicly oppose his father from a sense of filial duty. The backbone of the Congress was provided by lawyers and traders, professions where there was an exceedingly small number of Muslims. Even Sayyid Ahmad Khan might have thought better of the Congress if he had been 'a good English scholar'.[136]

The *Akhbar-i-Am* tried putting spanners in the wheels of both the Aligarh and the Arya Samaj bandwagons when it dismissed the former as 'no more represent[ative of] the social and political views of the Indian Muhammadans ... than the Diyanand Anglo-Vedic College ... [was] of the Hindus [sic]'. It was ironic that Sayyid Ahmad Khan, pronounced by the *ulema* to be an infidel, should have the audacity to declare Muslims who joined the Congress traitors to Islam. Seizing upon the principal contradiction in the contending strands of the narrative of Muslim identity, it maintained that if Muslims of the 'old school' were the 'true followers of Islam and those of the new school the reverse', then 'the first sect that deserves to be excluded from the pale of that religion are the followers of Sir Sayyid Ahmad Khan'.[137] Defining the rules of inclusion and exclusion in the community of Islam was not an appropriate vocation for a paper closely associated with the opinion of urban Punjabi Hindus. But by now Muharram Ali Chishti, the disputatious editor of the *Rafiq-i-Hind* had ditched Sayyid Ahmad and hitched his wagon to the Congress instead. In Chishti's opinion, Muslims of the Aligarh school 'did not represent the Indian Muhammadans' who regarded them as heretics. The sudden volte face of so vocal a defender of Sayyid Ahmad was attributed to Chishti's success in wangling his way to an important position in the pro-Congress Anjuman-i-Numaniya of Lahore.[138]

[134]Badruddin Tyabji to Sayyid Ahmad Khan, 18 February 1888, in Malik (ed.), *Political Profile of Sir Sayyid Ahmad Khan*, p. 392.

[135]Cited in Hardy, *The Muslims of British India*, p. 131.

[136]*Paisa Akhbar*, Lahore, 5 September 1897, *Punjab Native Newspaper Reports*, L/R/5/180, IOL, p. 534 (henceforth *PNNR* followed by IOL serial number and page).

[137]*Akhbar-i-Am*, Lahore, 15 January 1897, ibid., p. 52.

[138]*Akhbar-i-Am*, Lahore, 7 December 1899, *PNNR*, L/R/5/183, IOL, p. 724.

Changing personal circumstances made it relatively easier for upper-class Muslims to break ranks with Sayyid Ahmad Khan. Since 1895 Shibli Numani had been publicly opposing his old patron's policy of Muslim non-participation in the Congress. Differences with his colleagues at Aligarh led Shibli to help found the Nadwat-al Ulema in 1898, an institution which he believed would give a fillip to his personal aspirations of greater status as an intellectual leader of India's Muslims.[139] In his post-Aligarh phase, Shibli was a frequent visitor at the Bombay residence of Begum Attiya Faizi, a woman whose superior intellect was to later charm no less a person than Muhammad Iqbal. Here Shibli befriended Badruddin Tyabji, a close relative of Attiya Faizi.[140] Shibli's exposure to the Tyabji family shaped his political thinking at a time when Sayyid Ahmad Khan's intellectual influence, if not legacy, was being overshadowed by reactions to Britain's imperial policies in the Muslim world.

If individuals could change horses in midstream, mustering support for the enlightened aims of the Congress among Muslims at large was no simple matter. Having done so much to mould the narrative on communitarian interests, individuals had far less autonomy than before in minimizing the impact of periodic Hindu–Muslim quarrels in urban centres and rural localities now that the print medium together with the railway and telegraph system was spreading news like wildfire. The formation of the Congress had seen a sharp deterioration in communitarian relations in the Punjab and the North Western Provinces. Highlighting the gap between noble utterances at select political gatherings and the ignoble bigotry of those warring in defence of their faith, the growing polarization along communitarian lines further embittered an already strained dialogue in the public arena. For all the talk about an inclusionary Indian nationalism, there was by now a flourishing discourse in the vernacular press on an exclusionary majoritarian Hinduism, impatient of Muslim 'yavanas' and 'mlechhas', derogatory Sanskrit terms for foreigners and barbarians respectively.[141]

Building on pre-existing idioms of their distinctive identity,[142] and also redefining them in the process, this exclusionary majoritarianism was

[139]Metcalf, *Islamic Revivalism in India*, pp. 340–1.

[140]Murad, *Intellectual Modernism of Shibli Nu'mani*, p. 114.

[141]*Bharat Jiwan*, Benares, 6 September 1886 and *Prayag Mittra*, Allahabad, 18 September 1886, *Selections*, L/R/5/63, IOL, pp. 634, 672.

[142]According to Romila Thapar, the terms 'yavanas' and 'mlechhas' initially did not have the religious connotation of the word 'Muslim'. Denoting India's historical links and familiarity with the peoples of western and central Asia, they were used to refer to Greeks, Arabs, Turks and Afghans, who were often accommodated as rulers or identified as those who like the lower-caste Hindu *jatis* were outside the brahminical defined *varna* system. (See Romila Thapar, 'The Tyranny of Labels', Zakir Husain Memorial Lecture, IX, 9 December 1996, Delhi: Zakir Husain College, pp. 7–15.)

virulently orchestrated by the Arya Samaj press in the Punjab and like-minded papers in the North Western Provinces. Linkages between local Arya Samaj activists engaged in cow protection and newspaper editors in both regions were reflected in attacks of unrelieved intensity on Muslims. The rejoinders of the faithful, particularly in the Punjab where the Arya Samaj onslaught took the heaviest toll on relations between the two communities, acquired an extra sting once Mirza Ghulam Ahmad (1839–1908) of Qadian in Gurdaspur district appeared on the scene as the self-appointed messiah of Islam. Notwithstanding the rebarbative overtones of Ghulam Ahmad's claims for most Muslims, it was his targeting of the Arya Samajists which infused a fresh dose of poison into an already bigoted public discourse in the Punjab.

Even without the messiah of Qadian there was enough happening in the public arenas of the Punjab and the North Western Provinces which flew in the face of pious efforts to ignite the spirit of inclusionary nationalism. The more so since the ferocity of exchanges between the protagonists of Hindu and Muslim interests overlaid vicious internal assaults on recalcitrant elements within both communities. Unity was a favourite theme in the narratives of contested identities, not least because it eluded the champions of Hinduism and Islam alike. The *Hindi Pradip* of Allahabad and the *Bharat Jiwan* of Benares had a point when they charged Hindus for the continued slaughter of cows by Muslims. Ordinary Hindus seemed more interested in taking out Muharram *tazias* than in celebrating Ram-lila and did nothing to stop Muslims from sacrificing kine during Id. Such men did 'not deserve to be called Hindus'.[143]

An amusing view of the way in which some Hindus were exploiting the cow, and making an issue out of a non-issue, was provided by a Muslim who published five hundred copies of an Urdu pamphlet on the subject. Speaking for itself, the cow makes a personal plea to the government denouncing those who were using it for sectional purposes:

I am loved by all like life itself
Everyone holds me in affection like a dear friend
Never am I spoilt by anyone's influence
Like water I merge with all colours.

The cow cites the *shastras* to deny that animal flesh is proscribed for Hindus. After thousands of years of being left alone, new exigencies in the country had metamorphosed it into 'Mata' or mother. Though flattered by the honour, the cow begs for reprieve as this elevation had increased the intensity with which knives were turning against it. Hindus in any event forced it to perform all manner of demeaning tasks; no sooner had the milk dried out that its hide was used to make items of daily necessity. This was hardly a way to treat

<hr>

[143]*Hindi Pradip*, Allahabad, September 1886 and *Bharat Jiwan*, Benares, 22 November 1886, *Selections*, L/R/5/63, IOL, pp. 688, 802.

'Mother Cow'; there was nothing to the cry that it was a sacred animal. It was the refusal of Muslims to endorse the Congress's policies and the material concerns of wealthy Hindu traders which had resulted in the sudden furore over its fate. The wise cow concludes with an impassioned appeal for social harmony between Hindus and Muslims. Encouraged by his own creativity, the author ends the pamphlet with the imaginative prediction that if Muslims voluntarily stopped cow sacrifice, Hindus would next try to put a stop to their call to prayer and then to the saying of prayers in mosques.[144]

Fears of the 'other' were intended to kindle a communitarian spirit among Muslims just as the cow-slaughter issue was deployed to alert Hindus to a unity which for all too long had eluded them. While entailing the targeting of the other community, such narratives of identity were aimed at an internal audience. Muharram Ali Chishti's *Mullah Dopiaza* castigated Muslims who watched as silent spectators while their co-religionists were trampled by Hindus:

Can you bear to see the days of cruel Yazid and Hajaj come again? If your swords have become rusty, can you still decide your destinies .... Can there be no unity among you even in religious matters? Can you throw your old fame in the Ganges? Have you become so ... degenerated that the sense of honour has become quite extinct in you? Cannot even religion stir up enthusiasm among you now?[145]

According to the *Chaudhwin Sadi*, Muslims were suffering more at the 'hands of their brethren in faith than from the followers of other religions'. While a Hindu official would bend over backwards to assist another Hindu, Muslims in the employ of the colonial government were chary of coming to the aid of a co-religionist for 'fear of being denounced as bigots'. And this despite the fact that 'the Aryas urge the expulsion of the followers of the Prophet from the Aryavarta'. This attitude was based 'on the supposition that ... [Muslims were] rebellious and disobedient and d[id] not learn the art of flattery from the Hindus'. The only inference to be drawn from all this was that 'the

[144]*Har dil hoon aziz zindagani ke tara
Piyari hoon sabhoonko yar jani ke tara
Hoti he nahin mukhil kise sobat mein main
Har rang main miljati hoon pani ki tara.*

ہر دل ہوں عزیز زندگانی کی طرح
پیاری ہوں سبھوں کو پیارِ جانی کی طرح
ہو تی ہی نہیں مخل کسی محبت میں میں
ہر رنگ میں ملتی ہوں پانی کی طرح۔

(Munshi Abdul Karim, *Hindu Musalmanon ke Mazhabi Khiyalat Ka Numuna* (or unusual answers to conflictual writings), Moradabad, 1896, UT. 1221, IOL.
[145]*Mullah Dopiaza*, Lahore, 3 November 1886 , *Selections*, L/R/5/63, IOL, p. 789.

Muhammadan community is at its last gasp; for when a Muhammadan will not help a Muhammadan, the days of the community must be numbered'.[146]

The *Sat Dharm Paracharak* of Jullundur exclaimed that 'strange things' were 'constantly happening now-a-days among the Muhammadans'. An attendant at the grave of the Holy Prophet and a Muslim from Rampur claimed to have had the same vision. They had seen the Prophet declaring that of seventeen lakh Muslims who had died only seventeen died in true faith as the rest had disobeyed his commands. This proved that 'paradise cannot be attained by embracing Islam and following the Prophet, but by doing good actions'. The only logical course for Muslims was to 'join the Aryas, adopt their religion, and *form one nation* as was the case before they embraced the religion of the Prophet'. True salvation was possible only by 'following the holy Vedas'.[147]

Such inflammatory writings alarmed a few innocents in the newspaper industry. Market trends indicated that sensationalism paid better than circumspection. While clamping down on papers taking a stand on sensitive political matters, the Punjab government remained unfazed by the rising crescendo of religious bigotry in the vernacular press. Deeply troubled by the 'fire of fanaticism' burning in the Punjab, the *Taj-ul-Akhbar* of Rawalpindi named the *Punjab Patriot*, the *Punjab Observer*, the *Tribune*, the *Arjuna*, the *Akhbar-i-Am*, the *Chaudhwin Sadi* and the *Wakil* as the main culprits. The villain of the piece was the Arya Samaj's English language paper, the *Tribune* of Lahore, which had done incalculable harm to relations between Hindus and Muslims in the province.[148] The tragedy of a press settling personal scores in the name of communitarian interests was one from which the Punjab never recovered. While defending himself, Munshi Sirajuddin Ahmad, editor of *Chaudhwin Sadi*, claimed that the 'responsibility' for the 'disunion prevailing between the two communities rest[ed] with the Hindu Press' which for 'the past twenty or more years ... [had been] attacking the Muhammadans'. Now that a few Muslim papers had begun giving 'publicity to the facts of the case', Hindus accused them of creating discord. In a revealing statement, Sirajuddin Ahmad declared that 'a man who undertakes to represent a nation is bound to write something on behalf of his followers'; it was completely 'wrong to infer from this that ... he is guilty of causing a breach between the two communities'.[149]

Expectations of a semblance of peace in the Punjab met a severe setback with the assassination in March 1897 of the Arya Samaj propagandist Pandit Lekh Ram. A calamity for inter-communitarian relations, the murder was seen as a conspiracy involving the entire Muslim community even though the assassin was never apprehended. The responsibility for this perception lay in

---

[146]*Chaudhwin Sadi*, Rawalpindi, 1 October 1896, PNNR, L/R/5/180, pp. 606–7.

[147]*Sat Dharm Paracharak*, Jullundur, 27 November 1896, ibid, pp. 714–15 (my emphasis).

[148]*Taj-ul-Akhbar*, Rawalpindi, 15 August 1896, ibid., pp. 506–7.

[149]*Chaudhwin Sadi*, Rawalpindi, 8 January 1897, PNNR, L/R/5/181, IOL, p. 33.

no uncertain measure with Mirza Ghulam Ahmad who had an uncanny knack for correctly foretelling the death of his opponents, including Lekh Ram. In a rare shift from their immersion into a collective discourse, one Muslim paper after the other decried the attempt to hold the entire community to ransom for the act of an unknown individual.[150] Police sweeps of the premises of Lahore's Islamia College and houses belonging to the secretaries of the Anjuman-i-Himayat-i-Islam and the Anjuman-i-Numaniya delighted Hindus and offended Muslims. In a most remarkable commentary on the fragility of social relations in the Punjab, a complete trade boycott was instituted by Hindus and Muslims against each other while Sikhs joined the fray furious at attempts by some Hindu papers to compare the martyrdom of Lekh Ram with that of Guru Govind Singh.

Lekh Ram's murder gave the Arya Samaj press in the Punjab the pretext to pull out all stops in the campaign calling for the expulsion of Muslims from India. The *Paisa Akhbar* accepted that Aryavarta belonged to the Hindus and that Muslims were 'like unwelcome guests in the land'. Yet, where could they 'go to after the lapse of several centuries' and whatever happened to the loud exhortations by Hindus on the need to form a joint front, it enquired somewhat disingenuously.[151] There was for the moment no hope of the Punjab nailing its colours to the Congress's banner of an inclusionary nationalism. The situation was not much better in the North Western Provinces where cow protection *sabhas* had been fomenting tension. But instead of playing a supportive role as in the past, the Punjab in the closing years of the nineteenth century had stolen the thunder of its neighbouring region in crafting the narratives of an exclusionary nationalism.

The idea of a 'true union' among Hindus and Muslims was denounced on the grounds that it was impossible to reconcile the religious beliefs and customs of two communities that were more like oil and water than milk and honey. The majority would 'suffer a great loss by such a union' since once the British left India, Muslims were certain to 'call the aid of Kabul, Persia and Turkey and annihilate the Hindus'.[152] According to the *Arya Gazette*, every follower of the Vedic faith earnestly hoped that the British flag would fly over Kabul and Kafiristan so that 'Hindus may be able to reconvert the Kafir to their ancestral religion, from which they have been turned at the point of the sword'.[153] There was a stark contradiction between the notion of Muslims as foreigners or '*yavanas*' and the rage over their forcible conversions by the armies of Islam. These narrative slips were less important than the determination of the more frenzied among Punjabi urban Hindus to resist

[150]See for instance, *Paisa Akhbar*, Lahore, 17 March 1897 and *Chaudhwin Sadi*, Rawalpindi, 15 April 1897, ibid., pp.203–4, 318.
[151]*Paisa Akhbar*, Lahore, 20 March 1897, ibid., pp. 207–8.
[152]*Punjab Samachar*, Lahore, 24 July 1897, ibid., p. 655.
[153]*Arya Gazette*, Lahore, 30 September 1897, ibid., p. 864.

the implications in the Congress's call for an inclusionary nationalism. Translating the 'national' message of the Congress into a regional setting where accommodations with members of other religious communities, Muslims and Sikhs, entailed making concessions seemed a trifle unfitting for a fragment of a majority community so long denied its rightful place in Aryavarta. This was a mirror image of the Muslim *ashraf* classes, who never ceased mourning the lost privileges of sovereignty while carving out a niche for themselves in the colonial system. The regional minority interests of these advocates of an exclusionary majoritarian nationalism based on a glorified view of the Hindu past were to clash in louder dissonance not only with competitors for power and privilege within the Punjab but also many of their own co-religionists elsewhere in India.

For all the emphasis on the identity of religion, neither Muslims nor Hindus succeeded in throwing up the sort of politics that could eradicate ideological, class, sectarian and regional fissures within both communities. Conflict along communitarian lines in northern India as a whole, and the Punjab in particular, appeared to give substance to colonial and *ashraf* notions of an Indian Muslim 'interest' that needed articulation and representation. Incessant feuding with Hindus over places in educational institutions and government services, or battling with them for social space on issues like cow-slaughter or the taking out of religious processions during annual fairs, were giving Muslims more than a sneaking sense of their distinctive cultural identity. The recognition of a religiously informed cultural difference from an assertive Hindu 'other' did not cement the multiple internal cleavages among Indian Muslims. Apparent in disputes over leadership and debates over the political response most suited to the promotion of their interests, this hemorrhaging of a religiously bounded community was not a fleeting but a recurrent phenomenon.

These contestations among Muslims sabotaged otherwise concerted attempts to formulate a coherent strategy by a number of individuals professing to be moved by the appalling decline in the fortunes of the community. Despite a well-established epistemology of social enumeration and disbursement of political rewards based on privileging religious distinctions, even officials of the colonial state in the late nineteenth century desisted from using the essentializing terminology implicit in the notion of Muslim minority 'communalism'. By the same token, the idea of a majority 'nationalism' was as yet a feeble one. Better explicated were attitudes on the rules of inclusion and exclusion in the community of religion, whether Muslim, Hindu or Sikh. The turn of the century saw a sharpening of the fault lines within the communities of religion in what were efforts to dictate the terms on which Muslims, Hindus or Sikhs would make submissions to the colonial masters. In the case of Muslims these were exemplified in Mirza Ghulam Ahmad's controversies with various *maulvis* and sporadic Shia and

Sunni tensions in the North Western Provinces. Hindus were riven with dissensions between Arya Samajists and members of Sanatan Dharm *sabhas* while the Sikhs were divided among the Khalsa and the rest.

Processes of identity formation in the late nineteenth century were characterized by far more internal fluidities within collectivities defined by religion than has been conceded in retrospectively constructed nationalist pasts. *Qaum*, whether in the connotation of 'nation' or 'community', had not yet achieved the internal consistency or the rigidly defined external boundaries that it came to acquire during the course of the twentieth century. Conflicting discourses on religious community had contributed to the accentuation of cultural differences. Colonialism had invested religion with greater significance through its peculiar configuration of the domains of the 'public' and the 'private'. The growing sense of cultural differences did not translate into a politics of identity devoid of considerations other than that of the religious community. It was the divisive issue of language that further compounded the problem of cultural difference in the late nineteenth and early twentieth centuries.

Chapter 3

Common Languages, Contested Scripts, Conflicted Communities:
Shifting Identities of Urdu, Hindi and Punjabi

The role of language as a principal site of differential identity formation in north India and the Punjab has been more readily acknowledged than satisfactorily delineated. Proponents of Hindi versus Urdu in both regions and advocates of the regional vernacular in the Punjab were hard-pressed to explain what they meant by 'Hindi' and where the line with 'Urdu' or 'Punjabi' could plausibly be drawn.[1] Until the 1860s no specific religious community had sole proprietorship over any of these languages. Nor were there any criteria clearly according status to a language superior to the range of dialects with which it was affiliated. Disagreements over the identity of languages nevertheless led to a hardening of religiously informed cultural differences, underlining

[1]There are a variety of theories, some fanciful and others based on research, about the origins of the word and the language Urdu. Widely associated with the military camps established by Mahmud Ghaznavi and Muhammad Ghauri, Urdu in Turkish literally means an army camp. Some writers have argued that the word originates in the Sanskrit Urdaoo, which means two hearts, and came to refer to the fusion of Hindu and Muslim cultures—a process which everyone agrees was entirely indigenous to the subcontinent. Those dating the beginnings of the process to the Ghaznavid occupation of the Punjab have suggested that Urdu emerged from Punjabi dialects and took its literary form in the vicinity of Delhi. Sayyid Ahmad Khan thought the structure of Urdu was built under the Khilji dynasty and assumed the shape of a usable language under Shah Jahan. Muhammad Husain Azad thought *Brajbhasha* was the source of Urdu while most British and some latter-day South Asian scholars have held *Khariboli* or *Hindawi* to be the more important influence. (See Farman Fatehpuri, *Pakistan Movement and Hindi–Urdu Conflict*, Lahore: Sang-e-Meel Publications, 1987, chapter two and below.)

how existential fluidities were imparting epistemological rigidities to communitarian narratives in late-nineteenth and early-twentieth-century colonial India.

Quite as much as the categories 'Muslim' and 'Hindu', the designations 'Urdu', 'Hindi' and 'Punjabi' for a welter of locally specific dialects, some only nominally linked to classical Arabic, Persian and Sanskrit, would have been unthinkable without the presiding agency of the colonial state. Language, education and employment formed a continuum influencing the calculations of colonial officials and a vocal segment of Indian society. Yet language, script and religious community constituted a more contentious and disconnected spectrum, vitiating attempts to project Hindi and Urdu as symbols of a coherent Hindu and Muslim identity respectively.

A comparison of languages, as a medium of speech and as script, in the North Western Provinces and the Punjab underlines the limitations of both colonial policy and elite discourses attempting to redefine language for communitarian purposes in the public arena. It has the added merit of correcting the oft-repeated scholarly assumption that the dispute between 'Hindi' and 'Urdu' in the North Western Provinces spilled over into the Punjab with largely similar effects on relations between Muslims and Hindus. Punjab was also home to the Sikhs. But in demanding the adoption of Punjabi in the Gurmukhi script from the margins, the Sikhs are often merely seen to have complicated an already intractable problem.

The easy acceptance of Urdu as the language preferred by Punjabi Muslims, and Hindi by the Hindus, cannot go unchallenged. Urdu's linguistic roots are traceable to certain dialects of the Punjab. Yet the origins of a language as a medium of oral communication in the Punjab cannot be confused with its later development as a literary language in north India and the Deccan. Such a premise fails to distinguish a spoken language from a written script and simulates the disdain in which the regional vernacular of the Punjab was held by the colonial masters and the provincial elites. A recent study of language in fashioning communitarian consciousness in the North Western Provinces concedes the myriad internal fissures characterizing the Hindu–Hindi–Hindustan fusion of the rhetoric. But the strength of the approach in unpackaging categories is weakened by the acceptance, willy nilly, of religion as the basis for demarcating a 'majority' from a 'minority'. A small but articulate group championing Hindi in the Nagari script is seen to have successfully lodged its case with the colonial government given the larger numbers of Hindi speakers in the region.[2] Such an argument does not hold true for a province where the majority of the populace, whatever the extent of their familiarity with Urdu, spoke Punjabi irrespective of religious denomination.

[2]Christopher R. King, *One Language Two Scripts: The Hindi Movement in Nineteenth Century North India*, Delhi: Oxford University Press, 1994.

Unlike the North Western Provinces where the identity of language eventually metamorphosed into a language of identity for a religious 'majority', the same cannot be said to have occurred in neighbouring Punjab.

What accounts for the very different configurations of language as identity for religious communities inhabiting these two regions? An examination of the specific nexus between language and the colonial educational system in determining employment prospects has to precede any analysis of the subjectivity of religious communities in these regions. This was a subjectivity bestowed upon communities by entrenched interests which had something to gain from transforming language into a symbol of a distinctive communitarian identity. Many of the factors confusing the communitarian claims of the protagonists of Muslim and Hindu 'interests' also militated against any neat equation of language with any particular religious denomination. Language as identity for the vast majority of the populace was a lived cultural experience, not a label to adopt or discard to fit the selective subjectivity of differential discourses. In the North Western Provinces the exclusionary discourse of those demanding Hindi in the Nagari script created the conditions for a more tangible bond based on language as identity for a besieged Urdu-speaking Muslim minority. In the Punjab, Muslim proponents of Urdu had to contend with a sharp dichotomy between the spoken words of the many and the written scripts of the few. Here there could be no unswerving transition from the identity of language to the language of identity. The issue of language hit the public limelight in the North Western Provinces and the Punjab during the second half of the nineteenth century. But regional and class variations made certain that while the idea of Muslim cultural difference found a most forceful articulation in one, its not-unforceful echoes in the other were subject to some strong qualifications.

The Identity of Language, Education and Employment

Colonialism in its efforts to monitor and control the affairs of a sprawling empire selectively adapted pre-existing networks and patterns of social organization in the different regions of India.[3] But while indigenous institutions and ideas undoubtedly moulded the colonial impact, qualitative changes took place in virtually every aspect of Indian society. Nowhere was continuity and change more thoroughly imbricated during the transition to colonialism than in the overlapping domains of language, education and employment. The colonial takeover was facilitated by the pragmatic decision to minimize social dislocations. Segments of the old service gentry associated with the central Mughal administration and its regional successors found

---

[3]This is the organizing theme of Bayly's *Empire and Information;* for a discussion of language, see chapter eight.

new avenues of employment in the colonial state.

This was done by retaining Persian as the official language of government and, by extension, the educational system which produced the personnel for employment in the colonial service. By the turn of the nineteenth century, Fort William College was actively promoting the development of Indian vernacular languages, advertising the colonial resolve to replace Persian as the official mode of administration. In 1835, ready to embark upon a more concerted policy of change, the colonial state dropped Persian as the official language of government in Bengal. While the regional vernacular was adopted as the language of the lower courts, English was the medium chosen for higher levels of administration. Elevating Bengali as the language of the lower courts had more far-reaching social consequences since Indians could hope to find employment in the colonial state only at the lower levels of the administration. The switch in Bengal was one of language as well as of script. According official status to a language was a knottier issue in the North Western Provinces and the Punjab. By 1835 orders had been issued in parts of the North Western Provinces to replace Persian with Urdu or Hindustani in the Persian script, a shift of language rather than of script. There were as yet only marginal distinctions between Urdu and Hindi, and colonial officials designated both as Hindustani.

Hindustani itself was a composite of dialects such as *Brajbhasha, Khariboli, Awadhi* and *Bhojpuri,* all linked to Sanskrit in varying measures. Mir and Ghalib had called this linguistic compound *Rekhta* before colonial discourse named it Urdu. Though drawing on all the regional dialects, its Muslim antecedents were underlined by a surfeit of Persian–Arabic vocabulary. This finds its best demonstration in Ghalib's poetry, as he himself boasted:

If anyone asks how *Rekhta* can be the envy of Persian
Read him Ghalib's discourse just once to show how.[4]

Asserting Urdu's distinctiveness and, for some, superiority over Persian was simpler to do than to locate the language in the social setting of north-western India. Incorporating Urdu into Hindustani without separating it from Hindi identified it with Persian and Sanskrit alike.

Urdu's asset as an admixture of Persian and Sanskrit was also a potential liability. The colonial decision to privilege Hindustani written in the Persian script gave the official language an identity more linked to the Muslim past

---

[4] *Jo yeh kaheye 'Rekhta kiunkar ho rashk-i-Farsi'*
Guftta Ghalib aik bar parh key usey soona ke'Yuon'

جو یہ کہے کہ رِیختہ کیوں کہ ہو رشکِ فارسی ٭

گفتہ غالبؔ ایک بار پڑھ کے اُسے سُنا کہ یوں ٭

(Ghalib, *Nawa-i-Saroosh,* p. 399.)

than the one associated with the Sanskrit roots of either *Brajbhasha*, *Khariboli* or *Awadhi*. But what was Hindi? It may be a name of the popular form Sanskrit had taken in the North Western Provinces. No agreement could be reached on which of the many dialects spoken here should be considered Hindi. Urdu too had evolved into a regional language through the incorporation of the same dialects. If Urdu was not Hindi then which of the dialects could substantiate the latter's claims of origin in an ancient Hindu past? *Brajbhasha* with its evocative religious imagery outstripped *Khariboli* as the preferred medium of poetry written by Hindus over the centuries. But *Braj* languished behind *Khariboli* in the new prose writings. The pioneers of a more accessible type of Urdu and Hindi prose at Fort William College under John Gilchrist's direction opted for *Khariboli*, deeming it to be more amenable to expressing temporal as opposed to spiritual concerns.[5]

Identifying Hindi with *Khariboli* rather than *Brajbhasha* or *Awadhi* weakened the argument about its uninterrupted links with ancient Sanskrit literature. Yet most supporters of Hindi in the late nineteenth century came to associate the language with *Khariboli* even while conceding the older and more numerous literary contributions of *Braj* and *Awadhi*.[6] Hindi as *Khariboli* could be different from Urdu as *Khariboli* only if written in a script other than Persian. Discarding the Persian script was easy. But Hindi could be written in the Nagari or the Kaithi scripts and there was no agreement on how far to go in the direction of Sanskritization. Where Persian had left a stronger imprint, as in the western parts of the province, proponents of Hindi wanted to drop only the script and retain the vocabulary. Others showed their erudition by adorning their prose with overly long Sanskrit words. The more pragmatic preferred a simpler form of Hindi in order to preserve connections with the spoken language of the region. These disputes played themselves out during the course of the late nineteenth and early twentieth centuries. All three trends did much to boost the cause of Hindi in the North Western Provinces. So there at least contentions over the precise identity of language did not appear to be a formidable barrier to its deployment as a symbol of communitarian identity.

The situation was markedly different in the Punjab. Persian had been the official language of the Sikh court which had partially promoted Punjabi in the Gurmukhi script and presided over the continuing spread of Urdu or Hindustani in the urban areas. Whatever the claims of its proponents, Urdu in the Persian script was not exactly a replica of the various dialects of Punjabi spoken by the majority of the populace in the province. Already inclined to replace Persian with Urdu, officials in the Punjab went through the motions of soliciting opinion on which of the vernaculars ought to be systematized

[5] King, *One Language Two Scripts*, chapter two.
[6] Ibid.

and standardized to serve as the language of the lower levels of administration. Undertaken over a decade and a half after the induction of Bengali in eastern India, the process in the Punjab was intolerant in the extreme of the dominant vernacular of the region. It is true that Punjabi never made the transition from an oral to a literate tradition comparable to Bengali. But it never remained an exclusively oral tradition either. Nor was written Punjabi restricted to any specific religious community. Yet colonial officials associated Punjabi written in the Gurmukhi script with Sikh religious scriptures and denigrated it as a 'bastard form of Nagree'.[7] Their damning comments on Punjabi stemmed in large measure from administrative imperatives than concern for the needs and cultural sensibilities of the people.

On 11 April 1849 the Punjab board of administration sent out a circular requesting information on the linguistic characteristics of the different districts. The stated aim was to 'bring the people to pure and original language' by discard[ing] the Barbarous languages in vogue'.[8] Responses to the circular underlined the yawning gap between the language of administration and the language of the people. Persian found its strongest support in Multan and southern Punjab as well as Hazara district which, although closer to the Pushto-speaking tribal belt of the North Western Frontier, was administratively part of the Punjab. In Multan, 'people d[id] not understand Oordoo [Urdu] or very slightly' while most educated people and artisans knew Persian.[9] The majority spoke Seriaki, a dialect which was even more different than 'the common Punjabi of the north from Oordoo'.[10] Punjabi in the Multani style was also spoken in Dera Ghazi Khan where the 'common people ... [were] equally ignorant of Persian and Oordoo'. Baluchis living here spoke an entirely separate language. Only *munshis, maulvis* and the educated few had any knowledge of Persian. Since 'probably not a man' outside his establishment understood Urdu, the official plumped for Persian.[11] The district commissioner of Hazara pointed to the difficulties of deciphering the Urdu script, adding that 'Oordoo being a bastard language' it was 'impossible to say from what language any given word may have been borrowed'.[12]

Most district officers in southern Punjab rejected Urdu as a foreign language. Indian officials, 'invaluable for the knowledge of the country', knew

[7]Nazir Ahmad Chaudhry (comp.), *Development of Urdu as Official Language in the Punjab (1849–1974),* Lahore: Government of the Punjab, 1977, p. iii—henceforth *Development of Urdu in Punjab.*

[8]Ibid., p.iv.

[9]M.P. Edgeworth (commissioner, Multan division) to G.J.Christian (secretary, board of administration), 7 July 1849, ibid., p.11.

[10]Edgeworth to Christian, 27 July 1849, ibid., p.19.

[11]H.M. Van Mortland (deputy commissioner, Dera Ghazi Khan) to Captain D. Ross (commissioner, Leia division), 24 July 1849, ibid., pp. 15–16.

[12]Deputy commissioner, Hazara to G.J. Christian, 8 July 1849, ibid., p.13.

Persian rather than Urdu.[13] The administrative quandary was a real one. In two districts of Multan division, Jhang and Pak Pattan, Urdu was already in use while in Multan proper only settlers from the North Western Provinces understood the language. So Urdu was adopted in Jhang and Pak Pattan while Persian was retained in Multan. Urdu also replaced Persian in the Lahore and Jhelum divisions of the Punjab while Persian remained the language of administration in Peshawar and Hazara. Within two years district officers in Multan had come around to accepting Urdu on the grounds that familiarity with the language, if not necessarily its usage, had miraculously increased.

By 1854 a consensus had emerged within the Punjab administration in favour of making Urdu the official language not only in the southern districts but also Peshawar and Hazara. The changeover from Persian to Urdu was a product of administrative convenience. English officials had been learning Urdu and were not minded to grapple with Persian. Urdu may not have been the lingua franca for the whole of India yet it could become one through official patronage, enabling the colonial state to better administer its possessions. Ignoring the linguistic affinities of its overwhelmingly Pushto-speaking people, the commissioner of Peshawar believed it was 'desirable to encourage the spread of the Indians "Lingua Franca" [namely Urdu]'. It would 'hasten amalgamation of our trans-Indus Possessions' while Persian, the language of Kabul and also of 'the religions and least loyal class of our new subjects', had the 'tendency to retard it'.[14]

Education for Whom?

The colonial state's justifications for dethroning Persian are less liable to be faulted than the contradictory logic of its language and educational policies. After initial problems and some lingering ones for a destitute Muslim agrarian population in the eastern districts, Bengal soon overshadowed Persian and Urdu as the primary medium of vernacular education and the official language at the lower levels of the administrative system. Attempts by members of the old Muslim elite to revive the issue of Urdu, Persian and Arabic as languages of instruction were little more than statements of disaffection with their declining social status, especially as reflected in the relative share of the two communities in the colonial service.[15] The government of Bengal recognized that the vernacular language of the Muslims in the province was 'generally Bengalee, not Hindustani, far less Oordoo'. Muslims were attending Bengali schools even though they avoided the government's English schools. And

---

[13]I.Wedderburn (assistant commissioner, Khangurh) to Captain D. Ross, 25 July 1849, ibid., p.17.

[14]Major H.B. Edward (commissioner, Peshawar division) to P. Melvill (secretary to chief commissioner), 17 July 1854, ibid., p. 36.

[15]See Ahmed, *The Bengal Muslims*, pp. 119–32.

while Muslims had 'no desire to be instructed in an artificial Sanskritized Bengalee', they needed English rather than a dose of oriental languages to compete more effectively with Hindus for employment in the colonial state.[16] But Bengal was an exception which failed to disprove the norm. There were glaring ambiguities in the colonial state's language, education and employment policies in north-western India.

In the North Western Provinces the distinction between a common language and contested scripts led to the development of parallel systems of vernacular education. Already by 1845 schools teaching Hindi in the Nagari script or classical Sanskrit outnumbered those relying on Urdu, Persian and Arabic. The trend continued to gather momentum despite the attraction of learning English or Urdu as a means to government employment. In 1860, a mere 2.5 per cent of the students in the North Western Provinces were attending English schools. Hindi–Nagari and Sanskrit schools accounted for a walloping 62.1 per cent of the student population compared with 35.2 per cent receiving an education in Urdu, Persian or Arabic.[17] The educational system was churning out many more versed in Hindi and the Nagari script than could hope to find employment in the colonial state. This discrepancy contributed in no uncertain terms to the ferocity of the Hindi–Nagari movement in the North Western Provinces after the 1860s. Yet even in 1870 there were as many books in Urdu as in Hindi being published in the North Western Provinces. The director of public instruction thought the number of Persian publications was 'noteworthy'; it 'show[ed] how determinedly the old *Kayasth--Musalman* system of teaching [was] holding its own'.[18]

If vacillation was the operative word guiding the colonial approach towards language, education and employment in the North Western Provinces, there was a mulish quality about official attitudes towards these interrelated spheres in the Punjab. Here not just the script but the medium of instruction in government schools and the official language of administration was out of line with the regional vernacular. Periodic requests from officials to reconsider the language policy and make the educational system more responsive to the needs of the people were dismissed in a perfunctory manner. In 1862 one official suggested making Punjabi the language of the lower courts. The reaction was emphatically negative. There was absolutely 'no advantage' in the idea. Urdu had been embraced by the educated classes of the province and its use was increasing by virtue of it being taught in elementary schools

[16]C. Bernard, officiating secretary to the government of Bengal, to secretary, government of India (home department), 17 August 1872, 'The Education of the Muhammadan Community', in *Records*, V23/46, IOL, p.173.

[17]King, *One Language Two Scripts*, p. 99.

[18]There were ten more educational works in Hindi than in Urdu. Those in Persian were only a 'little less' than those in Urdu. (Report by M. Kempson, director of public instruction, NWP, 12 February 1870, in *Records*, V/23/129, IOL.)

and serving as the medium for court records. Punjabi was 'merely a dialect of Urd[u]' with 'no literature of its own' and made its appearance as a written language only in Gurmukhi which was a debased form of Nagari. There were in any case strong political reasons for patronizing Urdu as a 'common tongue' even in Pushto-speaking Peshawar and Hazara since this would expedite control over the 'wild border tribes'.[19]

The various dialects of Punjabi did not merit the status of a language. They were 'barbarian mixtures of Hindee and Persian of which Oordoo ... [was] the pure type'. Making local patois like Pushto, Multani, Derajatee or the variations of Punjabi spoken in the central districts of the province the language of evidence would put an end to the system of judicial appeal and 'the prospect of having a pure Provincial Language w[ould] be indefinitely postponed'.[20] Any such move would entail dismissing about half of the personnel employed in the courts and render the proceedings of one divisional bench unintelligible to another.[21] Even 'Punjabi' which had 'better pretensions than any other to be considered a distinct language' was 'dying out'.[22]

Punjabi was fading out only in the official mind. A Punjabi villager might understand simple Urdu better than 'indifferent Punjabee talked by foreigners'. It did not follow that in 'a few years Oordoo w[ould] be the language of the people'.[23] No one had a clue as to how this revolution was going to take place. Insisting that his objection to Punjabi was 'not founded on any prejudice', one colonial official went on to insult a language of which he had only desultory knowledge. Giving Punjabi the status of a court language was tantamount to establishing 'broad Scotch in the Courts north of the Tweed, or the barbarous patois of Summersetshire in the Courts'. Punjabi was 'inflexible and barren' and 'wholly incapable of expressing nice shades of meaning, and exact logical ideas so necessary for legal proceedings'.[24]

The official charge against Punjabi was that its many dialects made standardization impossible. Similar arguments had been used against making Bengali the language of the lower courts. There was no ostensible reason why Punjabi dialects should elude standardization any more than Bengali and

[19]Director of public instruction to secretary, government of the Punjab, 22 July 1862, in Chaudhry (comp.), *Development of Urdu in Punjab*, pp. 37–8.

[20]Commissioner of the Cis-Sutlej states to secretary, government of the Punjab, 17 June 1862, ibid., p. 43.

[21]Captain N.W. Elphinstone (deputy commissioner, Jullundur) to secretary, government of the Punjab, 8 July 1862, ibid., p.47.

[22]Colonel Lake (commissioner Trans-Sutlej states) to secretary, government of the Punjab, ibid., p.45.

[23]Captain E. Paske (deputy commissioner, Gujarat) to commissioner, Rawalpindi division, 23 June 1862, ibid., p. 52.

[24]Captain P. Maxwell (deputy commissioner, Goojaira) to Lieutenant. Colonel G.W. Hamilton (commissioner, Multan division), 23 June 1862, ibid., p. 60.

Urdu. The truth of the matter was that the colonial state had 'gone too far in the other direction' and its officials could not see 'any political advantage' in adopting Punjabi in the Gurmukhi character as the language of the courts and, in this way, 'keeping the Punjab more distinct from the N[orth] W[estern] Provinces'. If this was 'desirable' then the 'first step' had to be to 'do away with Oordoo and teach nothing but Punjabee in our Schools'. Why adopting Punjabi meant ousting Urdu is less obvious than the bureaucratic certitude about their inability to coexist.[25]

Spoken languages have a way of fighting back with a vengeance. Condemned to die an unsung death, the future of Punjabi was not decided at the margins of administrative analysis but at the centrestage of history by the people themselves. A similar fate had been foretold for Pushto. Here again any change of official language was seen as stymieing the 'growing prevalence of Urdu' which was believed to be 'greatly bound up with progress in civilization and amelioration of manners'.[26] Exiled from colonial schemes of vernacular education, the cultural resistance of Punjabi and Pushto has been remarkable for its persistence. Both have retained their indomitable hold on the psyches of their speakers despite being denied the status of official scripts. This is what makes the British patronage of Urdu in the Punjab and the Peshawar and Hazara divisions of the North West Frontier region particularly instructive.

In supporting Urdu as the medium of instruction in vernacular schools, colonial officials were fostering an educational system closely linked with the press and publications market. Needing some means of communicating with the 'vast class of Agricultural labourers', who were least willing to send their children to government schools, the Punjab government started official newspapers such as the *Sarkari Akhbar*. This would help promote adult literacy which some colonial officials considered more important than teaching young boys to read and write. Able to extend a type of education that was 'less repulsive less compulsory less methodical but a thousand times more influential', the 'press in its most popular form' could be 'a more forcible engine of popular instruction than the School'.[27] For all the good intent, the colonial state was better able to improve the spread of oral education than the written. Newspapers read out at gatherings of Punjabi villages could relay the government's message and much more since private presses were harping their own tunes out loud.[28]

[25]Commissioner, Rawalpindi division, to secretary, government of the Punjab, 3 July 1862, ibid., p. 55.

[26]Commissioner, Peshawar division, to secretary, government of the Punjab, 18 November 1862, ibid., p. 63.

[27]W.D. Arnold, director public instruction, Punjab to D.F. Mcleod, financial commissioner, Punjab, 13 March 1858, ibid., p. 70.

[28]As one memorial from the predominantly Muslim district of Jhang and Maghiana told the Hunter Commission on education in 1882, the fact that thirty out of thirty-three newspapers in the Punjab were in Urdu was being 'adduced as proof of that

An oral education, however, was no substitute for an effective system of mass education. The refusal to provide even a bare bones education in the mother tongue of the population did not fail to take its toll on the already low literacy rates in colonial Punjab. It was not as if colonial officials were oblivious of this problem. The establishment of various educational commissions to investigate the quality of primary-level instruction in the North Western Provinces and the Punjab made certain that the question of language turned up more often than anyone wanted. In 1853–4 a review of the vernacular educational system found the judicial commission highly complimentary towards a people whose spoken language had been ruthlessly sidelined. Punjabis of all religious denominations were responding to the educational system. There was 'less prejudice and fewer elements of passive hindrance or active opposition here than elsewhere'. The Sikhs were seen to be losing their inclination for 'fanaticism and political fervour'; Hindus in the Punjab were 'less superstitious and less priest ridden' while the Muslims were 'less bigoted and less bound by traditionary practice than their co-religionists in any part of India'.[29]

Such a rosy picture of relations between the three communities of the Punjab in the 1850s makes for a sharp contrast with the later part of the nineteenth century. Before considering the role of the vernacular press in disrupting the inter-communitarian balance with its flagrant writings on the Urdu–Hindi controversies, it is worth considering the structural effects of the colonial state's language policy on mass education in the Punjab. Convinced that 'Punjabi was an inferior language' that was 'degenerating into a mere provincial dialect', officials were against any move to 'promote it as opposed to superior Hindustani' or even to let its words fall into Urdu and Hindi usage. Quite the reverse was in fact happening. Urdu was being absorbed into Punjabi dialects, not the other way around. One Sikh memorial to the education commission in 1882 noted that since coming to the Punjab, Urdu had 'lost much of its force'. The 'Urdu used in this country is a Panjabi–Urdu, and seldom liked by Hindustanis'. These Sikhs were certain that 'after some time it [Urdu] w[ould] merge in Panjabi'.[30] This was not credible to the dominant colonial mindset adamant to keep Urdu immune from all 'superfluous' and 'vulgar characters' which were localized and 'semibarbarous in formation'.[31]

So, unlike Bengal and the North Western Provinces, the colonial state in the Punjab was not just establishing the identity of the regional vernacular.

---

language being the popular tongue of the province'. Signed by 1584 persons, the petition asked in bewilderment 'how this can be held to be a proof of Urdu being the language of the masses *who never read a paper*'. (See Ghulam Husain Zulfiqar [ed.], *Select Documents on National Language*, vol. i, part 1 [Report 1882], Islamabad: National Language Authority, 1985, p. 62.)

[29]Minute of the judicial commission, 1853–4, ibid., p.128.

[30]Memorial from Shri Guru Singh Sabha, ibid., p. 5.

[31]Chaudhry (comp.), *Development of Urdu in Punjab*, p.138.

For all its great leaps forward, Urdu was a literary vernacular, not a spoken language of Punjabis of any religious denomination. Urdu could be read and written but was rarely heard in the prattle of the bazaars or chitchats in the privacy of homes. The rural population did not speak it, nor did 'their wives, sisters, mothers, daughters ... speak or understand Urdu' and this was true 'not only of Hindu but of Muhammadan villagers alike'. Even in the key towns of the Punjab, Urdu had no place in the much talked about private domain. It was used 'only in public societies, courts and offices' since it was the medium of instruction for six or seven years and the mode of communication with the colonial administration.[32]

In the event, the equation between language, education and employment in the Punjab proved to be more a fitting barrier against mass literacy than conducive to the extermination of the spoken vernacular. It was a small elite versed in Urdu which in collusion with colonial officials dampened opposition to the language and educational policies decreed for the Punjab. There was 'unanimity of opinion ... among Muhammadan and Hindu gentlemen' about the merits of the government's educational system in the province. Exhibiting class rather than communitarian solidarity, Muslim luminaries saw no need for special schemes to encourage their co-religionists to partake of education. In 1872 Muslims attending government and government-aided schools accounted for 35 per cent of the student population while their total population was 53 per cent. The low proportion of Muslims was attributed to the fact that Brahmans and Khatris had 'hereditary prejudices against agriculture and manual labour' and looked to education 'as a means of livelihood'. But even if Punjabi Hindus were 'more alive to the advantages of a school education', the absence of Muslims was conspicuous only at the upper levels of the educational system. The system of vernacular education was more favourable to Muslims than Hindus. Most of the teachers at the primary level belonged to the 'Mulla class' since the languages taught were either Urdu or Persian. To give special grants-in-aid to Muslim educational institutions would 'throw the education of the masses into the hands of the priests'. This would have disastrous consequences in a province where 'even among the Hindus ... the influence of Muhammadan associations [was] so strong' that in 'correspondence, books, and newspapers the ideas and diction are Muhammadan in character ... when the language is Urdu'.[33]

[32]Statement of the pro-Hindi Delhi Literary Society in Zulfiqar (ed.), *Select Documents on National Language*, p. 58.

[33]C. Pearson, (officiating registrar, Punjab University College) to secretary, government of the Punjab, 8 July 1872, 'The Education of the Muhammadan Community', in *Records*, V23/46, IOL, pp. 198–201. A similar attitude marked the colonial state's educational policy in the North West Frontier. (See Robert Nichols, 'Settling the Frontier Land, Law and Society in the Peshawar Valley, 1500-1900', unpublished doctoral dissertation, University of Pennsylvania, 1997, chapter eight.)

Pleading with Officialdom

Within a decade the pro-Hindi lobby were voicing their demands in the Punjab, for the most part in the very Urdu language and script whose pre-eminent status they wished to equal or replace with Nagari. The common refrain was that the teaching of Persianized Urdu tended to 'Muhammadise the Hindus'.[34] Before the setting up in 1882 of the education commission headed by W.W. Hunter, meetings organized by *pandits* failed to muster support for Hindi in the Nagari script. The 'general opinion' was that 'the petition would not be heard' and so no submission was made.[35] There were continued rumblings of discontent among a section of Punjabi Hindus. This was attributed to the presence of Bengalis in the province, who seeing their prospects for employment in the colonial government undercut by the difficulties of mastering the Persian script thought they had a better chance learning Nagari. Educational institutions in Bengal were producing an estimated 2000 candidates annually for government employment. Footloose Bengalis eager for a place in the colonial government fanned out into the different parts of India throughout the second half of the nineteenth century. Believing Nagari to be more akin to their own script, Bengalis had already taken a lead in stoking anti-Urdu fires among Hindus in the North Western Provinces.[36]

This was not difficult considering the statistics to back their claims. Based on the colonial mind's inebriation with the religious category in enumeration, the 1881 census assumed that anyone whose self-definition did not fit the tenets of a recognized creed would be defined as Hindu. A Muslim deputation had challenged the notion of a Hindu 'majority', arguing that not all included in this category could be classified as Hindu.[37] But subtlety was not a virtue cherished by the colonial state's number crunchers. The religious accounting of the 1881 census showed that Hindus constituted over 86 per cent of the population in the North Western Provinces and Muslims an insignificant 13 per cent or so. But of the 54,130 Indian officials holding government jobs in the North Western Provinces, 35,302 or 65.2 per cent were Hindus while Muslims accounted for 18,828 or 34.8 per cent. The literacy rates of the two communities were only marginally different. Hindus had a literacy rate of 5.1 per cent and Muslims of 4.4 per cent. Based on their share of a total literate population of 11.8 per cent, Muslims were holding state employment nearly

[34]The opinion of Reverend C.W. Forman, Lahore, to the Hunter commission, 1882, Zulfiqar (ed.), *Select Documents on National Language*, p.18.

[35]The opinion of Pandit Bhuwan Das before the Hunter Commission, 1882, ibid., p.12.

[36]King, *One Language Two Scripts*, p. 73.

[37]Kenneth W. Jones, 'Religious Identity and the Indian Census', in Barrier (ed.), *The Census in British India*, p. 92.

three times than their proportionate population.[38] Statistically this was not a bad showing for an otherwise declining Muslim service gentry convinced that their fortunes had fallen appreciably under the new dispensation.

By the time the Hunter Commission began its deliberations in 1882 the idea of a 'majority' and 'minority' community had already impinged on the debate over language, education and employment. The memorial submitted by the National Muhammadan Association of Calcutta traced the decline of Muslims in eastern India to the abandonment of Persian as the court language. It protested the implementation in 1881 of an administrative decision taken in 1871 to introduce Hindi in the Kaithi script as the official language of the lower courts in Bihar. This amounted to throwing Muslims and Hindus of the Kayasth caste out of subordinate government jobs. The majority of Hindus in Bihar 'in their manners, their customs, and their modes of amusement' were like the Muslims from whom they derived their 'polish and culture'. Urdu was not unintelligible to the illiterate masses of Bihar and was by far the most popular language of communication among the educated. Unable to distinguish between Kaithi and Nagari, the memorialists claimed that 'Nagari' was a difficult script to master and therefore 'objectionable to all classes of people'.[39]

As it is Muslims were reeling under the impact of the decision to conduct official business in English at the higher levels of the administrative system. The more so since there had been no corresponding decision making English education compulsory. Until 1864 Muslims were being told that knowledge of their own classics was necessary for government employment and entry into the legal profession. But a couple of years later they discovered to their chagrin that examinations in English alone would qualify them for jobs in the higher levels of the judicial system. Before Muslims could wake up to the need for an English education, the doors of government employment were slammed shut on them.[40] Bengali Muslims in particular were hard done by the decision. On the basis of 1871–2 statistics, Muslims were 32.3 per cent of the total population in Bengal (including Assam) and 14.4 per cent of the students in schools.[41] They were doing no better in provinces where the regional vernacular was other than Urdu or Hindustani.[42]

In Sind where the state of education generally left much to be desired, a paltry 10,115 out of a total population of 1,354,781 were attending schools. Of this Muslims accounted for 31.8 per cent even though their proportion to

[38]Based on the 1881 census, these figures are taken from King, *One Language Two Scripts*, p. 108.

[39]Memorial of the National Muhammadan Association to Ripon, 6 February 1882, 'The Education of the Muhammadan Community', in *Records*, V23/46, IOL, p. 243.

[40]Ibid. pp. 239–40.

[41]See extract from Hunter Commission report, chap.ix, section 2, ibid., p. 355.

[42]Memorial of the National Muhammadan Association to Ripon, 6 February 1882, ibid., passim.

the rest of the population was four to one. Averse to studying English, Sindhi Muslims were trailing behind Hindus at the higher levels rather than in the educational system as a whole. Here Sindhi was the regional vernacular and Persian the mark of a gentleman from the middle and upper classes. Persian was taught in primary schools along with Sindhi and had an enthusiastic following among the villagers. The picture was not much different in Madras where although 6 per cent of the population, Muslims comprised only 4.4 per cent of the students in the province.[43]

Statistics examined by the Education Commission put the arguments of the Calcutta memorialists at a serious discount in the North Western Provinces and the Punjab. With a population of just a little over 13 per cent in the North Western Provinces, Muslims constituted 17.8 per cent of the students in schools. In Awadh with a population of only 9.9 per cent, the share of Muslims in schools was in the order of 25.3 per cent.[44] So Muslims by and large were doing well by the colonial government's language and educational policies in the North Western Provinces. In the Punjab, the Muslim share of the population was not reflected in the proportion of students at schools. In 1882 the total number of Muslim students in the Punjab had gone up from 35 per cent to 38.2 per cent largely due to increases in the higher rather than in the lower levels of the educational system.[45]

This was why upper-class Muslims in the North Western Provinces and the Punjab harboured reservations about the Calcutta memorialists' demand that Muslims as a community be granted special provisions in the domain of education. But they readily endorsed the memorialists' stance against Hindi in the Nagari script. Muslims of the *ashraf* classes in the North Western Provinces insisted that they had suffered a net decline in their share of the public services with the establishment of British rule. Manipulating figures to tot up a Hindu majority in these provinces took nothing away from the fact that Muslims were steadily falling behind in the competition for government employment. Support for Urdu in the Persian script was also powerfully voiced by the Anjuman-i-Islamia in Lahore. It deplored the developing opposition in the Punjab against Urdu started by 'some foreigners' and backed by some Hindus. If this succeeded it would mean 'a death-blow to the prospects of the Muhammadans'. The Anjuman hoped that the government would 'soon extinguish this wild fire' and ignore the memorial submitted by 'some "prejudiced" Hindus', a reference to Arya Samajists and Brahmo Samajists, who were spreading the 'revolutionary movement throughout the length and breadth of the Province'.[46]

[43]These statistics are for the year 1871–2. See extract from Hunter Commission report, chap. ix, section 2, ibid., pp. 355–7.
[44]Ibid.
[45]Ibid., p. 362.
[46]Muhammad Barkat Ali Khan (secretary of the Anjuman-i-Islamia) to the under secretary, government of the Punjab, 5 August 1882, ibid., p. 317.

But unanimity on the language question among upper-class Muslims in the two regions did not create the linguistic bond with subordinate social classes in the Punjab quite as neatly as in the North Western Provinces. For all the declarations about the healthy state of the colonial vernacular educational system in the Punjab, in 1882 a mere 4 per cent of the boys between ages five and fourteen were learning to read and write. The proportion among the Hindus was 12 per cent while for the Muslims it was a hopeless 3 per cent. Only 5.89 per cent of the entire male population in the province could read and write. Hindu commercial classes provided 17.8 per cent of literates; the agricultural classes a puny 1.44 per cent and artisans a dismal 0.88 per cent.[47] Intra-regional disparities indicated that the system of education was not nearly as successful as proclaimed by colonial officials. This was especially so in Derajat (Bannu and Kohat) and Peshawar divisions where although constituting 90 per cent of the population, the Muslim proportion in schools was 55 per cent.[48]

The sanguine conclusions of the education commission on the system of primary education in the Punjab accorded well with the opinions of an articulate group of Muslims belonging to the upper and middle classes. But the diversity of viewpoints expressed in memorials and representations heard by the commission points to greater contestation over language and much consternation about the appropriateness of the educational system than given credence by official and non-official protagonists of Urdu in the Punjab. The unresolved question of the identity of the regional vernacular was continuing to cast a menacing shadow on not just the sphere of education but, more broadly, on social and political relations between the three main religious communities. Intended for colonial ears, these points of views replicated the epistemological patterns set into motion by the privileging of the religious factor in Indian society.

Everyone conceded that Urdu was not the *bhasha* or spoken vernacular of the Punjab. But that was where agreement ended. Partisans of Hindi argued that the *bhasha* written in Nagari was a dialect of 'Hindi' and in Gurmukhi characters became 'Punjabi'. Urdu with nearly 80 per cent of its vocabulary derived from Persian and Arabic was wholly alien to the province. The real *bhasha* of the Punjab was an offshoot of Sanskrit and Prakrit. Teaching the regional vernacular in the Nagari script, the mother-tongue of the people, would boost primary education which was faltering on account of an inappropriate medium of instruction.[49] Others considered Punjabi to be wholly separate from Hindi and Urdu, both of which were foreign languages.

[47]Note by J. Wilson, (deputy commissioner, Shahpur), 21 April 1894, Chaudhry (comp.), *Development of Urdu in Punjab*, p. 169.

[48]Extract from Hunter Commission report, chap. ix, section 2 in 'The Education of the Muhammadan Community', in *Records*, V23/46, IOL, p. 362.

[49]See, for instance, the memorial submitted by some Hindu residents of Lahore in Zulfiqar (ed.), *Select Documents on National Language*, pp. 72–5.

This elicited protests from supporters of Urdu who maintained that the Punjab was the original birthplace of the language. Many Muslims accepted that Urdu was spoken only in very limited company. Only job seekers liked Urdu; 'all the rest like[d] Punjabi in their every-day dealings, but in the Persian characters'.[50] The proponents of Urdu could see no purpose in substituting it with Punjabi or Hindi since the existing educational system was attracting a fairly constant flow of students. A Muslim member of the select committee of the Anjuman-i-Punjab admitted that primary instruction in Punjabi would be 'a great improvement' and in time 'Urdu might reasonably be discarded'. But Persian and Arabic would still be necessary to translate books into Punjabi which was 'not so rich'.[51] Sikh memorialists for their part promoted Punjabi in the Gurmukhi script as the best means of popularizing mass education in the province. These conflicting stances on languages and scripts, seemingly coloured by notions of communitarian interests alone, were distinctly shaped by class biases among all three of the main religious denominations of the Punjab. Middle- and upper-class Muslims in particular were perfectly content to forgo mass education in order to secure and advance their own positions within the colonial system.

There were strong arguments in favour of including Punjabi as one of the vernacular mediums of instruction at the primary level. These were voiced most cogently by those whose religious denomination classified them as Sikh, but were reiterated by others whose nomenclature was Hindu. Muslim voices supporting Punjabi as a medium of vernacular instruction were not wholly absent.[52] It is remarkable to find that element of arrogance about the belief in a superior culture among educated Muslims of the Punjab which has come to be so strongly associated with the Urdu-speaking inhabitants of the North Western Provinces. That it had less to do with love for Urdu as with love for convenience is plain enough. The Muslim service gentry, enjoying a monopoly over a limited employment market for the colonial services, was one of the more entrenched interests in the Punjab. With the colonial bureaucracy on their side, this alliance could make common cause with the Urdu press, confirm the status quo and in the process deflect the challenge posed by supporters of Hindi. The cause of Punjabi as one of the mediums of primary instruction in a region where its speakers numbered well over 60 per cent was unthinkingly pushed to the backburner by the stalwarts of Urdu and Hindi in the Punjab.

[50]Abu Syad Muhammad Husain, member of the select committee of the Anjuman-i-Punjab, to the Hunter Commission, 1882, ibid., p. 55

[51]Dr Rahim Khan, member of the select committee of the Anjuman-i-Punjab, before the Hunter Commission, 1882, ibid.

[52]Mirza Fath Muhammad Beg of Kasur admitted that there was much to be said 'in favour of teaching the Panjabi dialect in primary schools' but this did not apply to higher education (ibid., p. 17).

Commenting on the Urdu–Hindi dispute, a joint memorial of the Hindu, Muslim and Christian residents of Lahore declared that the 'real movers of this agitation are some *Bengalis*'. They were appealing to the 'religious and national feelings of some young Hindus' by noting that 'Urdu and its present character are relics of those conquerors who were ... oppressors for centuries'. This clique had been successful in bringing together 'a party of youngmen', mainly members of local Arya Samajists and Brahmo Samajists who 'd[id] not in any sense represent the Hindu community.[53] Lieutenant-Colonel Holroyd in his capacity as the director of public instruction in the Punjab noted that 'a few highly educated Hindus' had long wanted to substitute Sanskrit for Persian and it had 'now become a class question'.[54] The merging of these two strands of thought among Hindus was registered in the Punjab press with the appearance of two papers under Bengali management. In 1881 the *Tribune* of Lahore was started as a weekly by the Arya Samajist Sardar Dyal Singh Majithia at the suggestion of Surendranath Bannerji. A lesser-known paper was the *Reformer* which along with its better-known rival formed the backbone of the Hindi agitation in the Punjab.

Many of the prejudices in the writings of these two newspapers found reflection in the arguments put forward by the Arya Samaj and Brahmo Samaj to the education commission. The gist of the Arya Samaj onslaught against Urdu was that it was 'written in perfectly redundant, imperfect, and unphonetic characters' which made it unpopular among agriculturists, traders and artisans. Students wasted an inordinate amount of time learning a language whose only value lay in its being a passport to government employment. The Brahmo Samajists showed more of a supra-regional spirit by arguing that adopting Hindi in the Nagari script as a medium of instruction would expedite communications at the all-India level.[55] A memorial by a group of Hindus in Lahore thought candour was the better part of valour. Muslims had 'no religious prejudices' against learning Nagari, just as they had 'no prejudice against eating ... [Hindu] food'. But the 'more religious among the Hindus have such prejudices against foreign character [sic]'.[56]

Proponents of Hindi in the Nagari script attributed Urdu's popularity in the Punjab wholly to government patronage. Muslims could have Urdu in the Persian script if they wanted. But it was unfair to prevent Hindus from building bridges with the larger Indian 'nation' by excluding Hindi from the official curriculum. Hindi in the Nagari script had to be brought on a par with Urdu at the primary level, especially where Hindus were in a majority. As justification for their demands, the pro-Hindi lobby noted that the

[53]Ibid., p. 5.
[54]Evidence of Lieutenant-Colonel W.R.M. Holroyd to the Hunter Commission, 1882, ibid., p. 25.
[55]Ibid., pp. 46–7, 51–2.
[56]Ibid., p. 74.

education of Hindu women, who rarely ever learnt Urdu in the Persian script, would receive a major stimulus if the educational system included instruction in Nagari. The *madari zaban* or mother-tongue of Hindus could only be the language spoken and understood by their women.

But the mother-tongue of 'the poor simple people', a series of Sikh deputationists stated passionately, was Punjabi which was neither Hindi nor Urdu. To say that Punjabi written in Nagari was Hindi was like saying that Persian written in English was English. Punjabi in the Gurmukhi script was 'used by every one of any race or creed who wants to write or read Punjabi' and the 'easiest, cheapest, and surest mode of imparting elementary instruction to all sorts of ... people'.[57] Making Hindi the vernacular would be 'killing the Punjabi language, the dearest language of the Punjab, and depriving the Punjabis of their mother-tongue'.[58] Moreover, Punjabi was not without a written tradition. Far from being a 'language destitute of literature or science' and restricted to Sikh religious texts, there were hundreds of books in Punjabi, including the fine arts and musical sciences.[59] Even Brahmins and Khatri shopkeepers wrote Punjabi in the Lunde characters which was not Nagari. Muslims used the Persian script for popular books in Punjabi such as *Pakki Roti* and *Baran Anwa* which imparted religious education to the lower classes and women.[60] Add to this the rich oral tradition of folk-tales or *qissas*,[61] a breath of heart-warming yet sublime mystical poetry, and Punjabi was not lacking in a literary heritage. One would look in vain at the government book depot for 'any book in Punjabi or any atlas even of the country itself in Punjabi'. Yet a visit to the booksellers would show 'hundreds of books [in Punjabi] on different subjects', composed not only by Sikhs but also Brahmins, Khatris and Muslims.[62] Unlike the proponents of Hindi and Urdu for whom the matter was really one of script, the Sikhs were ready to accommodate all sorts of written characters so long as the provincial vernacular attained its rightful place in the system of primary education.

Punjab officialdom opted to stand pat on the existing configuration of language, education and employment in the province. Urdu-knowing, if not

[57]Statement by Sardar Atar Singh, chief of Bhadour, to the Hunter Commission, ibid., pp. 101–3.
[58]Memorial from the Sat Sabha, Lahore, to the Hunter Commission, ibid., p. 106.
[59]Statement by Sardar Atar Singh, chief of Bhadour, to the Hunter Commission, ibid., p. 102.
[60]Memorials from Jhang and Maghiana to the Hunter Commission, ibid., p. 63.
[61]These were being transliterated into romanized Punjabi by Richard Temple in the 1880s. (See Richard C. Temple, *The Legends of the Punjab*, two vols, first published in 1884 [reprint], Islamabad: Institute of Folk Heritage, 1981.)
[62]Memorial from the Sri Guru Singh Sabha to the Hunter Commission, Zulfiqar (ed.), *Select Documents on National Language*, pp.114–15.

Urdu-speaking, Muslim elite of the Punjab, backed by a powerful press orchestra, were more concerned with warding off the threat of Hindi in the Nagari script than dabbling with notions of mass education. This despite the fact that with a 5.89 per cent literacy rate, Punjab was crawling well behind the North Western Provinces' comparable figure of 11.8 per cent. The discordance between the spoken language of the people and the literate training of a few had disastrous effects, not least on account of the gender dichotomy layering the schemes of colonial education. Lagging well behind their male counterparts, the women of the Punjab had done much to keep alive the oral literature in the colours and textures of their daily lives. The psychic disjunction created by a written script learnt for public convenience and the oral words spoken in private was not an ordinary one.

It took a woman, a missionary teacher in Ludhiana, Miss M. Rose Greenfield, to 'strongly advocate' that the teaching of Gurmukhi first in all village schools would 'open the minds of the children' and make them 'more intelligent'. They could then go up to the higher classes and learn the scripts closer to their religious identity—'Urdu for Muhammadans and Hindi for the Hindus'.[63] Her recommendation was rejected. Boys in government schools continued learning Urdu in the Persian script until 1917 when for the first time Hindi was included in the primary curriculum. The female population of the province for the most part spoke and wrote Punjabi in the Gurmukhi character. In some Hindu and Muslim households there were instances of women learning Punjabi in the Nagari and Persian scripts. Punjabi was the language of women, irrespective of religious denomination. Even a Muslim could not deny that women's education in the Punjab owed a great deal to the Gurmukhi script. 'Introduce Urdu instead of Gurmukhi' and the impulse for educating women would 'vanish all at once'.[64] Far from being confined to the rural areas and a few towns, 'all the lower classes, and the women of the higher', including 'foreigners' like Kashmiris and Kabulis used Punjabi as the primary means of interpersonal communication. Office babus who could 'talk highflown Urdu in court often leave it at the door of their own homes and resume the familiar colloquial'. The overwhelming importance of Punjabi as the more informal and more personal language in the private domain went completely unreflected in the public debate, perpetuating a gender-based dichotomy in educational skills. Women were not expected to learn Urdu. People asked if their 'daughters [were] to become Munshis and do "naukari" that they should learn Urdu?'.[65]

[63]Evidence of Miss M. Rose Greenfield, Ludhiana, to the Hunter Commission, 1882, ibid., p. 21.

[64]Mahomed Latif, secretary of the Anjuman-i-Rifai-Am, Jhang, to the Hunter Commission, ibid., p. 44.

[65]Evidence of Miss M. Rose Greenfield, Ludhiana, to the Hunter Commission, 1882, ibid., pp. 20–2.

Some British officials, for very different reasons, conceded the advantages of imparting primary education in the spoken language of the people. B.H. Baden-Powell, who knew the rural Punjab landscape better than most, was firmly of the opinion that the decision on dialect and script should be left to the local committees so as to better accommodate local requirements.[66] Underscoring the problem of language in the remapping of communitarian identities, G.W. Leitner noted that all 'advocates alike of Urdu, Hindi, and Punjabi speak on behalf of a people which has not itself been fully constituted'. Keeping the 'language question' separate from the 'religious difficulty' seemed to him to be the only reasonable way out. While Urdu in the Persian script would remain the official language, Muslim *maulvis*, Hindu *pandits* and Sikh *bhais* could keep alive the religious languages—Arabic, Sanskrit and Gurmukhi—by instructing pupils in their respective strictures.[67] Relegating the 'religious' aspects of the problem to the 'private' sphere was, on the face of it, a typical colonial posture. But the language controversy in the Punjab was about the material rather than the purely religious interests of the three main communities. Ignoring the more accommodative trends and seeing the problem of language as a zero-sum game, the colonial bureaucracy made sure that the supposedly private sphere of religion would continue inflaming the temporal debate in the public arena.

Romanized Punjabi and Mass Education

A last attempt to grasp the nettle in the late nineteenth century from within the Punjab administration found a lone district official facing implacable opposition from his colleagues. In April 1894, J. Wilson, the deputy commissioner of Shahpur district, proposed that primary education and the running of government be conducted in romanized Punjabi. This would rectify the 'serious faults in our system of primary education' owing to a 'foreign language' being the medium of instruction. The Punjabi boy attending school was at a grave disadvantage in the acquisition of cognitive skills. He was 'not taught to read the language he speaks, but a language many of the words in which he does not understand until they are translated for him into his own Punjabi'. Despite moves to simplify them, textbooks contained far too many 'pedantic words' from Persian, Arabic or Sanskrit which had to be translated into Punjabi before they could be understood. A boy at the primary level was taught Urdu in the Arabic character, but learnt it in Punjabi and went on to read a Persian classic like Sadi's *Gulistan* in the original. This was like teaching an English schoolboy 'French in the Hebrew character' and then moving to 'Virgil's *Aeneid* in Latin'. Punjabi was the mother-tongue of nearly sixteen

[66]B.H. Baden-Powell, commissioner of Lahore division, to the Hunter Commission, ibid., pp. 9–10.

[67]Evidence of Dr G.W. Leitner to the Hunter Commission, ibid., pp. 34–5.

million people who could never be properly educated until they were taught in the language they spoke.[68]

Wilson tried making a case for romanized Punjabi by arguing that the character 'developed by speakers of Aryan languages' was better suited to the 'genius of the Punjabi tongue' than Arabic with its plethora of Semitic words. The Gurmukhi and Nagari scripts may be more appropriate than the roman character for Punjabi, but these variants of the Sanskrit script could not express many Persian, Arabic and English words and would 'never be adopted by the Mussalman portion of the population'. The best hope of standardizing the many variants of Punjabi was to use the roman script. Banishing Urdu and the Arabic character as the medium of primary instruction would spread mass education into the rural areas and put it on a more general and a sounder basis.[69] These sprightly ideas on mass education were scotched by one official after another, parroting all the known arguments against Punjabi. The most persuasive was that Urdu was not as foreign to the Punjab as French was to England and could not be done away with in an instant. According to the 1891 census, 17 per cent of the people in the Punjab spoke Urdu and 62 per cent Punjabi. Urdu's advances were already impressive. Punjabi was 'an uncouth dialect not fit to be a permanent language'; the sooner it was 'driven out by Urdu the better'.[70] A Muslim employee of the colonial state admitted that it was 'the people who make and develop their languages and not committees'. But he was against Punjabi whose unwritten dialects formed 'the vehicle of thought' for the 'uneducated and uncivilized'. Efforts to write Punjabi ballads and sonnets ended up as examples of Urdu–Punjabi or Hindi–Punjabi.[71]

Denying Punjabi any sort of identity of its own was too inscribed in official thought to command further attention. As it is tempers were running high in the Punjab. No other matter had 'aroused religious antagonism so much in the Punjab as that of the language' or 'more properly that of the *character*'. Previously Urdu's status had remained 'unquestioned'. Now Hindus wanted Nagari and Muslims Persian, creating much bad blood between the two communities. Reason made way for sentiment and even a Hindu who was 'a good Persian scholar' would now 'affect to despise the character through which he gains his living' and refuse to let his children learn it 'simply because of Hindu prejudice'. Demands for the Nagari and Gurmukhi scripts by an assortment of Hindu and Singh *sabhas* showed 'religion as their motive'.[72]

[68]Note by J. Wilson, 21 April 1894, in Chaudhry (comp.), *Development of Urdu in Punjab*, pp. 169–76.

[69]Ibid., p. 176.

[70]Note by Judge Stogdon, 3 August 1894, ibid., p. 208.

[71]Khan Muhammad Hyat Khan, division judge, Jullundur, to the officiating registrar, chief court of the Punjab, 29 May 1895, ibid., pp. 214–15.

[72]J. Sime, director of public instruction, Punjab, to C.L. Tupper, officiating second financial commissioner, 17 September 1895, ibid., pp. 263–4.

Taking up Wilson's outlandish proposal of dumping all the indigenous scripts for romanized Punjabi was asking for trouble. Letting sleeping dogs lie seemed the best course of action. There was 'a very aggressive spirit' about the way in which Punjabis looked upon the issue of official script.[73] Nothing would torch it more than the strike of the Roman match.

The interconnections between language, education, employment and the press were already the subject of a raging controversy in the vernacular press in the Punjab and the North Western Provinces. For all the fanfare announcing its birth in the Punjab, Hindi in the Nagari script was never instituted in the province as a medium of instruction in the nineteenth century. By comparison, Hindi in the Nagari script had been edging out Urdu in the North Western Provinces in the numbers game since the 1860s. These regional variations had a different bearing on the Hindi–Urdu debate. It had been easier to controvert the identity of languages than to align them squarely behind narratives on the language or, more aptly, the script of religious identity. This was certainly true of the Punjab where the associations created with Urdu by the popular press excluded the spoken language of identity for the majority of the people. In the North Western Provinces, strident cries for Hindi were creating a sharper, if internally less strained, sense of Urdu as a language of identity. That there was ample material to make a bonfire out of the linguistic accord in both regions can be gleaned from the discourse on the language of identity in the popular press.

LANGUAGE AS IDENTITY: THE HINDI–URDU DISPUTE

Once the Hindi–Urdu issue had reared its head, seekers of fame in the name of doing good initiated an acrid narrative war of words on the linguistic affinities of religiously defined communities. The print media was a natural site for competing discourses on the language of communitarian identity. Far more intriguing than the inclusionary claims of 'communalism' or 'nationalism' were the exclusionary ideals implicit in the move to controvert the identity of Urdu and Punjabi and, in this way, invent a language of identity for religious communities.

Aimed at influencing the colonial state as well as Indian opinion, newspapers flexed their verbal muscles, trying to make a canonical issue out of a problem laden with a plethora of internal contradictions. There was truth in assertions that Urdu was neither Muslim nor Hindu, but a blending of the two as they accommodated themselves to each other as well as to a changing social ambience. As the proprietorships and editorships of the vast majority of the Urdu language newspapers in the North Western Provinces and the Punjab indicate, Hindus had by no means given up on the Persian script.

[73] Ibid.

Despite the increasing numbers educated in the Nagari script during the 1860s in the North Western Provinces, Urdu newspapers continued to outnumber those in Hindi. In 1870 there were fifteen Urdu newspapers with a circulation of 2050 compared to 384 for eight Hindi papers. About an equal number of books were being published in the Persian and the Nagari scripts. At the same time there was no denying the gathering momentum of opinion in favour of Nagari. It was seen by some colonial officials as 'indicative of a patriotic feeling on the part of the Hindoos'.[74]

But this patriotism had yet to give rise to a combination which could shore up the spirits of the more irrepressible believers of a religiously informed cultural nationalism, Hindu or Muslim. Men like Munshi Nawal Kishore, who had made a fortune publishing translations of Persian, Arabic and Sanskrit works into Urdu, had no reason to want to see the Persian script banished from the North Western Provinces. His Urdu newspaper *Awadh Akhbar* found it 'difficult to offer a correct opinion on the subject'.[75] The Urdu character would 'not be done away with', declared the *Muir Gazette*. It would be much 'like our own paper' with one column in Nagari and the other in the Persian script. The 'rights of Mussulmans will not suffer' as the 'true tongue of their religion is Arabic'. Not using Nagari hurt the religious sensibilities of Hindus.[76] To these gentler persuasions was added the sterner warning by the *Benares Akhbar* that the result of the dispute between Hindus and Muslims would hasten the 'takeover of English'. Hindi in the Nagari script was easy to master. Since Muslims had 'now no design of abandoning this country', they 'should learn the language of the country'.[77]

The *Jagat Samachar* published in Nagari graciously accepted that Urdu was not a bad language. But the Nagari script was not defective like the Persian. Adopting it would quicken the snail-like pace of the lower judiciary where legal documents were 'written one way, and read in another'.[78] The *Chashma-i-Ilm* thought it a mockery of justice that in courts using Urdu in the Persian script, litigants were 'seen standing like deaf and dumb animals' utterly 'ignorant' of what was being recorded as evidence. Short of adopting Nagari outright, Urdu had to be shorn of all complex Persian and Arabic words which were incomprehensible to the subordinate social classes. Unfortunately, *maulvis* and *pandits* had interfered so much with Urdu and Nagari that neither was 'pure, but a confused mixture of Sanskrit, Persian and Arabic words' depending on the 'particular fantasy of each advocate'. What had happened to the original languages of Hindustan was like the story of a man rendered bald by his two

[74]Reply of the NWP government to Kempson's report, 1 April 1870, *Records*, V/23/129, IOL, pp. 234–5.

[75]*Awadh Akhbar*, Lucknow, 27 January 1869, *Selections*, L/R/5/46, IOL, p. 64.

[76]*Muir Gazette*, Meerut (Urdu–Nagari), 7 May 1869, ibid., pp. 226–7.

[77]*Benares Akhbar*, 26 October 1876, *Selections*, L/R/5/53, IOL, p. 612.

[78]*Jagat Samachar*, Meerut (Nagari), 19 April 1869, *Selections*, L/R/5/46, IOL, p.198.

wives; the old wife had pulled out all his black hair and the young one all the white.[79]

What gave extra flight to resentments against Urdu was the sense of anticipation with which a segment of educated Hindus looked upon the new political dispensation. Now that Muslim colonialism was a thing of the past, they could revitalize Sanskrit, refine Hindi and reassert their distinctive religious identity. The decision to install Urdu in the Persian script as the official language of government gave the Muslim service gentry as well as Hindu Kayasths and Kashmiri Brahmans a monopoly on employment in the colonial services, placing many educated Hindus at a serious disadvantage. With statistics to back them, supporters of Hindi in the Nagari script in the North Western Provinces accused the British of insidiously trying to 'smother and stifle' Hindi by imposing a language that was 'almost as foreign to the people as English'. Not only were public offices 'closed to the Hindee-speaking and writing people of the country', but the educational department's 'insane craving for Oordoo' was undermining the 'little spark of vitality still left in ... Hindee'.[80]

Privileged by colonial policy, the supporters of Urdu could afford to be more moderate in making their counter-arguments. Yet arrogance born of cultural difference or a superiority complex made certain that Muslims who rose to the defence of Urdu made claims that smacked of exclusion. At a time when the pro-Hindi lobbyists were agitating for the inclusion of Nagari as an official script without upstaging Urdu, few Muslims saw the wisdom of permitting the coexistence of two scripts writing the same language. An exception to this general trend, significantly enough, was Sayyid Ahmad Khan's *Aligarh Institute Gazette* which before the establishment of the Congress periodically supported the introduction of Nagari in public offices.[81] In 1873 the paper openly called for government impartiality on the issue of language. Such a change might be 'distasteful to a certain class of Mahomedans'. Yet 'right-minded' Muslims would agree that 'a just Government cannot help displeasing the few when the interests of the many are at stake'.[82]

Sayyid Ahmad's capacity to sway his co-religionists had never been particularly impressive beyond a select circle of friends and admirers. Facing a concerted attack from the Nagari lobby, many Muslim supporters of Urdu thought their salvation lay in sticking firmly to their guns. But in emphasizing the commonality of Urdu as the language of Muslims and Hindus, few detected the irony of advancing an inclusionary argument with exclusionary tones. Even a man of Akbar Allahabadi's poetic flair and wit once asserted

[79]*Chashma-i-Ilm*, Patna, 16 February 1871, *Selections*, L/R/5/48, IOL, p. 74.

[80]*Harish Chandra's Magazine* (Anglo-Hindi monthly from Benares), 1874, *Selections*, L/R/5/51, IOL, pp. 72–3.

[81]*Aligarh Institute Gazette*, 23 April 1869, *Selections*, L/R/5/46, IOL, p. 195.

[82]*Aligarh Institute Gazette*, 15 August 1873, *Selections*, L/R/5/50, IOL, p. 544.

that unless everyone adopted Urdu, the affairs of the country could never be set right.[83] The partisans of Urdu were really angling for the absorption of Hindustani into the Persian script, a seemingly inclusionary strategy with exclusionary implications for Nagari. Muslims considered 'the abolition of that character humiliating to their pride and destructive of their national fame as [a] conquering race'.[84]

An imaginative piece written in 1873 appealing to the governor of the North Western Provinces personified both Urdu and Hindi. Urdu maintained that the Nagari and the 'Bhasha language' had 'formed a conspiracy' to exile it from the country by inventing various 'false charges' against it. In doing so they wanted to 'usurp the domain' which had been 'my uncontestable right from time immemorial'. These intriguers wrongly blamed Urdu for being a foreign encumbrance when everyone knew that Hindustan was its original birthplace. Over hundreds of years Urdu had been 'steadily increasing in civilization, refinement, and all kinds of excellencies'. With the exception of its adversaries and 'they too ha[d] become hostile only very recently', Urdu had been 'universally commended' and 'mentioned with approbation by all'. While some traced its origin to Sanskrit, others considered Arabic, Persian and Sanskrit as Urdu's common parents. This was no proof of Urdu being alien to Hindustan. Even if it was, these were no grounds why Urdu's 'ancient rights should be trampled under foot' and the language expunged from the country. It could just as well be argued that since the Europeans were a foreign people, they had no right to rule over India. Since foreignness was not a condition for illegitimacy, Urdu argued that it was 'quite a distinct language'. The mere fact that it appeared in the Persian character did not make it Persian any more than any of the regional dialects became Sanskrit simply by being written in that script. Claiming to be in 'the prime of my youth, if not in infancy', Urdu defended itself against charges that its character was illegible. This was 'no fault of mine', but of the writers. As for the aspersion that its script encouraged fraud and forgery, such dishonesty was possible in any written language. It was perverse to force the colonial state to append Urdu to the burgeoning list of 'criminal' characters![85]

During the later part of the 1870s there was a lull in the debate on Urdu's foreign or indigenous identity, notably in the Punjab. This was because unlike the North Western Provinces where English was the medium of higher education, vernacular languages had fared much better in the Punjab at the college level. In 1870 the establishment of the Punjab University College with the Oriental College as its most important division created the institutional structure for higher education in the vernaculars. During the rest of the decade educationists in the Punjab, led by G.W. Leitner and the

[83]Zulfikar (comp.), *Intikhab Kalam-i-Akbar*, p. 116.
[84]*Benares Gazette*, 17 July 1871, *Selections*, L/R/5/48, IOL, p. 413.
[85]*Agra Akhbar*, 20 July 1873, *Selections*, L/R/5/50, IOL, pp. 503–4.

Anjuman-i-Punjab, were primarily interested in persuading the colonial bureaucracy to elevate Punjab University College to the status of a university, independent of Calcutta University to which it was affiliated. Sayyid Ahmad Khan was virulently opposed to Leitner's policy since, in his opinion, educating Indians in the vernaculars could only produce petty clerks.

His appointment to the Hunter Commission in 1882 created the conditions for an alliance of convenience between educationists in the Punjab and the North Western Provinces. Wanting a separate university of their own, educationists in the North Western Provinces joined their opposite numbers in the Punjab to stress the distinctiveness of upper India from Bengal. People in these regions spoke 'very nearly the same language' and unlike the Bengalis had similar 'habits and sentiments'. Calcutta University could never 'sympathize with them or meet their wants'.[86] Bengalis were accused not only of arrogance and nepotism but of treating Hindustanis with 'great incivility'. There was 'no reason why able and well bred Hindostanees ... acquainted with the customs and manners of these parts of the country' should 'not be preferred to Bengalees for employment in these posts'.[87] Punjabis felt slighted and 'justly alarmed' by the colonial policy of privileging Bengalis 'without any apparent reason'.[88] Government departments in the North Western Provinces were overflowing with Bengali personnel. And this despite the fact that residents of the provinces were 'far cleverer than Bengalis'.[89]

The common interest in cutting the umbilical cord with Calcutta University and resisting Bengali encroachments in the services created the grounds for agreement between sections of society in the North Western Provinces and the Punjab. But the reappearance of the Hindi–Urdu dispute in the former and its reverberations in the latter showed up its fragility. Instead of a regional response, the battle of scripts made sure that formations constituted along lines of class and ideology paraded the colours of religious communities. Occasionally there were rifts in the ranks and even signs of willingness to be accommodating.

While charging Sayyid Ahmad Khan for fixing the membership of the Hunter Commission, the *Hindi Pradip* chided Raja Shiva Prasad for calling the Hindi of a newspaper, using complex Arabic and Persian words, the language spoken 'from Kashmir to the Narbada and the Bay of Bengal'.[90] If educated Hindus were agreed on Nagari, there was much contention on whether Hindi should lean towards Sanskrit or Persian and Arabic or stay true to the spoken languge of the people. Those unrelenting in their dislike of Persian influence published macabre stories, including one about a Kayasth

---

[86]*Agra Akhbar*, 20 June 1873, ibid., p. 452.
[87]*Jalwa-i-Tur*, Meerut weekly, 8 November 1873, ibid., p. 655.
[88]*Hindu Prakash*, Amritsar, *Selections*, L/R/5/51, IOL, p. 161.
[89]*Lawrence Gazette*, Meerut Urdu weekly, *Selections*, L/R/5/53, IOL, pp. 111–12.
[90]*Hindi Pradip*, August 1882, *Selections*, L.R/5/59, IOL, p. 580.

boy throwing himself into a well after being spurned by his beloved. His condition was diagnosed to have been caused by an overdose of Urdu love stories. This made it clear as daylight that 'Kayasths should first teach their sons Sanskrit, and not Persian, in order to save their morals from being spoilt'.[91] As the largest caste of Hindus in the government of the North Western Provinces, the Kayasths looked upon the rival claims of an increasing number of Khatri, Brahman, *bania* and Thakur candidates with greater disquiet than those of Muslims.[92] Difficulties in bringing the Kayasths to make common cause with other Hindus in the name of the larger religious community continued to bedevil the Hindi movement in the North Western Provinces in the late nineteenth century.

Even as literate Hindus self-consciously switched to the Nagari script, the power of a common language spoken by members of both religious denominations retained its ineluctable hold in the provinces. So in the larger oral domain of everyday life there was as yet no resolution in sight of controverting the identity of a language into one that demarcated the identity of distinctive religious communities. The continuing popularity in the North Western Provinces of the Urdu vernacular press, managed by Hindus as well as Muslims, is another reason to doubt the spread of the pro-Nagari wave beyond a select segment of educated society. Ensconced in the lower courts and taught in schools, Urdu in the Persian script offered allurements to not only Muslims but also many Hindus.

Nagari's sluggish advance to dominance in the North Western Provinces has commanded more than its share of attention and documentation. By comparison, far less has come to the forefront about the peculiar trajectory taken by the Hindi–Urdu dispute in neighbouring Punjab. It was at the time of the Hunter Commission that Hindi in the Nagari script made its advent as one of the contenders for official recognition in the Punjab. Only a superficial reading of the press can lead to the conclusion that contestations over language and script were unproblematically and unmistakably afforcing communitarian unity among Muslims, Hindus and Sikhs in the Punjab. Opposition to a language or script demanded by members of another religious grouping was fierce, but not sufficient to repair the ideological and class-based cleavages within communities. Staged solely for the purpose of the Hunter Commission, the commotion over languages and scripts in the Punjab press reeked of a subjectivity that was more calculating than intuitive. It was the close tie-up between newspapermen and would-be populists arguing the case of Hindi, Urdu or Punjabi which imbued the debate with far more communitarian logic than it deserved. Chopping and changing the identity of language was no guarantee of recasting it as the language of identity for religious communities.

[91] *Sitara-i-Hind*, Moradabad Urdu weekly, 28 February 1886, *Selections*, L/R/5/63, IOL, p. 204.

[92] King, *One Language Two Scripts*, pp. 111–16.

The editors of two weeklies, the Hindi *Mittra Vilas* and the pro-Arya Samaj *Reformer* (published in Urdu), were prominent among those who attended the meeting which led to the submission of a memorial to the Hunter Commission from certain Hindu residents of Lahore. Reporting the event, the *Mittra Vilas* declared that while government was unfairly promoting Urdu, it would be 'a great mistake' if anything was done to promote Punjabi which was not 'a separate language'.[93] Outraged by the dismissive tone, the *Gurmukhi Akhbar* curtly stated that Punjabi in Gurmukhi was 'the language of the people in the province'.[94] The *Panjabi Akhbar*, a paper under Muslim management, tried taking the wind out of the sails of the Hindi lobby by reiterating the charge that the movement was wholly extraneous to the province. Bengalis aided and abetted by educated Hindu youths had deceived people into signing the memorial by implying that Hindi and Punjabi were one and the same language. As far as it knew, Punjabi consisted of 'only a few thousand words'. Some 'thirty thousand words' would have to be imported into Punjabi to confirm its status as a full-fledged language. If these were taken from Arabic and Persian, Muslims would argue that this enriched Punjabi was none other than Urdu. Alternatively, if the words were borrowed from Sanskrit, a 'new language would be formed' which may be called 'Hindi' but would not be understood by the people of the province.[95]

The identities of languages were still more fluid than solid to justify fixating them to hard-and-fast colonial notions of religious communities. The stalwarts of Urdu and Hindi had no qualms about securing support from Hindus or Muslims to back their demands with the Hunter Commission. Muslims of Lahore who submitted a memorial pleading for Urdu were accused of getting Hindus to sign on it by arguing that 'their children would have no jobs' if Nagari was introduced. Conflating language and religion, the *Mittra Vilas* warned the Hunter Commission 'not to attach undue weight to the memorial simply because it bears the signature of some Hindus'.[96] The *Reformer* was delighted to find one Muslim *tehsildar* in Hissar who supported the adoption of Hindi.[97] Offended by the insinuation that Bengalis were instigating the agitation, it maintained that 'nothing could be a greater mistake than to ascribe the language controversy to religious motives'. This was evident from the fact that 'many Musalmans have signed memorials in favour of Hindi, and many Hindus have signed those in favour of Urdu'. It was the enemies of the people who tried sowing discord among 'the different masses'.[98]

[93]*Mittra Vilas,* Lahore (Hindi), 6 March 1882, *Selections,* L/R/5/59, IOL, pp. 162–3.
[94]*Gurmukhi Akhbar,* Lahore (Punjabi), 15 March 1882, ibid., p. 185.
[95]*Panjabi Akhbar,* Lahore, 29 April 1882, ibid., p. 289.
[96]*Mittra Vilas,* Lahore (Hindi), 12 June 1882, ibid., p. 374.
[97]*Reformer,* Lahore, 12 June 1882, ibid.
[98]*Reformer,* Lahore, 10 July 1882, ibid., p. 434.

Punjabis were clearly concerned about keeping fences mended with members of other religious communities. Amidst the claims and counter-claims of the partisans of Hindi and Urdu, the *Anjuman-i-Punjab* tried squaring the circle of differences by reiterating arguments about imparting education in the vernacular. That Leitner had a hand in shaping the paper's stance is a reasonable surmise. Under his influence the *Anjuman-i-Punjab* had 'fought a hard fight in the cause of the optional and voluntary as opposed to the compulsory and arbitrary method of education'. A firm believer in the 'freedom of choice' in the medium of instruction as well as subjects, the Anjuman considered the 'disregard' of this principle as the 'root [cause] of the people's indifference to the educational system'. The paper admitted the attractions of English and Urdu for some people, which it believed should be retained with the option of being written in Persian or Nagari. At the same time there was 'no reason' why a state-sponsored system of education should not cater to 'the natural desire' of the people to learn Hindi, Punjabi or Sanskrit, Arabic and Persian.[99] Going a step further, the Anjuman proposed that government's law reports should be translated in all the regional vernaculars, including Pushto, Baluchi and Sindhi.[100]

In a stark display of the contradictions which so often confused the debate on the language of identity, the *Anjuman-i-Punjab* asserted that the 'spoken language of a country' was the one used in its 'towns and cities and not the dialects used in distant agricultural tracts'. It followed that Urdu should continue to be promoted over and above other regional vernaculars. For all the open-mindedness about the possible equations between spoken vernaculars and schooling, the paper was decidedly against undermining the existing configuration of language, education and employment. Deploring the manner in which passions had been aroused by the Hindi–Urdu dispute, the Anjuman's message to its members was to curb the 'growing tendency' of turning language into an issue of 'race' and, thus, a 'burning political question'.[101]

These worries were not limited to a semi-government organ like the *Anjuman-i-Punjab*. There were reports of meetings attended by students and upper-class Hindus and Muslims to discuss how to prevent the Hindi versus Urdu exchanges from degenerating into verbal brawls. False rumours had been afoot that some people were trying to 'discourage dealings between the Hindus and Musalmans'. The power of rumour was not just holding out but actually broadening its scope now that the press had taken to fabricating news in print. Indication that many Punjabis may not have made up their minds on the matter, one meeting decided to limit discussions on the subject to the privacy of the homes.[102] Small wonder that most Punjabi-speakers

[99] *Anjuman-i-Punjab*, Lahore, 14 June 1882, ibid., pp. 375–7.
[100] *Anjuman-i-Punjab*, 27 September 1882, ibid., p. 653.
[101] *Anjuman-i-Punjab*, Lahore, 14 June 1882, ibid., pp. 376–7.
[102] *Kohinoor*, Lahore, 28 June 1882, ibid., p. 406.

tended to be more forthcoming about expressing feelings on the language of their identity in private than in public.

The Hunter Commission did more to ruffle feathers among the privileged upper crust of society than address the issue of the language of identity, much less redress the structural limitations of the colonial state's schemes for primary education in the Punjab. By giving a hearing to representations from Hindi, Urdu and Punjabi supporters, the colonial state heightened expectations without satisfying anyone. Supporters of Urdu may have won, but others thought they could live to see victory another day. Even more than their co-religionists in the North Western Provinces, Punjabi Hindus opted for Hindi in piecemeal fashion. There was very slow growth in Nagari newspapers in the Punjab until well into the first few decades of the twentieth century. This is not altogether surprising since Hindi in the Nagari character was not formally introduced into the Punjab curriculum until 1917. So Hindi as the language of identity for Punjabi Hindus had yet to become part of a lived cultural reality. Quite as much as the Muslims and the Sikhs, educated Hindus in the Punjab cherished their spoken vernacular in private but wrote in Urdu while talking about Hindi. Muslims similarly placed at least wrote and championed the same language. Yet Urdu was no more the language of Muslim identity in the Punjab than it was of the Hindus or the Sikhs. The impasse left the Sikhs comfortably positioned as far as the identity of spoken and written language was concerned. With the marginalization of Punjabi, however, the Sikhs could not capitalize on their success as the first religious community in the province to resolve the problem of its linguistic identity.

The utility of Urdu as a means to official employment in the Punjab strained the language of identity for all three communities. In 1897 the government thought of closing down Gurmukhi schools upon observing that few boys were willing to study Punjabi. The *Khalsa Gazette* ridiculed the government for dropping a subject simply due to the perceived aversion of students. Bengali, Marathi, Gujarati and many other regional vernaculars were being encouraged by the colonial state. It was a 'pity' that in Punjab the government was 'dealing a death blow to the study of Gurmukhi' which was 'another name for Punjabi'.[103] Yet such concessions as were made to the teaching of Gurmukhi in government and government-aided schools could not remedy the problem of spreading literacy in the spoken vernacular of the province, as many Punjabis irrespective of religious affinities must secretly have admitted within the confines of their home.

As the nineteenth century made way for the twentieth, the issue of language was appropriated more and more for communitarian purposes. For all the apparent confidence of the discourse on differential communitarian identities,

[103]*Khalsa Gazette*, Lahore (Gurmukhi), 15 December 1897, *PNNR*, L/R/3/181, IOL, p. 1063.

ambiguities about the identity of language continued to cast a lingering shadow on the language of identity for Punjabi Muslims and Hindus. In the North Western Provinces, the pro-Nagari movement which had been galvanizing support for Hindi among Hindus was proceeding in fits and starts with no immediate hope of a popular upsurge to shake the resolve of the colonial government. With language, script and religious community proceeding along an undulating and stony track, it was the agency of the colonial state that proved to be the decisive factor in defining the role of language as politics in both regions.

TURN-OF-THE-CENTURY POLITICS OF LANGUAGE

In April 1900 the decision of the North Western Provinces government to give Nagari equal status with Urdu served as catalyst in making the politics of language one of the primary manifestations of culture as difference. Lieutenant-Governor Anthony MacDonnell defended his decision on the pretext of doing justice to over 90 per cent of the people in the provinces, Hindus as well as Muslims.[104] Now that the government in the North Western Provinces had finally seen the light, it saw reason in deflecting the expected protests of the Urdu lobby. The more so since Muslims who mattered in government's eyes could be relied upon not to let matters come to such a pass that would entail clashing with the will of the colonial masters.

Showing how well they knew which side their bread was buttered, Muslim landlords in the provinces were notably absent from meetings held to discuss the implications of the decision. Many Hindus attended such gatherings in proof that Urdu was not, after all, the language of Muslims alone. The fact that Urdu in the Persian script was not actually being replaced with Hindi in the Nagari kept away many Muslims anxious not to get on the wrong side of the authorities. What killed the prospects of any sustained protest against putting Nagari on an equal footing with Urdu was the posture adopted by the Aligarh brigade after the death in 1898 of Sayyid Ahmad Khan.

The great bastion of Urdu, the Muslim Anglo-Oriental College at Aligarh was humbled by MacDonnell's threat of suspending all government funding for the institution. Whether Sayyid Ahmad Khan would have put up a more resolute fight in the interests of retaining Urdu's unchallenged status as the official vernacular in the provinces is a matter of conjecture. During his lifetime the *Aligarh Institute Gazette* had proposed putting Nagari on an equal footing with Urdu in the Persian script. Whatever his flaws as a conscientious servant of the Crown, the captain of Aligarh was a man who matched deeds and words better than his successors. As Akbar Allahabadi wrote on his death:

[104]Cited in King, *One Language Two Scripts*, p. 157.

Ours is just talk; the Sayyid did work
Don't forget the difference between those who say and do
Whatever anyone may say, I say Oh Akbar
God bless him, the departed had many qualities[105]

Preferring to prostrate themselves before a government directive, members of north India's Muslim *ashraf* classes demonstrated just how far they were ready to go against the grain of colonial policy in defence of their religiously informed cultural identity. Nawab Mohsin-ul-Mulk, secretary of the Muslim Anglo-Oriental College, was also president of the Urdu defence committee set up in response to the fears about the Nagari ruling. Once he had been tipped the wink, Mohsin-ul-Mulk resigned his office in the defence committee and flatly refused to sign its plea to the government. Other illustrious Muslims followed the same pattern with the result that the whole affair wound down to an ignominious end in the United Provinces (UP), as the North Western Provinces came to be known after the administrative rearrangements of 1901. If not for the Muslim-run vernacular press, no one would have guessed that the future of Urdu, if not its present, was an issue which divided communities along broadly religious lines in these provinces.

Taking the opportunity of breaking lose from the Aligarh clique, the Muslim-edited Punjab press reached new heights in its political uses of the language question. While Muslims were 'frightened out of their wits by the frowns of officials', wrote the *Vakil*, the Hindus preferred to become 'Congressmen rather than High Court Judges'.[106] A powerful condemnation of the Muslim *ashraf* classes of north India, it did not signal the beginnings of a more autonomous stance towards the colonial government. With a Congress enthusiast for an editor, the *Rafiq-i-Hind* lauded MacDonnell for his impartiality and sense of equity, condemning the 'political loafers' of Aligarh with no real following for attacking the governor in 'an unjust manner'. The 'great majority' of Muslims in the Punjab had nothing to do with the anti-government opinions appearing in print and wanted only to

---

[105]*Humari batein hi batein hain, Sayyid kam karta tha
Na bhulo farq jo hai kehnawalla karnawalla mein
Keha jo chahai koi, mey toh ye kehta hoon ah Akbar
Khuda bakhsay buhat see khubian thi marnawalla mein.*

ہماری باتیں ہی باتیں ہیں، سیّد کام کرتا تھا

نہ بھولو فرق جو ہے کہنے والے کرنے والے میں

کہے جو چاہے کوئی میں تو یہ کہتا ہوں اے اکبر

خدا بخشے بہت سی خوبیاں تھی مرنے والے میں۔

(Allahabadi, *Kulliyat-i-Akbar*, vol. i, p. 271).
[106]*Vakil*, Amritsar, 18 February 1901, *PNNR*, L/R/5/185, IOL, p. 131.

dissociate themselves from those in the United Provinces who 'maligned their rulers'.[107]

When it came to a head, it was the politics of loyalty and not the politics of language which had more blood than water. With the Urdu–Hindi dispute now in administrative incubation, the press in both regions quietly dropped the matter. As the *Bharat Partap* remarked sarcastically, there was no danger of Urdu being deposed by Hindi since with 'one hand it clutche[d] the beard of Islam and with the other the locks of Hinduism'. Indeed, Urdu had become the popular medium through which new religions were being promoted. The 'Prophet' of Qadian, Mirza Ghulam Ahmad, was bombarding the world with a 'battery of Urdu' revelations from God. And the Arya Samaj's crusaders, most of them unacquainted with Sanskrit, were 'demolishing Hindu scriptures' like the *puranas* in the same Urdu language which they roundly condemned as foreign.[108]

Indeed, once the Nagari agitation registered its triumph in the UP, it became evident that substantively little had changed. People continued to speak the same colloquial language in their daily interactions while the written forms were evolved to assume distinctively different appearances, one in the Nagari and the other in the Persian character. So in a sense the split between the spoken and the written languages in northern India roughly corresponded to the one in the Punjab. It was the similarity of the spoken and the written vernacular for many Muslims in the UP which helped foster a sense of Urdu as the language of identity. In the Punjab, by contrast, the discrepancy between the spoken and the written word continued to smudge the narratives appearing on Urdu as the language of Muslim identity.

By the time language struck a new chord of bitterness in the Punjab, the larger political scene had changed considerably. What upset the Punjab applecart on this occasion was the public defence by the new Lieutenant-Governor, Louis Dane, of Protul Chander Chatterji, the Bengali vice-chancellor of the Punjab University. Chatterji had erred gravely in the eyes of some Muslims by calling for instruction in the regional vernacular. There was nothing novel about these ideas. Coinciding with an acrimonious debate on the introduction of separate electorates under the Morley–Minto reforms of 1909, the controversy offers fascinating glimpses of the position which upper- and middle-class Muslims decided to affect on their language of identity. No less intriguing was the decision of many ardent supporters of Hindi to enlist their support for Punjabi.

Hoping to turn the tables on Urdu, the *Tribune* praised Dane and Chatterji with an unprecedented defence of Punjabi. Dane would 'earn the undying gratitude of the people of [the] Province' by scrapping the 'highly artificial

[107]*Rafiq-i-Hind*, Lahore, 6 July 1901, ibid., pp. 428–9.
[108]*Bharat Partap*, Delhi, April 1901, ibid., p. 480.

and unnatural system which stands like a stumbling-block in their way'; 'acts like a drag throughout their neck, pulverizing their natural faculties and checking their spontaneous growth and development'.[109] Agreeing wholeheartedly, the *Punjabi* lamented that there was a 'class' of Muslims who would have their 'own children' as well as those of others 'grow up in intellectual deformity' in order to be 'reminded of imperial traditions'. Muslims stuck on Urdu were 'men whom no logic c[ould] convince' and for whom the 'use of the horns comes most natural[ly'.[110] If some Hindus were coming to see the handicap of having a written language other than the spoken, the attitude of upper- and middle-class Muslims seemed palpably ostrich-like.

Mahboob Alam's *Paisa Akhbar* insisted that only 'Aryas and other classes of Hindus' who were 'inimically disposed towards Musalmans' liked Dane's speech. Before making such grand gestures, government should first consult the people. No one had asked Dane to introduce Punjabi at the primary level. Certainly not the one crore Muslims of the Punjab. With staggering reason, the paper argued that 'teach[ing] children at school the (Panjabi) words' which they already knew was the same as saying that government did 'not wish to impart any education to them'. The real point was that Chatterji was a Hindu Congressmen, 'actuated by feelings of bigotry', who wanted only to injure the cause of Urdu by luring Muslims into learning Gurmukhi and Hindi. Dane's intervention would encourage 'mischief-makers' to 'pit an uncouth and poor tongue like Punjabi' against 'a literary and rich language like Urdu'. This was a calculated move to ensure that neither Muslims nor, for that matter, Hindus would be able to communicate with anyone beyond Ambala.[111] Emboldened by their successes in northern India, some Hindus were seen as conniving to snuff out Urdu and, by implication, the distinctive culture of upper- and middle-class Muslims in the Punjab.

The *Akhbar-i-Am* thought the proposal would do 'more harm to Hindus than to Muslims'.[112] There was nothing wrong in giving Punjabi boys their 'first lessons in their mother tongue'. There was 'a fairly good stock of books' in Punjabi and its introduction as a court language would be 'a boon for the litigants'.[113] Women's education would make rapid strides. The *Tribune* spoke glowingly of Punjabi's 'richness, comprehensiveness and ... capabilities'; its 'musical diction'; 'harmonious flexibility' and 'capacity to reach the soul of the people'.[114] In an atmosphere of growing suspicion, these tributes to their spoken vernacular appeared to many educated Punjabi

[109]*Tribune*, Lahore, PNNR, L/R/5/190, 1909, IOL, p. 178.
[110]*Punjabi*, Lahore, 25 February 1909, ibid., p. 196.
[111]*Paisa Akhbar*, Lahore, of 4, 6, and 25 March 1909, ibid., pp. 219–21, 275.
[112]*Akhbar-i-Am*, Lahore, 23 March 1909, ibid., p. 274.
[113]*Akhbar-i-Am*, Lahore, 24 March 1909, ibid., p. 276.
[114]*Tribune*, 13 April 1909, ibid., p. 341.

Muslims as the velvet glove over the mailed fist. The *Akhbar-i-Am* contended that the only reason why Punjabi Muslims 'look[ed] upon Urdu and not Punjabi as their mother tongue' was that their 'newspapers [we]re entirely under the control of the Aligharites'. Unlike their Punjabi brethren, Muslims in Bombay, Bengal and Madras did not consider learning regional vernaculars an insult to their religious sensibilities. The attitude of educated Punjabi Muslims was utterly 'unnatural'. If they took 'pride in being called Punjabis', they could not 'regard their mother tongue with such contempt'.[115] Yet the Muslim disdain for their spoken vernacular had less to do with cultural sensibilities than with political concerns about the inwardness of the move on the part of some Hindus to advocate the case of Punjabi.

A letter to the editor of the *Observer* by a Muslim said it all in the rush of a few sentences. The call to introduce Punjabi was an extension of a deep-seated conspiracy against Urdu, which was the language of neither Muslims nor Hindus. Both had 'contributed their heart's blood' for the last three centuries. Yet despite its repository of knowledge, pleasing diction and the richness and elegance of its literature, Urdu was a language spurned by Hindus for narrow-minded reasons. By crying that Urdu was the language of the Muslims who would never abandon it, the Hindus had declared their 'complete isolation and change of front'. This was 'nothing less than a national calamity'. Forcing Muslims to adopt Punjabi as the literate language would throw them completely out of gear. They would have to create a new literature and a fresh reservoir of knowledge in Punjabi. There could not be a more masterful 'stroke of genius'. The call for Punjabi was 'a double-handed sword, a clever feat of killing the snake but saving the rod' and was one step closer to the goal of Hindu domination in India. Language had been the one tie which united Muslims and Hindus. Now that it had been severed, the very measures aimed at 'cement[ing] Hindu nationality' were 'injur[ing] the nationality of the Muslim community'.[116]

An unrelieved victim of contested narratives, language as identity became an appendage to the communitarian discourses of the early twentieth century. In the process of controverting the identity of language to fit regionally specific configurations of education and employment, the colonial state and an alert segment of Indian society, had created a definite niche for the politics of language. Yet this fell well short of settling the language of communitarian identities to permit essentializing religiously informed cultural differences. Individual, class, ideational and regional choices continued to undercut the equation of Hindu with Hindi and of Muslim with Urdu in everyday practice, if not so evidently at the level of discourse. Yet whatever the internal contradictions between language and communitarian identity, the issue had

[115]*Akhbar-i-Am*, 27 April 1909, ibid., p. 365.
[116]*Observer*, Lahore, 8 May 1909, ibid., pp. 450–1.

by the turn of the century ineluctably extended beyond the domain of culture into the maelstrom of politics where the ends justified the means. It was this changing context of politics which widened the breach between the dominant idioms of communitarian discourses constructed by the few and the multiple and shifting identities of the many whose interests they avowedly represented.

Chapter 4

Muslims as a Legal and Political Category: Subjecthood in Theory and Practice

The individual's first point of reference was undoubtedly the 'community'. But this 'community' could just as well be that of the family, the local kinship network, or the community of language, region or religion. Capping the relationship between the individual and community with the religious category in colonial schemes of enumeration did not mean that other associations fell by the wayside. Whether in conformity with or in resistance to the dominant discourse privileging religion, these relationships continued to influence an individual's attitudes and choices in life. The 'community' of the individual was more variegated and creatively experienced than suggested by the homogeneities enforced by inclusion in a religiously derived statistical category. This is amply borne out when communitarian discourses on identity are exposed to more rigorous analysis than permitted by colonial epistemology.

As it is, the certitudes of colonial knowledge often went against the grain of administrative practices. Building an impersonalized modern state structure based on rules and regulations in a society accustomed to personalized rulership was a tall order. This became evident once the Company state began adapting Mughal institutions for the administration of justice. Under Muslim rule, absolute sovereignty vested in Allah. In theory the ruler was not the master of the people but the humble servant of the Creator. As His viceregent–or the 'shadow of God on earth'–the sultan's ultimate responsibility was to Allah. The administration of law and order, intrinsic to legitimacy, was vital to fulfilling that responsibility given the Quranic emphasis on justice and equity or *adl*. In executing God's will, the ruler and his selected law officers like *qazis* and *muftis* had to appear to be doing what was just and right. The individual responsibility of the officers was the 'keynote of judicial interpretation of law in Muslim Indian States as well as in other Islamic countries'.[1] More than as an appointee of the ruler, it was the personal erudition and local stature of the *qazi* which imparted quality to the administration of justice in Mughal India.

In the context of a decentralizing Mughal state, Muslim law officers in conjunction with alternating local notables in certain regions came to exercise their judicial powers in an increasingly arbitrary fashion. The local autonomy of the *qazis* and the privatized conception of justice in Islamic criminal law militated against the Company state administering law and order under its centralizing authority.[2] Reluctant to tamper with the existing arrangements for the administration of justice, the Company state under Lord Cornwallis nevertheless began modifying Islamic criminal and civil law to better fit its own requirements. This was done by making a distinction between 'public' and 'private' law. One way to restrict opposition to judicial innovations was to undertake not to interfere in the personal laws of India's religious communities. Although consistent with pre-colonial practice, Muslim and Hindu sovereigns had never professed indifference towards religion. The legitimacy of temporal sovereignty had always depended on some measure of religious sanction. Muslim rulers, for the most part, acknowledged the supremacy of the *sharia* even while expanding their temporal authority under *qanun-i-shahi* or the law of the sovereign. Non-Muslims retained their personal laws but were subject to the *qanun-i-shahi* and aspects of Islamic criminal and civil law. So if a dichotomy marked the private and public laws of non-Muslims in Mughal India, no such distinction existed for Muslims prior to the establishment of the Company state. It was colonialism's marshalling of the existing sources of cultural legitimacy in late-eighteenth and early-nineteenth-century India which, in separating the public from the private, most profoundly effected redefinitions of social identities. In the case of the Muslims, this was done by gradually denuding the Islamic *sharia*—erroneously interpreted as an immutable code of law and not a set of moral precepts to be loosely applied according to local circumstances—of its civil and criminal components and defining it as Islamic 'personal' law. Colonial officials also began compiling, if not always codifying, the *shastras*, which were seen as the Hindu counterpart to the Islamic *sharia*.[3]

---

[1]While Jahangir regarded it as a sacred duty, Shah Jahan considered it to be the mainstay of his government. For Aurangzeb the 'garden of administration was watered by the rain of Justice'. (See Muhammad Basheer Ahmed, *The Administration of Justice in Medieval India*, Aligarh: Historical Research Institute, 1941, pp. 67–8.)

[2]For the steady dismantling of the Mughal system of criminal law by the colonial state, see Jorg Fisch, *Cheap Lives and Dear Limbs: The British Transformation of the Bengal Criminal Law, 1769–1817*, Wiesbaden: Franz Steiner Verlag, 1983, especially chapter two.

[3]For an extended discussion of these colonial manoeuvres in the legal domain, see J.D.M. Derrett, *Religion, Law and State in India*, New York: Free Press, 1968. For

Lending greater rigidity to both Muslim and Hindu personal law, derived from textual sources rather than actual social practices, may have been an unwitting result of the colonial state's search for a semblance of cultural legitimacy by appropriating aspects of Indian traditions. Yet there had to be a good deal of flexibility in the actual functioning of judicial institutions in order to accommodate regional and local variations. If Muslims in their different settings frequently defied the *sharia,* Hindu *shastras* were subsumed under a dizzying mosaic of local customary laws. Applying uniform personal laws to those categorized as Muslim or Hindu, colonial officials quickly realized, was impossible. This was why the personalized element remained a vital part of not only judicial but also other rule-bound institutions created by the colonial state, especially at the district level. Even the infusion of liberal ideas into colonial policy threw up curious concoctions. In creating a right to private property, for instance, the colonial state patted itself on the back for releasing individual initiative from communitarian restraints and giving stimulus to free market forces. But this concern for individual rights was negated by the decision to treat ancestral property as a collective asset which could only be alienated by a joint decision of the family.[4]

The incongruous logic underpinning the structural and ideational features of the colonial state at each step affected the theory and practice of subjecthood. While the theory was coloured by perceptions of religious distinctions in Indian society, its practice owed more to temporal realities in localities and regions. Britain conferred subjecthood, not citizenship rights, on Indians. The difficulties arising from efforts to replace personalized forms of rulership with impersonalized authority were addressed in vernacular newspapers. Apart from hinting at the nature of the public arena created by the colonial state, they underlined the disquiet which attended the shift to an impersonalized sovereignty and the corresponding reconceptualization of individual and collective rights. Indians were to be the subjects of the British Crown with fewer civic rights than religious. Forced to fall back on the religious community, Muslims as well as non-Muslims couched their demands for rights in terms of identifiable interests. Discussions on civic rights were for the most part marginalized by a public discourse claiming to project the identity and interests of religious communities.

Discrepancies between official discourse and social realities, even when seemingly effaced by the narratives of communitarian interests appearing in

---

equally incisive but more concise analyses, see Bernard Cohn, *Colonialism and its Forms of Knowledge: The British in India,* Princeton: Princeton University Press, 1996, especially chapter three and Michael Anderson, 'Islamic Law and the Colonial Encounter in British India', in David Arnold and Peter Robb (eds), *Institutions and Ideologies: A SOAS South Asia Reader,* London: Curzon Press , 1993, pp. 165–85.

[4]See David Washbrook, 'Law, State and Agrarian Society in Colonial India', *MAS,*15, 3 (1981).

print, continued to haunt the colonial bureaucracy at each level of the administration. Nowhere was this more apparent than in the domain of the colonial legal system where being Muslim did not entail the blanket application of Islamic law. Confronted with a welter of regionally and locally specific social arrangements governing the lives of their Muslim subjects, colonial officials pragmatically accommodated customary deviations from the Islamic *sharia*. This ensured that the Muslim remained more of an abstract legal category than a social entity whose life was ordered according to the precepts of religious doctrine.

So the theory of Muslim subjecthood in colonial India remained wholly at odds with its practice, compounding the difficulties of treating the individual's relationship to the religious community as the primary factor in the social organization of the faithful. In the absence of any systematic application of Islamic law for Muslims inhabiting the different parts of India, the overweening idea of the religious community was more a figment of the imagination than a coterminous reality shared by its constituent elements. Conceptually the dichotomy was fraught with consequences for the emerging discourse on a Muslim 'nation'. Intended for a public arena closely monitored by the colonial state, the discourse imputed common characteristics to the Muslims that were belied by uncommon facts on the ground. The actual operations of the colonial legal system reveal the full extent of the confusions surrounding the positing of a 'Muslim community' in singular and undifferentiated terms. A Muslim by birth might subscribe to the ideal of Islamic brotherhood and yet remain bounded by the localized affiliations and customs of the immediate community. The multilayered accretions influencing the lives of Muslims puts the privileging of the religious factor in colonial epistemology and communitarian discourses at a serious discount.

An exploration of the contradictions following attempts to apply the legal definition of an Indian Muslim in the British judicial system with special, but not exclusive, reference to the Punjab can be a fascinating exercise. It enables an analysis of the theory and practice of subjecthood in colonial India with reference to the administrative machinery established for disbursing justice. At the same time it furnishes a link between the ideas of identity and sovereignty and their implications for the apportioning of individual and collective rights in colonial India. Operating in different regional settings, the colonial state's hastily adapted infrastructure for policing and adjudicating the affairs of Indian subjects punctured many dictums of the communitarian discourse appearing in print. This in turn helps place the emerging narratives on the Indian 'nation', 'nationality' and 'citizenship' leading up to the construction of the political category of Muslims into a more meaningful perspective. Fashioned in response to the uneven spread of liberal ideals borrowed from the west, these were paralleled and even refuted by arguments more rooted in regional and local contexts. The class factor in combination with individual interests shaped by region and locale was firmly located in the clash of narratives on national identities, Muslim, Hindu or Indian.

COURTS, CUSTOMS AND COMMUNITIES

Quite as impelling as their liking for enumeration was the British penchant for law making. Perplexed by the reams of paper printed by government presses for their edification, Indians greeted the idea of impersonalized sovereignty with mixed feelings. The *Aligarh Institute Gazette* thought the Indian administrative code was utterly incomprehensible to the people. This was generating 'insecurity' and 'uneasiness' of the sort known under 'despotic tyranny'. Between the profusion of mutually contradictory legal edicts and the interpretations of pleaders, *munsifs* and judges, Indians were 'beginning to doubt whose authority they we[re] ultimately to look at'. Deepening rifts between rulers and ruled due to overregulation required more than the 'claptrap element' of English liberalism. Instead of 'burdening the memories and blunting the faculties of the local administrative officers' with a ceaseless 'list of martinet regulations unintelligible to the people', it was better to lay down some plain rules of conduct and allow personal discretion to those applying them. 'Natives love[d] justice' as much as their 'civilized brethren' but wanted it in a 'rough and ready way'. They would accept judicious interference from those whom they knew, even if a European. Yet they were suspicious when it reached them through a government circular order or an official gazette.[5]

If this was the view of Anglicized Muslims, a voice from the margins of urban Punjab derided them along with the colonial judicial system. The English seemed to think that 'Hindustanis ha[d] no fixed laws or rules'. But the wonder was that educated Indians thought the same and 'argue[d] as if they were born Englishmen' who had 'come to the country on a pleasure trip'. Law books were heaped upon the court official who could not 'keep them on his tongue' while to outsiders it 'all appear[ed] like a Freemason's lodge' where only the initiated could follow the proceedings. The 'meaning of justice' needed to be defined. Anyone who had 'sifted the dust of English Courts' knew that the 'justice of law' was 'no justice at all'. Not only was the system financially corrupt, it took an exasperatingly long time to get a decision. Embittered towards the *vakils* or lawyers who plundered the people, the paper believed there was 'no limit to the law'. Unfortunately the 'public generally' was 'not sufficiently learned to understand it'.[6]

Unable to seek justice without wagering their entire fortunes in the process, Indians were not exactly enamoured of the colonial legal system. Many

[5]*Aligarh Institute Gazette*, 3 July 1868, *Selections*, L/R/5/45, IOL, pp. 344–5.
[6]*Khair Khwah Punjab*, Gujranwala, 17 July 1868, ibid., pp. 369–70.

nostalgically recalled with 'feelings of love and esteem' their 'late rulers' who had established such 'perfect union and friendship' between 'the two nations' so that the 'rulers and the ruled became blended with one another'. Objecting to the entire tenor of British rule, the *Urdu Akhbar* thought India needed 'a permanent sovereign' and a settled European population, not peripatetic viceroys and footloose officials who came and went without eliciting an iota of trust and confidence from the people.[7] In popular perceptions the main difference between the old and the new sovereigns was that 'formerly rajahs ... loved the people as their own children' and their feelings were reciprocated. By contrast, the British were contemptuous of Indians, hardly a basis for amicable relations between the rulers and the ruled.[8]

Exaggerating the generosity and goodness of past sovereigns served to magnify the cracks in the emerging colonial edifice. Previously rulers provided for social welfare by 'squander[ing] large sums of money in gifts and charities'. The British did 'not consider support of the subjects as the duty of the ruling power'. Concerned with augmenting public revenues, they 'delight[ed] in encumbering the people' with local taxes and cesses. With few rights as subjects, Indians lacked any sense of civic responsibility. Even the nobles who used to spend lavishly on social causes shied away from philanthropic work on account of overregulation.[9]

The security offered by membership in local communities could partially compensate for the shrinkage in civic rights and responsibilities.[10] Yet a sense of rights derived from belonging to a community was not the same as one that evolved out of a civic sphere shared by all Indians. The colonial state's avowed policy of non-interference with the religious concerns of its subjects had in any case confused the public debate on temporal and spiritual matters. Packaging temporal needs in communitarian terms weakened the already feebly delineated rights and responsibilities of common subjecthood. It implied that Indians were first and foremost members of specific communities and only afterwards belonged to the same country. But cutting the field of subjecthood with the religious blade did not mean that the British had sewn up their ideas on how the rights of communities were to be upheld by the legal system they had created.

As administrative experience ought to have taught them, communities were moving targets in an individual's self-identification. There could not be a static notion of community in a social context where the family and the clan constituted the earliest fields of personal reference. Muslim *ashraf* classes

---

[7]*Urdu Akhbar*, Delhi, 24 December 1872 , *Selections*, L/R/5/49, IOL, pp. 12–13.

[8]*Kohinoor*, Lahore, 2 March 1872, ibid., pp. 147,149.

[9]*Akhyar-ul-Akhbar*, Lucknow, 11 March 1873, *Selections*, L/R/5/50, pp. 181–2.

[10]See David Washbrook, 'Progress and Problems: South Asian Economic and Social History, c.1720–1860', *MAS*, 22, 1 (1988).

in north India and elsewhere were evolving a discourse on a communitarian identity informed by a cultural and religious ethos that was self-consciously Islamic in its moorings. Disseminated by print technologies these were written for the better part in Urdu, a language which was distinct from the spoken vernacular in the Punjab. The decision against mass education in this region underlines the problems of treating communitarian discourse as the only referent of subcontinental Muslim identities. If language had become a class barrier in constructing an identity that was Punjabi as well as Muslim, customary practices in the Punjab and the North Western Frontier region were a bigger impediment to lending Islamic substance to the legal definition of an Indian Muslim.[11] The prevalence of custom in these regions indicates that conquests and conversions had not been followed by the adoption of the *sharia*.

With expediency and minimum disruption in the pre-existing mechanisms of collaboration and control as the motto, the colonial state introduced civil and criminal codes in India while simultaneously encouraging the compilation of both Muslim and Hindu law. But for all the sustained efforts in that direction neither the Islamic *sharia* nor the Hindu *dharmashastras* were relevant to the ordering of social arrangements in the Punjab and the North Western Frontier districts. In 1864 the decision to do away with Mughal law officials like *muftis, qazis* and *pandits* affected the regions differently. Unlike Bengal and northern India, the Mughals rarely managed to stretch their legal tentacles through the office of *qazis* into large parts of rural Punjab, especially in the western districts.[12] As in the North Western Frontier where the Muslim tribes had only the 'vaguest notion' of the Islamic *sharia*,[13] customary or tribal law in the Punjab superseded Muslim and Hindu personal law in matters to do with property, marriage and divorce. The domain of *qazis* and *pandits* was restricted to the purely religious or spiritual; they were not called upon to adjudicate over temporal affairs. By accepting the supremacy of customary practices in judicial decisions, the British institutionalized the hiatus between

---

[11]See David Gilmartin, 'Customary Law and *Shariat* in British Punjab', in Katherine P. Ewing (ed.), *Shariat and Ambiguity in South Asian Islam*, Berkeley: University of California Press, 1988, pp. 43–62.

[12]This is only partially qualified by J.S. Grewal's discovery that in matters to do with contract Hindus and Muslims presented their disputes to *qazis* in the rural areas all the way down to the village in the eastern districts of the Punjab. But while adjudicating on commercial matters, the *qazi* courts did not have jurisdiction in the personal law of non-Muslims. (See J.S. Grewal, 'The *Qazi* in the *Pargana*', in J.S. Grewal (ed.), *Studies in Local and Regional History*, Amritsar: Guru Nanak University, 1974, pp. 1–16.)

[13]Sir Charles Row, author of *Tribal Law in the Punjab*, cited in Diwan Paras, *Customary Law (of Punjab and Haryana)*, Chandigarh: Publication Bureau, Punjab University, 1978, p. 4.

the temporal and the religious community to a far greater extent in the Punjab than elsewhere.

Although classified as members of distinctive communities, Punjabi Muslims, Hindus and Sikhs in their everyday lives observed social customs which owed nothing to religious doctrines. Customary practices were based on the specific agricultural setting of clan–community networks in which property rights were held collectively rather than individually. There was no such thing as a 'common law' in the Punjab, nor for that matter *muqammi* or regional custom. *Rawaj* or custom in counter-distinction to law did not require the decree of a ruler. Individuals living in a rural locality were subject only to the customs of their family or *qaum*, which might refer to a 'tribe' but could be a looser association such as *biraderi*, literally brotherhood. These customs were considered transportable and informed court rulings even when the disputants had moved to a different rural or urban locality. Generally, however, those living in *qasbahs* and towns amended their customary laws which were often more personalized to the family than collective.[14]

Social convenience and individual choice, not an exclusive sense of identity with the larger religious community, determined a Punjabi litigant's preference for customary, personal or civil law. In one interesting legal battle, the plaintiff accused the defendant of running off with his wife. All the witnesses, including the *qazi*, substantiated the plaintiff's claim that the woman was his legal wedded wife. A Muslim extra assistant commissioner dismissed the case and handed the woman to the defendant. Illustrating the many possibilities for the carriage or miscarriage of justice afforded by the multiplicity of laws, he noted that the plaintiff was a raw youth of fifteen while the defendant had no faith in Muslim law and subscribed to 'the English law'. Moreover, the woman herself was unwilling to cohabit with her lawful husband.[15] Women were less fortunate than this unusual case seems to indicate. A handsome woman of the Oswal caste with her wits about her wangled a certificate from the state and started a 'system of plunder'. She was caught by the chief of the area. As was customary punishment for such crimes, she was paraded on an ass with her face blackened and eventually thrown out.[16]

In attempting to administer justice in the Punjab, the British ended up promoting a kind of legal anarchy qualified only by the requirement that litigants prove the existence of custom by satisfying the conditions of its antiquity, continuity and reasonableness. Once a customary practice was upheld in a court decision, the rule of precedent gave it the status of law, regardless of whether or not it conflicted with the laws of religious communities.

[14]See C.L. Tupper, *Punjab Customary Law*, vols i and ii, Calcutta: Government Printing Press, 1881. Paras, *Customary Law (of Punjab and Haryana)*, and Badruddin Quereshi, *Riwaj-i-Punjab* (Urdu translation of his *The Punjab Custom*), Lahore, 1912.

[15]*Vidya Vilas*, Jammu, 20 May 1871, *Selections*, L/R/5/48, IOL, p. 259.

[16]*Panjabi Akhbar*, Lahore, 4 March 1871, ibid., p. 85.

With a three-pronged legal system, individuals thronged the courts exercising their autonomy to decide which community of association they regarded as primary. Averaging at one case per ninety persons compared to a ratio of one to every 320 in Bengal, one to 390 in Awadh and one to 403 in the North Western Provinces, Punjab had a higher rate of litigation than anywhere else.[17] This was variously attributed to the fact of the Punjab being a non-regulation province, its relative wealth and the profusion of administrative departments. Yet the sheer bulk of litigation in the province was a direct product of the status accorded to custom by the courts. The primary sources of disputes in the Punjab were zan, zamin, and zar or women, land and money. Only a sixth of the cases before the courts were related to landed property.[18] Marital issues constituted the overwhelming majority of litigation, most of it based on settling conflicting claims arising from plaintiffs and defendants seeking recourse in customary, personal or civil law.

Customary marriages were often a euphemism for a flourishing slave trade in women. As the Kohinoor put it, the 'sacred contract of matrimony' was 'profaned' by being 'treated as little better than a sale transaction'. The rich and the powerful walked off with the women and the spurned husbands had to spend a good deal of money on stamp fees, pleaders and presents for the amlah, or law officers, to find justice in the courts. Justice was rarely forthcoming. All the losers could do was console themselves that they had done 'everything to preserve their izzat'. Land disputes took even longer and were no less 'perplexing and ruinous'. Litigants were tied up in knots from which they could not extricate themselves for a whole lifetime. Bribes to the police and the amlah often equalled the value of the claim so that the successful suitor was only nominally better off financially.[19]

Conditions were not significantly better in the North Western Provinces. Much as in the Punjab, the police was roundly abused for its corruption and indiscriminate recruiting. Police officials were accused of working hand in glove with local criminals. Thefts and dacoities had become common occurrences while the guilty were hardly ever apprehended and convicted. One newspaper thought the 'present age ha[d] eclipsed the fame of ages which ...[were] proverbially notorious for such crimes'.[20] Many preferred a return to the old chowkidari system than the disastrous new arrangements for policing. Answerable to the inhabitants of the locality, chowkidars patrolled the streets at night and served as a check on ordinary crime. Others charged the small cause courts in the provinces for operating on principles that were utterly 'bad' and 'indifferent'.[21]

[17]Panjabi Akhbar, Lahore, 24 to 31 January 1868, Selections, L/R/5/45, IOL, p. 45.
[18]Ibid.
[19]Kohinoor, Lahore, 2 March 1872, Selections, L/R/5/49, IOL, pp. 146–9.
[20]Akmal-ul-Akhbar, Delhi, 14 June 1871, Selections, L/R/5/48, IOL, p. 317.
[21]Jalwa-i-Tur, Meerut, 23 June 1871, ibid., p. 329.

There were suggestions that the small cause courts be entrusted to Indians or dispensed with altogether. Local *panchayats*, or councils of village patriarchs, would be better placed to keep tabs on crime and administer justice in terms understandable to the people. But this was an issue which divided opinion in both the Punjab and the North Western Provinces. The opponents pointed to the difficulty of finding men with integrity for the *panchayats*. In most cases, those connected with district officials secured appointments on village councils to carry out a reign of tyranny and oppression. Most people had 'little confidence' in their village elders. Despite the cost and time, Punjabi litigants sought recourse to public courts of law. These at least gave them the right to appeal adverse decisions while the verdicts of the *panchayats* were binding.[22] With such an endorsement from the 'people', the British had fewer reasons to be troubled by charges of corruption and mismanagement in the lower courts.

Qazis, Sects and Muslim Law

Disaffection with the colonial machinery for policing and administering justice led to intermittent calls for a revival of the Mughal legal system, particularly the office of the *qazi*. As the key law official in each city and town, and in certain regions also the rural areas, the *qazi* solemnized marriages and settled political, religious and social disputes among Muslims. English mechanisms of dispensation of justice had, for all practical purposes, rendered the office of the *qazi* redundant. But there were 'a great variety of suits' relating to inheritance and property which 'on account of being based on lineage and peculiar marriage rules and formalities, c[ould] only be fitly and justly decided by Qazees'. It was best, therefore, to select men who were 'pious, upright and well-versed in Mahomedan law' from the two main sectarian divisions in Islam. Sunni and Shia *qazis* would pronounce the *nikah*, the marriage oath, and settle all matters connected with divorce according to the laws of the two sects.[23]

Demands for restoring the office of *qazi* found support among educated Muslims cutting across regions and ideological divisions. This feeble effort to reinvoke the old world to redress the wrongs of the new was recommended as early as 1865 by the Anjuman-i-Punjab in a province where Islamic justice was virtually non-existent. The *Aligarh Institute Gazette* approved of the idea. In 1869 it was formally proposed by Bengali Muslims and strongly backed by those in Bihar. One of the main consequences of the displacement of Persian as the court language in eastern India, as various Muslim memorialists never ceased recording, was the dramatic decline in the status of *madrasas*. Reduced to the status of *maktabs* or grammar schools, the *madrasas* saw their

[22]*Kohinoor*, Lahore, 17 February 1872, *Selections*, L/R/5/49, IOL, pp. 115–17.

[23]This was the opinion of the *Roznamcha*, one of the first Urdu dailies from Lucknow. *Roznamcha*, 6 June 1873, *Selections*, L/R/5/50, IOL, p. 380.

clientele dwindling once the post of *qazi* and other Mughal law officers was abolished.

Socially the effects were unsettling for segments of Muslim populations, particularly in the urban areas. The *Shola-i-Tur* of Kanpur reported that many couples were not lawfully married since 'ignorant persons' who knew nothing of Islamic law presided over the ceremony. A proper system of registration headed by officially appointed *qazis* would reduce litigation on marriage and not be seen as 'an unjust interference' by the government in the 'religious affairs of Muslims'.[24] But restoring the former status of *qazis* amounted to opening up an Islamic can of sectarian worms. In 1871–2 the *Anjuman-i-Punjab* solicited the opinions of *maulvis* in various parts of India and the *qazi fazl* and *qazi alim* qualifying tests were instituted. In 1881 while welcoming the appointment of two *qazis* in Lahore, the *Anjuman-i-Punjab* regretted that the government had selected two Sunnis for 'a community composed of Sunnis, Shias and Wahabis'. With the exception of the Sunnis, no Muslim sect would let official *qazis* perform their marriages.[25]

Sectarian divisions were a bigger obstacle than customary practice to placing Indian Muslims under a single legal code. The multiplicity of sects in Islam, estimated to be over a hundred, meant that no one wanted to be subjected to rules other than those of their own choice. Ardent Shias believed they were not only distinct from the Sunnis but superior to them.[26] While many Sunnis disparaged Shias, they were themselves hardly a band of singing birds. The more puritanical, variously known as 'Wahabis', the Ahl-i-Hadith or the Ahl-i-Sunnat, attacked Sunnis of the dominant Hanafi school and the idiosyncratic Ahl-i-Quran for undermining the precepts of faith. By the time Mirza Ghulam Ahmad had created a new sect among the Muslims in the late nineteenth century, religious tract wars were competing with *munazaras* or polemical debates in their outreach. Exponents of one sect execrated all other sects in unspeakable language while purporting to prove them wrong in their interpretation of Islam. In one district in the Punjab, Sunni Muslims incensed by a Wahabi religious tract suspended all social intercourse with them. Wahabis were debarred from using Sunni wells or baking bread in their ovens.[27]

There were countless other such sectarian affrays. Colonial officials had to drop the rule of non-interference in religion into the waste paper bin in order

[24]*Shola-i-Tur*, Kanpur, 15 July 1879, *Selections*, L/R/5/56, IOL, p. 548.

[25]*Anjuman-i-Punjab*, Lahore, 16 August 1881, *Selections*, L/R/5/58, IOL, pp. 479–80.

[26]One religious tract abused Sunnis for holding anti-Islamic views. Citing stray *fatwas* by a Sunni *alim* to make a point about an entire sect, the author maintained that Sunnis considered the marriage of a man to his daughter as legitimate. According to another Sunni source a man could marry a mother as well as a daughter. (Maulvi Saiyid Sajjad Husain, *Ijaz-i-Daudi*, Delhi, 1912, VT 3788f, IOL, p. 384.)

[27]*Wakil-i-Hindustan*, Amritsar, 9 July 1875, *Selections*, L/R/5/52, IOL, p. 345.

to control their wayward Muslim subjects. In Delhi the local Ahl-i-Hadith had a long-standing rivalry with the Ahl-i-Fiqa. Though the doctrinal differences were minor, they 'hate[d] each other'. It required the commissioner's good offices to negotiate a compromise enabling members of the two sects to say prayers in the same mosque.[28] Like Hindu–Muslim tensions, sectarian conflicts were mainly over social space and power in local and municipal boards. With Muslims unable to agree with one another on issues, big and small, it required a miracle of faith to order their lives according to Islamic law. But the larger-than-life legal category of 'Indian Muslim' was reason enough for members of various classes and sects to try and gain some mileage by claiming to speak on its behalf.

In 1882 the memorial of the National Muhammadan Association pleaded for the appointment of *qazis*. English and Hindu judges were faulted for their scanty understanding of the *sharia* which resulted in the 'miscarriage of justice' for Muslim subjects of the Crown. With the abolition of the office of the *mufti* and the *qazi-ul-quzzat* or Chief Justice, Muslim law had virtually ceased to be publicly administered. The memorialists maintained that the bulk of the personal law of Muslims 'regulating ... domestic relations ... [was] not recognized by the courts of justice in India'.[29] Whatever the shreds of truth in this assertion, the bulging corpus of Anglo-Muhammadan law testifies to the fact that Muslim personal law far from falling into disuse received its greatest boost under British colonialism.[30] Beginning with Cornwallis it was a long process, culminating in the compilation of Muslim personal law by men like C. Hamilton, Neil B.E.A. Baillie, William MacNaghtan and Syed Ameer Ali.

British judges were not only confident of their understanding of Islamic law but believed they did a better job of interpreting it than retrograde and narrow-minded *qazis*. Prior to the memorial, they had never been 'taunted with ignorance of Muhammadan law' which to many seemed more straightforward than Hindu law.[31] Contrary to the charge of the memorialists, Muslims and Hindus were entitled to their personal law except when prevented by a legislative

---

[28]*Ataliq-i-Hind*, Lucknow, 19 October 1882, *Selections*, L/R/5/59, IOL, p. 719.

[29]Memorial of the National Muhammadan Association to Lord Ripon, 6 February 1882, 'The Education of the Muhammadan Community', in *Records*, V/23/46, IOL, p. 242.

[30]British judges set about applying the Islamic laws of inheritance rigidly against propertied Muslims trying to prevent the division of their assets by creating *waqfs*, literally religious and charitable endowments but in practice benefiting the creator's family. While public *waqfs* were deemed consistent with the *sharia*, the learned justices overturned many private *waqfs*. The clash between British and Muslim notions of 'public' and 'private' interests is documented in Gregory Kozlowski, *Muslim Endowments and Society in British India*, Cambridge: Cambridge University Press, 1985.

[31]Minute by Judge Bayley, 24 April 1882, 'The Education of the Muhammadan Community', in *Records*, V/23/46, IOL, p. 272.

enactment or by customary practice. In the few instances where Muslim law became applicable, there was no indication of any miscarriage of justice because of the judge's lack of knowledge of the *sharia*. There seemed no point in raising from the ashes a cadre of law officers who not very long ago had been 'condemned as useless, if not mischievous'.[32] If Muslims wanted their law offices, Hindu *pandits* would demand their share of the windfall. Seeing it as an employment generation scheme, British officialdom unanimously rejected the idea of appointing Muslim assessor judges.

There were other compelling reasons not to give credence to the memorialists' demands. Islamic law in comparison with civil and customary law was restricted in its application. In Bombay presidency, trading castes like the Khojahs and Memons formed a significant proportion of the Muslim population. Their rules of inheritance were of Hindu origin and it was 'quite common to find Mussulman litigants speaking of themselves as an undivided family'. A mere 2 per cent of the cases before the courts in the presidency related to Muslim law.[33] In the Central Provinces out of four hundred court rulings in twenty years only a dozen owed their reasoning to the *sharia*. Here the provincial laws imposed 'a substantial limitation on the applicability of Muhammadan law in cases between Muhammadans'. In some instances the courts did not recognize certain principles of the *sharia*.

Bombay and the Central Provinces were sparsely populated by Muslims. But a Muslim majority region did not necessarily mean the greater admissibility of Islamic law. At the time of its annexation, the Punjab had no 'authorised expositors of Muhammadan law'. Initially the courts dealt with Muslim personal law by referring to non-official *qazis* in whose *fatwas* the disputants had confidence. This was also the administrative practice in the frontier districts. In these areas custom superseded Islamic law on matters of inheritance. With few exceptions,[34] Muslim women were rarely allotted their assigned share in Islamic law. In special cases a Muslim woman without any sons could inherit the property of her deceased husband like a Hindu widow. The question of when Muslim law was superseded by custom arose only when a party claimed to be ruled by one as opposed to the other. Despite numerous departures in practice, Muslims of Peshawar and Derajat as well as Rawalpindi divisions claimed to follow Islamic rules of succession. Such assertions were

[32]This was the opinion of C.A. Wilkins, officiating registrar of the high court at Fort William. (Ibid., p. 283.)

[33]Minute by Justice Melville, Bombay, 2 April 1882, ibid., p. 269.

[34]Such as the Wattoo *qaum* in Montgomery and Bahawalpur districts, who had been converted to Islam by Baba Farid of Pak Pattan well over six hundred years ago. According to their custom, women became inheritors of their husbands' property although under Islamic law they were entitled to only a legal portion. (Quereshi, *Riwaj-i-Punjab*, p. 4.)

'partly dictated by bigotry and partly by ignorance'.[35] Outside a select circle, Muslims were more likely to 'feel aggrieved if their customs ... g[a]ve way to Muhammadan law' since *'they have never been accustomed to observe it'*. The problem was 'not so much to ascertain what the Muhammadan law [was] as to discover how far it [was] followed'.[36]

As Justice W.H. Rattigan explained, Muslim law scarcely mattered in the Punjab because the people themselves 'adhere[d] ... to a different system'.[37] After taking over the province, the British had tried to 'preserve the traditions both of Hindu and Muhammadan law'.[38] During the first twenty years, 'instead of superseding Muhammadan law' the British did 'a great deal to introduce it into a country where it was practically unknown'. But the Punjab Laws Act of 1872 gave primacy to custom in civil cases. George Campbell, the originator of the idea, defended it on the grounds that one out of a hundred Muslims in the Punjab was governed by the strict provisions of Islamic law. By privileging custom, Punjabi Muslims had voluntarily overlaid the *sharia*. Disputants seldom raised complex questions on Muslim personal law which were covered by the Punjab civil code of 1854.[39]

Cornered by the logic of its own categorization of the Indian Muslim and the expediency of accommodating local customary practices, the colonial state chose to contradict itself than engage in the unrewarding task of enforcing legal consistency where none existed. When it came to the machinery of law and justice, the British kept the guardians of legalist religion at a safe distance. Such reservations did not apply to census enumeration. For instance, Denzil Ibbetson had no qualms stating in the Punjab census report that conversion to Islam had an 'evil influence' on the inhabitants of the province as it made them 'proud, conceited, and extravagant'. Not fazed by Ibbetson's bumbling observations about its co-religionists in a neighbouring region, the *Aligarh Institute Gazette* instead objected to him 'ascribing these alleged characteristics of the Panjab Musalmans to their *religion*'.[40] The process of census enumeration in its more advanced stages included an increasing number of columns purporting to throw more light on the characteristics of Muslims, Hindus and Sikhs. In 1887 the Punjab government asked its commissioners to submit reports listing the inhabitants by religion along with information about their original

[35]This was the observation of Sir Charles Row, author of *Tribal Law in the Punjab*; cited in Paras, *Customary Law (of Punjab and Haryana)*, p. 4.

[36]Opinion of Justice D.G. Barkley, 'The Education of the Muhammadan Community', in *Records*, V/23/46, IOL, pp. 296–7 (my emphasis).

[37]Minute by Justice W.H. Rattigan, ibid., p. 298.

[38]W.M. Young, secretary to government of the Punjab, to secretary to the government of India (home department), 19 April 1883, ibid., pp. 293–4.

[39]This was the opinion of Justice G.R. Elsmie, ibid., p. 295.

[40]*Aligarh Institute Gazette*, 8 June 1886, *Selections*, L/R/5/63, IOL, p. 432 (my emphasis).

domiciles and educational qualifications.[41] This was further ammunition for those whipping up communitarian passions in the Punjab press. Nevertheless, as with the spoken vernacular, for all the hype about religious communities, no one wanted to give up the customs of their respective lineages.

Until 1937 there was no move to replace custom with the Islamic *sharia*. Even then agricultural property was kept immune from the amendment of the clause in the Punjab Laws Act of 1872 assigning greater weight to custom than Muslim law. So for all practical purposes, Punjabi Muslims continued wearing their customary badges, signifying their affinities with any number of *qaums* and tribes, while marching as foot soldiers under the Islamic banner towards the goal of Muslim nationhood. Given the multiplicity of communities permitted by the colonial legal system, a Muslim's identification with the army of the faithful was often undercut by fealty towards kith and kin of more localized standing. Narratives of a Muslim communitarian identity constructed in the public arena might try and side-step the legal dilemmas with their overarching claims. Yet the balance between individual and collective rights for large segments of Britain's Muslim subjects owed precious little to the grandiose ideas that were shaping notions of an Islamic identity or a common Indian nationality.

COMPARTMENTALIZING THE MUSLIM: POLITICS AS IDENTITY

By the turn of the century the idea of a distinct Indian Muslim interest that needed representing was being regularly flaunted in petitions to the colonial authorities. As yet there was no concerted move afoot to politically organize the faithful outside a select group consisting primarily of Urdu-knowing, if not Urdu-speaking, Muslims. Even as far afield as Bengal, it was Muslims from the *ashraf* classes with knowledge of Urdu and Persian who seemed most eager to make common cause with their co-religionists in northern India and the Punjab. When individual and regional interests did not obviate the commonalities of religion, class remained a formidable barrier in articulating interests jointly rather than severally. For the vast majority of Indian Muslims, outside the realm of privilege bestowed by the colonial state, the concerns and activities of Muslim *ashraf* classes were for the most part distant, if not altogether irrelevant.

This is not to deny that the press and publications market was making its presence felt over wider sections of the population. By 1905 some 1359 newspapers and journals boasted two million subscribers. Of these publications, 338 were in Urdu; 285 in English; eighty-two in English and a vernacular; seventy-eight in Hindi; seventy-four in Bengali; ninety-seven in

---

[41]The *Akhbar-i-Alam* (Meerut) of 5 July 1887 wondered why the preparation of such a statement had been ordered in the Punjab, *Selections*, L/R/5/64, IOL, p. 421.

Gujarati; ninety-three in Marathi; twelve in Punjabi; eleven in Sindhi; and the rest in other regional languages. Bombay with 320 had the largest concentration of newspapers and journals. There were 197 in the United Provinces and 263 in the Punjab, including the North Western Frontier region.[42] Notwithstanding the growing mobilizational potential of the press, it cannot be assumed that the direct impact extended beyond the intermediate strata of society. Word of mouth certainly aided the spread of information supplied by print. However, it was the immediacy of life and not the high-flown ideas expressed on paper which mattered most to those struggling to eke out a living.

There was no obvious connection between battles for social space in different localities and the narratives authored by a voluble group of newspapermen. But these occurrences provided the ammunition the newspaper guns needed for target practice. The community of the Muslims was an ideal even for those who adhered to it most strongly. As an examination of the press in the first decade of the twentieth century illustrates, its main utility lay in delineating a position that was oppositional to and distinct from that of non-Muslims, Hindus in particular. Irritated by what they saw as the exclusionary tactics of their fellow countrymen, to say nothing of the reactions to some of their own, educated Muslims in the Punjab, northern India and Bengal found solace in the colonial acknowledgement of them as a distinctive entity.

An identity forged in opposition to Hindus at the level of ideas was not sufficient to close Muslim ranks across class, regional and personalized lines. But even a negative identification could be a powerful unifying factor for a divided Muslim community. The more so since the notion of a Hindu 'majority' and a Muslim 'minority' was now deeply embedded in emerging narratives on the Indian 'nation', albeit not without some serious problems in empirical fact. According to the *Sat Dharm Pracharik* of Jullundur, educated Indians blamed English education for sowing the seeds of discord in the country. A mere 'forty years ago the Hindus and Muhammadans lived in peace and amity'. This was 'only natural' as 99 per cent of the Muslims were converts from Hinduism and still observed several of its rites and ceremonies. Western ideas of 'nation', 'nationality' and 'citizenship' had to contend with the reality of several sovereign Muslim countries in the world. Using the cover of these countries to offset their minority status in India, Muslims 'regard[ed] themselves as a separate nation and ... [sought] special rights and privileges'. Worse still, 'Rajputs, Bengalis, Panjabis, &c., also look[ed] upon themselves as so many separate nations' with the result that 'the disintegration of the Indian nation [was] complete'.[43]

[42]N. Gerald Barrier, *Banned: Controversial Literature and Political Control in British India, 1907–1947*, Columbia: University of Missouri Press, 1974, p. 9.

[43]*Sat Dharm Pracharik*, Jullundur, 14 June 1901, PNNR, L/R/5/185, IOL, p. 393.

Harping on the extra-territorial affiliations of Indian Muslims was an old dictum of the discourse on majoritarianism. Even before the formal granting of separate electorates to Indian Muslims in 1909, the discourse of Indian nationalism had become thoroughly infused with the presumption of 'majority' and 'minority' interests. The idea of a single Indian 'nation' was most powerfully expressed by the Bengali pen. Yet as educated Bengali Muslims noted with bitterness, the 'nation' had acquired overtones that were offensively exclusionary.[44] In 1898 the Muslim Educational Conference formally condemned the animosity towards Muslims found in Bengali literature. Novels and poems depicting Muslims as 'wicked, tyrannical, dissolute devils and hated lecherous dogs' drew the 'praise of countless Hindus'. Leading the attack was the popular Bengali novelist Bankim Chandra Chattopadhyay (1838–1894) whose creative imagination was not above dragging the daughters of Muslim rulers out of the harem to show them as 'desirous of the love of Shivaji', the 'devil' incarnate, 'mountain-rat and slayer of women'. Muslim women were seen 'languishing for the love of pig-eating Rajputs' or portrayed as 'handmaids' of 'Hindu slaves'. The delight with which such stories were staged and appreciated suggested that 'Hindu authors, orators, poets and novelists' believed they were 'born only to slay the *yavanas*'.[45]

Unless the term *yavana* was defined otherwise, Bengali Muslims would 'continue to take it as a terrible term of abuse' reserved exclusively for them. How could 'Hindus whiningly and brazenly' expect Muslims to like them while using derogatory terms like *yavana* and *mlechha*? Until they 'realised that internal dissensions' were the 'root of ruination', Hindu–Muslim unity would 'remain a mid-day reverie'.[46] While objecting to their lowly status in popular regional narratives, more Hindu and Bengali than Indian, upper-class Muslims debarred low-caste Hindu converts to Islam from attending their prayer meetings in addition to subjecting them to a range of discriminatory social practices. Conflict between the western educated and the rest was an even more unpropitious omen for an accord among Bengali Muslims. The western educated were caricatured as 'half Hindu and half

[44]That this has remained a problem can be seen in the exclusion of the Muslim dimension in works like Chatterjee, *Nationalist Thought*. Even within the narrower field of Bengali intellectual thought there is a curious absence of studies on Muslim political thought contending on equal terms with Bengali Hindu writings.

[45]This was the opinion of the *Islam-pracharak* in 1903 which was patronized by the loyalist Muslim landed gentry of Bengal; cited in Mustafa Nurul Islam, *Bengali Muslim Public Opinion as Reflected in the Bengali Press, 1901–1930*, Dacca: Bangla Academy, 1973, pp. 141–2. Bankim did not depict a Muslim woman desirous of the love of Shivaji. In his *Durgeshnandini* a Pathan woman named Ayesha falls in love with a Rajput prince Jagat Singh.

[46]The views of the *Naba Nur* and *Kohinoor* of 1903 and 1905 respectively, ibid., p. 109.

European' who went about crying 'you are Muslim'. They wore 'odd attire' despite 'possess[ing] such beautiful clothes'. Some of these 'rascals ridicule[d] the *Ulema* in turbans as large basket-carrying porters', such was 'the picture of our educated people'.[47]

Despite shared interests with co-religionists in other parts of India, Bengali Muslims flatly refused to replace Bengali with Urdu in the interests of a common Muslim nationhood. Muslim nawabs in the eastern districts were the strongest advocates of retaining the linguistic link with the rest of Hindustan. Yet unlike their counterparts in the Punjab, Bengali Muslim papers stuck firmly to their mother-tongue. As far as language and birthplace were concerned, Muslims were Bengali. As the *Kohinoor* was to put it in 1916, 'creat[ing] an All-India nationhood' on the basis of Urdu was 'as useless as trying to build a house in the sky'. The 'growth of nationhood' would 'not in the least be impeded if one releases the general public from the necessity of learning Urdu'.[48]

There was to be no shift from this position. Defending their mother-tongue against Urdu was seen as a logical concomitant to the 'welfare and salvation' of the Muslim 'nation' in Bengal. Bengali Muslims thought it 'preposterous' for anyone to ask them 'to weep in a foreign language'. They may 'hear the joyous laughter of Urdu from next door', but it brought 'no genuine joy or comfort'.[49] While resenting the Sanskritization of their language, Bengali Muslims did not rush to adorn their writings with Persian and Arabic vocabulary. Certain Muslim circles resented the efforts to make 'Bengali a second edition of Sanskrit'. Muslim admirers of the great Bengali poet Rabindranath Tagore, like Kazi Nazrul Islam were unfairly accused of rendering Bengali 'sickly and enfeebled'. What was needed to make Bengali 'strong, firm and heroic' was to 'teach it to parade and manoeuvre on the field of battle astride a spirited Arabian stallion, bearing an unsheathed scimitar'.[50]

These Bengali Muslim opinions on a linguistic identity that was different from the one represented by the equation of Muslim with Urdu foreshadow developments in a later period. Their utility here lies in pointing out how culture as difference could cut both ways. It could resist the dominant idioms defining the communities of religion and language even while acknowledging an affinity to either of these sources of identification. Culture as difference might at one moment highlight the religious affiliations of Muslims across class and region. Yet when it came to their linguistic identities, Muslims in one region could not agree with co-religionists in another. So there can be no

[47]This was the opinion of papers like *Kohinoor* and *Islam-pracharak*. See ibid., p. 253.

[48]Ibid., pp. 228–9.

[49]Ibid., pp. 231–2.

[50]This was the opinion in August 1923 of the *khilafat* organ in Bengal, the *Choltan*, ibid., p. 242.

straightforward interpellation of culture as difference and the politics of Muslim identity. Feelings of distinctiveness from Hindus in any given region did not create supra-regional bonds with an Indian Muslim community at an all-India level to enable a coherent politics of identity.

Ever since the formation of the Congress, one of the favourite hobby horses of the newspaper industry was discussing the implications of the lukewarm response of Muslims to India's only nationalist organization. Between 1885 and 1905 Muslims, constituting over a fifth of the population, accounted for one-tenth of the delegates to the Congress. Not in itself a meaningful indicator given the limited appeal of the Congress, it contributed to the hardening of the rift between Hindus and Muslims—the 'majority' and the 'minority' categories respectively in narratives of the nation-in-the-making. An analysis of the Punjab press bears out the extent to which an influential section of the Hindu 'majority' which was in a minority in one region was opposed to the tactics of a national organization seen to be carrying a distinctively Bengali impress.

Lahore's Hindu-managed *Akhbar-i-Am* stated the position in unequivocal terms. The Congress did 'not represent the public opinion of the country' and with the 'exception of a few lawyers' and a handful of others 'the entire population of the Punjab [was] opposed to the movement'.[51] Lacking any organization, enthusiasm for the Congress in the province was 'a periodical and spasmodic impulse of certain individuals' which tended to be less 'sustained and systematic' than went into the management of annual fairs in the province.[52] The *Khalsa Gazette* showed its contempt for the Congress by describing it as 'a society of beggars' who met annually 'to beg for various things from the Government of India'.[53] Punjabi Muslims were strongest in their rejection of the Congress. Muslims attending its meetings were seen as 'misguided adherents' of Islam; a 'few malcontents' who upon feeling 'inadequately honoured in their own community' had taken to seeking 'fictitious importance amongst a rival one'.[54]

Muslims needed their own political organization. It would not be 'directed against the Hindus' but 'owe[d] its origins to the necessities of the time' and MacDonell's Nagari resolution.[55] The writings of those who followed the 'Bengal School of Politics' was making it 'impossible for the two great sections of the Indian population to work together'.[56] A political platform of their own might deter Muslims from drifting towards the Congress whose 'principles ignore[d] the interests of the minorities' and which used suspect methods to attain its

[51]*Akhbar-i-Am*, Lahore, 15 January 1901, *PNNR*, L/R/5/185, IOL, p. 38.

[52]*Tribune*, Lahore, 5 September 1901, ibid., p. 550.

[53]*Khalsa Gazette*, Lahore, 28 January 1901, ibid., p. 78.

[54]*Punjab Observer*, Lahore, 7 August 1901, ibid., p. 497.

[55]*Paisa Akhbar*, Lahore, 28 September 1901, ibid., pp. 656–8.

[56]*Punjab*, Amritsar, 13 August 1901, ibid., p. 521.

aims.[57] Yet these Punjabi Muslims were equally determined not to hitch their wagons with the Aligarh coterie which had disgraced itself over the Hindi–Urdu controversy.

Despite opposition to the Congress, ideological and class differences prevented the emergence of an alternative political alliance among Muslims. In 1901 the Lahore-based newspaper *Sada-i-Hind* asserted that the opinions of the 'English-speaking Muhammadans' were not the 'united voice of the country' and giving the Aligarh party the lead in political matters was thoroughly 'undesirable'.[58] The *Tribune* at once hailed this a 'Revolt against Aligarh'.[59] Muslims' loyalty was the biggest barrier to their participation in the nationalist organization. The 'loyal and brave descendants of the Pathan and Moghul rulers of India' instead of 'joining the chattering "Babus" in their disloyal agitation' opted to 'strengthen the hands of the authorities'. Muslims would be more in 'consonance with their own traditions' if they were 'the guiding power in all political movements' and did not separate themselves in the interests of their own community. It was heartening that in the 'general body' of Muslims there was 'an awakening to a sense of national, as distinguished from sectional duty'.[60]

As the reaction to the partition of Bengal and the *swadeshi* movement after 1905 made all too apparent, the 'national' and 'sectional' dimensions of Muslim concerns were closely interwoven with individual choices. The Nawab of Dacca's brother, Khwajah Atiqulla, submitted a memorial signed by 25,000 persons to the government, arguing that as a community Muslims were opposed to the partition of the province. Atiqulla's relations with the nawab were less than cordial and he was promptly charged with 'selfish motives'.[61] In a significant demonstration of its position, most of the Muslim-managed press in Bengal did not join the agitation to unsettle the settled fact of partition. That the posture was due to its misgivings about the methods and aims of the *swadeshi* nationalists is well known. But even in the Punjab there was consternation about the spirit pervading the *swadeshi* movement. It seemed to suggest that Hindus did 'not wish Mussalmans well'.[62]

In December 1906 the formation of the All-India Muslim League to safeguard 'Muslim interests' widened the breach between the supporters and detractors of Congress's conception of the Indian 'nation'. With constitutional reforms on the anvil, these contestations instead of suggesting modifications to the western construct of the 'nation' worked to cast Indian differences into the mould of exclusionary communitarianism and inclusionary nationalism. As the debate in the vernacular press illustrates, the communitarian appeal to the

[57]Muhammad Shafi in the *Punjab Observer*, Lahore, 5 October 1901, ibid., p. 637.
[58]*Sada-i-Hind*, Lahore, 12 November 1901, ibid., p. 730.
[59]*Tribune*, Lahore, 26 November 1901, ibid., p. 760.
[60]*Tribune*, Lahore, 3 December 1901, ibid., pp. 775–6.
[61]*Watan*, Lahore, 15 March 1907, PNNR, L/R/5/189, IOL, p. 75.
[62]*Paisa Akhbar*, Lahore, 31 December 1906, ibid., p. 7.

'minority' was denuded of the inclusionary ideal largely as a reaction to the exclusionary nuances implicit in nationalist self-projections of the 'majority'.

Adding its bit to the political lexicon on 'majority' and 'minority' interests, the *Vakil* predicted that if self-government was granted 'Hindus would ... drive the Muhammadan *malechhas* out of the country'.[63] With the British about to initiate a fresh round of constitutional proposals, this was used to justify giving Muslims separate and adequate representation in the provincial and local councils under the new reforms. Instead of drawing upon normative Islamic political theory, Muslim upper classes took refuge in memories of a lost sovereignty. Assertions of a Muslim political identity were based on arguments that although fewer in number than the Hindus, Muslims derived their special importance from having been the 'rulers of India for seven hundred years' and continued to contribute a great deal towards the defence of the country. It followed that Muslims in the provincial legislative councils should be 'placed on a footing of equality with their Hindu fellow-countrymen'.[64]

Far from conceding them equality of status, some Hindu newspapers attacked Muslims for fawning before the British. The Urdu weekly *Akash* left no doubt that in its opinion the 'nation' was Hindu. Even among Hindus only the enlightened and the intrepid were true patriots of Mother India: 'Descendants of the great *rishis* .... who adorn the national pathways .... Sweep mean debauchees off the surface of the earth .... You, thirty crore descendants of *Maharishis*, come forward like brave men .... those who are cowed by fear are *others than ourselves.*' [65]

But the 'our' of the Hindus was itself contested. In the Punjab, Arya Samajists were pitted against the Sanatan Dharm in the battle for the leadership of the Hindu community. According to a prominent Arya Samaj leader, Lala Munshi Ram, 'unlike Islam and Christianity, the Vedic religion was meant for the whole world and ... did not concern itself with any particular country or people'.[66] This was anathema to many Hindus for whom a non-territorial conception of the 'nation' was inconceivable. Under the caption 'Victory to Hindus and defeat to the Dayanandis', one Sanatan Dharm paper cursed the Arya Samajists in a manner reminiscent of the attitudes of certain Muslim sects towards one another. 'The timid Dayanandis,' the paper bellowed, 'abuse Hindus and feel no shame in marrying their daughters to sweepers and *chamars.*' Hindus were 'calm and dignified like lions and care[d] nothing for the howling of jackals'.[67] Such ferocious exchanges among claimants to the leadership of the 'majority' provided the side show to more serious theatrics in which a detested 'minority' threatened to walk away with the prize.

[63]*Vakil*, Amritsar, 31 January 1907, ibid., p. 43.
[64]*Paisa Akhbar*, Lahore, 21 December 1909, *PNNR*, L/R/5/190, p. 6.
[65]*Akash*, Delhi, 31 December 1908, ibid., pp. 63–4.
[66]*Prakash*, Lahore, 2 December 1908, ibid., p. 74.
[67]*Hindu Sanatan Dharm Gazette*, Lahore, 19 May 1909, ibid., p. 500.

Race, Nation and Nationality in the Punjab Press

In 1909 the Morley–Minto reforms conceded the principle of separate electorates to Muslims at all levels of representation. The compartmentalization of Muslims into an all-India political category was a watershed event with disastrous implications for the Congress variety of inclusionary nationalism. A measure insisted upon by the All-India Muslim League, and conceded by the British, separate electorates assigned Muslims the status of a constitutional minority. Here was a minority differentiated along regional, economic as well as ideological lines with no history of organized political activity. It was expected to reap benefits from separate electorates in an imperial system of collaboration and control geared to localizing and provincializing political horizons. While local men of power and pelf were spared the trouble of competing with non-Muslims in elections to the reformed councils, separate electorates within an arena of formal politics based on a restricted franchise offered nothing to the majority of disenfranchised Muslims.

So separate electorates were effectively a class concession advanced in the name of a religious community. Since Muslims were in a majority in the north-western and the north-eastern extremities of the subcontinent, recognizing them as an all-India minority had large implications for regional discourses on communitarian interests and, by extension, on the politics of identity. In the Punjab where separate electorates in 1909 affected only one or two municipalities, discussions on the reform scheme saw Muslim and Hindu newspapers tailoring the debate on majority and minority rights to suit their own class and provincial purposes. By the time the dust had settled, Punjabis had fine-tuned the competing narratives on race,[68] nation and nationality that were communitarian in the regional rather than the supra-regional sense.

A number of Hindu newspapers faulted the Congress for this sorry turn of events. Its leaders were depicted as 'cringing and servile sycophants', 'slaves of the stomach', 'worshippers of mammon', 'cowards', 'title-hunters' and 'traitors to the nation'.[69] The influential Urdu weekly, the *Hindustan*, with a circulation of 13,000, impugned Congress leaders of 'desert[ing] their post at the most critical moment in the country's history'. Separate electorates would permanently cripple the notion of a common Indian nationality and have more pernicious effects on social relations than the partition of Bengal.[70] The *Punjabi* regarded the impending reform scheme as 'positively mischievous and deeply insulting

[68]The English translation of terms such as *qaum* and *millat* which have connotations other than purely racial.

[69]Such as the *Punjabi*, the *Akash*, the *Jhang* Sial and the *Haq Pasand*. (See *Report by the Criminal Investigation Department on the Native Papers Published in the Punjab for the Year 1909*, NCHCR, Islamabad, pp. 22–3.)

[70]*Hindustan*, Lahore, 12 March 1909, PNNR, L/R/5/190, IOL, p. 234.

to all non-Mussalmans' who wanted a united Indian nation within the British empire. Non-Muslim agitation against the scheme might fan 'racial dissension' and 'destroy the hope of national unity', but 'no race' could 'form part of the Indian nation' that 'arrogate[d] to itself superior importance', nor for that matter one which 'tamely submit[ted]' to being 'relegate[d] to an inferior position'.[71]

In a dangerous portent, a measure considered by some Muslims as a safeguard for their minority status was seen as an assault on the rights of the majority. Denying that Muslims were 'inimically disposed' towards their 'fellow countrymen', the *Watan* ascribed separate electorates to the exclusionary policies of Hindus. On the one hand they preached the doctrine of 'India for the Indians' and on the other treated Muslims like *shudras*. Muslims did not want to 'trample on the rights of any community' and merely wanted to ensure that their representation in the councils was 'real and effective'.[72] By denouncing Muslims for protecting their own interests, Hindus were 'betraying a spirit of malice, bigotry and hostility'. It was not for fear of the authorities that Muslims shunned the Congress. Far ahead of Muslims in education, wealth and influence, Hindus could only be relied upon to reserve all concessions won by the Congress exclusively for themselves.[73]

Given the logic of colonial political engineering, Punjabi Hindus considered themselves as worthy of preferential treatment as Indian Muslims. Numerically a minority in the province, and an economically important one at that, they had every reason to want political safeguards against a powerful Muslim majority. The passage of the Punjab Land Alienation Act of 1900, aimed at redressing the problem of rural indebtedness by restricting the transfer of land to moneylenders, was seen as a direct attack on urban Hindu commercial interests. And this despite the fact that the Act of 1900 bolstered Hindu and Sikh agricultural interests quite as much as those of the Muslim landed gentry. Finding their class interests threatened by the colonial policy of strengthening rural collaborative networks, urban Punjabi Hindus played the communitarian card with a special vengeance. Continued support of the inclusionary nationalism of the Congress stymied their provincial political prospects while exclusionary tactics promised solid gains.

The *Hindustan* was convinced that Hindus were 'greatly injuring themselves by their desire to create an Indian nation'. By portraying Hindus as trouble makers, Muslims had extracted special favours from the colonial masters. Hindus in other provinces had 'not yet opened their lips on the matter'. But those in the Punjab felt that Hindus should now 'eschew politics altogether' and, in what appears to be the first reference to the notion in these terms,

[71]*Punjabi*, Lahore, 6 March 1909, ibid., pp. 207–8.
[72]*Watan*, Lahore, 5 March 1909, ibid., p. 213.
[73]The *Paisa Akhbar* cited in the *Report by the Criminal Investigation Department on the Native Papers Published in the Punjab for the Year 1909*, NCHCR, Islamabad.

'safeguard their *communal interests*'. Recognizing that giving up politics may not be practicable, Punjabi Hindus proposed establishing 'a society after the model of the All-India Muslim League' to secure their political rights. Such an organization would neither interfere with the Congress's programme, nor jeopardize its existence.[74]

Friction between politicized Hindus and Muslims in the Punjab flowed from competing exclusionary communitarianisms, not abstruse ideas of inclusionary nationalism. In a mirror image of Muslim 'traitors' to the Indian 'nation', the Punjab Hindu Sabha demanded safeguards against the provincial majority in the allocation of seats on the viceroy's council. Unhappy with its Bengali stain, many Punjabi Hindus preferred seceding from Congress and setting up their own Sabhas.[75] But this did not mean giving up the pretence of representing the 'nation'. Only the 'blind and the enemies of the nation', the *Jhang Sial* vociferated, thought the Punjab was 'dead' to the nationalist cause.[76] A rich man's farce, the Congress had been created 'not by Indians but by the kith and kin of the authorities' and could not be the 'emblem of [Indian] nationality'. It operated as a 'theatrical company' which performed for only three days and slept the rest of the year.[77]

Having practically buried the Congress, if not the 'nation', in the lush plains of the Punjab, Hindu-owned newspapers decided to make a virtue out of separate electorates. After all, these had been granted only to appease a 'few selfish and vain Musalmans residing in cities'. They did not affect the sentiments of the vast majority of 'the Prophet's followers' in the smaller towns and villages who were 'bound to Hindus more closely than to their own brethren in faith'.[78] This was challenged on the grounds that the Hindu institution of *chhut* effectively debarred them from interacting with Muslims socially. With few exceptions, there was no interdinning between members of the two communities. Orthodox Hindus hastened to wash themselves if the shadow of a Muslim fell on them, not the happiest basis to inculcate feelings of fellowship.[79] The practice of social apartheid by upper-caste Hindu castes was not confined to Muslims. But its existence provided sufficient proof that the sole purpose of Hindus was to 'sweep the believers in the *Kalima* off the face of the earth'.[80]

The real reason for the social distance between Hindus and Muslims, the *Hindustan* contended, was the uneven distribution of wealth between the two communities. In ignoring this material fact, the Congress had ended

[74]*Hindustan*, Lahore, 26 March 1909, *Selections*, L/R/5/190, IOL, pp. 289–90.
[75]See *Hindustan*, Lahore, 23 April 1909, ibid., p. 383.
[76]*Jhang Sial*, Jhang, 23 April 1909, ibid., p. 386.
[77]*Jhang Sial*, Jhang, 22 May and 10 July 1909, ibid., pp. 495, 704–5.
[78]*Akhbar-i-Am*, Lahore, 26 May 1909, ibid., p. 497.
[79]*Paisa Akhbar*, Lahore, 2 June 1909, ibid., p. 516.
[80]*Nazim-ul-Hind*, Lahore, 4 September 1909, ibid., pp. 922, 928.

up becoming 'an apple of discord between the followers of Islam and Hinduism'. Calling it the 'Indian National Congress' was a misnomer. Once the two communities had organized themselves into Hindu Sabhas and Muslim Leagues, they could 'lay the foundations of a common Indian nationality' and make the Congress 'truly representative of the entire Indian nation'.[81] Whether a strategic volte face or a meek acceptance of a colonial fait accompli, some Hindu newspapers asked their co-religionists not to fret over the preferential treatment accorded to Muslims. Since Muslims had formally separated from the Congress, it could no longer be called 'national' and was at best a 'sectional' party.[82] Instead of screaming for self-government 'like children playing at King and Queen', the time had come for Congress to give up its 'pseudo-national character' and 'abstract patriotism' and convert itself into a Hindu movement.[83] Depicting its crisis of identity in the Punjab, a cartoon appearing in an Arya Samaj organ, the *Prakash*, showed the Congress as a two-faced female figure, one the face of a goddess and the other of a witch. With educated Hindu opinion divided over supporting or spurning the organization, the 'poor Panjabis d[id] not know ... [if] the Congress [was] a goddess or a witch and whether they should worship it or cruelly expel it from their home'.[84]

If only humour could have lightened Punjabi hearts, it may yet have been possible to put aspects of the new thinking to more productive uses. Most educated Punjabis of all religious denominations agreed that the Congress's idea of the 'nation' was in need of reformulation. Rather than pursuing the mirage of a single unified 'nation' it was worth considering ways of accommodating culture as difference and, in this way, releasing the politics of identity from the clutches of notional majorities and minorities based on religion. As some Punjabi Hindus realized, being part of the 'national majority' paid uncertain dividends in the provincial political arena. By the same token, Punjabi Muslims ran the risk of seeing the advantages of their provincial majority being undermined by linking their concerns with an all-India-based minority community.

This partly explains why Punjabis had no problems packaging exclusionary interests in an inclusionary idiom. Not given to leading or following others, the Punjab did steal the march over the rest of India in one important respect. Long before the Lucknow Pact of 1916 between the Congress and the Muslim League, Punjabi Hindus of their own volition had accepted the principle of separate electorates. An astute move, it justified their demands for preferential treatment as a provincial minority entitled to the same treatment as meted out to Indian Muslims. Less perspicacious than the Hindus and not nearly as wily

[81]*Hindustan*, Lahore, 8 June 1909, ibid., p. 537.
[82]*Punjabi*, Lahore, 29 June 1909, ibid., p. 618.
[83]*Punjabi*, Lahore, 1 July 1909, ibid., pp. 619–20.
[84]*Prakash*, Lahore, 7 September 1909, ibid., p. 919.

as their co-religionists in northern India, Punjab's Muslim elite myopically insisted on the extension of separate electorates only to lose their case for representation in proportion to population. Weighted representation for provincial minorities was an expense majorities had to bear for keeping separate electorates in place. With the benefit of hindsight, the practical inversion of the concept of majority and minority in the politics of the Punjab may have been a conceivable prelude to correcting the misrepresentations implicit in the numbers game at the all-India level.

Unfortunately its newspaper barons made sure that the Punjab's recipe of letting differences generate their own momentum for agreement became mired in communitarianisms so parochial and bigoted as to defy emulation. Punjab may not have had a literati and politicized middle classes comparable to Bengal, but it possessed a gutter press which made up for the province's relative intellectual deprivation and lack of radical politics by heaping insults on members of other communities. The close nexus between the networks of collaborative politics and the Punjab press effectively foreclosed a softening of the lines of communitarian divisions. As the *Akhbar-i-Am* predicted, the abusive nature of the exchanges between Arya Samaj- and Muslim-run papers were 'calculated to bring about more disastrous results than the throwing of a thousand bombs'. The majority of the newspapers were 'in the hands of rude and unmannerly persons' who exploited the communitarian card while in fact 'discuss[ing] nothing but personalities'.[85]

Individual animosities cloaked in communitarian colours was not a feature of public debate in the Punjab alone. In exercising their freedom of speech, such as it existed, Punjabis gave expression to a peculiar form of politics which while supposedly informed by religious concerns was strictly restricted to the parameters of loyalty set by the British raj. In an editorial on the 'real ingredients of Indian nationality', Mahboob Alam of the *Paisa Akhbar*, gave a perceptive and eloquent exposition of the Punjabi Muslim position. India might yet attain the goal of a common nationality if all the communities in 'the interests of Indian nationality' avoided 'injuring the individual existence, religious and communal feelings and traditions' of one another. He cited Aurobindo Ghose's paper *Karma Yogin* which said that treating Muslims as an insignificant part of the Indian nation was a gross error. But there was a price for inclusion. Muslims had to concentrate on India rather than their extra-territorial affiliations. Mahboob Alam concurred heartily, but demonstrated the quandary of his co-religionists by adding the proviso that this could be the Muslim posture only if the aim fell short of overthrowing British rule. Moreover, those who wanted Muslims to form part of the Indian nation had to treat them with love and justice.[86] So even a rare acknowledgement by a prominent Punjabi Muslim

[85]*Akhbar-i-Am*, Lahore, 1 December 1909, ibid., p. 1234.
[86]*Paisa Akhbar*, Lahore, 16 December 1909, ibid., pp. 1256–7.

paper of the merits of an inclusionary Indian nationalism was couched in the idioms of collaboration with a thin veneer of supra-regional communitarian interests.

Punjab's remarkable specificities notwithstanding, a combination of individual, class and regional concerns was shaping the discourse on Indian Muslim interests. With the annulment of the partition of Bengal in 1911, the crisis in the Balkans and the Kanpur mosque incident of 1913 these concerns were conveniently swept under the communitarian carpet. The shifting context of politics in colonial India during the 1910s also saw major reformulations in the discourse of upper- and middle-class Muslims spilling across regions. The attractions of exclusionary communitarianism had now to vie with the disappointing results of unflagging loyalty to the British raj, compounding the tensions in Muslim responses to a territorially bound inclusionary nationalism.

RECONFIGURING THE INDIVIDUAL AND COMMUNITY IN ISLAM

The primacy of the community over the individual in normative Islam gave Muslim narratives of identity a theoretical anchor, if not the means to translate the ideal into effective practice. With the privileging of religious differences by the colonial state, votaries of a communitarian Muslim identity used the print medium to craft an elaborate repertoire of shared idioms in an otherwise varied and internally contested discourse. As the operations of the British legal system in the different regional settings made plain, few Muslims felt compelled to align the temporal and religious dimensions of their identity by conforming to the principles of the Islamic *sharia*. The gap between the theory and practice of Muslimness was further accentuated with the institutionalization of Muslims into a separate category in a limited field of electoral politics. Despite their constitutional status as an identifiable community of interests at the subcontinental level, the politics of Muslims continued to be informed by local and regional requirements rather than affiliation to a common religion.

An abstract legal and political category, Muslims could evolve a common sense of nationality only through a conscious reconfiguring of their individual self-identification with the religious community. Until the turn of the century the narratives on communitarian identity projected by the press and publications market emphasized culture as difference without elucidating a distinctively Indian Muslim conception of 'nation' and 'nationalism'. Even those subscribing to the ideal of a universal Muslim *ummah* for political reasons, and scorned by western observers as pan-Islamicists, were more anti-colonial than anti-national in orientation. While rejecting the Congress, western-educated Muslims did not consider their extra-territorial loyalties to be an insurmountable barrier to forging a common Indian nationality. It was location in this nationality, not the concept itself, which most exercised the minds of Muslims who took it upon themselves to either question or accept the Congress claim to represent all of India.

Greater clarity, if not a dramatic shift, in Muslim ideas on 'nation' and 'nationality' developed out of a critique of certain variants of western nationalism spearheaded by Muhammad Iqbal (1873–1938), a middle-class poet and philosopher of Punjabi origin It has been said of Iqbal that he was a man of his age, a man in advance of his age and a man in disagreement with his age.[87] Hailed as a messiah who 'stirred the dead with life',[88] Iqbal was a poet of extraordinary passion, exquisite lyricism and exceptional complexity. His inspirational power, according to one scholar, lay in giving philosophic expression to what many upper- and middle-class Muslims were beginning to feel but could not themselves articulate.[89] He did much more than that. While sharing the concerns of his predecessors and contemporaries, Iqbal's thought was imbued with a vitality that activated the hearts and minds of co-religionists who he believed had abandoned the life of constant tension and struggle for one of inglorious passivity under colonial subjugation.

A Muslim, an Indian and a Punjabi of Kashmiri ancestry, all at the same time, Iqbal's own individuality and sense of community was shaped in equal measure by these multiple affiliations. Despite the overwhelming emphasis on the Islamic *ummah* in Iqbal's mature philosophy and poetry, the entire corpus of his work is marked by a celebration of individual freedom as much as of the Muslim community. In a poem written in 1903 entitled 'Zuhd aur Rindi' or continence and debauchery, Iqbal in a critically self-analytical mood recounts an exchange with his neighbour, a *maulana*, who berated him for deviating from the path of Islam. How could he be a paragon of Muslimness if in his eyes a Hindu was not an infidel? Iqbal admitted his heterodoxies and departures from societal conventions. He confessed to a liking for music and the company of prostitutes while adhering to the Quran as well as tenets of the faith. Iqbal's Islam was unlike anyone else's. The many variations in his philosophical worldview were incomprehensible even to himself:

Iqbal does not know Iqbal
By God, this is no joke.[90]

In one of the most profound statements of the paradox of the individual Muslim, Iqbal asserted that:

---

[87] See Reynold A. Nicholson's introduction to his translation of Muhammad Iqbal's Persian poem *Asrar-i-Khudi (The Secrets of the Self)*, first published in 1920. My reference is to the 1975 edition reprinted in Lahore, p. xxxi.
[88] Ibid.
[89] Smith, *Modern Islam in India*, p. 98.
[90] *Iqbal bhi Iqbal say aagha nahin hai*
    Kuch ise main tamaskhar nahin, wallah nahin hai.

اقبال بھی اقبال سے آگاہ نہیں ہے!

کچھ اس میں تمسخر نہیں، واللہ نہیں ہے۔

Dr Allama Mohammad Iqbal
Courtesy: Information Division, Embassy of Pakistan, Washington, D.C.

The religious bigot considers me an infidel
And the infidel deems me to be a Muslim![91]

Tensions between the internal norms of Muslim society and an externally imparted identity propelled Iqbal to posit a notion of individual autonomy circumscribed by membership in an ideal community of Islam. This was not the existential community chained to the worldview of the religious guardians of Islam. Iqbal ridiculed the Islam of the *mullah* whose misrepresentations of the faith had for all too long served as a drag on an individual Muslim's capacity to attain full potential as a conscientious member of the community. It was the liberating thrust of Iqbal's poetic vision of the ideal relationship between the individual

(In *Bang-i-Dara*, or the sound of the caravan bell, first published in 1923. There are multiple editions of Iqbal's collective works. My references are from *Kulliyat-i-Iqbal*, Karachi: Al Muslim Publishers,1994, p. 53.)

[91] *Zuhd taang nazar ne mujhe kafir jana
Aur kafir samajhta hai Musalman hoon main.*

زہد تنگ نظر نے مجھے کافر جانا

اور کافر سمجھتا ہے مسلمان ہوں میں۔

(Cited in Hakim, *Fiqr-i-Iqbal*, p. 121.)

and the community which explains his inspirational appeal for those aspiring to find a Muslim response to the challenge of western territorial nationalism.

Significantly, Iqbal began his poetic career as a strong proponent of the idea of *wataniyat* or love of the territorial homeland. His *Tarana-i-Hindi* or the Indian anthem composed in 1904 is still one of the most popular patriotic narrations on the national ideal:

Better than the whole world is our Hindustan
We are its nightingales; it is our garden of delights
. . .
Religion does not teach mutual discord
We are all Hindi, Hindustan is our homeland.[92]

In 'Naya Shawala' or the New Temple written about the same time, Iqbal taunts the Brahmin for being cantankerous and pays homage to Hindu–Muslim unity:

Begging your pardon, Oh Brahman, I shall speak the truth
Old and decrepit are the idols in your temples
They have taught you to hate your own kind
As if God preaches war and extermination!
Fed up, I abandoned temple and mosque
Left the preacher's sermons and your endless yarns
You see God in these stone idols
I see God in every particle of my homeland
Come let's tear down the curtains of alienness
Let's rejoin the estranged and efface differences
Long desolate has been the heartland
Let us build a new temple in this land
Our shrine should be the highest in the world
Its spires touching the skies
Every morning let us sing sweet mantras
Make all worshippers drink notes of sweetness

[92]*Sare jahan sey achchha Hindustan hamara
Hum bulbulein hain is ki, ye gulsitan hamara*
. . .
*Mazhab nahin sikhata apas mein bair rakhna
Hindi hain hum, watan hai Hindustan hamara.*

سارے جہاں سے اچھا ہندوستاں ہمارا

ہم بلبلیں ہیں اس کی، یہ گلستاں ہمارا

.....

مذہب نہیں سکھاتا آپس میں بیر رکھنا

ہندی ہیں ہم وطن ہے ہندوستاں ہمارا۔

(Iqbal, *Bang-i-Dara* in *Kulliyat-i-Iqbal*, p. 71.)

Strength and peace is there in the songs of the devout
In love lies the liberation of the inhabitants of this land.[93]

In various poems written before departing for Europe in 1905, Iqbal wrote feelingly about India and his despondency over the rising incidence of strife between Hindus and Muslims. Based in Lahore, Iqbal could hardly have remained unaffected by the caustic tone of the Punjab press. While in Britain Iqbal began reformulating his own views on *wataniyat* which along with western materialism struck him as a recipe for European disaster. In 1907 he wrote:

[93]*Sach keh doon aye Brahman? Agar tu bura na mane
Tere sanam-kadon ke buth ho gaye purane
Apnon se bair rakhna tune buthoon se seekha
Jang-o-jadal sikhaya waiz ko bhi khuda ne
Tang ake meine akhir dair-o-haram ko chhora
Waiz ka waaz chhora, chhore tere fasana
Pathar ki murton mein samjha hai tu khuda hai
Khak-i-watan ka mujhko har zara devta hai
Aa ghayriyat ke parde aik bar phir utha dein
Bichhron ko phir mila dein, naqsh-i-dui mita dein
Sooni pari hui hai muddat say dil ki basti
Aa ik naya shawala ise des main bana dein
Duniya ke tirthon say uncha ho apna teerath
Daman-i-asman say iska kalas mila dein
Har subah uth kai gayen mantar wo meethe meethe
Saray pujarion ko mai preet ki pila dein
Shakti bhi shanti bhi bhagatoon ke geet mai hai
Dharti kai basiyon ki mukti preet mai hai.*

سچ کہ دوں اے برہمن اگر تو نہ لڈنہ مانے   ترے صنم کدوں کے بت ہو گئے پرانے
اپنوں سے بیر رکھنا تونے بتوں سے سیکھا   جنگ و جدل سکھایا واعظ کو بھی خدا نے
تنگ آکے میں نے آخر پیرو حرم کو چھوڑا   واعظ کا وعظ چھوڑا، چھوڑے ترے فسانے
پتھر کی مورتوں میں سمجھا ہے تو خدا ہے
خاک وطن کا مجھو ہر زرہ دیوتا ہے
آغیرت کے پردے اک بار پھر اٹھا دیں   بچھڑوں کو پھر ملا دیں، نقش دوئی مٹا دیں
سونی پڑی ہوئی ہے مدت سے دل کی بستی   آ، اک نیا شوالہ اس دیس میں بنا دیں
دنیا کے تیرتھوں سے اونچا ہو اپنا تیرتھ   دامان آسماں اس کا کلس ملا دیں
ہر صبح اٹھ کے گائیں منتر وہ میٹھے میٹھے   سارے پجاریوں کو مے پریت کی پلا دیں
شکتی بھی شانتی بھی بھگتوں کے گیت میں ہے
دھرتی کے باسیوں کی مکتی پریت میں ہے۔

(Ibid., p. 75. For a translation of this and other selected poems of Iqbal in English, see Victor Kiernan (trs), *Poems from Iqbal*, London: John Murray, 1955.)

Men of the West! The country of God is not a shop
What you take to be real is a counterfeit coin
Your civilization will commit suicide with its own dagger
A nest built on a fragile branch cannot last long.[94]

Upon returning to India in 1908 Iqbal wrote poems extolling the Islamic conception of universal brotherhood and disparaging western nationalism as the source of bigotry, hatred and conflict. In a poem called *Wataniyat* he declared that of all the new gods, the biggest was the nation; whoever donned the nation's apparel wore the shroud of religion.[95]

Interestingly enough, the other great poet-philosopher of India—Rabindranath Tagore—began voicing his disenchantment with territorial nationalism at about exactly the same moment in history. In 1905 at the onset of the *swadeshi* movement in Bengal, Tagore had celebrated the glories of the mother-nation. By 1908 his mood had turned sombre at the hubris of the new nationalism. What they saw of communitarian bigotry in Bengal and Punjab as well as European rivalries of a murderous sort turned both Tagore and Iqbal into powerful critics of the western model of the territorial nation–state. Tagore's evocation of universal humanity was not devoid of a religious sensibility. By the same token, Iqbal's thought was not religious in the doctrinal or dogmatic sense of the term. His self-conscious adoption of purely Islamic idioms was not an overture to an exclusivity which justified religious bigotry. It was symptomatic of a desire to distance himself from the epidemic of 'isms' which circumscribed his own sense of individuality. He critiqued western materialism as the handmaiden of exploitative capitalism, excessive rationalism as the source of spiritual decay and nationalism as the breeding ground of a novel kind of fanaticism. Looking to counter these aggressive trends, Iqbal turned to Islam as a political weapon with which to give full play to his poetic prowess. In the *Milli Tarana* or the

---

[94]*Diyar-i-maghrib ke rahne wallo, khuda ki basti dukan nahin hai
Khara jise tum samaj rahe ho wo ab zar-i-kam aiyar ho ga!
Tumhari tehzib apna khanjar say ap he khudkashi kare ghi
Jo shakh-i-nazak pai ashiyana banee gha, na paidar ho gha.*

دیارِ مغرب کے رہنے والو خدا کی بستی دکاں نہیں ہے

کھرا جسے تم سمجھ رہے ہو وہ اب زرِ کم عیار ہوگا!

تمہاری تہذیب اپنے خنجر سے آپ ہی خودکشی کرے گی

جو شاخِ نازک پہ آشیانہ بنے گا، ناپائیدار ہوگا۔

(Iqbal, Bang-i-Dara in Kulliyat-i-Iqbal, p. 116.)
[95] *Ine taza khudaoon main bara sab say watan hai
Jo pyerhan ise ka ha, wo mazhab ka kafan hai.*

ان تازہ خداؤں میں بڑا سب سے وطن ہے

جو پیرہن ہے اس کا ہے وہ مذہب کا کفن ہے۔

(Ibid., p. 133.)

anthem of the Muslim community, Iqbal invoked the ideal of Islamic universalism when he wrote:

China and Arabia are ours, India is ours
We are Muslim, the whole world is our homeland.[96]

Iqbal was not cutting loose from India so much as appropriating it along with the rest of the world. As he let slip in 'Balad-i-Islamia', if *qaumiyat* or nationalism in Islam were delimited by space, then its boundaries would transcend not just India but also Persia or Syria.[97]

This was an ingenious way of parrying the growing disillusionment among his politically conscious co-religionists at being excluded or marginalized in the narratives of Indian nationalism authored by their more insensitive Hindu compatriots. As Mohamed Ali (1878–1931), another rising star on the Muslim horizon, put it in 1908 to the moderate Congress leader G.K. Gokhale, religious differences had not caused nearly as much bloodshed as territorial nationality. Pure territorialism appealed to the Hindu mind. The 'same intensity and fervour in their territorial patriotism' could not reasonably be expected of Muslims who for the past thirteen centuries had been 'a nation without a country'. Mohamed Ali regretted the insufficient thought given by the Congress to the matter of forging a genuine union among 'denominational interests' which in his opinion were improperly referred to as races, religions or sects. For three days in the year the Congress talked of nothing but 'fraternity and love' among territorial patriots. This was a 'false and factitious unity' since 'many of the patriots [we]re as narrow and selfish and as caste-ridden during the remaining 362 days as any Mosalmans whom they denounce as a fanatic'.[98]

Iqbal blamed this on the Hindu and Muslim predilection to imitate the west. Echoing the thoughts of Jamaluddin al-Afghani, Iqbal reinvoked the idea of the *millat* in a language intended to exhilarate his languid and dejected

---

[96] *Cheen-o-Arab hamara, Hindustan hamara*
Muslim hain hum, watan hai sara jahan hamara.

چین و عرب ہمارا، ہندوستاں ہمارا

مسلم ہیں ہم وطن ہے سارا جہاں ہمارا۔

(Ibid., p. 132.)
[97] *Hai agar qaumiyat-i-Islam paband-i-muqam*
Hind hi bunyad hai iseki, na Faras hai na Sham.

ہے اگر قومیتِ اسلام پابندِ مقام

ہند ہی بنیاد ہے اس کی، نہ فارس ہے نہ شام۔

(Ibid., p.122.)
[98] Mohamed Ali to G.K. Gokhale, 8 February 1908 in Shan Muhammad (ed.). *Unpublished Letters of the Ali Brothers*, Delhi: Idarah-i-Adabiyat-i-Delhi, 1979, pp. 9, 11.

co-religionists. Unencumbered by territory, race, caste, colour and nationality, the *millat* was the ideal community with antecedents going as far back as the Prophet of Islam. Abandoning faith, Iqbal warned, would spell the end of the Muslim community and the *millat*. Yet his readings of their history left him few illusions about the capacity of Muslims to approximate the ideal community of Islam.

In two of his most forceful and controversial poems, the 'Shikwa' and the 'Jawab-i-Shikwa' composed in 1909 and 1913 respectively, Iqbal traversed much the same road as Hali had done in the *Musaddas* while attempting to shake Muslims out of their moral and political stupor. Iqbal's 'Shikwa' or complaint takes the normative Muslim belief in the absence of any intermediaries between the individual and God to the extreme. Throwing all caution to the winds he boldly questions Allah's sense of justice in rewarding the faithful so poorly for their services in spreading the message of Islam throughout the world:

Before our time, a strange sight was the world You had made:
Some worshipped stone idols, others bowed to trees and prayed.
. . .
Do you know of anyone, Lord, who then took Your Name? I ask.
It was the muscle in the Muslim's arm that did Your task.
. . .
Whose world-conquering swords spread the might over one and all?
Who stirred mankind with Allah-o-Akbar's clarion call?
Whose dread bent stone idols into fearful submission?
They fell on their faces confessing, 'God is One, the Only One!'
. . .
Even so you accuse us of lack of faith on our part.
If we lacked faith, you did little to win our heart,
. . .
Your blessings are showered on homes of unbelievers, strangers all
Only to the poor Muslim, Your wrath like lightning falls.
. . .
Our lot is the strangers' taunts, ill-repute and penury;
Must disgrace be our lot who gave their lives for You?
Now on strangers does the world bestow its favours and esteem,
All we have been left with is a phantom world and a dream.'[99]

[99]*Hum say pehla tha ajab tera jahan ka manzar*
Kahin masjood thay pathar, kahin mahbood shajr
. . .
Tujhko malum hai leta tha koi nam tera?
Quwat-i-bazoo-i-Muslim nai kiya kam tera!
. . .

Chasing his own mirages in the desert of Islamic dreams, Iqbal went on to urge Allah to spread the rare commodity of love in India so that temple worshippers might convert to Islam.[100]

The poem generated a commotion among educated Muslims and infuriated many Hindus, though no one denied its literary quality. Charged with bigotry and heresy, Iqbal wrote a laudatory poem on Ram and tried placating orthodox Muslim *ulema* incensed by his impudence with the 'Jawab-

---

Kise ki shamshir jahangez jahandar hui?
Kise ki takbir say teri duniya bedar hui?
Kise ki haibat say sanam sehmay huwai rehte thay?
Moun ka bal gir kai Allah-o-Ahad kehte thay

. . .

Phir bhi hum say ye ghila hai ka wafadar nahin
Hum wafadar nahin, tuh bhi toh dildar nahin!

. . .

Rahmateen hain teri aghyar kai kashanoon par
Barq girti hai toh becharay Muslmanoon par!

. . .

Tahna-i-aghyar hai, roswai hai, nadari hai
Kiya tera nam pai marna ka ewaz kuwari hai?
Bani aghyar ki ab chhahanawali duniya
Rae ghi apna leya aik kheyali duniya!

کہیں معبود شجر   کہیں سجود تھے پتھر،   ہم سے پہلے تھا عجب ترے جہاں کا منظر

. . .

قوتِ بازوے مسلم نے کیا کام ترا!!   تجھ کو معلوم ہے لیتا تھا کوئی نام ترا؟

. . .

کس کی تکبیر سے دنیا تری بیدار ہوئی؟   کس کی شمشیر جہانگیر جہاندار ہوئی؟
منہ کے بل گر کے جو اللہ احد کہتے تھے   کس کی ہیبت سے صنم سہمے ہوئے تھے؟

. . .

ہم وفادار نہیں، تو بھی تو دلدار نہیں   پھر بھی ہم سے یہ گلہ ہے کہ وفادار نہیں

. . .

برق گرتی ہے تو بے چارے مسلمانوں پر   رحمتیں ہیں تری اغیار کے کاشانوں پر

. . .

طعنۂ اغیار ہے، رسوائی ہے، ناداری ہے؟
کیا ترے نام پہ مرنے کا عوض خواری ہے؟
بنی اغیار کی اب چاہنے والی دنیا   رہ گئی اپنے لئے ایک خیالی دنیا!

(Muhammad Iqbal, *Shikwa and Jawab-i-Shikwa (Complaint and Answer: Iqbal's Dialogue with Allah)*, translated by Khushwant Singh (third edition), Delhi: Oxford University Press, 1994, pp. 31, 37, 40–1, 44–5.)

[100]Ibid., p. 54.

i-Shikwa.' The substance of God's response was that Muslims themselves were
to blame for their debased condition. They had abandoned the teachings of
their Prophet and reverted to idolatrous practices. Despite a common set of
religious symbols, Muslims were hopelessly divided. From being the faithful
of yesteryear they had become the faithless of today. Instead of following in
the footsteps of their glorious forefathers, Muslims had adopted Christian
lifestyles and the culture of the Hindus:

You are Saiyyads as well as Mirzas, and you are Afghans—
You are all these, but tell us are you also Mussalmans?[101]

A people given to idling away their lives had no right to expect God to shower
tender mercies upon them. Islam was a religion of action, not empty words.
Only through struggle and individual initiative could Muslims as a community
regain their lost status in God's eyes and, therefore, in the world. The poem
concludes on an optimistic note:

The cry, 'Allah-o-Akbar', destroys all except God; it is a fire.
If you are true Muslims, your destiny is to grasp what you aspire.
If you break not faith with Muhammad, we shall always be with you.
What is this miserable world? To write the world's history, pen
and tablet we offer you.[102]

In 1910 while addressing an audience at Aligarh University, Iqbal offered an
early glimpse of his more mature political philosophy. The Muslim community
was unlike any other on account of its 'peculiar conception of nationality'
which had nothing to do with the unity of language or country or of economic
interest. Derived from 'a purely abstract idea' it was 'objectified in a potentially

[101]Youn toh Sayyid bhi ho, Mirza bhi ho, Afghan bhi ho
Tum sabhi kuch ho, batao toh Musalman bhi ho?

یوں تو سید بھی ہو، مرزا بھی ہو، افغان بھی ہو

تم سبھی کچھ ہو، بتاؤ تو مسلمان بھی ہو۔

(Iqbal, 'Jawab-i-Shikwa', ibid., p. 77.)
[102]Ma sawa Allah kai leya aag hai takbir teri
Tuh Musalman ho toh taqdir hai tadbir teri
Ki Muhammad say wafa tuh nai toh hum tera hain
Ye jahan chez hai kiya loh-o-qalam tera hain.

ماسوا اللہ کے لئے آگ ہے تکبیر تیری

تو مسلمان ہو تو تقدیر ہے تدبیر تری

کی محمدؐ سے وفا تو نئی تو ہم تیرے ہیں

یہ جہاں چیز ہے کیا لوح و قلم تیرے ہیں۔

(Ibid. p. 96.)

expansive group of concrete personalities' who identified with the *sunnah* or historical tradition associated with the Prophet of Islam. The subjective feeling of belonging to the community of the Prophet Muhammad gave Muslims a sense of nationality or *asabiyyat*. While creating a strong feeling for their own nationality, *asabiyyat* did 'not necessarily imply any feeling of hatred against other nationalities'. The Muslim community was structured by the religious ideal, though not by its 'theological centralisation' which would 'unnecessarily limit the liberty of the individual'.[103]

Iqbal juxtaposed the religious ideal against excessive rationalism which as purely intellectual analysis threatened to weaken communitarian solidarity. This was not a call for irrationalism, he explained, so much as an insistence on the need for a lived social synthesis based on shared spiritual and cultural values. Pitching his arguments at the level of ideals more than history, Iqbal believed Islam gave Muslims the world over a cultural uniformity. But Muslims in India might after all have something in common with other inhabitants of the country since Islamic civilization was a 'product of the cross-fertilisation of the Semitic and Aryan ideas'. Although specifically referring to the Persian contribution, he declared that Muslim culture had 'inherit[ed] the softness and refinement of its Aryan mother and the sterling character of its Semitic father'.

It was only while discussing the relationship between the individual and the community that Iqbal made clear his recognition of the difference between the ideal and the real. To become 'a living member of the Muslim community' an individual had to not just profess an 'unconditional belief in the religious principle' but 'thoroughly assimilate the culture of Islam'. This alone would create the uniformity of outlook and values which 'sharply defines our community and transforms it into a corporate individual ... [with] a definite purpose and ideal of its own'. Three types of individuals had moulded the nature of the Muslim community. The valiant, represented by Taimur, the liberal and generous of Jahangir's type and the ideal sort characterized by self-control such as Aurangzeb who in Iqbal's opinion was 'the starting point in the growth of Muslim Nationality in India'. But in describing the optimum conditions to 'secure ... continuous life to community', Iqbal was prepared to be flexible. Akbar Allahabadi also qualified as the ideal type of Muslim individual. What Muslim society needed were individuals who while holding fast to their own and resisting everything inimical to Islamic values selectively assimilated the good features of other communities.[104]

Sadly, Muslim youth had no knowledge of their own culture or the collective history of the community. These products of a purely secular education had in the process of imbibing western thought become 'thoroughly

[103]Iqbal in Abbas(ed.), *The Muslim Community*, pp. 16–17.
[104]Ibid., pp. 22–3.

demuslimised' and if not 'spiritually dead' were at best only half Muslims. Devotion to an alien culture was far worse than conversion to a new religion. Muslims owed a debt to the west intellectually. But they also possessed a 'unique culture' which a modern system of education could ignore only at the risk of 'denationalising' the Muslims. This would be a calamity for a community proud of its distinctive culture, not least because individuals versed in Muslim history and literature were needed for the 'ethical training of the masses' which was almost entirely in the hands of half educated and retrograde *maulvis* and public preachers. No such concern attended Iqbal's comments on women's education. He was candid enough to admit that he did not accept the principle of equality between men and women on biological grounds and also for the 'health and prosperity of the human family'. The emancipation of western women would cause 'incalculable harm'. Women needed education only to perform their 'duties of motherhood' which was their 'principal function'. Subjects which 'de-womanised' and 'de-muslimised' women should be weeded out of their educational curriculum.[105]

That Iqbal at times did not know Iqbal could pose serious problems. As his friendship with Attiya Faizi suggests, he not only enjoyed but solicited the company of educated and emancipated women. He once wrote to her complaining of his misery at having to cope with a woman he had never wanted to marry. 'They force my wife upon me,' Iqbal hollered. He had 'a right to happiness' as a human being; 'if society or nature deny that to me, I defy both'. Iqbal contemplated leaving India for good or committing slow suicide by drowning himself in liquor. There was no happiness to be found in 'dead barren leaves of books', but he had 'sufficient fire' in his 'soul to burn them up and social conventions as well'.[106] Taken to task by Attiya Faizi for his views on women, Iqbal denied that he was indifferent or a hypocrite. He was a mystery even to himself, but a secret that stood revealed before the world.[107]

A multi-sided mystery in a state of perpetual flux, Iqbal could not unveil himself in a flash. Intent upon forming himself as well as the community of his self-identification, it could hardly have been otherwise. Life as he put it was a forward assimilative movement, clearing away all obstacles by absorbing them. The essence of life was the continuous creation of desires and ideals which gave individuals the freedom to choose and by implication the power to reject.[108] For the Muslim this was conveyed by their creedal motto—*la ilah*

[105]Ibid., pp. 28–30.

[106]Iqbal to Attiya Faizi, 9 April 1909 in Bashir Ahmad Dar (ed.), *Letters of Iqbal*, Lahore: Iqbal Academy, 1978, p. 21.

[107]Iqbal to Attiya Faizi, 30 March 1910, ibid., p. 29.

[108]Reynold A. Nicholson 'The Secrets of the Self: A Moslem Poet's Interpretation of Vitalism' in Riffat Hassan (ed.), *The Sword and the Sceptre*, Lahore: Iqbal Academy, 1977, p. 265.

illa Allah—there is no God but God. Without the power of negation implied by the la there could be no real significance in the affirmative illa. It is the dialectical tension between the negative and the positive which is the stuff of human history.[109] Iqbal regretted that Muslims had lost the capacity to deploy the power of the negative to their positive self-realization. Outwardly upholding the unity of God without inwardly engaging in unified action was to misunderstand the crux of the Islamic creed.

Putting a premium on individual self-realization as a means to reaching God, Iqbal departed from the more esoteric aspects of the Islamic mystical tradition by stressing the importance of associating with others in collective social action. It was not enough to seek union with God through the annihilation of the self, but to turn the negation into positive affirmation so as to absorb the attributes of the Divine into individual personality. Only an individual who was closest to God, the insan-ul-kamal or the perfect human being, could through vigorous and fearless activity bestir a phlegmatic and disoriented community.[110] Nietzsche's influence on Iqbal's thought is undeniable. Yet unlike the German philosopher's iconoclastic vision of the superman with no constraints on his will to power, Iqbal's perfect individual finds inner strength through love of God and mankind while submitting solely to the authority of the Creator.[111] This was the basis for Iqbal's philosophic conception of a dynamic relationship between the individual and the ideal community of Islam through a constant process of negation and affirmation.

It found its most explicit statement in 1915 with the publication of his highly acclaimed Persian poem Asrar-i-Khudi or the secrets of the self. The Persian word khudi has negative connotations, implying selfishness or egotism. In Iqbal's poetry and philosophy the term has an altogether different meaning. He used khudi as self, personality and ego in a purely positive sense to put forward the idea of the dynamic individual.[112] Realizing that his message may not be immediately comprehended, Iqbal in the opening verses of the poem demonstrated the self-possessed arrogance which he extolled in his philosophy:

I am the voice of the poet of To-morrow
My own age does not understand my deep meanings.[113]

[109]Schimmel, Gabriel's Wing, pp. 89–91.

[110]See Hassan (ed.), The Sword and the Sceptre, especially articles by Hira Lall Chopra and Nicholson.

[111]Nicholson, 'The Secrets of the Self: A Moslem Poet's Interpretation of Vitalism', ibid., pp. 274–6. Also see Schimmel, Gabriel's Wing, pp.118–20, who argues that Iqbal was developing his notion of the perfect man long before he became familiar with Nietzsche's superman.

[112]Schimmel, Gabriel's Wing, p. 42.

[113]Asrar-i-Khudi, translated by Nicholson, p. 4.

He had become a firefly to illuminate secrets no one else dared tell:

Subject, object, means and causes—
All these are forms which it assumes for the purpose of action
The Self rises, kindles, falls, glows, breathes,
Burns, shines, walks and flies

. . .

'Tis the nature of the Self to manifest itself:
In every atom slumbers the might of the Self
Power that is expressed and inert
Chains the faculties which lead to action
Inasmuch as the life of the universe
comes from the power of the Self
Life is in proportion to this power

. . .

When Life gathers strength from the Self
The river of Life expands into an ocean.[114]

The core of Iqbal's message to the Muslims of India was individual self-affirmation, *khudi*, leading to purposeful collective action. This was a natural progression for a people whose religion demanded submission to none other than Allah and identification with the *millat* or the supra-territorial community of the faithful bound by the teachings of the Prophet Muhammad. Released of all material impediments, the individual and the community of Islam could through a process of perpetual spiritual renewal attain the heights ordained for them. Yet to make a difference Iqbal's invigorating thoughts had to first clear layers of cobwebs rooted in Muslim consciousness. As he knew all too well, these could prove far more obstinate than the barriers his philosophy had systematically tried breaking down. Seized by a gnawing sense that none of this might come to pass, Iqbal concluded the *Asrar-i-Khudi* imploring Allah:

Once more demand from us the sacrifice of name and fame
Strengthen our weak love

. . .

Though of the same family, we are strange to one another
Bind again these scattered leaves

. . .

In the midst of a company I am alone
I beg of Thy grace a sympathising friend.[115]

For a man who with his battery of winged phrases proclaimed the urgency of earthly action, Iqbal discovered more friends in words than in deeds. But

[114]Ibid., pp. 18–22.
[115]Ibid., pp. 141–8.

when words and deeds fail to match, differences implode quietly behind the fenced walls of agreement. As it was, intellectual disagreements meshed with personal jealousies to put a question mark on the validity of Iqbal's poetic vision. His critique of that strand in Islamic mysticism which advocated the annihilation of individual personality or *fana* as the final step in the quest for union with God kicked up a storm of protest among those who considered themselves the doyens of Sufi thought.[116] The more insecure among literary circles in Delhi and Lucknow resented this gifted Punjabi poet, seeing his emergence as an invasion of their space by someone who was not an *ahl-i-zaban* or a true speaker of Urdu. Despite many detractors, Iqbal's poetry even at this early stage of his creativity left an indelible mark on the consciousness of substantial segments of educated Muslims.

A poet whose primary aim was to egg on his co-religionists into concerted worldly action in defence of their religion did not find it easy to translate his own ideals into political practice. Instead of entering the political fray himself, Iqbal—who had to practice law to earn a living—preferred the quiet life of contemplation until later when he made a cautious entry into public life. This partly explains why his ideal conception of the relationship between the individual and the community of Islam made few concessions to political realities such as the identification of many Muslims to their spatial location within certain regions and, more broadly, to India. So while his poetic vision enthused many of his co-religionists, turning it into a dynamic principle of Indian Muslim identity meant exposing it to multiple interpretations and appropriations.

Iqbal wrote his most powerful poetry on Islamic universalism at a time when the attention of his co-religionists was rivetted on the reversal of the partition of Bengal, Italy's invasion of Tripoli, the war in the Balkans and the loss of many Muslim lives in a dispute over a mosque in Kanpur. His anguish at the impotence of Muslims symbolized by the European pincer movement against Ottoman Turkey was shared among others by Shibli Numani, Mohamed Ali, the editor of the *Comrade* and the *Hamdard*, Abul Kalam Azad (1888–1958) whose *Al-Hilal* appeared in 1912 from Calcutta and Maulana Zafar Ali Khan (1873–1956) who gave a new lease of life to Punjabi Muslim journalism through his organ the *Zamindar*. But there were also significant differences in the way each proposed to handle the practical issue of organizing and directing the Muslim community's response to the changing context of politics in India and the Islamic world at large.

[116]Iqbal's criticism of the great Persian mystical poet Hafiz in the *Asrar-i-Khudi* was a scarcely veiled attack on the inheritors of the Sufi tradition in India. It galvanized *pirs* and *sajjada nashins* as well as scholars like Khwajah Hasan Nizami of Delhi, forcing Iqbal to drop from subsequent editions of the *Asrar-i-Khudi* the couplets in which he had questioned Hafiz's conception of *tasawuff*, or the mystical path to union with God, the ultimate Beloved.

Shibli was not nearly as gifted a poet as Iqbal, but had a better grounding in Islamic history. This led him to admit the discrepancy that had always existed between the ideals of Islam and the historical practices of Muslims. While he too looked beyond the frontiers of India for ideational and spiritual nourishment, Shibli set his sights squarely on the predicament of Muslims within the spatial context of India. For him religion did not have to serve as the code for Muslim participation in politics. In a series of polemical poems he berated the All-India Muslim League for its servile posture towards the British raj. This contradicted the very spirit of self-government instituted by the colonial rulers. However nominally and inadequately, the subjects had every right to express their opinions and criticize the rulers. Politics by definition meant balancing the 'mutual demands of the government and the subjects'. It was decidedly not about the internal quarrels of the ruled.[117] Rejecting the notion of a separatist and loyalist politics, Shibli thought forging a joint front with Hindus was a better bet for Indian Muslims than entertaining hopes of uniting the *ummah*.

He blamed Sayyid Ahmad Khan for stunting the growth of political consciousness among Muslims and turning them into a 'nation' of cowards. By contrast, Hindus were making strides in the political field and extracting concessions from the colonial government. Shibli refused to dignify the League's mendicancy as politics. It was an upper-class *tamasha*, a circus sanctioned by the government and paid for by wealthy benefactors like the Aga Khan and a pack of grovelling Muslim landlords of northern India.[118] While accepting the Muslim League as an established fact, Shibli wanted to see it thoroughly reformed and taking bolder political stands. It could do so only by shedding its 'minority complex' and allying with the Congress to strike for substantive self-government.

Mohamed Ali was of a different opinion. One of the founding fathers of the All-India Muslim League, he chastised the 'nationalists' of the Congress school for refusing to accept that the only sort of patriotism 'in vogue in this country [wa]s exclusively Hindu or Muslim'. The educated Hindu 'communal patriot' had no qualms using the symbols of Hinduism for political mobilization and the construction of Indian 'nationality', ignoring the presence of seventy million Muslims in the country. Using *swaraj* as the 'war cry', the Hindu 'communal patriot' simply 'refuse[d] to give quarter to the Muslims unless the latter quietly shuffle[d] off [their] individuality and bec[a]me ... completely Hinduised'. For all the talk of nationhood and unity, the 'organs of Hindu "nationalism"' regarded Muslims as 'a troublesome irrelevance' as if there were 'no vital differences of feeling, temper, ideals and standpoints'. Muslims

[117]Murad, *Intellectual Modernism of Shibli Nu'mani*, p. 106.

[118]*Kulliyat-i-Shibli*, compiled by Sayyid Sulayman Nadwi, Karachi, 1985, pp. 106–16, 119–21.

were deemed to be a trifle 'too clannish', rapped on the knuckles for being lost in 'a world of unsubstantial shadows' and reprimanded for being only 'dimly aware' of 'such great secular causes as self-government and nationality'. Yet the goal of the Hindu patriot, Mohamed Ali charged, was nothing short of building a 'modern shrine' in India exclusively for his own purposes.[119]

Implicit in Mohamed Ali's flaming rhetoric was a view of Indian nationality that genuinely sought to accommodate cultural differences. An ardent admirer of Iqbal's poetry, and a believer of Islamic universalism by political choice, Mohamed Ali was not any less attached to things Indian. His was a challenge to a 'nationalist' agenda which surreptitiously, if selectively, absorbed the Hindu ethos while squeezing out the Muslim dimensions. Urdu was a case in point. In their desire for a common language for India, the Hindus were demanding the replacement of Urdu with the Nagari script. This was tantamount to depriving future generations of Muslims of the capacity to access their own religious and literary heritage and insulating India from other Asian countries. To turn the issue of language into a litmus test of patriotism was 'sheer imbecility'. 'Islam was neither insular nor peninsular', Mohamed Ali declared. If it was true that 'Muslims lacked something in their love for the land they lived in' then it was truer still that they had been 'charged with a little too much of it for the lands of others'. In adopting Urdu as their vernacular, a language which was not Islam's gift to India but vice versa, Muslims had given sufficient evidence of affection for the cultural mores of their adopted homeland. They would not renounce the language or the script to please the forces of 'narrow and exclusive "Nationalism" which ... [was] growing more and more militant every day'.[120]

Countering the charge of Muslim exclusivity by citing instances of Hindu exclusivity found a powerful rallying point in the ongoing debate over the future of Urdu. Even those given to less impassioned statements about their distinctively Muslim cultural identity regretted the efforts to stigmatize Urdu as an alien implant on Indian soil. The issue of Urdu demonstrated just how well culture as difference could serve the sense of Muslimness and Indianness at one and the same time. Abdul Halim Sharar (1860–1920), who began his career as a journalist and went on to establish himself as one of the foremost Urdu literary figures of the early twentieth century, defended the language of his identity while claiming a share of Indian nationality. On 30 September 1916 speaking at an Urdu conference in Lucknow, Sharar likened the development of the language to the life history of the *qaum's* greatness whose

[119]Mohamed Ali, 'The Communal Patriot', February 1912, in Afzal Iqbal (ed.), *Select Writings and Speeches of Maulana Mohamed Ali*, first edition 1944 (revised edition), Lahore: Islamic Book Foundation, 1987, pp. 75–7.

[120]Mohamed Ali, 'The Lingua Franca of India', first published in *The Comrade*, July 1912, ibid., pp. 31–50.

'branches came out, blossomed, separated, met, moved, grew, fought, collided and then again became one'. Deploying the Aryan race theory, he maintained that the coming of the Muslims to India had reunited the two branches of the Arya *qaum*. He objected to the enterprise which, in claiming that the people of Hindustan were the lost brethren of Europeans, presented the Muslims as an alien *qaum*. More influenced by the Persians than the Arabs, Indian Muslims did not trace their genealogy to the Semites and were part and parcel of the Arya *qaum*. Even the Arabs who made India their home adopted local languages and blended into its social ambience. Urdu was a symbol of centuries of interaction between Hindus and Muslims. The role of Persian and Arabic in the development of Urdu was that of the father while the linguistic antecedents of Hindi had mothered the child. To overlook this fact was to forget the era when friendship and close relations had existed between the two religious faiths. Sharar conceded that in retaliating against the promotion of Hindi, Muslims had begun claiming Urdu as their language. But Hindus had better claims to Urdu than Muslims since more of them had written in the language. Instead of destroying a common asset on account of petty jealousies, Hindus and Muslims should together rear their magnificent progeny.[121]

A supporter of the Congress, Sharar's pleadings underline the continuing attempts by some Muslims to situate themselves within mainstream Indian nationalism. One solitary individual who deserves a special mention in this respect is Mohammad Ali Jinnah (1876–1948), a Bombay-based lawyer with an uncommon aversion to all forms of Islamic orthodoxy. Firmly on the side of moderate nationalists in the Congress such as Gokhale, Jinnah was the only Muslim voice of repute that had opposed the granting of separate electorates. More cosmopolitan than communitarian in outlook, Jinnah's career exemplifies the constant reconfiguring of the balance between the individual and the community in Islam. Starting off on the outer margins of the Muslim community, Jinnah negotiated his space in all-India politics by becoming the 'ambassador of Hindu–Muslim unity' and then reconstituting himself as the foremost individual protagonist of the Muslim League's 'two-nation' theory. The trajectory of Jinnah the confirmed individualist to Jinnah the obdurate communitarian will unfold in subsequent chapters. It is a telling story of the proposition that the individual Muslim in praxis made or unmade his community of association without explicitly denying the ideal of the Islamic *ummah*, whether in its restrictive or expansive conceptions.

Another extraordinary tale of the infinite permutations taken by the individual in relation to the Muslim community is provided by the life and

---

[121]Abdul Halim Sharar, *Urdu se Hinduon ke Ta'alluq* (the Relationship of Hindus with Urdu), lecture given at the Urdu Conference at Lucknow, 30 September 1916, VT 3890g, IOL. The Aryan race theory, more mythical than historical, was a significant component of the emerging discourse on Indian nationalism within which Sharar was seeking to locate India's Muslims.

times of Abul Kalam Azad (1888–1958). Regarded by many as the most important of Muslim 'traditionalists', the shifting sands of Azad's religious and political beliefs convey the paradoxes of Muslim identity in the subcontinental context. Also an individualist like Jinnah, a comparison of the two men's roles in the history of the Muslims of India exposes the curiosity that passes as 'communalism' in South Asian historiography. Jinnah, the 'secularist' and 'nationalist' slips down a few notches when he begins opposing the mixing of religion and politics by the Gandhian Congress in the early 1920s and falls from grace altogether when he steals the mantle of the Muslim community in the mid-1930s. By contrast, Azad is showered with accolades in the tomes of Indian nationalist historiography for his steadfast opposition to the Muslim League's inexorable drift towards 'separatism' and 'communalism'.

Unlike Jinnah who never claimed much knowledge of Muslim history or philosophy, Islam was the vital component of Azad's identity and the main source of his intellectual and political orientation. In 1904 while still under the influence of Sayyid Ahmad Khan's reformist ideas, Azad once made a fleeting reference to the Congress as a Hindu body.[122] A precocious young man of exceptional learning, Azad's early ideas were laced with the very Muslim exclusivity which was to later disqualify many of his less Islamically inclined co-religionists from the nationalist mainstream. In a poem published in the *Al-Hilal* after the Kanpur massacre, Azad echoed Iqbal in a lesser vein while expressing alarm at European machinations against Muslims:

With whose blood is Tripoli flooded? Of the Muslims
Who, slain, lie quivering on the plains of Persia? The Muslims
Whose blood flows in the Balkan Peninsula? The Muslims
The land of Hindustan is athirst. It demands blood
Whose? The Muslims
At last it rained blood in Kanpur and the dust of Hindustan
is saturated with it
Oh you Muslims: Where will you now reside?[123]

Article after article in *Al-Hilal* finds Azad preaching the ideal of Islamic brotherhood, declaring Muslim participation in politics a religious duty and exhorting his co-religionists to organize themselves as a separate community under their own *imam* or *amir*. 'There will be nothing left of us if we separate politics from religion,' Azad wrote in his paper. More illuminating still was the categorical assertion that Muslims 'need not follow the Hindus to determine their political policy'; in fact they 'need not join any party' at all since they are

[122]See Ian Henderson Douglas, *Abul Kalam Azad: An Intellectual and Religious Biography*, edited by Gail Minault and Christian W.Troll, Delhi: Oxford University Press, 1988, p. 60.
[123]From N.B. Roy, 'The Background of Iqbal's Poetry', in Hassan (ed.), *The Sword and the Sceptre*, p. 103.

the 'ones to make the world join their party and follow their path'.[124] Almost replicating Iqbal's despondency in the (Shikwa) and (Jawab-i-Shikwa), he was crestfallen to see that Muslims were 'not united and organized as a community'; they had 'no *quaid* (leader)', a mere 'rabble scattered among the population of India' they were living an 'un-Islamic and irreligious life'.[125] An explicit exclusivism matched by an implicit sense of superiority was tempered only by Azad's consistently anti-colonial posture and support for the Congress.

With the exception of Azad and Iqbal, all the individuals mentioned so far hailed from provinces where Muslims were in a minority, UP in particular. Like Iqbal, Maulana Zafar Ali Khan belonged to the Punjab, a province known more for its parochialism and supine posture towards colonialism than for universalism and intrepid support for the nationalist cause. If Iqbal's Islamic universalism and implicit humanitarianism remained suspect on account of an exclusive concern with the ideal community of Islam and even led some of his more truculent critics to fault him for parochial excesses, Zafar Ali Khan's career belies most stereotypes of Punjabi Muslims. Brought up in a small rural hamlet of the Punjab, Karmabad near Wazirabad, Zafar Ali Khan was Iqbal's close associate and a peer of the dauntless Mohamed Ali with whom he had shared an education at Aligarh. Intellectually, Zafar Ali Khan was at one with Iqbal and politically in the same league as Mohamed Ali and Azad.

Under his courageous editorship the *Zamindar* became the foremost Urdu daily in the Punjab, attaining a circulation of well over 20,000 during the Balkan wars. Though not as prized a poet as Muhammad Iqbal, Zafar Ali Khan more than made up for it by putting the ideal of the self-affirming and dynamic individual into practice. His exhilarating public oratory and lively literary style were immensely popular among Punjabi Muslim youth. In contrast to Iqbal, Zafar Ali Khan managed to make himself understood to the unlettered in the Punjab and the Frontier Province some of whom paid two pice to buy a copy of the *Zamindar* and one anna to have it read out to them.[126] Small wonder that the *Zamindar* came to be regarded as the 'national organ of the Muslims' and its editor as a model for emulation.[127]

A proponent of Hindu–Muslim unity and a Congress supporter, Zafar Ali Khan's primary goal was nevertheless worldwide Muslim unity. His vitriolic writings against the British raj and its intrigues against the Ottoman empire

[124]Cited in Ali Ashraf, 'Appraisal of Azad's Religio-Political Trajectory', in Mushirul Hasan (ed.), *Islam and Indian Nationalism: Reflections on Abul Kalam Azad*, New Delhi: Manohar, 1992, p. 106.

[125]Ibid., p. 108.

[126]Ghulam Hussain Zulfiqar, *Maulana Zafar Ali Khan: Hiyat, Khidmat wa Asar*, Lahore: Sang-e-Meel Publications, 1994, p. 97.

[127]*Secret Punjab Police Abstract of Intelligence*, Lahore, 21 February 1944, vol.xxxvi. no.7, NCHCR, Islamabad, p. 116 (henceforth *SPPAI*, followed by date, volume and page number(s)).

kept him and his paper at sword's point with the Punjab administration. The *Zamindar's* anti-colonial stance resulted in the proscription of the paper on several occasions and the even more frequent confinement, if not actual incarceration, of its editor. There were public campaigns to raise money for the revival of the newspaper. These were not restricted to the Punjab but included a loyal readership in northern India. Along with Mohamed Ali and Azad, Zafar Ali Khan used the journalistic medium to condemn Britain's lack of support for Ottoman Turkey in the Balkan war. Together these three individuals gave pro-Turkish fervour a fresh boost among Indian Muslims. Zafar Ali Khan was in the vanguard of a campaign to collect donations for the Turkish cause. In June 1913 he personally delivered the amount to Sultan Muhammad in Constantinople along with a selection of Iqbal's poetry and a solemn plea that in the interests of Indian Muslims, who were his spiritual if not temporal subjects, Turkey should avoid getting trapped in a war with Britain.[128]

These thumbnail sketches of the ideological positions of key Muslim personalities who went on to play a leading part in Indian politics in the wake of the First World War are intended here only to underscore the many possible variations in the nexus between the individual and the community. In enunciating a dynamic conception of the individual Muslim's relationship to the community of Islam, Iqbal had drawn upon normative ideals rather than existential realities. Infusing an abstract legal and political category of Muslims with a self-consciously Islamic spirit aimed at internal regeneration was something of an advance on the communitarian narratives appearing in the press. Yet the all-important balance between the individual and the community of Islam had ultimately to be fashioned in response to shifting contexts shaped by an interplay of factors other than of a purely religious nature. If the religious demarcator was sufficient to establish a Muslim's sense of distinction from non-Muslims, divergences along lines of class, region, language and ideology militated against Muslims experiencing their communitarian identity in singular or monolithic terms. A religiously informed cultural identity might impel a Muslim to proclaim affiliation with the community of Islam as the single most important point of personal reference. Muslim self-identification, however, could be restricted to India or expanded to include the Islamic world, depending on individual need or preference. Together with the other dimensions in the life of an individual, the all-India and universal Islamic conceptions of the community left Muslims grappling uncertainly with alternative approaches to the idea of a common nationality.

The outbreak of the First World War put Muslim ideas of nationality to a serious test. With Britain and Turkey in opposite camps, Islamic sentiments had to be weighed against the imperatives of subjecthood in colonial India.

[128]Zulfiqar, *Maulana Zafar Ali Khan*, pp. 108–9.

Forced to face the implications of their extra-territorial affiliations in the light of changed circumstances, Muslims reacted according to their location within the colonial system. Those with a stake in the collaborative networks of the raj tried justifying their loyalist stance by pointing out that Britain was not directly waging war against Ottoman Turkey. Others like Mohammad Ali Jinnah took the opportunity to plump for Hindu–Muslim unity by engineering a working alliance between the Congress and the Muslim League known as the Lucknow Pact. Congress's acceptance of separate electorates opened up the possibility of Muslims voluntarily joining mainstream Indian nationalism. In the aftermath of war, the prospects of Muslim anti-colonialism leading to a united nationalist front seemed more promising than ever. Turkey's defeat and doubts about the future of the Ottoman Khilafat, the ultimate symbol of Islamic temporal and spiritual sovereignty, found the Muslims of India standing agitatedly at the threshold of new definitions of identity. By far the most dynamic moment in the history of colonial India, it saw the dialectic of inclusionary nationalism and exclusionary communitarianisms moulding individual Muslims in novel ways, prompting some of them to recast ideas of the community and the 'nation' in both their restrictive and expansive dimensions.

Chapter 5

Identity and Sovereignty in Muslim Consciousness:
The Khilafat Crescent and the Indian *Charkha*

Ever since the formal loss of sovereignty in 1857, the emerging discourse on Muslim interests had self-consciously projected the primacy of religious affiliation to emphasize a distinctive cultural identity. Yet the ubiquitous bond of Islam remained open to conflicting interpretations. Quite apart from the distance separating the upper crust from the lower echelons of the Muslim social order, there were ideological differences on how religion was to serve the needs of an internally heterogeneous community. In the absence of widely accepted mediational structures between the individual and Allah, the ultimate sovereign of the world, Muslims could in principle reject the authority of anyone whose opinion did not accord with their own. Containing diverse individual and sectarian beliefs, the community of Islam was a vast tapestry whose intricacies were not the less significant on account of being cut out of the same cloth.

The elusive balance between the individual and the community in Islam has been a product of the dialectic of fission and fusion inherent in the religious worldview of a Muslim. With submission to the will of none other than Allah as the first principle of Islam, the individual Muslim's identity assumes a transcendental quality. A feature of Allah's universal sovereignty, such an idea of identity is tempered by the imperative of fellowship with the community adhering to the teachings of the Prophet Muhammad. Non-territorial in its spread and rejecting barriers of race, colour, sect and class, the ideal community of Islam informs Muslim perceptions of identity at a spiritual and emotive rather than an existential level. More worldly than transcendental, the idea of Muslim identity in the second sense draws sustenance from the fact of sovereign countries inhabited and ruled by members of the Islamic community if not necessarily the precepts of the faith.

For Indian Muslims it was empathy with the trials and tribulations of co-religionists in sovereign and quasi-sovereign states in West and Central Asia which since the mid-nineteenth century had been a salient facet in the articulation of their communitarian identity. Inviting the charge of extra-territorial loyalties from their Hindu compatriots, these affinities based on religious sentiments had inspired the anti-imperialist discourse of those influenced by Jamaluddin al-Afghani as well as the adherents of Sayyid Ahmad Khan's line to uphold the legitimacy of subjecthood under British sovereignty. Until the second decade of the twentieth century the tussle between these competing yet overlapping conceptions of sovereignty and identity had captured the attention of a handful in a debate limited to a select few. Widespread socio-economic dislocations at the end of the First World War, colonial repression of discontents and the psychological impact of the dismemberment of the Ottoman empire altered the context of Muslim and Indian politics alike. The debate now was orchestrated in a broader public arena with the mass mobilization of Indians under two different sets of symbols, the *al-Hilal* or crescent of the Islamic *khilafat* and the *charkha* or spinning wheel of the Indian National Congress led by Mohandas Karamchand Gandhi (1869–1948). A consideration of the linkages between identity and sovereignty in Muslim consciousness at the normative level helps tease out the inwardness and ultimate significance of this rare blending of Islamic and Indian nationalist symbols.

HAKIMIYAT, THE UMMAH AND THE KHILAFAT

Sovereignty and identity have been so closely interconnected in normative Muslim thought that it is impossible to consider the one without the other. All Muslims subscribe to the *hakimiyat* or sovereignty of Allah over the entire world.[1] Together with the belief in the unity of God or *tauhid*, the notion of divine sovereignty lies at the heart of the Islamic view of universal brother-hood. It offers ideological justification for rejecting territorial nationalism and the separation of religion from politics. In theory no community or indi-vidual has a greater right to Allah's benediction: all are equal before the Crea-tor. But Islamic universalism, inextricably associated as it has been with the community of believers, could hardly avoid the strains of exclusivism. Sub-mission to Allah, the ultimate law-giver whose authority is absolute, all-per-vasive and inalienable, sets the Muslim apart from all others. Releasing the individual from all forms of human bondage except the community of the faithful, the message of Islam prompts Muslims towards an implicit exclusivism even while lauding the virtues of common humanity and univer-sal fellowship.

---

[1] For a discussion of this concept, see Parveen Shaukat Ali, *The Political Philosophy of Iqbal*, (second edition), Lahore: Publishers United Ltd, 1978, chapter three.

Far from being contradictory the twin dynamics of uni
exclusivism, both in their outward and inward manifestations,
in the thought of leading Muslim intellectuals since the incept
the Arabian peninsula. A perpetual overture to non-Mu:
universalism and its concomitant egalitarianism, played a role in the global
expansion of the faith. Yet the spread of Muhammad's religious message was
of necessity a political process. The imperatives of consolidating the gains of
conquest and conversion conferred limitations, more political than religious,
which were by nature exclusionary. In making the transition from propagating
the religion to creating a polity, the Prophet of Islam himself drew a distinction
between Muslims and non-Muslims under his jurisdiction. With the practical,
if not theoretical, separation of temporal and spiritual authority after the first
century of Islam, the politics of Muslim self-preservation relied more on
exclusivism than on the spirit of either universalism or egalitarianism.

As an ideal, universalism may have lost its appeal in relation to non-
Muslims but it continued to have profound relevance for the *ummah,* or the
worldwide community of Muslims. The principle of *hakimiyat* and
membership in the *ummah* provided the universal dimensions to an otherwise
exclusionary self-identity of Muslims living in specific territorial locations
such as India. Outnumbered by other religious denominations, Indian
Muslims could take comfort in belonging to the Islamic *ummah.* Exclusivism
aimed at emphasizing difference vis-a-vis non-Muslims was wholly consistent
with inclusion in a universal community of Islam.

A universal non-territorial identity was in line with the ideal of *hakimiyat.*
But the *ummah* was divided politically, raising questions about identity and
loyalty to temporal sovereignty. In normative Islam, divine sovereignty
devolved through the Prophet's viceregents or *khalifas* who were both the
spiritual and temporal bearers of authority. The bitter succession struggle
following the Prophet's death over the qualifications of the *khalifa* had split
the community down the middle. Constituting a majority of Muslims, Sunnis
accepted the legitimacy of all four *khalifas,* Abu Bakar, Umar, Usman and Ali
who assumed the mantle of leadership in the wake of the Prophet's death.
Shias contested the legitimacy of the first three *khalifas* on the grounds that
Ali, Muhammad's nephew and son-in-law, alone was the rightful heir to the
Prophet's spiritual and temporal authority.

In theory, the institution of the *khalifa* was not hereditary and had to be
decided upon by the *ijma* or the consensus of the community. Yet with the
establishment of the Ummaiyid dynasty by Muawiya in 656, the *khilafat* of
Islam became a hereditary monarchy which passed on to the Abbasids and
eventually became associated with the Ottoman Sultanate. Not all Sunnis
agreed with the principle of hereditary *khilafat* but accepted its *de facto*
existence. Shias, who established political power in Iran, continued to reject
the legitimacy of the Ummaiyid *khilafat,* and by extension of the Abbasids

and the Ottomans, paying allegiance only to the twelve *imams* or religious leaders directly descended from Ali. Unlike the Sunni *khilafat* the Shia *imamate* was divinely ordained and could not be elected by the consensus of the community. According to Shia belief, the twelfth *imam* disappeared mysteriously and would return as the *mahdi* or guide at an unspecified moment to save the world from evil and oppression. Although absent, the *imam* is seen to have a mystical presence and moulds the spiritual life of the Shia community through qualified representatives. Another variant of the theory of the *khilafat* or *imamate* was propounded by the Khwarijites, who after initially supporting Ali had broken with him due to disagreements about the role of the office. In the Khwarijite view, the *khilafat* was not a religious or political obligation. Anyone could assume the office, including slaves, non-Arabs and women.[2]

Even Sunnis, who formed the bulk of the Muslim population in India, were divided on the *khilafat* and *imamate* in Islam. Historically the spiritual and temporal authority of the *khalifa*, the *amir-ul-momineen* or the leader of the *ummah*, whether based in Damascus or Baghdad was symbolically acknowledged in varying measure by Muslim sovereigns in India. From the earliest period of Islam in the subcontinent, Muslim rulers typically sought the blessings of the reigning *khalifa*, considering themselves to be their *naibs* or subordinates in the exercise of temporal, though not spiritual, authority. This was a diplomatic way of keeping the Abbasid armies at bay while also bolstering the legitimacy of the sultan vis-a-vis a nobility consisting of foreign Muslim immigrants in the main. Some sultans tried enhancing their own status in the eyes of their Muslim subjects by striking coins bearing the name of the *khalifa* and mentioning him in *khutbas*.[3]

With the collapse of the Abbasids in Baghdad, the seat of the *khilafat* shifted to Cairo in 1261 where a descendant of the family assumed the religious leadership while temporal authority was exercised by the reigning Mameluke sultans. Two Muslim sultans of India sent deputations to the *khalifa* in Cairo to receive the formal investiture legitimizing their authority.[4] Following the subjugation of the Mamelukes by Selim I, the *khilafat* in 1517 was voluntarily

[2]The Sunni, Shia and Khwarijite conceptions of *khilafat* and *imamate* are well documented in a variety of sources. See, for instance, T.W. Arnold, *The Caliphate*, New York: Barnes & Nobles, 1965–6 and Syed Ameer Ali, *The Spirit of Islam: A History of the Evolution and Ideals of Islam with a Life of the Prophet* (first published in 1891, it has multiple editions), Lahore: Islamic Book Service, 1989, especially the chapter on the apostolic succession. For an overview, see Hamid Enayat, *Modern Islamic Political Thought: The Response of the Shii and Sunni Muslims to the Twentieth Century*, London: Macmillan, 1982.

[3]Sayyid Sulayman Nadwi, 'Khilafat aur Hindustan', in *Muqalat-i-Sulayman*, compiled by Sayyid Sabahuddin Abdur Rahman, no date and place of publication.

[4]Ameer Ali, *The Spirit of Islam*, p. 131.

transferred to the Ottomans, who simultaneously acquired guardianship over the holy places of Islam in Mecca and Medina. Without disputing the hereditary right of the Ottomans to the *khilafat*, the Mughals dispensed with ceremonial displays of their subordination to Constantinople, the *Dar-ul-Khilafat* or the seat of Islam. Royal coinage and *khutbas* invoked the name of the ruling emperor even though his sovereignty was more temporal than spiritual. The idea of the temporal and spiritual authority of the *khalifa* , however, continued to occupy a place in Indian Muslim normative thought. The great religious reformer of the eighteenth century Shah Waliullah while castigating the Mughals for their spiritual debasement and material decadence considered the *khilafat* a religious necessity for the Muslim community. But only a member of the Quraish, the family to which the Prophet of Islam belonged, could legitimately lay claim to the institution. On this view, the Ottoman sultan was not the *khalifa* of the Muslim *ummah*.

The matter remained unresolved at the normative level with barely any relevance for the majority of Muslims in India. So long as they were free to practise their religion, there was no need to seek the protection of an invisible sovereign somewhere in the distant horizon of West Asia. With the loss of formal sovereignty, the *khilafat* acquired new meaning for segments of Sunni Muslim *ashraf* classes who under the direction of some *ulema* began looking upon the Ottoman sultan as the temporal and spiritual leader of the *ummah*. This late-nineteenth-century posture was contested from within the community. Sayyid Ahmad Khan and his Aligarh associates dismissed Sultan Abdul Hamid's claims to the *khilafat*. Using Waliullah's argument, Sayyid Ahmad asserted that only a member of the Quraish could become the *khalifa*. Moreover, Indian Muslims were subjects of the British Crown and not of the Turkish sultan. He cited a famous Hadith in which the Prophet had predicted that the *khilafat* would survive him for thirty years before being replaced by *badshahat*, or kingship. It followed that temporal and not spiritual sovereignty formed the nub of relations between the rulers and the ruled. A *khilafat* to which Muslims were religiously bound to owe allegiance was plainly wrong.[5] Although a Sunni, Sayyid Ahmad's views dovetailed neatly with those of the Shias who had stronger religious objections to the Ottoman *khilafat*. Equally anxious to prove their loyalty to the British raj, Shias charged Sunni Muslims using the appellation *amir-ul-momineen* for the Turkish sultan with religious ignorance. Muslims in India enjoyed more peace, security and freedom of religion than Muslims in the Ottoman domains. So long as the British showed impartiality in the distribution of justice and patronage, it was mandatory for Muslims to be loyal subjects of the Crown.[6]

[5]*Aligarh Institute Gazette*, 10 July 1880, *Selections*, L/R/5/57, IOL, pp. 475–6.
[6]Ahmad Husain Shaikh, *Baz Musalmanon ki Afsosnak Ghalat Fahmi*, first published in 1897 (second edition), 2 March 1915, Muzaffarnagar, Urdu B. 14a, IOL.

This was political expediency vying with normative Islamic theory. Allegiance to the temporal sovereignty of the British gave an altogether different meaning to the identity of Indian Muslims than one derived from religious concepts like *hakimiyat*, *ummah* and the *khilafat*. Despite arguments against separating religion from politics in Islam, Muslims practised that duality while negotiating their relationship with British sovereignty. The *ulema* might carp and complain about the lack of religiosity among the faithful and bemoan that India was no longer a *Dar-ul-Islam*. But with few exceptions the learned men of Islam accepted subjugation to the raj by refusing to declare India a *Dar-ul-Harb*, or an abode of war. To do so would have made *jihad* or holy war obligatory for Muslims. But *jihad* without assurance of success was not a strategy to which the *ulema* of India were prepared to nail their colours. With the British guaranteeing their religious freedom, India was a *Dar-ul-Aman*, or the abode of peace, and loyalty to the established government incumbent upon all Muslims. If life under alien rule became unbearable, Muslims had the option of performing *hijrat* or migration instead of wasting blood in a *jihad* against a better-armed enemy. This rule of thumb, stated in a *fatwa* by Shah Abdul Aziz in 1765 and invoked by Maulana Abdul Bari in April 1915, was ignored by most Indian Muslims.

With a breath of pragmatism dictating their response to the British presence, Indian Muslims were hardly dogmatic about a religious identity shaped by three overlapping ideas of sovereignty—the divine, the spiritual and the purely temporal. Of these, God's universal sovereignty was the easiest to negotiate. There was also consensus on the principle of the *ummah*. But without a *khalifa* acknowledged as the legitimate viceregent of God and his Prophet by all Muslims, spiritual and temporal sovereignty assumed different meanings for the individual and, by implication, for the existential community. To be sure, the symbolic attachment to Ottoman Turkey, so vividly demonstrated in Muslim writings in the press as well as innumerable poetic compositions, was not the less genuine for being devoid of substantive reality. By dubbing this feeling 'Pan-Islamism', Anglo-Indian and Hindu newspapers raised a bogey invoking features of Islamic normative theory most Muslims had either readily or forcibly relinquished while adjusting to colonial rule.

Disagreements among Muslims on the *khilafat* highlight the myriad ways in which the normative ideal of Islamic universalism could be utilized to craft alternative conceptions of communitarian identity and politics. In a pamphlet reproducing his letters to the editors of three newspapers, one Haji Muhammad Ismail Khan in 1907 took umbrage at the propensity of some Muslim *ulema* to look beyond the borders of India. Worrying about the Islamic *ummah* and neglecting those at home was like 'dreaming about palaces from the confines of straw huts'. In crying about an illusory unity with the world of Islam, Indian Muslims in the style of Sheikh Chili, the inveterate conjurer of fantasies, were expecting others to come and solve their problems.[7] This dash of realism ignored the reasons for the undue emphasis some Indian Muslims placed on the universal community of Islam. For Mohamed Ali, Zafar Ali Khan, Abul Kalam Azad and also Muhammad Iqbal, holding firmly to the ideal of the Islamic *ummah* was effectively a defensive posture. It aimed at stressing Muslim cultural distinctiveness in the maelstrom of an Indian nationalism that was becoming increasingly suffused with the ethos of Hindu majoritarianism. While Iqbal rejected the Ottoman sultan's temporal and spiritual authority over the *ummah*, others took the opening presented by the end of the war not just to locate their co-religionists within mainstream Indian nationalism but to try and redefine its very basis.

They were assisted in their enterprise by a number of Sunni *ulema*, and even some Shia divines, who considered the defeat of Ottoman Turkey an unmitigated disaster for Islam. Signs that the British in combination with other western powers had no intention of saving the 'sick man' of Europe from impending death occasioned impassioned moves to stir up Muslim opinion in favour of preserving the Ottoman *khilafat*. Most alarming was the prospect of the League of Nations placing large chunks of the Ottoman domains, including the Arabian peninsula and Palestine, under British and French mandates. This directly contravened the Prophet's last will and testament that Arabia and the holy cities of Islam be kept immune from the presence of non-Muslim powers. The embarrassing fact that Muslim recruits to the British Indian army had contributed to the undoing of the Ottoman empire was not easy to live down. Blaming the raj for its misleading promises to preserve Muslim sovereignty over the holy places of Islam seemed the only way out of the impasse. With the war won, the British were accused of betraying the trust their Muslim subjects had reposed in them, a perfect weapon to channel injured religious sentiments to strike at the colonial jugular as recompense for unthinking deviations from the Islamic path. Even those who had misgivings about the legitimacy of the Turkish *khilafat* could now be brought around, given the threat to the holy places of Islam, arguably the more powerful reason Indian Muslims rallied behind the symbol of the crescent.

The intellectual content of the movement drew upon features in Islamic normative theory which pragmatism had placed at a discount in the history of Muslims in India for nearly four centuries. Quranic verses testified to the centrality of the *khilafat* in Islam. Muslims might quibble about who was to be *khalifa* or *imam*, but none could deny the religious significance of the institution. Fearing a British move to install their client, the Sharif of Mecca as the *khalifa*, various *ulema* in India came out openly in support of the Ottoman claim by elaborating upon the theory of the institution in the light of changed circumstances. In a departure from the past, political expediency guiding interpretations of normative Islamic theory at a time of crisis generated more

---

[7]Haji Muhammad Ismail, *Pan-Islamism*, Agra, July 1907, Urdu D. 3929, IOL.

agreement than disagreement among the intelligentsia and learned divines of Muslim India.

In an essay entitled 'Masla-i-Khilafat wa Jazirat al-Arab' published in 1920, Abul Kalam Azad relied on the authority of the Quran and the Hadith to outline his opinions on the subject. He took strong exception to the term 'Pan-Islamism' and its attribution to Sultan Abdul Hamid's claim in the late nineteenth century to be the *khalifa*. Muslims subscribed to the ideal of universal brotherhood and had a non-territorial conception of nationality. If this was 'Pan-Islamism', then its origins had to be traced to the beginnings of Islam and the Quranic revelation itself. While endorsing the Ottoman sultan's right to the *khilafat*, and making his authority mandatory upon all Muslims, Azad was more interested in the Indian aspects of the struggle. He admonished Indian Muslims for their part in destroying the only Islamic power which had for the last few centuries put up a semblance of resistance against western imperialism. Muslim support for Britain in the war was a monumental blunder and completely contrary to the teachings of their religion. Instead of empty protests, Indian Muslims could atone for their sins only by organizing themselves in defence of their religion. The individual without the community was nothing while a community as divided and disorganized as the Indian Muslims was a blot on Islam—shades of Iqbal.[8]

A lesser-known pamphlet by Maulana Abu Hasamat Nadvi of Azimgarh in UP is further illustration of the growing support for the Ottoman *khilafat* among Muslim scholars. In the author's considered opinion, the capacity to freely exercise the temporal and spiritual sovereignty vested in the *khilafat* was a more important qualification than membership in the Quraish family. This disqualified the Sharif of Mecca who, although a Quraish, had intrigued with the British against the Ottoman sultan. Drawing upon Shah Waliullah's ideas without privileging the claims of the Quraish to the *khilafat*, the tract listed four possible methods of appointment to the office. The first was through the community's *bait* or pledge in an allusion to Abu Bakar's succession to the mantle of the Prophet. Another was the designation of a successor by the previous *khalifa*. Equally valid was the appointment by the reigning *khalifa* of a group of men to select the best candidate. Finally, the *khilafat* might be acquired by an individual possessing superior force as long as his authority was endorsed by the *ulema*, the *umra* or the leaders and the community at large. If personal ability backed by the deployment of power was a legitimate basis for the leadership of the Muslim *ummah*, then anyone supported by the community with the requisite temporal power could qualify as *khalifa*. From this angle, the Ottoman sultan had the most meritorious claims to the *khilafat*.[9]

[8]Abul Kalam Azad, 'Masla-i-Khilafat wa Jazirat al-Arab' (1920), republished in *Intikhab-i-Khutbat-i-Khilafat,* compiled by Mahmud Elahi, Lucknow, 1988.
[9]Maulana Abu Hasamat Nadvi, *Khilafat-i-Islamia and Turks,* Delhi, 22 December 1920, Urdu D. 754, IOL.

Equating the preservation of the *khilafat* with their religious liberties, the leading spokesmen of Indian Muslim opinion on the question were against any move to limit the temporal authority of the Ottoman sultan. They wanted nothing short of clinching political victory from the jaws of military defeat.[10] However unrealistic, for men like Mohamed Ali and his brother Shaukat Ali (1873–1938), Zafar Ali Khan and, more calculatedly, Abul Kalam Azad, the dismantling of the *khilafat* along with the Ottoman empire was a personal and collective calamity for India's Muslims. Each in his own way was determined not 'to let the Khilafat go down unmourned, unhonoured and unsung'.[11] The politically myopic might view the spectacle of Muslim support for the *khilafat* an obscurantist attempt at turning a dead institution into a centrepiece of revitalized 'Pan-Islamism'; the cynical may wish to paint it as a wily effort to raise the Islamic crescent to the same heights as the Indian nationalist *charkha*, but the believer in Islamic universalism could see in it the realization of a long-cherished dream. There may have been a bit of all these and much more in the *khilafat* movement of 1919 to 1923. It seems prudent to postpone writing the epitaph on the *khilafat* as a normative ideal in Muslim consciousness until a more careful consideration of the motivations behind one of the most exciting agitations since the rebellion of 1857.

GOD, GOVERNMENT AND GANDHI

The *khilafat* movement has been the focus of some fine historical scholarship. Historians have differed in their emphasis on the Indian and Islamic motivations, individual as well as collective, underpinning the first effective mass mobilization against the British raj.[12] That there were shades of both in an agitation commanding support from an array of social groups, straddling class, ideological and regional lines hardly requires further elaboration.

[10]See for instance Mohamed Ali's speeches in London of 23 March and 22 April 1920 in Iqbal (ed.), *Select Writings and Speeches of Maulana Mohamed Ali*, pp. 267–99.

[11]Stated by Sayyid Husain, editor of the *Independent* (Allahabad) and member of the Indian Khilafat delegation which visited London. See ibid., p. 283.

[12]Those who have seen the movement as symbolic of Muslim identification with the larger world of Islam include Ahmad, *Studies in Islamic Culture in the Indian Environment*, and Hafeez Malik, *Moslem Nationalism in India and Pakistan*, Washington, DC: Public Affairs Press, 1963. A somewhat cynical view of the coming together of western-educated Muslims and the *ulema*, stressing the factional tears in the shifting alliance, is that of Francis Robinson, *Separatism Among Indian Muslims: The Politics of the United Provinces, 1860–1923*, Cambridge: Cambridge University Press, 1975. Gail Minault's *The Khilafat Movement: Religious Symbolism and Political Mobilization in India*, New York: Columbia University Press, 1982, gives more credence to the ideological underpinnings of the movement while also emphasizing the specifically Indian motivations.

More pertinent to a study of identity and sovereignty in Muslim consciousness was the nexus between the idea of Islamic universalism and an Indian nation, and the reasons for its successful or unsuccessful incorporation into mainstream nationalism of the Congress variety. Muslim anxieties about the *khilafat* coupled with post-war socio-economic and political discontents created a unique historical conjuncture for a broad-based anti-imperialist struggle. A crucial moment in Indian history, it offers rare insights into the practical prospects of accommodating religiously informed cultural identities and politics through a negotiated concord on national sovereignty.

The *khilafat* movement is commonly portrayed as heralding the entry of religion into politics. But these two realms had never been separate in any except a notional sense. British control on politics alongside a policy of non-interference in the religious affairs of Indians ensured that from the late nineteenth century the public discourse ventilated through the vernacular press and publications market became heavily imbued with communitarian idioms. Far from being a deviation from the norm, the years 1919–23 underscored the various possible blendings of religion and politics in colonial India. Given the strictures of colonial rule, it was relatively safer to package politics in religious idioms. Islamic normative theory, open as it was to multiple appropriations, in any case rejected the duality between religion and politics. It is better to be alert to the precise uses and meanings of Islamic symbolism in the politics of Muslims than to simplistically attribute an overarching religious impulse to the assorted motivations and aspirations which fuelled the *khilafat* movement.

This is not to devalue the Islamic sentiments of Muslims, however these may be interpreted, but to inveigh against an all-too-easy reification of religion at the expense of all other dimensions in the articulation of their politics. Such an approach takes into account the structural features of the colonial public arena which, together with the ideational aspects of Islamic normative theory, made the overlapping of politics and religion an intrinsic feature of Muslim consciousness. Quite as much as their religiously informed cultural identities, the religiously informed politics of Indian Muslims have to be placed within their spatial and temporal context.

The First World War and its aftermath introduced some novel features on the political horizon. An alliance of western-educated Muslims with a conglomeration of *ulema* and *pirs* as a prelude to the emergence of a rainbow coalition with the Congress under Mohandas Gandhi was an unprecedented development. An expression of growing Muslim disaffection with the old politics of loyalty, this grand coalition threatened the colonial state's system of control and collaboration even in hitherto relatively quiescent regions like the Punjab and Sind. Advertising the inadequacies of the colonial state's formal arena of politics, the *khilafat* and non-cooperation movements pushed the parameters of the public sphere to new limits, mobilizing elements through organizational networks that had previously been inconsequential or marginal to the national or communitarian agendas of the Congress and the Muslim League.[13]

A series of events internal and external to India set the stage for this remarkable transformation. Most notable amongst these was the rising graph of disillusionment among Muslim *ashraf* classes with their status under the British raj. The rejection in 1912 by the colonial government of the proposal for an autonomous Muslim University, coming hot on the heels of the annulment of the partition of Bengal, followed by successive wars in the Balkans and the Kanpur mosque incident in 1913 led to a fresh awakening among the younger generation of Muslims. Deploring the mendicancy of the Muslim League and the obsequious posture of the old guard at the Aligarh Muslim Anglo-Oriental College, men like Mohammad Ali Jinnah, Mohamed Ali, Shaukat Ali, Abul Kalam Azad and Zafar Ali Khan, to name only a few, tried in their different ways to chart a new course for Muslim politics in association with the Congress. Of these, Jinnah alone stuck to the methods of moderate constitutionalism, writing himself out temporarily from the pages relating the story of this stormy phase in Indian history. Moved by the ideal of Islamic universalism, the Ali brothers, Azad and Zafar Ali Khan, widened their respective spheres of influence through the journalistic medium in addition to establishing contacts with some leading *ulema* based at Farangi Mahal and Deoband.

By 1913 the Ali brothers had entered the inner circle of Maulana Abdul Bari (1879–1926) of Farangi Mahal. Bari became the president of their creation, the Anjuman-i-Khuddam-i-Kaaba, an umbrella organization designed to muster support among Indian Muslims for the protection of the holy places of Islam in the Arabian peninsula.[14] The Anjuman quickly won backing from leading *ulema* and *pirs* in northern India, the Punjab, the North Western Frontier and Sind.[15] This sort of networking aided and abetted the political ambitions of the Ali brothers and provided the religious guardians with supra-local organizational support and wider channels of communication.[16] To the extent that the *ulema* and *pirs* were for the first time

[13]For an account of how these networks were activated, see Minault, *The Khilafat Movement*, chapters one and two.

[14]Ibid., pp. 35–6 and Mushirul Hasan, *Mohamed Ali: Ideology and Politics*, Delhi: Manohar, 1981, p. 45.

[15]The Qadiri and Naqshbandi Sufi orders in the Punjab and Sind responded enthusiastically to the Anjuman-i-Khuddam-i-Kaaba.(*SPPAI*, 21 February 1914, vol. xxxvi, no,7, p. 116 and Sarah Ansari, *Sufi Saints and State Power: The Pirs of Sind, 1843–1947*, Cambridge: Cambridge University Press and Lahore: Vanguard Publications, 1992, p. 81.)

[16]According to Mushirul Hasan, the *ulema* were so 'unaccustomed to political life' that they leaped at the opportunity of allying with western educated Muslims. (See Hasan, *Mohamed Ali*, pp. 44–5.) Minault believes that it was the support of the

forging links beyond the circle of committed disciples, the intermeshing of their specifically religious concerns with those of the western educated can be seen as having altered the tenor of Muslim politics.

There can be no doubt that the end of the war found Muslims displaying an unusual degree of unanimity. The defeat of Ottoman Turkey, described by Abul Kalam Azad as the only Muslim power in the world that had wielded its sword and 'saved Islam from destruction',[17] could not be taken lightly. Their powers of empathy failing, the leading Muslim voices of the time belittled the forces of Arab nationalism, seeing in them a machiavellian western conspiracy to dismember the Ottoman empire. The unpopularity of the British-backed Sharif of Mecca was a direct product of this anti-imperial strand in Indian Muslim opinion. News of the Arab revolt in 1916 was received with disbelief by Maulana Abdul Bari and others who could not envisage why Muslims anywhere in the world would want to distance themselves from the Ottoman *khalifa*. Unlike the Arabs who had much to gain from exerting their national identity against the Ottomans, many Indian Muslims saw the preservation of the temporal power of Islam based in Constantinople as a necessary safeguard to their own political future.

So there was more logic than romance in Indian Muslim support for the crumbling Ottoman Khilafat. But one has only to delve below the surface of this apparent consensus to disinter the ideologically based tactical and strategic differences among them. There were multiple lines of fracture. Maulana Ahmad Raza Khan (1856–1921) of the Bareilly school of *ulema*, known as the Barelvis or the Ahl-i-Sunnat, opposed the *khilafat* movement and cooperation with Hindus on ideological grounds.[18] What eventually ferreted out the agitators from the co-operators, and linked Islamic universalists with Indian nationalists, was the triad of God, Government and Gandhi which came to inform an individual Muslim's political orientation and, by implication, identification with the community. This was true not only of western-educated Muslims associated with the Aligarh tradition, the religiously eclectic Barelvis and the heterodox Qadianis, but also of *ulema* linked with Deoband, Farangi Mahal and even the doctrinaire Ahl-i-Hadith. So long as the British government did not interfere with their religious freedom, there was no reason for them to explicitly invoke the sovereignty of God or the

---

ulema which enabled western educated Muslims to overcome the barriers between them and their less privileged co-religionists. (See Minault, *The Khilafat Movement*, passim.)

[17]*SPPAI*, 28 February 1914, vol.xxxvi, no. 9, pp. 139–40.

[18]Metcalf, *Islamic Revival in British India*, p. 313; M. Naeem Qureshi, 'The "Ulama" of British India and the Hijrat of 1920', *MAS*, 13, 1 (1979), pp. 49–50 and Syed Jamaluddin, 'The Barelvis and the Khilafat Movement', in Mushirul Hasan (ed.), *Communal and Pan-Islamic Trends in Colonial India* (revised edition), New Delhi: Manohar, 1985, pp. 400–13.

The Ali brothers
Courtesy: Nehru Memorial Museum and Library

spiritual and temporal authority of the *khalifa*. Even at the height of the movement a renowned scholar of Islam like Khwajah Hasan Nizami asserted that if the British embraced Islam, Muslims would have no difficulty accepting the King-Emperor as their legal *khalifa*.[19]

The *khilafat* could become a rallying point for a divided, dispirited and disorganized community only by transforming specific concerns about the fate of Ottoman Turkey into a general feeling that the government was trampling on the religious freedom of Muslims. Not an easy task under normal circumstances, it was facilitated by the disturbed conditions in India marking the end of the war. The government's wartime policies had fostered widespread socio-economic grievances in rural and urban areas alike. If there was enough combustible material waiting to be torched, a series of insensitive measures by the rulers inflamed the ruled. In 1918 the announcement of the Montagu–Chelmsford reform scheme sorely disappointed moderate nationalists who had set much store by the British accepting the Congress and Muslim League's Lucknow Pact of 1916 as the basis of the new constitutional arrangements. Indifferent to the subsistence needs of the subordinate groups and dismissive of the vocal and better-off segments of society, the colonial government chose to strengthen its powers of coercion rather than of persuasion. In March 1919 the Rowlatt Act perpetuating wartime emergency ordinances as draconian peacetime legislation provided provocation for a thousand mutinies. It was this scenario, more materially than spiritually electrified, which pitched the followers of God and Gandhi against loyalists of the government.

Even Muslims bracing themselves to battle with the government over the *khilafat* were uncertain whether the cause of God could be served by soliciting support from Gandhi and the Hindus. The years 1917 and 1918 had witnessed Hindu–Muslim conflicts in UP, Bihar and Bengal over cow slaughter and the eruption of local irritations during religious festivals. Such tensions posed problems for those pro-Congress Muslims who along with a group of *ulema* led by Abdul Bari were trying to take over the All-India Muslim League. On the eve of its eleventh annual session at Delhi in December 1918, despite efforts by Dr Mukhtar Ahmad Ansari (1880–1936) and Hakim Ajmal Khan (1863–1928), the *imam* of the Juma Masjid reprimanded the League for failing to assist Muslim victims of Hindu aggression. In his *khutbah* at the end of Friday prayers, he cited Quranic injunctions prohibiting Muslims from mixing with infidels. Ansari's supporters called him 'a Government spy, a man without honour and no Muslim'. An all-out scuffle ensued with Ansari screaming at the *imam* for being 'a lion against the Hindus, but a jackal when their quarrel was with the English'.[20]

[19]See Khwajah Hasan Nizami, *Government aur Khilafat*, Delhi, 15 March 1920, Urdu D.1197, IOL.

[20]*SPPAI*, 11 January 1919, vol. xli, no. 2, p. 19.

This set the tone for the League's annual session. With the Ali brothers, Zafar Ali Khan and Azad cooling their heels in jail, Ansari warmed the hearts of the *ulema* with a spirited speech in Urdu. Quoting profusely from the Quran and the Hadith, he virtually pronounced the death sentence on the Sharif of Mecca and threatened a *jihad* if Mesopotamia, Arabia and Palestine were not restored to Turkey. Pointing to British perfidy in violating the sanctity of the holy places, Ansari called for the independence of Muslims in North Africa and Central Asia, though, significantly, not of India.[21] The stalwarts of moderation—Jinnah, the Raja of Mahmudabad (1877–1931) and Sayyid Wazir Hasan (1874–1947)—were left eating humble pie. With the *ulema* in toe, the extremists took the League into the anti-imperialist camp, committing it to preserving the *khilafat* and restoring Muslim sovereignty over the holy places. Abdul Bari drove home the point by objecting to the presence of the British flag at a Muslim gathering. Denying any personal interest in politics, he accused those who refrained from speaking their minds of rebelling against God. But in a conciliatory gesture to the temporal sovereignty of the British, Bari announced that India would not be a *Dar-ul-Harb*, or the abode of war, if the religious rights of Muslims were respected.[22]

It was not clear what 'religious rights' meant in the context of British India. Abdul Bari was ready to give novel twists to the definition of 'religious rights', and of 'religious duties' too. A special League fund was set up to help the *ulema* propagate their views. As his opening shot, Bari in the last week of January 1919 circulated a *fatwa* in the form of an *istifta* or interrogatory, asking *ulema* of different schools of thought for their opinion on the *khilafat*, the geographical boundaries of Arabia and the duties of Muslims in the event of non-Muslims obtaining control over the holy places of Islam.[23] The *istifta*, designed to establish Bari's personal credentials as the pre-eminent theoretician of the *khilafat* movement, included his detailed views on the issues with an endorsement from the lesser fry of *ulema* at Farangi Mahal, all of whom were related to him.

The substance of the *fatwa* was culled out of well-known Islamic legal texts. Bari deemed it obligatory for Muslims to appoint an *imam* or *khalifa*, regardless of whether or not he belonged to the Quraish family. Arabia's territorial expanse was seen to include Mesopotamia and Palestine, making it incumbent upon Muslims to expel Christians, Jews and idolaters from these lands. Members of the *ummah*, jointly and severally, had to help the existing *khalifa* regain control of the holy places if Muslims in the neighbouring territories failed to assist the enterprise. Apart from Bari's henchmen, fifty-five *ulema* signed the *fatwa* which

[21]*SPPAI*, 1 February 1919, vol. xli, no. 5, p. 33. The speech was proscribed.
[22]Ibid., p. 34.
[23]*SPPAI*, Lahore, 15 February 1919, vol. xli, no. 7, pp. 63–4.

was forwarded to the viceroy.[24] His covering letter listed the difficulties facing Indian Muslims under Islamic law. Any diminution in the power of the *khalifa* would make it obligatory for Muslims to work for its restoration, especially if it led to the Sharif of Mecca claiming leadership of the *ummah*. If any part of the Arabian peninsula came under Christians or Zionist control, Muslims would have to undermine that power while also keeping Palestine and Constantinople free from non-Muslim rule. Looking to influence the outcome of the Peace Conference, Bari assured the viceroy that Indian Muslims were 'loyal subjects'. They were not bound by their religion to wage war on Britain or to assist her enemies and 'we have never done so'. But for this state of affairs to continue, the 'religious difficulties' of Muslims had to be addressed. He expressed 'fear' that 'some short-sighted persons' might 'betray the Islamic cause by pretences' and by 'lead[ing the] Government to interfere with our religion ... cloud the bright jewel of religious neutrality'.[25]

Putting a new spin on British non-interference in religion, Abdul Bari was covering his flanks while making extra-territorial political demands on a government whose jurisdiction was restricted to India. Here was Islamic universalism with its belief in the sovereignty of God testing the patience of a temporal authority subservient to the imperatives of a distant metropolis. Bari followed his missive to the viceroy with a series of announcements. The still-interned Ali brothers gave a fillip to Bari's claim to the spiritual leadership of Indian Muslims by vowing to accept his guidance in religious matters and 'give up everything in the path of God'. His *fatwa* to the viceroy aimed at asserting his political influence. Any adverse decision by the Peace Conference about the future of the Ottoman domains, and the Jazirat-ul-Arab in particular, would be seen by Muslims as 'a serious interference with religion *after which no agreement will remain an agreement* and no law will be a law'. Under such circumstances, it would be mandatory for Muslims to make necessary sacrifices without engaging in 'slaughter or *jihad*'. Holding up a veritable red rag to the government, Bari declared that passive resistance to the Rowlatt Act of the kind Gandhi had in mind was entirely consistent with the teachings of Islam.[26]

This signalled the beginnings of efforts to establish a common Hindu–Muslim front against the government. Much pageantry surrounded the theme of Hindu–Muslim unity. An exclusive focus on the activities of all-India leaders offers few insights into popular inclinations at the social base. A tactical

[24]Of these only one belonged to the Punjab. Among the prominent *ulema* who disagreed with Bari were Maulana Ashraf Ali Thanawi, Shamsul Ulema Maulana Abdul Hamid of Farangi Mahal, Maulana Ahmad Raza Khan of Bareilly and the *ulema* of Deoband. (*SPPAI*, 5 April 1919, vol. xli, no.14, pp. 131–2.)

[25]Bari's letter to the viceroy and the *fatwa* were published on 12 March 1919 in the Lucknow-based *Akhuwat*, an organ of pro-*khilafat* Muslims opposed to the group led by the Raja of Mahmudabad. (See ibid., pp. 132–3.)

[26]*Akhuwat*, Lucknow, 14 March 1919, ibid., pp. 133–4.

understanding between the top- and middle-ranking leaders of the two communities did not mark a strategic departure in the articulation of religiously informed politics based on mass mobilization. An analysis of the interactive processes linking the different levels of politics, all-India, regional and local, reveals the rarified nature of supra-communitarian unity and throws light on how internal divisions among Muslims and Hindus seriously hampered the first ever attempt at juxtaposing Islamic universalism with Indian nationalism.

The early phases of the movement show that there was no spontaneous upsurge in popular Muslim opinion about an impending danger to the temporal power of Islam. This had to be generated for the most part by middle-ranking leaders belonging to the newly established *khilafat* committees and the Jamiat-ul-Ulema-i-Hind through sermons on what constituted true religiosity. A meeting of the Anjuman Ahmadia Ishaat-i-Islam in Lahore[27] described the Ali brothers as the 'specimens of the Prophet of Islam'.[28] But the ultra conservative *Mashriq* of Gorakhpur chastised the radical nationalist poet Hasrat Mohani (1878–1951) for appearing at a Congress session with an 'uncovered face'. It was equally put off by the publication in the Anglo-Indian press of a photograph of Bi Amma, the revered mother of the Ali brothers. The 'so-called leaders of the Muslim Nationalists ha[d] lost every respect for their religion'.[29] The message was unambiguous: Muslims could strive for the preservation of Islam in the face of western machinations only by undergoing a thorough reform spearheaded by their religious leaders. By putting the fear of God in the hearts and minds of ordinary Muslims, the reformist strain in the *khilafat* agitation was looking to strengthen the leadership credentials of the *ulema*. It also served the purpose of keeping pro-Congress Muslims on a leash, lest they go over to the Hindus in their enthusiasm for national unity.

According to Dr Saifuddin Kitchlew (1884–1963), a middle-ranking leader with support among fellow Kashmiri Muslims in Amritsar city, it was the religious duty and legitimate right of all Muslims to protect the *khilafat* and the holy places of Islam. The government had wrongfully interfered in their religious liberty and Muslims could not be held 'responsible for their acts'. When it came to Hindu–Muslim unity, Kitchlew and his co-religionists were '*first* Indians and then Muslims'. This was contradicted by Maulvi Abdullah Minhas of the *Vakil*. Quranic teachings demanded that any follower of the Prophet of Islam should be '*first* a Muslim and then Indian'. He even asked Hindus to be 'first Hindus and then Indians'.[30] The question of the first identity of India's Muslims was a touchy one for many Hindus who for their own

[27]A Lahore-based splinter group of Ahmadis which accepted Mirza Ghulam Ahmad's claim to prophecy only in a metaphorical sense. It had broken away in 1914 from the Qadian party led by Ghulam Ahmad's son, Bashiruddin Mahmud Ahmad.

[28]*SPPAI*, 4 January 1919, vol. xii, no.1, p. 7.

[29]*Mashriq*, Gorakhpur, 30 January 1919 in *Selections*, L/R/5/95, IOL, p. 51.

[30]*SPPAI*, 8 March 1919, vol. xli, no.10, p. 68.

political purposes had come around to supporting the *khilafat* crescent though not the implications of Islamic universalism. Dr Satyapal, an Arya Samajist, advised Muslims in Amritsar on how to go about juggling their dual identity. As descendants of those who in the days of the great Mughal emperor Akbar walked alongside Hindus, they ought to be 'first Indians and then Muslims'.[31] Most Muslims preferred making their own decisions about the sequence of their identity. While in prison, Mohamed Ali reportedly told one of his potential defence lawyers that 'all Muslim leaders were Muslims first, and Indians second'. More disturbing was the alleged claim by the champion of Islamic universalism that if they could not find a Muslim ruler for India from within the subcontinent, they would try and get one from outside.[32]

There were layered meanings and multiple subtexts in the efforts to accommodate Islamic universalism within Indian nationalism. It all depended on how well individual Muslims operating at different levels of the political arena could play God's ace against the British king and the Gandhian joker in the pack. Occasionally they were dealt a splendid hand which obviated the problem of tactical errors. The Punjab government's decision to step up the reign of repression came as a boon for Congress agitators in a province harbouring an uncommon sense of alienation. Showing his knack for timing, Gandhi called for a nationwide *hartal* on 6 April 1919. The run-up to the strike saw an uncharacteristic display of fellowship among Punjabis, particularly in Amritsar where the economic grievances of cotton piece-goods traders and wholesale grain merchants converged with the pro-*khilafat* sentiments of a large and influential Kashmiri Muslim population.[33] Here Kitchlew and Satyapal led the Congress bandwagon expounding on the themes of nation, nationality and citizenship rights with extraordinary eloquence. On 29 March at Jallianwalla Bagh, the very site which was to provide the most famous martyrs of the non-cooperation movement, 13,000 people heard Kitchlew promoting *jazba-i-qaumi* or national sentiments and proclaiming that there was 'only one nation' in India. Contrary to their assurances, the British discriminated against Indians, rewarding loyalty with the Rowlatt Act, a punitive measure in the hands of an oppressive bureaucracy. Indians, Hindus and Muslims alike, were serving notice on government that the 'time had come' for them to 'live with equal rights'.[34]

The next day a meeting in the city was attended by 40,000 people, including a large number of women. Pandit Dina Nath, an influential Arya Samajist and editor of a string of newspapers, charged the bureaucracy with muzzling

---

[31] Ibid., p. 74.

[32] Extract from Central Provinces Police Abstract of Intelligence, 26 April 1919 cited in *SPPAI*, 3 May 1919, vol. xli, no.18, p. 146.

[33] *Memorandum on the Disturbances in the Punjab, April 1919*, first printed in 1920 by the Punjab Government Press, reprint Lahore: Sang-e-Meel Publications, 1997, p. 3.

[34] *SPPAI*, 12 April 1919, vol.xli, no.15, pp. 138–43.

opposition and spreading the 'poison of disunion into our bodies'. Fortunately 'Hindus and Muhammadans [we]re now walking on common ground'. They were not 'slaves' and would treat the 'chains' of the colonial masters as 'ornaments' and consider jails their *mandirs* and *masjids*. With Lahore and Amritsar taking the lead, most towns in the Punjab observed the *hartal* with aplomb. Large numbers of Marwaris closed down shops and joined the throngs attending protest meetings. In the remote districts there was some confusion among the populace as well as the local notables as to what they were protesting about. But no one doubted that the 'masses realise[d] that there [was] something wrong between them and the Government'. The 'opposition to the Rowlatt act and admiration of Gandhi [we]re practically universal'.[35]

While the administration kept the lid from blowing in Lahore, matters took a serious turn in Amritsar city after Kitchlew and Satyapal were interned. On 10 April, military troops fired on protesting crowds, killing some and injuring many more. Angry residents attacked government buildings, fatally assaulting a few Europeans. Rumours that the raj was at an end and the bazaars open to plunder saw villagers from neighbouring districts flocking to the city. Ignoring the Seditious Meetings Act, announced in the early hours of the morning of April 13, thousands gathered in Jallianwalla Bagh for a meeting to condemn government repression. As many as 379 were brutally gunned down and some 1200 injured when Brigadier General Dyer ordered his troops to fire without forewarning the crowd.[36] The atrocities in Amritsar and Gujranwala, which was subjected to indiscriminate aerial bombing, bolstered the Gandhian non-cooperation movement in the province.

April was the cruellest month for Punjabis. The imposition of martial law and widespread arrests were no ordinary occurrences in a province just opening its account in the annals of anti-imperialism in India. Attacks on symbols of government authority–railway lines, post and telegraph offices and police stations–were accompanied by inspired attempts to bury the hatchet of Hindu–Muslim animosity. Cow slaughter, instead of remaining an issue of mutual recrimination, became the basis for a national entente with Muslims volunteering to abstain from a practice which hurt Hindu sensibilities. Hindus reciprocated by agreeing to shut down *jhatka* shops. An example of this spontaneous outburst of Hindu–Muslim fraternization in the Punjab was the appearance in many districts of postcards with Om and Ali scribbled on them. People were entreated not to sell cows, a sin in God's eyes with penalty of hell. They should use *swadeshi* goods and forward eleven more cards of this sort to wash away the sin of killing as many cows. This relatively innocuous communication was intercepted by an irate administration on charges of sedition.[37]

[35]Ibid., pp. 152–4.
[36]*Memorandum on the Disturbances in the Punjab, April 1919*, pp. 5–11.
[37]*SPPAI*, 3 May 1919, vol. xli, no.18, p. 177.

But even in colonial prisons, Hindus and Muslims arrested for their part in the Punjab disturbances made a show of eating and drinking out of the same vessel. There were similar demonstrations of goodwill elsewhere and more concerted efforts to merge the spirit of Islamic universalism with that of Indian nationalism. Not only was the name of the Turkish *khalifa*, Sultan Muhammad VI, routinely mentioned in Friday *khutbas* but Hindus for the first time were invited to the prayer meetings. Letting Hindus into mosques angered some Muslims. A group of *ulema* in Farangi Mahal also disapproved.[38] But the objections were ignored in many areas. In Calcutta, Hindus and Muslims were taking '*sharbat* together' and sitting side by side for prayers. Muslim butchers in the city were considering giving up killing cows. In Bihar a movement was afoot to stop Hindus from selling cows to Muslims while in Lucknow sepoys were circulating snowball letters with the same message.[39]

A telling example of how political busybodies could undermine initiatives taken by people on their own was a statement by a pre-eminent leader of Hindu opinion. According to Pandit Madan Mohan Malaviya (1861–1946), 'Hindus had no objection to cow-slaughter throughout the year but interfered only during the Ba[qra]-Id festival'. He undertook to 'personally get cows slaughtered in his presence without any objection on the part of Hindus'.[40] This was in part why educated Muslims in Bihar 'doubt[ed] the sincerity of the so-called unity between the two communities'. There could be 'no reality in a unity based upon passion and a temporary feeling of resentment against the Government'. Under 'favourable circumstances' like the aftermath of the Punjab outrages and Muslim worries about the peace terms for Turkey, 'difficulties and differences may be softened' but an accord based on 'complete conciliation [was] impossible'.[41]

Keeping the principles of Islamic universalism and Indian nationalism on parallel tracks was awkward to say the least. With Hindus and Muslims in revolt against British authority, Amir Amanullah of Afghanistan saw easy pickings in India. In May 1919 his forces attacked British outposts on the north-western frontier, sparking off the third Anglo-Afghan war. The Afghan adventure was one of the more trivial instances of strategic miscalculation and proved to be an Islamic flash in the pan. Yet a Muslim ruler's foray into the subcontinent threatened the delicately poised balance between Islamic universalism and Indian nationalism. For many Hindus it revived memories of Muslim invaders of yesteryears. But Muslims by and large remained

[38]Extract from UP Abstract of 3 May 1919, *SPPAI*, 17 May 1919, vol. xli, no. 20, p. 208.

[39]Ibid.

[40]Extract from the Bihar Special Branch, 3 May 1919, ibid., p. 215.

[41]Extract from Bihar Special Branch, 10 May 1919, *SPPAI*, 24 May 1919, vol. xli, no. 21, p. 229.

apathetic, with some describing the Amir's action as egregious and irrelevant to their concern for Turkey and the holy places.

This is the more remarkable given the Afghan efforts to curry support for the invasion. In the North West Frontier Province posters announced the formation of a 'Hakumat-i-Mawaqatta-i-Hind' or a provisional government of India to replace the 'present treacherous, usurping and tyrannical Government'. It was signed by Obaidullah, a reference to Obaidullah Sindhi who had been involved in the Silk Letters Conspiracy of 1916.[42] Indians, irrespective of caste and creed, were promised peace and a life of honour. But they had to 'kill the English', desist from helping them with 'men and money' and 'continue to destroy rails and telegraph wires'.[43] A leaflet in Pushto and Persian spoke of 'glad tidings for the Frontier Afghan'. Kabul was described as *Dar-ul-Aman* and Amanullah as 'a great King' who was 'freeing the whole Pathan race and the people of the Frontier Province and India' from the 'clutches of tyrants'.[44]

Indian Muslims thought even less well of the Amir than before. There was a 'shade of resentment at his presumption in meddling with India's domestic affairs and imagining that Afghan rule would be acceptable to any class'.[45] Educated Muslims in Lahore confessed that while 'Pan-Islamism' was 'a distinct ideal', 'few wish[ed] to replace [the] British by any other rule'.[46] By the end of May, however, attempts to foster Hindu–Muslim unity in the Punjab were running aground. Apart from the dampening effect of the Anglo-Afghan war, the punishments meted out under martial law had been unduly harsh. Women in Gujranwala whose male family members had been arrested and convicted abused the agitators and the leaders.[47] Many thought that the last *hartal* had been 'a Hindu movement' while Muslims had 'reaped the greater share of punishment'. If this was the opinion of the relatively privileged, Hindu–Muslim unity among the 'lower classes ... [was] nearing dissolution'.[48] Local *maulvis* in their *khutbas* held Gandhi 'responsible before God for the loss of so many lives'. Muslims had 'erred in following Gandhi'.[49]

Opposition to the British was by no means evaporating.[50] Events on the

---

[42] A Sikh convert to Islam, Obaidullah was a follower of Maulana Mahmud al-Hasan of Deoband. In 1915 both men left India to secure Afghan and Turkish support for an invasion of the subcontinent.

[43] *SPPAI*, 14 June 1919, vol. xli, no. 24, p. 278.

[44] *SPPAI*, 12 July 1919, vol. xli, no. 27, p. 337.

[45] *SPPAI*, 31 May 1919, vol. xli, no. 22, pp. 251–2.

[46] *SPPAI*, 5 July 1919, vol. xli, no. 26, p. 310.

[47] *SPPAI*, 24 May 1919, vol. xli, no. 21, p. 239.

[48] *SPPAI*, 5 July 1919, vol. xli, no. 26, p. 308.

[49] *SPPAI*, 19 July 1919, vol. xli, no. 28, p. 356.

[50] Reports from the canal colonies suggested that unless martial law continued, the government would have difficulties collecting land revenue. (*SPPAI*, 14 June 1919, vol. xli, no. 24, p. 276.)

north-western frontier and Afghanistan had found the Mahatma dithering on the issue of a general strike. But he confessed that if he did not give in 'some of the people might break away from control'.[51] And indeed the impending dismemberment of the Turkish empire was agitating a widening circle of Muslims. Especially abhorrent was the 'idea of the Jew—the Yahoudi—lording it over the follower[s] of the Prophet' in Palestine. Among informed sections of Muslim opinion, neither the territorial nor political reductions of the former Ottoman domains was causing as much resentment as the anticipated loss of the *khalifa*'s religious authority over the holy places of Islam.[52] The Urdu press was doing its utmost to counter any slackening of fervour for Ottoman Turkey. A lone woman proprietor of the Allahabad-based *Muslim Herald* conveyed the mood when she complained bitterly of financial difficulties in trying to run an honest business. No one bought her paper unless it published explosive articles.[53]

Writings in the Urdu press, and the chain of rumours sparked off by them, were pointing to the mood prevailing among the unlettered and less privileged Muslims. In a local mosque in Matiari, Sind, there was fairly persistent talk of the appearance of the 'Imam Mehdi-i-Islam' within two or three years. Gandhi's name was being mentioned in this connection. News of non-Muslim occupation of the holy places in the Arabian peninsula was eliciting innovative local reactions. The Pir of Luwari, Muhammad Zaman whose *murids* or disciples numbering nine lakh were concentrated in Sind, Cutch and Kathiawar, announced that visitations to his shrine would now qualify as the Muslim *haj*. All proclamations of *jihad* were to proceed directly from the *pir* while the letters *alif, lam, mim* of the Quran were to be deemed as signifying Allah, Luwari and Muhammad Zaman. In northern India, an updated version of an old prophecy by Hazrat Naimatullah Shah was focus of local discussions.[54] Muslims from the subordinate social classes in Ferozepur district were 'extremely perturbed' about Turkey and consulting their local *maulvis* on whether or not to wage a *jihad*. Even staunch loyalists were condemning the government. Unless 'early action' was taken 'religious frenzy' could 'assume dangerous forms' since 'the whole country and even the villages' were being told by the newspapers that 'the Christian Government [was] bent on crushing Islam'.[55]

Not content with leading from the margins, many Urdu newspaper editors attended meetings in key cities, small towns and remote districts to educate

[51]Extract from Bombay Abstract, 17 May 1919, *SPPAI*, 31 May 1919, vol. xli, no. 22, pp. 248–9.

[52]*SPPAI*, 5 July 1919, vol. xli, no. 26, p. 311.

[53]Shahzadi to Saifuddin Kitchlew, 25 May 1919, intercepted letter in *SPPAI*, 14 June 1919, vol. xli, no. 24, p. 279.

[54]Extract of Bombay Abstract, 21 June 1919, *SPPAI*, 19 July 1919, vol. xli, no. 28, p. 357.

[55]*SPPAI*, 20 September 1919, vol. xli, no. 37, p. 494.

Muslims on the issue of the Turkish *khilafat*. With the Ali brothers, Azad and Zafar Ali Khan still in detention, a second string of leaders was making its presence felt through *khilafat* committees and the Jamiat-ul-Ulema-i-Hind. In addition, various *anjumans* had mushroomed all over India with the aim of propagating Islam and whipping up support for Turkey.

By 21 September 1919 when the Muslim League sponsored-All-India Muslim Conference met at Lucknow to chalk out a joint Muslim programme, lesser known individuals and organizations had succeeded in mobilizing opinion on the *khilafat*. Disagreements on who should preside signposted the perennial Muslim quandary over who was to lead and who was to follow. Over a thousand participants, including 300 delegates from outside UP, were split on whether to take the Raja of Mahmudabad's advice and humbly petition the government or join Abdul Bari in a mass agitation. Amidst expressions of remorse over Muslims killing their co-religionists and being poorly rewarded by the British, Bari triumphed easily. Muslim sovereignty directly linked to the Ottoman Sultan was a dominant motif. Mahbub-ul-Haq of Burdwan wanted 'the Muslim races to be made autonomous under the suzerainty of the Sultan'. Others could not conceive of the *khilafat* without control over the holy places.

Sections of the audience wept profusely when Sulayman Nadwi described the conference as 'a house of mourning' where Muslims were 'crav[ing] shelter for the remnant of Islamic culture and moral and material grandeur'. They could either become 'homeless like the Jews' or wake up and 'change their hopeless and degrading condition'. Invoking the crusades, Nadwi reminded his co-religionists that the holy lands, 'flooded with the blood of their ancestors', were where the 'bones of their forefathers were buried'.[56] A collection of poems entitled *Zakhm-i-Jigar*, or the wounded soul, by Maulvi Aqil-ur-Rahman urged Muslims to agitate against European injustices and Greek aggression against Turkey.[57] The conference concluded with a series of predictable resolutions on the *khilafat* and the holy places of Islam. An All-India Khilafat Committee was established with headquarters in Bombay. Those eager to escalate the agitation had their moment when the delegates voted to hold an all-India *khilafat* day on 17 October 1919. Despite appeals for Hindu support, it was Muslims who carried the day with prayers, fasts and a *hartal*. It was altogether an impressive display of the increasing capacity of Muslim leaders to reach out to a wider audience. The effort also helped identify areas of more muted support which were targeted for heightened propaganda in the aftermath.

In parts of the Punjab, such as Amritsar, where Muslims remained relatively unenthused, local *maulvis* tried stirring emotions to awaken the spirit through

[56]*SPPAI*, 11 October 1919, vol. xli, no. 40, pp. 548–52.
[57]Ibid.

khutbas at mosques and street preaching in sparkling Urdu. As a prelude to holding a League session in the city, the district organization sprang into action with speakers declaring that the time had come for Indians to demand their rights. Pro-Congress Muslims tried shaming Muslims into joining the agitation by likening them to pawns on the government's chessboard and dispelling the impression that the Congress was a Hindu movement. Others equated the Muslim League with Islam, billing those opposed to it as infidels. One of the loudest and most effective voices to emerge on the Amritsar scene at this stage was that of Maulana Ataullah Shah Bukhari (1891–1961), a Deobandi by choice, who had an exceptional way with words.[58] Bringing his special touch to bear upon an otherwise staid meeting of the district League, Bukhari threatened to murder the Sharif of Mecca since a Muslim was obliged to kill anyone who rebelled against the lawful *khalifa*. By far the most memorable of his statements was that no Muslim could let 'persons fed on bacon and liquor to walk in streets where their Holy Prophet [had] lived and walked'.[59]

While the *maulanas* were on a rampage in Amritsar, Mian Fazl-i-Husain (1877–1936) and Muhammad Iqbal were addressing meetings in Lahore urging the boycott of the peace celebrations scheduled by the government in December. Iqbal told a gathering outside Mochi Gate that the principle of self-determination was not an invention of the Peace Conference but originated with the Muslims who had to remain self-reliant, make sacrifices and trust in God. The meeting concluded with the formation of the city Khilafat Committee with Fazl-i-Husain as president and Iqbal as secretary.[60] It was a short-lived association with the *khilafat* for the two men, both of whom withdrew from the limelight once Gandhi ensconced himself at the helm of the movement.

The Mahatma was well poised to steal the mantle of leadership of the first organized mass movement of Indian Muslims. In November 1919 he attended the All-India Khilafat Conference in Delhi where one-third of the participants were Hindu. Muslims from UP dominated the proceedings to the exclusion

[58]One of his biographers portrays him as a man of extraordinary spiritual understanding and worldly knowledge gained from personal experience. A descendant of the great spiritual leader Khwajah Baqi Allah of Delhi, Ataullah Shah Bukhari was never educated at Deoband. But he considered himself a *mujahid* of Deoband and never failed to uphold its cause. A master of Punjabi and its Seriaki variant, he mesmerized mass audiences in the Punjab for hours on end with the power and poetry of his oratory. He is estimated to have given ten thousand speeches in his 26-year-long struggle to banish the British from India. (Shorish Kashmiri, *Syed Ataullah Shah Bukhari: Swanah wa Fikar* (third edition), Lahore, Mutbuat-i-Chitan, 1994, pp. 38, 50–1.)

[59]*SPPAI*, 29 November 1919, vol. xli, no. 46, p. 669.

[60]*SPPAI*, 20 December 1919, vol. xli, no. 49, pp. 720–1.

of all except Gandhi who used more stick than carrot to check their influence. At his behest, the resolution on non-cooperation did not include the boycott of English goods. He also vetoed efforts to link the grievances of the Punjab with the *khilafat* agitation to secure Hindu cooperation. When the opposition tried making the principle of majority opinion the basis of decisions, Gandhi 'cowed his opponents into submission' by threatening to resign. He insisted that the *khilafat* was a Hindu question because it mattered to Indian Muslims. In a line which did not endear him to his co-religionists, he ruled out the option of trading Hindu support with Muslim renunciation of cow slaughter. This drew the approbation of Abdul Bari who said that 'Gandhi had converted him to opposition to cow sacrifice'. Showing political acumen, the Muslim divine gave the newly accepted principle of conscientious objection in Europe an Islamic turn, thus avoiding the charge of sedition. Serving a government which 'compelled them to become infidels' was worse than death. Muslims had to decide whether they wanted to become *kafirs* by killing their own kind or remaining true to their faith.[61]

Identifying what constituted Muslimness was the main preoccupation of the top- and middle-ranking leaders, resulting in some marvellous elisions of Islamic exclusivism and universalism. In Amritsar where preparations were underway for the holding of simultaneous sessions of the Congress and the Muslim League, the irrepressible Ataullah Shah Bukhari told a meeting at a local mosque that it was not enough to be Muslim. A Muslim was merely a follower while a *momin* was a 'firm believer and sincere lover of God'. If Muslims became *momins*, the whole world would be at their feet. Continuing his vicious attacks on the Sharif of Mecca, Ataullah announced that given the conditions in Arabia where a renegade from Islam was in command, *haj* would be invalid for Muslims.[62] On another occasion, Ataullah donned the hat of Islamic universalism in the true sense of the word when he declared that Muslims and Hindus were brothers as they were 'descendants of the same Adam and Eve created by God'. There was at present 'no distinction between Hindus and Muslims, as both had shaved off their beards'.[63]

While differing from Ataullah on many counts, Saifuddin Kitchlew was also interested in strengthening cooperation with Hindus by underplaying Muslim exclusiveness. He told an audience at Allahabad that for 150 years efforts had been made to separate Hindus and Muslims. And this despite the fact that most Muslims were of Aryan descent. Kitchlew spoke at length about the ancient glory and culture of India and Islam which had taught the principle of republicanism and democracy for the last thirteen hundred years. The Aryans and their Muslim descendants had established a rule of sympathy

[61] Ibid., pp. 716–18.
[62] Ibid., p. 724.
[63] *SPPAI*, 3 January 1920, vol. xlii, no.1, p. 15.

with the inhabitants of the subcontinent. By contrast, 'the Europeans merely come and take money and go back again'. He regretted that Muslims had not participated in the Holi festivities. It was their duty to do so since Hindus were supporting the *khilafat*. After bundling religion, culture and politics together, Kitchlew betrayed his own ideology by telling a rapt audience that 'every Hindu and Muhammadan should become a Bolshevist'.[64]

All arguments at this stage aimed at fostering cooperation with Hindus and weakening Muslim loyalty to the government. In the Punjab, memories of the April disturbances and the excesses of the martial law administration provided 'handy tools to stir up popular feeling'. With most of the leading politicians vegetating in jail, extra-provincial patriots arrived in droves to lend the needed stimulus. The setting up of a government commission to investigate the recent troubles came as 'a climax to lower substantially the prestige of the Englishman' in this most loyal of provinces.[65] There was a distinct 'change in the tone and discipline of educational institutions, a newly found rudeness on the part of the masses towards the officials of Government' as well as 'a general attitude of discontent and sullenness among all classes of people'.[66]

In December 1919, the Congress, the Muslim League, the All-India Khilafat Committee and the Jamiat-ul-Ulema-i-Hind met simultaneously in Amritsar. It was a rare spectacle of Indian unity with more people attending the Congress and the League session than ever before. The recently released Ali brothers gave an emotional tenor to the League's proceedings. Shaukat Ali wept while recounting how Muslim sepoys had 'degraded themselves' for a mere Rs 10 to Rs 12 per mensem to fight against Turkey. An impassioned Mohamed Ali asserted that 'Government did not belong to anybody but to God alone'. Muslims were 'the subjects of God and not of Great Britain'.[67] These utterances of Muslim autonomy from temporal authority were being made from the platform of a party which had not only 'become a mere appendage of the Congress' but seemed 'content to play second fiddle' to its better-organized counterpart. The meeting marked the metamorphosis of the League from a party priding itself as the vehicle of Islam to one counselling Muslims to give up cow sacrifice. Yet the merging of the League and the Congress barely disguised the continuing differences. While speakers used the Congress podium to dilate on the virtues of Indian nationalism and the ills of British oppression, the League session was infused with the spirit of Islamic universalism. There was talk of *jihad* and, following Bari, emphasis on 'the duty of every true Mussalman to choose between God and the Government'.[68]

[64]Extract, UP Abstract, 6 March 1920, *SPPAI*, 20 December 1919, vol. xli, no. 49, p. 188.

[65]The findings were published as a *Memorandum on Disturbances in the Punjab*.

[66]*SPPAI*, 10 January 1920, vol. xlii, no. 2, p. 42.

[67]*SPPAI*, 31 January 1920, vol. xlii, no. 5, pp. 69–70.

[68]*SPPAI*, 10 January 1920, vol. xlii, no. 2, pp. 42–3.

Anti-British feelings supplied the common thread to two otherwise distinct meetings. A noticeable feature of the League session was the presence of the 'poor' as well as students and shopkeepers. The spirit was 'fanatical and fiercely *anti*-Government'. British officialdom was loathe to 'admit the wonderful cleverness of the Congress manipulator' who had used the 'ferment over the *khilafat* question to estrange Muslim feeling from the Government' and the 'unscrupulous tactics' of Islamic universalists who had 'succeeded in giving a religious colouring to a mundane problem'. The Amritsar Congress was equally unique. Catering to an audience containing large numbers of women, villagers and *zamindars*, speeches abusing the colonial masters were given in the regional vernacular. A popular Punjabi song of the time gloated over the Turkish successes:

Ghazi Kamal Pasha's arrows are fantastic
Killing Greek goats like Muslim butchers.[69]

To the agents of the colonial state the gatherings advertised the 'waking of a new spirit in the land'. Not only had the 'people's point of view ... changed' but 'their aspirations ha[d] undergone a striking expansion' which would 'require both tact and firmness to keep within reasonable bounds'.[70]

The vitriolic tone of the vernacular press was impressing the 'minds of the townsfolk' to such an extent that it could be said that 'every newspaper reader [was] an extremist'.[71] By the beginning of 1920 unlikely individuals were asking Muslims to forsake cow slaughter in return for the support Hindus were lending to the *khilafat* movement. As Ataullah explained, 'no power in the world' could force Muslims to give up their religious obligations. Abstaining from cow sacrifice was 'due only to their love for the Hindus' who should come forward and settle, once and for all, disputes over the Muslim call to prayer. Other pro-Congress Muslims propagated giving up cow sacrifice from 'an Indian national point of view'.[72]

On visiting the province, the Mahatma chided Punjabis for misinterpreting the meaning of *satyagraha*. If banks and churches had not been burnt and people not killed, there would have been no martial law. In his inimitable way Gandhi tried placing the idea of Hindu–Muslim conviviality into perspective. He 'strongly deprecated' the notion prevalent in certain quarters that 'inter-dining and inter-marrying were a necessary adjunct to Hindu–

[69]*Ghazi Mustafa Pasha Kamal dey teeran door bullayan*
     Kar bakray Unani halal dey beybadaang qasayan.
     (Cited in Janbaz Mirza, *Karavan-i-Ahrar*, Lahore: Maktabah-i-Tabsirah, 1975–83 [in eight volumes], vol. i, p. 415.)
[70]*SPPAI*, 10 January 1920, vol. xlii, no. 2, p. 43.
[71]*SPPAI*, 14 February 1920, vol. xlii, no. 7, p. 109.
[72]*SPPAI*, 31 January 1920, vol. xlii, no. 5, p. 76.

Muslim unity'. The British and the Germans despite interacting socially were the deadliest of enemies. There was no point in 'outward fraternity and inward aggression'. True union was imperative for India's independence, but could not be achieved 'at the expense of religious observances'.[73] This was just the sort of argument deployed by local *mullahs* opposing the anti-cow sacrifice lobby. After Friday prayers in Amritsar, Maulvi Abdus Salam told one thousand Muslim worshippers to launch a *jihad* against Gandhi and his supporters for interfering in their religion by demanding the abandonment of cow sacrifice. The martial law arrests of the past year had furnished ample evidence of 'the treachery of Hindus', who conveniently 'blame[d] the Muslims ... to save their own brothers'. In the *maulvi's* opinion, God forbade Muslims to befriend those who did not believe in the Quranic message. Opposition to Hindus, therefore, was a religious duty.[74]

The power of local *mullahs* with only a rudimentary knowledge of Islamic precepts was a double-edged sword which could be blunted only by their intellectual superiors in the religious hierarchy. By January 1920, Maulana Azad was back in circulation after a three and a half year internment. He soon established himself as one of the leading theoreticians of the *khilafat* movement, overshadowing Bari's influence in certain quarters. While Azad focused on providing a religious justification for combining the *khilafat* with Indian nationalism, Mohamed Ali spent the better part of 1920 pleading the case of Muslim 'religious rights' with the British public.[75] It was a fitting division of labour between two men of quite different dispositions. Looking to strengthen Mohamed Ali's hand, Shaukat Ali, Abdul Bari and Azad urged Gandhi to sanction another all-India *hartal*. It was only reluctantly that the Mahatma gave his approval. Held on 19 March 1920, the all-India *khilafat* day was a paler version of the two *hartals* in April and October 1919. Punjabi Hindus were less sympathetic. In the smaller towns the *hartal* went unobserved. Incensed at being snubbed so soon after they had warmly embraced their compatriots, Muslims in parts of the province advised their co-religionists to sever all links with Hindus.[76] Keeping up the semblance of cross-communitarian unity while pushing the cause of the *khilafat* now required a more delicate balancing of tactical means and strategic goals.

Striking for Rights: Hijrat or Non-cooperation

Needing new and imaginative ways to shore up support for the *khilafat* and non- cooperation, which had yet to receive the imprimatur of either the All-India Khilafat Committee or Gandhi, Muslims prompted by Azad's theological

[73]*SPPAI*, 14 February 1920, vol. xlii, no. 7, pp. 134–6.
[74]*SPPAI*, 13 March 1920, vol. xlii, no.11, p. 180.
[75]See M.Naeem Qureshi, *Mohamed Ali's Khilafat Delegation to Europe (February-October 1920)*, Karachi: Pakistan Historical Society, 1980.
[76]*SPPAI*, 3 April 1920, vol. xlii, no.14, p. 212.

arguments began dabbling with the idea of *hijrat* as a substitute for *jihad*. A protest against the British curtailing their religious rights, the proposal to leave India raises intriguing questions about Muslim notions of identity and legitimate sovereignty. Taken at face value, the willingness of an estimated sixty thousand Muslims[77] to migrate seems to indicate their insufficient attachment to India. More than one scholar has attributed the *hijrat* drive to the pervasiveness of religious sentiments among Indian Muslims.[78] It is scarcely possible to deny the religious aspects of the movement. The motivations and composition of the *muhajirin* or refugees who abandoned home and hearth for an uncertain future in Muslim Afghanistan deserves better explanation. The fact that it was Azad, backed by the Jamiat-ul-Ulema-i-Hind, who issued the *fatwa* declaring it an 'Islamic obligation' for Muslims to 'quit India' might suggest the primacy of religion.[79] But in so far as *hijrat* aimed at highlighting British oppression in India, it was inextricably linked with a conception of rights which though couched in a religious idiom included the entire gamut of civil, political, social and economic entitlements.

One of the main refrains of Mohamed Ali's public speeches in Britain was the paradox of Indians enjoying rights in the metropolis that were denied to them within the juridical limits of the colony. Given the restrictions on civil liberties in India, Mohamed Ali considered himself a subject and not a citizen of the British empire. The right of citizenship was something he might appreciate in Britain, but could not relate to 'in my own country, where I can be interned or imprisoned without charge or trial'. He condemned British officialdom for hypocritically wooing Indians as 'equal partners' to extract sacrifices for war and tyrannizing them for exercising their right of independent opinion in the making of peace. Muslim subjection had 'always been strictly conditional'. If the pledges of 1858 were broken with respect to the *khilafat*, Indian Muslims would not remain loyal to the Crown.[80]

In view of Muslim arguments about the denial of religious liberties, widely defined, the *hijrat* movement was as much about temporal as spiritual matters. The idea is said to have gathered impetus with the return to India in June 1920 of the Sheikh-ul-Hind, Maulana Mahmud-ul-Hasan of Deoband.[81] But

[77]Based on a calculation by Qureshi, 'The "Ulama" of British India and the Hijrat', *MAS*, p. 57.

[78]See, for instance, Minault, *The Khilafat Movement*, p. 107.

[79]Azad's *fatwa* is cited in Mushir U Haq, *Muslim Politics in Modern India, 1857–1947*, Lahore: Book Traders (no date), p. 124.

[80]Mohamed Ali's speech in London, 22 April 1920 in Iqbal (ed.), *Select Writings and Speeches of Maulana Mohamed Ali*, pp. 287–90.

[81]As Mohamed Ali put it, the Maulana had 'migrated to Mecca, the sanctuary where, at least, Muslim conscience is expected to be safe from outrage and coercion'. (See Mohamed Ali's speech in London, 23 March 1920, ibid., p. 270.) On returning to India from jail in Malta, with his student Maulana Husain Ahmad Madani, the

already by April second rank leaders were mooting the question in many small towns and cities in India. In February 1920 the Amir of Afghanistan with an eye on gaining leverage in peace negotiations following the Anglo-Afghan war, offered refuge to Muslims and Hindus wishing to migrate from India. To prove his bona fides to the Hindus, the Amir banned cow slaughter within his domains. The British failure to call the bluff was a tactical error since the Afghan sovereign had no intention of honouring the 'invitation'.[82]

Some Indian Muslims saw in the Afghan offer an opportunity to embarrass the British. There was much excitement as newspapers dilated on the significance of the Amir's speech. In April the Khilafat Workers' Conference met in Delhi to discuss non-cooperation. It was here that the idea of *hijrat* was first debated publicly. Prominent *ulema* were conspicuous by their absence. The editor of the *Dastoor* invoked the principles of equality and liberty while blasting the anti-Islamic policies of the raj. The meeting concluded with the majority favouring *jihad* and *hijrat*.[83] All that was required to legitimize the migration was a *fatwa* from a respected religious divine.

Significantly, Maulana Abdul Bari was not enthused with the prospect of trainloads of Indian Muslims disappearing into the wilds of Afghanistan. His brief telegraphic comment on *hijrat* being consistent with Islamic principles was leaked to the press and flaunted as a *fatwa*. With its antecedents in the famous *fatwa* of Shah Abdul Aziz in the eighteenth century, Bari's slip of the pen was seized upon with consummate zeal. The *maulana's* subsequent clarification that *hijrat* was commendable but not mandatory exposed him to a barrage of criticism from the Ahl-i-Hadith.[84] With Bari refusing to retract, Azad came to the aid of those championing *hijrat* by issuing a *fatwa* sometime between the end of April and early May 1920.[85] By then rabble-rousers like Ataullah Shah Bukhari had given up their initial resistance to the idea, seeing in it a stick with which to challenge the British guns in the Punjab.

An analysis of the *hijrat* propaganda sheds light on one of the more fascinating and intricate layers in the nexus between identity and sovereignty in Muslim consciousness. The provinces most affected were the Punjab, UP, Sind and later the Frontier Province where local *maulvis* used the network of mosques to frighten Muslims with hellfire if they did not flee the accursed rule of the British. Bukhari's theatrics in the Punjab easily take pride of place for their entertainment value. In late April he told an audience at Hoshiarpur

---

Sheikh-ul-Hind was elected president of the Jamiat-ul-Ulema-i-Hind. Among his more notable deeds was laying the foundation stone of the Jamia Millia University in Delhi. (Kashmiri, *Syed Ataullah Shah Bukhari*, pp. 52–3.)

[82]Qureshi, 'The 'Ulama' of British India and the Hijrat', *MAS*, p. 45.

[83]Extract, Delhi Abstract, 24 April 1920, *SPPAI*, 15 May 1920, vol. xlii, no.19, pp. 296–9.

[84]See Qureshi, 'The 'Ulama' of British India and the Hijrat', *MAS*, pp. 47–9.

[85]Ibid., p. 50, fn. 46.

that all Muslims should wear beards lest the Afghans invade India and mistakenly kill them as Christians. He urged Muslims to leave their wives and children under Hindu protection and go off to Afghanistan in silence as they were destined to return 'shouting victory'. Even Hindus could perform *hijrat*. Anticipating the future, Bukhari predicted that if the *khilafat* fell, 'the English would make Muhammadans work as sweepers' and use the 'Holy Places as stables for their horses and donkeys'[86]

Here was a loaded allegory designed to convey to illiterate Muslim audiences the likely effects on their social status if the *khilafat* was dismantled. Muslim identity and rights were intrinsically connected to the temporal and spiritual sovereignty of the *khalifa*. 'In the absence of a *Khalifa*', Bukhari announced, 'there cannot be any Muhammadans' because like the scum of the earth a 'sweeper has none to whom he can look for support'. *Hijrat* was necessary for Muslim self-preservation. They could not launch a *jihad* since martial law had taken away even their *lathis*. By emigrating they might secure German munitions in Afghanistan and be better placed to declare a *jihad*. Sacrificing their all for the future glory of Islam, Muslims should 'go on caravans, bare-headed and bare-footed ... not expect grapes, but live on barley and curb [their] appetites'. Only six lakh were needed for the purpose, but an angel had told him that twelve lakh should be sent. Declaring his own inability to leave India where his valuable services were required, Bukhari totted up the figures required in Kabul to three million—a nightmare for the Afghan authorities. Muslims who sat twiddling their thumbs might as well 'throw the *Quran* into the river' along with themselves since it was 'better that you were drowned than suffered so to live'.[87]

This was a powerful play on the imagination of Muslims whose fragile livelihoods were just a touch short of the status of the proverbial sweeper. By late May the Delhi *muhajirin* office was publicizing the Amir's generous promise to confer social welfare benefits on non-citizens from India. Each migrant would be given free living quarters, eight *jaribs*[88] of revenue-free land for three years, one maund of flour per month and all kinds of work to earn a living.[89] Lured by the prospect of a better standard of living, Muslims hard hit by the cumulative effects of wartime and post-war economic distress responded enthusiastically to the call for *hijrat*.

Even as several lower- and middle-class Muslims began toying with the idea of abandoning their homes, there were others bewildered by the proposition. Some confessed their inability to perform this religious duty for private reasons. There was consolation for them since the *hijrat* issue had created a serious breach in the ranks of the leadership. Saifuddin Kitchlew, Bukhari's *bete noir* in

[86]*SPPAI*, 15 May 1920, vol. xlii, no.19, pp. 300–1.
[87]Ibid., pp. 306–7 and *SPPAI*, 22 May 1920, vol. xlii, no. 20, p. 328.
[88]One *jarib* is equal to sixty yards of land.
[89]*SPPAI*, 19 June 1920, vol. xlii, no. 24, p. 376.

Amritsar, proposed non-cooperation as an alternative to the religious necessity of migrating. If India's eight crore Muslims could be accommodated in Afghanistan, they should all go there with their movable property.[90] Since *hijrat* had not been sanctioned by the majority of the *ulema*, he advised Muslims not to follow any single individual. Kitchlew was promptly contradicted by the pugnacious Bukhari who reiterated his wish to migrate and said that '*before doing so, he would, if he could, kill three or four English in their bungalows*'.[91]

Such bravado was difficult for others to emulate. Most of the top- and middle-ranking leadership were at best ambivalent about the wisdom of quitting India in God's name. On 14 May 1920 the announcement of the peace terms for Turkey showed how little the *khilafat* agitation had influenced Britain's larger strategic calculations. Affronted, the *khilafatists* wanted to scuttle British rule in India. As the seasoned political agitator Maulana Zafar Ali Khan, now back in action, told an audience at Saharanpur in UP, *hijrat* was 'not wise' at a time when boycott and non-cooperation were on the anvil.[92] But with people lining up at railway stations to cheer trainloads of *muhajirin* from Sind, dismally poor cultivators or *haris* in the main,[93] even Zafar Ali changed his tune. At a small meeting in Mochi Gate, the political nerve centre of Lahore, he likened wealthy Muslims to 'lickspittles' who entertained government officials but went numb in the hand when it came to matters of religion like the *khilafat* and *hijrat*.[94] Becoming an ardent supporter of *hijrat*, he declared that 'if the king ... practised oppression on his subjects, it was their duty to obtain redress by ... going to the country of a just king'.[95]

The emergence of *hijrat* as an alternative to *jihad* and non-cooperation flushed out class, regional and ideological differences among Muslims, underlining the role of individual autonomy in judging how best to contribute to collective activity. As the more prominent leaders wavered, neither endorsing nor defusing the *hijrat* fervour, tens of thousands of *muhajirin* drawn from the lower social classes began converging on the Afghan border. Against this backdrop, the All-India Khilafat Committee met at Allahabad in early June to dot the i's and cross the t's of the non-cooperation programme. There was much consternation about the consequences of *hijrat* on the Hindu population if the *muhajirin* returned to India with an Afghan or a Bolshevik army. Dr Ansari thought Hindus were justifiably apprehensive about an Afghan invasion; those emigrating were among the

[90]*SPPAI*, 22 May 1920, vol. xlii, no. 20, pp. 319–20.

[91]*SPPAI*, 19 June 1920, vol. xlii, no. 24, pp. 376–8 (my emphasis).

[92]Ibid., p. 382.

[93]For an account of how the *pirs* of Sind played on the economic insecurities and religious sentiments of the landless poor to get them to perform *hijrat*, see Ansari, *Sufi Saints and State Power*, pp. 88–9.

[94]*SPPAI*, 31 July 1920, vol. xlii, no. 30, p. 481.

[95]Ibid., p. 482.

most spirited and should stay in India to make a success of the non-cooperation movement.[96]

With the majority of the Congress Committee at Benares opposing non-cooperation, Gandhi took a middle-of-the-road position. He offered to support the items on the non-cooperation programme relating to the renunciation of titles, boycott of the reformed councils and resignation from government service. The remaining two called on Indians to resign from police and military service and refuse to pay taxes. This was less than what Gandhi had agreed upon. Abdul Bari 'interrupted him fiercely'; he had with great forbearance 'endured the behaviour of his co-religionists who had taunted him for having joined hands with *Kafirs*'. If Gandhi continued hedging his bets on non-cooperation, Bari swore to 'make up his mind not to listen to him anymore'. Upon being accused of breaking his word, Gandhi demurred. He had only expressed his 'personal opinion'. While some 'friends' favoured a more limited non-cooperation programme, he was ready to go further.[97]

Gandhi's compromise could not iron out the creases in the grand coalition of Home Rule Leaguers, Congress Hindus and the *ulema*–politician combine among Muslims. Annie Besant backed by Madan Mohan Malaviya was solidly opposed to non-cooperation while Bepin Chandra Pal and Satyamurti considered mere expressions of 'sympathy for the Muhammadans ... a mockery and a hoax'. Malaviya wanted Muslims to place their case for non-cooperation before the Hindus when the Congress met at Calcutta. Motilal Nehru concurred, appealing for more time to deliberate. A delirious Shaukat Ali stated that Muslims were ready to go it alone if Hindus refused to cooperate with them. When Jamnadas Dwarka Das accused him of intimating that Hindu opinion was irrelevant for the Muslims, Shaukat Ali saw tactical sense in backing down.[98]

The Central Khilafat Committee's manifesto reiterated the importance of preserving an understanding with Hindus. Muslims wanted to serve their religion and the country of their birth at the same time. They did 'not desire to oust England and introduce a Muhammadan or any other power to rule over India'. While Muslims wanted to 'realize the highest national aspiration in association with the British', they would end that connection if it 'hamper[ed] India's advance' or 'affront[ed] cherished religious sentiments'. Muslims would work alongside Hindus but 'reserve[d] the right to take such other and further steps' enjoined by their religion.[99] If an Islamic cause could bring Hindus and Muslims together, then it could also provide the basis for something very close to equality of status.

The *khilafatists* were fighting for a permanent place in the constellation of

[96]Extract, UP Abstract, 12 June 1920, *SPPAI*, 19 June 1920, vol. xlii, no. 24, pp. 383–4.

[97]Ibid., p. 384.

[98]Ibid., pp. 385–6.

[99]Ibid., pp. 386–8.

nationalist forces based on an articulation of identity and sovereignty that was uniquely their own. If the bond with God released them from the fetters of an unsympathetic government, then that primary association could also provide the pretext for breaking with Gandhi and the Congress if their 'religious rights' were not safeguarded. This has been interpreted all too easily as religious zeal, pure and simple. Few have actually ventured to explain what religion meant in a context where Indian nationalism and Islamic universalism were not deemed to be antithetical alternatives. In making tactical use of Islamic idioms, an improbable coalition of Muslim propagandists were strategically aiming at the whole question of rights for a group claiming not only a distinctive identity but also propounding a conception of sovereignty which lay outside the narrowly defined notion of western nationalism that was coming to dominate the Congress. If a common religious identity was the one irrefutable facet of the Muslim minority accepted by the British and the Hindu 'majority' as legitimate, then it could become the mainspring for claiming the right to seek location in as well as refashion the discourse on the Indian nation.

This explains why a diehard anti-imperialist like Hasrat Mohani saw no contradiction in letting a Muslim power invade India to expel the British. If that were to happen, Indian Muslims would 'join forces in order to drive away the enemies of Islam'. Mohani's statement created a sensation. Malaviya, a nationalist of unimpeachable credentials, thought it was unconstitutional and anti-government and demanded a full explanation of the Muslim attitude towards an invasion. Outraged by the insinuation of Muslim disloyalty, Shaukat Ali shook his fist at the *pandit*. The holy places of Muslims had been taken away and attempts were being made to obliterate Islam. If a Muslim invader came to India 'to punish British injustice and high-handedness the Musalmans would join hands with them'. He then 'burst into tears and sat down'. A more composed Zafar Ali Khan argued that a Muslim invasion of India would not be against Hindu interests. If this came to pass, Indians would join hands and support the invaders 'with good intentions, whether they were Afghans or Bolsheviks'.[100]

Lala Lajpat Rai, a key voice among Punjabi Hindus, said Muslims were deceiving themselves if they believed 'Hindus were ready to give them unlimited help'. The question before the Hindus was 'purely political' while for the Muslims it was 'first a religious question and only indirectly political'. Hindus were ready to assist Muslims in the interests of India. But they could never tolerate an invasion and would 'counteract the dangerous policy adopted by the Muslims'. Raza Ali from UP was 'at a loss to understand what mischievous devil induced the Hindus to fear a foreign invasion'. They were baiting Muslims for something that was 'not coming at all'. Fearing the near collapse of the entire edifice, Seth

[100]Ibid., pp. 388–9.

Ahmad Mian Chotani of the *khilafat* movement from Bombay, tried assuaging both sides by adopting the usual nationalist Muslim position. On matters concerning co-religionists in other countries, 'they were Musalmans first and Indians afterwards' but in matters closer to home 'they were Indians first and Musalmans afterwards'.[101]

It was a close shave which clearly spelt out the distance separating the various protagonists of a single Indian nation. Gandhi reassured Muslims of Hindu support. He did not agree with either *hijrat* or *jihad*, but would not stand in the way if Muslims wanted to go beyond the non-cooperation programme. The price for his unflinching faith in Muslims was a declaration that they would proceed with non-cooperation irrespective of Hindu support. To his co-religionists, the Mahatma's advice was to continue supporting Muslims 'as long as they were certain that the cause of India as a nation was not in jeopardy'. He was less conciliatory when it came to outlining his plans to direct the non-cooperation movement. While consulting with *khilafatist* Muslims, he would pursue his personal directives through 'a Martial Law Committee'. Even Malaviya had expressed satisfaction that the Mahatma was 'leading the Muhammadans'. Gandhi had told the *pandit* that 'it would be a great thing for Hindustan to help Islam and display its tolerance in a just cause'. If the Muslims chose to break away, he would watch their activities in silence.[102]

For all the double talk, the Allahabad meeting of the Khilafat Committee endorsed all four stages of the non-cooperation movement which was to commence on 1 August, a month ahead of the special Congress session called to discuss the issue. This was achieved by permitting only the thirty members of the Khilafat Committee to vote although some 150 participants had followed the deliberations. Shaukat Ali who masterminded the final result gave the press a 'roseate picture of concord and harmony'. Hindu-edited newspapers were unconvinced. The *Leader* of Allahabad noted the hollowness of the claim that the non-cooperation movement had general Hindu–Muslim support. The programme had been 'watered down almost to vanishing point'. Moreover, not a single Hindu had been given a place on Gandhi's special committee.[103]

Whatever the misgivings of influential segments of Hindu opinion, the *khilafatists* had succeeded in creating an illusion of support for non-cooperation.[104] Having retained his veto power, Gandhi insisted that the *khilafat* was a 'righteous' and 'sincere religious cause'. It was 'an opportunity for ... Hindus' to 'prove faithful to the Muhammadans and to bridge the gap that once existed between the two communities'. Short of killing anyone,

[101] Ibid., p. 390.

[102] Ibid.

[103] Ibid., p. 396.

[104] For an account of the uneasiness among Gandhi's Hindu supporters see B.R. Nanda, *Gandhi: Pan-Islamism, Imperialism and Nationalism*, Delhi: Oxford University Press, 1989, especially chapters eleven and twelve.

which his religion did not permit, Gandhi was ready to 'walk side by side with ... Muhammadan friends'.[105] It was not going to be a pleasant stroll for the Mahatma. Shaukat |Ali made no bones about the fact that 'lay[ing] down their lives and kill[ing] others' was a religious obligation for Muslims while the 'Mahatma's religion taught him to sacrifice his own life without doing any harm to the opponent'.[106]

This left the Mahatma acutely vulnerable to the charge of giving a moral face to his opportunistic alliance with the *khilafatists* and endangering the cause of Indian nationalism. But if Gandhi the moralist had not abandoned his will to persuasion, Gandhi the dictator was determined to stamp his personal authority on the non-cooperation movement. He had emerged from the Allahabad session as the undisputed leader of the *khilafatists* and was not ready to throw away the advantage in the vain hope of winning accolades from his co-religionists. Touring the Punjab to muster support for non-cooperation and his impending bid to seize the leadership of the Congress, Gandhi accepted that he was 'termed mad by many public men in India'. But such people had forgotten the incidents of the previous year. As for the general public, their excitement was like the 'effervescence of soda water'. He told a gathering of 20,000 outside Delhi Gate in Lahore that the Muslims were not going to get their way on the *khilafat* by 'crying like babies' or flying the *hijrat* kite. They would have to make sacrifices without committing any excesses.

Shaukat Ali who accompanied him during the jaunt through the Punjab asked Muslims to 'look upon Mahatma Gandhi as the King of India and their Ruler'. But the uncrowned sovereign of India could be a trifle too temperamental. In Jhelum, Gandhi refused to leave his train compartment to address a huge crowd that had gathered to give him a thunderous welcome. Disgusted more than tantalized by the Mahatma's sudden recourse to *purdah*, the Punjabi *ryot* went berserk. Terms of 'open abuse were flung' at the great man who instead of invigorating support for non-cooperation 'thoroughly dampened the spirits of the people'.[107] Gandhi in the Punjab was less than a resounding success. His choppy Hindustani could not send Punjab's rural populace into an agitational whirl.

This left the field wide open to Gandhi's self-appointed propagandists, men like Ataullah Shah Bukhari and Zafar Ali Khan for instance who could combine Urdu with Punjabi in speeches so intemperate as to put the leader's message to shame. While Zafar Ali made a pretence of not needling the authorities unnecessarily, Bukhari harangued and taunted the alien rulers with feminine epithets like 'Bibi Britannia'. As a rule, speakers played on religious sentiments in the expectation of moving people to tears, if not organized action of the sort

---

[105]*SPPAI*, 31 July 1920, vol. xlii, no. 30, pp. 472–3.
[106]*SPPAI*, 7 August 1920, vol. xlii, no. 31, p. 494.
[107]Ibid., p. 500.

Gandhi had in mind.[108] An example of this was a long poem published in the form of a pamphlet celebrating the awakening of Muslims on the *khilafat* and lauding the Turks as the ultimate defenders of Islam with scarcely a mention of India or Hindus.[109]

Even if it were possible, which it was not, the Mahatma-turned-commander-in-chief of the *satyagraha* campaign had no reason to curb his foot soldiers from excesses in the name of religion. In many districts of the Punjab where the networks of collaboration were firmly in place, the *khilafatists* won over the populace and, in this way, instilled the fear of God in the hearts of local officials of the colonial state. In Attock, Zafar Ali Khan's speech sufficed to turn the people on *zaildars*, *lambardars* and *chowkidars*. They were bluntly told to resign their posts, failing which they would be denied admission into mosques and *hujras*. No one would attend their funeral ceremonies and they would face complete excommunication. British officials wryly noted that the 'fear of being termed *kafir* and being ostracized ha[d] shaken almost all the leading men of the district'. The deputy commissioner hoped that the *khilafat* debacle would 'set the dupes of these gentlemen against them', but nevertheless thought they ought to be 'muzzled' before they led British collaborators further astray.[110]

In the Frontier Province where support for *hijrat* was stronger than in the Punjab, colonial officials were stunned by the popular response to what they superciliously regarded as pernicious propaganda. Peshawar district saw 'an alarming increase' in those wishing to emigrate to Afghanistan while in certain parts the 'exodus at one time threatened to become a stampede'. The movement also gained support in Hazara, Bannu and Dera Ismail Khan. Between May and August 1920, an estimated 24,000 people 'animated in a high degree by religious enthusiasm' had crossed the border into Afghanistan. There was consolation for the British in the knowledge that 95 per cent of the emigrants were 'ignorant dupes' whose 'religious enthusiasm was stirred to a pitch closely resembling frenzy'. Yet quite a few 'educated men went with their eyes open', convinced that the 'religious oppression of the British and Indian Governments left them no course but to emigrate'.[111] The inspector general of police in Mardan was emphatically of the opinion that the movement was 'purely economic' and had 'started ... before the question of *hijrat* had been mooted at all'.[112]

Expecting an effusive welcome at the Afghan border, many *muhajirin* had

[108]See *SPPAI*, 21 and 28 August 1920, vol. xlii, nos. 33 and 34, pp. 526–7 and 537.

[109]Malik Lal Din Ahmed Qaisar Lahori, *Chand ghon se nikal aiya*, Lahore, 27 July 1920, Urdu D.858, IOL.

[110]*SPPAI*, 4 September 1920, vol. xlii, no. 35, p. 547.

[111]'The Khilafat Movement in the North West Frontier Province', Officials Records of NWFP Tribal Cell, National Documentation Centre [henceforth NDC], Islamabad, p. 4.

[112]Ibid., pp. 4, 70.

sold off their meagre belongings to crafty neighbours for a pittance. Sadly enough, their first brush with Islamic glory came in the form of rapacious Pathan tribesmen who stripped them of the few items in their possession. The tragedy reached a climax when on 9 August 1920 the Amir ordered his officials to stop the flow of immigrants. Their dreams of a better livelihood under Muslim sovereignty shattered, approximately 75 per cent of the *muhajirin* managed to return to India more destitute and desperate than before. Many lost their lives through disease and exhaustion. Those who survived either stayed on in Afghanistan or fanned into Turkey and Russia.[113] Neither the learned divines nor the political agitators are known to have taken any responsibility for this human disaster in the name of Islam.

By the time the non-cooperation programme was formally adopted, the *hijrat* bubble had exploded in the face of its enthusiasts. In August 1920, the Treaty of Sevres put paid to all reasonable hopes of preserving the temporal sovereignty of the *khalifa* over the Arabian peninsula. Doubts about non-cooperation were being aired more forcefully in certain quarters, especially in the Punjab and Bengal, the two provinces where Gandhi had not made the impact he had elsewhere. Yet there was no let up in *khilafatist* support for non-cooperation, vindicating Gandhi's endorsement of their cause. As Gail Minault has correctly noted, continued participation in the anti-imperialist struggle was seen by key Muslim leaders as an opportunity to permanently align their interests with the forces of Indian nationalism.[114] But if proponents of Islamic universalism were indeed keen to preserve and strengthen their bonds with Indian nationalism, what factors prevented them from achieving the goal?

Writing in the *Independent* of Allahabad on the eve of the special Congress session at Calcutta, Bepin Chandra Pal identified the main obstacle to Hindu–Muslim unity.[115] He did not question the 'sincerity of the Hindu solicitude for the integrity and independence of the *khilafat*'. But while Muslims were 'moved by profound religious feelings', Hindu backing for the agitation was actuated by 'no less strong political motives'.[116] The danger was that if the

[113]Qureshi, 'The 'Ulama' of British India and the Hijrat', *MAS*, pp. 57–8.

[114]Minault, *The Khilafat Movement*, pp. 109–10.

[115]For an account of the opposition by Pal and other prominent politicians of Bengal like C.R. Das to the Congress adopting the non-cooperation resolution passed by the Khilafat Committee, see Rajat K. Ray, 'Masses in Politics: The Non-cooperation Movement in Bengal 1920–1922', (*IESHR*), 11:4 (December 1974), pp. 352–8.

[116]Gandhi, however, regarded the *khilafat* claim to be 'just and reasonable' which only derived greater force because it was backed by Muslim 'religious sentiment'. He would have rejected 'any religious doctrine that d[id] not appeal to reason and [wa]s in conflict with morality'. On 'Gandhi's reason' for taking up the *khilafat* cause, see Sugata Bose, 'Nation, Reason and Religion: India's Independence in International Perspective' in *Economic and Political Weekly* (henceforth *EPW*), vol. xxxiii, no. 31, August 1–7, 1998, pp. 2090–7, especially pp. 2093–4 for quotations from Gandhi writing in *Young India*.

khilafat issue could be settled to the satisfaction of the Muslims, 'they would not continue the movement simply for the sake of winning India's freedom'. There was 'a body of non-Muslim opinion ... which look[ed] upon the new friendship between the Indian politicians and the *khilafat* leaders with considerable uneasiness'. Pal detected 'an unpleasant feature in the frequent expressions of gratitude of Muhammadans to Hindus for their support' which 'betray[ed] an inner consciousness of the *absence of identity of interests*, wherein l[ay] the weakness of the whole movement'. For Gandhi to 'force the hand of the Congress' on non-cooperation was not only unjust but 'fatal to the cause of Indian unity and Indian freedom'.[117]

These cautionary words were drowned by impassioned speech making and the bullying tactics by pro-Gandhian *khilafatists* led by Shaukat Ali. At the Calcutta Congress, the moderates were sidelined and the extremists of the *swadeshi* era chastened into going along with the Mahatma.[118] But it was only at the Nagpur Congress in December 1920 that Gandhi managed to deploy the weight of the *khilafatists* to ram his way to complete success.[119] Even C.R. Das who came to Nagpur to oppose Gandhi saw sense in changing tack.[120] Having finally grabbed the Congress trophy, the Mahatma ushered in a new phase of the movement in which the *khilafat* crescent slipped to second place as the nationalist *charkha* became the pre-eminent symbol of anti-imperialist protest. The shift in symbolism, however, was not nearly as transparent as the altered balance of power between *khilafatists* and Gandhian non-cooperators. Instead of pushing Gandhi into taking a position, the *khilafatists* had now to reckon with the conflicting pulls of Islamic universalism and Indian nationalism. Divisions within their own ranks coupled with the strains of building mass support for a boycott of government schools, courts and the reformed councils put the *khilafatists* to a test for which they were not nearly as well equipped as their rhetoric suggested.

Mobilizing support for non-existent rights on the basis of religion was quite different from forcing a broad cross-section of society to make material sacrifices for the political goal of obtaining *swaraj* within a year. This is precisely what had troubled men like Pal who, apart from questioning the timing of non-cooperation, were sceptical of a Hindu–Muslim entente withstanding the pressures of an all-out political struggle against the raj. And indeed, once Gandhi assumed the Congress leadership such reservoirs of goodwill as existed between the two communities dried up in many regions, most notably the Punjab. The

[117]*Independent*, Allahabad, 9 September 1920, *Selections*, L/R/5/95, IOL, p. 305 (my emphasis.)

[118]See Ray, 'Masses in Politics', *IESHR*, pp. 355–9.

[119]For an analysis of the Gandhian takeover see Judith M.Brown, *Gandhi's Rise to Power: Indian Politics 1915-1922*, Cambridge: Cambridge University Press, 1972, pp. 250–304.

[120]Ray, 'Masses in Politics' *IESHR*, pp. 364–7.

interface of God, Government and Gandhi in this Muslim-majority province was rather more fluid given the fragile balance between classes and communities than in UP and Bengal where socio-economic discontentment among a peasantry reeling under the impact of the post-war slump could be channelled to give a respectable face to the non-cooperation movement.

Similar tactics were employed by agitators in the Punjab, but far less successfully than in 1919 or even 1920. One reason for this were the attractions of entering local and provincial councils under the Montagu–Chelmsford reforms. Although the non-cooperation programme had ruled out the possibility, local khilafat committees in the Punjab openly debated the issue. Such meetings often became an occasion to accuse Hindus of defrauding Muslims with the myth of non-cooperation. The anti-cow killing agitation had also lost its thrust with many more Muslims resenting the prohibition. To add to the woes of the agitators, the khilafat committees in the province were rocked with financial scandals and a corresponding decline in the people's willingness to contribute funds. It was apparent that in the Punjab the Congress's formal adoption of non-cooperation had come well after the passing of the anti-imperialist storm.

Unwilling to allow a repetition of the events of 1919, the Punjab administration girded its loins against the non-cooperators. This was not too difficult once the first elections under the 1920 reforms had been held. Pro-government Muslims alleged that the khilafat issue was not 'a religious one but ... a cloak for political agitation'. Government-sponsored publicity leagues sought to 'acquaint the poor villagers with the disadvantages of non-cooperation'. Propagandists invoked Indian history and legends to argue that loyalty to the king was part of the indigenous tradition.[121]

It was to offset such invidious propaganda that in February 1921 Gandhi with Abul Kalam Azad at his side toured the Punjab to revitalize enthusiasm for non-cooperation. Their message was one of open revolt against the government. Azad proclaimed that any Muslim who took up arms against his co-religionist ceased to be a Muslim. So Muslims had to stop enlisting in the army to avoid mixing with their sworn enemies and instead cooperate with Hindus who were their brothers. Embroidering the point with his own preferred imagery, a local Congress leader added that Hindus and Muslims were like Ram and Lakshman and should bring home swaraj in the same way as the two brothers brought Sita back from Lanka. The khilafat was in tatters but Hindus and Muslims had become one and would soon repair the damage done to this most sacred of Muslim institutions. In the meantime, people should demonstrate their lack of confidence in the government by taking their disputes to local panchayats and ignoring the police.[122]

[121] SPPAI, 29 January 1921, vol. xlii, no. 6, pp. 51–2.
[122] SPPAI, 5 March 1921, vol. xlii, no. 9, p. 99.

Punjabi audiences were visibly less interested in the political extravaganzas orchestrated by the Mahatma and his top associates. Azad did not help matters by contemptuously noting that the Punjab was 'lagging behind other provinces in following the policy of non-cooperation'. As Gandhi was learning first hand, insistence on the renunciation of government titles and efforts to raise funds were sorely resented by some Punjabis. In-laws in particular were infuriated over young brides giving away their precious ornaments as donation. In Rohtak the Mahatma was given a rough time by women when he visited the Arya Samaj temple. Some openly 'abused him' for creating so 'much trouble'. One woman who lost her bangle 'accused Gandhi of being the cause of it'.[123] Furious with the response, Azad scolded an unsuspecting audience in Amritsar which had at least taken the trouble of gathering together to cheer the great leader. They were 'not fit to be addressed', he stated imperiously, and had not only 'disgraced the name of their motherland by obeying humiliating orders during martial law' but 'entirely forgotten their Almighty Creator and regarded the present Government as their idol'. Non-cooperation with the government, he told his co-religionists, was a religious duty and friendship with Jews and Christians strictly forbidden.[124]

None of this had a salubrious effect on Punjabi minds caught between the jaws of the government and the Gandhian nutcracker. Rebuking Punjabis for their political backwardness and indiscipline was not the best formula for raising the tempo of Gandhian agitation in the province. In Hoshiarpur the Mahatma's entreaties created an unfavourable impression while the trip to Haryana ended in a fiasco. Upon arriving in Haryana to inaugurate a national school, Gandhi was accosted by a crowd which demanded that he address them by the roadside as they could not pay the entry fees for the meeting. Pandemonium ensued when people were told that they could enter the meeting free of charge. Kasturba Gandhi lost her shoes and had 'the misfortune to stumble and fall in the general excitement'. Events took a turn for the worse when the Mahatma, hailed by two Jat Sikhs as 'his holiness' and their 'saviour', fainted and had to be fanned back to consciousness. After recovering from the shock of such adulation, Gandhi promptly left Haryana without opening the school. In an upbeat mood, police informers thought the Mahatma's visit to the Punjab had been 'beneficial in removing any ideas as to his being a superman'. The more astute observation was that Gandhi's 'oratory ha[d] been called into question and his knowledge of the vernacular ... subject[ed] to adverse criticism'.[125]

Determined to squash the non-cooperation movement, the Punjab administration was busy mopping up the leading trouble makers. In October

[123]Ibid., pp. 101–2.
[124]*SPPAI*, 15 March 1921, vol. xlii, no.10, p. 135.
[125]*SPPAI*, 26 March 1921, vol. xlii, no.11, p. 184.

1920, Zafar Ali Khan had been arrested on charges of sedition. He had made a speech at Hazro, a key recruiting ground, detailing the religious arguments against Muslims serving in the British Indian army. Towards the end of March 1921, the rebarbative Ataullah Shah Bukhari was also put away. With two of their most effective speakers in gaol, the Punjab *khilafatists* were left facing an uphill task. Calls for a *hartal* to protest against Ataullah's incarceration found the Hindus in no mood to oblige. This heightened recriminations between the two communities with Muslims blaming Hindu duplicity for the failure of the strike. The Lahore Khilafat Committee's call to boycott the annual *mela chiraghan* or festival of lights at Shalimar gardens went unheeded with nearly 20,000 people joining in the celebrations.[126] In desperation the *khilafatists* turned to student recruits to sustain interest. But the sight of student agitators patrolling the streets singing national songs of a 'seditious' kind took nothing away from the fact that the non-cooperation movement in the Punjab was proceeding without its former populist spark.[127]

If the movement was losing momentum in the Punjab, there were signs of a bigger crisis looming at the all-India level. Eager to turn non-cooperation into a vehicle for establishing *shariat* rule, and by the way their leadership of Indian Muslims, the *ulema* demanded that the Central Khilafat Committee spell out the parameters of unity with the Hindus according to the religious tenets of Islam. This exposed the fragile basis of the alliance between Muslim politicians and the *ulema*. So long as the focus remained on the *khilafat*, Islamic universalism could find a tactical accommodation with Indian nationalism. But in their determination to commit the *khilafatists* into implementing Islamic law in India, the *ulema* were encroaching upon space which Muslim politicians had never conceded to them. The dilemma was a real one. It was conveniently averted by events in Anatolia where Mustafa Kemal Pasha's forces were locked in grim battle with the Greeks. British sympathy for the Greeks gave the Ali brothers, Abul Kalam Azad and other key *khilafatists* a fresh round of ammunition to blast the government in the name of God without actually renouncing Gandhi.

They had never denied their differences with the Mahatma on the issue of non-violence. With Turkey again confronting real danger, Muslims had to set aside their internal quarrels for the sake of Islamic brotherhood. This was a phase of the non-cooperation movement in which leading *khilafatists*, especially the Ali brothers, in open defiance of Gandhi advocated violence in defence of their religion. In April Mohamed Ali revived the controversy about an Afghan invasion by publicly stating that Indian Muslims would hail such an eventuality. With the British contemplating action against the Ali brothers for intemperate speech-making, Gandhi at Malaviya's insistence intervened

---

[126]*SPPAI*, 9 April 1921, vol. xlii, no.14, p. 244.
[127]*SPPAI*, 23 April 1921, vol. xlii, no.16, p. 273.

in May 1921 to extract a formal apology from them.[128] There was a loud public outcry against the two brothers who in order to avoid another stint in jail were seen to have meekly repented and solemnly promised to adhere strictly to non-violent non-cooperation.

In July 1921, addressing the All-India Khilafat Conference at Karachi, Mohamed Ali vociferously denied that he or his brother had been cowed into making the apology and characterized their relationship with Gandhi as 'a magic drug which cures all diseases'.[129] This was expected hyperbole from Mohamed Ali now that the Khilafat Conference had found a panacea for Muslim ills in the form of a unanimous or *mutafiqa fatwa* by a group of prominent *ulema* belonging to the Jamiat-ul-Ulema-i-Hind. Intended to accelerate the pace of non-cooperation beyond what Gandhi envisaged, the *fatwa* pronounced that the 'worst sin' for Muslims was to hold military and civil posts in the colonial government since they were expected to fire on their co-religionists. Muslims were also forbidden to join the reformed councils, receive education in government schools, practise law or accept honorary posts and titles as this created undue attachment with the enemies of Islam. By the same token, the use of British goods was *haram*. Social interaction with non-Muslims was permitted by the *shariat* so long as they were not hostile to Muslims. Most interesting, and evidence of Azad's influence, was the view that Muslims could act on 'any pious suggestion of a non-Muslim' so long as it was 'not opposed to the injunctions of the *Sharia*'.[130]

This was a declaration of war on the government which banned the *fatwa* under the Indian Press Act of 1920. The Ali brothers were arrested along with five others for sedition after the Karachi meeting of the Khilafat Conference. By then copies of the *fatwa* were in circulation and the focal point of public discussion. The confiscation of the *fatwa* was seen as amounting to the 'proscription of the *Quran*' but nothing could 'stop the passionate current of Islamic verses flowing in ... [Muslim] veins'. Any cooperation with the British would 'stigmatize' Muslims as *kafirs*. Undaunted by the government crackdown, middle-ranking leaders urged Muslims in the army and police to quit serving masters who had the gall to impound their holy book. If Muslims in government service did 'not realise the insult', all social interaction with them had to be suspended. Vows were taken to republish and distribute the *fatwa*. A government order meant nothing to Muslims, most of whom knew the Quran by rote and could fearlessly reproduce the *fatwa*. Superintendents of police were among the first to be sent copies of the new edition. The *fatwa*

[128]See Minault, *The Khilafat Movement*, pp. 142–3.

[129]*Civil and Military Gazette*, Lahore, 13 July 1921 cited in K.K.Aziz (ed.), *The Indian Khilafat Movement 1915–1933: A Documentary Record*, Karachi: Pak Publishers, 1972, p. 183.

[130]See appendix to the *SPPAI*, 1 October 1921, vol. xlii, no. 38.

was reprinted and distributed to thousands of Muslims who shouted slogans of 'Allah-o-Akbar' and denounced government service as haram.[131]

There was evidently still an undercurrent of anti-imperialist feeling which required just the right sort of nudge to burst into the open. Gandhi's message of non-violent non-cooperation was not nearly as inspiring as the one charging the government with infringing the religious rights and obligations ordained by God. The incarceration of the Ali brothers was another sore point, not least for being portrayed as a classical example of an infidel government's lack of regard for Muslim religious sensibilities. Using the idiom of religious rights to justify Muslim insubordination within the military was an explosive mix which neither the colonial government nor Gandhi could look upon with equanimity. It might generate more support for the khilafatists' variant of non-cooperation but could seriously compromise efforts to keep Islamic universalism and Indian nationalism on parallel tracks.

Declaring military service unIslamic was potentially fraught with consequences for the Punjab, the home of Britain's most favoured martial races. Fortunately for the colonial state, here the movement had been slipping out of the grip of khilafat agitators despite sharper attacks on Muslims who placed government above God and Gandhi. Ordinary sepoys and police constables were charged with perpetuating foreign rule and oppression for trivial sums of money. Muslims had to 'follow M. Gandhi's behest' and 'no[t] ... put the word of a paltry constable on a level with the orders of God'. Carrying out a jihad was a religious duty since the sacred places of Islam had been 'fire[d] upon by the kafirs'.[132] But instead of advancing the anti-colonial struggle in the Punjab, the non-cooperators were facing a more concerted attack for letting Gandhi pipe away Muslim dreams of rights.

In a stinging pamphlet, one Maulvi Abdul Hakim set about proving that Gandhi was not a well-wisher of the Muslims. After hurting Muslim trading interests in South Africa, Gandhi on arriving in India had lost no time undermining their main cultural symbol, the Urdu language. His policy of boycotting government educational institutions was hurting Aligarh and other centres of Muslim learning. While asking Muslims to give up cow slaughter, Gandhi had never told Hindus to make such concessions. This was proof positive that once swaraj was achieved, the Hindus would prohibit cow slaughter and impinge upon the few rights enjoyed by Muslims. Showing his Punjabi stripes, the author charged the Mahatma for surreptitiously encouraging Hindus in their nefarious designs to force the repeal of the Land Alienation Bill of 1900, the government's 'gift' to Muslim zamindars. Duped by the notion of an imaginary unity with Hindus, Muslims were in the unenviable position of not knowing which part of their body was being amputated. Unconcerned

---

[131]SPPAI, 15 October 1921, vol. xlii, no. 39, pp. 494–5.
[132]SPPAI, 9 July 1921, vol. xlii, no. 26, pp. 388 and 390.

about the *khilafat*, Gandhi and the Hindus were using Muslims to promote *swaraj*—a code word for undiluted Hindu raj.[133]

If this was a bad portent for Hindu–Muslim accommodation in the Punjab, the prognosis was not appreciably better in other parts of India. In late August 1921 a bloody revolt in which mainly Hindu landlords were hacked to death by the predominantly Muslim Mappilla peasants of Malabar dealt a decisive blow to the non-cooperation movement. Reports of forced conversions of Hindus by Muslim peasants emboldened by *khilafatist* propaganda of an Afghan invasion was a disastrous omen for Indian unity. Efforts by *khilafatists* to distance themselves from the revolt or attribute it to long-standing agrarian discontent cut no ice with large segments of Hindu public opinion. They were fed up with all the loose talk about an invasion from the northwest and utterly convinced that Gandhi had blundered in giving an irresponsible band of Islamic universalists their head. Azad, who had taken over as secretary of the Central Khilafat Committee following Shaukat Ali's arrest, tried intervening through his recently launched organ *Paigham* from Calcutta. His belief that if forced conversions had taken place then the Mappilla Muslims had acted contrary to the teachings of Islam did nothing to allay the outrage felt by Hindus at being violated in their own backyard.[134] The Jamiat-ul-Ulemai-i-Hind's refusal to accept the stories of mass conversions as reliable only made matters worse.[135]

The Mappilla rebellion pushed relations between the two communities to an all-time low, illustrating how stray developments in the localities could rip the patchwork quilt of Hindu–Muslim understandings at the all-India level. But it also made the stalwarts of non-cooperation more resolute than ever to save the concord form being blown to smithereens. One of the most carefully delineated arguments aimed at reconciling Islamic universalism and Indian nationalism came from the inimitable pen of Abul Kalam Azad. Detailing the history of the *khilafat* and non-cooperation movements in the *Paigham*, Azad reminded his readers that it was the Muslims who had persuaded Gandhi and the Congress to embark upon the anti-imperialist struggle. It was the *khilafatists* who had strengthened the movement for *swaraj*. The 'real solution of the *khilafat* problem was the freedom of Hindustan'. Indians had to work under the direction of the Congress—the 'united organization of all the *qaums* in the country', Hindu and Muslim alike.

While conceding that the work initially done by the *khilafatists* was now being done by the Congress, Azad opposed the disbandment of the *khilafat*

[133]Maulvi Abdul Hakim, *Mr Gandhi Musalmanon ke hargis khairkhwah nahin*, Lahore. August 1921, Urdu D.1264, IOL

[134]*Paigham*, Calcutta, 23 September 1921, p. 5. The complete files of the paper were reprinted in New Delhi in 1988. (References to the paper are followed by date and page number.)

[135]*SPPAI*, 3 December 1921, vol. xlii, no. 46, p. 550.

committees. The *khilafat* movement had imposed two kinds of duties on Muslims, one relating to India and the other to the Islamic world. Internally, Muslims had to struggle for the attainment of rights by fortifying non-cooperation and externally they had to keep watch and ward on the problems facing their co-religionists in other countries. Although Congress was in control of non-cooperation, Muslims needed the *khilafat* committees to address issues outside India's borders. Even internally, the *khilafatists* had to ensure that Muslims did not fall behind in participating in the national movement. They had to show more enthusiasm than any other *qaum* to claim their rights more effectively. There had to be more *charkhas* spinning *khaddar* in Muslim than in Hindu homes. *Khilafat* committees had to make sure that Muslims enrolled as members of the Congress so as to make their presence felt.[136] And as for Muslims accepting Gandhi's leadership, Azad reiterated that this was entirely consistent with the teachings and history of Islam.[137]

In charting the path to Muslim incorporation into mainstream Indian nationalism, Azad used copious quotations from the Quran and the Hadiths to prove that the followers of the Prophet could not live under a government which impeded their religious freedom. This was his way of defending the Karachi seven on trial for sedition and also Maulana Zafar Ali Khan facing similar charges in a separate court in the Punjab. Azad emphatically endorsed the arguments of Mohamed Ali and Zafar Ali Khan that they were conscientious objectors whose religion forbade the killing of their own co-religionists. After all, he had pioneered this line of argument but had not been arrested.[138] Azad had discovered a Hadith according to which if a Muslim was poised to behead a non-Muslim who responded by reciting the *kalima*, it became illegal for the former to kill the latter. If the Muslim ignored the non-Muslim's acceptance of Islam then he would lose his religion while the new convert would make a pragmatic entry into the fold of Islam.[139]

At the Karachi trial, Mohamed Ali tried putting the matter more simply. In asking Muslims not to serve in the army, he had only acted on his religious beliefs. In Islam ultimate sovereignty vested with none other than Allah. After God and the Prophet, it was the duty of every Muslim to obey the authority of the *khalifa*. The dictates of divine, spiritual and temporal sovereignty were categorical and there was no room for a Muslim or anyone else to question them. As a Muslim, he knew that it was legal to eat pig's meat to avoid death by starvation. But it was absolutely prohibited for a Muslim to kill another

---

[136]*Paigham*, 23 September 1921, pp. 5–7.

[137]*Paigham*, 9 December 1921, p. 7.

[138]*Paigham*, 4 November 1921, pp. 4–5, 18 November 1921, pp. 4–9, and 25 November 1921, pp. 6–7.

[139]*Paigham*, 11 November 1921, p. 6.

Muslim. Such clarity was nowhere apparent in British legal texts. There was a glaring contradiction in the colonial legal system which could charge a man for sedition when he was merely exercising the religious freedom guaranteed by the British sovereign in 1858.[140]

The religious freedom of Muslims could not be confined to praying in mosques. Islam as a complete way of life had certain rules which had to be observed by Muslims if they wanted to remain within its pale. In appealing to their co-religionists to quit military service lest they be called upon to kill other Muslims, the *khilafat* leaders were merely carrying out their religious duty. If this translated as disloyalty, then the confusion lay on the British side and not with Muslims whose sense of identity flowed from a clear sense of obligations based on a tripartite conception of sovereignty. Simply put, the fault was not of Muslim agitators in calling upon their brethren to eschew military service but of the British legal system which contravened the orders of its own sovereign.[141] Unfortunately for Mohamed Ali and his co-defendants as well as Zafar Ali Khan, the British judges were not impressed. The opinion of the British sovereign was not above the rule of law.

It has always been relatively easier for Muslims to fiddle with normative Islam than to strike the right chords to produce some measure of harmony between theory and practice. This has been attributed widely to an almost congenital inability to accept the leadership of any single individual or institution whose interpretations of Islam could be deemed binding by all Muslims.[142] Not surprising considering that Muslims can draw upon three different though equally valid notions of sovereignty to assert their sense of a common religious identity. Whereas the idea of *hakimiyat* gives maximum leeway to an individual's judgement, the spiritual and temporal dimensions of sovereignty are invoked to temper that autonomy with responsibility to the Muslim community, both as an extra-territorial and territorial entity. The demands of spiritual and temporal sovereignty for Muslims have been as much a source of contestation as of consensus. Even after the *khilafat* movement had seemingly settled the issue of spiritual authority, the imperatives of living under the juridical rule of the British continued to militate against an unambiguous relationship between temporal sovereignty and Muslim identity.

If Muslims were to continue striving for rights by recourse to religious

[140]Mohamed Ali, *Bayan-i-Hurriyat*, Amritsar, 2 February 1922, Urdu D.1365, IOL.

[141]Mian Mohammad Abdul Ghafoor (comp.), *Marika-i-Siyasat wa Khilafat yani Muqadama-i-Karachi - Mukammal Ruidad*, Amritsar, 2 February 1922, Urdu D.1371, IOL.

[142]For two stinging internal critiques of the whole gamut of Muslim leaders, religious and lay, see Mumtaz Husain Sayyid, *Risala-i-Kafn-Posh Lidaran-i-Qaum*, Amroha, 8 July 1915, VT 3858k, IOL and Akbar Shah Khan Najibabad, *Akhbar-i-Qaum*, Lahore, 3 March 1920, Urdu D.997, IOL.

idioms and yet locate themselves within mainstream Indian nationalism, someone had to try and untangle the extra-territorial from the territorial conception of temporal sovereignty without vitiating their sense of Islamic identity. This could only be done by an individual or a select group whose authority was acknowledged by large segments of the Muslim population. Despite internal jockeying for position by the more ambitious, the alliance of convenience between the *ulema* and Muslim politicians had skirted around the issue in order to present a common front against the raj. But the question of who spoke for the Muslims most authoritatively had to be addressed if Islamic universalism was to be accommodated within Indian nationalism.

One man who had been conscious of this problem was Abul Kalam Azad. Ever since his *Al-Hilal* days, he had considered the lack of leadership and organization among Muslims a principal weakness. Upon joining the *khilafatists*, Azad had worked behind the scenes to marshall the support of the disparate divines constituting the Jamiat-ul-Ulema-i-Hind for his bid to takeover as the *amir* of India's Muslims. His unsolicited *fatwa* on *hijrat* had been part of the same enterprise. With the Ali brothers facing a two-year prison term and none of the prominent *ulema* capable of pulling together, Azad found an opening to make a concerted bid for the leadership of the Muslim community. In September 1921 he had circulated a proposal to the Khilafat Committee meeting in Tanjore for the appointment of provincial *amirs* and an all-India *amir* or the *imam-i-shariat*. The matter was not debated due to serious 'divergence of views on the subject among the leaders'. This is highly significant given the nature of the proposal. The main principle underlying it was to institute a mechanism for the enforcement of strict obedience by Muslims to the *ahkam-i-shariat* or religious ordinances and, in this way, ensure 'the perpetual preservation of Islamic Nationality and democracy'. If this were achieved, the *imam-i-shariat* would have the sole authority to pronounce a *jihad*. This was seen as vesting inordinate power in the hands of a single individual. So although there was broad agreement on implementing the *shariat*, there was considerable disagreement about the powers and responsibilities of the *amir* and whether or not an oath of allegiance to him was compulsory.

Azad—who fancied himself as the prospective *amir-i-hind*—and his cronies not only favoured the oath but threatened anyone refusing to take it with excommunication. Even the Ali brothers, Abdul Bari, Hakim Ajmal Khan, to mention only a few, were fiercely opposed to enthroning a veritable dictator and that too in the form of Azad. As they correctly realized, Azad's scheme if accepted would reduce their own influence over Muslims to vanishing point and enable the all-India *amir* and his provincial underlings to emerge as the undisputed centres of authority. When Abdul Bari challenged the *amir-i-hind's* right to exercise such unbridled power on democratic grounds, he was 'threatened with murder' by Azad's followers. And so the proposal was quietly shelved.[143]

Disappointed but undeterred, Azad continued his three-year-long effort to become *amir-i-hind* at the Jamiat-ul-Ulema-i-Hind's annual meeting at Lahore in November 1921. He flaunted his qualifications for the office with a speech in Arabic which impressed the audience even though it was completely unintelligible to most of them. To his dismay, some of the *ulema* were less keen on appointing an *amir* than objecting to the prohibition on cow slaughter, 'a religious right for which they had made many a sacrifice'. But Azad and the majority of the Jamiat had a common interest in wanting to rivet control over the Indian Muslims. The meeting resolved to print 100,000 pledge forms asking Muslims to commit themselves to 'act blindly on the [*mutafiqa*] *fatwa* of the *Jamiat*' which among other things proclaimed the illegality of military service. But if this was a step in the direction Azad wanted to move, his opponents manoeuvred to make sure that the Jamiat merely approved the idea of an *amir* as the 'spiritual leader' of India's Muslims. The final decision was to be taken by a select committee which included Abdul Bari. Azad was arrested in early December 1921. An honour for so dedicated a non-cooperator, he nevertheless felt belittled when instead of the two-year sentence handed to the Ali brothers his was limited to one year.

By the time Azad was released from jail the proposal to select or elect an *amir-i-hind* had gone down the well-worn road of Indian Muslim unity. If even the *ulema* who wanted *shariat* rule were reluctant to support it, many Muslims preferred their religion without let or hindrance from the learned divines. The Muslim individual might in principle concede to the will of the community, variously defined, but was less than amenable to being dictated to by a co-religionist claiming authority on account of a superior knowledge of Islam. If he had understood the obstacles to Muslim unanimity and participation in the nationalist cause, Azad was still in the dark about the psychological effects of a religious doctrine in which authority could be everywhere and yet nowhere both at the same time.

In a blistering attack on the entire idea, one shrewd observer noted that the very term *amir-i-shariat* was alien to Indian Muslims. Those who claimed the Islamic mantle were organized along sectarian lines and so deeply opposed to one another as to want their rivals pushed out of the community of Islam. Such a divided lot could never agree on a single *amir-i-shariat* since the authority flowing from that office would be purely religious and utterly devoid of any political basis. The Jamiat-ul-Ulema-i-Hind would have to set up ten or even twenty individuals as *amir-i-shariat* given the multiple sectarian differences in

[143]Report from the Criminal Investigation Department, Madras, 5 September 1921, *Khilafat Movement in NWFP, Afghanistan and Bombay*, Official Records of NWFP Tribal Cell, NDC, p. 25.

Indian Islam. Before taking the idea any further, it was vital to establish which sect the *amir-i-shariat* would be drawn from and what the rules of election were going to be. Any ad hoc appointment of the *amir* instead of uniting Muslims would divide them even more.[144]

It was equally important to decide who among Muslims were going to exercise their right of choice. Certainly not the ordinary folk, most of whom could barely recite the *kalima*. If the educated were to make the decision then it had to be clear which sect they belonged to and whether that choice would be binding on Muslims who did not share their religious beliefs. Knowing Muslims as well as he did, the author's educated guess was that Sunnis would want a Sunni *amir*, the Shias one of their own kind and the same would be the case for the Wahabis and the Qadianis. Even in the unlikely event of all the Muslim sects settling on a single *amir*, the problem would not end with the election. The *amir* would be in the odious position of making decisions for all the sects. If he chose an interpretation of the law, one sect or the other was bound to repudiate his authority. The educated would have myriad ideas as to which source was more authentic for a particular decision. In short, the *amir-i-shariat*'s authority would be unenforceable. It was conceivable that a competent *amir* might come up with a set of principles acceptable to all Muslims. But here was the twist. The rules arrived at would not be those of the Shariat-i-Muhammadi but of a hitherto non-existent Shariat-i-Ittahadi, literally the law of unity.[145]

Appealing to the Sunnis, the author warned that any attempt to create a united and true body of Muslims would mean excluding all those deemed to be non-religious or at best not adequately religious. He had no doubt that the so-called *'qaumi* leaders' and *'qaumi* maulanas' were exploiting Muslims in the name of religion. The institution of the *amir-i-shariat* aimed at extracting additional funds from the people which instead of being spent on good causes would be frittered away by the leaders in the pursuit of luxurious lifestyles. Alternatively they would be utilized for a 'damned Hindu–Muslim unity'. In his considered opinion, Muslims would do well to steer clear of an *amir*—an allusion to Azad—who told them to embrace people who attacked their religion and the Prophet.[146]

There were far too many sectarian and ideological divisions, to say nothing of regional and class differences, among Muslims to allow for the emergence of a single leader or an institution deriving legitimacy exclusively from Islam. Azad's failure to press his claims as the *amir-i-shariat* was symptomatic of the internal fractures within a community which although defined by a universal

[144]Irtiza Hussain Hasani Qadari, *Tehrik-i-Imarat Sharia pai ak Tanqidi Nazar*, Etawah, 1921, Urdu F. 237, IOL.

[145]Ibid.

[146]Ibid.

religion had never overcome the particularities of contextual location or the intricacies of personalized faith. So an altogether poor prospectus for that elusive accommodation between Islamic universalism and Indian nationalism which the *khilafatists* in their different ways had been trying to achieve. By the time Gandhi decided unilaterally to call off the non-cooperation movement on 5 February 1922 after hearing news of the burning alive of twenty-two policemen by an angry crowd of peasants at Chauri Chaura in the Gorakhpur district of UP, the cracks in Hindu–Muslim unity had widened into open breaches. Communitarian narratives, pushed to the margins though never wholly repressed, were back in ascendance even as dyed-in-the wool *khilafatists* and their allies in the nationalist camp continued to see in the lingering shadows of anti-imperialist sentiments the lost tracks to substantive Indian unity.

CULTURAL DIFFERENCE AND NATIONAL ACCOMMODATION

Though the years 1919 to 1921 saw unprecedented displays of Hindu–Muslim goodwill, the experience of the first mass-based anti-imperialist struggle had done much to sharpen animosities both between and within the two communities. Even before the eruption of violent conflict along communitarian lines in different parts of India, strident assertions of cultural difference had begun muffling the pleas for accommodation. Opponents of a national concord had never ceased sniping from close range at the extraordinary alliance Gandhi had helped fashion. Bringing virulent Arya Samajists, western-educated Hindus and Muslims as well as the *ulema* of Farangi Mahal and Deoband on a common platform had been no ordinary feat. Lacking solid gains on either the *khilafat* or the *swaraj* fronts, the will to unity crumbled rapidly. It was not just the sense of despondency that comes of abandoning cherished goals, but the urge to recriminate while facing the consequences of a painful post-mortem.

Blaming Gandhi's non-violent philosophy for the setback was a common refrain among *khilafatists* led by Maulana Abdul Bari. But none had the courage of one's convictions to openly break with the Mahatma and take on the government to prove their undying faith in God. This gave some leverage to diehard Congressites like Hakim Ajmal Khan and Dr Ansari for whom the main purpose of the *khilafat* movement had been Muslim solidarity and Indian unity. In their opinion, the *khilafat* was irrelevant now that Muslims had taken the initial steps towards national accommodation. By blowing their cover prematurely, these men lost their line with the *ulema* for whom the *khilafat* remained intrinsic to their goal of establishing *shariat* rule. Without the religious divines to keep up the semblance of mass support, Muslims within the Congress ranks were a weak reed. The problem of sustaining the alliance between western-educated Muslims and the *ulema* had come out fully into the open.[147]

With the top leadership in the grips of a crisis, the suspension of non-cooperation was an opportunity for individuals to voice dissent on matters decided on behalf of the community in the absence of real debate. In UP where non-cooperation had made headway, a bitter tract war was initiated on cow slaughter. Prohibiting it negated the *shariat*, turning what God had decreed as *halal* or permissible into *haram* or forbidden. Lower class Muslims would not only lose their entitlement to healthy nutrition but also their faith. This was too high a price to pay for Hindu–Muslim unity. Scoffing at Muslims who looked upon Hindus as brothers, one tract writer pronounced the non-cooperation movement a grand deception. Hindus had a visceral hatred for Muslims and would stop at nothing short of complete dominance over them.[148] Another polemicist proclaimed the Mahatma a 'fake'; he had neither saved the *khilafat* nor attained *swaraj*. If Muslims followed the Ali brothers, Dr Ansari and Hakim Ajmal Khan, they would almost certainly end up as cow worshippers. It was preposterous for newspapers like the *Mashriq* and the *Taj* to tell Muslims to treat cow's and pig's meat as one and the same or better still become vegetarian. All this was contrary to nature and ordinary Muslims had no sympathy with the pro-Gandhian activities of such men.[149]

Religiously informed cultural differences were being invoked once again to score political points against Muslims who had hitched their wagons to Gandhi's leadership. In Bengal where more Muslims advocated cooperation with the Congress than before, doubts about the alliance had been a recurrent feature of the public debate. In 1921 the *Muslim Bharat*, to which the poet Kazi Nazrul Islam was a key contributor, spelled out how the problem of identity, sovereignty and rights was bedeviling the minds of its co-religionists. 'Are we first of all Muslims, or inhabitants of India?', it asked. If the representatives of the *khilafat* invaded India, would it not be the duty of Muslims to oppose them? After all, 'we are not the only inhabitants of India' and no one had 'the India' and no one had 'the right to hold in subjection all those countless Hindus, Buddhists and Christians of India'.[150]

If this was an unusually sophisticated understanding of the obligations of common citizenship, some Bengali Muslims were offended by the Hindu overtones of the *khilafat* and non-cooperation movement. The *Islam-darshan* in 1920 berated Muslims for extolling Gandhi's personality; it was improper

[147]See Minault, *The Khilafat Movement*, pp. 187–8.

[148]Maulana Abdul Hadi Muhammad Zahid, *Adalat Gawshala Parastan*, Jubbulpore, 29 July 1922, Urdu D.1192, IOL.

[149]Hafiz Abdul Hamid, *Azad Gao*, Jubbulpore: Anjuman Zahirin Alal Haq, 21 July 1922, Urdu D.1193, IOL.

[150]*Muslim Bharat* of 1921 cited in Islam, *Bengali Muslim Public Opinion*, p. 68.

for them 'to adulate any one but Allah and the Prophet'. Muslims in imitation of Hindus were hanging photographs of Hindu and Muslim leaders in their homes. Particularly off-putting was a popular poster portraying Draupadi as mother India suffering humiliation at the hands of Duhshasan or the British. Gandhi appeared as Krishna while the Pandavas included such luminaries as the Ali brothers, C.R. Das, Lala Lajpat Rai and Motilal Nehru. Another poster depicted Gandhi in Brindaban as Krishna in the famous *tribhanga* pose piping the flute of non-cooperation. The Ali brothers, Das, Rai and Nehru were shown as young cowherds engaged in a wild *charkha* dance with cowherd maidens. While it was 'not unnatural for Hindus to see such pictures', the editor was 'mortified to see representations ... of Mohamed Ali, Shaokat Ali and Abdul Kalam (Azad) who bear the title of *Maolana*'.[151]

Educated Punjabi Muslims like their Hindu counterparts had opposed political alliances which ignored the fractures at the social base. They now took the lead in discounting the very possibility of a national accommodation. Published for the third time in 1921, a pamphlet by a convert from Hinduism, explained how his abhorrence for the social institution of *chhut* or untouchability had led him to adopt Islam. As a young boy his parents had stopped him playing with Muslim neighbours since contact with a *'mlechh qaum'* would pollute an upper-caste Hindu. It was shocking that a Hindu could eat food taken from a dog's mouth but not if it had been touched by a Muslim. With the enthusiasm of a convert, the author urged Muslims to enforce a total trade boycott of Hindus and instead open their own shops.[152] Another trenchant critic of unity without genuine social accommodation deployed the poetic medium to caution Muslims of deceitful Hindus who constantly admonished them for saying their prayers in mosques. A high school teacher, the poet linked the decline in Muslim social status and rights to the loss of sovereignty and lamented that former slaves were behaving like masters. Muslims could make their presence felt by attending mosques in ever larger numbers and praying to God, the ultimate sovereign and benefactor.[153]

Such arguments had been around since the late nineteenth century. In the political atmosphere of the early 1920s they exposed the brittleness of national accommodation in the absence of any significant shift in social psyches. In their efforts to rustle up popular support, the *khilafat* and non-cooperation movements had done much to legitimize the political articulation of religiously informed cultural identities. Short of appropriating these to negotiate an alternative form of Indian nationalism, one which went beyond the morass of majoritarian and minoritarian narratives to project a vision of equal citizenship

[151]Cited in ibid., pp. 78–80.
[152]Shaikh Abdur Rahman, *Risala Safina-i-Najat*, Amritsar, 25 June 1921, Urdu D.744, IOL.
[153]Master Mohi-ud-Din, *Faryad-i-Muslim*, Amritsar, 16 November 1921, Urdu D.1212, IOL.

rights irrespective of cultural difference, the architects of a united Hindu–Muslim 'nation' were unwittingly strengthening the hands of their opponents. Simply put, the only way of imaginatively cohering two quite different sets of symbolisms in the construction of a single Indian nation was to abandon the dominant discourse on religiously based majority and minority communities derived from colonial categories of enumeration for one based on the ideals of common citizenship. An admittedly difficult enterprise in a context where Indians were colonial subjects, not individual citizens of a sovereign nation-state, it nevertheless captures the quandary of those wishing to reconcile Islamic universalism with Indian nationalism.

Nationalist Muslim tracts of the period are strikingly oblivious of the tension between the exclusive connotations of Islamic symbolism and an apparently inclusive approach to the Indian nation. If Islamic symbols were the bait intended to pull Muslims behind the larger cause of anti-colonial nationalism, they could also inflame sentiments and militate against identification with the Congress. Without a corresponding change in the dominant nationalist idioms, symbolism alone was a precarious basis for an effective link between Muslim and Indian identity. In early 1922 a series of pamphlets published from a press in Madras tried making political capital out of the imprisonment of the Ali brothers. Steeped in Islamic symbolism focusing on the *khilafat*, these celebrated the heroism of the brothers, bringing in the gender dimension by harping on the pain of separation felt by the women of the Ali family. One tract depicted Mohamad Ali's daughter longing to see her father's face. But in the true spirit of Islamic sacrifice she asks him to suffer his ordeal with fortitude and patience. At her mother's insistence she had taken to wearing *khaddar* and appeals to the 'mothers of the nation' to instruct their children to do the same.[154] Shaukat Ali's wife exhorts *khilafatists* to perform their duty through earnest 'national effort'. Everyone had to give up European goods and wear *khadi*. 'Forge connections with the Shariat', she tells the Muslims, and 'break relations with European ways'. Muslims could demonstrate their pride and concern for the 'nation' by working for their religion.[155] Mohamed Ali's wife entreats her husband to give his life for the *khilafat* since martyrdom was preferable to a life of subjugation.[156]

Apart from creating a personality cult around the Ali brothers and Gandhi, a number of tracts promoted the *charkha* as the pre-eminent symbol of non-cooperation. Another pamphlet from Madras delineated the multiple virtues of the spinning wheel in the form of a popular ode: the *charkha* would instruct the heart; liberate the people; destroy the enemy and revive a ruined country. It would also save the *khilafat* and get rid of colonial rule.

---

[154]*Sada-i-Dukhtar*, Madras, 12 March 1922, Urdu D.1228, IOL.
[155]*Piyam-i-Begum*, Madras, 8 February 1922, Urdu D.1232, IOL.
[156]*Sada-i-Begum*, Madras, 8 February 1922, Urdu D.1233, IOL.

Women were asked to promote *swadeshi* and create a sense of national pride by wearing *khaddar*.[157]

Nationalist tracts published in UP both during and after the halting of non-cooperation also reproduced Islamic symbolism with hortatory appeals to heed the call of the Ali brothers and Gandhi. A vast majority of these were in extended verse form and invariably sought to combine Islamic universalism and Indian nationalism. One poet reiterated the notion of Hindus and Muslims belonging to the same Aryan race who after long separation had reunited once again in Hindustan. If only they could expunge bigotry from their midst they would become one nation. He opposed cow slaughter since the vast majority of Muslims could not afford the luxury. After sharply critiquing the lifestyles of the rich who were after government employment, the poet advised Muslims to turn to their religion while at the same time adopting the national symbol of *khadi*.[158] Religion as the basis of participation in Indian nationalism found voice in another pamphlet which began with *bismillah* and went on to sing praises of the *charkha* and *khadi*. By destroying the economic basis of British imperialism, Indians could achieve the goals of *khilafat* and *swaraj*. But to do so they had to follow Shaukat Ali and Gandhi and court death if necessary.[159]

In the Punjab, Zafar Ali Khan's *Zamindar* had played a leading role in presenting the *charkha* and *khadi* as nationalist symbols consistent with the principles of Islamic universalism. An opponent of cow slaughter, the paper surpassed its provincial counterparts in promoting the cause of national accommodation. Even with its editor serving a five-year prison sentence, it remained an ardent supporter of the *khilafat* and Hindu–Muslim unity. The *Zamindar* was also in the forefront of intra-Muslim controversies and attacks on Hindus for their misinterpretations of Islam. In January 1922 Zafar Ali Khan published a poem designed to embarrass Muhammad Iqbal who had maintained a conspicuously low profile after Gandhi gained control over the non-cooperation movement:

[157]*Charkha dil ko shad karega*
   Bandoon ko azad karega
   Dushman ko barbad karega
   Ojaara des abad karega.

چرخہ دل کو شاد کریگا   بندون کو آزاد کریگا

دشمن کو برباد کریگا   اُجاڑا دیس آباد کریگا

(Khwaja Mohiyuddin Sahib (Muhammad), *Bahar-i-Charka*, Madras, 25 February, 1922, Urdu D.1227, IOL.)
[158]Hasan Mirza, *Jazabat-i-Qaumi or Gandhi ki Jai*, Lucknow, 1 May 1921, Urdu B. 648, IOL.
[159]Wali Muhammad, *Gandhi ka Charkha*, Saharanpur, 1 July 1922, Urdu B. 649, IOL.

Go tell Hazrat Iqbal, oh gentle breeze
No one compares with you in eloquence
What is the reason for your silence these days
Why no warmth of flight in your lofty thoughts
The gathering says that ever since you ceased chanting
There is no melody or rhythm anywhere
Do you have no themes to piece together
Or is the flow not there for the moment
What day goes by without some calamity
What night passes without a thunderstorm
Is there a place where there is no mourning
Or a corner devoid of some upheaval
Not a locality has any regard for the Prince
Not a city in the country of Hind without a strike
If in your eyes these issues are obsolete
At least the cause of the *khilafat* has not decayed
With this knowledge come and perform *jihad*
The *sharia* demands no material sacrifice from you
When has expediency ever stopped passion
Why then have you forgotten your own truths today
Do not turn away from your own in these times of crisis
You are the wealth of Islam, not the infidel's Iqbal.[160]

[160]*Arz kar Hazrat-i-Iqbal say ja kar ye saba*
Ahe ke duniya-i-sukhan mein tera tamshal nahin
Majara kiya hae ke kuch rooz say khamosh hai tuh
Garam parwaz tera fiqr-i-sabak bal nahin
Bazam kehti hai ke tuh jab say nahin zamzama sanj
Kise ahang mein wo sur nahin wo tal nahin
Bandhnein ke liya mazmoon nahin milta tuj ko
Ya rawani pae teri tabah he fil hal nahin
Konsa din hae ke sar pae kui bijli na giri
Konsi shab hai ke aya kui bhunchal nahin
Konsa goosha hae matam nahin jis me barpa
Konsa khita hae jo muztarab-u-lhal nahin
Shahzade say aqidad nahin kis basti ko
Kishwar-i-Hind kae kis shahr mein hartal nahin
Yeh mubahis tere nazdik hain farsooda agar
Toh khilafat ke mazamin toh pamal nahin
Ine muharaf he say kar aake jihad-i-akbar
Shira ko tuj say taqazah-i-zar-o-mal nahin
Kab junon maslahat andesh hua karta hai?
Aaj kuin yad tujhe apnay he aqwal nahin
Tanth ke waqt apnoon se na mon pher ke tu
Daulat Islam ki hae, kufar ka Iqbal nahin

Very much the individual standing judgement on the community with his winged turns of the phrase, Iqbal whether in anticipation or in response to this query wrote:

If the country goes out of the hands then so be it
Do not betray God's commands
Are you not familiar with history
You have taken to begging for the *khilafat*
What we do not buy with our own blood
Disrobed is that sovereignty for the Muslim.[161]

Elsewhere Iqbal made light of all forms of sovereignty other than that of God:

What Scriptures sets forth riddlingly
Of Kings, let me impart:

عرض کر حضرتِ اقبال سے جا کر یہ صبا   اے کہ دنیائے سخن میں تری تمثال نہیں
ماجرا کیا ہے کی کچھ روز سے خاموش ہے تو   گرم پرواز ترا فکرِ سبک بال نہیں
بزم کہتی ہے کہ تو جب سے نہیں زمزمہ سنج   کسی آہنگ میں وہ سُر نہیں وہ تال نہیں
باندھنے کے لیے مضموں نہیں ملتے تجھ کو   یا روانی پہ تری طبع ہی فی الحال نہیں
کونسا دن ہے کہ سر پر کوئی بجلی نہ گری   کونسی شب ہے کہ آیا کوئی بھونچال نہیں
کونسا گوشہ ہے ماتم نہیں جس میں برپا   کونسا خطہ ہے جو مضطرب الحال نہیں
شاہزادے سے عقیدت نہیں کس بستی کو   کشورِ ہند کے کس شہر میں ہر تال نہیں
یہ مباحث ترے نزدیک ہیں فرسودہ اگر   تو خلافت کے مضامیں تو پامال نہیں
ان معارف ہی سے کر آ کے جہادِ اکبر   شرع کو تجھ سے تقاضائے زر و مال نہیں
کب جنوں معلحت اندیش ہوا کر تا ہے؟   آج کیوں یاد تجھے اپنے ہی اقوال نہیں
تخت کے وقت اپنوں سے نہ منہ پھیر کہ تو
دولت اسلام کی ہے کفر کا اقبال نہیں۔

(Cited in Zulfiqar, *Maulana Zafar Ali Khan*, pp. 204–5.)
[161]*Agar mulk haton say jata hae jae
Tuh ahkam-i-haq say na kar bewafai
Nahin tuj ko tarikh say agahe keya?
Khilafat ke karna laga tuh goodai!
Kharideen na hum jis ko apna laho say
Musalman ko hae nang wo padshahi!*

اگر ملک ہاتھوں سے جاتا ہے جائے   تو احکام حق سے نہ کر بے وفائی
نہیں تجھ کو تاریخ سے آ گمی کیا؟   خلافت کی کرنے لگا تو گدائی!
خریدیں نہ ہم جس کو اپنے لہو سے   مسلماں کو ہے ننگ وہ پادشائی!

(Iqbal, 'Daryuizah-i-Khilafat', in *Bang-i-Dara* in *Kulliyat-i-Iqbal*, p. 206.)

In towering empires sovereignty
Is all a conjurer's arts—

. . .

None with dominion's orb invest
But the Most High alone:
He is the sovereign, all the rest
Are idols carved from stone.[162]

Taking a dig at those of Zafar Ali Khan's ilk, Iqbal quipped that if everyone was indeed one and the same then why engage in endless discussions about the 'other'. He impishly asked his co-religionists whose romantic bent of mind made them dearly love idols what their quarrel with Brahmins was about.[163] In a more serious vein, Iqbal predicted in April 1922 that future generations would look upon the history of this period with amazement.[164]

The poetic visionary had a point. A source of inspiration for Mohamed Ali and Zafar Ali Khan, Iqbal had parted company with them in the heat of the *khilafat* and non-cooperation struggle for practical, ideological and political reasons. He had never thought much of the Turkish *khilafat* and still less of Gandhian non-cooperation. In his opinion, 'no sincere Muslim could join [the *khilafat* movement] for a single minute'.[165] In November 1922, Iqbal was among the few who acclaimed the Turkish Grand National Assembly's decision to abolish the sultanate and appoint a new *khalifa* stripped of any temporal authority. Seeing it as the correct exercise of collective as opposed to individual *ijtihad*, Iqbal later declared that among the Muslim countries of the world 'Turkey alone ha[d] shaken off its dogmatic slumber, and attained ... self-consciousness' through the exercise of 'her right to intellectual freedom'. Muslims in the rest of the world, including India, were

[162]*Aa bataoon tujhko ramzaya en-al-mulk*
Sultanate aqwam-i-ghalib ke hai aik jadogari

. . .

Sarwari zeba faqt use zat-i-behemta ko hae
Hukmaran hae ik wohi, baqi butan-i-azari

آبتاؤں تجھ کو رمز آیہ اِن الملوک
سلطنت اقوامِ غالب کی ہے اک جادوگری

. . . . .

سروری زیبا فقط اس ذاتِ بے ہمتا کو ہے
حکمراں ہے وہی باقی بتانِ آزاری۔

(Iqbal, 'Sultanat' in ibid., p. 212, trs. by Kiernan, *Poems from Iqbal*, pp. 20–1.)
[163]Muhammad Iqbal, *Kulliyat-i-Iqbal*, p. 234.
[164]Iqbal to Muhammad Akbar Munir cited in Zulfiqar, *Maulana Zafar Ali Khan*, p. 204.
[165]Cited in Schimmel, *Gabriel's Wing*, p. 47.

'mechanically repeating old values, whereas the Turk ... [was] on the way to creating new values'.[166] If the *khilafatists* were devastated by the Turkish action, they were already on the ropes licking their wounds when in January 1923 Iqbal accepted the grant of a knighthood from the British.

By then the movement had collapsed both in substance and in spirit. This was formally registered in December 1922 at Gaya when the Congress split between the no-changers, or those still loyal to Gandhi's agenda, and the *swarajists* led by C.R. Das and Motilal Nehru who believed that since non-cooperation had been called off it made sense to try and wreck the reformed councils from within. While men like Dr Ansari wagered on Gandhi's side in the hope of securing the road to future Muslim participation in the nationalist cause, the Jamiat-i-Ulema-i-Hind stunned by events in Turkey clung to the *mutifiqa fatwa* which had plumped for non-cooperation. But what the *khilafatists* and non-cooperators did now was less relevant than the activities of the multifaceted opposition to them.

Having used religious symbols and themes to mobilize Muslims as a first step to national accommodation, the learned divines and the dwindling ranks of their allies among the western educated were susceptible to the charge of turning Islam into an expendable cog in the extremist Hindu wheel. The Hindu Mahasabhites[167] and the Arya Samajists had lost no time trying to counter the advances Muslims had made in getting their voices heard through the channels of the Gandhian Congress. Determined not to let Indian nationalism lose sight of the majoritarian will as defined by them, the followers of Dayanand at their exclusionary best had been touring the localities of the Punjab and UP since the Mappilla riots of August 1921. A leading Arya Samajist from the Punjab, Swami Shradhanand (1856–1926) masterminded the *shuddhi* movement through which Muslims on the farthest fringes of Islam along with the lower castes were to be purified and brought back into the Hindu fold. This aimed at ensuring that the Islamic universalist fervour of the previous years would never again be allowed to queer the pitch of the Hindu nation's quest for freedom and supremacy. Since the Hindu nation was unacceptably divided, Lala Lajpat Rai and Pandit Madan Mohan Malaviya turned to establishing the *sangathan* or unity movement.

With the Hindu–owned press jubilantly reporting the successful 'conversions' of Malkana Rajput, Jat and Gujar Muslims in western UP and the Punjab, the scales were tipped decisively against the *khilafatists* and the non-cooperators. Under serious challenge from the Arya Samajists, they were

---

[166]Muhammad Iqbal, *The Reconstruction of Religious Thought in Islam*, edited and annotated by M. Saeed Skeikh, Lahore: Institute of Muslim Culture and Iqbal Academy (reprint), 1989, pp.128–9.

[167]Founded in 1919 the Hindu Mahasabha, literally the great assembly of Hindus, aimed at defending Hindu interests, political as well as religious.

torn to pieces more effectively by their own co-religionists, furious at being misled on to the prickly turf of Hindu–Muslim unity. One tract powerfully conveyed the feelings of Muslims, stung by the rise of aggressive Hindu revivalism so soon after all the heart-warming talk of brotherhood. To liken the teachings of the Quran and the Hadith with Gandhi's scheme of non-cooperation was to insult Islam and misuse it to secure fame and political power. A leading religious scholar like Maulana Ashraf Ali Thanawi had declared the Gandhian-led agitation a *fitna*.[168] Questioning the legitimacy of the *mutafiqa fatwa*, the author wondered whether Abdul Bari would swear by the Quran that its five hundred signatories were well versed in Arabic. There was widespread opposition among a section of *ulema* in Lahore and Delhi to '*be-dini*' or irreligious Muslims who were sacrificing the teachings of the Quran and the Hadith at the Gandhian altar. The *khilafat* volunteers were paid hoodlums and criminals who had adopted the cause for material advancement. Instead of freeing Mecca and Medina, they were telling Muslims that the independence of the Ganga and Jumna as well as Hardwar was a religious duty. Neither *swaraj* nor *swadeshi* had anything to do with the *shariat*. History was testimony to the fact that the *qaum* which emulated the ways of another ended up getting absorbed or eliminated. Azad in one of his Friday *khutbah*'s at a Nagpur mosque had likened Gandhi to a saint. And an editor of a Lucknow-based newspaper had ventured the opinion that if prophethood had not ended with Muhammad, peace be upon him, Gandhi would have been the last prophet. This was grist to the mill of the Aryas whose goal was to conquer the *kaaba*. *Swaraj* would mean the 'death of the Muslims' and the 'departure of Islam from India'. Hindu leaders were playing a waiting game, confident of avenging Mahmud of Ghaznavi's conquest once British rule had ended. It was plainly *haram* for Muslims to join Hindus in forcing the expulsion of the British from India.[169]

So all in all a tragic countdown to the concluding moments of a phase in Indian history when cultural differences seemed capable of finding accommodation in mainstream Indian nationalism. Yet the final epitaph on the *khilafat* and non-cooperation was not written at the level of discourse alone. Events in the localities of the Punjab during 1923 and 1924 serve as an eye-opener for confirmed sceptics of elite discourse parading as peoples' history. A focus on the Punjab is justifiable on practical and conceptual grounds. The province was the seat of the more virulent manifestations of communitarian-based rivalries of which those between Muslims and Hindus took on murderous proportions. More important, given the binary opposition between nationalism and 'communalism' in South Asian historiography, especially in recounting events after the early 1920s, the story of the Punjab

---

[168]Al-Basar, *Ghoor Karna ki Baten*, Lucknow, April 1923, Urdu F.496, IOL, p. 3.
[169]Ibid., pp. 7–9, 11–13.

in the final leg of the *khilafat* and non-cooperation movements serves as a useful corrective.

THE EMBARRASSMENTS OF NATIONALISM IN THE PUNJAB

A microcosm of the all-India Hindu–Muslim equation in reverse, the Punjab more than any other province had been the hub of contending narratives of identity since the late nineteenth century. Without the most respectable of nationalist credentials it had nevertheless provided the best-known moments and martyrs of the Rowlatt *satyagraha* which catapulted India into a movement of anti-imperialist resistance under Mohandas Gandhi. True to its pivotal location in the British imperial system of collaboration and control, the Punjab was also the first to take the sting out of the non-cooperation movement and put it back into relations between Hindus and Muslims. Even before the Congress split of December 1922, Multan in southern Punjab had been hit by violence along communitarian lines with matters not looking appreciably better in other parts of the province where Arya Samaj activists were working dexterously to undermine local equations.

Increased Arya Samaj activity in the Punjab marked a sharp decline in Congress fortunes. In 1921 there were 713 Congress committees with links to 163 *panchayats* and boasting 313,000 members in the Punjab. By 1922, the number of Congress committees had slumped to 487 while the membership had shrunk to 187,000. Of the fifty-three *panchayats* associated with the Congress, only nineteen were actually functioning.[170] The rise and fall of the Congress in the Punjab is explicable only in terms of the initial support lent by Arya Samajists to non-cooperation and their withdrawal from the movement following the Mappilla uprisings of the late summer of 1921. By early 1923 a mere 350 paid workers were engaged in Congress propaganda, most of whom refused to take orders from a divided provincial leadership.[171]

The rapid depletion of Congress ranks had seen a corresponding replenishment of local Hindu Sabhas, some of which included the word 'Raksha' in their nomenclature to underscore their concern with protecting the adherents of Hinduism from the aggressive followers of Islam. In Multan which had been the scene of disturbances in September 1921, the Hindu Raksha Sabha was directing its co-religionists to boycott Muslim labourers and shopkeepers. Muslims retaliated by refusing to eat anything touched by a Hindu.[172] Individual appeals by relatively unknown tract writers were finding expression in collective action through the mushrooming of local Hindu Sabhas and their Muslim counterparts.

[170]*SPPAI*, 13 January 1923, vol. xlv, no. 2, p. 16.
[171]Ibid., p. 11.
[172]*SPPAI*, 27 January 1923, vol. xlv, no.4, p. 30.

Tensions between Hindus and Muslims in the Punjab were not entirely manipulated by determined agitators. But even relatively autonomous happenings in the localities needed some measure of organization to orchestrate collective grievances, fears and aspirations. Locally constituted, the Hindu Sabhas and a variety of Muslim *anjumans* drew upon a range of issues, some purely religious, others more political and economic, a few utterly fatuous and ephemeral to bring individuals in line with the concerns of the community. The very process of imbuing a pre-existing sense of cultural difference with more pronounced communitarian overtones tended to exacerbate social tensions, strengthening arguments about the impossibility of Hindu–Muslim coexistence. Contextualizing the local irritations which were erecting seemingly insurmountable walls between Punjabi Hindus and Muslims shows the twists and turns of lived history which an exclusive reliance on the narratives of distinctive identities can all too easily metamorphose into the immutable truths of communitarian discourses.

What embittered social relations in the Punjab to an extraordinary degree was Swami Shradhanand's much-trumped-up conversion of Muslim Malkana Rajputs in Agra and Mathura in UP. They were declared victims of forced conversion by the Mughal emperor Aurangzeb. In Shradhanand's estimation there were at least six and a half lakh Hindus who mistakenly thought they were Muslims. Others put the figure at millions and some considered the entire Muslim population of India as products of forced conversion. But the Swami's gameplan was more specific. He wanted to use the 'noble example' of the Malkana Rajputs to make an impression on 'other apostates' and in this way unite the Hindus. Without this, he argued, there could be no 'lasting union between the two communities'.[173] Lala Lajpat Rai's *sangathan* or organization movement was specifically aimed at enabling Hindus to hold their own against the Muslim majority in the Punjab.

The Ludhiana Hindu Sabha on its own initiative had appealed for subscriptions to assist the casualties of Muslim colonialism to return to their original faith. Hindu merchants readily made donations, convinced that the Muslim majority in the city municipal committee was favouring its own co-religionists in collecting octroi duty.[174] Muslims who asked the local Khilafat Committee to intervene were blandly told that the provincial headquarters would disapprove of any such move and withhold the salaries of its paid workers. So Muslims in Ludhiana settled for their own fund-raising drive and formed the Tabligh-i-Islam Committee to counteract the Hindu Sabha.[175] In Rawalpindi, Muslims accused Hindus of using their majority on the municipal committee unfairly. Reactions to the conversions in UP were made worse by

[173]*SPPAI*, 24 March 1923, vol. xlv, no.12, p. 93.
[174]*SPPAI*, 10 March 1923, vol. xlv, no.10, p. 80
[175]*SPPAI*, 17 and 24 March 1923, vol. xlv, nos. 11, 12, pp. 87, 93.

religious debates between Arya Samajists and local *maulvis*. Even the president of the city Khilafat Committee felt compelled to say that the Hindus had befriended Muslims only to convert them. Their real purpose was to establish Hindu raj. Arya Samaj propagandists were abusing Islam and making false accusations against Muslims. Despite the president's efforts, the Congress Committee had refused to curb the tongues of the Aryas. This made it 'obvious that the Congress and the Arya Samaj were one and the same party'. Hindus considered Gandhi to be a great man although he had 'prayed for forgiveness with folded hands' after Chauri Chaura. Most troubling was the claim by some Arya Samajists that 'Mecca had in former times been a Hindu temple which had been forcibly snatched from them by the Muhammadans'. How could Muslims 'associate with the Aryas' without 'being considered traitors to their faith'.[176]

Over the years Amritsar city had fluctuated between displays of unity and intense political and commercial rivalries between Hindus and Muslims. Perched between Lahore and Delhi, it had always attracted a two-way flow of itinerant *maulvis*. The conversions in UP had wounded the bearded men of Islam to the core. One visitor from Ludhiana claimed that Muslims had given up cow slaughter to please Hindus but would now kill four cows for every one sacrificed in the past. A set of local divines concurred; they wanted no part of *swaraj* if it meant interference in religion. A notice issued by the Anjuman-i-Muin-ul-Muslimin maintained that with the coming of *swaraj*, the community of Islam would be expelled from India just as poor Muslim shopkeepers were being turned out of Hindu bazaars in the city. So Muslims had to sever ties with the Hindus and make generous subscriptions for the upkeep of a deputation of *ulema* who would go to Agra and put an end to the wicked practices of the Aryas.[177]

With the Arya Samaj preachers on the loose, and the Punjab Khilafat Committee reluctant to formally take up the cause of the Malkana Rajputs, the *maulvis* of north India were in action as never before. Finding the Khilafat Committee's stance hypocritical, many defected to join the roving bands of religious divines who were doing the rounds of various cities and towns in the Punjab and UP. The race to convert and reconvert damaged the few remaining threads of goodwill between the two communities in the Punjab. It was a dismal manifestation of inverted pride on both sides of the religious divide. Conducted in the name of Hindus and Muslims, the bigotry was no less individual for being cast in communitarian idioms.

In Multan one prominent Arya Samajist imported from Lahore nearly succeeded in sparking off a second round of violence in a city still recovering from the one six months ago. Pandit Dharm Bhikshu exemplifies the individual

[176]Ibid.
[177]*SPPAI*, 24 March 1921, vol. xlii, no. 12, p. 94.

bigot who ends up implicating the entire community merely by claiming to speak in its defence. At a meeting of the Hindu Sabha, he fulminated against the ungrateful Muslim who had repaid his compatriots for supporting the *khilafat* by perpetrating violence in Malabar and Multan. But it was the *pandit's* knowledge of history that impressed the audience the most. Citing instances of Hindu supremacy in the past, he noted that they were 'at the present moment stronger than the Muhammadans and could turn them out of India' but refrained from doing so due to the 'ties of relationship'. The real howler was the assertion that the Prophet of Islam was 'originally a Hindu and the original Quran was composed from a Hindu book in the possession of Muhammad'. Unfortunately the book was lost and so 'Muhammad composed a fresh Quran'. Muslims had been 'following a false religion' all along. They should convert to Hinduism, 'failing which they should leave India'. Exclusion was to be matched by inequality in status. According to the *pandit*, if 'a Muhammadan struck a Hindu once, the latter should strike the former twice'.[178] But nothing could quite compare with Bhikshu's contention in Ferozepore that Mecca was 'originally a Hindu temple'. There could be 'no union' with the Muslims until the Hindus took Mecca back from the Muslims.[179]

Alarmed by the turn of events in the Punjab, a number all-India leaders rushed to the province with appeals for communitarian harmony. These included such weighty names as Motilal Nehru, Abul Kalam Azad, C.R. Das, Mrs Sarojini Naidu, Hakim Ajmal Khan and Dr Ansari. But the ideals of nationalism expounded by them fell on deaf Punjabi ears. The Jamiat-ul-Ulema-i-Hind did not help matters by issuing a circular calling for the collection of ten lakh rupees to undo the reclamation work done by the Aryas in UP.[180] Efforts by Arya Samajists to spread the conversion movement in the Punjab encouraged Muslims to do the same, hardening social divisions as the communities boycotted each other's shops and campaigned to start their own in many parts of the province. *Shuddhi* and *tabligh* had replaced *swaraj* as the main emblems in popular consciousness. Instead of non-cooperation with government, the emphasis was on ensuring suspension of all dealings between the two communities. By mid-1923 the Provincial Khilafat Committee had split on whether or not to divert funds to counter the *shuddhi* movement. This was the beginning of the end for the few remaining outposts of anti-imperalism and Hindu–Muslim accommodation in the Punjab.

Towards the end of April there was mayhem in Amritsar and Multan. The Amritsar troubles were preceded by bitter exchanges between Hindu and Muslim propagandists. This inspired some 4000 lower class Muslims to arm themselves with *lathis* and parade the bazaars singing songs urging their co-

[178]*SPPAI*, 7 April 1923, vol. xlii, no.14, p. 108.
[179]*SPPAI*, 19 May 1923, vol. xlii, no.19, p. 156.
[180]*SPPAI*, 21 April 1923, .vol. xlii, no.16, pp. 127–8.

religionists to break off all ties with Hindus. Offers by the all-India leadership to intervene and negotiate a compromise were briskly rejected by the local bigwigs. The actual violence was sparked off by an alleged insult to a young Hindu girl by Muslim toughs. Although scotched by British troops, the outbreak gave a fillip to the policy of boycott. Muslims opened up their own shops.[181] Hindus retaliated by threatening to import non-Muslim labour from Jammu and the hill tracts.[182] In Multan efforts to start Muslim businesses and the ensuing stoppage of commercial exchange resulted in individual assaults and a steep deterioration in social relations.[183]

Both communities tried imposing restrictions on the movement of women. In Amritsar, local *maulvis* told Muslims not to let their women go to the bazaar lest they be abused or molested. Hindu women in Gujrat faced similar curbs while the men were instructed to take physical training in preparation for an impending battle with the Muslims. In some districts, the two communities were known to be arming themselves with *lathis*. Not to be left behind, some Hindu landlords threatened to eject their Muslim tenants.[184] There were also tensions between Muslims and Sikhs over *jhatka* shops. It was altogether a sorry state of affairs.

Obscene and abusive language was used to denigrate the social customs and religious beliefs of the other community. Muslim preachers likened Swami Shradhanand to General Dyer, the butcher of Jallianwalla Bagh, arguing that so long as the existing divisions persisted there would be no *swaraj* for the next hundred years.[185] Warning the Swami of terrible consequences, Pir Jamaat Ali Shah vowed to convert thirty-two crore Hindus to Islam. The Aryas retorted that they would 'only stop their endeavours when the Muhammadans had handed over all who had embraced their creed since the days of Muslim rule'. In Lahore where the trade boycott had not proceeded as far as in the smaller cities, preparations were underway to open Muslim shops, shun Hindu fairs and festivals and boycott the Congress. More disquieting was the increased Hindu–Muslim bitterness among the subordinate social classes. The 'idea of Hindustan for the Hindus' was 'gaining favour in Hindu circles' with 'every Hindu ... becoming obsessed with the dream of a Hindu Swaraj'.[186]

Attacks on the nationalist leadership were another cherished theme for the zealots of Islam and Hinduism. Local *maulvis* never ceased telling Muslims that they had harmed themselves irreparably by accepting Gandhi's lead.

---

[181]Ibid., p. 127.

[182]In Amritsar a large number of Muslim labourers were out of work. Hindus were also boycotting Muslim barbers, milk-sellers, vegetable-sellers and cart-drivers. (*SPPAI*, 5 May and 2 June 1923, vol. xlii, nos. 18, 21, pp. 146–7, 171.)

[183]*SPPAI*, 19 May 1923, vol. xlii, no. 19, p. 156.

[184]See Ibid., pp. 155–6.

[185]*SPPAI*, 26 May 1923, vol. xlii, no. 20, p. 165.

[186]*SPPAI*, 2 June 1923, vol. xlii, no. 21, p. 172.

Muslims now learnt that the Quran prohibited them from befriending non-Muslims.[187] The Ali brothers were condemned for saying that Gandhi was as big a personality as the Prophet Muhammad.[188] Strong exception was taken to statements by Hakim Ajmal Khan and Abul Kalam Azad against letting the apostasy movement jeopardize Hindu–Muslim unity. Such men, one propagandist asserted, were 'not leaders but jackals' who had no respect for their own religion. Muslims were told to refuse to be led in prayers by men who held the teachings of the *shariat* in such disdain.[189] The Aryas were no less trenchant in their critiques of nationalist leaders, particularly Gandhi. Pandit Dharm Bhiksu cited the Vedas to justify his opposition to the kind of Hindu–Muslim unity preached by the Mahatma.[190] From the Arya angle, the goal of *swaraj* could be attainable only by converting Muslims to Hinduism.[191]

Spouting hatred in the name of their respective religions came easily to these crusaders. As ever, divisions between Hindus and Muslims were mirrored by growing internal tears within the two communities. Aryas and Sanatan Dharm Hindus fought for the allegiance of the new converts while Muslims opposed to the *khilafatists* and non-cooperators abused their co-religionists mercilessly. There was much consternation among the Sanatan Dharm Hindus as well as Muslims over sharing wells with recently purified untouchables like *chamars* and *banjaras* whom the Aryas had won over to their side.[192] This showed the extent to which class and caste undercut the balance of differences between Hindus and Muslims in the Punjab. Sectarian differences were another factor undermining communitarian unity. The defenders of Islam could not resist sniping at the Qadianis who were among the most truculent opponents of the Aryas.

The war against internal others, however, had to await the successful conclusion of the one against the perceived oppression of the external enemy. This is why the multiple fractures along caste, class and sectarian lines in Punjabi society have been so easily swept aside by communitarian interpretations. Habits of perception die hard. Amidst heightening tensions it was difficult to separate the causes of one social fracas from the other. An incident in Lahore illustrated the trend. A Hindu shopkeeper in the Kasera bazaar had secured the municipal committee's approval to carry out certain improvements involving the removal of a staircase and the demolition of a room which gave access to a shop owned by a Muslim woman. When the woman's male relatives protested a scuffle ensued causing minor injuries to both parties. Seeing this as a Hindu–Muslim quarrel the shopkeepers in this as well as the adjoining bazaars closed their

[187]*SPPAI*, 5 May 1923, vol. xlii, no. 18, p. 147.
[188]*SPPAI*, 9 June 1923, vol. xlii, no. 22, p. 180.
[189]Ibid., pp. 181–2.
[190]*SPPAI*, 23 June 1923, vol. xlii, no. 24, p. 196.
[191]Ibid., p. 197.
[192]See for instance *SPPAI*, 16 June 1923, vol. xlii, no. 23, p. 189.

shops. The incident was greatly exaggerated in the Punjab press as yet another instance of communitarian tensions. And this despite the fact that 'inter-communal feeling had nothing to do with the origin of the fight' which would have taken place regardless of inter-communitarian relations. But in demonstrating how 'so small an affair' could be 'so quickly bruited about as a Hindu–Muhammadan riot', it provides an indication of 'the highly electrical state of the atmosphere and the uneasy apprehensiveness of the public mind'.[193]

Realizing that the situation in the Punjab was out of the hands of the provincial and the all-India leadership, Madan Mohan Malaviya visited the province in the hope of patching up differences and exonerating himself of the charge of being at the root of the problem. The strained atmosphere of Lahore found Malaviya in a conciliatory mood. He lectured on tolerance, deprecated the exaggeration of trivial differences and exhorted Punjabis to once again develop a sense of Indian unity and independence. They had to put the good of India before that of their own religion. Malaviya recommended setting up citizens' associations in every *mohalla* to settle disputes on the spot. But seeing specks of red in Malaviya's white flag, many Muslims in the audience jeered at a speaker who lauded this champion of unity and peace. The meeting ended abruptly, allowing the *pandit* to make a hasty exit. Nowhere near the execration in which the Muslims held Shradhanand's name, Malaviya's presence in the Punjab gave a fresh edge to Hindu–Muslim bitterness.[194]

The tone and substance of Malaviya's approach suggested a recognition on the part of all-India leaders that the Punjab could not be allowed to continue its rudderless drift through the fires of Hindu–Muslim differences. Unfortunately, there was a wide gap between intention and credibility. In Amritsar where relations between the two communities had curdled after a hard boil, local opinion placed the onus on Malaviya along with Azad, Ajmal Khan and Ansari. Muslims were warned not to let these men lead them further into the trap of deception laid by Hindu infidels. After rancorous debate among members of all three communities in which each accused the other for the state of disunion, it was decided to let bygones be bygones. Committees consisting of four members from each community were to be established which would visit any future scenes of disturbance and try to bring about a settlement. The press was to refrain from publishing any news of incidents until after the submission of the committees' reports.[195]

For the remainder of 1923 various moves made to restore some semblance of civility in Hindu–Muslim relations came to naught. In August the release of the fervent Muslim Congressman Saifuddin Kitchlew temporarily raised hopes of an accord between the two communities. Kitchlew began by holding out an olive branch to the Arya Samajists. On *shuddhi* and *sangathan*, he held

---

[193]*SPPAI*, 7 July 1923, vol. xlii, no. 26, p. 210.
[194]Ibid., pp. 211–12.
[195]Ibid.

that Hindus had a right to do what they wanted. He personally thought
Muslims should be allowed to join the *sangathan* movement to attain *swaraj*.
But he conceded that if the Hindus were not prepared to cooperate with the
Muslims, then the latter should form an organization of their own.[196] On
bad terms with Lala Lajpat Rai, it did not take long for Kitchlew to establish
the Jamiat-i-Tanzim. He had originally intended this to serve as the vehicle
for Muslim participation in the broader nationalist movement. The
overlapping politics of the Punjab and UP, however, buried any prospects of
a Hindu–Muslim rapprochement. During Muharram there was violence in
the western UP towns of Saharanpur and Agra. Preferring to survive in the
maelstrom of Punjab's politics rather than shooting in the dark for Hindu–
Muslim accommodation, Kitchlew took a stiff stance against both the *shuddhi*
and *sangathan* movements.

With even the most ardent nationalists among Punjabi Muslims turning
into Arya bashers, there was no prospect of the province springing into another
burst of pro-Congress activity. There was a touch of nationalist embarrassment
interspersed with remorse in Mohamed Ali's admission to Nehru soon after
his release from jail that the Punjab was 'an eternal puzzle' for him. The
leaders in Lahore were 'hopelessly narrow-minded' and it was difficult to
find anyone who had truly imbibed the Gandhian message.[197] Himself an
unlikely follower of the Mahatma, what had brought Mohamed Ali into the
Congress camp was his unflinching belief in Islamic universalism as a
necessary concomitant for genuine Muslim affinity with Indian nationalism.
This was precisely what the Aryas were challenging through the *shuddhi* and
sangathan movements and the Muslims countering with *tabligh* and *tanzim*. A
safe distance away from the Punjab might have given these activities the
appearance of petty politics. The post-non-cooperation phase in the Punjab
inadvertently placed the barriers to Gandhian *swaraj* into much sharper relief
than all the platitudes about nationalist unity put together.

As Mohamed Ali's presidential address to the Congress at Cocanada in
December 1923 revealed, there was a world of difference between the Islamic
universalist and the Indian nationalist mindset. In giving an all-too-extensive
justification of the history of Muslim politics in India, Mohamed Ali did his
Punjabi and Bengali co-religionists proud by defending separate electorates.
This political arrangement, accepted by the Congress as long ago as in1916,
was 'the consequence, and *not* the cause of the separation between Muslims
and their more numerous Hindu brethren'. India's greatest hope for the future
lay in becoming a 'federation of faiths', not in a 'misleading unity of opposition'.

[196]*SPPAI*, 8 September 1923, vol. xlii, no. 35, pp. 279–80.

[197]Mohamed Ali to Nehru, 7 November 1923, in Jawaharlal Nehru, *A Bunch of Old Letters (written mostly to Jawaharlal Nehru and some written by him)* (second edition), Delhi, Oxford University Press, 1988, pp. 31–2.

But when it came to chalking out a path for the future, Mohamed Ali could come up with no better suggestion than continued non-cooperation with the government through a unity of opposition captured in the dictum 'To you your faith, to me mine'.[198]

Offering a non-solution to the Hindu–Muslim problem may have been a politic way to conclude a controversial speech. Sadly for Mohamed Ali and also his brother, who in his keynote address at the Khilafat Conference had insisted on the continued relevance of the *khilafat* issue, their moment in history was on the verge of a total eclipse. In June 1923 the Lausanne settlement had seen the Turks relinquishing all claims to spiritual and temporal sovereignty over the Arabian peninsula. This was followed in October with the declaration of Turkey as a republic, a short step away to the final abolition of the *khilafat* in March 1924. This left the Islamic universalists holding their heads in shame and, depending on their political proclivities, facing the abject prospect of endorsing or rejecting the equally lost cause of Gandhian non-cooperation.

Even before the Turkish National Assembly hammered the last nail into the coffin of the *khilafat* movement, the clashing politics of regionalism tilted the balance against those looking for all-India solutions, dimming whatever prospects still remained for an accommodation between Islamic universalism and Indian nationalism. What the all-India Congress's rejection at Cocanada of C.R. Das's political tour d'force in concluding a pact with Bengali Muslims suggests is that partisan narrow-mindedness was not the monopoly of the Punjab alone. Moreover, it underlines why leaving everyone to his own faith posed a danger to sustaining the myth of *swaraj* and uncontested sovereignty under the banner of a single Indian 'nation'. Das had gone over the heads of strident Hindu opposition to forge an alliance with Muslims in Bengal. Not only did Bengali Muslims retain separate electorates, they were also given representation proportionate to their population in the province. Confined to a mere 40 per cent by the much-vaunted Lucknow Pact of 1916, Muslims in Bengal could look forward to 55 per cent of the seats in the provincial legislative assembly. Unwilling to accept a 15 per cent cut in their representation, many Bengali Hindus were even more averse to conceding 55 per cent of all future government appointments to Muslims. In an attempt to promote religious accommodation, the pact prohibited the playing of music before mosques and granted Muslims the right to slaughter cows.

That many vocal Bengali Hindus considered the pact a sell-out is understandable. But for the premier nationalist organization to intervene and censure Das for injecting altruism into politics is indefensible given the high-

---

[198]Mohamed Ali's presidential address at the Indian National Congress at Cocanada, 26 December 1923 in Iqbal (ed.), *Select Writings and Speeches of Maulana Mohamed Ali*, pp. 370–2, pp. 406–7, p. 419.

sounding talk about Hindu–Muslim unity as a necessary prelude to *swaraj*. Desperately in need of a similar display of political foresight, Punjabi public opinion on the Bengal pact as manifested in the vernacular press was neatly divided along communitarian lines. Encouraged no doubt by the stance taken by the Congress, Hindu-owned newspapers damned Das's method of accommodating the cultural and political differences between the two communities. The *Milap* sarcastically commented that the noble goal of union would be achieved sooner if all Indians embraced Islam; this would solve the problem of cow slaughter once and for all. In addition, Turkey and Afghanistan should be invited to take possession of India and everyone should start viewing slavery as freedom. By contrast, Muslim-edited papers such as the *Zamindar*, the *Vakil* and the *Paisa Akhbar* thought all provinces should follow the Bengal example. The Sikh paper *Akali-te-Pardesi* took a neutral position by asserting that the pact was in line with the circumstances pertaining in Bengal.[199]

Determined to scuttle Das's formula, a Congress subcommittee consisting of Lajpat Rai and Dr Ansari cobbled together an ill-fated all-India arrangement for a Hindu–Muslim settlement. A barometer of urban Punjabi Hindu opinion, the *Tribune* welcomed the Congress-sponsored effort as a just solution of the vexed question of religious liberty but disapproved of the continuation of separate electorates for Muslims. The *Muslim Outlook* took strong exception to the clause requiring Muslims to take an oath against cow slaughter throughout the year except on the occasion of Baqra Id. This was establishing Hindu raj, 'not Swaraj in which all Indians may be common sharers'. Muslims would rather 'cut off their hands' than sign away their rights. The pro-Congress *Zamindar* thought it was 'intended for some country inhabited entirely by Hindus and provide[d] for the total extinction of the Mussalmans'.[200]

Congress's repudiation of the Bengal pact and support for the Lajpat–Ansari proposal appeared to demonstrate the extent to which it was tied to the chariot wheels of a notional majority defined by individuals associated with the *shuddhi* and *sangathan* movements. A number of Punjab Muslim newspapers condemned the underhand manner in which the Congress was merging the formal and informal arenas of politics. The last thing the Punjab needed was for the Congress to give its imprimatur to a view of nationalism defined wholly in terms of majoritarian and minoritarian interests. As the *Zamindar* put it, by discarding the Das pact the Congress was coming to the aid of Punjabi Hindus who wanted 'to control everything even in a province where they [we]re in a minority'. This 'deviation ... from the right path at the

[199]See *Milap*, 21 December 1923; *Zamindar* (29 December); *Vakil* (22 December); *Paisa Akhbar* (24 December) and *Akali te-Pardesi* (29 December) in *Note on the Punjab Press for the Week Ending 5 January 1924*, Lahore, NCHCR, Islamabad, p. 6 (henceforth NPP followed by date and page numbers).

[200]*Tribune*, 28 December 1923; *Muslim Outlook* (22 December) and *Zamindar* (7 and 29 December), ibid., p. 7.

instance of the Hindu majority ... [would] prove a message of death' for the Congress. Disappointed and disillusioned with the Congress, it supported the Jamiat-ul-Ulema-i-Hind's appointment of a committee to draw up a report on Muslim rights.[201] The *Paisa Akhbar* for its part reprimanded Congress Muslims for shirking responsibility at a critical moment. It was relentless in attacking the Ali brothers who had 'greatly injured the best interests of the Muhammadans' by persisting in their efforts to ally with the Hindus who wanted to eliminate Islam from the subcontinent.[202] The subsequent retraction of the Bengal Swarajist Party on the Muslim share in government service did not help Congress in the Punjab. It merely reinforced many Punjabi Muslim's opinion that *swaraj* was not worth fighting for unless their place in an independent India had been put on 'a fairly uniform level of political power and resourcefulness' with the Hindus.[203]

Haggling over the price of political unity while promoting trade boycotts reveals how well Punjabis could tell their left hand from their right. Some of the most unconscionable attacks on Islam and Hinduism nevertheless carry Punjabi thumbprints. Supplementing the revivalist ardour of the Aryas and Muslims engaged in *tabligh* and *tanzim*, these writings reveal an almost cussed determination not to settle differences until the principles of communitarian primacy had been spelt out, if not accepted. Yet it would be an historical error to attribute purely religious motivations to the hatred Punjabis seemed to harbour against one another. Efforts to rupture the existing pattern of exchange relations in the marketplace had strong material overtones. Together with the poisoned narratives appearing in print, these trends in the informal arenas were relatively more autonomous of politics in the reformed councils than in Bengal. The Bengal Swarajists not only dominated the reformed councils but enjoyed a support base among the disenfranchised in urban and rural areas alike. By contrast, the Muslim, Hindu and Sikh agricultural interests constituting the Punjab Unionists led by Mian Fazl-i-Husain were drawn from the collaborative networks built by the colonial state in the countryside.

The divergence, though by no means insularity, of informal and formal politics in the Punjab had important ramifications for Indian nationalism. For one thing, those engaged in the construction of communitarian narratives, Hindu or Muslim, tended not to be the direct beneficiaries of the constitutional reforms. For another, the Arya Samaj activists and their Muslim counterparts who had orchestrated the *khilafat* and non-cooperation agitation in the Punjab had by 1923 turned to *shuddhi–sangathan* and *tabligh–tanzim* respectively. As for the Unionists, they had no reason to untie themselves from the government's apron strings. This left no room for the kind of nationalist politics propagated

---

[201]*Zamindar*, 6 and 10 January 1924, ibid., p. 16.
[202]*Paisa Akhbar*, 5 January 1924, ibid., p. 16.
[203]*Muslim Outlook*, 16 March 1924, ibid., p. 112.

by Gandhi, imagined by Mohamed Ali and negotiated by Das. The provincial Congress, such as it existed, was deeply infected with the communitarian plague. Lala Lajpat Rai, Swami Shradhanand, Saifuddin Kitchlew and Ataullah Shah Bukhari were singing the tunes of anti-imperialism and communitarianism in varying measures, indicating the extent to which Indian nationalism was imbricated with its pejorative other—'communalism'.

While the Arya Samajists could project their communitarianism as consistent with a majoritarian view of Indian nationalism, the politics of cultural difference articulated by Punjabi Muslims was to be consigned to the ignoble category of 'communalism'. This bifurcation between 'good' and 'bad' communitarianism was not a Punjabi invention. In 1923 the appearance of Vinayak Damodar Savarkar's book, *Hindutva*, had set the terms of the debate for at least a segment of India's population. According to Savarkar who founded the Rashtriya Swayamsewak Sangh a few years later, a Hindu was 'a person who regarded this land of Bharatvarsha' extending from 'the Indus to the Seas, as his Fatherland as well as his Holy land' or the 'cradle or land of his religion'. The concept of Hindustava incorporated the 'depths of thought and activity of the whole being of our Hindu race'. On this view Hindus were a 'nation'; the Muslims merely a community.[204]

Until now the communitarian discourse had spoken of *qaums*, inaccurately translated into the English term 'nation'. With Savarkar's intervention, the unequal status of Hindus and Muslims was made explicit in the distinction between 'nation' and 'community'. In the British Indian political system where separate electorates encapsulated the minority status of Muslims, transforming the Hindu *qaum* into a 'nation' was inherently problematic. Instead of negotiating the terms of accommodating cultural differences within the Indian nation, those excluded from the definition of a 'Hindu' had either to seek incorporation by adopting a territorially based religious identity or go in the opposite direction through a self-generated process of separation. Seen against this backdrop, *shuddhi* and *sangathan* as well as *tabligh* and *tanzim* take on deeper shades of meaning.

Sharing the common motto of aggressive defence, both sets of activities aimed at converting and organizing as many Hindus and Muslims as possible. For Punjabi Hindus this was the best hope of reclaiming their edge in the numbers game while Muslims felt the need to protect and advance their provincial dominance against an economically powerful minority that was part of an all-India majority. The theme of unity was naturally the main fatality. An example of this was the *Arya Gazette*'s offensive comment on a series of articles in the *Siyasat* stressing the importance of Hindu–Muslim unity on

---

[204]V.D. Savarkar, *Hindutva*, p. 4 cited in Afzal Iqbal, *Life and Times of Mohamed Ali: An Analysis of the Hopes, Fears and Aspirations of Muslim India from 1878 to 1931*, (second edition), Lahore: Institute of Islamic Culture, 1979, p. 312.

the authority of the Quran. Instead of wasting so much ink and paper, the writer would 'have done better if he had got expunged from the Quran the odious verses' regarding non-Muslims. So long as the Quran contained 'abominable epithets' and taught its adherents to 'hate non-Muslims' it was 'futile to expect any lasting unity between Hindus and Muhammadans'. Furious at such wanton provocation, the *Vakil* remarked that 'no sensible person' could 'use such insolent language towards the revealed book of a *numerically very strong community*'. This brought the *Akash Vani* into the melee with the complaint that 'Punjab Muhammadans ha[d] a sort of mania to crush the Hindus of this province and establish Muslim rule'. It referred to a letter by the Delhi-based Islamic scholar Khwajah Hasan Nizami inviting Gandhi to embrace Islam. Delving into history the paper noted that Aurangzeb had offered his daughter in marriage to Shivaji's son Sambhaji if he converted to Islam. A religion which tried inducing people into its fold through 'the bait of wealth, women or *jagirs*' was not worthy of respect.[205] These acerbic exchanges are a reflection of the rumours rife in certain Muslim circles of the 'speedy conversion to Islam of Mahatma Gandhi, Shradhanand and Malaviya'.[206]

Bolstering their numerical strength was only one aspect of Muslim and Hindu preoccupations in the Punjab. The more serious problem for the future were the ongoing efforts to expand the trade boycott against Hindus. Leading the *tanzim* movement in the Punjab, Kitchlew exhorted Muslims to take up trade since 'unity was impossible with the Hindus when ... [they] were so much richer'.[207] Zafar Ali Khan agreed. He had come out of jail to discover that no one in the Punjab was interested in reviving the *khilafat* movement.[208] So it made sense to join the flow and propagate *tanzim* and trade among the Muslims. Attaining commercial equality with the Hindus was now deemed a necessary concomitant to unity between the two communities. The sight of Zafar Ali Khan—a great Islamic universalist—and Saifuddin Kitchlew—a hardened Congress nationalist—advocating the material advancement of their co-religionists through the setting up of Muslim banks and credit organizations signposted the end of a moment in history where the convergence of the crescent and the *charkha* had raised hopes of an emerging Indian nation with inclusionary rather than exclusionary bearings.

While the responsibility for this turnabout has to be shared by the paragons

---

[205]*Arya Gazette*, 15 May; *Vakil* (18 May) and *Akash Vani* (18 May), *NPP*, 24 May 1924, p. 191 (my emphasis).

[206]*SPPAI*, 13 September 1924, vol. xlii, no. 36, p. 190.

[207]*SPPAI*, 20 September 1924, vol. xlii, no. 37, p. 192.

[208]In Attock, Zafar Ali Khan asked an audience to raise their hands if they would join him in revitalizing the *Khilafat* Movement. He was crestfallen when 'no one responded'. *SPPAI*, 6 December 1924, vol. xlii, no. 49, p. 240.

of Islamic universalism and Indian nationalism, one man's voice needs special airing. Swami Shradhanand, the architect of *shuddhi*, did much to engineer the reversal of such gains as were made towards accommodation between Hindus and Muslims during the heyday of the *khilafat* and non-cooperation movement. He accepted that Hindu–Muslim unity was a precondition for Indian independence. But the Congress had squandered that opportunity by not properly investigating the causes of communitarian violence in Malabar and Multan and was responsible for the subsequent troubles in UP and the Punjab. Swayed by Islamic sentiments, it had been expending its energies on matters outside India, ignoring the gravity of the situation within. Evidence of the Congress pandering to Muslims was its outright condemnation of *shuddhi* and *sangathan*. Instead of booking Muslim murderers and bandits, the Congress was pointing an accusing finger at those working for the uplift and organization of Hindus. *Shuddhi* and *sangathan* were a quest for the religious rights of Hindus and no one, not even the Congress, could prevent them from protecting themselves against Muslim aggression. Calling for the suspension of these activities was tantamount to eliminating Hindu identity and letting Muslims make outlandish demands.

The real danger to communitarian unity, Shradhanand roared, came from Muslim leaders who packaged their faith in terms of *jihad*, collected funds from Hindus for the *khilafat* but used them for propagating Islam. It was intolerable for Abul Kalam Azad to misuse his privilege as Congress president to demand the abandonment of *shuddhi* and *sangathan*. This showed how far the Islamic impulse had come to pervade the political spirit of the times. With too many Muslims in its midst, the Congress had become incapable of protecting Hindu interests. So Hindus had every right to form their own organizations to safeguard their property and women from the predatory Muslims. Since arriving in India, Muslims had been converting Hindus forcibly and slaughtering cows. Yet Gandhi had taken up the *khilafat* issue as if it were the Muslim cow. Although Hindus had supported the Muslim cow both morally and materially, their holy cow continued to be killed. Such an unequal exchange was no basis for unity with Muslims. Now that the Muslim cow was well and truly dead, the Swami wanted all *khilafat* committees disbanded since they were a mere cover for *tabligh* and *tanzim*.[209]

The flip side to the embarrassment of nationalism in the Punjab was the province's contribution in supplying some of the more jarring idioms for its hidden subtext. As developments in this veritable war zone of contending communitarian narratives during the next few decades made clear, the inversion of the all-India majority and minority equation in the Punjab far from being an irritating side-show was very much at the centrestage of the

[209]Shri Swami Shradhanand, *Hindu Muslim Itihad aur Congress ka aik Tarikhi Warq*, Delhi, July 1924, Urdu D.435, IOL.

ongoing struggle between nationalism and imperialism. By keeping the curtain drawn on the Punjab, the binary modes of nationalism and communalism can only continue confusing rather than clarifying the thorny issue of accommodating religiously informed cultural differences within a nationalist discourse of uncontested sovereignty and equitable rights of citizenship.

Chapter 6

Contested Sovereignty in the Punjab:
The Interplay of Formal and Informal Politics

'Let it not be forgotten,' the Bengali radical Manabendra Nath Roy had written in 1926, 'that the Punjab is the centre of the Hindu–Moslem conflicts that radiate from there to all other parts of India.'[1] The second half of the 1920s saw social and political currents in the Punjab receding from the ideal of an inclusionary nationalism towards an apparently unbending kind of exclusionary communitarianism. This has encouraged at least one historian to depict the decade as a 'prelude to partition'.[2] Yet the Punjab in this period can just as well be seen as providing alternative visions of nationalisms which seriously challenged the notion of one nation and undivided sovereignty propagated by the Congress. The rebarbative overtones notwithstanding, assigning Punjabi politics the pejorative label of 'communalism' serves the retrospectively constructed agendas of secular and Muslim nationalisms better than the purposes of analytical history. If one is to avoid perpetuating the tyranny of imperialist knowledge, especially the misleading rigidities of its favoured classifications of Indian society, dismantling the dominant assumptions of its main derivative—the nationalist discourse itself—seems to be in order.

Punjab in many ways is a perfect burial ground for the hubris of Indian nationalism. In its discourse, if not in its practice, the pre-eminent view of Indian nationalism has been that of an inclusionary, accommodative, consensual and popular anti-colonial struggle. This has entailed denigrating

---

[1]M.N. Roy, 'Punjab Money-lenders' Bill', in Sibnarayan Ray (ed.), *Selected Works of M.N. Roy*, vol. ii, 1923–7, New York and Delhi: Oxford University Press, 1988, p. 439.

[2]See David Page, *Prelude to Partition: The Indian Muslims and the Imperial System of Control 1920-1932*, Delhi: Oxford University Press, 1982, 1987, passim.

the exclusive affinities of religion as 'communal' in an imagined hierarchy of collectivities crowned by the ideal of a 'nation' unsullied by bigotry. By implying that religious affiliations are, if not necessarily bigoted, then certainly less worthy than identification with the 'nation', Indian nationalism comes dangerously close to trampling over its own coattails. The cultural roots of Indian nationalism owed far more to religious ideals, reinterpreted and reconfigured in an imaginative fashion, than has been admitted. According to Partha Chatterjee, who takes the cultural fragment represented by certain Bengali Hindu middle-class intellectuals to illuminate the consciousness of the Indian nation as a whole, religion provided the spiritual stores for resisting and negotiating the inherent materiality of both western modernity and British rule. While giving more respectability to religious sentiments and symbols than they have tended to enjoy in the past, Chatterjee does so by invoking a dichotomy between an autonomous inner spiritual and a dominated outer material domain.[3] This unfortunately skirts around the problem of dismantling the binary opposition between 'secular nationalism' and religious communalism on which so much of the ideological edifice of the post–colonial Indian nation–state has rested.

The imperatives of the post-colonial state and its nationalism cannot be allowed to dictate the agendas of historical scholarship. Commenting on what he calls the 'nationalist transition', Partha Chatterjee asserts that 'relations between the people and the nation, the nation and the state, relations which nationalism claims to have resolved once and for all, are relations which continue to be contested and are therefore open to negotiation all over again'.[4] Since his project is to explore the construction of the nationalist hegemony, albeit with an excessive reference to the Calcutta middle classes, Chatterjee glosses over the unresolved tensions and continued contestations that marked the terrain of both region and religion. While acknowledging that 'the real difficulty was with Islam in India' which gave 'rise to alternative hegemonic efforts than the one based on the evocation of a classical Hindu past', he stops short of considering the substance of these other alternatives.[5] What such an investigation of the cultural roots of nationalism leaves unexamined are the myriad subaltern contestations of an emerging mainstream nationalism which like its adversary, colonialism, may well have achieved only dominance without hegemony.

[3]Chatterjee's curious dichotomy between the inner spiritual and outer material realms is both analytically and empirically unsustainable. But this in no way detracts from his many invaluable insights. He notes for instance that the culture of the Bengali middle classes who played a constitutive role in the formative phase of Indian nationalism 'was, and still is, in its overwhelmingly cultural content, "Hindu"' (Chatterjee, *The Nation and its Fragments*, p. 74).

[4]Ibid., pp. 154–5.

[5]Ibid., pp. 73–4.

To call this dominance hegemony is to confuse the claims of one strand of nationalist discourse with its ability to ensure cultural, not to mention, political acquiescence. It also underplays the exclusionary aspect of this nationalism which only succeeded in eliciting a stronger reaction from its sceptics and critics. This was particularly true of the Indian Muslims, engaged in redefining their religiously informed cultural identity in the face of a modernity underwritten by the fact of British sovereignty. The extension of the representative principle since the late nineteenth century and, in the 1920s, the extension of separate electorates to most elective institutions in the Punjab exacerbated the political bifurcation between majority and minority communities defined by religion.

Continued recourse to the colonial privileging of religious distinctions thwarted many well-meaning attempts at accommodating differences within a broad framework of Indian nationalism. So long as the dominant discourse among Indians drew upon notions of religious majoritarianism and minoritarianism there could be no hard and fast separation between 'nationalism' and 'communalism'. This was amply apparent in the Punjab where the Arya Samajists' rejection of 'minority' status, and the stolid defence of their 'majority' by articulate Muslims, gave impetus to acrimonious debates on rights and privileges of social groups defined by religion. These trends in Punjabi discourse and politics inflected the all-India postures of the Congress as well as the *khilafat* committees and the Muslim League throughout the remaining decades of the British raj. Recognizing the multiple and shifting ways in which individuals identified with the collective, whether as community or nation, helps to tease out why contending discourses on cultural differences emanating from the province instead of being accommodated ended up transforming the very idioms of an all-India nationalist politics.

Such an epistemological shift needs a matching empirical one. Most historical studies of the Punjab have tended to dwell on the formal arenas of politics while conceding the growing 'communalization' at the social base.[6] These have made admirable contributions to an understanding of the colonial state's networks of collaboration and control. Yet the preferred emphasis overstates the scope of politics in the reformed councils at the expense of neglecting the relatively autonomous activities in the informal arenas. What has been missing in scholarly analyses of the province is a nuanced and textured assessment of exchanges among Punjabis as they jostled for advantage vis-à-vis one another in the process of seeking a privileged hearing from the colonial state. Some of these related to representation in elective institutions and government services. But there were others squarely rooted in battles for social space and status at levels so fragmented and

---

[6]See, for instance, Page, *Prelude to Partition* and David Gilmartin, *Empire and Islam: Punjab and the Making of Pakistan*, Berkeley: University of California Press, 1988.

localized as to defy treating them as mere extensions of the more self-consciously communitarian discourses appearing in the press and publications market. Since the inadequate representative institutions of the colonial state were not designed to reflect the concerns underpinning larger social dynamics in the province, the historical focus has to turn more emphatically to the informal arena and its interplay with formal politics in the Punjab.

THE POLITICS OF UNION AND DISUNION

One of the main reasons for the early demise of the *khilafat* and non-cooperation movement in the Punjab was the success of the colonial state and its collaborators in forging a loose alliance of agricultural interests, Muslim, Hindu and Sikh. Known as the Unionist Party, this combination dominated the provincial ministry after the first elections to the reformed councils in 1920. Led, ironically enough, by an urban-based Muslim lawyer, Mian Fazl-i-Husain, the Punjab Unionists working the Montagu–Chelmsford reforms validated the faith reposed by the raj in the landlord element. Protected by the Punjab Land Alienation Act of 1900, the rural overlords had a mighty stake in the colonial dispensation. Whatever their personal views on God or Gandhi, it was the Government which promised them the greatest security with minimum risks. The disjunction between the networks of collaboration and agitation in the Punjab accounted in no uncertain way for the sharpening of communitarian identities and a corresponding polarization in the informal arenas.

Denied direct access to the colonial state and its channels of patronage, urban-educated Punjabis belonging to the intermediate strata in the main sought to make their presence felt by rustling up support among segments of the subordinate social classes. When this could not take the form of political rallies and meetings, the usual method was to craft stirring newspaper articles and pamphlets. The stridency of the authors tended to be in inverse proportion to their effectiveness in influencing the policies of the colonial state and the Unionist ministry. So the limited politics of union sponsored and promoted by the British in the Punjab had as its obverse a potentially more broad-based politics of disunion, aimed at undermining the system of collaboration and control quite as often as scoring debating points against rival communities. Put differently, the colonial state's decision to restrict the cross-communitarian alliance to a specific class left those outside this charmed circle with no option but to try and elbow for political space by unleashing a volley of narratives based on idioms of exclusionary communitarianism. A political necessity, if not always the most accurate measure of private predilections or social interactions, the pitched wars of communitarianism in the Punjab surpassed those in neighbouring UP where Hindus and Muslims were far from living in the bliss of social harmony.

There were, admittedly, fleeting moments when self-correcting mechanisms seemed to be at work. For all their disunion, Punjabis did not cease dreaming of union. The barriers to its attainment were commonly attributed to the colonial state and its policies of keeping the communities divided. A good illustration was the reaction in 1924 to the government's decision to enhance the water rates. Coming at a time of much bickering between Hindus and Muslims over *shuddhi, sangathan, tabligh* and *tanzim*, the debate in the vernacular press hinted at a growing realization among segments of the provincial literati of the merits of fashioning a politics of union autonomous of the colonial system of collaboration. The Sikhs for their part were in a belligerent mood due to the Shiromani Gurdwara Prabandhak Committee's agitation to gain control of the *gurdwaras* from British-backed *mahants* or temple keepers. So Hindu, Muslim and Sikh papers were at one in condemning the arbitrary increase in the tax burden on the rural populace. The provincial bureaucracy reappeared as the principal villain of the piece in much the same way as during the Rowlatt *satyagraha*.

Burying the communitarian hatchet and displaying a more-than-usual empathy for the landed classes, the Muslim-edited *Vakil* declared the new water rates 'a fresh calamity for the already afflicted Zamindars'. An article in the *Tribune* by a member of the Lyallpur municipal committee considered the tax hike 'a great opportunity for the Congress to win the sympathy of the Punjab Zamindars and use the unity of Hindu, Sikh and Muhammadan agriculturalists to remove communal disunion in this province'. The *Akali* thought gains could be made 'by showing a (bold) front to Government and ... not let opportunities slip through our fingers'.[7] The discomfiture of Punjabi *zamindars* and peasant proprietors could enable 'the Congress ... [to] regain its lost prestige'.[8] Before any of this could materialize the British wisely reduced the water rates.

The Unionists were seen as the main obstacle to the regeneration of nationalism in the province. A proposed amendment of election rules for the municipal committees, tabled by Fazl-i-Husain, was condemned as a transparent device to keep Congress and *khilafat* workers out of the formal political system. The Arya paper *Milap* accused the leading Unionist minister of 'danc[ing] to the tune of Government' which wanted to 'clear Municipal Committees of political workers'. In moving the amendment 'the Mian ha[d] afforded yet another proof of his being [a] traitor to the country'. For once the attack on Fazl-i-Husain was not motivated solely by communitarian prejudice. By tinkering with election rules he was ensuring that 'the best brains and servants of the Punjab ... ha[d] no part in local self-government' and only those willing to 'act as puppets' served on the municipal committees.[9]

---

[7]*NPP*, 21 June 1924, pp. 222–3.

[8]*NPP*, 5 July 1924, p. 233.

[9]*Islah*, Ludhiana, 28 June 1924 and *Milap*, Lahore, 2 July 1924, ibid., pp. 233–4.

Many newspapers held the provincial bureaucracy and colonial collaborators culpable for the spate of Hindu–Muslim conflicts. The Sanatan Dharm paper *Bharat* alleged that attempts had been made during the non-cooperation movement to incite Hindus by calling Muslims *mlechhas* and cow killers. Stories were circulated about the oppression of Muslim rulers and the razing of Hindu temples to the ground. Muslims in turn were told that Hindus were idolaters and infidels who ought to be boycotted. Consequently, 'simple-minded persons got entangled in this net'. Yet 'neither cow-killing nor the playing of music before mosques wa[s] the real cause of the strained relations between the two communities'. The 'evil' was 'ascribable to the bureaucracy and its henchmen', namely 'some selfish people who constitute[d] an obstacle in the way of Hindu–Muslim union'.[10] The *Bande Mataram* assailed the colonial state's unconscionable stance towards abusive propaganda conducted under the rubric of religion. It was convinced that 'speeches and writings on communal matters alone ha[d] led to the recent Hindu–Muslim riots'. The troubles could have been nipped in the bud. But British officers acted to 'punish hooligans only when the life of an Englishman [was] in danger'.[11]

With the more rabid Arya Samajists campaigning against Muslims, it was difficult to keep the attack focused on the colonial bureaucracy. The *Milap*, which competed with the *Pratap* in kindling communitarian ill-will in the Punjab, had no qualms publishing an article in which the author paraded his knowledge of history while mourning that 'civil wars in India [had] turned this Elysium-like land into hell'. It was 'D[u]aryodhan's feelings of jealousy' which had paved the way for the 'destruction of the Aryan race by *malechhas*' while 'Jai Chand's enmity with Prithvi Raj allowed a barbarous race to secure a footing in India'. As a result, 'dacoits and tyrants' like Taimur, Babar, Qasim, Mahmud, Aurangzeb and Nadir Shah had established their supremacy. It was ludicrous to maintain that tales of 'rapine, desecration of temples, outrages on women, forcible conversions and the carrying off of Hindu slaves chronicled in Indian history ... [were] fictions invented by European historians'. The historical proof was the current behaviour of Muslims who while claiming to be peaceful 'carried out the most barbarous attacks on their neighbours'.[12] Feeling burnt by the inexhaustible fusillade at the disposal of the Aryas, the *Muslim Outlook* reiterated that Hindu–Muslim outbreaks of violence originated in 'the methods of Hindu revivalists with their jeering pamphlets' and the 'new and sudden attachments to such cults as *arti*'. The 'real mischief' lay in a Hindu conspiracy to deprive Muslims of government employment and monopolize the higher and the lower services.[13]

According to this view, religious differences as such were not the primary

[10]*Bharat*, Amritsar, 4 October 1924, *NPP*, 11 October 1924, p. 325.
[11]*Bande Mataram*, Lahore, 19 October 1924, *NPP*, 25 October 1924, p. 337.
[12]*Milap*, Lahore, 5 October 1924, *NPP*, 15 November 1924, p. 363.
[13]*Muslim Outlook*, Lahore, 14 October 1924, *NPP*, 18 October 1924, p. 331.

cause of the troubles. It was the category of religion used in colonial enumeration and the narratives spun around them which had set Punjabis at each others' throats. All the quibbling over representation in electoral institutions or government service was really about using population percentages to justify a larger share for those who like the protagonist happened to fall into the same column in the census data. But while such technical matters could preoccupy those with an eye on the formal arenas of politics, marshalling popular support required translating them into a language accessible to a largely illiterate populace. The Arya Samaj's *shuddhi* and *sangathan* and the Muslim *tabligh* and *tanzim* movements were trying to win the colonial numbers game by taking advantage of the rulers' self-proclaimed non-interference in the cultural and religious affairs of their subjects. Their presumed indifference never prevented the British from keeping tabs on what went on under the guise of religion. Assessing the Arya Samaj's purification and social uplift campaign in the Punjab a few years later, a police intelligence report found it 'difficult to resist the conclusion that since the reforms the main object of shudhi ha[d] been to swell Hindu voting strength in anticipation of democratic Government'.[14]

To ward off such an eventuality the politically astute among Punjabi Muslims were anxiously shoring up the claims of their numerical majority. There were rumblings in some quarters about the injustice done by the Lucknow Pact of 1916. This was why so many educated Muslims had hailed the Bengal Pact. Even a committed Congressman like Saifuddin Kitchlew had felt compelled to concentrate on organizing the Muslims. His organ the *Tanzim* took strong exception to an article by Lala Hardayal advising Indians to become one nation by 'making them study Hindu history and adopt the Hindi language and the Hindu mode of living'. In advancing such an 'impracticable suggestion', the Lala was seen as luring his 'fellow countrymen to fall into the abyss of slavery'.[15]

For many influential urban Hindus the experience of the Montford reforms seemed like a dress rehearsal for an unmitigated 'Muslim raj'. Every step taken by Fazl-i-Husain was invariably interpreted as tilting the balance of advantage in favour of the Muslims. Husain's adoption of affirmative action in the domain of higher education and the extension of separate electorates to the municipalities and local boards did pass on benefits to Muslims. Whether these stemmed from 'communal' motives alone has remained a moot point.[16] It was the vehemence and flair with which Punjabi Hindus assailed Fazl-i-Husain's brand of politics as 'communalism' that needs underlining. Under separate electorates only Muslims voted for Muslims. In so far as elected Muslim representatives had to try and cater to the interests of their constituents,

[14]Supplement to *SPPAI*, 2 February 1929, vol. li, no. 5, p. 51.

[15]*NPP*, 22 November 1924, p. 367.

[16]See Mushirul Hasan, 'Communalism in the Provinces: A Case Study of Bengal and the Punjab 1922–1926', in Hasan (ed.), *Communalism and Pan-Islamic Trends*, pp. 268–72 and Page, *Prelude to Partition*, pp. 68–72.

there was nothing to prevent their detractors from tarring them with the brush of 'communalism'. So an elected Muslim had to lose his constituency to escape being a 'communalist'. By contrast, anyone belonging to the Hindu 'majority' community and elected on the basis of general electorates could appropriate the colours of 'nationalism', irrespective of the content of the political agenda.

For instance, the introduction of the Moneylenders' Registration Bill by a Muslim member of the legislative council sent the Hindu-edited press into spasms of anger in defence of the class interests of an influential segment of their co-religionists. Charges of Muslim 'communalism' reverberated as the Punjab Hindu Sabha allied with Hindu members of the council to scotch a bill intended as a palliative for debt-ridden Punjabi agriculturists. It was attributed to Fazl-i-Husain, the evil genius whose 'brains invent[ed] new plans to harm Hindus'. If passed, the legislation would 'paralyse' Hindu *sahukars* or creditors and dramatically shrink the amount of credit available to the *zamindars*. Apart from being 'impracticable, premature and unreasonable', the bill unfairly placed urban moneylenders in the same rack as rural creditors although the former had no direct dealings with agrarian society.[17] Kabuli Pathans who charged interest at the rate of four annas per rupee and resorted to dreadful measures to realize their due were excluded from the ambit of the legislation. The *Hindu* wondered whether this was because 'the Kabuli usurers [we]re Mussalmans?' *Milap* thought 'the real object' of the bill was to 'destroy what little power was left to the Hindus under the Land Alienation Act'.[18]

The *Karam Vir* damned the bill for placing 'restrictions on the freedom of citizens' and punishing Hindus for supporting *swaraj*. Especially revealing was the prediction that 'Muslim tenants in Western Punjab ... [would] witness Islamic rule under the British Government' and social peace as well as rural credit would disappear. Joining the hysteria, the *Sangathan* noted that whenever arrangements were being made for 'crushing Hindus, our Mussalman friends' pleaded 'in a transport of ecstasy' that the issue should not be given 'a religious colour'.[19] The *Tanzim* deemed the bill necessary to save agriculturists, and not just Muslims, from ruin. And the *Siyasat* while supporting the bill felt it did not go far enough in protecting *zamindars* against 'blood-sucking moneylenders'. What Punjab's debt-ridden *zamindars* and peasants needed was for the government to fix the rates of interest.[20]

Evidence of the close interplay between formal and informal arenas of

[17]This was the opinion of the Lahore-based papers *Milap* and *Bande Mataram* of 3 November 1924, NPP, 8 November 1924, p. 257.

[18]See *Hindu*, Lahore, 7 November and *Milap*, Lahore, 12 November, NPP, 15 November 1924, p. 363.

[19]*Karam Vir*, 22 November 1924 and *Sangathan*, 26 November 1924, NPP, 29 November 1924, pp. 378–9.

[20]*Tanzim*, 7 November, NPP, 15 November 1924, p. 363 and *Siyasat*, 24 November 1924, NPP, 29 November 1924, p. 378.

politics, the debate on the Moneylender's Registration Bill shows how class issues could be draped in 'communal' or 'national' hues. There were powerful undercurrents of sub-denominational identities which scarcely fit the patterns of religious communitarianism displayed in the mainstream vernacular newspapers. The press itself was one of the primary media for collective articulation in the sub-denominational as opposed to an overarching communitarian mode. The *Muslim Jat Gazette* from Ludhiana was only concerned with reforming the social condition of Muslim *Jats*.[21] An Urdu weekly called *Gaur Brahman* started in Rohtak had a similarly limited objective and is just one example of the innumerable newspapers started by Hindus and Sikhs to advance their specific caste-based interests. Much the same was true of Muslims. The *Piam-i-Ittihad*, an Amritsar Urdu monthly, described itself as 'a caste organ of Sheikhs'.[22] Another Amritsar-based Urdu monthly, the *Jamaat* was an organ of the Hanafi sect of Muslims. But those in disagreement with its management started the *Hanafi*, from the same city, in a demonstration of the intra-sectarian accord among Muslims of this caste.[23] Some Muslims belonging to the Qadiri sect launched the *Al-Qadar Naushahi* in Gurdaspur to propagate their views on Islam. And the Shias, who had a spread of newspapers and journals in the province, found a new advocate in the *Al-Muslih* of Sargodha.[24]

These localized tendencies flew in the face of attempts at the regional and all-India levels to conjure up generalized narratives of identity in the communitarian or the nationalist vein. So the Punjab in the 1920s was not simply drifting inexorably towards an undifferentiated and essentialized form of communitarianism. If anything the multifarious and conflicting strands in the informal arena were undercutting the self-confident narratives authored by the doyens of Punjabi communitarianisms. It was precisely because the hierarchy of collectivities gave the individual multiple points of reference that sub-denominational identities were articulated so vigorously, offering multiple options to those who had yet to empathize fully with either religious communitarianism or the more laudable sentiment of Indian nationalism.

This was why the contest for the allegiance of the individual between communitarian and nationalist propagandists had to be couched in uncompromising terms. It was not the lack of choice but too much of it which explains the unseemly nature of the narratives of collective identity composed in the Punjab. But the Punjabi trademark on the narratives of differential identity loses much of its bite and novelty if restricted to exchanges within the province. It was the contrast with those engaged in projecting the ideal

[21]*NPP*, 19 January 1924, p. 38.
[22]*NPP*, 22 March 1924, p. 118.
[23]*NPP*, 21 June 1924, p. 224.
[24]*NPP*, 22 November 1924, p. 371.

of an Indian nation that gave the discourse on contending identities in the Punjab its distinctiveness and unenviable status of being the most politically obdurate in the British Indian provinces.

REGIONAL, RELIGIOUS OR NATIONAL RIGHTS?

Anyone subscribing to the Congress vision of an inclusionary Indian nationalism had cause to be exasperated by the exclusionary overtones of the political discourse emanating from the Punjab. More than one all-India leader who came to the province trawling for support was chastened by the experience. Not the hub of the nationalist movement but in many ways its most effective foil, the nexus between region and religion in the Punjab nevertheless had a decisive bearing on the larger question of accommodating communitarian differences within the framework of a unified nation. If the Punjab generated a particularly virulent brand of politics, it was also the locus of some of the more interesting ideas on how the rights of religious communities might be reconciled with the imperatives of Indian unity.

Historians of Indian nationalism have generally regarded the role of the Punjab in the making of Indian independence as marginal, characterizing its politics variously as collaborationist, particularistic and, most commonly, communalist. This has relegated the revolutionary anti-colonialism of the Bhagat Singh variety to the footnotes of history while the story of religiously informed political conflicts in the Punjab has been left to a specialized academic task force looking for 'communalism'.[25] It is no ordinary matter—certainly not something that can be proscribed to the back shelves of history—that the first call for the partition of the Punjab into Muslim and non-Muslim-majority areas was given by Lala Lajpat Rai. A firm believer in the Arya Samaj doctrine of social reform, a cohort of Madan Mohan Malaviya in organizing the *sangathan* and president of the Hindu Mahasabha, he had foretold the future in a chilling confirmation of M.N. Roy's warning about the radiation qualities of Punjabi politics. Implicit in Lajpat Rai's proposal was the vision of Hindu and Muslim India. He left it to the Bengalis to decide if they wanted a federation of autonomous Hindu and Muslim states. An India with Punjab and Bengal divided may have seemed unimaginable in the 1920s. But if there is to be some semblance of balance in apportioning responsibility

[25]Punjabi reactions to the 'terrorist' methods of Bhagat Singh and his associates are discussed below. My article 'Exploding Communalism: The Politics of Muslim Identity', in Sugata Bose and Ayesha Jalal (eds), *Nationalism, Democracy and Development: State and Politics in India*, Delhi: Oxford University Press, 1996, provides a quick survey of the implications of the term in a context of contested sovereignties based on narratives of 'majority' and 'minority' communities. For an in-depth analysis, however, see the present work.

for the partition of India, the allusion to it so early on cannot escape the glare of historical analysis.

The battle for sovereignty in the Punjab was waged with verve by Muslims and Hindus alike. As the erstwhile sovereigns of the Punjab, the Sikhs were not above brandishing their own claims. Reflecting the three-cornered struggle in the formal and informal arenas of politics, the Punjab press continued disseminating barbed narratives of communitarian identity and, in the process, shaping the emergent discourse on contested sovereignty. Using the press to air his ideas, Lala Lajpat Rai is as good a guide as any to the thinking that was gaining ground among Punjabi Hindus confronted with the prospect of Muslim-majority rule. It tells in essence why a regionally based minority community, a component of a larger entity that was a Hindu majority 'nation', could not countenance the thought of a Muslim-dominated Punjab.

In late 1924 Lajpat Rai berated his Arya Samaj allies in the Punjab for being intolerant and bigoted. Many of the 'ablest and most patriotic' among the younger generation of Muslims and Hindus had become 'obsessed' with the idea of absolute rights. All rights were relative and there was no question of 'any individual or ... community forming part of a nation' claiming absolute rights. This 'pernicious doctrine of rights' was a direct product of Gandhi's pandering to Muslim religious sensibilities which had emboldened some Hindus to make far-fetched demands in defence of their faith.[26] After resigning from the Congress, Rai wrote a series of articles in the Lahore *Tribune* between 26 November and 17 December 1924, explicating his views on rights and lamenting the very real damage done by the Mahatma's tactic of mixing religion with politics. True communitarian union demanded separating the essentials from the non-essentials of religion. Without specifying how such a distinction was to be made, he rejected communal electorates as 'the negation of nationalism'. The supremacy of the state over religion was the only basis for a united India. An alien government in consort with a handful of self-seeking Muslim leaders was undermining that prospect by driving a wedge between Muslims and Hindus. The three major Punjabi communities had their 'separate clubs, separate organizations and separate colleges'. Religion was being used for political ends although there was 'a certain amount of genuine religious element in it'.[27] In a more explicitly political vein, Lajpat Rai rejected the Gandhian message of non-violence. It was 'lawful' to resort to violence in 'defence of one's own self, family and nation'. But this did not mean attacking others with impunity. If any 'foolish person or *badmash* [bad character] abuse[d] a religion or its great man we should not act similarly in replying to him'. The Arya Samaj had failed to 'prevent its preachers from paying back the assailants

[26]Lala Lajpat Rai, 'On the Hindu–Muslim Problem', in Ravindra Kumar (ed.), *Selected Documents of Lala Lajpat Rai, 1906–1928*, vol. iii, New Delhi: Anmol Publications, 1992, pp. 149–56.
[27]Ibid., p. 184.

Lala Lajpat Rai
Courtesy: Nehru Memorial Museum and Library

of their religion in the same coin' and, therefore, was 'to some extent responsible for the evil consequences ....'[28]

In an atmosphere shot through with communitarian animosity, it was easy to ignore Rai's rebuke of the Aryas and focus instead on his largely justifiable criticisms of the socially disruptive role of Muslim itinerant preachers. The more so since Lajpat Rai's enlightened notions of harmonious social relationships between Hindus and Muslims were coloured by stereotypical notions of Islam and Muslim history. Convinced of the inherent tolerance of Hinduism, Rai saw a singular absence of the trait in the Muslims. 'Religious intolerance of the severest kind,' he stated authoritatively, 'has been a handmaid of chivalry, bravery, zeal, learning and piety among the Muslims throughout Muslim history.'[29] He was nearer the mark in noting that no organized body of Muslims, whether in India or outside, had any 'legal right or authority to bind other Mussalmans'. The hallmark of laws was that they changed with the law-makers. It was pointless hammering out agreements. Muslims needed 'a change of heart'; their leaders had to spend their energies 'removing the idea that the Hindus are *Kafirs*'.[30]

Failing that, the only solution to the problem of difference and contested sovereignty in the Punjab was to partition the province which might in turn open the way to a possible federation of autonomous Hindu and Muslim states in Bengal. A logical outcome of communal electorates, such an arrangement seemed unavoidable now that some Punjabi Muslims were raising a storm against the 'insufficiency and unfairness of the Lucknow Pact' which had left them with fewer seats in the provincial legislature than warranted by their population.[31] No purpose would be served by pushing for an elusive unity of opposition if this meant forcing one community against its will to accept the rule of another.[32]

An extreme solution to the problem of accommodating the politics of religiously informed cultural differences, Lajpat Rai's proposal was not a call for the partition of India, but a laboured attempt to forestall such an eventuality. A divided Punjab was to remain part of a united India under Hindu-majority rule. As he explained, communal electorates once institutionalized could be eliminated only through civil war. In rejecting Muslim rule over the whole of the Punjab, the Hindus were not asking for 'any special favours', merely seeking 'justice and fairplay'. Punjabi Hindus were willing to 'subordinate ... [their] communal life to national life'. But not if the quest for an artificial unity meant

[28]*Bande Mataram*, Lahore, 1 and 2 December 1924, *NPP*, 6 December 1924, p. 388.
[29]Lala Lajpat Rai, 'On the Hindu–Muslim Problem', in Kumar (ed.), *Selected Documents of Lala Lajpat Rai*, vol. iii, p. 162.
[30]Ibid., p. 168.
[31]Ibid., p. 184.
[32]Ibid., p. 198.

surrendering to the dictates of a community whose leaders never ceased threatening a *jihad* against the Hindus.[33]

Here was a declaration of war by one of the champions of the regional rights of Punjabi Hindus. It drew comfort from the fact of a Hindu majority at the all-India centre guaranteeing their national rights. Religion was the premise of both the regional and national rights of Punjabi Hindus. And yet Lajpat Rai claimed to be an indefatigable opponent of mixing religion with politics. He was anticipating the arguments of later-day Indian nationalists in upholding the supremacy of the state over religion. Predicated on the separation of the spiritual from the material realm or, alternatively, of religion from politics, it sought to construct an idea of equal citizenship in an independent modern nation–state of India. Apparently consistent with the western concept of citizenship, the notion sat well in the fanciful realm of the ideal. It crumbled instantly in the light of socio-political dynamics in regions like the Punjab. The idea of equal citizenship left the spiritual or religious realm out of its conception of legal and political rights. This posed difficulties in a situation where the political debate and electoral representation were both cast in the mould of religiously informed cultural identities.

Even a sub-denominational paper like the *Muslim Rajput* was rattled by the drift of Rai's thinking. It was outraged at the suggestion that 'Maulvis, Maulanas and Muslim associations' were the cause of the 'present deplorable tensions between the two communities' as if 'his own co-religionists were angels'. Announcing the increasing convergence between developments in the Punjab and the princely state after which it was named, the *Kashmiri* protested Lajpat Rai's 'filthy attacks on Islam and Muhammadans' and condemned his articles on Hindu–Muslim unity for being 'permeated by a spirit of bigotry and mischief'.[34] Whatever else the Punjab in the 1920s may have been, it was not in a mood for non-partisanship. This rather than the overly simplistic stamp of an undifferentiated communitarianism seems to be the more accurate reading of the province's see-sawing between the politics of union and disunion.

Given an all-India discourse on the virtues of nationalism, the complex nuances of Punjabi politics have been lost in the fog of interminable communitarianism. If Lajpat Rai's recipe for settling differences through division was unpalatable to many Punjabi Muslims, they were equally averse to the ideas of an Islamic universalist venturing forth as an Indian nationalist. After his political career had been short-changed by events in Turkey, Mohamed Ali took refuge in journalism by reviving his Urdu paper *Hamdard*. Still a fervent admirer of the Mahatma and in close communion with the rising star of Indian nationalism, Jawaharlal Nehru, the mercurial Muslim propagandist from UP

[33]Ibid., p. 201.
[34]*Muslim Rajput*, Amritsar, 10 December 1924 and *Kashmiri*, Lahore, 12 December 1924, *NPP*, 20 December 1924, p. 404.

was not about to discredit himself by taking too sympathetic a view of Punjabi communitarianism. And so he remained the leading voice in the vanguard of nationalist Muslims, albeit with slips of the pen too flagrant to escape the more astute among the brigade commandeering the war camps of the rival community as well as his own co-religionists in the Punjab.

Explicating his ideas on Hindu–Muslim unity, Mohamed Ali denied that Islam required its followers to force their own government upon non-Muslims. Nor was it necessary for Muslims to turf out a non-Muslim government since they acknowledged the sovereignty only of Allah. It was incumbent upon a Muslim to resist the authority of anyone who went against the dictates of Allah. Invoking his dead hobby horse, Ali noted that so long as the Islamic requirement of safeguarding the religious rights of Muslims vested in the *khalifa*, the faithful could be indifferent to living under a non-Muslim government. Now the only religious requirement for Muslims was to ensure that *swaraj* did not undermine their religious rights. It was inconsequential if *swaraj* perpetuated non-Muslim rule since an independent Indian state would guarantee non-interference in all religions. Muslims who wanted their own rule were 'not capable of living in India'. Similarly Hindus who wanted 'Hindu rule should leave India and go to another country where they could live with their narrow mindedness and small heartedness'. Such individuals gave religion a bad name. They had to be defeated so that India could achieve *swaraj* with equal protection for all religious creeds.[35]

In a more calculated attack on his co-religionists in the Punjab, Mohamed Ali defended Gandhi after the *Muslim Outlook* charged him with duplicity. He regretted the bad taste in which a paper representing educated and respectable Punjabi Muslim opinion had made a personal attack on the Mahatma.[36] It was sheer stupidity to reject the Congress as a Hindu body if Muslims refused to join it in proportion to their population. Reiterating the main nationalist charge against his co-religionists, Mohamed Ali was ashamed to find Muslims biding time like the proverbial fox who claimed its share of the lion's prey after sitting pretty during the hunt. Although many Hindus had deserted the Congress in preference for partisan politics, the disgrace was greater for Muslims who were answerable only to Allah. Yet Mohamed Ali excused Muslims for nurturing ties with the Islamic world. The Hindu objection to this was based on a misunderstanding of the Muslims since their religious places such as Mathura and Kashi were not outside Hindustan. Muslims could feel passionately about the Islamic world and still be patriots and nationalists.[37] Punjabi Hindus involved in *sangathan* like Bhai Parmanand accused the Congress of being partial

[35]*Hamdard*, 30 December 1924, in Sabahuddin Omar (comp.), *Intikhab Hamdard*, Lucknow, 1988, pp. 61–2.

[36]See *Hamdard*, 13 January 1925, ibid., pp. 70–4.

[37]*Hamdard*, 19 November 1925, ibid., pp. 102–6.

to Muslims. But Congressites and Swarajists were not bigoted like the Hindu *Sangathanis*. If Congress could be charged with partiality towards Muslims, most of whom regarded it as a Hindu organization, it only proved that the party included segments of all religious denominations and was the only representative voice of the country and the nation.[38]

This was the kind of idealism which turned a series of negatives into an affirmation of a positive nationalist creed. A few years later Muhammad Iqbal gave the idealism of Islamic universalists like Mohamed Ali fresh philosophical meanings. Disregarding the troubling fissures among Indian Muslims, Iqbal provided an inspired, dynamic and markedly different interpretation of the relationship between religion and politics in Islam. The great believer in the individual will and visionary of the ideal community of Islam declared it a 'mistake' to presume that 'the idea of State is more dominant' in Islam.[39] A corrective to the mainstream nationalist view searching for political power at the apex of the colonial state, this was a perspective from the lofty heights of philosophy by a man who was a Muslim, a Kashmiri, a Punjabi, and an Indian under the subjecthood of the British Crown. For someone who was to go on to give the first, albeit politically incomplete, conception of what came to be associated with the demand for a 'Pakistan', Iqbal's notions of the state in Islam and the place of religion in the temporal activities of the individual and the community merit deeper analysis.

According to Iqbal, the spiritual and the temporal domains were not distinct in Islam since 'the nature of the act, however secular in its import, is determined by the attitude of mind with which the agent does it'. He was alluding to the Muslim belief in Islam as a complete way of life and locating it within the concept of *tauhid* or the belief in the unity of God. The implications of his conclusions were more fraught with significance than Lajpat Rai's pedestrian separation of the essentials from the non-essentials of faith or, for that matter, Mohamed Ali's pious hope that non-interference in religion would be sufficient accommodation for religiously informed cultural differences. Rejecting the post-enlightenment misperception of the binary opposition between the spiritual and temporal as 'two distinct and separate realities', Iqbal affirmed both the 'unity of man' and Islam as 'a single unanalysable reality' in which the religious and political aspects depended on positionally specific observations. The 'working idea' of *tauhid*, the binding principle of a Muslim's submission to Allah, was 'equality, solidarity and freedom'. It was incumbent upon the state 'to endeavour to transform these ideal principles' into reality by constructing 'a definite human organization' based on Islamic precepts.

'It was in this alone,' the leading intellectual light in Muslim India noted, 'that the State in Islam is a theocracy'. This was not a form of government

[38]*Hamdard*, 18 November 1925, ibid., p. 98.
[39]Iqbal, *The Reconstruction of Religious Thought in Islam*, p. 122.

'headed by a representative of God on earth who can always screen his despotic will behind his supposed infallibility'. An Islamic 'theocracy' was one which sought to 'realize the spiritual in a human organization'. In other words, the purpose of the state was only to ensure the conditions enabling the realization of the spiritual needs of the individual and the collectivity in temporal activity incorporating the natural, material or the secular.[40] Giving a wholly different spin to what has come to be associated with the term 'secular', to say nothing of its ideological formulation, Iqbal's philosophical vision aided by an understanding of Islam collapsed the meaning of sacred and profane. The secular was 'sacred in the roots of its being'. An act was temporal or profane if it was done in a 'spirit of detachment from the infinite complexity of life' and 'spiritual if it is inspired by that complexity'. Modern thought's 'greatest service' had been in recognizing that the material had no meaning without being grounded in the spiritual. There was 'no such thing as a profane world'.[41]

This was why assimilation by Turkish nationalists of the European idea of the separation of the church and state bordered on profanity. 'Such a thing could never happen in Islam,' Iqbal asserted, 'for Islam was from the very beginning a civil society, having received from the Quran a set of simple legal principles which, like the twelve tables of the Romans, carried ... great potentialities of expansion and development by interpretation.' The principle of *ijtihad* or independent judgement allowed Muslims to constantly adjust themselves to social change without abandoning the Islamic path. In contrast to the religious scholars, Iqbal believed that since the institution of the *khalifa* had ceased to exist the right of *ijtihad* should be vested in an elected Muslim assembly which 'in view of the growth of opposing sects' in Islam was the 'only possible form Ijma can take in modern times'.[42] In opting for the republican form of government and collective *ijtihad* by the Grand National Assembly, the Turks alone among the Muslims had asserted the right of intellectual freedom conferred by Islam.[43]

But in separating the state from religion, the Turks had gone too far. Iqbal alerted Muslims to the dangers of becoming overawed by the currents of western liberalism. As he put it:

The light of foreign wisdom does not dazzle me
The kohl lining my eyelids is the dust of Mecca and Najf.[44]

Iqbal's principal critique of western enlightenment philosophy was that it

[40]Ibid., pp. 122–3.
[41]Ibid.
[42]Ibid., pp. 123, 138.
[43]Ibid., p. 128.
[44]*Khara na kar saka mujhe jalwa danish-i-farang*
Soorma hai meri ankhon ka khak-i-Madina wa Najf
(Iqbal, *Bal-i-Jabrial* in *Kulliyat-i-Iqbal*, p. 34.)

had taken free thinking to such extreme limits as to deny that 'all human life is spiritual'. Islam on the other hand was 'an emotional system of unification' which 'recognizes the worth of the individual' and 'rejects blood-relationship as a basis of human unity'.[45] Emerging at the moment of the disintegration of western civilization, Islam 'demand[ed] loyalty to God, not to thrones'. Since God was the 'ultimate spiritual basis of all life', loyalty to Him was loyalty to one's 'ideal nature'. Any such conception of reality had to strike a balance between permanence and change. There was no greater sign of God than change. By denying change, Muslims had become stagnant. The 'principle of movement in the structure of Islam' was *ijtihad*. Rejecting the unnatural closing of the doors to independent judgement, proclaimed by a handful of jurists in the early Islamic era, Iqbal gave a thumping endorsement to the principle.[46] *Khudi* or the self for Iqbal constituted the spiritual being who through *ijtihad* finds emancipation in the world. Acknowledging his admiration for Nietzsche, but also recording his dissent, he wrote:

If that prophet of the west had been around in this age
I would have explained to him the place of God.[47]

The Quranic insistence on the immutability of key tenets like *tauhid* was balanced by an emphasis on adapting to social change through the exercise of *ijtihad*, the principle of movement in Islam. Any collectivity needed a core of principles to survive the flux of historical time. But eternal principles did not mean excluding any possibility of change to the point of complete stagnation. In Iqbal's opinion, 'Europe's failure in political and social science' lay in its rejection of a permanent code of ethics while the 'immobility of Islam during the last five hundred years' was due to the incapacity of Muslims to keep pace with historical change.[48]

If Iqbal had discerned the opportunities afforded by Islam to accommodate change, he had nothing to say about how the Muslim community in India was to overcome its divisions and translate these into practice. He confessed that in India the exercise of *ijtihad* could pose serious difficulties since it was 'doubtful whether a non-Muslim legislative assembly' could be vested with

---

[45]Iqbal, *The Reconstruction of Religious Thought in Islam*, p. 116. He cites J.H. Denison, a modern historian of civilization who had painted a gloomy picture of the western world about the time when Islam emerged on the historical stage: 'Was there any emotional culture that could be brought in, to gather mankind once more into unity and to save civilization?' The world needed 'a new culture' and in Iqbal's view this was what Islam provided.

[46]Ibid., pp. 117–18.

[47]*Agar hota woh majzoob-i-farangi ise zamana mein*
To Iqbal useko samjhata muqaam-i-kibriya kiya hai.
(Iqbal, *Bal-i-Jabrial*, in *Kulliyat-i-Iqbal*, p. 46.)

[48]Iqbal, *The Reconstruction of Religious Thought in Islam*, p. 117.

this power of independent judgement.[49] Iqbal did not rule out Muslims participating in a parliament alongside non-Muslims and using their right of independent judgement on matters related to their faith. Nor did he elaborate on whether the idea of sovereignty in Islam necessitated Muslim rule. What Iqbal's philosophical reconstructions of Islamic thought made evident was the chasm between a view of Indian nationalism based on keeping religion out of politics and the normative Muslim conception of treating the spiritual and temporal domains in non-oppositional terms.

Clashes at the ideological level often do not translate into stark distinctions in the realm of practical politics. Those propagating the nationalist creed were not always successful in keeping their religiously informed cultural identities separate from politics. By the same token, Muslims professing belief in Islam as a complete code of life rarely acted according to the tenets of the faith when it came to politics. Far from being the main obstacle to any sort of united anti-imperialist struggle, religion in Indian conditions could be used to justify a wide spectrum of political differences flowing from the class, regional or ideological location of the protagonists.

What then was the precise significance of religion in the politics of colonial India? Religion's role in the regional politics of the subcontinent cannot be understood through an arbitrary bifurcation of nationalism and communitarianism. In so far as religion in the Indian context was primarily a demarcator of identity, the boundary between these two constructions was at the very least porous if not a figment of individual imaginings. The nexus between region and religion in the Punjab could prompt Lajpat Rai to advance arguments on rights based on the separation of the essentials and non-essentials of faith in one breath and conflate the interests of the Hindu community with those of the Indian 'nation' in the next. Punjabi Hindus were prepared to accept a division of religion and politics in the national interest. But this political posture was a product of their sense of belonging to a larger national whole in which their religious denomination gave them a numerical majority. The separation of religion and politics expounded by Congress nationalists and rejected by 'communalists' like Iqbal assumed very different connotations at the regional and all-India levels. Religiously informed cultural differences had to be emphasized to claim regional rights but, following nationalist ideas of equal citizenship, became illegitimate if insisted upon by a geographically disparate numerical minority as the criterion for the distribution of national rights.

It was this contradictory logic that gave religion the handle it came to enjoy in the politics of late-colonial India. As region interacted with an emerging conception of the nation, variously appropriated by the votaries of the majoritarian community, those reduced to minority status by virtue

[49]Ibid., p. 138.

of their religious affiliation had grounds for apprehension. Emphatic assertions of an inclusionary nationalism based on separating the spiritual from the material, the religious from the political and the emotional from the rational seemed to marginalize the problem of cultural difference, not give it the centrality it had come to occupy in the discourse and politics of communitarianism. If fragments of the majority community could present their demand for regional rights in the language of religiously informed cultural differences, then members of a 'national' minority could hardly be expected to do otherwise. By clinging more obstinately to the politics of cultural difference, a statutory minority might extract some safeguards. After all, 'the respect for cultural diversity and different ways of life finds it impossible to articulate itself in the unitary rationalism of the language of rights'.[50] But it had to do so on a collective basis if it was to get a hearing from a colonial state whose tinted spectacles saw India in terms of essentialized but not adequately existentialized religious blocs. To be sure, individual interests combined with claims of representing the established communities of colonial discourse to throw up a welter of ideas on rights.

Fed on a curious blend of an indigenized liberal democratic theory and occasional spots of bigotry, the idea of rights had found an interesting manifestation in the worldview of one of the leading voices among the Punjab Hindus. With shades of the individual and the collective underlining the logic, Lajpat Rai had pieced together a political jigsaw for India which was practically a blueprint for the post-1947 configuration of the South Asian subcontinent. Using religion to advance a claim for rights at the regional level and denying the very relevance of religious difference at the national level made a travesty of political consistency. It did not require much intelligence on the part of urban Punjabi Muslims to realize the significance of a scheme to partition the province if the matter of Hindu representation to the legislature and the government services proved impossible to settle. Punjabi Hindus were emphatically opposed to Muslim-majority rule without weighted safeguards. But safeguards for minorities defined by religion meant denying those whom colonial discourse classified as majority community the right to their share of political representation. Whatever the advantages gained by the upper crust of Muslim *ashraf* households in northern India through weighted representation, the principle placed their co-religionists at a severe disadvantage in the Punjab. Lagging behind Hindus in higher education and government employment, Punjabi Muslims were finding the consequences of generosity towards co-religionists in other regions a trifle painful.

---

[50]Partha Chatterjee, 'Secularism and Toleration', *EPW*, 9 July 1994, p. 1773. The notion of a blend of individual and collective rights was available in the realm of Muslim political philosophy which had reached beyond the rigid boundaries of a unitary colonial rationality.

Playing notes borrowed from liberal democratic theory in the communitarian key, Lajpat Rai had issued an ultimatum to Muslim Punjab that separation may have to be the price for majority rule premised on religion. He was of course perfectly correct that separate electorates for Muslims and the matching 'communalization' of government through religiously defined quotas would serve a devastating blow to the homogenizing claims of an inclusionary nationalism. But it was his equally impassioned defence of the rights of Punjabi Hindus which betrayed to many Muslims the hollowness of the nationalist discourse. The bait of equal citizenship in an independent India carried the price tag of singularity and homogeneity which was rudely at odds with narratives steeped in the language of cultural difference. They were expected to rally to the call of a unified and uncontested sovereignty which conferred upon them minority status with no prospect of relief in their regional majority. Inequality in the terms of representation could not be expected to produce the conditions for equality of citizenship. It was this sense of denial that stoked the fires of Punjabi Muslim fears and found expression in assertions of Islamic supremacy.

Under the circumstances, adopting a nationalist discourse which sounded like a variant of Hindu communitarianism was tantamount to committing political suicide. Even if the issue of cultural difference could be settled through negotiations on the quantum of state intervention in religion, there was no guarantee that Hindu-majority rule would not try and efface the marks of the Islamic impact on the subcontinent. Imbued with the wonder of a union of the Mother Goddess with the territorial homeland, Hindu India's vision of *Bharatvarsha* was dramatically at odds with the individual and collective Muslim belief in the absolute sovereignty of a universal God. That it could give rise to a rich variety of ideas on identity and sovereignty was evident in the views of two men wedded to the universalist pledge in Islam who chose initially at least to occupy different niches in the politics of Indian Muslims. If Mohamed Ali put forward an argument on the possibility of Muslim citizenship in a non-Muslim state, Iqbal veered the very parameters of the debate away from the sterile, and European-born, idea of the separation of the spiritual and material domains.

Iqbal's intervention had the added advantage of being more relevant to India's political and intellectual legacies than a discourse on nationalism shaped by Europe's history of the formation of nation–states. As he put it in one of his *zarifana* or humorous verses:

We Eastern innocents have entangled our hearts with a West
Where there are crystal chalices and here only an old earthen pot
All will perish in this era except the one
Who is established in way and firm in conviction
Oh Sheikh and Brahman, do you hear what the scriptural say
From what high heavens nations have fallen

Here it is either conferences on mutual love: the ways of love were established
Or disputes over Urdu and Hindi, cow sacrifice and *jhatka*.[51]

Derisive of the pitiful absence of any fellow feeling among the different
communities, Iqbal had made a scathing statement on the poor judgement
of those who accepted the liberal premise of a separation between the material
and the spiritual. He had shown shades of the democratic spirit in his
conception of the ideal Islamic state, albeit one that had yet to be foregrounded
in the history of India. This was to be the product of a later period when the
poet and philosopher began dabbling directly in active politics. A look at
Iqbal's ventures into the politics of the Punjab must await an examination of
how his ideas impinged on the question of identity and sovereignty.

'Iqbal is a great preacher; his talk wins the heart', but this 'warrior of language'
could not 'conquer character'.[52] What had been left out of Iqbal's philosophical
conceptions were the sectarian and other differences among Muslims and the
problems they posed for collective action. His preference for an elected
parliament as the only response to sectarian divisions among the faithful made
no mention of how representation was to be shared by these different Muslim

[51] Hum mashriq kai maskeenon ka dil maghrib mein ja atka hai
Wahn kantar sab buloori hain yahan aik purana matka hai
Ise duor mein sab mitt jain ghai, haan baqi woo rahe jai gha
Jo qaim apni rah pai hai aur paka apni hat ka hai
Aie Sheikh o Brahman! Suntay ho kya ahl-i-baserat kahte hain
Gardoon nai kitne bulandi saay oon qaumoon dai patka hai
Ya baham piyar kai jalse thay; dastoor-i-muhabat qaim tha
Ya bahis mein Urdu-Hindi hai, ya qurbani ya jhatka hai.

ہم مشرق کے مسکینوں کا دل مغرب میں جا اٹکا ہے

واں کنڑ سب بلوری ہیں یاں ایک پرانا مٹکا ہے

اس دور میں سب مٹ جائیں گے، ہاں باقی وہ رہ جائے گا

جو قائم اپنی راہ پہ ہے اور پکا اپنی ہٹ کا ہے

اے شیخ و برہمن! سنتے ہو کیا اہل بصیرت کہتے ہیں

گردوں نے کتنی بلندی سے ان قوموں دے پٹکا ہے

یا باہم پیار کے جلسے تھے، دستور محبت قائم تھا

یا بحث میں اردو ہندی ہے، یا قربانی یا جھٹکا ہے۔

(Iqbal, *Bang-i-Dara* in *Kulliyat-i-Iqbal*, p. 234.)
[52] Iqbal bara padeshik hai, maan batoon mein moo layta hai
Guftar ka ye ghazi to bana, kirdar ka ghazi ban na saka.

اقبال بڑا اپدیشک ہے من باتوں میں مو دیتا ہے

گفتار کا یہ غازی تو بنا، کردار کا غازی بن نہ سکا۔

(Ibid., p. 239.)

groups. A considered omission to sustain his philosophical scheme, it cannot be glossed over in a study of Muslim identity, sovereignty and related notions of citizenship aimed at balancing the individual and the collectivity at both the discursive and the practical level.

SATANIC PROSE AND THE DIFFERENCE WITHIN

Presenting a coherent picture of the political entity, the Indian Muslim, on the basis of religious affiliation was an exacting task. Muslims bitterly disagreed on matters of religious interpretation. The Shia–Sunni schism flowing from the doctrinal and the historical dynamics of relations between these great branches of Islam was just one among many. Ahl-i-Hadith locked horns with the Wahabis; Barelvis with Deobandis. The appearance of Mirza Ghulam Ahmad's followers in the Punjab with Qadian as their local base upset the denominational balance among Muslims. Anti-Ahmadi tracts found an enthusiastic market among a community riddled with sectarian differences.[53] With the Arya Samajists on the offensive, Punjabi Muslims in their serried ranks saw in Ghulam Ahmad's teachings an insidious plot to alter an immutable tenet of Islam, namely the finality of Muhammad's prophethood. Attacks from without and fears within merged to produce the Punjabi Muslim variant of anti-colonial nationalism in both its bigoted and enlightened varieties. As with the Arya Samajists, this was a form of bigotry which found multiple niches through narratives of hatred laced with suspicion.

To some, the incapacity of Muslims to agree on an individual leader or establish a collective basis for authority seemed like the handiwork of a satanic will. In 1925 Satan in the form of a human pen at the Aligarh Muslim University conceded his role in instigating the downfall of Indian Muslims. This startling confession was made by Iblis in a presidential address delivered after an absence from India since the revolt of 1857.[54] Convinced that the aftermath would enmesh the rulers and the ruled in a grim battle, Iblis had turned to plotting the decline of Muslims in Ottoman Turkey and Iran.

---

[53]An example of this genre was an anti-Ahmadi tract published in 1913 by the Anjuman-i-Taid-ul-Islam at the Brahman Steam Press, Lahore. Rejecting Mirza Ghulam Ahmad's claim to be working to replace the worship of Christ and the Trinity with Islamic unitarianism, it noted that Christians were becoming stronger and Muslims had been killed in lakhs and rendered homeless. 'Was then Mirza Ghulam Ahmad the promised Messiah or a dire calamity for Islam', seeing that 'he wrought the ruin of the Muslim world'? Some Muslims were forcibly converted to Christianity while the rest, with the exception of 20,000 Ahmadis, were driven out of the pale of Islam by the Mirza and branded infidels. 'A liar', Ghulam Ahmad 'having failed to win over Christians, Aryias, Brahmos, Siks, & c., to his die [sic]' had 'opened the shop of *gurudom*' and taken to 'miracle-working' (*SPPAI*, 6 December, 1913, vol. xxxv, no. 47, p. 767).

[54]Iblis is the Muslim name for Satan.

After the Young Turks had damaged Islam beyond repair, Iblis had returned to his favourite prey, the Indian Muslims. On last visiting India in 1909 he had found the situation less than perfect but well poised to assist the Muslims in their self-destruction. Developments at the Aligarh Muslim University had prompted the author to invoke the satanic spirit in his evaluation of Indian Muslims.

Iblis ka Khutbah-i-Sadarat or Satan's presidential address published a second time in 1927 may have been an exercise in black humour.[55] But it gave a strikingly accurate picture of the Indian Muslim condition. In a series of historical shifts, the devil recounted how he had planned the destruction of Muslims and of those in India in particular. Among his aces was to confuse Islamic universalism with the colonial view of 'Pan-Islamism' and encourage Indian Muslims to take pride in their Persian and Arab ancestry. Designed to generate unpatriotic feelings among Muslims towards their adopted homeland, this was a bar to any notion of a common nationalism leading to participatory citizenship. Focused on politics in the Islamic world, they would empathize with the inhabitants of Turkey, Iran, Egypt and Morocco, diverting their energies from matters of practical importance in India. Muslims, as Satan knew from experience, preferred the world of ideas more than the reality. The 'Pan-Islamic' movement was Satan's India special. He delighted in the fact that the Islamic veneer of the movement would forever ensure the anonymity of its founder.[56] The tract deliberately exaggerated the extra-territorial dimension in the Indian Muslim character. Few had ever argued that an affinity with the holy lands of Islam was incompatible with patriotism towards the homeland. Denying that Muslims were uninterested in India, the Bengali paper *Saogat* asserted in 1926 that there was 'absolutely no truth in this allegation by Hindu nationalists'. Indian Muslims had 'failed to establish themselves in India'; their 'own country ha[d] turned them into aliens'. Impediments were being placed in the way of Muslims by members of the other community with the result that they sought relief for their frustration by clinging to the thought of Muslims outside India.[57]

So the secret of the Indian Muslims' political quandary may well lie in their failure to evolve any kind of agreed ethics on the principles of leadership. If he had bluffed on the first, Satan pulled three aces out of the second draw. His bid was to ensure that no mature Muslim leadership survived the stratagems of a young and impatient new generation of lawyers-cum-politicians. Unsuccessful in life, this despondent brigade of young men could be relied upon to do down any Muslim leader who through genuine work for the community seemed capable of attaining a position of leadership. Satan proudly claimed this as his

[55]'*Iblis ka Khutbah-i-Sadarat*', first published in 1925 at the Aligarh Muslim University. This edition by the Nizami press of Badiyaun in 1927, pp. 19–25.

[56]Ibid., pp. 21–2.

[57]Cited in Islam, *Bengali Muslim Public Opinion*, pp. 36–7.

personal achievement. He had promoted younger leaders and helped organize lowly campaigns of personal attack against the proven ones to deprive Muslims of a worthy leadership. Everyone knew that when an individual lacking in real ability failed in life he became more intent on finding other means to reach the heights. Such people were past masters in *abro-raizi*, or making personal attacks. They deployed this technique not only to chalk out their own path to the top, but against those more capable than them. If any well-meaning and brave soul came forward for public service, he ran away after a few days of being abused and tied up in endless arguments.[58]

To cap it all, Iblis had imbued Muslims with the spirit of *hurriyat* or freedom which, in the absence of any capacity for collective political action, could turn deadly. He recounted the story of a Muslim congregation where, Omar, the second *khalifa*, asked how the faithful would react if he did not rule according to the principles of Islam. An Arab bedouin drew out his sword on the *khalifa* and said that he would bring him back into line.[59] Individual freedom encumbered only by the limits set by God and the Prophet could rightfully resist and even dismiss authority if it undermined the Islamic way of life. A poignant insight into the relationship between the follower as individual and the leader as the symbol of collective political authority, it underlines just how well someone had charted the plan for perpetual Muslim political disarray. Lacking in organization, both spiritual and temporal, Indian Muslims could choose whatever interpretation of Islam they liked, support whichever political alignment they wanted and resist anyone who impinged upon their religious freedom. While this may be true of other communities, the singular incapacity of Muslims to build institutions and run them efficiently or accept the authority of any one individual or party suggests the work of a wilier mind.

Satan's masterly moves against Muslims had worked with clockwork precision with the onset of modernity. He had aided the process by which Muslims were tempted away from the spiritual and religious dimensions of life towards science and philosophy. Faith clashing with reason had been the undoing of the Muslims. Thanks to him, none of the Muslim leaders of yesteryear or today cared about the tenets of their faith. The leadership of the Aligarh movement and the Muslim League had always been in the hands of men who cared nothing about religion. But Satan knew that seducing Muslims away from the Islamic path was not enough. Planning for their total destruction also meant depriving Muslims of the capacity for self-improvement. According to the Quran, God never improved the lot of a people who did nothing to change themselves. Devoid of religiosity and steeped in western rationalism, Muslims had seen education, wealth and sovereignty

[58]*Iblis ka Khutbah-i-Sadarat*, pp. 22–3.
[59]Ibid., pp. 24–5.

slipping from their hands. No nation in the world could surpass them in degeneracy and ignominy.[60]

None of this was a historic coincidence. It was a tribute to Satan's constant vigilance and carefully thought-out moves against the Muslims. The annulment of the partition of Bengal, the Kanpur mosque incident, heightening Shia–Sunni differences at the Aligarh Muslim University, the Lucknow Pact of 1916 and the *khilafat* movement were all due to his intrigues. At his behest, the Hindu Mahasabha had rejected the Congress–League agreement substituting Muslim majorities in the Punjab and Bengal with weighted representation for their co-religionists in the minority provinces. Taking a simple view of the equality principle, it followed that what was good for Muslims could not be all bad for Hindus. So Hindus in Muslim-majority provinces were given seats on the provincial legislative assembly disproportionate to their population. By inciting the Mahasabha against the accord, Satan had beguiled Muslims into thinking that a political arrangement depriving them of their due share of representation was in their interest. There could not be a more ingenious way of misleading Muslims into seeing disadvantage as advantage and squandering the few opportunities available to them to ameliorate their political status in India.[61]

It would have been harmless enough if the theme of Muslim disunity were limited to this genre of Satanic satire. The storm brewing in the teacups of the editorial rooms at Zafar Ali Khan's *Zamindar* leading to the breakaway of two key editors, Ghulam Rasul Mehr and Abdul Majid Salik, may not have been revolutionary in the ideological sense. Formed primarily to voice the opinions of the '56% group', [62] the *Inqilab* kept alive the personal element in the politics of the province by engaging in a lowly war with the *Zamindar*. As Zafar Ali put it wryly:

With labels 'Hajji', 'Hinduzai' and 'Nehruvani'
My faith needed one symbol
The picture of me drawn by Salik
Is shocking and the sense of amazement has meaning
My affections are repaid in messages of cruelty
And the vivaciousness of the pen depends on bad feeling
May God keep alive Mehr's and Salik's journalism
Through this sacrifice comes recognition for me
Its [*Inqilab's*] poetry and prose mirror the feats of the personal
But in this [*Zamindar*] also shines some family decency.[63]

[60]Ibid., p. 6.

[61]Ibid., passim.

[62]The name given to Punjabi Muslims demanding their proportionate share of elected representation. They were supported by Muhammad Iqbal.

[63]*Laqab 'Haji' bhi hai, 'Hinduzai' bhi, 'Nehruani' bhi*
Mera iman ko akhir chahiya thi aik nishani bhi

If attacking their boss gave a personal angle to the campaign, the *Inqilab* group spent the better part of their energies communicating the Punjabi Muslims' sense of betrayal at the terms of the Lucknow Pact of 1916. Pieced together by Mohammad Ali Jinnah, the agreement between the Congress and the Muslim League had given Muslims 45.1 per cent of the seats in the Punjab legislative assembly. Needed to secure weighted representation in the Hindu-majority provinces, the arrangement undermined the principle of representation by community. With the government controlling one-third of the provincial council seats through nomination, no community could dominate the legislature under the Montford reforms. To the chagrin of Punjabi Muslims, they were given only 34 per cent of the elected seats. They could hope to improve the figures through government nomination. But many Punjabi Muslims were loathe to accept Hindu-majority rule under the all-India nationalist umbrella of the Congress and a principle of weightage which denied them their share of political representation in the province.[64]

Morqay mein meri tasveer Salik nai woo khainchi hai
Kai dang arsang hai aur pekhar-i-hayrat hai maani bhi
Sila meri wafaoon ka diya payam jafaoon say
Aur ise par mustazad ise shookh ki hai bad zabani bhi
Khuda abad rakhe Mehr o Salik ki sahafat ko
Kai ise kay sadqay main hoti hai meri qadardani bhi
Hai use ki nasr o nazm aina jauhar hai zati ka
Magar ise mai chamkti hai sharafat khandani bhi.

لقب "حاجی" بھی ہے "ہندوزئی" بھی "نہروانی" بھی

مرے ایماں کو آخر چاہیے تھی اک نشانی بھی

مرقع میں مری تصویر سالک نے وہ کھینچی ہے

کہ دنگ ارزنگ ہے اور پیکر حیرت ہے مانی بھی

صلہ میری وفاؤں کا دیا پیم جفاؤں سے

اور اس پر مستزاد اس شوخ کی ہے بدزبانی بھی

خدا آباد رکھے مہر و سالک کی صحافت کو

کہ اس کے صدقہ میں ہوتی ہے میری قدردانی بھی

ہے اس کی نثر و نظم آئینہ جوہر ہائے ذاتی کا

مگر اس میں چمکتی ہے شرافت خاندانی بھی۔

(Zulfiqar, *Maulana Zafar Ali Khan*, pp. 239–40.)

[64]Sharing the misery with Bengali Muslims was cold comfort. Under the Lucknow Pact, Bengali Muslims received 40 per cent of the elected seats against 60 per cent for Bengali Hindus. This gave Muslims 27.9 per cent and Hindus 32.9 per cent in the Bengal legislative assembly. Only in the Central Provinces where non-Muslims constituted 95.4 per cent were the elected members of the majority community classified as 'Hindus' able to dominate the legislature. For the statistical details of the Lucknow Pact, see Page, *Prelude to Partition*, pp. 32–3.

If only the Punjabi Muslims had had the political organization to take advantage of their right of representation, matters might have been different. Satan may well have condemned Muslims to forever disagree on any sort of binding authority, whether of the religious or temporal kind.[65] Sectarian differences compounded the problem of deciding who was more Muslim than the other and which of the religious interpretations was to assume dominance. An Ahmadi tract attributed a saying to the Prophet that only one sect among the Muslims would gain entry into heaven. When Muslims had subdivided into seventy-two sects, an *imam* would appear to lead the one conferred with the privilege. This was seen as validating Mirza Ghulam Ahmad's claim to being a prophet and establishing the Ahmadi community as the sect which alone would avoid hellfire.[66]

The Prophet's remark was open to multiple interpretations. If only one sect in Islam could qualify for the ultimate prize—a place in heaven amidst the promised *houris*—then it was obligatory for each one of them to individually and collectively work to eliminate the other one hundred or so subdivisions among Muslims. The concern assumed entirely new proportions in the context of separate electorates for Muslims. Sections of the urban Hindu population might complain of the grave damage done by separate electorates to Indian nationalism, but it was far worse for the Muslims. To get ahead a Muslim had to push his co-religionist aside rather than a non-Muslim. Sustained Hindu opposition to separate electorates kept this aspect of Muslim politics under wraps. Under the constitutional arrangements of the British raj, *ashraf* Muslims who monopolized government employment and political representation detected merits in restricting the contest further. As Satan had hinted, individuals lacking in the ability to advance in life on their own resources invariably tried blocking the more capable by sponsoring personal assaults through an unethical press. From here it was only a short distance to excluding Muslim sects that offended the sensitivities of Islamic orthodoxy. The Punjabi Muslim elite may not have fully understood the politics of numbers, but their instinctive response to a resurgent Hinduism was to take a sterner view of the Ahmadis. Hurling them out of the community might lose Muslims a few percentage points in the national ratings but would reaffirm the tenets of Islam without which the immutability principle could not continue to be operative.

Once the precedent of exiling one sect from the community was established, those remaining in the fold could step up their activities to turf out the others. The Muslim penchant for using the words *kafir* and *la-dini* (irreligious) for each other is a manifestation of this tendency. Through a

[65]For an example of the Muslim view of their leadership, religious and lay, see Najibabad, *Akabar-i-Qaum*, 3 March 1920, Urdu D.997, IOL.

[66]Sardar Abdul Rahman, *Sawal-o-Jawab Imamat wa Khilafat*, Wazir-i-Hind Press, Amritsar, 14 June 1922. Urdu B. 255, IOL, p. 30.

destructive logic of exclusion, the object of every Muslim sectarian group in colonial India seemed to be to eradicate others. This was the best insurance to a heavenly hereafter and a no less divine gift of capturing the Islamic mantle in the subcontinent. The intense sectarian differences in Indian Islam had as much to do with the colonial state's social engineering as with multiple interpretations of the *sunnah* or tradition of the Prophet, to say nothing of Satan's ruses.

It was this devilish blemish which made certain that the crystallization of Iqbal's thoughts on state and religion in Islam would remain forever out of line with the dynamics at the social base. The shifting alignments of the *khilafat* era had heightened Muslim unwillingness to accept the religious leadership of one of their own numbers. Although contrary to their fabled concern with religious identity, this meant relinquishing the hope of any unity of spiritual and temporal authority in Indian Islam. The field was left open for anyone who could seize upon Indian Muslims being a separate and identifiable political category. This was another reason why Muslims had to regularly denounce sectarian divisions within their community. Mirza Ghulam Ahmad's crime was not his new fangled ideas on prophethood; it was the construction of a new sect within Islam. With the exception of a few bitter exchanges, through most of his lifetime Ghulam Ahmad remained unruffled by the denunciations of the more voluble *ulema*. A brief look at the Ahmadi community and its links with an existing and emerging leadership among Punjabi Muslims clarifies the close interconnections between contested sovereignty and an exclusionary notion of identity fostered by internal sectarian divisions.

The Ahmadi 'Heresy'

On 26 February 1914 a notice appeared in Simla signed by a local shopkeeper named Abdul Qadir. It complained bitterly of the Ahmadis who by 'preaching their false doctrines and rationalistic heroics' were 'endeavouring zealously day and night to seduce orthodox Muhammadans'. Not a month passed without the circulation of a handbill appealing to people to accept Mirza Ghulam Ahmad's message. Qadir deplored the apathy of the *raises* of Simla. While aware of his own limitations, he had after looking at 'things for a long time ... lost ... power of self-control'. The thought 'possessed' him that although he was 'not a learned man' and had 'no acquaintance at all with our religion', it was mandatory for him as a Muslim to put 'trust in God' and place before his 'brethren in religion the stock of informations [sic]' he had 'gathered from the writings of the learned'. He vowed to present a paper every Sunday after mid-afternoon prayers at the Jamia Masjid hall on how Muslims could avoid becoming 'the dupes of aliens (?unorthodox people) and thus spoil our record of good deeds'.[67]

[67]*SPPAI*, 12 July 1919, vol. xli, no. 27, p. 136.

An extreme reaction to proselytizing by the Ahmadis, it had not yet assumed the ferocity which periodically led Muslims to institute a social boycott of the Hindus. This mode of collective social censure had first made an appearance in 1893 after the assassination of Pandit Lekh Ram.[68] Muslims and Hindus enforced a commercial boycott of each other and engaged in some of the more abominable exchanges in the press. Punjabis, however, also showed their capacity for mending communitarian fences. During the first two decades of the twentieth century there were fewer flare-ups in which the religious factor played a direct part.[69] But what the Punjab never recovered from was the bigotry of some great men of the province ever since the emergence of the press as a channel of mass communication in the colonial public arena.

In the words of the deputy inspector-general of the Punjab police's criminal intelligence department in 1928, 'Mirza Ghulam Ahmad proved to be a greater danger communally than religiously owing to his prophecies foretelling the death of his opponents'.[70] For this uncanny knack of predicting the demise of his key enemies, including Lekh Ram, Ghulam Ahmad incurred the wrath of many Punjabi Hindus. The arrival of Ahmadis on the historical stage as Hindu bashers made them more acceptable to Muslims. Despite doctrinal differences, Muslims interacted with members of the Ahmadi community with whom they shared a common language—Punjabi—a regional culture and, not infrequently, family ties. It required a temporal issue of an intra-communitarian nature to spark off battles for social space between Ahmadis and other Muslims. Among the potential catalysts was the impression among some Punjabi Muslims that the Ahmadis were in the pay of the British.

Charges of collaboration, if not conspiracy, on the part of the Ahmadis are difficult to establish conclusively. Mirza Ghulam Ahmad was a scion of a family that traced its origins to a Mughal clan from Samarkand. The family lost political status during the Sikh ascendancy but regained it under Ranjit Singh. While resuming the family *jagirs*, the British assigned a modest pension to Ghulam Ahmad's father. That the family rendered 'excellent services during the mutiny' was hardly exceptional for the Punjab. In 1876 Ghulam Ahmad came to notice for claiming he had received revelation. Giving a modernist twist to the Quranic *surah* telling Muslims that God had sent *nabis* (literally

[68] An ex-police constable in the North West Frontier Province, Pandit Lekh Ram had been discharged in 1884 for immorality and neglect of duty. Indication that Satan's potions also entranced members of the Hindu community, the disappointed constable found a healthy alternative in abusing Muslims. (See *The Ahmadi Sect: Note on the Origin, Development and History of the Movement up to the Year 1938*, Government of the Punjab, 1938, NDC, Islamabad.)

[69] Until 1926 there were fewer deaths related to communitarian violence in the Punjab than in UP.

[70] *The Ahmadi Sect*, NDC, pp. 1–2.

prophets) throughout the ages, he argued that while Muhammad was the seal of the prophets, his task had to be continued by others. Some of those ordained for the job were vested with such divine favours as revelation but did not have canonical powers. The Ahmadis have continued to observe the rituals of Islam with the strictest orthodoxy, underlining their view of Ghulam Ahmad as a *nabi* rather than an apostle with law-giving powers.

Like Muslims of other denominations, the Ahmadis are not of a single mix. An important source of disagreement has been their interpretations of Ghulam Ahmad's claim. Many accept him as a spiritual preceptor while bestowing the highest honours upon the Prophet of Islam. Occasionally the celebration of their founder led the Ahmadis to transgress the limits. This might put off some Muslims but there was room for accommodation with many more. Although he created a commotion with his claims, Ghulam Ahmad and his followers were by and large absorbed into the community of Islam in the Punjab. Until his death in 1908 Ghulam Ahmad 'continued to propagate his faith with *remarkably little opposition from orthodox Muhammadans*'. As late as 1928 colonial officials had not found a 'single incident on record' of Ahmadis being 'molested' or denied the use of mosques in Muslim burial grounds. The only exception to this rule was in Cuttack where some Ahmadis infuriated Muslims when they tried changing the code of worship in the town mosque.[71]

So allegations of complicity with the British appear to have been a product of a different set of perceptions. In 1895 Ghulam Ahmad had published a pamphlet denouncing *jihad* and urging loyalty to the raj. At the time this was the stance of most individuals, whatever their community or religious affiliation. Whether Ghulam Ahmad was planted by the British, especially those seized by the missionary fever, or a localized response to the increase in Christian and Hindu religious preaching may well depend on positionally specific observations. In the absence of any concrete evidence to prove their disloyalty to Islam and the Muslim community, it might be historically more informative to consider how the locale of Qadian interacted with larger political currents at the regional and national levels.

After Ghulam Ahmad's death, Hakim Nuruddin succeeded him as the leader of the community. This was contrary to the Mirza's instructions that his authority over the community be vested in a collective body such as an *anjuman*. Nevertheless, Nuruddin remained *khalifa* until his death in March 1914, after which time it proved impossible to keep the Ahmadis from splitting in two. One group was led by Ghulam Ahmad's son, Bashiruddin Mahmud Ahmad in Qadian, and the other by Muhammad Ali, who formed the Ahmadia Anjuman-i-Ishaat-i-Islam in Lahore. The Lahori party, as the latter came to be known, consisted mainly of educated Ahmadis who did not consider Ghulam

---

[71] Note by E.W.C. Wace (assistant to the deputy inspector-general of police, criminal investigation department), 2 June 1928, ibid., (my emphasis).

Ahmad a prophet in the literal sense of the word but accepted the metaphorical significance of his claim. This allowed for their continued association with other Muslims in various social and political affairs. The assimilation of the Ahmadis in the Muslim community seems to have been seriously disturbed by the local politics of Qadian where Bashiruddin Mahmud was experimenting with unifying temporal and spiritual authority.

Bringing the family's association with the founder to bear upon his authority over the Ahmadi community in Qadian had required firm rule on Bashiruddin's part. A scholar of religion in his own right, he overstepped the bounds acceptable to Muslims of other sectarian denominations. Many egos were battered and many more sensibilities mauled. Running the local administration on the lines of an Ahmadi mafia, Bashiruddin found bitter enemies among a diverse collection of Sunni *ulema* from the Deoband seminary or influenced by it, who had risen to prominence during the *khilafat* agitation. Notable among these was Maulana Ataullah Shah Bukhari, a Sunni of the Hanafi *fiqh*, who even in the early 1920s rarely missed an opportunity to rail against Ahmadis. But it was not until the formation of the Majlis-i-Ahrar with men like Bukhari and other publicists in their midst that the dispute between Ahmadis and others over Qadian came to the fore. Accusing Bashiruddin Mahmud of discriminating against non-Ahmadis, the Ahrars in the 1930s embarked upon a public campaign to expel the sect from Islam.[72]

Janbaz Mirza, the prolific official historian of the Majlis-i-Ahrar, in his eight-volume set gives special place to the campaign against the Ahmadis. He concedes that initially neither Mirza Ghulam Ahmad nor his disciples were regarded as a threat by other Muslims. When the claim to prophecy was first made, only the *ulema* of Ludhiana issued a *fatwa* declaring Ghulam Ahmad a *kafir*. The rest of the *ulema* thought it best to ignore the matter.[73] Purportedly quoting from the Royal Commission led by W.W. Hunter in 1870, Janbaz Mirza maintains that the idea of a Muslim claiming to be a prophet had grabbed the colonial masters as an artful way of dividing the community of Islam in the subcontinent. The notion of intercession may have been contrary to the teachings of Islam since the emphasis on the individual's personal relationship with God is an undeniable one.[74] But the idea of prophetic intercession is firmly rooted in the Muslim psyche and finds expression in the veneration of the Prophet of Islam.[75] Encapsulating a mosaic of beliefs

[72]See the note on 'The Ahmediya Sect' prepared by G. Ahmed, assistant to the deputy inspector-general of police, Lahore, 15 October 1938, ibid. For the Ahrar point of view, see Mirza, *Karavan-i-Ahrar*, passim.

[73]Mirza, *Karavan-i-Ahrar*, i, p. 375.

[74]For an interesting, comparative view of the issue in terms of the Christian belief in the idea of God, especially in the personality of Jesus, see Nicholson, *The Idea of Personality in Sufism*, especially lecture one.

[75]For an excellent study of this dimension of Muslim identity see Annemarie

in the unitary ideals of Islam, the love of Muhammad attains its ecstatic heights in Sufi poetry, the oral renderings of which at *qawwali mehfils* provide spiritual diet to many ordinary Muslims and non-Muslims. One way of demolishing the edifice of the Muslim worldview was to challenge one of its main pillars: the belief in the finality of Muhammad's prophethood.

It was the view of Muhammad as the seal of the prophets that bound the Muslim, individually and collectively, to Islam. According to this view, Muhammad's essence was present in all the earlier prophets, only he was the last one in God's line of *nabis*. As an Indian Muslim poet put it:

Certainly, Adam is God's special friend, Moses the one with whom God spoke, Jesus is even the spirit of God—but you are something different.[76]

The adoration of Muhammad is as central to the Muslim as that of Christ for the Christians. In the words of the nineteenth-century poet Amir Minai:

God bless him, and give him peace,
The leader of Moses, the guide of Jesus.[77]

Despite evidence of a more flexible Muslim attitude towards spiritual intercession, Janbaz Mirza accuses the British of purposefully promoting the claims of those who contravened the belief in the finality of the Prophet. If the first immutable pillar came crashing down, the edifice would follow soon after. After Sayyid Ahmad Khan, Mirza Ghulam Ahmad was the man chosen for the task. Unflinching loyalty to the raj meant that between the revolt of 1857 and the annulment of the partition of Bengal, Muslims were unable to raise their heads on matters of significance to the Islamic world.[78] It was this line of argument that found the ear of Punjabi Muslims who implicitly or explicitly supported the Ahrars in charging the Ahmadis of conspiring with the British in Kashmir and, more deceitfully, luring poor Kashmiri Muslims into their fold.

Until the Ahrars kicked up a storm over Ahmadi activities in Kashmir, the sect continued to be accommodated within the broader community of Muslims in the Punjab. In December 1927, a meeting of the Ahmadia Anjuman-i-Ishaat-i-Islam of Lahore attended by Muhammad Iqbal, Khwajah Hasan Nizami, Muhammad Shafi and Maulana Zafar Ali Khan denied that Mirza Ghulam Ahmad was a prophet.[79] Coinciding with the controversy surrounding the appointment of an all-white Royal Commission under Sir John Simon,

---

Schimmel, *And Muhammad is His Messenger: The Veneration of the Prophet in Islamic Piety*, Lahore: Vanguard, 1987.

[76] Alam Muzaffarnagari cited in ibid., p. 64.

[77] Ibid.

[78] Mirza, *Karavan-i-Ahrar*, i, pp. 379–90.

[79] *SPPAI*, 7 January 1928, vol. l, no. 1, p. 8.

this may have been a prelude to the activities of those Punjabi Muslims who decided to co-operate with the government in the face of stiff Congress opposition. There were other reasons for the presence of the Punjab's literary and political luminaries at the meeting of the Lahore Ahmadi group. It was an affirmation of Punjabi Muslim unity in the aftermath of two particularly ugly episodes in the history of communitarian relations in the province. These provide the connecting threads to why doctrinal differences with the Ahmadis were less serious for Punjabi Muslims than the threat posed by Arya Samaj propagandists and an emerging Hindu and Sikh political concord.

In 1924 the publication of an offensive book by Rajpal, provocatively entitled *Rangila Rasul* or the colourful prophet, cut Muslims to the quick. Mounting communitarian tensions did not need much provocation to spark off disturbances. In May 1926 Lahore was the scene of a major conflagration over the alleged rape of a young Sikh girl by a Muslim. As if this was not enough, Swami Shraddhanand was murdered in Delhi by a Muslim, Abdur Rashid, in December of the same year. In this charged atmosphere, the Punjab High Court under Justice Dilip Singh acquitted Rajpal in June 1927. With the *Milap* and *Pratap* conducting a fierce campaign against their intolerance and bigotry, the judicial exoneration of Rajpal incensed Punjab's Muslims. Here was ready ammunition in the hands of anyone looking to capture the leadership of the community in the province.

In 1926 a second round of elections to the reformed councils had seen Muhammad Iqbal entering the political fray and winning a seat to the provincial legislative council from Lahore. Wearing the politician's hat, the poet and philosopher joined the Muslim delegation which met the Punjab governor to demand a judicial review or, failing that, an amendment in the law. After the government agreed to reopen the Rajpal case, Iqbal drafted the resolution of the Punjab council declaring it illegal to publish anything which hurt religious sensibilities. At a meeting on 8 July 1927, he tried to dissuade the provincial Khilafat Committee from starting a civil disobedience campaign. Despite a shared belief in *tauhid*, unity had always eluded Muslims. But now an attack on the Prophet had brought them on a common platform. While he might have personally disagreed with the methods of Ataullah Shah Bukhari and Khwajah Abdur Rahman Ghazi who had been arrested for mobilizing opinion against Rajpal, there was no denying their contribution to Islam.[80] A few days later Iqbal told a congregation at the Badshahi mosque that Muslims had to seal their internal divisions to stop other communities from maligning the Holy Prophet.[81] After a reconsideration, the Punjab High Court convicted Rajpal for wounding Muslim sentiments. But on 6 April 1929, he

[80]*Inqilab*, Lahore, 10 July 1927 cited in Muhammad Rafiq Afzal (comp.), *Guftar-i-Iqbal*, Lahore: Research Society of Pakistan, 1969, pp. 39–40.
[81]*Inqilab*, 13 July 1927, ibid., pp. 41–6.

was murdered by a young Muslim, Ilim Din, who after his conviction and hanging by the British authorities acquired the esteemed title of *ghazi*, or holy warrior. Henceforth, the word *ghazi* was respectfully affixed to the name of any Muslim who murdered a Hindu or a Sikh in defence of Islam.

There was not much hope here of a negotiated settlement for religiously informed cultural differences. This made the issue of internal differences relatively more manageable. As Iqbal had observed, the vilification of the Prophet by non-Muslims guaranteed Muslim solidarity.[82] With the Ahmadis under Bashiruddin Mahmud taking a lead in propagating the way of life, and the work and character of the Prophet, there was no immediate danger of Muslims collectively turning upon enemies within. Individual Sunni Muslims might resent Ahmadis spearheading the veneration of the Prophet, but with one of Punjab's most indefatigable public speakers, Ataullah Shah Bukhari, temporarily in jail for creating a breach of the peace, there was for the moment no prospect of a concerted popular campaign against the Qadian faction. Gatherings organized by Ahmadis to celebrate the Prophet of Islam drew friends and detractors as well as the police, which frequently had to muscle its way in to keep order.[83]

With their considerable intellectual and organizational abilities, the Ahmadis were useful allies. Iqbal was by far the most important associate of both the Lahori and the Qadiani Ahmadis. Unlike the Ahmadis, the Punjabi Muslim intermediate strata had singularly failed to link their spiritual and material worlds within any kind of organized local, far less regional, setting. Averse to buying a basket of lemons in the name of the Congress's inclusionary nationalism and equal citizenship, Punjabi Muslims had neither a strategy nor political organization with which to counter the demands of rival communities. More pragmatic than doctrinaire in his approach to politics, Iqbal was not about to flail at an organized group of Muslims like the Ahmadis, far less prove his anti-imperialist bona fides in the vain hope of extracting concessions from the colonial rulers.

While the arrival of the Simon Commission with no Indians on board seriously insulted anti-imperialist sensibilities, it did nothing to assuage the communitarian rift. In rejecting civil disobedience and allying with the Unionists, Iqbal was conveying his anxiety about the sharply deteriorating communitarian relations in the province. It would be a banal reiteration of

[82]Throughout the Muslim world the 'sublime and unique position' of the Prophet is acknowledged with reverence and best efforts made to protect him against 'slander, contempt, and defamation'. (Schimmel, *And Muhammad is His Messenger*, pp. 64–5.)

[83]Meetings in praise of the Prophet attracted thousands in Lahore and Kasur. In Amritsar local roughs tried disrupting a gathering by accusing Ahmadis of British loyalty. Yet at a similar meeting in Multan, the pro-Congress and Islamic universalist editor of the *Siyasat*, Sayyid Habib made an appearance alongside Ahmadis. (*SPPAI*, 23 June 1928, vol. l, no. 24, p. 279.)

the old nationalist and communalist debate about the strength of his anti-imperialism to saddle him with the label of collaboration. But expedient it certainly was for a thinker who in a moment of bad judgement had entered the hurly burly of mass politics without any sort of organizational support. Contextualizing Iqbal, the poet and philosopher, and Muhammad Iqbal, the greenhorn politician, illuminates some of the problems posed by his high-flown ideas on the inseparability of the spiritual and material realms and notion of Islam as civil society.

Press Incivility and Public Culture

If Muslims could fume about a judicial decision which disregarded their religious sensibilities, Hindus were bound to deplore the killing of human beings in the name of Islam. Zafar Ali Khan did not help matters by arguing in the *Zamindar*, of 17 November 1927, that in certain circumstances it was legitimate for Muslims to commit religious murders. Whatever his real intention, this could be interpreted as justifying Abdur Rashid's murder of Shraddhanand the previous year. Muslims have never agreed on whether the *sunnah* of the Prophet and his companions is absolutely binding. They in any case have first to consult several Hadiths deemed to contain sound traditions laid down by the Prophet, select the most appropriate and then work to establish their claim to be complying with the *tariqa-i-Muhammad* or the way of Muhammad.[84] Indian Muslims were far from being on any *tariqa* remotely akin to the Prophet's way of life. For them the *sunnah* was more an ideal, a model of reality they might aspire to but never fully emulate. This did not mean that there was no occasion for illusion. It was the imbalance between the ideal and the real which tended to find its way into the pages of the Muslim press, smacking of ill-will towards other communities.

Their Hindu counterparts were more than a match. Combining duties in the editorial room with active politics came naturally to Punjabi journalists. In Lahore, the hub of the provincial press, the Hindu Sabha was 'frankly communal'. It made clear that 'the Hindus of the Punjab ha[d] no intentions of standing aside while the Muhammadans press[ed] their claims' with the British. Hindu bigotry was displayed not at a meeting to whip up support for the Simon Commission, but at the jubilee celebrations of the Arya Samaj in Lahore during late December 1927. With Mahasha Krishen, editor of the *Pratap*, playing stage manager, Mahasha Basant Ram read a hair-raising poem. If Hindus 'united they could defeat Muhammadans' and 'kill the tyrants in fair fight'. Painting a

[84]These have been compiled by Sahih al-Bukhari (d. 870), Muslim (d. 875), Ibn Da'ud (d. 888), al-Nasai (d. 915), al-Tirmidhi (d. 892), and Ibn Maja (d. 886). Richard Bulliet notes the importance of the Hadiths in conversions to Islam prior to the eleventh century. By the thirteenth century the process of compiling the authoritative Hadiths had been completed. (See Richard W. Bulliet, *Islam: The View From the Edge*, New York: Columbia University Press, 1994, p. 19 and fn.20.)

gory spectacle of Muslims being slain like goats and kicked into the sea, he announced that 'with the dagger of *Shuddhi* all Muhammadans would be converted to Hinduism' while the 'stick of *Sangathan*' would force them 'to ask forgiveness for their assaults on Hinduism'. Sensing bedlam, the president urged his co-religionists 'not ... to besmear their hands with the blood of others'; they should 'remove the sting of the scorpion but not ... kill it'. This did not deter two joint editors of the *Bande Mataram* from reciting anti-Muslim poems. Another poem declared that if not for the services rendered by the Arya Samaj, 'cows would have disappeared and the "muck-eaters" would have preponderated everywhere; the *Kalma* would have replaced the *Gayatri*, and Hindu women would have been known by Muhammadan names'. Another poem objected to Hindus supplying milk to the 'reptiles of Muhammadans'. By far the most accurate assessment was that Shraddhanand's murder had done more to 'popularise the Arya Samaj than all the work of the previous 20 years'. Hopes were expressed that the departed soul might reappear in a new incarnation to 'suppress the Muhammadans'.[85]

It was not just extremist Hindus like Bhai Parmanand who raised cries of Muslim bigotry. Diwan Chand, principal of the Dayanand Arya Vedic College, Kanpur, 'criticised the narrow-mindedness of Indian Muhammadans', arguing that 'real progress was impossible so long as their social customs were controlled by religious institutions'. The Turks had opted for democracy, 'Afghanistan was an example of liberalism'. It defied common sense 'why the Muhammadans of India remained in their old groove'. But some of his own co-religionists showed themselves in even lesser light. Kanwar Vidyasagar read a poem to an audience of 2000 to the effect that 'butchers would become cowherds'; *shuddhi* would save the cows and 'those who shouted *Allah-o-Akbar* would one day worship Ram and Krishan'. If this was not provocation enough, the poet confidently predicted that one day Zafar Ali Khan and Khwajah Hasan Nizami would 'cut of their beards and wear the Hindu sacred tuft of hair'. Once the Aryas had 'converted the whole of India they would ... turn to Mecca'.[86]

Congenitally inclined to give a Muslim twist to the idea of his tuft, Zafar Ali Khan had only the day before declared at the meeting of the Khilafat Committee in Lahore that he was 'not afraid of the Hindus'. After 1000 years in slavery Hindus were less able to resist alien rule than Muslims who had been enslaved for only a 150 years. According to this logic, 'the Hindu mentality was inferior to Muslim mentality'. Punjabi Muslims did not need the Hindus to 'get their birthright'. It was just as well that the fight was not with the Hindus but with the British. Shades of the nationalist line were evident in Zafar Ali's denunciation of the Simon Commission. Contemptuous of

[85]*SPPAI*, 7 January 1928, vol. l, no. 1, p. 1.
[86]Ibid., pp. 5–7.

Muslims cooperating with an all-white commission, he pronounced Muhammad Shafi, 'a sycophant'.[87] Zafar, a gifted man who carried the colours of the Muslim *hurriyat pasand* or lover of freedom in a sharper hue than Iqbal and comparable to Mohamed Ali, must secretly have known that what the communitarian tangle in the Punjab really needed was a Solomon's decision.

The historical actors seemed to have placed their trust in a Satanic prose on difference. This made it even more difficult to accommodate religiously informed perceptions of cultural identity within the emerging ideal of the Indian nation. The Achilles' heal, it must be reiterated, was the principle of majorities and minorities defined by religion. Khwajah Hasan Nizami, the copious author from UP, told a meeting in Lahore attended by a thousand people that 'Muslims had the right to be fully represented in the administration of India as they were the race from which the British had wrested the government of India'. Azad Gul, editor of the NWFP paper *Afghan*, thought the Hindu claim to a majority was unsustainable since the number included twenty-two crore untouchables. If Punjabi Muslims 'united' with the Pathans, '*Shudhi* and *Sangathan* would have a short life'.[88]

To avert this catastrophe the Lahore Hindu Sabha stepped up its activities following the announcement of the Simon Commission in November 1927. On 8 January 1928, a meeting attended by the editors of *Pratap* and *Milap* warned the Congress against any pact with the Muslims that undermined the interests of Punjabi Hindus. Despite having their fair share in the Lucknow Pact, Muslims wanted representation according to their population in the Punjab and Bengal, the separation of Sind from Bombay and the extension of the reforms to the NWFP and Baluchistan. At both its Lahore and Calcutta sessions, led by Muhammad Shafi and Jinnah respectively, the All-India Muslim League had unambiguously demanded 'communal superiority in five Provinces so as to be in a position to avenge any attacks on Muhammadans in Provinces where the Hindus were in a majority'. There was no question of letting 'Congress ... sacrific[e] the interests of Hindus in those Provinces ... for the sake of a so-called national boycott'.[89] If the split in the Muslim League reflected the difficulties of reconciling the interests of Muslims in the majority and the minority provinces, the Punjab Hindu Sabha's posture posed a bigger problem for the inclusionary nationalism of the Congress. Satanic prose and differences within had coalesced to the detriment of broader equations at the all-India level, pointing to the hazards of turning a deaf ear to the communitarian bugles sounding the Punjabi revolt against any move to sacrifice regional and religious rights at the altar of national unity.

[87]Ibid., p. 9.
[88]Ibid., pp. 9–10.
[89]Ibid., p. 17.

The Delhi Proposals, the Nehru Report and Simon's un-Solomonic Paper

There can be no understanding of the dynamics of Indian politics at this crucial conjuncture without taking into account the emerging dialogue between the region and the centre. After all, the central apex of power was the prized trophy sought after by an array of nationalists, whatever their level of social support. Mohammed Ali Jinnah, put in the shade by the religious divines and politicians at the local and regional levels of society, could see his moment in history with the setting up of a Royal Commission. It was regrettable that the British considered Indians incapable of arriving at an impartial view of how best to shape the future of the subcontinent. But giving the commission a royal snub did not mean ignoring its presence. The prospects of a new spate of constitutional reforms had reopened the possibility of forging a common, if not necessarily united, national front, irrespective of religious distinction. This afforded Jinnah an opportunity to get his stocks quoted in the central assembly where after the 1926 elections he was an independent member without a following.[90]

Mohammad Ali Jinnah is a telling example of the individual interacting with an amorphous Muslim collectivity. Prior to 1926 he had been the leader of the Independent Party in the central legislative assembly, holding the balance between the government and the Congress. Tossed into the political wilderness, Jinnah tried turning the emblem of his Indian identity to advantage. He was a Muslim and a beneficiary of separate electorates. Having played a good hand at the time of the Lucknow Pact, Jinnah was a man with a sense of possibility.[91] Seeing the opening, Jinnah before the appointment of the Simon Commission had tried solving his problems in the assembly by associating himself with the Indian Muslim political category. The Delhi proposals which he helped draft in the presence of other Muslims[92] offered to give up separate electorates if four conditions were met. These asked for Muslim representation in the Punjab

---

[90]See Page, *Prelude to Partition*, pp. 145–6 for the background to the Delhi proposals. My own account owes a debt to him. But while Page looks mainly at the formal arenas of politics, provincial and central, this chapter is concerned with drawing out the links between the formal and informal arenas and their impact on the refashioning of regional, communitarian and national identities.

[91]Jinnah initially tried aligning himself with the Muslim group in the assembly led by Sir Abdul Qaiyum. That proved impossible given the Qaiyum group's pro-government posture. The problem was greater for the Congress leadership in the assembly. Marred by divisions within, they needed a way of winning over the Muslims.

[92]Of the twenty-nine Muslims present, sixteen were members of the central legislative assembly and two of the state council. The rest consisted of pro-Congress Muslims, Islamic universalists and those interested in all-India constitutional arrangements. There were only three Muslims from the Muslim-majority provinces.

and Bengal according to population; the creation of a new province of Sind; the extension of the reforms to the NWFP and Baluchistan; and 33 per cent of the seats in the central legislative assembly. There was no mention of weightage for provincial minorities, a significant omission considering its centrality in the framing of the 1916 accord.

If this explains the Mahasabhite opposition to the proposals, it underlines the Muslim realization, even in minority provinces, that separate electorates were at best a poor relief with the further extension of the representative principle in India. Fudging the numbers and turning majorities into minorities in the name of weightage had been overborne by the march of events. The prospect of a real devolution of power in the localities and the provinces had shifted the focus from the numbers game to one of regional political dominance. By far the most important outcome of Jinnah's Delhi proposals was the Congress Working Committee's decision at its Delhi session on 31 March 1927 to accept this Muslim point of view. Unfortunately neither Jinnah nor the Congress had the support of all those belonging to the categories 'Muslim' and 'Hindu'. Jinnah's success turned out to be a pyrrhic one precisely because he had not cared to understand politics at the regional level. Ready to promote the regionalization of Muslim dominance in five provinces, Jinnah the constitutionalist quite as much as Iqbal the poet was an individual without the organized following of the community.

If Iqbal occasionally echoed the sentiments of urban Punjabi Muslims, Jinnah was palpably in the dark about the real workings of the Muslim psyche. More interested with power at the centre, he had completely overlooked the Punjabi Muslim's dread of general electorates. That some of their fears may have been justified is suggested by the counter proposals put forward by Malaviya on behalf of the Hindu Mahasabha. Presented on 21 April 1927, these among other things demanded constitutional safeguards for the distribution of religious rights and the representation of religious divisions. This was warmly endorsed the next day by the Punjab Hindu Sabha. In an insolent telegram, the provincial Sabha instructed the Congress high command to cease claiming to represent Hindus when it came to dialogue with the Muslims. If it did, the decisions would not be binding on the Hindus. To the horror of Punjab's Muslims, a few days later Sardar Mangal Singh, a spokesman of the Sikhs, endorsed the Mahasabha's demands.

So the plot had thickened even before the establishment of an all-white commission in November 1927. Its impending arrival marked the Punjabi

---

(See Page, *Prelude to Partition*, p. 146, fn.6.) Posing a problem for the principle of representation, it captured the gulf dividing the regional and the national vision. Chalking out the future shape of the centre in smoke-filled rooms was easier than marketing the product to a divergent and disorganized Muslim community. For an account of these divisions and their impact on all-India politics, see Mushirul Hasan, *Nationalism and Communal Politics in India, 1916-1928*, Delhi: Manohar, 1979.

breakaway from the All-India Muslim League. Left only with Muslims present at the time of the Delhi proposals, Jinnah in December 1927 presided over the All-India Muslim League session in Calcutta. In contrast to his centralist reading of the political dynamics, the provincial dimension was in the ascendance in the Punjab. The Shafi League in the Punjab bore the hallmark of collaboration. But the reasoning that led Muhammad Iqbal to join the Punjabi band owed more to the contest for regional, religious and national rights in the province. If Punjabi Muslims ditched Jinnah at the centre, they did so with a reason.

On 31 December 1927 a meeting of the Shafi All-India Muslim League in Lahore with 500 present heard Nawab Zulfiqar Khan censuring 'Mr Jinnah [for] continu[ing] to face inter-communal antagonism with serene unconcern'. Invoking the principle of self-determination, Zulfiqar Khan asserted that India's problem was 'not national but inter-national'. The 'slogan of Indian nationality was raised only by interested people for the purpose of impressing foreigners in India or for exploiting minorities'. Shafi attacked the agitation against separate electorates as 'artificial' and 'injurious' to the 'cause of Indian nationalism'. The Lucknow Pact was a 'grievous injustice to the Muslim community'. Muslim interests had to be accommodated since 'in the India of the future the Central Government would be permanently in the hands of Hindus'. Despite efforts by flag-waving *khilafatists*, only nineteen votes were cast against 184 in favour of working with the Simon Commission. All the delegates from UP, the NWFP, Bengal, Bombay and Delhi present voted for cooperation. Elections to the top positions in the party saw the elevation of Muhammad Shafi as permanent president—an ominous title for any party to confer upon an individual—with Muhammad Iqbal as secretary and Hasrat Mohani as joint secretary.[93]

The proposals submitted to the Simon Commission on behalf of the Punjab legislative council had the support of the Shafi group. Bearing the Unionist stamp, these demanded separate electorates and a majority for Muslims of one seat over other communities in the reformed legislature. Traitors in the eyes of the remaining *khilafatists* in the province, the Shafi League was not without support in the Punjab. Whatever the postures of the nationalist spokesman on the central stage, there had been an alarming increase in communitarian tensions in the districts between Hindus and Muslims, and Muslims and Sikhs over the usual issues: control of religious places, cow slaughter and music before the mosques. In this situation, the prospects of a Congress–League agreement based on joint electorates looked bleak. Jinnah's main support in the Punjab came from Zafar Ali Khan, Kitchlew and Malik Barkat Ali who wanted to advance the cause of freedom now that Congress had recognized Muslim claims. All that was required was to substitute the false security of separate electorates with the solid advantages of provincial dominance.

[93]*SPPAI*, 7 January 1928, vol. l, no. 1, p. 10.

The controversy over the Delhi proposals and the provincial demands put forward by Muslims in the Punjab and UP to the Simon Commission were drowned by reactions in August 1928 to a report prepared by a special Congress committee under Motilal Nehru with his son Jawaharlal as secretary. Instead of full independence, its stated goal was dominion status with a complete transfer of all departments of the central government to a responsible Indian legislature. The government structure envisaged by the Nehru report was unitary rather than federal in form. If this was a potential source of disagreement, the report's efforts to accommodate Muslim political interests opened up a can of worms. Influenced in the main by Jawaharlal Nehru, the Congress committee recommended the elimination of separate electorates. This was the price Muslims had to pay for securing their majority in the Punjab and Bengal without weighted representation for the minority communities. Muslims in Sind and the NWFP also had reason to be gratified; the former was to be separated from Bombay and the latter brought on par with other provinces in British India. The Muslim demand for 33 per cent of the seats in the central legislature was rejected, a serious defect from Jinnah's point of view.

The centralist politician nevertheless chose not to condemn the Congress initiative out of hand. The Nehru report was by far the most radical statement of Indian nationalist ambitions at the centre to date, albeit one which had compromised on the issue of full independence. But without accommodating provincial interests, bitterly divided along communitarian lines, the Nehruvian vision of India's future was destined for the waste-paper bins of history. The rejection of separate electorates meant certain Punjabi Muslim opposition. Moreover, with the *Tribune* hailing it as 'an epoch-making report' and Lajpat Rai rushing to endorse its verdict on communal electorates, the Punjab Hindu Sabha denounced it as an unmitigated disaster. According to its vice-president, Bhai Parmanand, the report would 'divide the country permanently into two hostile parts'.[94] The Sikhs were alarmed at the summary dismissal of their claim to a separate identity. On 20 August the Punjab Provincial Congress Committee accepted the Nehru report while declaring its preference for complete national independence. It did so without bothering to consult those on whose behalf it was advancing its provincial and all-India claims. Backing for the Nehru report among Punjabi Muslims was provided by old *khilafatists* and young radicals of the Nau Jawan Sabha founded in March 1926 by college students in Lahore.

Khilafatists, Nau Jawans and the Nehruvian Ideal

All that had remained of the *khilafat* committees in the Punjab was a network of individuals without any formal organizational backing. This militated against any unanimity in their response to the Nehru report. The Lahore Khilafat

[94]*SPPAI*, 18 August 1928, vol. l, no. 32, p. 345.

Committee gave a warm welcome to Ataullah Shah Bukhari after his release from prison in connection with the *Rangila Rasul* episode. Instead of supporting the Nehru report, a fighting-fit Bukhari landed a straight volley in the Hindu camp, 'deprecat[ing] the attitude of Malaviya, Moonje and Gandhi who had never advised their co-religionists to play fair with Muhammadans'. Habibur Rahman of Ludhiana inched closer to the jugular, proposing that 'Muslims should not rely upon the Hindus but ... lead a separate existence from them'.[95]

At a meeting of the Lahore Khilafat Committee, Habibur Rahman joined Kitchlew, Zafar Ali Khan, Muhammad Daud Ghaznavi and Choudhury Afzal Haq in giving a good bill of health to the Nehru report. In Amritsar, Kitchlew defended joint electorates as a means to ending communitarian tensions.[96] The Nehru report gave fresh urgency to the battle for control of the *khilafat* committees, facilitating their demise and leaving much of the organizational work in the informal arenas of politics to the Majlis-i-Ahrar. The mystery surrounding the fate of the Khilafat Committees, left unaddressed by historians, can be pieced together only by keeping the cursor on men like Zafar Ali Khan, Kitchlew, Ataullah, Habibur Rahman and Choudhury Afzal Haq.

Focusing on individuals does not mean neglecting the broader picture. For instance in Amritsar city, internal rivalries resulted in two different Khilafat Committees. The immediate reason for the break was Bacha-i-Saquo's revolt against Amanullah in Afghanistan. Many Punjabi Muslims suspected a British hand in Saquo's *fitna*, who in turn was believed to be influenced by Pir Karam Dad. Sheikh Hissamuddin, another future Ahrar leader, told the meeting of the old Khilafat Committee that the new Khilafat Committee was a creature of the *pir* who was 'neither Muhammadan nor Indian' but of 'Lawrence of Arabia fame'. Backed by the British, he had worked to heighten divisions in Afghanistan, especially among Shias and Sunnis. Not to be done in by this low-lying attack, the new Khilafat Committee passed a resolution supporting Amanullah's restoration to the throne. Sayyid Habib of the *Siyasat* defended the new *khilafat* committee in the city on the grounds that the old one 'had supported the Congress and not followed the principles of Islam'.[97]

In other instances the *khilafat* committees provided a forum for those who had their own reasons for wanting to support the Nehru report. Zafar Ali Khan could not bring himself to make terms with the British government. So he told a *khilafat* committee meeting in Amritsar that the 'Muslim community was in a very critical condition'. Hindus, whom they regarded as cowards, were taking a lead in politics and had issued an ultimatum to the government. Taking time out from purely communitarian considerations, Zafar Ali extolled the courage of Bhagat Singh and other revolutionary

[95]Ibid., p. 347.
[96]Ibid., pp. 389–91.
[97]*SPPAI*, 8 June 1929, vol. li, no. 23, p. 285.

'terrorists'. He lamented that Muslims had not produced a young man like Bhagat Singh.[98]

The comment was in keeping with Zafar Ali Khan's attempts to press the Congress to endorse the demand for complete independence. Once the provincial Congress gave its approval, the Nau Jawan Sabha began trying to hijack the organization. The rift between an older generation of Congress politicians and the *nau jawans* of the Punjab administered a radical tonic to the communitarian miseries of the province. Zafar Ali and Kitchlew warned that if Gandhi's programme of non-cooperation did not result in dominion status by the end of December 1929, they along with the younger element would adopt revolutionary means to oust the British. But capturing the Provincial Congress Committee from their broken *khilafatist* base was more difficult than they had imagined. During the public debate on the Nehru report, it was easier for Zafar Ali Khan to go to Congress meetings than to stay there. At a meeting of the Lahore Congress Committee, he regretted that 'interested people were creating a gulf between the Hindus and Muhammadans which would soon be impossible to bridge'.[99] At another Congress meeting, however, Zafar Ali Khan hurled abuses at Hindus for not accepting Muslim majorities in the Punjab and Bengal despite their preponderance in India. There was 'much confusion and uproar' in the audience, forcing the *maulana* to walk out in protest. The colonial police's intelligence department thought the 'incident' would 'effectively kill any hope the Hindu leaders still cherished' about 'win[ning] over the support of the Muhammadan community to the Congress cause'.[100]

Barely capable of holding his ground in the Congress or rallying Punjab's fractious *khilafatists*, Zafar Ali Khan cuts a sorry figure in another story about a dynamic individual's interactions with the community of Islam in India, both in its expansive and restricted senses. An Islamic universalist, his Punjabi Muslim identity was located in India in the political sense. What distinguished Zafar Ali Khan from his fellow co-religionists was the sustained support he lent to the Congress cause in the Punjab. But this confirmed anti-imperialist rejected Kitchlew's suggestion that everyone should be first a nationalist, and then a Hindu, Muslim or Sikh. Zafar Ali had 'decided once for all' that he was 'a Musalman first, second and last'. He also took issue with Kitchlew's contention that the 'observance of religion should be confined to the ... homes as in the outer world they were Indians alone'. This was 'doing immense harm to the Congress cause'.[101] Zafar Ali Khan was ready to test Congress's commitment to accommodating religiously informed cultural differences. At its forthcoming session at Lahore, he proposed to not only push the complete

[98]*SPPAI*, 6 July 1929, vol. li, no. 27, p. 342.
[99]*SPPAI*, 24 August 1929, vol. li, no. 34, p. 457.
[100]*SPPAI*, 21 September 1929, vol. li, no. 38, pp. 529–30.
[101]*SPPAI*, 2 November 1929, vol. li, no. 44, p. 630.

independence resolution but ensure that the proceedings were suspended to give Muslims time to say their afternoon prayers.[102] An ardent supporter of the younger Nehru, whose promotion of the complete independence resolution along with the popular Bengali leader Subhas Chandra Bose is legion, Zafar Ali might have appeared to be confusing political goals with cultural differences. Yet, convinced of the inseparability of the spiritual and the temporal, he could not comprehend the logic of inclusionary nationalism of the Congress being propounded by Jawaharlal Nehru.

The reasons are easy to discern. In mid-April at a meeting of the Nau Jawan Sabha at Lahore's Mochi Gate attended by a thousand people, mostly Hindus, the architect of post-independence India's secular nationalism argued against letting religion swamp intelligence. Having implied that the religious were unintelligent, he concluded by urging the audience to give intelligence preference over religion. Sunam Rai declared Hindu–Muslim unity impossible so long as religion held sway in India. Religion was the opiate of the ignorant and the best religion was the attainment of freedom. When M.A. Majid rose to speak, some Muslims asked 'what degree of Islamic faith he possessed'. After difficulty in disciplining the audience, Majid supported the separation of religion and politics in Kemalist Turkey. 'Indians,' he stated, 'should regard religion as an article of personal property.' Unconvinced, Muslims at the meeting voted solidly as a community against a resolution calling for the separation of church and state.[103]

The Nau Jawan Sabha's proposal to 'disassociate religion from politics' faced 'considerable Muslim opposition'. A meeting of the Khilafat Committee in Lahore condemned the 'sacrilegious and profane' propaganda of the *nau jawans* which was 'opposed to the spirit of Islam'. The Nau Jawan Sabha was constrained by its association with the Communist Party's affiliate, the Kirti-Kisan Party consisting of Sikhs committed to revolutionary change.[104] Dependent on a radical fringe of the Sikhs, the *nau jawans* were thought to have 'alienated the sympathies' of those who preferred 'constitutional changes in the land revenue system' while their 'extreme politics' and 'communistic doctrines ha[d] alarmed land-holders'.[105]

Members of the Nau Jawan Sabha had to take an oath putting the interests of the country before those of the community. One of its prominent leaders,

---

[102]Ibid., p. 631.

[103]*SPPAI*, 21 April 1928, vol. l, no. 16, p. 179.

[104]In December 1927 at Madras the Punjab Kirti-Kisan Party had formally associated itself with the Communist Party of India. By January 1928 the Shiromani Akali Dal, the premier Sikh party, was supporting the Kirti-Kisan Party. The decision to work closely with the Nau Jawan Sabha was taken in April 1928. There were similar links between revolutionary and agrarian groups in Bengal. (Supplement I to the *SPPAI*, 5 May 1928, vol. l, no. 18, pp. 195–200.)

[105]Supplement II of ibid.

Kidar Nath Sehgal, wrote a biting pamphlet against Lajpat Rai. This was seen as the 'beginning of the end of the Sabha'. After a lull, the Sabha got back on its feet in March 1928, well in time for the Congress' famous Lahore session of December 1929 where the resolution calling for complete independence was finally adopted. Matters took an ugly turn when the Kirti-Kisan Party, 'alarmed at the opposition aroused by the *anti*-religious and *anti*-communal propaganda of the Sabha', tightened its purse strings.[106] Congress extremists in the province were promoting the Hindustani Sewa Dal which in addition to trying to organize people talked about setting up national clubs to help improve their physique.[107] In 1929 there were 255 Congress committees in the province with a membership of only 18,881. The quota for the Punjab was 51,712 and even after a membership drive by September of the year the total Congress membership just touched 28,000. The provincial *nau jawans* were furious at Motilal Nehru's refusal to let the Allahabad session of the all-India Congress discuss Bhagat Singh's imprisonment in the Lahore conspiracy case.[108]

So there was a hollow ring to the Lahore Khilafat Committee's appeals to the people to join the Congress in driving the British out of India. There had never been much hope for the Congress in the Punjab. By the summer of 1929 the provincial police was convinced that 'the large majority of Muhammadans ha[d] little use for the kind of constitution outlined by the Nehru report'.[109] Neither the ramshackle *khilafat* committees nor the financially and ideologically strapped Nau Jawan Sabha fared very well in promoting Nehruvian ideals in the Punjab. This was apparent in the debate on the Nehru report from perspectives other than those of the *khilafatists* and the *nau jawans*.

Punjabis on the Nehru Report

True to character, Punjabis of all religious denominations had conflicting opinions on the Nehru report. Coherent discussion and a detailed examination of the proposed constitution was scotched by the communitarian bugbear. Matters came to a head soon after the All Parties Conference in Lucknow unanimously approved the report. Such a rare consensus had been possible only through the device of excluding those Hindus, Muslims and Sikhs who disagreed with the Nehruvian vision. Neither Jinnah nor the Ali brothers were present at this select gathering of Indian nationalists. A section of the Punjab *khilafatists*, including many of the future Ahrar leaders, endorsed

[106]The Kirti-Kisan Party refused to help finance the two Amritsar papers *Akali* and the *Akali-te-Pradesi*—the main organs of the Akalis—unless they desisted from communitarian propaganda. (*SPPAI*, 23 June 1928, vol. l, no. 24, p. 260.)

[107]*SPPAI*, 16 June 1928, vol. l, no. 23, p. 249.

[108]*SPPAI*, 24 August 1929, vol. li, no. 34, p. 456.

[109]*SPPAI*, 6 July 1929, vol. l, no. 27, p. 341.

the Nehru report in Lucknow. But neither the *khilafatists* nor the *nau jawans* could provide a solid phalanx of support for the Congress.

At a provincial political conference in Lyallpur organized to secure support for the report, Lajpat Rai and Ansari had a hard time explaining away the 'communal objections of their co-religionists'. Using 'specious arguments', Rai tried skirting around the issue by making 'a clever oratorial appeal to Hindu consciousness'. This could work only if Muslim and Sikh trouble makers were excluded from meetings organized to secure backing for the Nehru report. But it was difficult keeping everyone out. Even the Kirti-Kisan Party believed that the Nehruvian constitution would 'only replace one set of bureaucrats by another set represented by the so-called "all-India leaders", who w[ould] pay as little regard to the interests of peasants and workers as the present Government ...'[110] The insight was lost upon a Punjab in the throes of communitarian enmity. With the Punjab Hindu Sabha leader, Bhai Parmanand, bitterly opposing its provisions, and a vocal section of the Muslims describing it as a Hindu document, there was no future for the Nehru report. Mangal Singh, one of the few Sikhs allowed to participate in the proceedings, urged his co-religionists to accept the Nehru formula. If the Muslims tried establishing their rule, he personally would 'oppose them with the sword'. This led the unsung *ghazi* of Islam, Zafar Ali Khan, to retort that 'there certainly would be an Islamic *raj*' in the Punjab but one that would 'teach equality, justice and the oneness of God to the people'. If Mangal Singh opposed Muslim rule, Zafar Ali vowed to 'correct him with his bludgeon'. But he would also 'break the head of any Muslim who disrespected a Hindu woman'. Zafar Ali Khan blamed British propaganda for portraying a Muslim as someone 'armed with a sword in one hand and a copy of the *Quran* in the other'.[111]

Lajpat Rai conceded that 'Hindu rights could not be safe so long as the mentality of the Muslims remained what it was'. He had always argued that separate electorates for Muslims were the root of the problem in the Punjab. Now he learnt to his dismay that this opinion was not shared by Punjabi Hindus who disliked the idea of giving up their weightage. Rai could see that it was 'difficult to give up any concession'. What puzzled him was the refrain in certain Hindu quarters that the Nehru constitution would initiate Muslim rule in the Punjab. He for one believed that there was 'already a Muslim *raj*' in the province. But at least there would be 'a Hindu *raj* in other provinces'.[112] This was why he failed to understand why Hindus in the Punjab were opposed to the separation of Sind when Sindhi Hindus approved of it.[113] In Lajpat Rai's opinion, those who opposed the report had 'not considered it from the

[110]*SPPAI*, 22 September 1928, vol. l, no. 37, p. 405.
[111]Ibid., p. 420.
[112]Ibid., p. 445.
[113]Ibid., p. 422.

all-India point of view'. Even if the Nehru constitution 'ruined the interests of Hindus and Sikhs of the Punjab', there was 'no reason' why they should 'ruin the rest of India'.[114]

These were the last entreaties of a man who in 1924 had produced a set of cogent, if controversial, arguments on the regional, religious and national rights of Punjabi Hindus. On 17 November 1928 Lajpat Rai died in Lahore of heart failure. This was within weeks of his being subjected to *lathi* blows by the provincial police. Many Punjabis attributed his death to the incident. While some of his ideas had been adopted by his co-religionists, the political direction they had taken was radically different from the one presented in the Nehru report and dangerously close to that which pointed to the extreme solution of dividing the province into two. In the words of Parmanand, 'no Hindu in his senses would accept the report'. Certainly, no member of the Punjab Hindu Sabha had been present in Lucknow when the All-Parties Conference ratified the Nehru report.[115] But he 'admitted that the Hindus were divided into two camps over the Nehru report'. The difficulty was that Muslims wanted the lion's share. Describing the Lucknow Pact as a 'communal curse', he held it responsible for the poor state of Hindu–Muslim relations. If Hindus succumbed to pressure on the separation of Sind and reforms in the NWFP and Baluchistan, the Muslims would up the ante. Hindus had no choice except to reject the 'fatal report drawn up by the Nehru Committee'. The Nehru report would divide the country into 'two communal camps'. All-India Hindu leaders had 'foolishly co-operated with Muslims' on the question of Sind's future. As a result, Muslim demands were 'more tainted with communalism than at any time before'.[116]

Supporters of the Nehru report thought its conception of the political future would root out 'communalism' from India. The term's etymological origins in the granting of separate electorates to Muslims notwithstanding, it was coming to be deployed as a weapon against other communities. At its meeting in Lahore, Dr Moonje, who had close links with the Rashtriya Swayamsevak Sangh leader Dr Keshav Baliram Hegdewar in the Central Provinces, denied that the Punjab Hindu Sabha was 'a communal body' which 'promoted communalism'. Its sole object was 'to defend the rights of Hindus' and it had been established 'because other communal institutions were already in existence in India'. In a giveaway, Moonje asserted that 'the perfecting of separate communal organizations would lead to national solidarity'. He placed special emphasis on *sangathan* since Hindus were 'in reality weaker than the Muslims' owing to the subdivisions of castes. It was his hope that after India's freedom Hindus and Muslims would develop 'a diplomatic friendship'. But there was always 'danger in such friendships' and Hindus had to organize

[114]*SPPAI*, 20 October 1928, vol. l, no. 40, p. 422.
[115]*SPPAI*, 22 September 1928, vol. l, no. 37, p. 421.
[116]Ibid., p. 407.

themselves to 'defend their country', if not with swords then at least with *lathis.*[117]

Fear parading as chauvinism is not a novel occurrence. The creation of the RSS in 1925 by Hegdewar had provided a paramilitary front for the paragons of Hindu majoritarianism with origins going back to the late nineteenth century. Moonje's flitting about the concentric circles of the Mahasabha, the Arya Samaj and the RSS on the one hand, and contacts with all-India Congress leaders of Gandhi's stature on the other, suggests that the *sangathan* of the Hindus was more of a political *sangam* of independently constituted organizations. Too little attention has been paid in the historical scholarship to the network of individuals who served as channels of communication between the Congress and various Hindu nationalist organizations. The intermeshing of these two apparently dissimilar strands had far greater consequences for identity, sovereignty and citizenship in the subcontinent than the nationalism–communalism paradigm has permitted historians to explore.

A Hindu nationalist from Nagpur, Dr Moonje considered India his sovereign domain. For one felled by *lathis*, Lajpat Rai represented another kind of Hindu nationalist with moorings in the Punjab. With an idea of regional rights safeguarded by national rights drawing upon the colonial conception of religious communities, Rai had campaigned ceaselessly against the extension of separate electorates to the Punjab. To his credit, he supported the Nehru report, accepting a Punjabi Muslim majority in a province that was part of a larger Indian whole. He even avoided reiterating his formula for partition from public platforms. A nationalist at heart and a communitarian regionalist in deed, Rai thought the constitutional arrangements envisaged in the Nehru report were effective safeguards for Punjabi Hindu interests. Indeed, he accepted Muslim majorities in five provinces of British India as a fair exchange for dominating the rest of India from the centre.

If Lajpat Rai was compelled to rebuke his co-religionists for their stance on Sind's separation from Bombay, Kitchlew had to do much the same with Punjabi Muslims. Flying a flag he secretly realized could never be hoisted in the Punjab, this Kashmiri lawyer who had made an impact in Amritsar politics thought 'all communities were treated equally in the report'. He could not understand the Punjabi Muslim opposition to Nehru's constitution 'when their co-religionists in Bengal and Sind had approved it'.[118] At a meeting of 3000 people in Jullundur on 10 October 1928, he supplied statistics on voting patterns in district board elections. These showed Muslims holding a majority on twenty-eight district boards. Quite evidently, 'Muslims ha[d] no fear of joint electorates for Council elections'. Decrying the logic of exclusionary communitarianism, Kitchlew maintained that the 'communal leaders were

---

[117]*SPPAI*, 26 January 1929, vol. li, no. 4, p. 63.
[118]*SPPAI*, 20 October 1928, vol. l, no. 40, p. 443.

afraid of joint electorates because they would have to work for their seats'. It was 'foolish' for Muslims to be 'afraid of Hindu *raj*' since 'under the reformed constitution there would be no communal parties'.[119]

A leading activist in the *tanzim* movement, Kitchlew was far removed from the sort of bigotry reflected in Parmanand or Ataullah Shah Bukhari. It was his personal intervention which had resolved a dispute involving a Hindu woman in Amritsar, who after converting to Islam and marrying a Muslim, decided to return to her faith. She left her home and went to an Arya Samaj worker. The abandoned husband's cause was taken up by his friends and relatives and snowballed into a communitarian issue. With Kitchlew's mediation the woman was allowed to exercise her individual right of judgement in the matter of religion and marriage.[120] It was to rein in forces of bigotry among Muslims that Kitchlew recommended control over the 300 mosques in Amritsar on the same lines as Sikh *gurdwaras*. Advertising his disdain for the religious divines, he 'stigmatised *Maulvis* as traitors'.[121]

In a lesser known tale of the individual striving for the support of the community to join a larger whole, Kitchlew fared relatively better than many of his contemporaries. But his social background and political location within the Congress undermined his provincial standing. In October 1929 a mere 600 were present at a Congress meeting in Lahore. Mainly students, they greeted Kitchlew's arrival with slogans of 'Inqilab Zindabad', long live the revolution.[122] Within days he was preaching freedom and advising people to read their religious books. 'The Nehru report,' he now asserted, was 'a mere scrap of paper meant to compromise ignorant people.' [123] Just a few weeks before the all-India organization's session in Lahore chucked the Nehru report into the river Ravi, Kitchlew was hailed as the 'King of India' at a meeting of the Gujranwala Congress. In a glaring demonstration of his impatience with the policy of non-violence, Kitchlew characterized Gandhi as 'a weak-hearted man, who now that the country was prepared for liberty, was deserting them'. But he was still prepared to give the Mahatma one last chance.[124] Unfortunately the Punjab had lost its enthusiasm for the Mahatma. With the all-India leaders shifting their political positions, no one imbibing the daily diet of being a Muslim, Hindu or Sikh was prepared to forsake a religiously informed cultural identity for an uncertain political future.

If the Nehru report brought out disagreement in the Punjab along communitarian lines, reactions to the Sarda Act of 1929 raising the legal age of

[119]Ibid., p. 444.
[120]*SPPAI*, 3 November 1928, vol. l, no. 42, p. 481.
[121]*SPPAI*, 7 July 1928, vol. l, no. 26, p. 290.
[122]*SPPAI*, 19 October 1929, vol. li, no. 42, p. 593.
[123]*SPPAI*, 2 November 1929, vol. li, no. 44, pp. 630–1.
[124]*SPPAI*, 23 November 1929, vol. li, no. 47, p. 697.

marriage from twelve to fourteen years showed that Muslims and Hindus were internally divided on whether the British had the right to lay down the legal age of marriage. The Muslim campaign against the act was particularly vigorous in Sialkot, Ludhiana, Gurgaon and Lyallpur. *Inqilab*, the organ of the '56% group' appealed to its readers to send telegrams of protest to the governor. It was the posture of the Muslim divines, many of whom were associated with the Congress since the *khilafat* days, which rudely disturbs the neat assumptions of an idea of equal citizenship rights based on separating the religious and the temporal domains.[125] Ataullah Shah Bukhari was hell bent against the act. So too was the Jamiat-ul-Ulema-i-Hind which described the Sarda Act as 'a flagrant interference with the Muhammadan religion'.[126]

Local branches of the Sanatan Dharm Sabha also condemned the act. By contrast, at a meeting of the Punjab Hindu Young Men Sammelan in Jallianwalla Bagh attended by 700 including women, Bhai Parmanand defended the Sarda Act. And yet his speech was steeped in the politics of cultural defence. It was 'impossible for Hindus to exist in the Punjab with a Muhammadan government over them' as 'contemplated by the Nehru report'. Ready to back the Sarda Act, this prominent spokesman of Punjabi Hindus stated that he was 'not prepared to accept that form of *swaraj* which entailed the abolishment of religion [sic]'. The next day, Moonje in his presidential address took an ostensibly contrary view. He 'emphasized that ... all the inhabitants of India were Indians no matter what their creed'. But this apparent concession to the idea of equal citizenship was not devoid of partisanship. Shades of the Aryan race theory were present in Moonje's statement that if Hindu youth improved their physique they could wrest *swaraj* without the Muslims.[127]

Such narratives of communitarian difference could not possibly corroborate the sameness implicit in an idea of equal citizenship rights. To interpret the opinions of Parmanand and Moonje as proving the necessity of maintaining the distinction between Indian nationalism and communalism would be an error. Conferring labels does not resolve the problem of accommodating self-definitions of religiously informed cultural differences within an inclusionary nationalism not free of the majoritarian and minoritarian principle. So while the term 'communalism' had by now acquired most of the connotations associated with the concept in South Asian historiography, it seems appropriate to consider the nexus between individual bigotry and a politics of exclusionary communitarianism. A return to this unseemly dimension in the politics of the Punjab reveals how provinces could and did shape the nationalist agenda.

The debate on the future constitution had taken place against the stark

[125]See *SPPAI*, 16 November 1929, vol. li, no. 46, p. 682.
[126]*SPPAI*, 23 November 1929, vol. li, no. 47, p. 700.
[127]Ibid., p. 696.

backdrop of two of the worst episodes in the history of communitarian relations in the Punjab. Rajpal had lit the fires of cultural self-defence among Punjabi Muslims, especially those belonging to the lower middle and middling social classes. These Muslims from the intermediate strata had some educational qualifications but not necessarily cushy jobs in the colonial government services. Many were absorbed into the press and publications market, while others took to political activism or, resources permitting, commerce. The interconnections between commerce, consisting of a range of retail stores and small businesses, and the torrent of Muslim communitarianism in the Punjab cannot be underestimated. Muslim social boycott of Hindu shops had been one of the more marked features during times of intense communitarian tensions.

When the Nehru report reached the public circuits, economic boycotts of Hindu shopkeepers were being carried out in many of the smaller towns. In Gujranwala district, the Anjuman-i-Himayat-i-Islam had been formed with the objective of forcing Muslim women to boycott Hindu shops and helping Muslim shopkeepers and traders. Multan was another city where a similar campaign was underway.[128] The Anjuman also undertook to hire the services of Muslim experts in Sanskrit to more effectively counter the Arya Samaj's propaganda through the *tabligh* movement.[129] If to the bazaar politics one adds the role of pro-Deobandi *ulema* like Ataullah Shah Bukhari the picture becomes rather more charged. A marathon speaker who once spoke continuously for seventeen hours, Ataullah Shah is one of the more intriguing examples of the link between the individual and collective in Indian Islam.

Ever since his rise to fame during the *khilafat* agitation, Ataullah rarely missed an opportunity to demonstrate his exclusionary communitarianism despite a pro-Congress stance in politics. But he was better at running down his co-religionists than in helping forge the unity which was the elusive goal of Indian nationalists. The Nehru report, which he personally disliked, gave Bukhari the pretext to settle scores with Zafar Ali Khan. Harbouring Ahl-i-Hadith sympathies, Zafar Ali was among the five *ulema* of Lahore who had bestowed the title *amir-i-shariat* on Ataullah Shah Bukhari. In a poetic vein he had said:

Bukhari's songs are blowing in our ears
The nightingale is singing in the Prophet's garden.[130]

128*SPPAI*, 28 January 1928, vol. l, no. 4, p. 39.
129*SPPAI*, 14 April 1928, vol. l, no. 15, p. 154.
130*Kanon mein goonjate hain Bukhari ke zamzamay*
Bulbul chahak raha hae Riaz, Rasul mein.

کانوں میں گونجتے ہیں بخاری کے زمزمے

بلبل چہک رہا ہے ریاض، رسولؐ میں۔

(Cited in Mirza, *Karavan-i-Ahrar*, i, p. 272.)

Within five years Zafar Ali Khan had conferred the title of *amir-i-millat* upon Pir Jamaat Ali Shah and insulted Bukhari with a couplet deprecating his confrontational tendencies.[131] In April 1929, Ataullah at a meeting of Muslims in Jullundur attacked Zafar Ali Khan's 'conciliatory attitude towards the Hindus'.[132] Hindus would never trust a descendant of Aurangzeb who had built mosques on the ruins of their temples. Gandhi was not a Mahatma but 'a coward' who had 'betrayed India at Bardoli'. Bukhari had no time for the '56% group'. Islam did not teach Muslims to beg.[133]

Without the services of one of their leading propagandists in the Punjab, the Congress had to occasionally enlist Arya preachers to liven up its proceedings. Pandit Atma Ram, imported from Aligarh, told a Congress meeting in Hissar district to stop buying goods from Muslim shops. Muslims were 'chiefly responsible for the slaughter of cows' and should be 'turn[ed] ... out of India'. In the meanwhile the 'beards and moustaches of Muhammadans should be pulled and ... their houses and shops ... set on fire'. He believed that Muslims 'did not eat pork' because 'the pig was a dangerous animal which could show fight'. It followed that 'Hindus should act like a powerful pig and overcome the Muhammadans'. The *pandit* had to be booked for his statements.[134]

Such inflammatory speech making was not designed to help the Congress achieve its aims among Punjabi Muslims. At a meeting to recruit Muslims in Ambala, Muhammad Alam was interrupted by two Muslims who 'announced that their community had no use for the Congress'. One of them denounced the Nehru report as 'entirely pro-Hindu', pointing to the absence of Muslim leaders like the Ali brothers at recent Congress meetings. Duni Chand, who had organized the meeting, was reminded that he had resigned from the local municipal committee to protest the election of nine Muslims. How could Muslims have any 'expectations ... from a man of this type'? This was greeted by shouts of *Allah-o-Akbar*.[135] Congress had reason to be 'perturbed at the lack of public enthusiasm' as 'very few genuine workers [we]re forthcoming'.[136]

It was the Arya Samaj and the Hindu *sabhas* that commanded the attention of Punjabi Hindus. Meetings and newspapers associated with these organizations insisted that Hindus did not need Muslims to win *swaraj*. One Manu Datt of Delhi asserted in Ambala that expecting Muslims to protect Hindus was like letting 'a cat ... guard a vessel containing milk'.[137] More provocative still was a song composed by Gulshan Rai about how the 'Aryas would spread

---

[131]Ibid.

[132]*SPPAI*, 6 April 1929, vol. li, no. 14, p. 171.

[133]Ibid., p. 176.

[134]*SPPAI*, 20 April 1929, vol. li, no. 16, p. 211.

[135]*SPPAI*, 21 September 1929, vol. li, no. 38, p. 537.

[136]*SPPAI*, 9 November 1929, vol. li, no. 45, p. 653.

[137]Several Hindus joined Muslims in condemning these remarks, forcing the speaker to leave the meeting. (Ibid., p. 661.)

their religion all over the country and in time ... convert the people of Mecca'.[138] Mahasha Krishen, the proprietor of the *Pratap*, believed Hindus 'could not ignore their rights in their fight for freedom'; 'peace in the country would only be attained when other religions had been absorbed in Hinduism'.[139] At an Arya Samaj gathering in Hoshiarpur, a visitor from UP ruled out unity with Muslims. Referring to Ilim Din's murder of Rajpal, he fulminated against the Muslims whose religion taught them to exterminate *kafirs*. While moderate Punjabi Hindus had refrained from holding the entire Muslim community responsible for the act of a solitary individual, this would-be leader from UP wanted his co-religionists to 'select seven crores of their numbers' to assist 'Muhammadans fight their way to heaven'. This would allow the 'remaining 14 crore of Hindus in India ... [to] live in peace'.[140]

Exposed to such vicious onslaughts, more and more Muslims were becoming obsessed with the idea of making a show of their religiously informed cultural identity. While many saw Hindus as the main enemy, Zafar Ali Khan took a more sophisticated view of the matter without compromising his beliefs. He played a prominent role in getting the jail authorities to release Ilim Din's body so that he could be given a proper Muslim burial. On this issue, he made it known that the Muslims' quarrel was with the British and not the Hindus.[141] This lone ranger in the Congress cause in the Punjab, however, was unable to persuade his co-religionists to stop objecting to such triflings as Hindus playing music before mosques.[142] The stiffening of Punjabi Muslim attitudes on cultural differences moulded their reactions to the Nehru report. It was, after all, the realm of politics which ultimately mattered if there was to be any concerted attempt to prevent the Aryas from fulfilling their dream of 'hoisting the banner of *Om* on the walls of Medina'.[143] Whatever their internal disagreements, Punjabi Muslims recognized the importance of dominating the provincial councils. However, not all were prepared to go as far as the '56% group' in demanding a fair share of political power in the province. Directed by the *Inqilab*, the movement for maximum regional power as a means of safeguarding Muslim rights was more political than religious in nature. Their main objection to the Nehru report was that the Congress had become 'a representative merely of the *Hindu Maha Sabha*'.[144]

[138]*SPPAI*, 30 November 1929, vol. li, no. 48, p. 719.

[139]*SPPAI*, 28 December 1929, vol. li, no. 51, p. 785.

[140]Ibid., p. 290. For moderate Hindu reactions to Rajpal's murder see, *SPPAI*, 13 April 1929, vol. li, no. 15, pp. 183, 188. But Khushal Chand 'Khursand', editor of the *Milap*, condemned Muslims for honouring Ilim Din and 'eulogiz[ed] Rajpal as a national martyr'. (*SPPAI*, 7/14 December 1929, vol. li, no. 49, p. 743.)

[141]*SPPAI*, 16 November 1929, vol. li, no. 46, p. 673.

[142]*SPPAI*, 9 November 1929, vol. li, no. 45, p. 661.

[143]*SPPAI*, 3 November 1928, vol. l, no. 42, p. 482.

[144]*SPPAI*, 21 December 1929, vol. li, no. 50, pp. 761–6.

The taunt came at a time when all eyes were fixed on the annual session of the Congress in Lahore. Once again it was Zafar Ali Khan who tried pacifying his provincial co-religionists with the bait of full independence from British rule. Better rooted in a Punjabi Muslim religiously informed cultural ethos than those cooperating with the Simon Commission, the firebrand editor of the *Zamindar* in February 1929 gave a memorable speech to the Lahore Students' Union. He bluntly said that 'if Gandhi could not keep the banner of freedom which had been entrusted to him, it would be snatched from him and given to Jawah[ar] Lal Nehru'.[145] Non-violence was not only inconsistent with the dream of independence, but made a mockery of anti-imperialist politics when it took positions on the fate of youthful heroes turned 'terrorist' like Bhagat Singh. As the poet Zafar put it, with attention rivetted on Bhagat Singh's trial in the Lahore conspiracy case in the Punjab:

When the blood of the homeland's martyrs reveals its essence
Through every part of it shines forth Bhagat Singh
In Iran Mansur went to the gallows for saying 'An-al-Haq' (I am the truth)
Delight is upon hearing a similar song by one of India's own stars
How many young men have the Muslims produced
Whose upbringing was in the spirit of freedom .... [146]

An immensely popular poem, it was accompanied by a more poignant one:

Cast away the ashes of someone in the waves of Sutlej
Torture another corpse in dust and blood beyond the Attock
The end of this government cannot be avoided
Embattled as it is with its own people.[147]

[145]SPPAI, 9 February 1929, vol. li, no. 6, p. 64.
[146]Shaheedan-i-watan kae khoon-i-nahaq ka joost nekle
Toh ise kae zarae zare say Bhagat Singh nekle
Charha Iran mein Mansur An-al-haq kahe ke sooli par
Maza jab hae kae tara-i-Hind say aisey hi geet nekle
Musalmanoon ne kitne naujawan ab tak keya paida
Jo azadi ke ghewarae mein pa kar tarbiyat nekle.

شہیدانِ وطن کے خونِ ناحق کا جوست نکلے
تو اس کے ذرے ذرے سے بھگت سنگھ نکلے
چڑھا ایران میں منصور انا الحق کہہ کے سولی پر
مزا جب ہے کہ تارِ ہند سے ایسی ہی گیت نکلے
مسلمانوں نے کتنے نوجواں اب تک کیے پیدا
جو آزادی کے گہوارے میں پا کر تربیت نکلے ...

(Cited in Mirza, *Karavan-i-Ahrar*, i, p. 109.)
[147]Baha dena kise ki rakh ko Sutlej ki mojoon mein
Kise ki laash Attock ke par khak-wa-khoon mein tarpana

Zafar Ali Khan continued exhorting Muslims to join the Congress. At a Congress meeting in Jhang he announced that Gandhi's 'policy of non-violence' had 'failed' and 'unless India was granted *swaraj* before the end of 1929 the party would raise the national standard in Lahore'.[148] On 19 December 1929 when Motilal Nehru came to Lahore on a preparatory visit, he was told by the leaders of the Nau Jawan Sabha that they had the 'power to carry' out their programme 'even in the face of the opposition of the elder leaders'. The older Nehru expressed consternation over the hostile attitude of the Sikhs towards the Congress as well as the activities of the '56% group'.[149] But he had preferred to concentrate on the arrangements at the Congress session where his son was to preside.

The adoption of the full independence resolution by the All-India Congress Committee at Lahore was a major milestone in the history of Indian nationalism. Yet the fallout which attended the Congress's abandonment of the Nehru report created far more ripples in Punjabi politics. It was widely seen as a concession to Sikh interests. Those who had wagered so much to get the document approved were thoroughly disillusioned. These included the Punjabi *khilafatists*—Choudhury Afzal Haq, Maulana Abdul Qadir Kasuri, Maulana Habibur Rahman, Maulana Mazhar Ali Azhar and Sheikh Hissamuddin—who had accepted the report at the All-Parties Conference in Lucknow. With most Punjabi Muslims adamantly opposed to the Nehru formula for political advance at the centre, there was nothing to prevent immediate provincial considerations from triumphing over a misty vision of the future. In one of its final acts before disappearing from the political scene, the Punjab Khilafat Committee in July 1929 expelled all those who had endorsed the Nehru report. If this was a hammer blow to pro-Congress Muslims in the province, the AICC's decision to scrap the document sounded the death knell. The all-India Congress leadership did not even deign to consult its *khilafatist* allies, greatly saddening Muslims who had risked their co-religionists' anger to strike for national independence.[150]

This was a crucial turning point in the history of the interaction between

---

Zawal ise sultanate ka tal nahin sakta taley say
Ke apni hi rayaya say para ho jis ko takarana.

ہمارا یہ کسی کی راہ سنگ کی موجوں میں !

کسی کی لاش انک کے پار خاک و خوں میں تڑپانا

زوال اس سلطنت کا ٹل نہیں سکتا ہے تلے سے

کہ اپنی ہی رعایا سے پڑا ہو جس کو ٹکرانا۔

(Cited in ibid., p. 110.)

[148]*SPPAI*, 20 April 1929, vol. li, no. 6, p. 226.

[149] *SPPAI*, 21 December 1929, vol. li, no. 50, p. 761.

[150]Mirza, *Karavan-i-Ahrar*, i, p. 80–2.

formal and informal politics in the Punjab. Spurned by the Congress, many *khilafatists* felt the need for their own political organization. At the Lahore session of the Congress, Abul Kalam Azad advised his erstwhile *khilafatist* allies to form their own party. On 29 December 1929 at a meeting chaired by Ataullah Shah Bukhari, the Muslims present agreed that they had to participate in the anti-imperialist struggle.[151] But they needed an organization of their own. The result was the establishment of the Majlis-i-Ahrar with a significant base of support among men of commerce in the bazaar, educated lower to middle classes and a network of *ulema* trained at Deoband. Unable for the most part to gain entry into the colonial state's limited system of electoral representation, the Ahrars offered an alternative view of Muslim politics with consequences for region, religion as well as the 'nation'–a theme addressed in the next chapter.

This chapter on Punjabi politics has shown that at the level of both discourse and politics, fissures within the Punjabi Muslim community were far more complex than has been conveyed by the rural–urban divide in the province. If not sectarian differences, then class and ideological contradictions riddled Punjabi Muslims. While agreeing on the need to unite against the Arya warriors, considerations of cultural defence were easily undercut by political differences within. This made it more difficult for Punjabi Muslims to present a coherent view of how cultural differences might be accommodated within a framework for the whole of India.

Just as the British had calculated, provinces like the Punjab did stymie the nationalist challenge. Not one to submit to colonial machinations, Jinnah had tried rescuing the spirit from the dead letter of the Nehru report. But his demands on behalf of Muslims–four in 1927, six in 1928 and fourteen in 1929—failed to break the political stalemate.Their incapacity to agree proven yet again, Indians were left to run their angry fingers through the Simon Commission's paper. Few had to read the provisions to know that the nationalist ambition of securing real power at the centre had been indefinitely postponed. While conceding the principle of provincial autonomy, the authors expressed their doubts about a federal system in India. For Muslims the recommendations were a mixed bag. They were promised separate electorates with weightage in the provinces until such time as they chose to give them up. That was the good news. The bad news was the denial of Muslim majorities in the Punjab and Bengal. Sind's separation was made contingent upon evidence of its economic viability while extension of the reforms to the NWFP and Baluchistan found no support at all.

Effectively rejecting the main thrust of Muslim demands, the Simon Commission had delivered an unacceptable verdict. Realizing the limitations

---

[151]They included those who had been stripped of their membership of the Punjab Khilafat Committee as well as Zafar Ali Khan, Khwajah Abdur Rahman Ghazi and Maulana Muhammad Daud Ghaznavi. (Ibid.)

of their damage-control techniques, the British announced that Indians would be invited to a series of round table conferences in London before the constitutional arrangements were finalized. Not many believed that talking in the presence of the final arbiters of their destiny could facilitate the forging of a united Indian front. Jinnah certainly preferred the peace of the wilderness than the humdrum of political life in India. But in opting to live in London's Hampstead Heath, he showed his understanding of where the political pendulum had momentarily come to rest. Those situated in the British-controlled networks of collaboration, the Unionist leader Fazl-i-Husain for instance, turned to extracting maximum concessions for their provincial co-religionists, irrespective of the nationalist agenda or the interests of Muslims in the minority provinces. The contest for sovereignty in the Punjab was entering a new phase with visible effects not only in the formal and informal arenas of provincial politics but well beyond. Communitarian narratives and politics in conjunction with individual bigotry were creating a nexus between region and nation where notional majorities and minorities defined by the religious distinction had to envisage the future shape of the centre. If a single centre required a common language of rights, the signals radiating from the Punjab were discomforting. With religious idioms—Hindu, Muslim and Sikh—a cardinal feature of regional politics, the failure to accommodate them in a conception of equal citizenship relying on a homogenizing narrative of inclusionary nationalism could potentially leave India without a unified centre.

7

Between Region and Nation:
The Missing Centre

T
he emergence of the region as the highest rung in the British colonial system where Indians could expect to exercise power in the foreseeable future had a decisive bearing on the continuing interplay of discourse and politics. While much of the discourse drew on communitarian conceptions of identity and sovereignty, the liberal democratic idea of separating the religious and the temporal domains was coming to be projected by the Congress as the basis of equal citizenship rights in an independent India. Reactions to the Sarda Act of 1929 underlined the unwillingness of many Muslims and Hindus to countenance interference in their religiously informed cultural practices. On the face of it, Congress's inclusionary nationalism left religion out of the affairs of the state. Mere declarations of religious impartiality did little to assuage fears roused by the evocation of majoritarianism in the more potent concoctions of communitarian bigotry. It was the exclusion by obfuscation implicit in the more moderate blendings of community and nation which did most to steel Muslim resistance to Congress's inclusionary nationalism.

Parroting the colonial state's disputable claim of non-interference in the religious and cultural concerns of its subjects seemed a politic way of acquiring power at the all-India centre. But this entailed losing sight of developments unfolding in the regions and taking refuge in a conception which came dangerously close to abolishing the fact of difference. Accustomed to the state conferring favours on communities of religion, Indians were expected to embrace a form of inclusionary nationalism promising equal citizenship rights, irrespective of community, caste or class. The abstraction may have been a reasonable solution to the problem of cultural difference in India. But the obstinate adherence of regional peoples to their communitarian identities was at odds with a construct of homogenizing nationalism imported from the west. It was precisely because they had not given up thinking of themselves as part of an Indian whole that the idea of majoritarianism seized the imaginations of Hindus and Muslims alike. Small wonder that their aspirations and fears were not very different.

Punjab reveals in stark fashion the importance of majorities in claiming regional, religious and national rights. The connections between region and nation mapped out in Lajpat Rai's arguments on rights were entirely in accord with his religiously informed sense of cultural identity. Since Hindus were fortuitously in a 'majority' in India, a Punjabi Hindu of Rai's ilk could comfortably adopt the idea of separating the religious and the temporal realms. For Muslims reduced to being a permanent minority, the formulation reeked of deceit. Despite internal differences, Muslims agreed that their communitarian rights had to be safeguarded in any future constitutional arrangement. They could counter majoritarian diktat more effectively by opening up channels of communication with the government. It might lead to a more judicious resolution of differences than co-operation with the Congress and its network of Hindu allies. The principal obstacle to Muslim support for a future constitution was not separate electorates but the demand for provincial majorities.

Having proclaimed the 'secular' to be sacred to the core, Muhammad Iqbal upon entering the formal arenas of politics in the Punjab declared that 'agreement on only religious matters would not eliminate all the differences'.[1] The mantra of rights being chanted by the Hindus, and echoed by the Sikhs, entailed extending them reservations in government service and representative bodies—temporal issues that impinged on the exercise of 'secular' state authority. So Iqbal avoided the issue of minority rights in a Muslim-dominated Punjab. Nor was he prepared to let Muslims in the rest of India impose joint electorates on the Punjab. He deplored the readiness of 'nationalist' Muslims like Jinnah to exchange separate electorates for a place in a national movement informed by Hindu communitarianism.[2]

While concerned with the rights of Muslims, and those of the Punjab specifically, Iqbal continued emphasizing the compatibility between an Indian and an Islamic identity. It was 'completely wrong' to say that 'the Muslim psyche was devoid of any spirit of love for the homeland'. Besides love of the homeland, Muslims felt passionately about Islam. This was what brought together disparate individuals of the community.[3] When more focused on politics in India, Iqbal supported Jinnah's fourteen points. These advocated a federal system of government, the retention of separate electorates and Muslim majorities in the

[1]Statement on the Simon Commission, *Inqilab*, 12 November 1927, in Afzal (comp.), *Guftar-i-Iqbal*, p. 51.

[2]Ibid., pp. 53–73.

[3]*Inqilab*, 10 September 1929, ibid., p. 91.

Punjab and Bengal, the separation of Sind, reforms in the NWFP and Baluchistan and one-third representation at the centre. The remaining points demanded an adequate share for Muslims in ministries and the government services. Muslim religious rights were to be protected against non-Muslim interference in the *sharia*, confined to personal law, as well as Islamic culture and education.

Convinced that the Nehru report had 'struck a death blow' at the 'Muslim majority in the Punjab',[4] Iqbal was equally resentful of efforts by Jinnah and other pro-Congress Muslims to deny Punjabis their democratic voice in the All-India Muslim League. The attempted merger in March 1928 of the Shafi and Jinnah Leagues in Delhi had left the Punjabi contingent fuming in the lurch. Certain of tipping the scales, they were only allowed to fill a few vacant seats available in the All-India Muslim League committee. Handpicking an All-India Muslim League through political exclusion could not prevent the setting up of alternative Muslim forums. Kept out of the All-India Muslim League, Iqbal rallied behind the newly formed All-India Muslim Conference. In what was an indication of the government angling for Punjabi Muslim support, the Unionist leader Fazl-i-Husain became one of the driving forces in the organization after his appointment in 1930 to the viceroy's executive council.[5] Between 29 December 1928 and 1 January 1929 the All-India Muslim Conference in Delhi met under the presidency of the Aga Khan to formally approve Jinnah's fourteen points. Applauding the decision, Iqbal alluded to the Quranic verse stating that the *ummat* of Allah never congregated on misguided issues.[6]

In the event, it was not Muslim gatherings but the colonial state's channels of communication with the metropolitan establishment that saw Fazl-i-Husain ramming the Punjabi view into the Government of India Act of 1935. Beyond such safe channels there were others in the monitored public arena with their own ideas about the regional community and the nation, none of which fitted well with the requirement of a unified centre exercising authority throughout the subcontinent.

PUNJAB: A VIEW FROM THE 'WHOLE'?

To many the Punjab of the late 1920s appeared to be on the precipice of calamitous happenings. This unenviable location also gave it a cutting edge

---

[4]Cited in Page, *Prelude to Partition*, p. 207.

[5] Displaying sound political sense, Fazl-i-Husain placed the demands of Muslims in the minority provinces and Bengal before those of the Punjab. With help from an efficient, well-connected and experienced working secretary like Maulana Shafi Daudi, the Muslim Conference was assured a wider network of support. (See ibid for details, especially chapter four.)

[6]*Inqilab*, 1 January 1929, in Afzal (comp.), *Guftar-i-Iqbal*, p. 73.

in refashioning perspectives on the centre. The political debate on region and nation among Punjabis was closer to the idea of 'absolute rights' than to any conceivable notion of equal citizenship rights. There were of course exceptions. It was in many ways the problem of a missing centre which lays bare the difficulties in accommodating religiously informed cultural differences within an inclusionary framework of nationalism. In the Punjab, the inability of Muslims, Hindus and Sikhs to find an equitable arrangement for sharing power created the additional complication of tackling the issue of majority and minority rights at the provincial level. A consideration of how individual members and communitarian organizations envisaged their rights serves as a corrective to the claims of inclusionary nationalism.

Underscoring the Ahmadi community's identification with the political category of Muslim, both in its religious and regional senses, the *Sunrise* of Qadian dubbed the attitude of the Hindu delegates at the first Round Table Conference to the idea of a federal system in India 'a fraud'. This crafty manoeuvre did not fool Punjabi Muslims.[7] The *Zamindar* heaved a sigh of relief that the conference was 'at last dead'. But the British were warned that it was 'altogether impossible to gag a nation which demands its freedom'.[8] Making an unabashed distinction between the nation and its others, the *Bande Mataram* blamed the political stalemate in London on the 'eloquence of selfish communalist lawyers'.[9] Muslim editors fiercely contested being designated 'communalists' while reiterating their commitment to India's independence. The *Inqilab* expressed disquiet about the apparent jubilation in certain quarters upon the failure of a Hindu–Muslim rapprochement. Those who hoped the problem would disappear after the winning of *swaraj* were sadly mistaken. If the Delhi resolutions of the Muslim Conference were accepted, Muslims would be 'prepared to do everything for the liberation of India'. Alternatively, they would 'keep quiet'.[10]

Well before Muhammad Iqbal's presidential address to the All-India Muslim League in December 1930, Lahore was rife with a press-inspired campaign to hold a conference of Muslims from the Punjab, Sind, NWFP and Baluchistan. So the logic of exclusion first employed by Punjabi Muslims derived from the contradiction between regional majorities and religious minorities, not from any pulsating hatred of sects within Islam. Political and not religious considerations led Iqbal, the great Islamic universalist, to propose leaving Muslims in the minority provinces to their own devices. Upon hearing that the first round table conference was on the verge of finding an all-India

---

[7] *Sunrise*, Qadian, 19 December 1930, *Report on Newspapers and Periodicals in the Punjab, 3 January–27 June 1931*, NCHCR, p. 4—(henceforth *RNPP*, followed by date and page number/s).

[8] *Zamindar*, Lahore, 25 December 1930, ibid., pp. 4–5.

[9] *Bande Mataram*, Lahore, 25 December 1930, ibid., pp. 5–6.

[10] *Inqilab*, Lahore, 23 December 1930, ibid., p. 6.

agreement based on joint electorates, he categorically told the Aga Khan that if Hindus rejected the demands of the Muslim Conference, the Muslim delegates should simply leave.[11]

On 23 November 1930 at a meeting in Lahore, Iqbal gave his blessings to a conference of Muslims from 'upper India' as a preparatory step to organizing themselves for the attainment of their 'Islamic rights'.[12] Much in the same way as other communities, this claim for 'religious' rights covered both the spiritual and the material dimensions of individual and collective life. Furious at the attacks on their religion and cultural practices by the adherents of the Hindu–Hindi–Hindustan triad, Muslims were insistent that their communitarian rights as a statutory minority had to be assured in any constitutional framework for an independent India. It was convenient that Islam provided them with an alternative way of reconciling the religious and the temporal dimensions of Muslim identity. On 19 December 1930, Iqbal, in a joint appeal signed among others by the editors of the *Muslim Outlook*, *Siyasat* and the *Inqilab*, asked Muslim representatives from the NWFP, Sind and Baluchistan to join their Punjabi co-religionists at a conference to be held in Lahore in late January 1931. Muslims of the majority provinces had to counter the machinations of 'neighbouring communities' and the British. God had willed Muslim majorities in north-western India to ensure the protection of Islam and Muslims in India. This was possible only on the basis of the fourteen points chalked out by Jinnah as the highest common denominator of Muslim political differences. Iqbal and his associates deplored the political chess being played in the name of minorities in India. It was a clever, if transparent, subterfuge to prop up the Sikhs and, in this way, more effectively fell Punjabi Muslims.[13]

Iqbal's Vision of 'Muslim India'

The selection of a Punjabi Muslim to preside over the All-India Muslim League's twenty-first session in Allahabad signified where the balance of political advantage was coming to lie. Speaking in English in the heartland of Urdu speakers may have been Iqbal's way of making a point. He could just as well have been speaking in Punjabi given the explicit regional bias of his proposal. Speaking as an individual, he declared, 'I lead no party; I follow no leader.' His sole qualification to address a Muslim gathering was that he had 'given the best part of ... [his] life to a careful study of Islam, its law and polity, its culture, its history and its literature'. A 'constant contact with the spirit of Islam, as it unfolds itself in time' had given him an 'insight' he wished to share with fellow Muslims. The purpose was 'not to guide' Muslims but 'the humbler task of bringing clearly to ... [their] consciousness the

---

[11]*Inqilab*, Lahore, 18 November 1930, in Afzal (comp.), *Guftar-i-Iqbal*, p. 109.
[12]*Inqilab*, Lahore, 25 November 1930, ibid., pp. 111–12.
[13]*Inqilab*, Lahore, 23 November 1931, ibid., pp. 112–16.

main principle' which ought to 'determine the general character of the[ir] decisions'.[14]

He chided the new generation of Muslims who were inspired by European political thought but ignorant of European history. The life of Islam in India had depended on 'a social structure regulated by a legal system and animated by a specifically ethical ideal'. This nurtured the 'basic emotions and loyalties' that could 'gradually unify scattered individuals' and 'finally transform them into a well-defined people, possessing a moral consciousness of their own'. By contrast, in Europe Christianity had been 'a purely monastic order' which later developed into 'a vast church-organization'. Martin Luther's protest was against the church, 'not ... any ... polity of a secular nature'. He could not have foreseen that his revolt would end up displacing 'the universal ethics of Jesus' with the mushrooming 'of a plurality of national and hence narrower systems of ethics'. The 'break up of the one into mutually ill-adjusted many', entailing the 'transformation of a human into a national outlook', took concrete historical form in 'recogniz[ing] territory as the only principle of political solidarity'. If one 'conce[ives] ... religion as complete other-worldliness', then there was nothing unusual about what had happened to Christianity in Europe. For the European, 'religion [wa]s a private affair of the individual' which had 'nothing to do with ... man's temporal life'. Islam did 'not bifurcate the unity of man into an irreconcilable duality of spirit and matter'. One was not 'the citizen of a profane world' that had to be 'renounced in the interest of a world of spirit situated elsewhere'.[15]

A Luther, even with Iblis's help, was unimaginable in Islam. Without a church there could be no destroyer. The teachings of Islam were poorly reflected in the lives of Muslims because of 'our legists' want of contact with the modern world'; they needed 'renewed power by adjustments'. No gazer of crystal balls, Iqbal refused to predict the 'final fate of the national idea in the world of Islam'. It might be assimilated and transformed by Islam or through sheer force bring about a 'radical transformation' of Muslim societies. If trends were anything to go by, the 'national idea' had started 'racializing the outlook of Muslims' and 'materially counteracting the humanizing work of Islam'. Yet the visionary had 'not despaired of Islam as a living force' capable of 'freeing the outlook of man from its geographical limitations'. Religion was 'a power of the utmost importance in the life of individuals as well as of states'. Islam for Iqbal was 'itself Destiny'; it could 'not suffer a destiny!'.[16]

This was described by one enthusiastic newspaper as the 'manliest note in

[14]Muhammad Iqbal's presidential address to the All-India Muslim League at Allahabad, 29–30 December 1930, Syed Sharifuddin Pirzada (ed.), *Foundations of Pakistan, All-India Muslim League Documents: 1906–1947*, Karachi: National Publishing House, 1969–70, ii, p. 154.

[15]Ibid., p. 154.

[16]Ibid., pp. 155–6.

a manly address'.[17] This gendered reading of a vision moored in Islamic thought and Indian political realities does not detract from its significance. For Iqbal, Islam was the highest ideal humanity could hope to attain. With constitutional reforms on the anvil, and the suppositions of Congress's inclusionary nationalism before them, Muslims had to decide whether autonomy in religiously informed cultural practices, confined to the domestic sphere under the provisions of the *sharia*, was an adequate safeguard for their conception of identity, sovereignty and citizenship.

Was it possible 'to retain Islam as an ethical ideal and ... reject it as a polity' in order to embrace the idea of 'national polities' in which religion played no part? All Muslims knew that the religious life of the Prophet of Islam was an 'individual experience creative of a social order'. The individual was an organic whole whose cognitive capacity to differentiate between spiritual and material concerns did not mean separating the two realms in everyday life. It was, as Iqbal had said in his lectures in the early 1920s, the attitude of mind one brought to bear on action which mattered. For the individual the secular at the core was sacred. And for the Muslim individual Islam was a 'polity' with specific 'legal concepts' whose 'civic significance' could not be 'belittled merely because their origin is revelational'. If the civic life of India's Muslims was emptied of Quranic principles then 'the rejection of the one' would 'eventually involve the rejection of the other'. Keeping the religious and spiritual dimensions of life in the domestic corner to qualify for equal citizenship in a decidedly ungodly nation-state was incompatible with Muslim identity. It was 'unthinkable' for Muslims to subscribe to the 'construction of a polity on national lines' by abandoning 'the Islamic principle of solidarity'. Referring to Ernest Renan's definition of a nation as the expression of a collective 'moral consciousness', Iqbal observed that the affinities of caste and religion in India had resisted 'sink[ing] their respective individualities in a larger whole'. Despite internal divisions various groupings in India were unwilling to pay the price of fashioning a common national moral consciousness if this meant the extinction of their cultural distinctiveness. It was imperative to 'recognize facts' and 'not assume the existence of a state of things which does not exist'.[18]

Whatever the claims of inclusionary nationalism, there was a veritable absence of any inter-communitarian trust and scarcely any checks on nurturing hopes of dominating one another. No one wanted to give up on 'monopolies'. It was all too easy to 'conceal ... egoism in the cloak of nationalism, outwardly simulating a large-hearted patriotism, but inwardly as narrow-minded as a caste or tribe'. Indians could never forge a nationality by talking about dominating and conquering their internal others. Muslims would be 'ready

[17]*Light*, Lahore, 16 January 1931, *RNPP*, 3 January–27 June 1931, pp. 66–7.
[18]Iqbal's presidential address to AIML in December 1930, Pirzada (ed.), *Foundations of Pakistan*, ii., pp. 156–7.

to stake ... [their] all for the freedom of India' if the principle of each group living according to its 'own culture and tradition' was made 'the basis of a permanent communal settlement'. This, Iqbal quickly explained, was 'not inspired by any feeling of narrow communalism' due to animosity towards other communities. There were 'communalisms and communalisms'. A mere taunt, the term was propaganda of the lowest kind. Iqbal had 'the highest respect for the customs, laws, religious and social institutions of other communities'. At the same time he was fervently attached to his Islamic identity: ' ... *I love the communal group which is the source of my life and behaviour; and which has formed me what I am by giving me its religion, its literature, its thought, its culture ... thereby recreating its whole past, as a living operative factor, in my present consciousness'.*

Even the Nehru report had conceded that the separation of Sind was not a concession to 'communalism' or contrary to the spirit of 'nationalism'. To deny this amounted to saying that the cause of internationalism militated against the existence of separate nations. Just as it was impossible to 'create the international State' by rejecting 'the fullest nationalist autonomy', there could be no 'harmonious nation' without cultural autonomy. The 'communalism' Iqbal deemed to be of the best sort was one sensitive to culture as difference.[19]

Since Congress's inclusionary nationalism effaced this in an attempt to present a unified anti-colonial struggle, Iqbal felt obliged to articulate a powerful alternative grounded in Islam. But the tone and substance of his presidential address in 1930 was different from his philosophical reconstructions of Islamic religious thought in one important respect. Geared to the political situation in India on the eve of another set of British constitutional reforms, it lacked the careful method and clarity of his scholarly lectures. But if one reads Iqbal in his proper context, it is impossible to miss the resonance of Indian imperatives on his political reasoning. As far as he could see, the 'principle of European democracy c[ould] not be applied to India without recognizing the fact of communal groups'. In his opinion 'the Muslim demand for the creation of a Muslim India within India' was 'perfectly justified'. The resolution adopted by the Muslim Conference at Delhi was 'inspired by the noble ideal of a harmonious whole which, instead of stifling the respective individualities of its component wholes, affords them chances of fully working out the possibilities that may be latent in them'.[20]

Punjab, the NWFP, Sind and Baluchistan were the components of the Indian whole which Iqbal wanted to see develop according to their own possibilities. None of this, he emphasized, should 'alarm the Hindus or the British'. In a sentence which puts paid to any suggestion of a partition based on bordered separation, Iqbal dubbed India 'the greatest Muslim country

[19]Ibid., p. 158.
[20]Ibid., p. 159.

in the world'. A northwest Indian Muslim state minus the Ambala division was to remain within the subcontinental whole. The exclusion of Ambala would make the proposed state 'more Muslim in population' and allow for 'more effective protection to non-Muslim minorities within its area'. Far from calling for the partition of India, Iqbal thought the 'centralization' of Muslim-majority areas in the northwest, whose military and police services were indispensable to British rule, would 'eventually solve the problem of India as well as of Asia'.[21] The demand was not actuated by a desire to hold the future independent government of India to ransom. Its purpose was to let Muslims living in these provinces develop freely, a prospect which was 'impossible under the type of unitary government contemplated by the nationalist Hindu politicians' who were angling to establish 'permanent communal dominance in the whole of India'. Iqbal emphatically denied that such a Muslim state would result in 'the introduction of a kind of religious rule'. Explaining the meaning of the word religion in the Muslim context, he repeated that Islam was not a church but a contractual state whose citizens were spiritual beings with rights and duties in society. He noted with approval that previous Muslim states in India had not banned the collection of interest. A 'consolidated Muslim State' in India would permit innovations in Islam and 'rid it ... of the stamp that Arabian imperialism was forced to give it'. This would bring Muslims into 'closer contact' with the 'original spirit' of Islam as well as 'the spirit of modern times'.[22]

However one might interpret Iqbal, there can be no denying the cultural defence inherent in his proposal. As a Muslim individual relegated to being a member of a minority community, he rejected the western liberal model of the 'nation' as a 'universal amalgamation'. It was the right of the 'communal entity' to 'retain its private individuality'.[23] There was no room in the homogenizing claims of inclusionary nationalism for incorporating the assertion of cultural difference based on an imbrication of religious faith and political need. The insistence on keeping religion apart from politics may have been the logical corollary of such a conception of nationalism, but it was not one which tallied well with realities at the social base. India's cultural differences required a political solution. If his recipe for the territorial consolidation of Muslim power in the north-western regions proved unacceptable, Iqbal wanted nothing less than the acceptance of the 'Muslim demands' adopted by both the Muslim Conference and the All-India Muslim League.[24]

Despite strenuous attempts to prove that Indian Muslims were more of a piece than any other community, and therefore closest to being a 'nation',

[21] Ibid., p. 159.
[22] Ibid., p. 160.
[23] Ibid., p. 161.
[24] Ibid., p. 166.

Iqbal had no illusions about his co-religionists. At the end of a stirring speech, he pleaded for unity among Muslims. If the spirit could not move them to achieve it, then he was prepared to let material factors prod them to the unity prescribed by Islam. After all, at 'critical moments in their history', it was 'Islam that ha[d] saved Muslims and not *vice versa*'. If Muslims embraced Islamic precepts they might yet find a way of 'pass[ing] from matter to spirit', thereby attaining the highest goals of their faith which offered a 'superb conception of humanity' based on an organic equipoise of the individual and the community.[25]

The explicit Muslimness of Iqbal's proposal drew fire from many non-Muslims. His own co-religionists in the minority provinces also had no real reason for cheer. In so far as this was a solution to the problem of cultural difference in India, there was nothing here for those excluded from Iqbal's territorial conception of the Muslim community. Muslims in the minority provinces might take comfort in the thought that Iqbal's state was at least part of India. But for non-Muslims, especially in the Punjab, Sind, the NWFP and Baluchistan, the very conception seemed like an Islamic conspiracy to diddle them out of their share of power at the regional level. That they were not alone in thinking this can be seen from the sharp reaction to Iqbal's ideas in Britain. Edward Thompson, the reputed author and a friend of India, in a letter to the London *Times* came close to charging Iqbal with 'Pan-Islamic Plotting'. He regretted that anyone calling for a 'fair consideration' of 'the Hindu case (which has been shockingly mismanaged)' ended up being 'branded ... anti-Muslim'. Islam may be more democratic than Hinduism and vastly superior to Christianity in its 'practice of human brotherhood'. What irked Thompson was that Iqbal's consolidated Muslim state was akin to a confederation 'within or without the Indian Federation'. One had only to 'look at the map' to realize that the rest of India would be left with an indefensible frontier.[26]

Iqbal was not only quick to the defence but consciously played to the British gallery, exposing himself once again to the charge of collaboration. Such labels hang poorly on Iqbal, an intellectual powerhouse who was attempting to lend some coherence to an inchoate, and hopelessly divided, community. In venturing forth his opinion, Iqbal had spoken as an individual first and last. The balances and imbalances in his address flowed from efforts to woo the community, not from contradictions inherent in his philosophical thrust and political objectives. This becomes clear when one reads the *Bal-i-Jabrial*, or Gabriel's wing, which Iqbal was composing during the time of his presidential address and the second round table conference. As he said it:

[25]Ibid., p. 171.
[26]Edward Thompson to the London *Times*, 3 October 1931, Dar (ed.), *Letters of Iqbal*, p. 216.

Listen to my entreaties whether or not they have an effect
This free being is not seeking appreciation.[27]

A confirmed critic of the west, Iqbal was not enamoured of British imperialism.
He declared:

The culture of modernity has granted me that freedom
Which apparently is freedom, but unintelligibly arrest![28]

Commenting on his own and, by implication, the fate of his co-religionists,
he wrote:

The foreigner has taught me infidelity
Why are the mullahs of this era the disgrace of Muslims?[29]

Iqbal's views on the impact of colonial subjugation in India are contained in
the following lines:

What is slavery? Deprivation from appreciating beauty
Whatever free beings call beautiful, that is beauty
You cannot rely on the prudence of slaves
It is only that in this world the noble man alone is blind
He is the enlightened one who with his endeavours
Pulls from the world's ocean the light of the individual.[30]

A believer in the sovereignty of Allah and the unity of being, Iqbal asserted
his freedom over and over again:

[27] Asr kare na kare sone toh le meri faryad
Nahin hae dad ka talib ye banda-i-azad!

اثر کرے نہ کرے سُن توُلے مری فریاد

نہیں ہے دادکا طالب یہ بندۂ آزاد!

(Iqbal, Bal-i-Jabrial in Kulliyat-i-Iqbal, p. 8.)
[28] Mujhe tehzib-i-hazar nae atta ke hae wo azadi
Ke zahir mein toh azadi hae, batin mein giraftari

مجھے تہذیبِ حاضر نے عطا کی ہے وہ آزادی

کہ ظاہر میں تو آزادی ہے، باطن میں گرفتاری۔

(Ibid., p. 32.)
[29] Mujhko sekha di hae afrang ne zindaqi
Ise dor ke mullah hain kuin nang-i-Musalmani

مجھ کو سکھادی ہے افرنگ نے زندیقی

اس دور کے ملا ہیں کیوں ننگِ مسلمانی!

(Ibid., p. 17.)
[30] Ghulami kiya hae? Zooq-i-hosan-i-zebai say mehroomi
Jise zeba kahin azad bandeh. Hae wohi zeba!

In the world of the soul I have found no foreign rule
In the world of the soul I have seen neither Sheikh nor Brahman.[31]

He appealed to Muslims to ask their own hearts, not the mullahs, why the sanctuary had been emptied of God's men.[32]

Life in the public arena may have required speaking to the collective more often than to the individual. As the above verses indicate, Iqbal continued celebrating the individual in his poetic outpourings. Indeed, his best-known statement on the power of the individual comes from *Bal-i-Jabril*:

Why should I ask the wise men: what is my beginning?
When I am busy worrying: what will be my end?
Raise the self to such heights that before the realisation of each destiny
God asks the human being: 'Tell me, what is your will'.[33]

Hinting at Iqbal's personalized sense of sovereignty based on devotion to a universal God, this was not an emotion he wanted to keep under wraps. He had taken the big step of entering the political arena at a crucial time in Indian history. The experience had convinced him that his conception of freedom was better, for him certainly and potentially also for the Muslims, than the one patented in the west and marketed in India. His aversion to the western conception of nationalism requires no further evidence beyond this striking composition:

Bharoosa kar nahin sakte ghulamoon ki baseerat par
Ke duniya mein faqt mardan-i-hur ke hae ankh beena!

غلامی کیا ہے؟ ذوقِ حسن و زیبائی سے محرومی

جسے زیبا کہیں آزاد بندے، ہے وہی زیبا!

بھروسا کر نہیں سکتے غلاموں کی بصیرت پر

کہ دنیا میں فقط مردانِ حر کی آنکھ ہے بینا!

(Ibid., p. 22.)
[31] *Mann ke duniya me na paya mein ne afrangi ka raj*
Mann ke duniya mein na dekha mein ne Sheikh wa Brahman

من کی دنیا میں نہ پایا میں نے افرنگی کا راج

من کی دنیا میں نہ دیکھے میں نے شیخ و برہمن۔

(Ibid., p. 27.)
[32] *Ah Musalman! Apna dil say puchh, mullah say na puchh*
Ho giya Allah ke bandoon say kiun khali haram?

اے مسلمان! اپنے دل سے پوچھ، ملا سے نہ پوچھ

ہو گیا اللہ کے بندوں سے کیوں خالی حرم؟

(Ibid., p. 28.)
[33] *Khurdmandoon say kiya puchhoon kae meri ibdada kiya hae*
Kae mein ise fikr mein rahta hoon, meri intaha kiya hae!

Whether it be the majesty of royalty or a democratic circus
If religion and politics are separate, all that remains is autocracy![34]

Not surprisingly, Iqbal accused Thompson of misunderstanding the substance of his proposal. He had not put forward a demand for a Muslim state outside the British empire, 'only ... guess[ed] at the possible outcome in the dim future of the mighty forces now shaping the destiny of the Indian sub-continent'. Vehemently opposed to the creation of a 'cockpit of communal strife' in central Punjab, Iqbal preferred 'a re-distribution of India into provinces with effective majorities of one community or another'. His recommendations for the Muslim provinces merely carried forward ideas expressed in the Nehru and the Simon reports. As far as he could see, 'a series of contented and well-organised Muslim provinces on the North-West Frontier of India would be the bulwark of India and of the British Empire against the hungry generation of the Asiatic mainlands'.[35]

But the proverbial wolves which most worried Iqbal's non-Muslim compatriots were the Muslims of India. The Hindu press in Lahore predictably slammed Iqbal for being bigoted and 'communal' minded. Labelling the entire address 'unpatriotic' and 'anti-national', the *Bande Mataram* considered Iqbal's consolidated Muslim state a 'deadly poison for the peace of India'. A 'separate Muslim state within India', according to the *Milap*, seemed designed to 'ridicule' the nationalists.[36] The *Pratap* wondered why a compromise was needed with 'communalist Mussalmans'. 'What sacrifice had they made for the country?', it asked disingenuously. While thousands were in jail, Muslim 'communalists' were 'making merry by realising from the Government the price of their treachery to the country'.[37] The *Tribune* spotted some silver linings

---

Khudi ko kar buland itna kae har taqdir say pehele
Khuda bandeh say khud puchhe 'bata teri raza kiya hae'!

خرد مندوں سے کیا پوچھوں کہ میری ابتدا کیا ہے

کہ میں اس گھر میں رہتا ہوں، میری انتہا کیا ہے

خودی کو کر بلند اتنا کہ ہر تقدیرے سے پہلے

خدا بندے سے خود پوچھے، بتا تیری رضا کیا ہے!

(Ibid., p. 45.)
[34] *Jalal-i-padshahi ho kae jamhoori tamasha ho*
Juda hoon din siyasat say, toh rehe jati hae changezi!

جلال پادشاہی ہو کہ جمہوری تماشا ہو

جدا ہو دیں سیاست سے، تو رہ جاتی ہے چنگیزی!

(Ibid., p. 34.)
[35] Iqbal to Thompson, *Times,* 12 October 1931, Dar (ed.), *Letters of Iqbal,* p. 217.
[36] *Bande Mataram* and *Milap,* Lahore, 31 December 1931, RNPP, 3 January–27 June 1931, pp. 13–14.
[37] *Pratap,* Lahore, 18 January 1931, ibid., p. 64.

to the clouds. Seldom had an address been more roundly 'condemned' by respectable Indian journals and 'sane Muslim politicians'. The nub of the matter, as the *Sunday Times* put it, was that Iqbal's proposed state was a more fitting component of 'a big pan-Islamic federation than of [a] British Indian federation'. Its only 'saving grace' was that it had 'expose[d] the hollowness' of Muslim 'communal demands'.[38]

Insulted by the abusive connotations of the word 'communalism', one Muslim-owned newspaper after the other objected to such a categorization of their demands. Encouraged by Iqbal's negative affirmation of the term, they agreed that the charge of 'communalism' was a way of discrediting those opposed to a Hindu majoritarian vision of an independent India. Someone like Edward Thompson might find this more acceptable than the Muslim insistence on the inseparability of politics and religion. Yet the two domains had never been more intermeshed than in late-colonial India. The implicit majoritarianism of Congress's inclusionary nationalism rendered it difficult for politically honed Muslims, especially from the Punjab, to swallow the ideal with any measure of equanimity. Based equally on principles of western democracies and the colonial enumeration of majority and minority religious communities, it compounded the problem of Muslim identity in India.

A reading of the Punjab press indicates just how warmly Iqbal's address was received by sections of the urban Muslim population. One paper thought the speech was 'a masterpiece of clear reasoning and courageous outspokenness'. Iqbal had persuasively defended the right of Muslims to live freely according to their own culture and tradition.[39] The *Light* of Lahore lauded Iqbal for making the 'greatest contribution' to a 'much-muddled controversy'. His proposal had the 'good of India as a whole at heart'. Instead of a notional Hindu–Muslim unity, Iqbal had put forward the concrete idea of 'Hindu–Muslim adjustment'. It was 'wrong' to tarnish this legitimate aspiration of the Muslims with the charge of 'narrow communalism'.[40]

The *Inqilab* deplored the hostile reaction of the Hindu journalistic community. If Moonje and Parmanand called for 'the establishment of a purely Hindu raj, the entire Hindu Press shower[ed] praises on them'. Yet 'if a Muslim leader simply demand[ed] the protection of the culture and religion of his community', the Hindu press kicked up a storm. How could India be 'liberated with such a mentality?'[41] There was 'hardly a Hindu' who had 'not spurt venom' against Iqbal's ideas—'the first successful attack on the Hindu conception of "nationality" or the establishment of Hindu Raj in India'. Iqbal's only crime was that he had 'exposed the machinations of the Hindus to

[38]*Tribune*, Lahore, 4 January 1931 and the *Sunday Times*, 5 January 1931, ibid., pp. 15, 36.
[39]*Muslim Outlook*, 31 December 1930, ibid., p. 14.
[40]*Light*, Lahore, 1 January 1931, ibid., p. 14.
[41]*Inqilab*, Lahore, 3 January 1931, ibid., p. 15.

deprive the Muslim majorities of their rights'. This had 'shown to the world that the Hindus [we]re not influenced by nationalism or principles of democracy'.[42] Endorsing this interpretation, the *Light* hailed Iqbal for courageously taking up the 'gauntlet of atheistic nationalism'. His was 'a bold challenge to the forces of irreligion masquerading as nationalism'. Muslims had to 'plunge into the thick of the struggle' against this 'false nationalism'. This alone could ensure that India would 'not only be a free India but a Godly India as well'. The world might call the proposed state in the north-western extremities of the subcontinent 'Muslim India within India'. But the Muslim right to majority rule was the only way of 'sav[ing] humanity from the reign of a Godless, narrow, self-seeking, aggressive nationalism ... inaugurated by the West'.[43]

If this was putting too much of bad religion into the good idea of self-determination, other Muslim newspapers applauded Iqbal from quasi-Marxist as well as nationalist and democratic perspectives. The *Rahnuma* of Rawalpindi blasted the Hindu delegates at the first round table conference. They had revealed 'their narrow-mindedness' and demonstrated to the world that 'the Indian Congress was a body of capitalists' who had 'no sympathy with minorities or labourers' and only wanted 'Hindu raj in India'.[44] The *Sunrise* of Qadian ridiculed the charge that 'Muslim anxiety to see their religion and culture progress and thrive side by side with Hindu culture and Hindu religion [was] contrary to the ideas of true democracy'. Tongue in cheek, the Ahmadi organ remarked that Muslims were only asking for their 'just rights' as they knew perfectly well that their '*bania* counterpart[s]' were 'physically and temperamentally incapable' of generosity.[45]

The Sikh Factor, the Depression and Denominational Assertions

What made the political deadlock in the Punjab a particularly knotty one to resolve constitutionally was the presence of a third community styling itself as heirs of sovereigns from whom the British had inherited state power in the region. Muhammad Shafi had worked out a formula by which Punjabi Muslims were to get 49 per cent seats through separate electorates and pick up another 2 per cent through special constituencies. But the Sikhs, a mere 12 per cent or so of the population demanded nothing less than 24 per cent, which left the Hindus, who accounted for 32 per cent, with something like 27 per cent. Evocatively named Sikh newspapers defended their demands as just and rightful. A gauge to the pain of a disinherited community, the *Asli Qaumi Dard* wanted Sikhs in the Punjab to be treated on the same footing as Muslim minorities in the rest of India. Emphatically opposed to Muslim-majority rule, the *Kirpan*

[42]*Inqilab*, Lahore, 11 and 15 January 1931, ibid., p. 65.
[43]*Light*, Lahore, 16 January 1931, ibid., pp. 66–7.
[44]*Rahnuma*, Rawalpindi, 28 January 1931, ibid., p. 102.
[45]*Sunrise*, Qadian, 13 March 1931, ibid., pp. 229–30.

Bahadur vowed 'not to let a bigoted communal administration ... run for a single minute'.[46]

With the communities counting the duration of each others' rule in days and minutes, there seemed to be little prospect of an amicable solution of the Punjab problem. Muslims had long suspected a Hindu hand in the Sikh demands, seeing it as a device to scuttle the chances of a Muslim majority. And, indeed, attempts to accommodate the Sikhs posed some serious mathematical dilemmas. The *Mauji* reported that the ante had been upped to 30 per cent. If representation was to be on a population basis, Sikhs wanted Dera Ghazi Khan, Dera Ismail Khan and other Muslim districts separated from the Punjab. If this proved unworkable, central Punjab would be claimed as a Sikh province. The descendants of Ranjit Singh could never agree to become slaves and would disrupt the workings of any constitution that assigned them this status.[47]

An old campaigner of the '56 per cent group', the *Inqilab* scoffed at the Sikh demand for a one-third share in the Punjab. It was the 'height of stupidity' and 'posterity' would 'laugh at their demand till eternity'.[48] For the moment, however, there was more reason to scream than smile. The prospect of receiving less representation than merited by their population had left the campaigners of Punjabi Hindu rights clutching their handkerchiefs. Consider the *Pratap*'s woeful lament on the 'strange ... fate' of Punjab's Hindus; everyone wanted to 'usurp their rights'.[49] But with Sikhs targeting Muslims, there was hope yet for this hapless fragment of a larger majoritarian whole. Tensions were high in the districts and the bitterness between Sikhs and Muslims greater than between Hindus and Muslims. The breaking point was expected to be reached after the final distribution of power in London.

The growing strain in communitarian relations in the Punjab coincided with the impact of the great depression and the Gandhi-led Congress's civil disobedience movement. By the early 1930s widespread agrarian distress, increasing student and labour radicalism in Bombay, to say nothing of sporadic terrorism of the heroic kind, found Gandhi issuing an ultimatum to the British. Unless his eleven demands were accepted, he threatened a civil disobedience campaign. Many Indians were furious with the Mahatma for not including as one of his demands a stay on Bhagat Singh's death sentence. A folk-hero in the Punjab and beyond, Bhagat Singh had assassinated a British police officer in 1928. A bomb hurled upon the central legislative assembly in 1929 landed the young Sikh radical in jail. By the early 1930s Bhagat Singh had become a nationalist icon. So while the spectacle of the great man leading the Dandi march to the western coast of India

[46]*Asli Qaumi Dard*, Amritsar, 3 January 1931 and *Kirpan Bahadur*, Amritsar, 11 January 1931, ibid., p. 32.

[47]*Mauji*, Amritsar, 19 January 1931, ibid., pp. 64–5.

[48]*Inqilab*, Lahore, 31 January 1931, ibid., p. 102.

[49]*Pratap*, Lahore, 17 January 1931, ibid., p. 45.

electrified many people, there were others who had seen through the Mahatma.

Gandhi's ultimatum was a damp squib compared to the excitement generated by the Congress's *purna swaraj* resolution of December 1929. He shocked Indians further by abruptly calling off the civil disobedience campaign following a tactical agreement with Irwin in March 1931. This gave the Mahatma the excuse he needed to attend the second round table conference in London. But if the rumblings of discontent were any indication, it seemed likely that in the event Gandhi's popularity waned, his disciples in the Punjab would be among the first to dump him. Declared illegal in June 1930, the Punjab administration was only too eager to further tighten the screws on the Congress which was spared complete embarrassment in north-western India when Pathans in the Frontier Province rose to the occasion in April of 1930.[50] With the Congress organization virtually in the hands of the Nau Jawan Sabhas, Gandhi's inability to enthuse young radicals was a serious drawback for his disobedience campaign in the Punjab. As it is, the radicalism of the Nau Jawan Sabhas was hardly reflective of rural realities. The crisis of the depression in the Punjab saw the interlocking of religious identity with material life. Individuals belonging to one or the other of the communities recognized in colonial enumeration were, willy-nilly, coming to accept their religious identity as the key determinant in political preferences. The role of the Punjab press in fanning religious sentiments was surpassed only by the provocative language used by itinerant preachers and *imams*. Local irritations combined with not-so-localized religious passions were a deadly potion for a province reeling under the effects of a worldwide economic depression.

As an instance of how organized violence along communitarian lines was imported into otherwise relatively peaceful towns, the story of Bewal is a revealing one. A small township of 1200, half Muslim and the other half Hindu and Sikh, it had never seen violence of this sort or scale. As in other similarly placed towns in the province, Hindus and Sikhs formed the bulk of the moneylenders and shopkeepers. A small boarding school owned by a wealthy Hindu was the site of the primary conflict. Offended by the cooking of beef at the school, Hindu and Sikh boys had allegedly 'thrust pigs' bones' into the mouths of their Muslim peers. The rumour was spread by local *imams* of the mosques to neighbouring villages. Bewal itself remained tranquil. On 30 January 1931, an ensemble of about a thousand men arrived from villages as far as fifteen miles 'armed with sticks and axes ... beating drums and shouting [N] *ara-i-Takbir*'. They invaded the bazaar, ransacked several shops, setting fire to three which led to the death of a Sikh shopkeeper. The Muslim insignia was all too visible. A cow was slaughtered and the corpse left behind. It was

---

[50]According to one estimate, compared to 10,000 arrested in the NWFP, 5000 were picked up in the Punjab, many of them Ahrar volunteers. (Mirza, *Karavan-i-Ahrar*, i, p. 106.)

by coincidence that two policemen arrived in the town and managed to restore order. The attack had been planned with such 'amazing secrecy' that the local police knew nothing of what was brewing.[51]

Reactions to this and other disturbances indicate how localized incidents were embellishing communitarian narratives. It was one thing to reproach 'Muslim hooligans' for destroying the peace of Bewal. Besmirching them as 'traitors to the country' who had 'sprinkled salt on the afflicted hearts of the Hindus' may have been stretching the point. Equally searing was the charge that such troubles confirmed the Hindu impression of the Muslim as a 'bigoted plunderer'.[52] Muslim recrimination was not long in coming. A *hartal* called by the Congress to commemorate the sacrifice of Bhagat Singh led to forcible closure of Muslim shops in Mirzapur district in UP, followed by a massacre of Muslims in Kanpur. While both sides condemned the police for its non-action, they missed no opportunity to abuse each other. The *Zamindar* charged Congress volunteers for using strong-arm tactics against Muslim shopkeepers. It regretted the short memory of the Hindus. When Mohamed Ali 'Jauhar' succumbed to an untimely death in London on 3 January 1931, Muslims did not coerce Hindus to join the *hartal* and express grief.[53] In what must surely have been a foreboding, the deceased soul had said:

A whole world is envious of the death of Jauhar,
But this is a gift of God; He gives to whosoever He pleases.[54]

A poem carried by the *Siyasat* spoke of the Muslim sense of betrayal at the massacre in Kanpur:

Alas! How cheap the Muslim blood has become!
It is being wasted over the *hartal* question.
Dead bodies are lying and none cares for them.
Every street and lane of Cawnpore is presenting the spectacle of doomsday.
Those who attended on the Muslims are now murdering them with daggers.
Would that the ignorant man opened even now and washed all the
stigmas of humiliation in his own lifetime.[55]

---

[51]*SPPAI*, 7 February 1931, vol. liii, no. 6, pp. 88–9.

[52]*Siani Kashatri*, Lahore, 13 and 21 February 1931, *RNPP*, 3 January–27 June 1931, p. 171.

[53]*Zamindar*, Lahore, 28 March 1931, ibid., p. 278.

[54]*Hae rashk aik khaq ko Jauhar ke mot pae*
Yae use ke din hae, jise parwardigar de!

ہے رشک ایک خلق کو جوہر کی موت پر

یہ اس کا دین ہے جسے پروردگار دے!

(Cited in Iqbal, *Life and Times of Mohamed Ali*, p. 400.)

[55]*Zamindar*, Lahore, 28 March 1931 and *Siyasat*, Lahore, 2 April 1931, *RNPP*, 3 January-27 June 1931, pp. 278, 293.

Economic distress was giving added impetus to religious zealotry. Anti-Hindu moneylender sentiment, which translated as hatred for the *bania*, was given a fillip by the sudden shrinkage in available credit. To pay revenue, some Punjabi cultivators were reportedly selling cattle, women's ornaments, children and, in cases of extra hardship, even their daughters.[56] But the revenue demand was not nearly as crushing a burden as the pressure to meet the usurer's interest payments. One estimate put the interest at nearly fifteen times the multiple of land revenue.[57] A poem tried to convey the feelings of the cultivators and landless labourers:

O God! The peasant is oppressed, grieved and helpless.
O God! The English will set India free,
But the Congress will ruin us
The *Sahukars* [moneylenders] have reduced the peasants to straitened circumstances. These sympathisers of the peasants have sucked their blood.
O God! Relieve the peasant of the disgrace of debt.
So that I may pass my life in comfort.
I will never have anything to do with the *Sahukars*.
I will keep these beastly usurpers at an arm's length.[58]

Attacks on Hindu shops and the account books kept by moneylenders were becoming more frequent. The *Milap*, not known for balanced reporting, claimed that as many as forty Hindu moneylenders had been murdered in rural Punjab.[59] Muslims were obvious suspects, but Jat farmers were equally agitated. Seeing the Congress as an arm of capitalism, they called upon their kin to organize to push for their rights. The *Jat Gazette* from Rohtak—a stronghold of the Punjab Unionist minister, Chhotu Ram—bemoaned the fate of the debt ridden:

This world of loans and the victims of interest—
The world of the zamindars is a hell.
Here capitalism rules.
This world is of poverty-stricken people,
Here labour does not bring fruit.
This is the world of helpless people like us.
No one listens to the poor.
This world belongs to the capitalists.[60]

Growing distress in the countryside did force the colonial government to reduce land revenues. No one was persuaded that this went far enough, least of all non-agriculturists facing the prospect of fresh taxes at a time of slumping

[56]*Inqilab*, Lahore, 24 June 1931 and *Zamindar*, Lahore, 25 June 1931, ibid., p. 532.
[57]*Light*, Lahore, 24 June 1931, ibid., p. 533.
[58]*Daur-i-Jadid*, Lahore, 24 January 1931, ibid., p. 117.
[59]*Milap*, Lahore, 10 July 1931, ibid., p. 589.
[60]*Jat Gazette*, Rohtak, 8 July 1931, ibid., p. 589.

job opportunities and a massive credit crunch. The *Insaf* bewailed the fate of non-agriculturists: 'Are we not the inhabitants of the Punjab? Are we not the subjects of the Government? Are we not the creatures of God? Are we born like sheep and goats, so that these wolves may eat us? Shall we always be kicked by them? Shall we be reduced to sorry plight day by day?'[61] Creditors had no insurance against defaulters which made the collection of dues extremely difficult during an economic depression. Attacks on Hindu shopkeepers and *sahukars* were accompanied by local scuffles in Sikanderabad, Mianwali and Ferozepur. For the Punjab press these occurrences were a boon. The melee that gripped Sikanderabad in Jhang district was likened to the 'Pillage of Nadir Shah's time under British rule'. Others thought Muslim hooliganism now ruled the Punjab. In Jhang, Mianwali and Muzaffargarh, where the police was wholly Muslim, Hindus were in a 'tight corner' since *maulvis* were 'spurt[ing venom] against the Sahukars and shopkeepers'. Muslim papers insisted that the disturbances were not premeditated. They had been caused by the construction of a mosque in Sikanderabad and prohibition on Muslim women from going to Hindu shops.[62] Police intelligence reports attributed the attacks on Hindu shopkeepers to economic factors. *Sahukars* had taken grain from *zamindars*, promising to advance money for revenue payments and then reneged on the understanding. Tensions between creditors and debtors were not unusual in the western districts of the Punjab.[63] During an economic slump and heightened political activity, they could easily flare up into violent encounters along communitarian lines.

With the Congress trying to make the most of the agrarian distress, the colonial administration in the Punjab became more vigilant than ever. The role of the local arms of the colonial state in worsening, if not actually fomenting, some of the communitarian conflicts seems plausible. Colonial imperatives in combination with constitutional issues were shaping the politics of sub-denominational groups at the social base. By far the 'most striking' new development was the manner in which hereditary menials and outcastes were making their voices heard. Unlike other parts of India the disabilities of the depressed castes or classes[64] had not been 'a prominent feature of the sociology of the Punjab'. Dispersed throughout the province, they were 'almost entirely unorganized'. However, with census enumeration under way, and the emergence of B.R. Ambedkar as the pre-eminent spokesman

---

[61]*Insaf*, Lyallpur, 13 June 1932 , ibid., p. 517.

[62]*Insaf*, Lyallpur, 11 July, *Hindu*, Lahore, 13 July and *Inqilab*, 12 July 1931, ibid., p. 634.

[63]*SPPAI*, 1 August 1931, vol. liii, no. 30, p. 486.

[64]'Depressed classes' constituted the formal colonial category in which were included most of the 'untouchable' castes. Popular discourse used the terms depressed classes and depressed castes interchangeably. For reasons of clarity, the term 'depressed castes' is used in this section.

of the 'depressed castes' at the all-India level, they were expressing opinions
with remarkable unanimity. The 'angling for voting strength by the major
communities' was one reason for the new-found assertiveness. Seeing the
opportunity of improving their lot, members of the downtrodden castes were
demonstrating 'the shrewdness and blunt out-spokenness of the typical Punjab
peasants among whom they live[d]'. Their strongest condemnation was
for 'the caste Hindus' and they regarded 'Congress as an essentially caste
organization'. Indication that the colonial administration had encouraged
the meeting, two hundred sweepers in the Punjab congregated in Lahore to
'expose ... the sham sympathy of the Congress' but ended their speeches with
the slogan 'Government ki jai'.[65]

Not all meetings of subordinate caste associations can be attributed to
colonial engineering. Punjab's main depressed castes—Churas, Chamars,
Ahirs and Sansis—were commonly grouped together as *Ad Dharmis* or
Balmikis. Over 5000 attended a meeting in Lahore presided by a labour
leader, M.A. Ghani. 'No nation,' he said, 'ha[d] ever subdued its aborigines
so ruthlessly'. The depressed castes bitterly resented attempts by Hindu and
Sikh activists as well as some census enumerators to forcibly include them
into one or the other of the two main non-Muslim communities of the
Punjab.[66] Muslims were clearly not alone in resisting the Hindu majoritarian
claims implicit in Congress's inclusionary nationalism. Yet the incipient
Muslim and depressed caste alliance in the Punjab was showing itself up as
a pro-government posture quite as much as an anti-caste Hindu stance. Some
three hundred Muslims, one hundred *Balmikis*, and another hundred Hindu
sweepers were present in Lahore where the main nationalist speakers
included the labour leader, M.A. Ghani, Dr Shujaullah of the Jamiat-i-
Shabtan and members of the Arya Swarajya Sabha. Although his Jamiat
had recently supported the Congress, Shujaullah described it as a band of
'dacoits and capitalists'. Disclaiming any connection with *swaraj*, the
president argued that the *Balmikis* were only interested in 'extort[ing] their
rights from the Hindu'. He was greeted with cries of 'Angrez raj zindabad'.[67]
If this was evidence of colonial manipulation, there were also hints of
depressed caste subjectivity in their increased recourse to public activity.
The All-India Ad Dharm Mandal's meeting in Lyallpur resolved to oppose
swaraj until Congress gave them full political rights.[68]

Echoing B.R. Ambedkar's arguments, the depressed castes were decidedly
against the British devolving power into the 'hands of a clique ... an oligarchy,
or ... a group of people, whether Muhammadans or Hindus'. It had to be

[65]*SPPAI*, 14 March 1931, vol. liii, no. 11, pp. 170–1.
[66]*SPPAI*, 21 February 1931, vol. liii, no. 8, pp. 120–1
[67]*SPPAI*, 21 March 1931, vol. liii, no. 12, p. 191.
[68]*SPPAI*, 18 April 1931, vol. liii, no. 16, p. 258.

'shared by all communities in their respective proportions'.[69] Ambedkar charged the Congress of neglecting social reforms and excluding the depressed castes with its slogans of inclusion. The leader of the Mahars in Bombay presidency was raising the standard of separation that was more threatening than anything the Muslims could expect to throw up. He deemed Hinduism to be 'incompatible' with social union and 'the greatest obstacle to Hindu unity' since it 'create[d] an eagerness to separate'.[70] A 'political shoe-maker', Gandhi's campaign for the elimination of untouchability was 'a fad if not a side-show'.[71]

By the time of the second round table conference in London, Ambedkar had pieced together an extensive set of demands for the depressed castes. His memorandum to the minorities committee laid down the conditions on which the depressed castes might consider Hindu majoritarian rule in India. Couched in the language of citizenship rights, these rejected the position of 'hereditary bondsmen' in a future independent state. Before majoritarian rule could be established, untouchability had to be abolished and the depressed castes given equal rights of citizenship. Ambedkar advocated adequate representation with separate electorates for the depressed castes for a period of ten years, adding the proviso that joint electorates would be accepted only with universal adult franchise.[72]

Since Gandhi vehemently opposed separate electorates for the depressed castes, Ambedkar thought the Congress could not have chosen 'a worse person ... to guide India's destiny' at the second round table conference. Portraying himself as 'a man full of humility', the Mahatma was a 'failure' as 'a unifying force'. His autocratic behaviour at the conference confirmed his 'petty-minded[ness]'. 'A curious complex of a man' with a 'rather queer trait in his character', Gandhi refused to budge on issues which savoured of 'pure prejudice'. And yet he could make 'the worst compromises on ... matters of fundamental principle'. The abolition of untouchability, according to the Mahatma, was an 'indispensable condition for the attainment of full freedom'. It constituted the Congress's claim of being 'national in every sense of the term'.[73] The Congress had, however, done nothing to ameliorate the lot of the depressed castes. Instead Gandhi challenged Ambedkar's capacity to represent the depressed castes. This was 'a declaration of War by Mr Gandhi and the Congress against the Untouchables'. However representative, Ambedkar was not prepared to give Congress or Gandhi plenipotentiary powers to 'bind' the depressed castes.[74]

[69]B.R. Ambedkar, *What Congress and Gandhi Have Done to the Untouchables*, first printed by Bombay: Thacker & Co., 1945; reprinted by Lahore: Classic, 1977, p. 66.
[70]Ibid., p. 187.
[71]Ibid., pp. 274–5.
[72]Ibid., chapter three, pp. 41–52.
[73]Ibid, p. 56.
[74]Ibid., p. 58.

Such bold assertions flustered Gandhi the more when they received a friendly hearing from Muslim participants at the conference. Ambedkar and the Muslim delegates were on the verge of cementing an agreement which Gandhi had to torpedo. On the evening of 12 November 1931 the document was handed to the British prime minister as an understanding representing 46 per cent of the population of British India. At the meeting of the minorities committee the next day, the Aga Khan argued that 'all parts of the agreement [we]re interdependent and agreements stand or fall as a whole'.[75] The document came to be known as the minorities pact. If implemented it would cut the Hindu community's share of political power. Turning a Hindu majority into a minority was anathema to Gandhi. Separate electorates would 'throw the apple of discord between the "Untouchables" and the orthodox'. It already had in the case of Hindus and Muslims. Gandhi was prepared to 'tolerate the proposal for special representation' for Muslims and Sikhs, but 'only as a necessary evil'.[76]

The same pernicious logic could not be permitted to hive off a sizeable chunk of a self-styled Hindu community at long last poised to acquire power at the helm of affairs of the colonial state. And so the Mahatma resorted to desperate efforts to buy himself Muslim support by appearing to accept their fourteen demands. Fielding in the slips, the Mahatma bent over backwards to take the depressed caste catch. This sealed the fate of the minorities pact and the second round table conference. With the pieces out of line with the whole, the future constitutional arrangement was unlikely to be a steady one, whatever the final tabulations of the figures. A more important outcome of Gandhi's stonewalling tactics in London lies in the singular logic which was coming to fashion India's Hindu–Muslim problem. The Congress leader was ready to concede Muslim demands in principle if he could keep the sub-denominational politics within the Hindu community at bay. This was additional confirmation, as if Muslims needed it, of their exclusion from the majoritarianism inherent in Congress's nationalism. But here was the rub. Gandhi was prepared to accept the reasonable demands of Muslims only if they were the 'unanimous' opinion of the whole community. With a plethora of sub-denominational identities, Muslims had to close ranks to make a concerted bid for power at the regional and the all-India levels. For the parts to fit the all-India whole, Muslims had to try and conjure up the spirit, if not the substance, of unanimity and uniformity.

RELATING THE MUSLIM PARTS TO A 'WHOLE'

Punjabi Hindus had much to answer for in turning Muslims against the Congress brand of nationalism. Looking to strike political gold with a

[75]Ibid., pp. 67–8.
[76]Ibid., pp. 70–1.

minoritarian status rooted in a majoritarian whole, they had convinced many urban Punjabi Muslims that there was no future for 'unity' between two maladjusted parts. Iqbal's idea of adjustment was less innovative as a political formula than in its attempts at accommodating the problem of cultural differences for some parts of the whole. Dismissing this as the pipe dream of a poet and philosopher in the solitude of his private study would be a poor reading of the historical trends. The demand for political power and representation in the services proportionate to their population was surfacing among wider segments of society in the Punjab. For all its parochialism, the Punjab did not remain immune to developments in other parts of the Indian whole. Politics in UP never ceased to find their echo distorted across the border in the Punjab. Administratively and politically, the NWFP and Sind were also inextricably tied to the province. One relationship which had yet to make an appearance on the political stage, broadly defined, was that between segments of the provincial configuration of Punjabi Muslims and the north Indian princely state of Kashmir.

The story of Punjab's intensely emotive relationship with the state of Jammu and Kashmir requires a separate sub-section. Assessing the political mood in the province around the time of the round table conferences in London is necessary for a meaningful evaluation of the efforts by some Punjabi Muslims to create a larger 'whole' in order to better negotiate terms with the Indian whole. Kashmir formed a vital part of this conception, popular among Muslims of the intermediate strata for whom the colonial state's formal arenas of politics offered few opportunities of immediate advance. Kashmir, praised by a succession of poets as *jannat nazeer* or heavenly spectacle, and known for the autocracy of Dogra rulers over a predominantly poor Muslim population, was as enticing in conception as in its exquisite natural attributes. Unable to command political heights in the Punjab, stragglers from the *khilafat* committees and the Congress in the 1920s were coming to set their sights on Kashmir. Desperation or determination, the motivation behind the Majlis-i-Ahrar's sallies into Kashmir had everything to do with the politics of the Punjab.

Yet the nerve centre of one of the more formative events in Punjabi Muslim consciousness was located in UP. While the Kanpur killings shook Muslims to the core, Jawaharlal Nehru's efforts to dress down Muslim victimization in the Congress enquiry report was the last straw. The report proffered evidence of how the 'Hindu majority [wa]s trying to screen a deep and horrible conspiracy of its community by freely using the Congress platform for this purpose'. Undeterred by the charge of 'communalism', Muslims had to take cognizance of the 'true facts as well as the mentality of the Hindu majority'. The 'mentality' of Congress Muslims was no less 'deplorable' as it aimed at 'conceal[ing[true facts'.[77] An outraged *Siyasat* maintained that 'our new masters desire that when

[77]*Inqilab*, Lahore, 5 April 1931, *RNPP*, 3 January–27 June 1931, p. 313.

they murder us we should not tell people that our men are being murdered'. It was certain that violence in Kanpur and in other parts of UP was the work of 'Congressites and Mahasabhites'. Congress ended up 'reprimanding both the oppressors and the oppressed by describing the high-handed assaults of the Hindus as communal riots'.[78] The *Qaumi Daler* considered the very epithet 'communal riot' for the incident in Kanpur to be a falsification of reality. 'Gandhiji, notwithstanding his mahatmaic breadth of human sympathies' was by no means 'free from the taint of communalism'.[79]

More damaging to the Congress in the Punjab was the widespread allegation that its reactions to communitarian violence in UP substantiated 'the Muslim view' that it was 'under the thumb of the Hindu Maha Sabhites'.[80] Many papers blamed the Vanar Sena, the monkey arm of the Congress, for the killings in Kanpur. Convinced of Congress connivance with the Mahasabha, the *Muslim Outlook* predicted the imminent genocide of Muslims. The violence in Kanpur was the 'outward manifestation of the Hindu policy of clearing the land of the Muslims'. This 'happy idea', it commented wryly, had been concocted by the Mahasabha and 'inwardly applauded by Hindu leaders'. What made the Kanpur disturbances different from those in the past were the attacks on helpless women and innocent children. According to the paper: 'Women whose sex and incapacity alone, should have been their protection, were brutally done with, their breasts cut off and their bodies mutilated and mangled, were shamelessly exposed on the roads. Innocent babies and young children, blissfully ignorant of the political issues at stake, were rent in twain.'[81]

Colonial officials noted that the 'uncompromisingly Hindu outlook of the Congress' had 'deeply affected the feelings of all Muhammadans'.[82] The All-India Congress meeting at Karachi in March 1931 was a blow for Muslims like Zafar Ali Khan who had wagered their prestige on trying to show that cultural differences could be accommodated under the umbrella of a single nationalist organization.When Zafar Ali recommended suspending the proceedings to permit Muslims to say their prayers, he was laughed out of court. Gandhi intervened to say that no important matters would be discussed without the Muslims. But the formal position was that Muslim delegates absent from the meeting would forfeit their voting right. Snubbed by an organization to which he had devoted so much of his life must have been sobering for Zafar Ali Khan. He was not alone in feeling the cold winds of exclusion through marginalization. The dominant 'impression' conveyed by the Congress meeting

[78]*Daur-i-Jadid*, Lahore, 7 April 1931 and *Siyasat*, Lahore, 10 April 1931, ibid., pp. 330, 332.

[79]*Qaumi Daler*, Amritsar, 1 and 8 April 1931, ibid., p. 330.

[80]*Siyasat*, Lahore, 17 April 1931, ibid., p. 333.

[81]*Muslim Outlook*, Lahore, 12 April 1931, ibid., p. 334.

[82]SPPAI, 18 April 1931, vol. liii, no. 16, p. 253.

in Karachi was that 'the Hindu leaders were confidentially planning a Hindu *raj*' in the blissful certitude that once it had been established they could do 'what they like[d]'.[83]

For Zafar Ali the ultimate rebuff came when he was denied a place in the Congress working committee to make room for Dr Muhammad Alam. Disqualified by his politics from a place at the round table conference, the old campaigner had to pause and reconsider. He did so, according to one view, by 'abandoning his ultra-nationalist opinions for something that w[ould] gain him the support from the majority of his own community'.[84] This placed him somewhere 'midway between the *anti*-Congress mass of his own community and the pro-Congress Muslim'. Zafar Ali's new stance was believed to have an 'appreciable following'. His main opponents, Dr Muhammad Alam and Malik Lal Din, did not have significant support among Punjabi Muslims. If this did not seal the fate of the Congress in the province, there were more portentous signs on the political horizon. Ataullah Shah Bukhari, who had 'long been a salaried Congress speaker', was becoming 'decidedly communal and critical of the Congress'.[85] While stepping up propaganda in the rural areas, 'not a single Congress leader [wa]s making the slightest attempt to promote co-operation'. They were either busy quarrelling over power and profit, as in Amritsar, splitting Congress ranks, 'turning to communalism', surreptitiously organizing for a future revolutionary campaign, sponsoring enquiries that heightened 'racial bitterness' over the cremation of Bhagat Singh or sitting pretty at home. Attempts to give momentum to a lethargic civil disobedience campaign had merely accentuated differences—communitarian, sub-denominational and personal.[86]

With Muslims looking towards government-sponsored *Aman Sabhas*, or peace leagues, the stresses and strains in communitarian relations were assuming alarming proportions. In Ludhiana, Hindus were collecting *lathis* in large numbers while Muslims were trying to find out where they were stored.[87] Matters were not helped by the Akali leader, Master Tara Singh, who threatened rivers of blood if Muslim majority rule was established in the Punjab.[88] Muslims complained bitterly that Hindu leaders, once considered the 'soul of the Congress', were preparing for violent confrontations under the auspices of the Mahasabha. Even women were being offered 'train[ing] in target shooting and wielding the sword'. Congress was allegedly raising an army, making nonsense of its non-violent creed. Muslims 'enamoured of the Congress' were strictly 'kept away from these

[83]*SPPAI*, 4 April 1931, vol. liii, no. 14, p. 226.
[84]*SPPAI*, 25 April 1931, vol. liii, no. 17, p. 271.
[85]*SPPAI*, 18 April 1931, vol. liii, no. 16, pp. 253–4.
[86]*SPPAI*, 25 April 1931, vol. liii, no. 17, p. 263.
[87]Ibid., p. 269.
[88]*SPPAI*, 4 July 1931, vol. liii, no. 26, p. 421.

military arrangements'.[89] The Sikh willingness to forgo their claim to 30 per cent representation if joint electorates were conceded was 'a move to hoodwink the Mussalmans out of their due rights'.[90] But the Muslim demand for separate electorates and representation in proportion to their population was seen by other communities as a ploy to establish Islamic rule not only in the Punjab but over the whole of India. The *Tribune* thought this was 'inimical to the evolution of Indian nationhood'. It charged Muslim 'communalists' of wanting to divide the country and then seeking to reunite it for common purposes which were beneficial to them but utterly detrimental to the non-Muslims.[91] If nationalist Muslims were worth their salt, they had to work hard to drive 'communalism' out of India, here and now.

In April 1931 an All-Parties Nationalist Muslim Conference at Lucknow under Sir Ali Imam's direction tried strengthening Gandhi's hand just prior to his departure for London by plumping for joint electorates. The *Tribune* depicted it as a first step to 'reconcile the demands of communalism with those of nationalism'. Yet, in endorsing the rest of Jinnah's fourteen points, even these Muslims who were a cut above the rest of the community in patriotism had fallen 'lamentably short of the high standard of nationalism'. By insisting on the 'fair share of each community in the public services', the Conference had 'adopt[ed] a frankly communal point of view'. The suggestion that residuary powers be vested in the constituent units demonstrated 'a fundamental misconception of the position of the Provinces *vis-a-vis* the Nation'. Equating the 'centre' with the 'nation', the *Tribune* took strong exception to the proposal for a reservation of seats for minorities of less than 30 per cent in federal and provincial legislatures. This was all very well for Muslims in provinces where they were in a minority. But 'why should ... Hindus in Bengal and the Punjab alone of all minorities ... be denied a privilege which the Muslim nationalists believe to be needed for the protection of ... minorities'?[92] The *Hindu Herald* attacked the Lucknow proposals as 'a compromise between nationalism and communalism drafted with Muslim interest in the forefront'. The difference between Muslims posing as 'nationalists' and their 'communalist' brethren in the Muslim Conference was 'not more material than between Tweedledum and Tweedledee'. Giving up separate electorates was a clever subterfuge to strengthen the 'Pan-Islamic Federation'.[93]

So even contrasting stands on the future electorate did not always ferret out the 'nationalist' Muslim from the 'communalist'. In the heat of political battle, internally divided Hindus and Muslims tended to perceive each other in

[89]*Al-Fazl*, Qadian, 25 April 1931, *RNPP*, 3 January-27 June 1931, p. 384.
[90]*Muslim Outlook*, Lahore, 20 April 1931, ibid., p. 350.
[91]*Tribune*, 19 April 1931, ibid., pp. 348-9.
[92]*Tribune*, Lahore, 23 April 1931, ibid., pp. 351-2.
[93]*Hindu Herald*, Lahore, 23 April 1931, ibid., p. 352.

undifferentiated terms. This is where the continuing distinction between 'nationalism' and 'communalism' reveals its logic with stunning bluntness. The main advantage of using 'communalism' to denounce those with whom political differences outweighed all other considerations was in establishing the legitimacy of a 'nationalism' suiting one's own angle of vision. In a context where multiple identities had been forced into monolithic communitarian moulds and had given rise to an embittered discourse on contested sovereignties, the binary did more than that. It effectively erected a notional wall between a 'nationalism' advocated by the Congress and the rest, mostly Muslims, who did not subscribe to its agenda. Even those anxious to keep the nationalist organization at arm's length resented the derogatory connotations of being classified as 'communalists'.

A leading crusader of the Punjabi Muslim cause in the English language, the *Muslim Outlook*, noted that while the 'entire Muslim press ha[d] repudiated the "Nationalist" Muslims', Hindus had 'hailed them as the real representatives of the Muslim community'. Hindus were none too pleased with those they called 'nationalist' Muslims. They were afraid of the implicit agreement among Muslims on all constitutional issues except the issue of the electorate. The *Tribune*'s intimation that 'nationalist' Muslims should avoid negotiating with other Muslims showed how pro-Congress Muslims were being 'used as pawns in a sinister game' to keep the community divided.[94]

The explicit communitarianism should not detract from the regionalism inherent in Punjabi Muslim reactions to the attempted coup d'etat by a group of minority-province Muslims in Lucknow. Try as they may, neither Ali Imam, nor Mukhtar Ahmad Ansari and Abul Kalam Azad had much hope of aligning their co-religionists to the Congress mast. In the Punjab even diehard Congressmen like Ataullah Shah Bukhari and Choudhury Afzal Haq had jumped ship on the question of the electorate. Many Punjabi Muslims shared the *Inqilab*'s opinion that the 'nationalist' Muslims were hired hands of the Congress. The All-India Muslim Conference alone represented the Muslims.[95] The *Sunrise* thought Ansari, Azad and 'their henchmen and proteges' had 'played false with Islam and Muslims' merely to win the approval of Hindu leaders.[96] Sensing failure, Ansari made a last-ditch attempt in Faridpur to arrive at a modus operandi with the Muslim Conference. Muslims in Punjab and Bengal were assured that under joint electorates their majorities would not be reduced to a position of equality, far less a minority. This provoked a biting response from the Punjab Hindu Sabha leader Bhai Parmanand. Ansari had 'once for all established the truth that no Muslim organisation, be it the Muslim League, the Khilafat Committee or the Nationalist Muslim party c[ould] ever look at

[94]*Muslim Outlook*, Lahore, 25 April 1931, ibid., p. 353.
[95]*Inqilab*, Lahore, 23 and 24 April 1931, ibid., p. 354.
[96]*Sunrise*, Qadian, 26 June 1931, ibid., p. 529.

the question of the future of India from a nationalist point of view'. The man whom Congress projected as a 'truly nationalist Muslim leader in the country' was nothing but a 'Muslim first and Muslim last'. To press claims for a religious majority was the very 'negation of democracy'.[97]

The great harbinger of democracy in an independent India thought better than to stop negotiating with Muslims. Gandhi had set the tone of the Congress's attitude towards the Muslims by asking for a unanimous set of demands. He did not have to bank on the sectarian divisions among Muslims since the interests of those in provinces where they were in a majority or a minority were dramatically contradictory. This in large part explains why the designation 'nationalist' applied to fewer Muslims from the Punjab than to those of UP and Bihar. While men like Ansari and Ali Imam might see virtue in giving up separate electorates for an agreement with the Congress at the all-India level, the Ali brothers had broken with the Nehrus precisely on this point. As the president of the hastily revived All-India Khilafat Conference made plain in Bombay, the demands of the Muslim Conference adopted in Delhi were the 'irreducible minimum'. Shaukat Ali and Shafi Daudi were present when Maulana Abdul Majid Badauni declared that the Muslims would not accept any constitution which did 'not adequately safeguard their rights'. Badauni 'refused to believe' that the 'plea for separate electorates [wa]s incompatible with nationalism'. If Gandhi had 'the larger interest of the country' in mind, he should accept the Muslim demands.[98] Muhammad Iqbal deplored the attempts of the Gandhian Congress to veto an understanding with the Muslims by insisting that they produce a united set of demands. Whatever their religious differences, the Muslims were at one politically with regard to the future constitution. With irreligious nationalism gaining currency, he warned the younger generation, Muslims could expect nobody to ensure the survival of their distinctive Islamic identity in India.[99]

For a variation on the Punjabi view of the whole, it is worth turning to the eastern fringes of the subcontinent. Bengal after all constituted the other major pillar in the Muslim demand for regional majorities. One of its emerging political stars, Hussain Shaheed Suhrawardy told an All-India Muslim Volunteers Conference in Bombay that he was appalled by the dismissive attitude of Hindus towards the reasonable demands of Muslims. His Hindu friends did 'not attempt even to understand' them while the Hindu press damned them as 'communal'. Muslims wanted an India in which no community would 'run the risk of being tormented, exploited and oppressed by the others'. Hindus considered themselves a nation and wanted their own rule. The 'communalism of the

[97]*Tribune*, 15 July 1931, *RNPP*, 4 July-12 December 1931, pp. 607–8.
[98]*Tribune*, 2 June 1931, press clippings in *Khilafat Movement in NWFP, Afghanistan and Bombay*, NDC, p. 89.
[99]*Inqilab*, 5 May 1931 in Afzal (comp.), *Guftar-i-Iqbal*, pp. 116–18.

Muslims mean[t] encroachment on the vested interest' Hindus had acquired.[100] By claiming to be 'denominated Nationalists', Congress Muslims might pretend to be the only ones concerned about the welfare of the Indian nation. But they were 'wrong' since this was also 'the ambition of all the Muslims', only the latter disagreed with the solution proposed by the Congressmen. Suhrawardy was convinced that separate electorates could 'create an Indian nation while joint electorates would mean disintegration and Hindu domination'. Congress Muslims had 'no right to call themselves Nationalists' when they subscribed to the same views as the 'leader of the Mahasabha' who was 'not ashamed to declare that by Hindu he mean[t] Indian'.[101]

Undeterred by such onslaughts, Ansari continued his efforts during the summer of 1931 to piece together an agreement between the Congress and the Muslims. But he ended up offering the Sikhs more than the Nehru report had. Such generosity on the part of a UP Muslim seemed egregious to Punjabi Muslims. Many of the best-known Congressmen in the province had by now opted for the Majlis-i-Ahrar, an organization which included anti-imperialists, Islamic universalists and communitarian bigots of varying measures. The Ahrars demonstrated that their first affinity was with their regional interests. Gandhi was warned of grave consequences if he supported the 'nationalist' Muslim formula for joint electorates.[102] An Ahrar rally at Lahore presided over by Maulana Habibur Rahman of Ludhiana was an indication of how regionalism was making sure that protestations of 'nationalism' would be 'strongly overlayed with communalism'.[103] His support for separate electorates exposed him to the *Pratap*'s charge that there was plainly 'no difference between the Nationalist and the toady Mussalmans'.[104] Mazhar Ali Azhar, a leading light of the Ahrars, was convinced that Hindus and Sikhs were 'the social enemies of the Muhammadans'. Separate electorates had to be retained until Hindus abandoned their aggressive posture. A resolution to the effect was passed with only ten dissenting voices among six hundred. Dr Muhammad Alam and Saifuddin Kitchlew, 'the sole remaining champions of nationalist Muslims' in the Punjab, could do 'nothing to stem the tide of sectarianism'. With this, the 'last shred of support' for joint electorates in the province had 'gone'.[105]

Without substantial support from pro-Congress Muslims, Ansari could make little headway in the Punjab. As it was, the non-Muslims were in no mood for a compromise. A minorities conference of Hindus, Sikhs and Christians came out firmly against separate electorates and Muslim-majority rule in the province.

---

[100]*Tribune*, Lahore, 4 June and *Muslim Outlook*, Lahore, 17 June 1931, press clippings in *Khilafat Movement in NWFP, Afghanistan and Bombay*, NDC, p. 91.

[101]Ibid.

[102]*SPPAI*, 4 July 1931, vol. liii, no. 26, p. 421.

[103]Ibid., p. 433.

[104]*Pratap*, Lahore, 13 July 1931, *RNPP*, 4 July–12 December 1931, p. 605.

[105]*SPPAI*, 18 July l 1931, vol. liii, no. 28, p. 455.

Even the *Zamindar* saw this as an attempt to 'trample underfoot the rights of the Mussalmans'. Could those who were Hindu 'if not by religion but by nationality' actually 'believe that a nation whose individuals regard not only others but their own brethren as unholy ... accept the idea of joint nationalism'? More poignantly, would 'a community which regards others as *malechas* form an alliance with *malechas*'? The paper had been stung by the rejection of adult suffrage and a proposal to divide the Punjab into two parts which was designed 'to ruin the Muslim majority in the Punjab'.[106] If this was the opinion of Zafar Ali Khan's paper, Malik Barkat Ali's critique of the Punjab Minorities Conference decisions elicited an interesting diatribe from the *Tribune*. 'No man with even an elementary knowledge of things' could fail to note that 'Mr Barkat Ali's conception of nationalism, democracy and *Swaraj*' was 'fantastic and perverse' and 'essentially medieval and anti-modern'. Barkat Ali had opposed separate electorates in the past. His support for Muslim-majority rule in the Punjab proved that he was 'a pure communalist who, by accident and ... the exigencies of his position ... [had] strayed into the nationalist fold'.[107]

By the early 1930s an increasing number of Punjabi Muslims were finding it difficult to sustain their presence in nationalist circles. Zafar Ali Khan tried keeping his options open. But even he had come out in support of separate electorates since universal franchise, the precondition for Muslims accepting joint electorates, was nowhere on the political horizon. Adamant to move forward on the basis of joint electorates, the Congress Working Committee in July 1931 published its blueprint for a solution of the communitarian problem. Universal franchise was a thing for the future. What Congress wanted in the interim was joint electorates with uniform reservations for religious minorities. Reactions to the Congress proposal followed the usual trajectory. The *Tribune* applauded it as a 'compromise between proposals based on undiluted nationalism and those based on undiluted communalism'.[108] The *Hindu* assailed the Congress Working Committee for having 'lowered the position of the Hindus of the Punjab to that of a pariah'. Unless Punjabi Hindus fought for their rights, they would be 'blamed by future generations'.[109] This invited a flurry of schemes to redistribute the provincial boundaries. These ranged from schemes to separate the Ambala division from the Punjab and merging it with UP or Delhi[110] to a variety of Sikh proposals to chew up the province in moth-like fashion.[111]

[106]*Zamindar*, Lahore, 10 July 1931, *RNPP*, 4 July-12 December 1931, p. 583.

[107]*Tribune*, Lahore, 11 July 1931, ibid., p. 584.

[108]*Tribune*, Lahore, 17 July 1931, ibid., p. 610.

[109]*Hindu*, Lahore, 3 August 1931, ibid., p. 710.

[110]A move supported by Muhammad Iqbal, this would increase the Muslim population to 62 per cent and make separate electorates irrelevant. It was fiercely opposed by the *Akali* and the *Akali-te-Pardesi* of Amritsar which appealed to Sikhs, Muslims and Hindu Jats to oppose the merger of Ambala with Delhi province. (Ibid., pp. 996, 1041.)

[111]One Sikh proposal was to extract Lyallpur from the Multan division and remove

If there were hurdles to a resolution of the majority–minority equation in the region, greater difficulties attended the problem at the all-India level. Ansari's hopes could have materialized only if pro-Congress Muslims like him had been given pride of place at the second round table conference. But Gandhi failed to secure an invitation for Ansari. Indication of Fazl-i-Husain's influence over the viceregal lodge was the selection of Shaukat Ali, Shafi Daudi and Muhammad Iqbal—all supporters of separate electorates. The collapse of the second round table conference effectively put paid to the possibility of Indians arriving at an agreement on a formula for communitarian representation and rights. Punjabi Muslims thought they would do better if the terms were laid down by the British. Months before the second round table conference, the *Muslim Outlook* recommended that 'the Mussalman community should now ignore the Hindu community, the Gandhis and the Nehrus and the Malaviyas and try to canvass the British delegation in their favour'.[112]

Historians of this period have focused rather more on the doings of men like Fazl-i-Husain, the Aga Khan and others in railroading Muslims to safety in the constitutional negotiations in London. Not all Muslims could influence the future course of events in the same way as a Fazl-i-Husain. Unable to command attention from within the confines of the colonial state's system of representation, those without pelf or privilege could make an impact only through propaganda and agitation in the informal arenas of politics. These campaigns for political ascendancy reflect the personal, class and ideological divisions among Muslims more accurately than the discourse on their communitarian interests. Stretching the contours of the Muslim 'whole' seemed the best hope of negotiating terms with the Indian whole, but there was no agreement on who should dictate the terms everyone else was expected to obey. For all the talk about minimum constitutional safeguards for their cultural self-defence, the question of leadership and legitimate authority continued to bedevil the politics of India's Muslims. In the quest for new horizons, nothing gripped the imaginations of Punjab Muslims more than Kashmir—the *jannat nazeer* turned into a slough of despond. Small wonder that so many staked their reputations on the will-o'-the-wisp of liberating the downtrodden people of Kashmir.

Kashmir Jannat Nazeer: Ahrar Reds and Ahmadi Blues

Kashmir's legendary beauty meshed awkwardly with the destitution, illiteracy and infirmity of the vast majority of its people. Ever since March 1846 when the British 'sold' it for seventy-five lakh rupees to the Dogra warlord Gulab Singh, predominantly Muslim Kashmir together with its sister state of Jammu

Montgomery, Sheikhupura and Gujranwala from the Multan bar. (*Eastern Times*, Lahore, 29 October 1931, ibid., p. 1018.)

[112]*Muslim Outlook*, Lahore, 13 June 1931, *RNPP*, 3 January–27 June 1931, p. 491.

and the frontier districts including Buddhist Ladakh experienced unmitigated autocratic rule. A succession of maharajas, nurturing ties with a small group of Hindu *pandits* in the Kashmir valley and a more extensive network of Dogra kinsmen in Jammu, wilfully trampled on the rights of their subjects. Protests against Dogra depredations made for stirring newspaper stories but rarely succeeded in pushing an insensitive state administration to adopt even the most nominal of reforms. Extreme poverty, exacerbated by a series of famines in the second half of the nineteenth century, had seen many Kashmiris fleeing to neighbouring Punjab.

Kashmiris settled in other parts of India, especially Punjab and the NWFP, retained emotional and familial links with their original homeland. Like most diasporic movements, that of Kashmiri Muslims drew upon the myth of return and the vision of a free and prosperous Kashmir. Since the turn of the century, the Kashmiri Muslim Conference had been serving as a venue to ventilate grievances against the Dogra administration and bemoan the lack of equal opportunities in their adopted homes. In 1913 the fourth annual meeting held in Gujranwala urged Maharaja Pratap Singh to recruit Muslims into his army and redress their educational backwardness. A resolution was simultaneously passed calling for promoting education and recruiting Kashmiris in the Punjab into the army. Another complained that Kashmiris engaged in agriculture were disqualified from taking advantage of the Punjab Land Alienation Act. One speaker conceded that Punjab was not the *watan* of the Kashmiris. Under international law anyone resident in a place for more than five years enjoyed the same rights as its indigenous inhabitants. Yet Kashmiris settled in the Punjab for centuries faced discrimination. This was because of the improper use of the term Kashmiri which did not refer to a special *zat* but to the inhabitants of Kashmir who were nothing less than a *qaum*. Unfortunately the Kashmiri sense of their distinctive *qaumiyat* had suffered on account of dismal educational qualifications.[113]

As one of the most highly educated Kashmiris in the Punjab, Muhammad Iqbal supported the Kashmiri cause through the Anjuman-i-Himayat-i-Islam and the lesser known Anjuman-i-Kashmiri Musalman. His poetry demonstrates a keen sense of belonging to Kashmir, the magnificent valley which the cruel hands of fate had allowed men of bestial disposition to reduce to abject slavery and benightedness.[114] In Iqbal's words:

[113]According to the 1911 census there were 177,549 Kashmiri Muslims in the Punjab; the figure went up to 206,180 with the inclusion of settlements in the NWFP. In the Punjab a mere 3.2 per cent were reported to be educated. (*Kashmiri Conference ke Chauthe Salana Jalse ki Ruidad*, 26 and 27 April 1913, Gujranwala, Lahore, 1914, VT 3890d, IOL.)

[114]Iqbal's sympathy with the Kashmiri cause and his poetic renderings on the issue are detailed in Saleem Khan Gami, *Iqbal aur Kashmir*, second edition, Lahore: Universal Books, 1985, pp. 63–150.

Oh God, break this tyrannical grip
Which has mauled the spirit of Kashmiri freedom[115]

Among the other notable Kashmiris based in the Punjab who kept alive hopes
of turning the tide of Dogra despotism was Mohammad Din Fauq, editor of
the *Kashmiri Magazine*. In a poem celebrating his beloved homeland, Fauq
wrote:

Every corner of Kashmir is like heaven
Each part of Kashmir holds the secrets of nature

...

Every particle of my Kashmir is hospitable
Even the stones along the way gave me water.[116]

But even the most inspired poetry could not incite a rebellion against the
indomitable Dogra fortress. Sporadic unrest was crushed with brutal
determination. Compared with the Maharaja's whimsical exercise of
personalized sovereignty over his hapless subjects, the people of British India
seemed to be living in relative bliss. Religious freedom, ostensibly one of the
main tenets of the contract between the colonizers and the colonized in British
India, was for the most part limited to the ruling family and their courtiers.
Movements demanding rights for the subjects of princely states often assumed
a religious dimension. In Jammu and Kashmir, where not only the legitimacy
of Dogra sovereignty but also the orbit of privilege was defined by the symbols
of Hinduism, the tendency could acquire dangerous proportions.

Here religion was neither a private nor a temporal matter. With few
exceptions, most of the Muslim religious places were in the possession of the
state. The conversion of a non-Muslim to Islam entitled the Maharaja to
confiscate the individual's property. Religious preaching by Muslims was
strictly controlled and, when aimed at non-Muslims, punishable by law. Cow
slaughter was illegal and entailed ten years in prison and a hefty fine. These
religious restrictions may have been bearable if not for the long shadow they
cast upon every aspect of the subjects' existence. Practically no form of
economic activity, not even prostitution, escaped taxation. Muslims were
debarred from expressing their opinions freely, virtually excluded from the
army and poorly represented in the government services. The state claimed

[115]*Tor ise dast-i-jafakesh ko yarab jisne*
Ruh-i-azadi-i-Kashmir ko pamal kiya.

تو اس دستِ جفاکش کو یارب جس نے
روحِ آزادئ کشمیر کو پامال کیا۔

(Cited in ibid., p. 93.)
[116]*Adabi Duniya*, vol. vi, no. 19, March-April 1966, special issue on Kashmir,
pp. 190–1.

exclusive ownership of the land. Landlords had no proprietary rights and required official permission to cut down a tree or build a residence on their own premises. Most of the produce of the land was seized by the state while cultivators paid hefty taxes. *Begar* or forced labour was rampant as was corruption among state officials. As an insurance against revolt, the state banned Muslims from keeping arms and ammunition.[117]

Remarkably little organized resistance was put up by Kashmiri Muslims until the third decade of the twentieth century. Efforts by Kashmiris in the Punjab to raise the standard of revolt against Dogra oppression added fresh layers of enmity to the ongoing controversies between Muslim- and Hindu-owned newspapers. The Anglo-Indian press periodically cited instances of maladministration in Kashmir to goad the government of India to extend direct control over the state. This would secure British strategic interests against Russian infiltration and, more concretely, allow Europeans to circumvent the prohibition against acquiring property in the state. As a rule, the Hindu-owned press defended the Maharaja while most Muslim and Anglo-Indian papers condemned Dogra rule as iniquitous and inhuman. In 1889 the British did curtail the powers of the Maharaja by establishing a council of administration. While creating tensions between the Maharaja and his imperial benefactors, cosmetic changes at the top were no substitute for the massive facelift needed at the social base.

Against the backdrop of a worldwide economic depression, heavy taxation of agricultural and commercial activities tightened the noose on an emaciated and dejected populace. Mounting economic distress and political disaffection found a ready outlet in Jammu where a police constable carried out a wanton act of sacrilege against the Quran. This incident, which occurred on 6 June 1931, created a commotion whose impact exceeded the expectations of the state authorities. Reactions were sharp in Muslim-majority Srinagar where young Kashmiri leaders like the Aligarh-educated Sheikh Mohammad Abdullah had recently established a reading group as a first step to raise popular consciousness. On 21 June Muslims assembled at the Srinagar Jamia mosque heard stringent critiques of the Dogra administration. Abdul Qadir, a cook from the NWFP in the service of an English officer vacationing in Kashmir, who happened to be present, suddenly gave an inflammatory speech. He was immediately arrested, which transformed him into a popular hero. When on 13 July Qadir was sentenced, a crowd of Kashmiri Muslims outside the jail demanding to see him were fired upon by the state forces. Twenty-two perished on the spot, giving impetus to a long-delayed internal struggle for rights in Jammu and Kashmir.[118]

Cashing in on events, Punjabi Muslim newspapers outdid one another

---

[117]Mirza, *Karavan-i-Ahrar*, i, pp. 172–4.
[118]Ibid., p. 178 and Gami, *Iqbal aur Kashmir*, pp. 60–1.

in sensationalizing Dogra atrocities. Their Hindu counterparts charged them of the malicious intent to destabilize Maharaja Hari Singh and encourage the introduction of cow slaughter in Kashmir. Condemning the 'savage oppression' of its co-religionists, the *Inqilab* nevertheless insisted that the troubles in Srinagar were 'not a riot between Hindus and Mussalmans' who had been living cheek by jowl in relative harmony for centuries. The uprising was a reaction to the 'tyrannies of a high-handed and oppressive Government' which was 'ruin[ing] its 95 per cent subjects by depriving them of human rights'. Hindu newspapers gave the 'Srinagar riot a communal tinge'.[119] The *Muslim Outlook* 'refused to believe' that the 'Maharaja [wa]s actuated by anti-Muslim prejudice'; rather, he had 'surrounded himself with counsellors' who were 'saturated with the hatred of Mussalmans' and 'blind to the signs of the times'.[120]

Accusing the Maharaja's ministers of religious bigotry was another way of calling for the appointment of more Muslims in the higher echelons of the state administration. Given the appalling educational standards in the state, this meant employment for footloose and ambitious Muslims of British India. There was much ado about state officials arbitrarily prohibiting Id sermons and recitations of the Quran. Punjabi Muslims also learnt that many mosques in Jammu and Kashmir had been 'converted into granaries, magazines, stables and ... received harsher treatment than was meted out to churches in France during the revolution'.[121] But none of these complaints were seen as fanning the fires of communitarian animosities. Instead Hindu papers were blamed for 'introduc[ing] communalism in every matter and giv[ing] a communal colour to every difference of views'. The contest was between 'the Kashmiris and the Dogra Government', the erstwhile 'sycophants of the Sikhs' who with the advent of the British had become 'traitors'. Hindu papers were 'busy saying that the Mussalmans ha[d] risen against the Hindus'. These papers wanted to 'enlist the sympathy of the entire Hindu community in India' and, in this way, 'conceal the atrocities of the Dogras'.[122]

Not to be outdone, the *Milap* ascribed the tensions in Srinagar to an intrigue concocted in Lahore. A 'scheme' had been prepared whereby 'Hindu rule in Kashmir' would be 'replaced by Muslim rule'. Consequently, 'people from outside went to Srinagar and started an agitation against the Government'.[123] The *Tribune* detected 'two sinister ideals' at the 'bottom of this essentially engineered agitation'. First, to divert attention from India's constitutional problems and, second, 'to further the professed aim of [the] Iqbal school to

[119]*Inqilab*, Lahore, 14 and 19 July 1931, *RNPP*, 18 July 1931, pp. 623–4, 659.

[120]*Muslim Outlook*, Lahore, 19, 20, 24 and 25 July 1931, ibid., p. 657.

[121]*Muslim Outlook*, Lahore, 30 July and 1 August 1931, ibid., p. 694.

[122]*Sardar*, Lahore, 25 July 1931, ibid., p. 699.

[123]*Milap*, Lahore, 21 July 1931, ibid., p. 664.

have a chain of Provinces and States under Muslim Raj in the North-West of India'.[124] A Sikh paper concurred: the disturbances in Srinagar were part of 'a conspiracy to establish an Islamic Government in Northern India'. Others were more specific in identifying Afghanistan as the prospective occupier of Kashmir.[125]

If there was a grain of truth in some of this, it was tinged with rivalries among Muslims in the Punjab for the privilege of hoisting the Islamic flag in the Dogra domains. Desperately seeking a reversal of fortunes, the Majlis-i-Ahrar moved swiftly to nail its colours to the cause of liberating thirty-two lakh Muslims in Kashmir. A meeting under Ataullah Shah Bukhari issued a call for money to send *jathas* or volunteers into the state. Protest rallies by the Ahrars, dressed in red shirts in memory of the martyrs of the Khissa Khani bazaar massacre in Peshawar in April 1930, drew Muslims in their thousands. The best attended were in towns with substantial numbers of Kashmiri settlers, notably Sialkot where some 15,000 congregated to express anger and sorrow at the insouciant killing of Muslims in Srinagar.[126] But the Ahrar bid for leadership of the anti-Dogra agitation misfired when on 25 July a select gathering of prominent Muslims, Muhammad Iqbal among them, met in Simla and created the All-India Kashmir Committee. To the chagrin of the Ahrars, Bashiruddin Mahmud, leader of the Qadian section of the Ahmadis, was appointed president of the committee on Iqbal's recommendation.[127]

The move was ascribed to Mian Fazl-i-Husain, whose pre-eminent position in the collaborative networks of the colonial state had long been anathema for the Ahrars. Whatever else the Ahrars may have been capable of, they could not be enamoured of the British and their wealthy and titled allies. Class differentials overlaid by political and ideological disagreements militated against such a possibility. Needing an issue like Kashmir to wrest back the glory of the *khilafat* era, the Ahrars had reason to be put off by the development at Simla. The fact of an Ahmadi at the helm was an excuse to damn the All-India Kashmir Committee as a British plant to sabotage efforts to enlist Kashmir into a larger Muslim whole.[128] Strapped for funds, the Ahrars could not contend with the economic and political clout of the Kashmir Committee. Discrediting the committee as an outpost of Qadian proved ineffective since at most only nine of its sixty-three members could be identified as Ahmadis.

[124]*Tribune*, Lahore, 8 August 1931, ibid., p. 726.

[125]Ibid., p. 728.

[126]*SPPAI*, 1 August 1931, vol. liii, no. 30, p. 485.

[127]Among the other founding members were Nawab Zulfikar Ali Khan, Khwajah Hasan Nizami and Abdur Rahman Dard, an Ahmadi, who took over as secretary. Later the editors of the *Inqilab* and the *Siyasat*, Ghulam Rasul Mehr and Sayyid Habib respectively, also joined the Kashmir Committee.

[128]For an elaboration of the theme, see Mirza, *Karavan-i-Ahrar*, i, pp. 181, 249.

Even the Jamiat-ul-Ulema-i-Hind decided to co-operate with the Kashmir Committee. After consulting with their political godfather, Maulana Abul Kalam Azad, the Ahrars opted to go it alone until conditions were ripe to seize control of the Kashmir agitation.[129]

While the Kashmir Committee concentrated on extending legal aid to those incarcerated in connection with the troubles in Srinagar and making representations to the Maharaja and the British authorities, the Ahrars stepped up efforts to recruit volunteers in the Punjab. By mid-August, Maulana Mazhar Ali Azhar became 'dictator' of the Ahrar agitation in Kashmir. But after an initial burst of fervour for their suffering brethren in Kashmir, Punjabi Muslims seemed reluctant to support a cause which instead of acquiring a clear political direction was rekindling the fires of sectarian hatred among them. In Amritsar and Sialkot, Muslims were split down the middle between 'those who follow[ed] the *Ahrar-i-Islam* and those who t[ook] their orders from Qadian'.[130] With their hold over the Kashmir agitation slipping, the 'extremist bigots' of the Ahrars revived their agitation against the Hindu principal of the Maclagan Engineering College in Lahore for his allegedly disparaging remarks against the Prophet of Islam. At the same time, Bukhari made a vicious speech against Bashiruddin in Sialkot which led his Ahrar underlings to attack Ahmadi volunteers headed for Kashmir.[131]

Posturing as defenders of Islam against Ahmadis and Hindus alike may have been an Ahrar speciality. But without magnanimous donors, there was no guarantee of either sustained or expanding popular support. The large number of volunteers rallying under the Majlis-i-Ahrar banner to free *jannat nazeer* from the clutches of Dogra infidels created the impression that it was 'a much more powerful body than it really [wa]s'. The eagerness to don Ahrar reds owed much to the high level of unemployment in the province during the depression. The Ahrars nevertheless were trailing behind the Ahmadis in the first round of the Kashmir agitation. Renewed clashes in Srinagar were instigated by an Ahmadi volunteer in direct contact with Qadian. As if this was not enough to 'keep the *Ahrar* party and orthodox Muhammadans quiet', there were rumours that Mazhar Ali and his party had been lavishly entertained and bribed by the Dogra authorities. Upon returning from his sojourn in Kashmir, where he was housed in the state guest house, the great 'dictator' dismissed reports of the ill-treatment of Muslims in Kashmir as hugely exaggerated. This put a spanner in the works for the Ahrars with the result that even 'nationalist' Muslims like Malik Lal Din and Muhammad Alam

[129]This was revealed by Maulana Habibur Rahman in his book, *Rais-ul-Ahrar*. (Cited in Sheikh Abdul Majid, *Iqbal aur Ahmadiyat* [Critique of Javed Iqbal's *Zinda Rawad*], Lahore: Choudhry Irshad Ahmad Wark, 1991, p. 436.)

[130]*SPPAI*, 29 August 1931, vol. liii, no. 34, p. 530.

[131]*SPPAI*, 19 September 1931, vol. liii, no. 37, p. 558.

began angling for a place in the Kashmir agitation. Proof of disarray was in evidence at an Ahrar meeting where one speaker told his audience to 'join the Congress in such large numbers as completely to control it'.[132]

That there may have been more to this exhortation is suggested by the counter moves by Punjabi Hindus through the Arya Swarajya Sabha. Its aim was to get Hindus to gird their loins and 'show that the real object' of the Muslim agitation was 'not the emancipation of their Muslim brethren in Kashmir, but the desire for a Muslim State in northern India'. They had apparently 'succeeded in winning over a number of nationalist Muhammadans' who had been 'induced to form an association called the *Anjuman-i-Hamdard-i-Mussalmin* ... financed by Hindu money'. The Anjuman's purpose was to 'dampen down the Muhammadan agitation about Kashmir'.[133] Such an alliance was not nearly so bizarre given the bitter history of relations between Ahmadis and Hindus, not to mention the 'nationalist' pretensions of the Ahrars' star players. Since the Ahmadis were seen to have edged ahead of everyone else in the Kashmir agitation because of British support, differences could momentarily be buried for the sheer satisfaction of calling a halt to a common enemy's perceived gains. The *Kesari* recalled that over the years the Ahmadis had 'lost no opportunity of setting Hindus and Muslims by the ear and causing them to shed each others' blood'. Their sole purpose in creating 'mischief' in Kashmir was to get New Delhi to meddle in the affairs of the state.[134] The *Al-Adl* was convinced that the Kashmir Committee had been formed at British insistence since 'the Ahmadis never participate[d] in movements which criticise[d] the policy of Government'.[135]

Giving a sectarian tinge to class differences dovetailed nicely with the Ahrar position. British officials noted that 'jealousy and distrust' of the Ahmadis had made 'other Muhammadans cautious about taking up the agitation'. This, together with the 'desire of each to lead' had made co-operation impossible between the Kashmir Committee and the Ahrars. Personal rivalries further complicated matters. Ahrar leaders envious of Mazhar Ali's new-found prominence tried ousting him from the leadership. The effort came to naught once Azhar was arrested by the Kashmir authorities. With the Congress loyalist Muhammad Alam eager to intervene, and a confusing chain of individual and collective machinations as well as 'efforts by a variety of sharks to get at the State Treasure chest', the prospects of Punjab providing organized muscle power for the liberation of Kashmir's subjugated people looked all too dreary.[136]

Small batches of Ahrars pouring into Kashmir were more an irritation than

[132]*SPPAI*, 26 September 1931, vol. liii, no. 38, p. 570.
[133]*SPPAI*, 22 August 1931, vol. liii, no. 33, pp. 523–4.
[134]*Kesari*, Lahore, 17 August 1931, *RNPP*, 18 July 1931, p. 778.
[135]*Al-Adl*, Gujranwala, 9 August 1931, ibid., p. 776.
[136]*SPPAI*, 3 October 1931, vol. liii, no. 39, p. 585.

a threat to the Dogra authorities since the stragglers could be made to change tack for a pittance. With such unpromising assistance from across the border, Kashmiri leaders under Sheikh Abdullah's direction thought it better to co-operate with the reform commission under Bertrand James Glancy appointed in November 1931 by the Maharaja. They were also ready to welcome financial and legal help from the All-India Kashmir Committee. This led to the further marginalization of the Ahrars. After being released from prison, a 'disgruntled' Mazhar Ali Azhar returned to the Punjab to announce that the Ahrars had 'broken' with the Kashmiri Muslim leadership for refusing to plump for a legislative assembly responsible to the people. The situation was not much better in the Punjab where more Ahrar volunteers instead of sneaking into Kashmir ended up in prison. Reduced to a semi-immobilized condition, Ahrar volunteers had to be kept busy picketing liquor stores and brothels. Internal feuds over funds added to Ahrar discomfiture, leaving them seething with hatred for both the Ahmadis and the government.[137] To keep up morale, the Ahrar volunteers were ordered to engage in physical exercises in every *mohalla* and get young Muslim men to parade with swords and *lathis*.[138]

Shunned by Abdullah and their volunteers hit by a spate of arrests, the Ahrars refused to stop posturing as the ultimate saviours of Kashmir. Mazhar Ali Azhar made light of the criticism that it was 'unfair to agitate' while Kashmiri Muslim demands were under consideration. It was 'the duty of every human being to save even a stranger from drinking a cup known to be poison'. Attacks on Dogra rulers now took second place to scurrilous attacks on Ahmadis who were condemned as *kafirs*. In Amritsar, ex-Ahmadis disgruntled by the Qadian leadership were paraded to advertise the insidious nature of the sect, while in Sialkot police confiscated effigies tagged 'Jhuta Rasul' or false prophet. The Ahrars had transformed the Kashmir agitation into a holy war against the Ahmadis. In late October 1931 when negotiations in Srinagar collapsed, the Ahrars resumed their tactic of despatching volunteers to Jammu and Kashmir. By then they had established nineteen district committees in the Punjab. Since the central committee of the Majlis-i-Ahrar had a mere Rs 700 in its kitty, local committees had to give the funds to send the *jathas*. Consequently, there was 'dwindling enthusiasm' among the volunteers who 'promised support on the condition that the agitation be brought to a definite conclusion'.[139]

The Ahrars were more adept at moving their targets in the Punjab than calling the shots in Kashmir. Beginning with attacks on Punjabi Hindu supporters of the Dogras, they had concentrated their fire on the Ahmadis. The only constant in their agitation was the charge of Ahmadi complicity with the British and their Unionist collaborators, especially Fazl-i-Husain

[137]*SPPAI*, 24 October 1931, vol. liii, no. 41, p. 1111.
[138]*Durr-i-Najaf*, 26 October 1931, *RNPP*, 26 September 1931, p. 1053.
[139]*SPPAI*, 31 October 1931, vol. liii, no. 42, pp. 619–20.

and his younger lieutenant, Sikander Hayat Khan. This appealed to Zafar Ali Khan whose paper threw its weight behind the Ahrars at a time when the *Inqilab* and the *Siyasat* were aligned with the All-India Kashmir Committee. In the *Zamindar*'s opinion, the Maharaja could 'conquer the hearts of his subjects' by expelling Ahmadis who were 'spreading mischief in the State' and 'urg[ing] Kashmiri Pandits to give up their hostile attitude towards the Mussalmans'.[140] Hardly a typical 'communal' stance, it signifies how schisms within Islam could override the politics of religious difference.

Far from hedging his bets, Zafar Ali Khan was acting as the 'liaison between the Congress and the *Ahrars*'. In early November 1931 the eruption of violence in Jammu and resultant death of an Ahrar volunteer 'intensified the already deep and widespread feelings of sympathy felt by Muslims of all classes for their brethren in Kashmir'. Above all it gave 'the political adventurers of the *Ahrar-i-Islam* their chance' as never before. The erstwhile 'henchmen of the Congress', the Ahrars were 'men whose reputation was besmirched in the eyes of their co-religionists'. But the excesses of Dogra troops coupled with 'widespread distrust' of Kashmiri *pandits* saw Muslims from all walks of life being 'drawn into the ranks of the *Ahrar-i-Islam*, or at least into sympathy with them'. This meant more funds and manpower for the Ahrars. The decision to send British troops into the state was by and large hailed by Punjabi Muslims in general and by the Kashmir Committee in particular. The Ahrars echoed the opinion of many Hindus that the move was an attempt by British imperialism to gain a foothold in the state. There was now a greater tendency among the Ahrars to project their agitation as anti-British. The Congress was only too eager to exploit the opening. With Zafar Ali acting as broker, the Congress was trying to bring the Ahrars back into its fold.[141]

A higher political profile offered greater possibilities of arrest. By the second half of November the Punjab police had jailed 15,756, including many of the top Ahrar leaders.[142] Thousands more were arrested in Jammu and Kashmir. Stories about the jail authorities ill-treating prisoners from the lower classes generated considerable sympathy for the Ahrars at a time when they were looking for a face-saving device to call off the agitation. After harvesting operations in the Punjab were over, the 'rural classes' began replacing the 'bobtail of the towns' in substantial numbers, lending 'surprising virility' to the campaign. A succession of Deobandi *maulvis* arrived from Delhi and UP as replacements for the incarcerated Punjabi leaders.[143] Just when they least expected it, popular trends were favouring the Ahrars as the party of the poor pitted against the rich and well-connected All-India Kashmir Committee. In the centre of the Ahrar agitation in Sialkot, women wearing red *dupattas* and

[140]*Zamindar*, Lahore, 26 September 1931, *RNPP*, 26 September 1931, p. 925.
[141]*SPPAI*, 7 November 1931, vol. liii, no. 43, pp. 625–6.
[142]*SPPAI*, 14 November 1931, vol. liii, no. 44, pp. 637–8.
[143]*SPPAI*, 21 November 1931, vol. liii, no. 45, pp. 645–6.

shirts were feeding volunteers and boosting their morale in 'unprecedented numbers'.[144]

By December two influential *pirs* of Alipur and Multan as well as many occupational *pahalwans* or wrestlers had clambered on board the Ahrar bandwagon. Growing support for the Kashmir agitation outside the Punjab led to the opening of Ahrar branches in Calcutta, Bombay and Nagpur. Closer to home in the NWFP, the Khudai Khidmatgars or Red Shirts under Abdul Ghaffar Khan were reportedly considering joining forces with the Ahrars. The Jamiat-ul-Ulema-i-Hind factions in Kanpur and Delhi also threw their weight behind the Ahrars and there were unconfirmed rumours of the venerable Abul Kalam Azad planning to lead a *jatha* into Kashmir from Bengal. Certain of Gandhi reviving the civil disobedience campaign, Ataullah Shah Bukhari threatened to boycott foreign cloth unless the government changed its policy. In a fresh departure, Ahrar propagandists now insisted that their movement was not 'communal'. But 'if the Hindus want[ed] perfect unity' they would have to 'help the Muslims' whose 'assistance' was crucial for the success of the civil disobedience movement.[145]

This was a bait Congress could ill-afford to resist. It had been dismayed by Jawaharlal Nehru's opinion that the 'work of the Congress in the Punjab was a disgrace to the rest of India'.[146] It was of course one thing to lure the Ahrars back into the Congress corral and quite another to reckon with the bickerings within. Far from being an optimistic development, the formation of a Congress Ahrar Party by Zafar Ali Khan and his coterie served to further mar the prospects of organizational unity. The new formation was the old district Congress Committee over which Zafar Ali gained control by 'out-manoeuvring the Hindus'. Booked for the non-payment of income tax and his paper proscribed, this was Zafar Ali's response to the Punjab government's efforts to spike the Ahrar guns. Without Hindu backing, a Congress and Ahrar alliance added to precious little. In any case, the provincial working committee of the Congress was on the verge of suspending all connections with 'communal bodies' like the Arya Swarajya Sabha and the Ahrars.[147] This set the pattern for the future. Individuals holding dual, even multiple, affiliations kept informal lines open with organizations espousing creeds that were in such obvious conflict as to make any sort of overt association palpably embarrassing.

The story of the Congress's unofficial support of Ahrars in the Punjab for the most part has been kept under wraps. Needing something of a base among Muslims in the province, the Ahrars were an obvious choice. Azad had gilded

[144]*SPPAI*, 28 November 1931, vol. liii, no. 46, p. 656 and Mirza, *Karavan-i-Ahrar*, i, p. 228.

[145]*SPPAI*, 5, 12 and 19 December, nos.47, 48, 49, pp. 677, 687, 701.

[146]*SPPAI*, 3 October 1931, vol. liii, no. 39, p. 582.

[147]*SPPAI*, 5, 12 and 19 December 1931, vol. liii, nos. 47, 48 and 49, pp. 685, 691 and 697.

the lily once communitarian and regional interests combined to alienate many *khilafatists* from the Congress. It was an astute move. Class oppositions among Punjabi Muslims could only grow in a political system geared to rewarding affluence and loyalty, qualifications not at the disposal of a party drawn mainly from the lower- to middle-class urban strata. While eager to capitalize on Ahrar successes in the informal arenas, the Congress was careful not to sully its credentials by coming too close to a camp capable of astounding displays of bigotry. This did not ruffle the Ahrars unduly. Having survived the ignominy of being bested by the Ahmadis in the contest for Kashmir, the Ahrars were not prepared to be dictated to by others. By January 1932 they felt confident enough with their organization in Jammu and Kashmir to start a movement for non-payment of taxes in Mirpur and Poonch. After Sheikh Abdullah's formal dissociation with the civil disobedience campaign, the Ahrars charged him for being on the payroll of the Kashmir Committee and, more damagingly, a henchman of the Ahmadis. Refuting the accusations as plainly sinister, the Kashmiri leader maintained that he was proud of being a member of a non-sectarian organization devoted to the welfare of the persecuted.[148] These disclaimers did nothing to mollify the Ahrars, even as Abdullah's stature rose after he was jailed for an additional six months by the Dogra administration.[149]

Facing stiff opposition in Kashmir, pro-Ahrar newspapers in the Punjab, including their newly launched mouthpiece *Ahrar*, spun elaborate yarns of Ahmadi and British intrigues in collusion with the Maharaja. According to their official historian, the 'bigotry of Kashmiriyat' and greed for Ahmadi money deterred those at the helm of the popular movement in Jammu and Kashmir from allying with the Ahrars. Abdullah's key associates were alleged to be avid followers of Mirza Ghulam Ahmad. The father of Choudhury Ghulam Abbas, the man in control of affairs in Jammu, was identified as a member of the Lahori group of Ahmadis while Maulana Muhammad Yusuf, the Mir Waz of Kashmir, had been told that he would face the fury of the Maharaja by joining the Ahrars.[150] Further proof of the Ahmadi stranglehold in the state was said to be the presence of Khwajah Jamaluddin, the inspector of the department of education and the brother of Khwajah Kamaluddin of the Lahori party of Ahmadis.[151] Despite this, the non-Ahmadi members of the All-India Kashmir Committee continued working under the direction of Bashiruddin Mahmud. Expecting the Maharaja to meet them half way once the Glancy Commission had completed its report, they chose to ignore the Ahrars. By the time Maharaja

---

[148]See Sheikh Muhammad Abdullah, *Flames of the Chinar: An Autobiography*, translated from the Urdu by Khushwant Singh, New Delhi: Viking, 1993, chapter five.

[149]Mirza, *Karavan-i-Ahrar*, i, pp. 250–2, 255.

[150]Ibid., pp. 189–90, 278.

[151]Ibid., p. 178.

Hari Singh agreed to accept the recommendations of the reform commission and confer certain rights on his subjects, 34,000 Ahrar volunteers had filled the jails in Punjab as well as Jammu and Kashmir.[152]

An indication that the Ahrar effort had been in vain was the categorical rejection of their demand for a responsible legislature. The Maharaja's Muslim subjects were instead granted religious freedom, including the right to give the call to prayer. Certain key shrines were placed under Muslim control. Some of the properties forcibly confiscated by the state were restored to the original owners. Educational improvements were promised with a view to increasing literacy rates among Muslims. The state also undertook to appoint Muslim teachers and officials in the department of education. Recruitment to the government services was to be proportional to the population. Some tax relief was offered and an oppressive agricultural levy, *laghan*, reduced from 50 per cent to 5 per cent. For the first time in history of Kashmir, the state agreed to confer land rights on the actual cultivators. On the political front, the Maharaja's subjects could look forward to forming parties and bringing out newspapers according to the provisions of the press act operative in British India.[153]

It was in the face of these newly won rights that on 23 October 1932 the Muslim Conference was established with Sheikh Abdullah as president and Choudhury Ghulam Abbas as general secretary. Denied credit for their part in forcing the Maharaja's hand, the Ahrars took serious note of Abdullah's visit to Amritsar where he stayed with a prominent Ahmadi family. This confirmed Ahrar suspicions of a concerted Ahmadi plot to keep them out of the running. Graduating from the political margins of the Punjab to the inner fringes of Jammu and Kashmir, the Ahrars had in September 1932 signalled their future plans by forming the All-India Majlis-i-Ahrar. The meeting resolved to focus on the social and economic problems of Muslims in British and princely India. This was an advance on the mainly constitutional concerns of the All-India Muslim Conference and the virtually moribund All-India Muslim League, though not an altogether surprising one. The limited space available to the Ahrars within the formal structures of the raj left them with no real option except to take the path of agitation in the name of defending poor and underprivileged Muslims. MacDonald's Communal Award in October 1932, preserving separate electorates and giving Punjabi Muslims two seats more than other communities, restricted the franchise to the moneyed classes, landlords in particular. If the Ahrars intended to be the vanguard of movements to wrest rights for the Muslim dispossessed, especially in states under Hindu rulers, their prospects in the Punjab depended on campaigning against the Aryas and the Ahmadis.

[152]Ibid., p. 277.
[153]Cited in ibid., p. 268 and Majid, *Iqbal aur Ahmadiyat*, pp. 455–6.

A marriage of ostensibly progressive agitations with blatantly bigoted and sectarian ones could only be a stormy one. Unable to resolve their internal dilemmas, the Ahrars turned to flushing out those they disapproved of in the Muslim community. Fazl-i-Husain was first to come under attack for recommending a learned and capable Ahmadi, Choudhury Zafrullah Khan, as his temporary replacement on the viceroy's executive council. Sections of the Punjab press led by the *Zamindar* and others in the Ahrar mould accused the Unionist leader for patronizing Ahmadi infidels over true Muslims like Muhammad Iqbal. The poet and philosopher himself refrained from making a public comment, though he was evidently disappointed at being passed over for the highest office an Indian could occupy in the colonial system. Sensing their moment, the Ahrar leaders Choudhury Afzal Haq and Ataullah Shah Bukhari held a series of meetings with Iqbal and urged him to ditch Bashiruddin who was allegedly using his leadership of the Kashmir Committee to bring Kashmiri Muslims into the Ahmadi fold. Bukhari, whom Iqbal respectfully referred to as 'Pirji' or spiritual mentor, chided him for supporting Ahmadi infidels and endangering the future of Islam not only in Kashmir but the whole of India. This did the trick. Iqbal obediently agreed to let the Ahrars assume direction of the Kashmir agitation.[154]

On 4 May 1933 the *Civil and Military Gazette* reported that some members of the All-India Kashmir Committee wanted a non-Ahmadi as its president.[155] Three days later at an emergency meeting, Bashiruddin was forced to step down and Iqbal was elected as temporary president of the Kashmir Committee. The move was condemned by all the prominent leaders of Kashmir, including Sheikh Abdullah, Ghulam Abbas and Bakshi Ghulam Mohammad, who implored the deposed *khalifa* of Qadian to continue working for their cause.[156] In the Punjab itself, few were convinced of Iqbal's ability to carry Bashiruddin's mantle. The editors of the *Inqilab* and *Siyasat* regretted the change while the Unionist leader Ahmad Yar Daultana remarked that Iqbal had never got things done in the past and would not be able to do so now.[157] They had a point. Iqbal was at the beck and call of the Ahrars. On 18 June 1933 at the very first meeting of the Kashmir Committee under his presidentship, Iqbal startled everyone by resigning, alleging that its Ahmadi members were willing to accept the authority only of their own *khalifa*. He instead called upon India's seven crore Muslims to form a new Kashmir Committee whose membership would not be open to Ahmadis.[158] The committee was dismantled soon afterwards.

Iqbal's first and final fling with sectarianism was described by the *Inqilab*

---

[154]Ejaz Ahmad, *Mazloom Iqbal: Chand Yadeen, Chand Tasarat*, Karachi, 1985, pp. 202–3.

[155]Ibid., p. 203.

[156]For Abdullah's reaction, see his *Flames of the Chinar*, p. 32.

[157]Majid, *Iqbal aur Ahmadiyat*, pp. 444–6.

[158]Ibid., pp. 450–4, 456–62.

as a 'very big *fitna*'.[159] Instead of projecting a Muslim whole through expansion and inclusion, a frustrated and politically ambitious band of men were pushing for the more dangerous course of deeming exclusion a precondition for self-preservation. The demand to eject the Ahmadis from the Muslim community had been simmering on the backburners of Punjabi politics for decades. It was brought to a boil by the Ahrars seeking to avenge their failure to outshine everyone else in the contest to incorporate Kashmir into a larger Muslim whole. The paradox of enlarging the Muslim political universe through a process of exclusion has been attributed to their irreconcilable doctrinal differences with the Ahmadis. Yet Mirza Ghulam Ahmad's followers had been practising and preaching their creed for nearly half a century before anyone sensed the urgency of declaring them non-Muslims.

The spectacle of an ideologically disparate intermediary strata rallying behind the Ahrars to ostracize a sect that identified with the community of Islam is inexplicable without reference to the class antagonisms in Punjabi Muslim society. These assumed an altogether new dimension once the implications of the new constitutional reforms were signposted by the Communal Award. While creating the conditions for Muslim dominance in the Punjab, the award perpetuated the British policy of keeping at bay those vocal urban segments which, apart from playing a leading part in fashioning the narratives of communitarian identity, tended to be in the forefront of anti-colonial movements. Unable to effectively challenge the colonial state so long as the collaborative systems remained intact, these urban groups needed some way of expressing their grievances without exploding the myth of communitarian interests. Raising the specter of a handful of relatively more educated and better-off Ahmadis securing jobs in government and representation in the electoral bodies was one way of getting heard, even if it did not assure greater opportunities for advancement.

It was this strained logic which allowed the Ahrars to prevail upon Muhammad Iqbal to take the momentous step of calling for the exclusion of the Ahmadis from the Muslim community. No ordinary feat, it was not accomplished without significant psychological pressure. For someone who execrated the orthodox for their bigotry, Iqbal's somersault on the Ahmadi issue has been the subject of much partisan controversy. Some have argued that he was an ardent admirer, if not a disciple, of Mirza Ghulam Ahmad. Others more mischievous have insinuated that following the family tradition, Iqbal adopted the Ahmadi creed which explains his positive estimation of their contributions to the Muslim community. His son and official biographer has categorically denied Iqbal's associations with the Ahmadis.[160] While underscoring the delicate nature of the issue for Muslim self-projections, this rash of charge and counter-charge fails to do justice to

[159]Cited in ibid., p. 461.
[160]Javed Iqbal, *Zinda Rawad*, vol. iii, Lahore: Iqbal Academy, 1984, chapter twenty.

the changing historical context which prompted Iqbal to extol and then denounce the Ahmadis.

Prior to 1935 Iqbal considered the Ahmadis a sect within Islam and once described Mirza Ghulam Ahmad as 'probably the profoundest theologian among modern Indian Muhammadans'.[161] In 1911 he declared the Ahmadis to be the perfect exemplars of the Islamic *sunnah*. Iqbal even sent his eldest son, Aftab, to a school in Qadian to acquire religious training.[162] Although he himself never converted, Iqbal's paternal uncle and a cousin to whom he was especially close were fervent Ahmadis. An indication that his links with the Ahmadis were not coincidental was the favourable opinion he held of the sect's role in propagating Islam to non-Muslims.[163] Despite strident Ahrar propaganda that the Ahmadis were using the All-India Kashmir Committee to multiply their numbers in Kashmir, Iqbal did not withdraw support for Bashiruddin. And with good reason. In 1931–2, when the Ahmadis were accused of furtively proselytizing in Kashmir, a mere sixty-seven Muslims in the state were actually reported to have entered the Ahmadi fold.[164]

What then were the reasons for Iqbal's sudden change of heart? There have been various theories, ranging from the pedestrian to the sublime. The guardians of Muslim orthodoxy and Ahrar sympathizers consider Iqbal's volte face as the falling into line of a prodigal son whose escapades into religion had most often been misguided. Those occupying the middle ground are inclined to view the turnabout as a tragic conclusion to a brilliant career when declining health got the better of an otherwise thoughtful individual's judgement. Ahmadi writers have charged the Ahrars of playing the Congress's game in the Punjab and Kashmir, disrupting Muslim unity and bamboozling an otherwise well-meaning Iqbal. They have also stressed Iqbal's personal disappointment at being overlooked in favour of Zafrullah Khan as Fazl-i-Husain's replacement on the viceroy's executive council.[165] The viceregal decision was not finalized until October 1934 by which time Iqbal had joined forces with the Ahrars to excommunicate the Ahmadis from his ill-fated All-India Kashmir Committee. What cannot be denied, however, is that Iqbal's attacks on the Ahmadis as the bane of the Muslim community acquired an uncharacteristic stridency once Zafrullah formally took his seat on the viceroy's council. It may be more prudent to give credence to Iqbal's own analysis of the issue to cull out the reasons that propelled him to take a stand alongside the bigoted Muslims he consistently harangued and humoured in his poetry.

In a series of articles written during and after the summer of 1935, Iqbal

---

[161]This was stated by Iqbal in an article which appeared in the *Indian Antiquary*, Bombay, vol. 29, 1900, p. 246, cited in Ahmad, *Mazloom Iqbal*, p. 195.

[162]Ibid., p. 196.

[163]Ibid., pp. 196–8.

[164]Majid, *Iqbal aur Ahmadiyat*, p. 434.

[165]See ibid., pp. 344, 346 and Ahmad, *Mazloom Iqbal*, pp. 206–8.

deployed theological and political arguments to justify expelling the Ahmadis from the Indian Muslim community. As he confessed in a letter to Jawaharlal Nehru: 'I myself have little interest in theology, but had to dabble in it a bit in order to meet the Ahmadis on their ground.'[166] This suggests that Iqbal allowed himself to be guided by those he regarded as more proficient in theological matters. Whatever his private assessment of Ataullah Shah Bukhari's and Zafar Ali Khan's theological knowledge, Iqbal had the highest respect for the religious scholar Maulana Syed Muhammad Anwar Kashmiri. A firm believer in the *khatma-i-nubaut*, or the finality of prophethood in Islam, Kashmiri avoided all social contact with Ahmadis. After the formation of the Kashmir Committee in 1931, the *maulana* refused to visit Iqbal's home because of his association with Ahmadi heretics.[167] Such a stringent form of social censure could hardly have failed to affect Iqbal, susceptible as he was to the charge of harbouring pro-Ahmadi sentiments.

Staged controversies have a way of foisting the stamp of partisanship on ordinary bystanders. And Iqbal was in the thick of the dispute over the leadership of the Kashmir Committee. Using received theological arguments to defend his political decision to oust the Ahmadis may not have been characteristic of Iqbal the individual. But speaking on behalf of the community required compromises, even if that entailed contradicting earlier positions and undermining personal convictions. Iqbal had 'no hesitation admitting' that his views on the Ahmadis had undergone a dramatic change. A quarter of a century ago he had 'hopes of good results following from this movement'. He became 'suspicious' upon discovering that the Ahmadis were not merely proclaiming their founder as a prophet, but conferring upon him a status 'superior even to the Prophethood of the Founder of Islam' and reproving Muslims as *kafirs*. These doubts made for 'positive revolt' when he heard an unnamed Ahmadi deriding the Prophet of Islam. A 'living and thinking man' had the 'privilege of contradicting himself'.[168]

This could not be said of a living religion like Islam whose outer parameters were perfectly defined and eternal. It was the belief in the finality of Muhammad's prophethood which distinguished a Muslim from a non-Muslim.[169] While there was 'freedom of interpretation' in Islam, there could be no disputing this fact. Islam gave wide berth to differences of opinion which 'far from working as a disruptive force' had 'actually given an impetus to synthetic theological thought'. Historically doctrinal differences in Islam were no more than 'heresy below heresy'. Indeed the idea of heresy, in the sense of turning anyone out of the fold, was alien to the 'conceptual structure

[166]Iqbal to Nehru, 21 June 1936 in Nehru, *A Bunch of Old Letters*, pp. 187–8.
[167]Mirza, *Karavan-i-Ahrar*, i, pp. 346–7.
[168]Iqbal's rejoinder to the *Light*, Qadian, in Sherwani (ed.), *Speeches, Writings and Statements of Iqbal*, pp. 168–9.
[169]Iqbal's letter to *The Statesman*, 10 June 1935, ibid., p. 172.

of Islam'. It was unfortunate that the *mullahs* through sheer 'intellectual laziness' regularly condemned their theological opponents as *kafirs*.[170] Iqbal sneered at the Ahmadi notion of Mirza Ghulam Ahmad being a *buruzi* prophet, or one who was like the Prophet of Islam in spiritual qualities. He did not reject the possibility as such, only objected to the insinuation that the founder of the Ahmadis was last in the line of those who could aspire to such a status. This amounted to saying that Ghulam Ahmad and not Muhammad was the last of the prophets.[171] Such blasphemous thinking would destroy the Muslim community in India and encourage other 'religious adventurers' to press their claims. The only safe option was to place the Ahmadis outside the pale of Islam. If this happened, Muslims would tolerate them like any other religious community, not work to eradicate the Ahmadis for contravening one of the principal tenets of Islam.

If abstract theology was not Iqbal's forte, his appreciation of the practical dimensions of the problem carried the impress of urban middle-class Muslim politics in the Punjab with greater conviction. In his opinion, the future of the Ahmadis was not merely a religious question but of the highest political importance for Punjabi Muslims. The British had to 'understand the mentality of the average Muslim' on a matter that was 'absolutely vital to the integrity of the community'. Invoking the doctrine of modern liberalism may be consistent with the colonial policy of non-interference in religion, but the policy was eating into the roots of Muslim unity in the Punjab. By promoting 'ambitious political adventurers' and perpetuating the invidious distinction between rural and urban Muslims, the British had 'crushed all hope of a real leader appearing in the province'.[172] Iqbal was alluding to the common charge that the Ahmadi doctrine provided 'a revelational basis' for abject surrender to colonial rule.[173] No Muslim true to his faith could accept such a dastardly proposition. Moreover, the Ahmadis could not insulate themselves from other Muslims and expect to remain within the community. They not only avoided saying congregational prayers with other Muslims, but refused to intermarry with them. It did not take 'any special intelligence' to see why despite their ritual and social boycott of Muslims the Ahmadis were so 'anxious to remain politically within the fold of Islam'. A mere 56,000, they could not qualify for a single seat in the provincial legislature or secure jobs in government as a separate political community. Muslims were 'perfectly justified' in calling for 'the immediate separation' of the Ahmadis who were being used to 'effectively damage the already marginal majority of Punjab Muslims in the local legislature'. After

[170]Muhammad Iqbal, 'Islam and Ahmadism' (originally published in *Islam*, 22 January 1936), ibid., pp. 180–2.
[171]Ibid., p. 183.
[172]Iqbal, 'Qadianism and Orthodox Muslims', ibid., pp. 164–6.
[173]Iqbal, 'Islam and Ahmadism', ibid., p. 187.

all, in 1919 the British had not waited for the Sikhs to make a formal request to separate from the Hindu community.[174]

When it came to the crunch, the politics of class rather than purely doctrinal differences swayed Iqbal into throwing his weight behind the Ahrar demand for expelling the Ahmadis. For a man projecting the idea of a Muslim state in the northwest of India, the illustrious Allama dodged the problems which an exclusionary definition of Muslim identity could pose for the related notions of sovereignty and citizenship. Locked in grim battle with other religious communities for power and privilege, Muslims in the Punjab had begun extending their political horizons into neighbouring regions. But the quest for a larger communitarian 'whole' had accentuated class differences at the regional level once it came to calculating the practical implications of the new constitutional reforms. Instead of an inclusionary and expansive communitarian vision with which to challenge the claims of majoritarian nationalism, Iqbal had ended up championing the exclusion of an existing part from a yet-to-be constructed Muslim 'whole'. This may have been consistent with the hope of enabling a few urban middle-class Punjabis to better their chances against a small but influential sect in securing access to government employment and public office. It was a strange logic to apply in the great numbers game where addition and not subtraction seemed to be the Muslim community's best guarantee to claiming a substantial role on both the regional and the all-India stage. In the event, the proposed formula failed to win a hearing from the colonial masters. With its flaws untested, it merely served to set a dangerous precedent by which different Muslim sects could try and discredit, if not actually oust, their rivals in order to gain the upper hand in the affairs of the community. Heartened by Iqbal's endorsement of their mathematical innovation, the Ahrars bided time until the moment was right to wage a holy war in Lucknow against Shias, who in refusing to accord the first three *khalifas* of Islam the same respect as they did to Ali, deeply offended Sunni sensibilities.

So the search for a Muslim 'whole' heightened internal contestations among the different parts along class, sectarian, regional and ideological lines. Basing Islam's much-vaunted unity in difference on the logic of internal exclusion was a novel invention for which Punjab's urban middle-class leadership can rightfully claim credit. Their foremost strategist had a point when he argued that the false separation of religion and politics advocated by idealistic nationalism would annihilate cultural difference. Not drawing any distinction between the two, as he had also implied, could mean succumbing to the bigotry of *mullahism* so as to make nonsense of not just individual but also collective faith. Islam rejected the separation of religion and politics at the level of ideas— there was no metaphysical dualism of spirit and matter as in Christianity—but acknowledged the division as necessary for the practical functioning of the

[174]Iqbal's letter to *The Statesman*, 10 June 1935, ibid., p. 173.

state.[175] Subtle distinctions between metaphysical propositions and practical requirements could be easily blurred as Iqbal's dallying with religious theology for political effect had made all too plain. With the first elections under the Government of India Act of 1935 in the offing, the time for metaphysical discourses on Muslim identity was running out.

THE TOSS-UP FOR THE CENTRE AND COMMUNAL-NATIONALISM IN THE REGION

The Communal Award of 1932 was condemned by the Hindu Mahasabha and the Congress in unison. Gandhi's heroic fast saved the day, momentarily weakening Ambedkar's resolve to take the depressed castes out of the Hindu community.[176] The Poona Pact, safeguarding the principle of a Hindu majority against the sub-denominations of caste, was a triumph for Congress's inclusionary nationalism. But nothing could mollify the Mahasabha, diluting hopes of the new constitution ushering in a fresh phase in Indian politics. It was a missed opportunity since, barring a few voices in the political wilderness, Indian Muslims generally welcomed the award. Separate electorates had been retained. Muslims in the Punjab and Bengal were denied outright statutory majorities but given more seats in the provincial legislature than any other community. With provincial autonomy just round the corner, the likelihood of Sind separating from Bombay and the extension of reforms in the NWFP, the Muslim position in the northwest of India had never been better. But the regional consolidation of Muslim power—the ultimate 'communal' fantasy—was the nationalist nightmare unless a way could be found to align it with Congress's purposes at the all-India centre.

The containment of 'communalism', however defined, was imperative if the nationalists were to wrest power at British India's unitary centre. The 'communalism' which the Congress chose to contest was that of the Muslims, who mostly deplored its conception of a liberal and secular nationalism. By conceding separate electorates as a necessary evil, Gandhi had ducked a bouncer, not secured his own or the Congress's innings. Perpetuating the political distinction between Muslims and non-Muslims at the level of electoral representation without modifying the ideal of a singular homogenizing nationalism could create greater difficulties when it came to finally sketching the political map of India. To be fair, the Mahatma was only acknowledging

[175]Iqbal, 'Islam and Ahmadism', ibid., p. 195.

[176]By October 1935 Ambedkar was urging the scheduled castes to convert to another religion. This excited the Majlis-i-Ahrar's hopes of bringing an estimated fourteen to fifteen lakh scheduled castes in the Punjab into the Islamic fold. (Mirza, *Karavan-i-Ahrar*, i, p. 280.) Villagers in the main, these outcastes of Hinduism would more than make up the difference in numbers caused by the exclusion of the Ahmadis.

a consistent demand in Muslim communitarian narratives and politics. Even Muslims prepared to countenance joint electorates insisted on the prior granting of universal adult franchise.[177]

An electorate enlarged to no more than thirty-five million in a population of nearly four hundred million was a very restricted one indeed. The tilt towards Britain's loyal allies in the rural areas had left urban groups to rue their paltry numbers. Most did by turning the census into a political primer. Muhammad Iqbal's curious entanglement with the Ahrars cannot be fathomed without accounting for the individual and collective frustrations of the urban Muslim middle strata, denuded as they had been of any real influence in the formal arenas of politics. Punjab's version of communal–nationalism may have been unique among the Indian regions. But it offers a harvest of insights into the depths of communitarian bigotry which liberal democratic nationalism tried and failed so miserably to check.

Punjab's Political Breakdown: Progressive Bigots Versus Reactionary Liberals

The Punjab in the second half of the 1930s might be likened to a three-dimensional jigsaw puzzle of exasperating complexity. Making sense of the jumbled mosaic by invoking the teleology of partition and focusing on the formal arenas of politics has highlighted certain aspects and distorted or omitted others. Recognizing the ambiguous relationship of the different pieces to one another as well as the all-India whole permits a closer approximation of the regional political landscape. An enigma at the best of times, Punjab on the eve of full provincial autonomy was perilously adrift, subverting as ever the distinction between 'communalism' and 'nationalism' and in the process defining its own notions of a 'progressive' and a 'reactionary' politics.

A vital component of the British covenant, the province had one of the most stable networks of control and collaboration anywhere in colonial India. But the very reliability of its formal structures made the informal arenas of the Punjab that much more prone to bizarre and, occasionally, explosive political mixtures. The politics of consistency, if not principle, was restricted to the privileged few awarded the Unionist badge. For the rest it was primarily a free for all, depending on which flag and political canon temporarily offered

---

[177]The Shia Conference's decision to plump for joint electorates was a political gambit which failed. It merely drew attention to the sect's determination to remain apart from the rest of Muslim India. Support among Sunni Muslims for the Ahrars' *Madha-i-Sahaba* (literally praise of the Prophet's companions) agitation against the Shias of Lucknow was a reaction to this tendency. Offended by the alleged defamation of the first three *khalifas* of Islam by the Shias, Sunni Muslims in Punjab joined their opposite numbers in Lucknow to recite public praises of the first four *khalifas* of Islam. The agitation began in July 1936 and continued sporadically until April 1941. (For details, see Mirza, *Karavan-e-Ahrar*, ii, pp. 412–15, 460–3; iii, pp. 122–5; v, p. 54.)

the quickest rewards. His Unionist credentials conferred and denied in rapid succession, Iqbal had buckled under pressure to support the Ahrars peddling an interesting amalgam of goods. In a forewarning of things to come, these middle-class Muslims covering a cross-section of educated and commercial groups had taken out the skeletons from the communitarian closet in a dramatic campaign of hatred against the Ahmadis. There is no comfort in conceding that the anti-Ahmadi virus had spread more deeply and widely among those whom Iqbal had consigned to the category of 'orthodox'.

A pamphlet, *Char Ahamm Masail Par Tabsirah*, or a commentary on four important issues, written by a woman, lays bare the fascinating juxtaposition of 'progressive' and 'bigoted' opinions.[178] The tract rails against the press for spreading a thick web of lies.[179] The centres of journalism resembled shops selling fraudulent goods varnished with gold water. Newspapers might pretend to be concerned with religious causes. But like the political leaders, their main objective was personal interest and money making, not the welfare of the *qaum* or religion. Cow slaughter was a glaring example. If Hindus were truly beholden to the holy cow, they ought to cease trading in leather goods and dispense with their shoes, saddles and suitcases. Genuine faith demanded erecting shelter houses where cows would be well fed and looked after. Only by treating the cow with utmost respect could Hindus force Muslims to give up a right decreed by Allah. If defending the rights of the cow disguised implicit biases, there was no such restraint when it came to the internal others of Islam. The pamphlet ferociously attacked Ahmadis and called for their total social boycott. Faced with ostracization, people would think twice before professing such an offensive creed and the sect would go into decline. Showing her sense of realism, the author derided Muslims for wanting Congress to incorporate Quranic law into the future Indian constitution. Without practising what they preached, Muslims could not expect others to accept their laws as natural, far less consistent with the objectives of the Congress.[180]

This bald critique of the press, politicians and politics as well as religious attitudes is only one example of progressive thinking overlapping with flashes of communitarian bigotry. That the Ahmadis had offended Muslim sensibilities by their enthusiasm for Mirza Ghulam Ahmad cannot be denied. As Iqbal once regretted, few had cared to understand the phenomenon in its psycho-historical dimensions. Least of all the Ahrars who won the top prize for ingenuity in blending 'progressive' thought with bigotry hands down.

[178]*Char Ahamm Masail Par Tabsirah*, no authors name. Lahore, 1936, PIB. 145, IOL. On p. 15 it becomes apparent that the author is a Muslim woman.

[179]On 9 August 1935 the Ahrars started their own paper, *Mujahid*, to counteract the *Zamindar*'s defamatory pieces against them. According to their official historian, 'if the *Zamindar* published one lie the *Mujahid* made up four lies for publication'. (Mirza, *Karavan-i-Ahrar*, i, p. 259.)

[180]*Char Ahamm Masail Par Tabsirah*, PIB. 145, IOL.

Confirmed anti-imperialists, they had since their formation in 1929 remained loosely linked to the Congress even while taking up causes which smacked of social conservatism and bigotry. It was the Ahrars who first thought of agitating against a film which they believed undermined Islamic morality.[181] They were also the sworn enemies of the Arya Samaj, the suspected hand behind incidents involving the denigration of the Prophet of Islam. Murderers of Hindus charged with irreverence to the Prophet were glorified by the Ahrars as *ghazis*.

At the same time they took great pride in providing the only real opposition to 'reactionary' Muslim toadies huddled under the Unionist umbrella. Their efforts bore fruit in August 1933 when Choudhury Afzal Haq won a by-election to the Punjab assembly from the Muslim rural constituency of Ludhiana and Hoshiarpur. By early 1934 there were two other Ahrar members in the provincial legislature, including Mazhar Ali Azhar. Buoyed by these electoral successes, the Ahrars decided to take on the Ahmadis in their own stronghold in Qadian. The Ahrar–Ahmadi stand-off in this remote town had wider repercussions. On 29 August 1934, Habibur Rahman, then president of the Majlis-i-Ahrar, formally demanded the removal of Zafrullah Khan from the viceroy's council on the grounds that he was a *kafir*.[182] In October 1934 the Ahrar conference in Qadian was graced by religious luminaries like Maulana Husain Ahmad Madani of Deoband and Mufti Kifatullah of Delhi. It was here that Zafar Ali Khan moved a resolution calling for the exclusion of Ahmadis in all future head counts of the Muslim community.[183] By January 1936, the Ahrars were urging all Muslim organizations to expel their Ahmadi members.[184]

This was the unseemly scenario which confronted Mohammed Ali Jinnah after he had failed to make any headway with Fazl-i-Husain on an electoral understanding between the Unionists and the newly revived All-India Muslim League. Total rejection by a province which along with Bengal held the key to the future balance of power at the all-India centre was not something Jinnah could countenance. 'I shall never come to the Punjab again,' he had quipped, 'it is such a hopeless place.'[185] Since it could not be left out of his political calculations, he turned to Muslims who were sworn enemies of the Unionists. This promised him a mixed crop of fruits, one more sour than the other. The reasons are not surprising considering the political tendencies among Punjabi Muslims on the outer margins of the colonial structures of patronage and support. Dependent on the British, the *pirs* and landlords of the Punjab were not men who could electrify literate Muslims in the urban areas.

[181]Mirza, *Karavan-i-Ahrar*, i, p. 352.

[182]Mirza, *Karavan-i-Ahrar*, ii, p. 61.

[183]Ibid., p. 87.

[184]Ibid., p. 328.

[185]Jinnah on leaving the Punjab after a humiliating attempt at putting together a Muslim League parliamentary board in the province. (Cited in Azim Husain, *Fazl-i-Husain: A Political Biography*, Bombay: Longmans, Green & Co. Ltd, 1946, p. 311.)

No one of course put it better than Iqbal. He once asked why the homes of the supposed spiritual leaders of the Punjab were better lit than his. In a different vein he told the inhabitants of the Punjab that though the fire in them had been buried in dust for thousands of years, the call to prayer now had been given. It was time to awaken.[186] In a poem dedicated to the *pirs* of the Punjab, Iqbal lauded the courage of those individuals who refused to bow their heads before the emperor Jahangir and whose spirit still fired the Ahrars.[187] He even hinted at the reasons the Ahrar had struck a chord with Punjabi Muslims. Temperamentally inclined to look for religious variety, they adopted one creed and passed on to another. A hunter with a trap was needed to prevent them from flying in yet new directions.[188]

An inventory of the political groupings in the Punjab makes for dizzying reading. Apart from the Ahrars who modelled themselves on the Red Shirts led by the 'Frontier Gandhi', Abdul Ghaffar Khan, a new paramilitary organization had appeared in the form of the spade-carrying Khaksars. In the thinking and activities of their leader, Khan Inayatullah Khan 'Mashriqi', one finds an uncanny brew of undoubtable genius and eccentric determination.[189] In a healthy corrective to the Ahrars, though still in imitation of the Red Shirts in the Frontier, the Khaksars aimed at performing social service through the organization of all Muslims, irrespective of sect. Despite its 'thinly disguised' anti-communal stance, 'Inayatullah Khan's own political opinions [we]re decidedly anti-Congress'. He wanted the 'coalescence of the Muslims lest they should be totally annihilated from India as they were in Spain'. Mashriqi was interested in 'securing control of petty trade by opening Muslim shops in the villages'.[190]

If Mashriqi was too idiosyncratic for Jinnah's liking, lesser known outfits like the Fidayan-i-Islam and the Khuddam-ul-Islam with their localized and socially disruptive anti-Hindu activities were too hot for the constitutionalist to handle. This left the Ahrars and Zafar Ali Khan's Ittihad-i-Millat, a one-man show which had come to the limelight in the dispute between Muslims and Sikhs over the Shahidganj mosque.[191] With help from Iqbal, Jinnah solicited Ahrar support to set up a Muslim League parliamentary board in the Punjab.

[186]Iqbal, 'Punjab ke Dahekan Saay', *Bal-i-Jabrial*, in *Kulliyat-i-Iqbal*, p. 128.

[187]Iqbal, 'Punjab ke Pirzadaon Saay', *Bal-i-Jabrial*, ibid., p. 134.

[188]Iqbal, 'Punjabi Musalman', *Zarb-i-Kaleem*, ibid., pp. 58–9.

[189]This is not to deny Mashriqi's many qualities. His tactics are discussed in the next chapter. For a highly complimentary view of the Khaksar leader, see Syed Shabbir Hussain, *Al-Mashriqi: The Disowned Genius*, Lahore: Jang Publishers, 1991.

[190]*SPPAI*, 17 October 1931, vol. liii, no. 40, p. 593.

[191]The mosque had been built in the seventeenth century by Muhammad Abdullah, an employee in Dara Shikoh's kitchen. It had been taken over by the Sikhs under Ranjit Singh and turned into a *gurdwara*. Muslims had been demanding the return of the mosque for some time.

But in August 1936 the Ahrars officially broke with the League's parliamentary board. The ostensible reason was their refusal to pay the stipulated sum of money to cover election expenses. But the more controversial demand, and one Jinnah wisely resisted, was that provincial assembly candidates taking the League oath should vow to expel the Ahmadis from the Muslim community.[192]

A courageous stand to have taken, it reflects Jinnah's understanding of constitutional law and the imperatives of citizenship in a modern state. Exclusion in any case was not going to help Muslims keep pace with, far less win, the numbers game. Moreover, setting the standards of inclusion in a community that was utterly disjointed in the legal and the political sense amounted to suicide. If Jinnah had been a Punjabi, he might conceivably have taken a different position. That he was not made all the difference. He saw no reason to strip the Ahmadis of their Muslim identity simply on account of a doctrinal dispute. For Indian Muslims, it postponed the day of reckoning for a question that had a critical bearing on their identity and, by extension, on their ideas of sovereignty and rights of citizenship. The mood in the Punjab was turning against the Ahmadis. Not only Muslims but also Hindus and Sikhs were accusing the Ahmadis of having set up a state within a state in Qadian.

Although the Muslim League adopted the Shahidganj mosque issue, Jinnah's efforts to woo Zafar Ali Khan were unsuccessful. A Congressman, an Ahrar and, of late, a Khaksar, the editor of the *Zamindar* had a reputation for changing his parties on a daily basis. His consistent passion was hatred of British imperialism and the Ahmadis. The rancorous *maulana* and the stiff-upper-lipped man made for strange bedfellows. An extension of the *Zamindar*'s office, the Ittihad-i-Millat had few roots among those with a right to vote. A mosque turned into a Sikh *gurdwara* might stir Muslims into wanting to restore their sovereignty over religious places. It could not make two dour men like each other.

This brought the future Quaid of India's Muslims close to making a humiliating compromise with the Jamiat-ul-Ulema-i-Hind, a disparate group of divines whose worldview on most matters contradicted his own. The *ulema* were prepared to do the League's propaganda work in the Punjab from their headquarter in Deoband.[193] The disadvantage of courting the intermediary strata, as Jinnah had learnt at a cost, was that potential candidates instead of pouring resources into the party depleted its funds without winning the elections. With next to nothing in its coffers, a Muslim League relying on the

---

[192]Mirza, *Karavan-i-Ahrar*, ii, pp. 425–6. Candidates were expected to cough up Rs 500 for the privilege of the Muslim League's parliamentary board considering their applications and an additional Rs 150 on being given the ticket. This was more than the Ahrars could afford.

[193]For details, see Ashiq Hussain Batalvi, *Iqbal ke Akhari Do Saal*, Lahore: Iqbal Academy, pp. 327–8.

support of urban middle-class Muslims was a losing proposition. If this inclined Jinnah to look on the 'reactionary' landlords of the Punjab and UP more favourably, there were others better endowed and only too willing to mobilize this vocal strata to their own advantage. The Congress for one was eagerly exploring possibilities of making electoral gains against the Unionists. A fortnight of negotiations in Lucknow between Abul Kalam Azad, acting as the link between the Congress and the Jamiat-ul-Ulema-i-Hind, the Ahrar leader Habibur Rahman and the Muslim League's trouble shooter in UP, Khaliquzzaman, produced a three-cornered electoral agreement. The Congress leader Pandit Pant agreed to finance the Muslim League's candidates by paying the Jamiat-ul-Ulema-i-Hind its stated price.[194]

Even with tactical support from the Congress and the verbosity of the Deobandi *ulema*, the Muslim League came nowhere near striking distance of the Unionist castle. It did marginally better in the provinces where Muslims were in a minority, UP in particular. But with a better showing than anyone had expected, the Congress superciliously asked Jinnah to disband the Muslim League and join its ranks. Despite separate electorates, the All-India Muslim League polled a dismal 4.4 per cent of the total Muslim vote. In Bengal an electoral adjustment with the United Muslim Party gave the League a nominal title to thirty-nine members of the provincial assembly. In the Punjab assembly of 175, the Unionists seized ninety seats, seventy-six representing Muslim constituencies. Congress was restricted to twenty-nine with only two Muslim members in the assembly. The Hindu Nationalist Party won ten seats, the Ahrars and the Ittihad-i-Millat secured two apiece while the Muslim League had one lonely member, Malik Barkat Ali, heeding its call in the provincial legislature.[195]

Party labels in any case are deceptive. The Unionists' impressive showing had to do with the 'personal prestige' or 'tribal influence' of candidates who 'spent considerable sums of money'. Party organization, such as it existed, was 'unable to direct and control the course of voting to any appreciable extent'.[196] A Unionist victory had been on the cards. It was the extent of the sweep which infuriated the urban classes of all religious denominations. Reflecting the disappointment, one paper attributed the Unionist success to 'official influence' and 'the slavish mentality of the public'. With the future in the hands of 'a party known for its conservatism and reactionary attitude', there was 'no hope of the progressive parties being able to offer a strong opposition to it'.[197] The formation of a Unionist ministry gave fresh vitality to urban Punjab's political permutations and combinations. If the fallacies of the 'nationalism' versus 'communalism' dichotomy in the province have been flushed out, the distorting nature of its

[194]Mirza, *Karavan-i-Ahrar*, ii, p. 389.
[195]*SPPAI*, 20 February 1937, vol. lix, no. 8, p. 122.
[196]Ibid.
[197]*Ihsan*, Lahore, 18 February 1937, *RNPP*, 20 February 1937, p. 73.

purportedly 'progressive' and 'reactionary' politics requires more careful delineation. The Ahrars were among those who considered the Unionists to be the bulwarks of 'reaction' and their own agenda as the harbinger of 'progress'. The main item in the Ahrar gameplan was the demand that Muslim members of the Punjab legislative assembly pass an act declaring the Ahmadis a non-Muslim community. Other than exacerbate ill-will against the Ahmadis, Ahrar propagandists failed to prevent Unionist 'reactionaries' from taking a 'liberal' stance on the matter. Ironically, they had a better chance of forging an alliance with Sikh and Hindu 'nationalists', enraged by Ahmadi attempts to appropriate Guru Nanak as a Muslim. Since communitarian bigotry was not the monopoly of the Ahrar or Ahmadi Muslim, the non-Muslim counter-attack led by the Arya Samaj concentrated on proving that Mirza Ghulam Ahmad was a Hindu. There was scope here for an informal agreement between the Ahrars and the Aryas. It was just that the communitarian bigotry of the Ahrars and the Aryas was not restricted to making life difficult for the Ahmadis alone. Against this backdrop the All-India Congress Committee's decision to embark upon a Muslim mass contact movement added a new twist to the already tortured course of 'progressive' politics in the Punjab.

Communal Means for Nationalist Ends

Deeming its support base among Indian Muslims to be inadequate, the Congress at Jawaharlal Nehru's behest took the unprecedented step of trying to advance its nationalist purposes through outright communitarian mobilization. By appointing Dr Kanwar Muhammad Ashraf, a staunch communist, to co-ordinate the movement at an all-India level, Nehru showed his ideological touch more than its reach. The choice further alienated the Congress right wing under Vallabhbhai Patel who saw no reason to complicate their life by increasing the party's Muslim membership. Its left wing was equally unhappy. Through the 'political kidnapping' of Muslims, Congress was 'perpetuating the vicious principle that the approach to a particular religious unit must be through its co-religionists'.[198]

By legitimizing the very tactics it roundly condemned as 'communal', the Congress simply strengthened the forces of communal–nationalisms. Most Punjabi Muslim papers attacked the Congress initiative as a design to polarize the community. It was about time the Congress abandoned 'this mad course of action' and avoided being 'misled by the few Maulanas of the Jamiat-ul-Ulema' who because they were on its payroll 'play[ed] the tune it chooses to call'.[199] Such outright rejection was fortified by challenging Congress's assurances on the freedom of religion. This was not too difficult since Dr Ashraf, 'a Congress hireling', had the gall to assert that there was 'no such

[198]SPPAI, 12 June 1937, vol. lix, no. 23, p. 318.
[199]Light, Lahore, 24 April 1937, RNPP, 1 May 1937, p. 172.

thing as Muslim culture'.[200] The *Inqilab* took umbrage at the suggestion that all Muslim political parties should cease to exist and allow the Congress to speak on their behalf. By giving ministerial slots to its Muslim 'henchmen' and 'encouraging Hindus' instead of the stated policy of Indianization, the Congress had 'at the very outset falsified its claims that it [wa]s above communalism'. The All-India Muslim League had no option but to 'expose the communalism of the Congress'.[201]

Dismissing these arguments as evidence of Muslim 'communalism' did little to take the sting out of the charge. The provincial wing of the Congress suddenly found itself richer by Rs 30,000 to conduct propaganda among Muslims. Not prepared to let the opportunity pass them by, the Majlis-i-Ahrar's Shoba-i-Tabligh promptly decided to come to the Congress's aid while retaining its separate identity. This signified the Ahrar intention of continuing the virulent campaign against the Ahmadis while multiplying support among Muslims by waving the nationalist wand. They denied that 'Muslims had no sympathy with the Congress'. Organizations like the Red Shirts under Ghaffar Khan in the Frontier province and individuals such as Abul Kalam Azad 'bore ample testimony to the fact that the Muslims, no less than the Hindus, entertained the desire to liberate the country'. The main obstacles were the 'narrow minded policy of Mr Jinnah' and the provisions of the new constitution which had further ensconced the Unionists. But Muslims were ready and able to co-operate with any progressive elements to defeat the reactionaries.[202]

Unfortunately for them, the Ahrars were not the only 'progressives' scrambling for influence in the Punjab. Zafar Ali Khan embarrassed his old party when he 'warned the Muslims against joining the Congress'.[203] In a measure of his political strength, he forced the Congress candidate for the central assembly from the Lahore Muslim constituency to withdraw from the contest at the eleventh hour. His supporters called the Congress an appendage of the Mahasabha and the provincial boss, Dr Satyapal, 'a fanatical Hindu'.[204] A meeting of the Ittihad-i-Millat at Lahore attended by 5000 celebrated Zafar Ali's victory as 'the greatest defeat of the Congress' which was nothing but 'a communal body'.[205] A paradoxical accusation, considering that the main preoccupation of the Ittihad-i-Millat and its leader at the time was to protest against Hindu attempts to demolish walls around mosques or whip up Islamic fervour over the Shahidganj dispute. 'Once a mosque, always a mosque' was a slogan popularized by Zafar Ali Khan.[206] With the League taking a stand on

---

[200]*Eastern Times*, Lahore, 29 April 1937, ibid., p. 174.
[201]*Inqilab*, 25 July 1937, RNPP, 31 July 1937, p. 304.
[202]SPPAI, 29 May 1937, vol. lix, no. 20, pp. 291–2.
[203]SPPAI, 15 May 1937, vol. lix, no. 19, p. 262.
[204]SPPAI, 5 June 1937, vol. lix, no. 22, pp. 305–6.
[205]SPPAI, 12 June 1937, vol. lix, no. 23, p. 315.
[206]SPPAI, 31 July 1937, vol. lix, no. 30, p. 389.

Shahidganj and the Congress dithering, Zafar Ali's relations with the Ahrars hit an all-time low.

Active opposition from Zafar Ali Khan was awkward for the Congress's mass contact movement, not least since the Ittihad–League combine had found a useful symbol in Shahidganj to shore up popular support. Riding on the back of the Ittihad may not have been Jinnah's idea of widening the League's base in the Punjab. But with the Ahrars backing the Congress, he had little choice in the matter. The editor of the *Zamindar* was only too eager to oblige. Giving a non-existent Muslim League a higher profile than it deserved was not nearly as threatening as letting the Ahrars surge ahead under the Congress banner. Fancying himself a greater opponent of colonialism than the Congress henchman in the province, Zafar Ali projected his own version of communal–nationalism. As he roared before a crowd of 4000, 'every brick of the Shahidganj mosque was more sacred to the Muslims than ten British Governments'. He chastised the *ulema* for failing to give Muslims a lead at a critical juncture, implying that they were on the Congress payroll. With the audience crying 'maulvis are devils', Zafar Ali lashed out at the Congress for refusing to mediate between Muslims and Sikhs. Purporting to be India's premier nationalist organization, the 'Congress consisted of hungry dogs living on the bread of Jawahar Lal Nehru' who was 'one of the Kashmiri Pandits ... sucking the blood of the poor in Kashmir State'. And Gandhi, mistakenly called the Mahatma, was 'a traitor' and the main stumbling-block in the path of freedom.[207]

Like its 'communalisms', there were many intriguing varieties of home-grown Indian nationalisms in the Punjab. Those preferring hard-and-fast definitions of the two concepts would do well to take a closer look at the evidence. Flashing his communitarian identity, Zafar Ali Khan had no qualms celebrating the murder of anyone accused of vilifying the Prophet of Islam. It was proof that 'Muslims would stop at nothing to vindicate their religious rights'. Even an Ahrar of Bukhari's oratorial skills could not have put it more forcefully. Where the similarity between the two men ends, however, is of vital importance in grading their communitarian bigotry and nationalist zeal. An Ataullah Shah Bukhari could publicly brandish a sword and express regret at the law prohibiting him from using it against the Ahmadi leader, Bashiruddin.[208] A Zafar Ali Khan, on the other hand, interjected at a meeting where poems 'exhorting Muslims to massacre all non-Muslims and usurp their Gurdwaras and temples' were being read. Apart from being in sheer bad taste, this was contrary to the spirit of Islam.[209]

So long as he clung to the Congress cause, Bukhari's anti-Ahmadi rhetoric and attempted breach of peace could be ignored by the doyens of the Hindu

---

[207]*SPPAI*, 17 July 1937, vol. lix, no. 28, p. 376.

[208]*SPPAI*, 12 June 1937, vol. lix, no. 23, p. 316.

[209]*SPPAI*, 14 August 1937, vol. lix, no. 32, p. 407.

press. Muslim sectarianism was apparently not inconsistent with Congress nationalism. The same rules did not apply to Zafar Ali Khan, who apart from inducing his co-religionists to join the Muslim League was considering organizing a Muslim National Congress to counteract the Congress. His fulminations against those accused of voicing or writing blasphemous remarks about the Prophet earned him the labels of 'fanaticism' and 'communalism' while Ahrar bigots were considered 'nationalists'. Commenting on the increase in the murders of Hindus and Sikhs blamed for reviling the Prophet, the editor of the *Pratap* told the Unionist premier that Muslim fanaticism would have to be contained if he genuinely wanted to banish 'communalism'.[210] This occasioned a gem of a response from the *Zamindar*. It observed that 'as new and novel interpretations' could be 'put on a single view point and idea' it was becoming 'difficult to determine what communalism' actually meant. The Punjab needed to give a definition to the word so that everyone could act accordingly. What the Hindu press regarded as the 'worst form of communalism' was the 'cry of the Muslim against the disregard shown to his rights'. If separate electorates were the main cause of 'communalism', then the Unionist government—the main beneficiary of the Communal Award—was the single biggest obstacle in the way of 'joint nationalism'. Yet Sikander Hayat was going out of his way to appease the Hindus in the name of pursuing a supra-communal policy.[211]

With each political grouping preferring to rely on its own lexicon, popular discourse in the Punjab was riddled with confusions in terminology. Even the Congress found itself being hoisted by its own petard during the Muslim mass contact movement.[212] Only the hazy-eyed in Delhi and UP could have hoped for a fair run in the province. These nationalists of a different hue had, in the opinion of Punjab's foremost literary figure, allowed their 'political idealism' to 'kill ... [their] sense of fact'.[213] And indeed there seems to be something immensely wrong about the Congress decision to despatch a communist ideologue like Dr Ashraf to a province dazed by its own narratives of communitarian identities and contested sovereignties. A mere 700 turned out in Jallianwalla Bagh to hear the chief of the Muslim wing of the All-India Congress despite the attraction of listening to music played by an Ahrar band. It was perhaps just as well that few heard Dr Ashraf proselytizing that 'true

[210]*Pratap*, Lahore, 13 August 1937, *RNPP*, 14 August 1937, p. 328.

[211]*Zamindar*, Lahore, 14 August 1937, ibid., p. 328.

[212]While refusing to take up the Shahidganj issue, the Punjab Congress fervently opposed the construction of a slaughter house in the Lahore cantonment, convincing many Muslims that it was the Hindu Mahasabha in disguise.(*SPPAI*, 11 September 1937, vol. lix, no. 36, p. 451.) The project was abandoned once the Congress agitation assumed 'gigantic proportions'. (*SPPAI*, 4 and 18 September 1937, vol. lix, nos. 35, 37, pp. 439, 457.)

[213]Iqbal, 'Islam and Ahmadism', in Sherwani (ed.), *Speeches, Writings and Statements of Iqbal*, p. 177.

democracy in India could only be found under the Red Flag', the banner of revolution. [214] Lahori Muslims did not let these radical preachings go without a characteristic barb. Speaking in the provincial capital at the conclusion of an exhausting tour, the learned doctor fumbled badly when asked why the Congress was not settling the Shahidganj issue.[215]

It was no wonder that some Ahrars had serious misgivings about promoting the Congress cause in the Punjab. Hissamuddin in his presidential address to the provincial Ahrar conference at Multan had referred to the Congress as a Hindu party. Congress tactics of making accommodations with individual Muslims rather than established leaders of Muslim parties like the Ahrar and the Jamiat-ul-Ulema-i-Hind had destroyed hopes of a common front. The setting up of a separate Muslim mass contact department was almost comical. Ashraf, a Congress courtier, and a communist, denied that Muslims had a distinctive culture.[216] With a section of the Ahrars opposing it, the provincial Muslim mass contact committee found the going especially rough. Azad and Ghaffar Khan had to be deputed to give the Congress's lacklustre mass contact movement a Muslim polish. The few still willing to do the Congress's biding were for the most part salaried Ahrar workers, and, of course, the Red Shirts of the Frontier. But the red revolution also had the green of Islam, which was more focused on attacking certain Muslim sects. At a conference in Multan district, the Shoba-i-Tabligh of the Ahrars were not in the least interested in sowing Jawaharlal Nehru's socialist oats. They instead assailed Ahmadis, Wahabis and the Shias.[217] Choudhury Afzal Haq, tipped as one of the Muslim candidates for Congress president in the Punjab, Mian Iftikharuddin of the Arian clan of Lahore being the other, went about attacking the Ahmadis. Considered as being for the Ahrars what Gandhi was for the Congress, Haq believed that India could 'never be free until the *Ahmadis* were destroyed'.[218]

Internal discord within the communities was not restricted to Muslims in the Punjab. Tensions between the Aryas and Sanatan Hindus were recurrent in certain districts. Even the Ahmadis were hit by dissensions, resulting in the excommunication of recalcitrant members of the sect by Bashiruddin. But heightened political activity had affected Muslims the most. Apart from sharp disagreements over the Shahidganj mosque, there were Shia–Sunni differences in Jullundur while in Ferozepur district the Ahrars had drawn fresh battlelines against the Ahl-i-Hadith. In Amritsar the Ahl-i-Sunnat was pitted against the Ahl-i-Hadith. Maulvi Sanaullah, the Ahl-i-Hadith leader, suffered serious head injuries after being attacked with a chopper by a member of the opposing sect.[219]

[214]*SPPAI*, 12 June 1937, vol. lix, no. 23, pp. 317, 319.

[215]*SPPAI*, 19 June 1937, vol. lix, no. 24, p. 328.

[216]Mirza, *Karavan-i-Ahrar*, iii, pp. 78–86.

[217]*SPPAI*, 11 September 1937, vol. lix, no. 36, p. 452.

[218]*SPPAI*, 25 September 1937, vol. lix, no. 38, p. 469.

[219]*SPPAI*, 6 November 1937, vol. lix, no. 43, p. 535.

These murderous urges among rival sects of Islam found the Muslim League, unbeknown to itself, 'steadily gaining ground in the Punjab' while Ahrar efforts to bolster their organization had 'met with little success'. According to one astute observer, if the 'strength' of the Ahrars was their hatred of Ahmadis, it was also their main weakness. They were 'never able to live down their refusal to sponsor the Shahidganj agitation'. Their failure to 'convince Muslims that fraternization with the Congress [wa]s in the best interests of the community' came as no big surprise.[220] Stated in the aftermath of Jawaharlal Nehru's most recent visit to the Punjab, this reading of the Muslim response to the Congress overture, if correct, underlines the problems of relying on political ideals with no real appreciation of the situation on the ground. Propagating the Congress creed while flying the flag of their Muslim identity gave some marvellous touches to the internal discourse among Muslims. Mazhar Ali Azhar told a gathering of 4000 at Batala in Gurdaspur district that those raising a hue and cry over Shahidganj were 'the same people who sided with the British Government in bringing about the ruination of Turkey'. Casting Zafar Ali Khan in the camp of British loyalists was a trifle unfair. But he had the political skills to force Mazhar Ali to eat humble pie for saying that 'neither justice nor honesty demanded that the Shahidganj Mosque should be restored to the Muslims'. He was immediately refuted by Maulvi Aziz Ahmad Khan, a member of the UP legislative assembly. Muslims could not conceivably join the Congress. Elements of the Congress now in power 'consisted of more or less communally-minded persons'. A small minority of Congressmen were 'sincere workers'. But their 'creed' was 'communism and communism was opposed to religion'. Unless Congress shed its anti-religious complex, Muslims were better off 'consolidat[ing] their own progressive organisations' and 'inculcat[ing] in themselves the revolutionary spirit to fight capitalism.[221]

Similar concerns motivated Iqbal to write to Jinnah, urging him to help organize Punjab's Muslims.[222] He feared that with the Ahrars to light the fires, the Congress might blaze its way to Muslim hearts in the Punjab.[223] More importantly, Iqbal thought the 'Indian Nationalist' of the Congress mould was 'intolerant of the birth of a desire for self-determination in the heart of north-west Indian Islam'.[224] Looking at the Muslim–Hindu political

[220]SPPAI, 9–16 October 1937, vol. lix, no. 40, p. 485.

[221]SPPAI, 30 October 1937, vol. lix, no. 42, p. 42.

[222]See Syed Shamsul Hassan Collection/Press and Publications, vol. 1, in All-India Muslim League Papers, National Archives of Pakistan, Islamabad, also Muhammad Iqbal, Letters of Iqbal to Jinnah, Lahore: Sheikh Muhammad Ashraf, 1943.

[223]An official estimate put the Congress membership in the Punjab at 128,765. Of these, 34,060 were urban and 94,705 rural. (SPPAI, 27 November 1937, vol. lix, no. 46, p. 561.)

[224]Iqbal, 'Islam and Ahmadism', in Sherwani (ed.), Speeches, Writings and Statements of Iqbal, p. 177.

equation through his regional spectacles, he asked Jinnah to take up bread and butter issues and ignore the Muslims of the minority provinces.[225] Jinnah shattered Iqbal's hopes in October 1937 by striking a deal with the Unionist premier which came to be known as the Sikander–Jinnah pact. A red rag for urban Punjabi Muslims like Iqbal, this was Jinnah's response to the bedlam of bigotry that had broken loose in the Punjab. His decision to opt for the 'reactionaries' over the 'progressives' was a product of pragmatism and, to a lesser extent, personal preference.[226]

Lacking organization, money and leadership, the Muslim League was finding it difficult to carry out any sort of propaganda. The Unionist bosses at least had their own resources to eventually deliver something to the League. For Sikander Hayat Khan the agreement was the best insurance for warding off the Muslim League.[227] He was immensely successful in driving a wedge between Jinnah and the handful of urban Punjabi Muslims who stuck by the League despite its electoral debacle. Their sense of despair was reflected in the comment that the all-India high command had failed to give a clear lead as to whether Muslims should co-operate with Hindus, play the role of 'the proverbial dog in the manger' or 'strive for the establishment of a separate state of their own'.[228]

Iqbal may have been the originator of the idea of a separate state in north-western India but by 1937 the notion was coming to acquire a life of its own. In the journalistic imaginings of the *New Times*, Muslims in north-western India had distinctive national characteristics. In their 'religion, culture, history, tradition, economic system, laws of inheritance, succession and marriage' they were a world apart from the inhabitants of Hindustan. There could be 'no peace and tranquillity in the land if the Muslims [we]re duped into a Hindu-dominated Federation where they c[ould] not be masters of their own destiny and captains of their own souls'. Instead of an all-India federation of the sort Iqbal had envisaged in 1930, this maverick of Punjabi Muslim nationalism in the late 1930s wanted 'separate national status' with a 'separate Federal Constitution from the rest of India'.[229] These ideas emanating from the margins of the Punjab press long before the Muslim League was clearly in the picture underscore the continuing disjunction between Muslim discourse and politics. During the remaining years of the 1930s various schemes by Muslim politicians and intellectuals tried resolving question of how power was to be

[225]See Iqbal to Jinnah, 28 May and 21 June 1937, *Syed Shamsul Hasan Collection/ Press and Publications*, vol. 1.

[226]For urban Punjabi Muslim reactions, see Batalvi, *Iqbal ke Akhari Do Saal*, pp. 472–80, 489–568 and his *Hamari Qaumi Jid-o-Jehd: January 1939 Saay December 1939 Tak*, Lahore: Pakistan Times Press, (no date), chapter five.

[227]See Ibid.

[228]*Truth*, Lahore, 19 October 1937, *RNPP*, 23 October 1937, p. 436.

[229]*New Times*, Lahore, 20 June 1937, *RNPP*, 26 June 1937, p. 256.

shared at the all-India level after the British withdrawal.[230] No one explicitly advocated severing all links with the rest of India, even as they sought to consolidate Muslim power in regions where they were in the majority. What they all had in common was the apprehension that they would be swamped by a Hindu majority in the absence of adequate safeguards for Muslim interests, however defined. There was as yet no strategy of how divided and disorganized Muslims were to be brought under a single political banner.

The new constitutional arrangements merely intensified class, sectarian and ideological differences both within and across regions. If a sense of exclusion was by now driving a segment of Punjabi Muslims to an incipient form of 'separatism', there were as yet no signs of the sort of convergences which might connect the region with the wider 'nation' of Islam, a necessary concomitant to a 'centre' for the north-western provinces. While claiming a Muslim 'whole' may have been sufficient to emphasize differences with other communities at the discursive level, converting it into a viable political strategy for asserting the religiously informed cultural identity of Muslims required overcoming structural contradictions within the British Indian system.

Highlighting the dilemma were the contradictory legal implications of two seemingly unconnected issues—the passage of the *shariat* bill by the central assembly in September 1937 and the Lahore High Court's ruling on the disputed Shahidganj mosque in January 1938. Introduced in the central assembly on 9 September 1935, the *shariat* bill was the first attempt to dispense with the varied customary practices in the different regions and make Islamic law binding on all Indian Muslims. Since it covered not only marriage and divorce but also inheritance, including agricultural land, the bill was debated for two years before its adoption on 16 September 1937. Muslim members of the assembly like Sir Muhammad Yamin tried arguing that the bill was unenforceable as the word *shariat* meant different things to different sects in Islam.[231] A comment on the inconsistencies between the political and legal identities of India's Muslims, such objections were easier to counter than the prospect of extending the Islamic law of inheritance to agricultural property. Under the customary law practised among other places in the Punjab, Muslim women did not inherit agricultural land. A bar against the fragmentation of land, this contravened the *shariat* which gave women the right to inherit half the familial property given to their male siblings. Jinnah rescued the bill from oblivion by arranging to omit agricultural property from its purview, an intervention which won him kudos among Muslim landlords in Punjab and UP.

A sleight of hand by an able parliamentarian like Jinnah saved the protagonists of a coherent political and legal Muslim identity from acute embar-

---

[230]See below and Jalal, *The Sole Spokesman*, chapter two, for a discussion of some of these schemes.

[231]Cited in Mirza, *Karavan-i-Ahrar*, iii, pp. 159–60.

rassment. But within a matter of months the Lahore High Court's decision on the Shahidganj mosque pulled the rug from under their feet. With the exception of Justice Din Muhammad, all justices ruled in favour of dismissing the petition that the mosque be restored to the Muslims. They conceded that under the *shariat* a mosque always remained a mosque. Yet since 1872, the Punjab Laws Act had overruled Muslim personal law. Consequently, the Muslim claim to the mosque could not be upheld with reference to the *shariat*.[232] With Lahori Muslims in a tizzy over the adverse ruling, Zafar Ali Khan invited Jinnah to help resolve the dispute. The would-be champion of the Muslim community could do little in the face of Sikander Hayat Khan's stonewalling. Punjab's premier was not about to risk his alliance with Hindu and Sikh landlords to appease his urban Muslim opponents. Despite a closing of ranks by the Muslim League, Ahrars and the Ittihad-i-Millat, Jinnah wisely chose not to waste his energies trying to contest the supremacy of British law over the *shariat*.

If the *shariat* bill of 1937 was a pyrrhic victory for the paragons of the religiously informed cultural identity of the Muslims, the Shahidganj mosque dispute symbolizes the as-yet incomplete transition from discourse to politics. Only through innovative and concerted attempts at linking the region with the nation could Muslims in the Punjab trace a path to the missing centre. But until they could agree on how to go about reconciling internally differentiated interests, the Punjabi Muslim trek could lead to any number of destinations. It was the plethora of options available, not the teleology of the partition of 1947, which help unravel the historical dynamics leading to the denouement which settled the fate of the Punjab and, consequently, of India as a whole.

[232]Ibid., pp. 237–9.

Chapter 8

At the Crossroads of 'Pakistan':
Muslim Imaginings and Territorial Sovereignty

Until the fateful parting of ways signalled by Mohammad Ali Jinnah's call to Muslims to observe a 'Day of Deliverance' upon the resignation of Congress ministries, an amicable settlement between the All-India Muslim League and the Indian National Congress was not beyond the pale of possibility. Writing to Jinnah on 18 October 1939, Jawaharlal Nehru thought it was 'a tragedy that the Hindu–Muslim problem' had 'not so far been settled in a friendly way .... [f]or after all, the actual matters in dispute should be, and indeed are, easily capable of adjustment'. He spent the next decade turning what should have been a simple matter to resolve into one extraordinarily difficult, if not impossible, of resolution. Already in 1939, Nehru was 'terribly distressed' and 'ashamed of [him]self' that he had 'not been able to contribute anything substantial' to the solution of the Hindu–Muslim problem. 'I must confess to you,' he wrote, 'that in this matter I have lost confidence in myself, though I am not usually given that way.' Developments in India during the past few years had left him feeling like 'an outsider ... alien in spirit'.[1]

Nehru's faltering resolve was ominous for the future. The assertion of religiously informed cultural identities and the politics of contested sovereignty in certain regions posed the single biggest challenge to Congress's calculations at the all-India centre. Many Muslims were averse to the Nehruvian brand of nationalism. But if they could still be persuaded in the interest of keeping India united, there could be no denying them their regional dominance in the Punjab and Bengal. By conceding defeat before the battle had been lost, the rising star of the Indian nation struck a grievous blow to the hopes for a

[1]Nehru to Jinnah, 18 October 1939, in Nehru, *A Bunch of Old Letters*, pp. 402–3.

negotiated accommodation of differences in a territorially united subcontinent. His 'own mind move[d] on a different plane and most of [his] interests l[ay] in other directions'.[2] If Jawaharlal Nehru, adulated by a considerable number of Muslims, could not resist the pull of his interests against the push of his ideals, others were nurturing dreams of adjustments on an imaginative and expansive scale. Muhammad Iqbal merely fired the first salvo; he did not try to etch the historical trajectory or define the character of a Muslim state in north-western India. An assertion of territorial sovereignty based on cultural differences, the scheme avoided laying down precisely how adequate safeguards for one large segment of India's Muslims would bear upon the interests of their co-religionists in the rest of India or of those non-Muslims who might end up living in the new state.

Such important omissions notwithstanding, Iqbal's example was emulated by others who came forward with their own ideas on the various possible permutations and combinations of Muslim identity and territorial sovereignty. Blazing the trail of the visionary, these echoed the deafening silence on individual and collective rights of citizenship in a more glaring fashion than those marking the Congress discourse on the issue. Whatever its idealistic formulations, the content of citizenship rights has everywhere been shaped by historically specific interactions between states and societies. India's colonial subjects on the threshold of citizenship tended to envisage their rights in absolute rather than relational terms. This was a habit fostered by the need to get a hearing from the colonial state. But absolute demands are also the best insurance against absolute solutions. If Indian differences invited absolute conceptions of cultural rights, their layered multiplicities mitigated the prospects of absolute political solutions. The disjunction between an exclusivist discourse on cultural rights and the indeterminacy of political possibilities has to be recognized and its implications explored.

Subjecting Muslim projections of identity and matching claims of rights to close scrutiny illuminates their historically contingent nature and the incapacity to endorse an absolute division of India. In contesting their part in relation to the whole, Indian Muslims like other religious groupings were asserting absolute rights to territories based on religiously informed cultural identities. A tactical stance necessitated by Congress's insistence on representing the whole of India, it did not mean foreclosing negotiations leading to mutually acceptable accommodations. Muslims seeking to wrest their share of political power on grounds of cultural difference were still mainly challenging the Congress's right to indivisible sovereignty, not rejecting any sort of identification with India. There were contradictions and indifference to other people's sense of difference. Yet schemes using religiously informed cultural differences to stake political claims for territorial sovereignty offer a marvellous canvas on which to explore

[2]Ibid., p. 402.

Muslim imaginings. These in their different ways were trying to keep alive the idea if not the reality of an India extending from the Khyber Pass in the north-western marcher regions to the Bay of Bengal in the east, and from the city of exquisite monuments evoking the spirit and memory of the Sultanate and the great Mughals to the southernmost tip of Kanyakumari.

'MUSLIM SCHEMES' OF THE LATE-1930s RECONSIDERED

By the late 1930s Muslim anxieties about the community's constitutional future in an independent India found expression in a spate of schemes imbued with imaginative notions of power sharing by religiously enumerated 'majorities' and 'minorities'. If the novelty of the proposed 'solutions' lay in claiming national status for the Muslim community, now deemed to be on a par with the numerically preponderant Hindu community, their primary defect invariably was in identifying areas over which territorial sovereignty could realistically be asserted. Giving a territorial basis to a heterogeneous community turned homogenous 'nation' was a more vexed issue than is borne out in those historical studies which, informed by the teleology of 1947, chart a linear course to the achievement of Muslim statehood.

A consideration of the balance between individual and community, alongside an examination of the schemes published by Muslims from different regions and social backgrounds is a profitable enterprise. While expressing their sense of cultural difference with Hindus, statements of Muslim identity in the late 1930s were also directed at Congress's dictatorial tendencies. The Congress's refusal to form a coalition ministry in UP, a province where it had done the best electorally, gave a new lease of life to the All-India Muslim League. Jinnah made political capital of Nehru's tactical stumble while pursuing his more narrowly focused regional interests. The impetuous call to disband the Muslim League and join the Congress was denounced in Muslim circles, most markedly in the Punjab. Ironically a province which had never needed and still did not need a Muslim League was coming to spearhead a cause which after the 1937 elections seemed a practically lost one. That a mere 4.4 per cent Muslim voters heeded its call was a bitter blow to the All-India Muslim League. The rage at Congress's refusal to have any truck with the only all-India organization claiming to speak on behalf of all Muslims saw the revival of a party which had remained in the political woodworks at crucial moments of self-definition like the *khilafat* movement.

With a longer history on paper than on the ground, the All-India Muslim League did come to play a crucial role in the negotiations of how power was to be shared after the British quit India. Whatever the Congress's claims, sharing power in an independent India ultimately required making accommodations not just between communities of faith living in the different regions but also individuals with multiple associations. The question of future

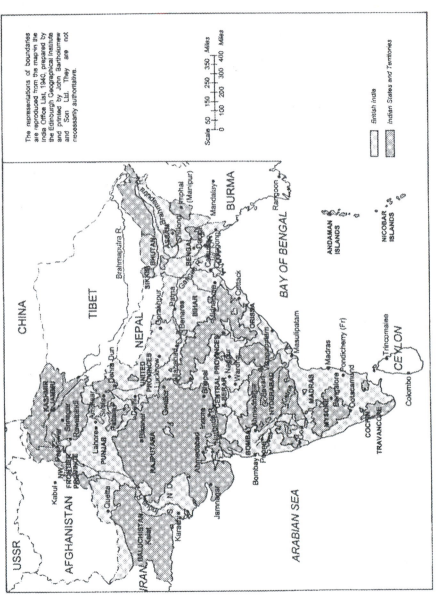

The representations of boundaries are reproduced from the map in the India Office List, 1940, prepared by the Edinburgh Geographical Institute and printed by John Bartholomew and Son Ltd. They are not necessarily authoritative.

Scale 50   150   250   350   Miles
0   100   200   300   400   Miles

British India

Indian States and Territories

India before partition c. 1940

citizenship had remained unsettled despite Congress's adoption of the liberal framework of democracy. Studded with home-grown illiberalities, particularly in the Punjab, the formula for equal citizenship rights based on separating the material and cultural domains was unacceptable to most Muslims. Once the prospect of a 'Hindu raj' dressed in Congress's secular colours began looming large in New Delhi, regions increased their efforts to strengthen the provincial autonomy granted to them under the Government of India Act of 1935. Punjab's vital role in any future all-India equation found it rife with ideas about how power was to be shared among the regions. Far from being uncompromisingly 'separatist', most of the solutions put forward were compatible with eventual all-India arrangements provided an acceptable resolution of power sharing could be worked out between centre and region, and within the region among the different communities of religion.

There was no notion of secession in the conception of a 'United States of South Asia', put forward by the Aga Khan in the mid-1930s.[3] If minority communities were to 'become citizens of self-governing provinces' then the Muslim Conference wanted safeguards from the 'majority' community before settling on *swaraj*. This gave a constitutional lawyer of Jinnah's calibre the political opening that had long eluded him. With the focus shifting to all-India political arrangements, Jinnah was better placed to align the Muslim-majority provinces with his concerns at the centre. These aimed at covering all Indian Muslims. Punjabi Muslims might generate their own logic of exclusion while projecting the idea of a Muslim 'community' or 'nation'. But Jinnah had no doubts about how to play the numbers game to achieve his larger purposes.

Donning the democratic garb, Jinnah in the spring of 1937 called the Congress Working Committee a 'grand fascist council'.[4] In December 1939 he made a point of saying that the 'Day of Deliverance' was targeted at 'Congress raj' and not the entire Hindu community.[5] Ambedkar's public support of the League's day of deliverance gave moral weight to Jinnah's posture.[6] But it was the backing of Sikander Hayat Khan, the Unionist premier of the Punjab, that lent political potency to his charge against the Congress. Even hopelessly divided Muslims were coming to agreement on certain matters. Minority status at the all-India level coupled with restrictions on the exercise of their provincial majorities in the Punjab and Bengal was out of the question. This was certainly the opinion of Sikander Hayat who, taking the cue from Fazl-i-Husain, advocated Punjabi nationalism in preference to any of the purely Muslim or Indian varieties. Speaking in Gurdaspur in May 1939, Sikander stated that he

[3]See Jalal, *The Sole Spokesman*, p. 52, n.31.
[4]Cited in Batalvi, *Hamari Qaumi Jid-o-jehd*, p. 20.
[5]*Civil and Military Gazette*, Lahore, 19 December 1939, cited in ibid., pp. 295–6.
[6]Ibid., pp. 288–9.

was 'first a Punjabi and then a Muslim'.[7] But with the Congress on a romp, playing provincial rights against a future conception of a centre which could diddle Muslims out of the power-sharing equation required coming to terms with Jinnah at the all-India level.

The impetus for this had been provided by the formation in July 1937 of Congress ministries in initially six and subsequently eight British Indian provinces. Eager to further strengthen provincial autonomy, Sikander struck a deal with Jinnah to resist the kind of centralized rule the Congress could bring to bear upon the provinces. The inauspicious removal of Dr N.B. Khare, the premier of the Central Provinces, followed by the undemocratic ouster of Subhas Chandra Bose as party president did not help the Congress's democratic credentials.[8] A few days after declaring Punjabi as his primary identity, Sikander Hayat was humming a Muslim tune in Bombay. Ignoring his own authoritarianism in preventing the League becoming a thorn in his provincial side, he told the Provincial Muslim League that 'the big leaders of the Congress' spoke of 'democracy' but took the 'path of dictatorship'. Congress's extraordinary electoral success had unsettled its leadership. On a high horse, they were surpassing the autocracy of Mussolini and Hitler whom they publicly condemned.[9]

Sikander went on to trash the idea of a Hindu 'majority'. If scheduled castes were excluded, Hindus would be reduced to a minority. This was why the Congress used tropes like the Muslim mass contact movement to divide Muslims. Such undemocratic practices augured poorly for a federal democracy in a Congress-dominated India. An Indian federation with the Congress ruling from a strong centre would effectively be unitary in its operations. The Congress might threaten to destroy the federal arrangements proposed by the 1935 Act, but if push came to shove, it would grab any opportunity to seize power at the existing British unitary centre.[10] Sikander Hayat proposed maximum autonomy for individual units of the federation. Strong provinces and a weak federal centre was the best hope for those looking at the all-India political equation from the perspective of Muslim-majority regions.

The search for a Muslim 'whole' based in the Muslim-majority regions of the northwest had boomeranged on its Punjabi proponents. While wanting strong provinces, non-Punjabi Muslims had no intention of letting a Punjabi-dominated 'whole' encumber their autonomy. The conference of Muslims from 'upper India' proposed by Iqbal in late 1930 was never held. However, in 1933 a Punjabi Muslim student at Cambridge, Choudhary Rahmat Ali, had coined the name 'PAKISTAN', an acronym for Punjab, Afghanistan

[7]Ibid., p. 127.

[8]For a Muslim opinion on Khare's expulsion and Bose's discomfiture in the Congress, see ibid., chapters one and two.

[9]Ibid., p. 100.

[10]Ibid., pp. 104–5.

(including the North West Frontier Province), Kashmir, Sind and Baluchistan].
Literally, the 'land of the pure', the 'Pakistan' scheme was scoffed at in the
formal arenas of British Indian politics.[11] But the 'Pakistan' idea, variously
appropriated, filtered more widely in the informal arenas. While its protagonists
remained largely unorganized, the opponents acted concertedly to nip it in
the bud. Opposition to a Muslim state of 'Pakistan' dominated by the Punjab
was not confined to non-Muslims. At the height of the public debate on the
separation of the province from Bombay presidency, the Sindhi Muslim leader
Ghulam Hussain Hidayatullah dismissed the idea of one large Islamic province
in the northwest. In July 1934 he told a meeting of the Sind Azad Conference
that it would be a political blunder for Sindhi Muslims to group with Punjabi
Muslims. 'Our interest in the separation of Sind', Hidayatullah remarked,
was 'only this that we should be owners of our own home'.[12] The Khudai
Khidmatgars, or servants of God, in the NWFP led by Abdul Ghaffar Khan also
asserted their autonomy even while preferring to deal directly with the
Congress.

There was much ado in 1938 when the Sind Muslim League, a mere label
for an assortment of individuals, met at Karachi and passed a resolution calling
for the division of India into Muslim and non-Muslim states. While invoking
the religiously informed communitarian affiliations of Sindhi Muslims, the
resolution was an expression of their regional aspirations. The desire for strong
provinces and a weak federal centre was perfectly consistent with rejecting a
subordinate position in a Muslim state. It was this disjunction between
religious and territorial identity which hampered Jinnah's efforts to build a
solid Muslim phalanx against the Congress's aims at the all-India level. The
emphasis on 'grouping' of provinces and 'zonal schemes' flowed from the
uneasy equation between Muslim identity and territorial sovereignty. Only
by bringing the combined weight of the Muslim provinces to bear on
discussions at the all-India level could Jinnah and the League hope to influence
future constitutional arrangements. But as Jinnah had always feared, the fumes
emanating from the Punjab could seriously cloud his broader calculations.

Blurring the distinction between outright Muslim 'separatism' and the
search for better terms in an all-India whole results in unacceptable teleology.
Even the author of the scheme best remembered for its 'separatist' overtones
was concerned about Muslims in the rest of India. Having introduced the
idea of 'Pakistan' into the public discourse, Choudhary Rahmat Ali proposed
setting up a 'Bangistan' or 'Bang-i-Islamistan' by grouping Bengal and Assam.
But his most innovative blending of identity and territorial sovereignty was
reserved for areas where Muslims were in a minority. 'Osmanistan' was the

[11]See Choudhary Rahmat Ali, *Pakistan: The Fatherland of the Pak Nation*, Cambridge:
Foister and Jagg, 1947.
[12]Reported in *Inqilab*, Lahore, 31 July 1934, cited in Mirza, *Karavan-i-Ahrar*, ii,
p. 62.

name given to a would-be sovereign state of Hyderabad Deccan. Colourfully named Muslims states like Sadiqistan, Faruqistan, Muinistan, Mappallistan, Safistan and Nasiristan, were to be carved out of an area covering British and princely India as well as present-day Sri Lanka.[13] Rahmat Ali's 'Pakistan' was nothing less than the territorial embodiment of the Muslim notion of a worldwide *ummah*. Creating half a dozen Muslim states in India and consolidating them into a 'Pakistan Commonwealth of Nations' was only the first step to his 'original Pakistan'. The Muslim commonwealth was eventually to be integrated with Central and West Asia.[14]

This may have been an excessively impracticable vision. There were more sober attempts by other Muslims claiming varying measures of territorial sovereignty in defence of their religiously informed cultural identities. The significance of Rahmat Ali's 'original Pakistan' lies in its underlining the expansive and constrictive dimensions of Muslim identity and the ensuing ambiguities in claiming territorial sovereignty. Inclined to taking a less-than-precise view of formal boundaries, Muslim notions of sovereignty have historically tended to be more fluid than rigid. Absolute claims to territory without defining relations with non-Muslim areas might suggest the exclusionary, even 'separatist', nature of the 'Pakistan' scheme. But if Muslim states in Hindustan were to survive, 'Pakistan' and 'Bang-i-Islamistan' had to retain something of an all-India conception without necessarily abandoning hopes of reviving the *khilafat* in an era of modern nation–states. As ever, the Indian and Islamic aspects of subcontinental Muslim identity meshed in an intriguing fashion. The period after the late 1930s is more aptly seen as a political crossroads in the articulation of Muslim nationhood rather than a sharp bend on a well-defined path to sovereign statehood.

Sikander Hayat Khan's 'zonal scheme' for an Indian federation consisting of seven constituent units replaced the exclusive emphasis on religious community with regional conglomerates. The Punjab was placed in a zone encompassing not only Sind, the NWFP and Baluchistan but also Kashmir, the Punjab princely states as well as Bikaner and Jaisalmer. Each zone was to have its own autonomous legislature whose members would collectively form a federal assembly. Muslims would enjoy one-third of the representation at the centre and in the zonal ministries.[15] But the scheme made no allowance for Indian aspirations to be free. Sikander envisaged a government of India with a British viceroy as the presiding authority. This was less than what even the All-India Muslim League could accept. There were nonetheless tips here for Jinnah as he turned his attention to the League's special committee examining the various Muslim schemes.

Although a member of the League's constitutional committee, Sikander

[13]See Rahmat Ali, *Pakistan: The Fatherland of the Pak Nation*, pp. 309–10.
[14]Ibid., cited in Jalal, *The Sole Spokesman*, p. 53, n. 34.
[15] For details of the scheme, see Batalvi, *Hamari Qaumi Jid-o-jehd*, pp. 152–5.

Hayat communicated his ideas through the press and publications media. So did the authors of other noteworthy schemes. One by 'A Punjabi' proposed a confederacy of India based on sovereign Muslim and Hindu federated zones. Attributed to Mian Kifayat Ali and financed by Nawab Shahnawaz Khan of Mamdot, it explicitly rejected the word 'Pakistan' since it had come to signify an entity outside the framework of India. The northwest zone outlined in this scheme consisted of the four main Muslim-majority provinces, minus the Ambala division, along with Kashmir, Bahawalpur, Amb, Dir, Chitral, Khairpur, Kalat, Las Bela, Kapurthala and Malir Kotala. Hindu-majority areas in eastern India were to be extracted from Bengal and Assam and appended to Bihar and Orissa. If the scissor-and-paste method fell short of consolidating Muslim power in north-western and north-eastern India, separation from the rest of India was the preferred solution.[16]

Schemes with secessionist undertones remained the hobby horse of Punjabis in the main. Beginning with Hasrat Mohani's proposal in 1927 for separate Muslim and Hindu states sharing power at a common federal centre, schemes by Muslims from the minority provinces were inclusive, not exclusive of the Muslim-majority areas of the subcontinent. The best known was entitled 'The Problem of Indian Muslims and its Solution' associated with two professors from Aligarh University. It carried Dr Afzal Husain Qadri's signature and Dr Syed Zafrul Hasan's input. In his covering letter, Qadri described it as the outcome of 'the hardest and most serious thinking' on whether Muslims could 'live as a free and honourable nation in India'. After this calculated jab at the unitary calculus informing Congress's nationalist demands, the professors illustrated what leaps in logic were required to configure the 'ideal of a *free Muslim Nation*' with that of a '*free National Home*'.[17] Scattered throughout the subcontinent, the Muslim 'nation' could not be confined to a single territorial homeland. But even half a dozen national homelands could not surmount the problem of cohering Indian Muslim identity with territorial sovereignty. This left open the possibility of a layered union with multiple levels of sovereignty sharing between regions as well as communities living within them. For the moment, however, it was the willingness to chop and change the hallowed administrative boundaries of colonial India which merits attention.

The justification for this apparent act of sacrilege was the 'perpetual domination of a Hindu majority at the centre' and the cry of a single nation which augured ill for those with a sense of distinctiveness. Establishing an all-India federation on these principles would 'within the space of a generation, bring about a total annihilation of the specific Islamic outlook, culture, and language'. Muslims had to 'win freedom and equality' and not 'acquiesce in

---

[16]'A Punjabi', *Confederacy of India*, Lahore, 1939.

[17]Mohammed Afzal Husain Qadri to Jinnah, 2 February 1939, in Quaid-i-Azam Papers (henceforth QAP, followed by file number), file no. 135.

their subjugation', whether engineered by the Hindus, the British or even 'Hinduised anti-British Muslims'.[18] This tried mopping the floor clean for a sticky scheme outlining how Muslims in the minority provinces could secure their 'separate religious, cultural and political identity' with the 'full and effective support ... [of] the Muslim majority provinces'. For this to happen, it was necessary to 'repartition' India into 'three wholly independent and sovereign states' with adequate arrangements safeguarding the interests of 'our nationals living in Hindu India'.[19] 'Pakistan' was to consist of the Muslim-majority provinces in the northwest and the princely states of Jammu and Kashmir, Bahawalpur, Kalat, Khairpur, Patiala, Jhind, Nabha, Kapurthala, Malir Kotala as well as the hill stations of Faridkot and Simla. There was to be a self-governing Muslim state in a Bengal shorn of Howrah, Midnapur and Darjeeling but including Bihar's Purnea district and the subdivision of Sylhet in Assam. Muslims elsewhere in India were to be bundled in a number of new-fangled administrative units. They were to be considered 'a nation in minority' that was part of 'a larger nation inhabiting Pakistan and Bengal'.[20]

On the more expansive scale was the call to amalgamate Hyderabad Deccan with Berar and Karnatak to form an autonomous state. The cheekier suggestion was the creation of two new provinces in Hindustan, the name given to those parts of the subcontinent not claimed by the protagonists of India's freshly minted Muslim nation. Delhi's provincial status was to be bolstered territorially by adding the districts of Meerut, Rohilkhand and Aligarh where Muslims lived in appreciable numbers.[21] Malabar was to be grouped with the southern part of Madras presidency, an area where Muslims had substantial trading interests. Turning to Muslims in other parts of Hindustan, the Aligarh professors proposed conferring the status of a borough or 'free city' upon all towns with populations of over fifty thousand. Extricating these urban pockets from the clutches of Hindu-dominated provincial and central governments was not enough. Muslims living here were to have their own police and magistracy and preferably legislative powers. Those in the rural areas of Hindustan were to be encouraged to move to villages where Muslims already had a preponderance.[22]

If extravagant territorial demands on behalf of the Muslim nation smacked of exclusion, there was some sense of the relational nature of workable power arrangements in subcontinental conditions. In the Aligarh view, the independent states would forge alliances on matters of common interests. There had to be

[18]Qadri, 'The Problem of Indian Muslims and its Solution', ibid., p. 2.
[19]Ibid., p. 3.
[20]Ibid., p. 8.
[21]In the new province of Delhi, Muslims would still form only 28 per cent of the population. But this 'highly cultured and educated' Muslim minority would use its proximity to 'Pakistan' to safeguard its interests. (Ibid., p. 6.)
[22]Ibid., p. 7.

reciprocal safeguards for both sets of minorities, Muslim and non-Muslim. Just as the Muslims in Hindustan were to be seen as belonging to a larger nation in north-western and north-eastern India, religious minorities in 'Pakistan' and Bengal could derive security from sharing a common nationality with co-religionists dominating the non-Muslim state. Given the difficulties in equating 'nationhood' with 'statehood', Muslims and non-Muslims had to remain linked to a larger Indian whole, albeit radically re-articulated in form and substance by virtually independent self-governing parts.

Outright secession was clearly not an option for minority-province Muslims chalking out 'national homelands' on the blackboard of cultural difference. Like his counterparts in Aligarh, Dr Syed Abdul Latif, a professor of English at Osmania university in Hyderabad, laboured hard to balance the relative power of Muslim- and Hindu-majority areas through a drastic redrawing of the internal boundaries of the subcontinent. He contemplated creating five Muslim and eleven Hindu cultural zones with corridors connecting them. Princely states could join any zone with which they shared cultural affinity and geographical proximity. There was to be a free movement of individuals and collectivities to cultural zones of their choice.[23] Thinking of a single Indian federation, Latif demonstrated how the problem of cultural difference required intricate power-sharing arrangements, not the establishment of separate Muslim and Hindu national homelands.

It was this morass of proposals which the All-India Muslim League's constitutional committee had to pare down to arrive at a demand on behalf of all Indian Muslims. Not an easy enterprise to be sure, it was facilitated by the commonality underlying schemes characterized by significant differences in perspective. Whatever their angle of vision, Muslims rejected a Congress-dominated all-India federation in which they would be a perpetual minority. It followed that Muslims, regardless of numbers, were henceforth to be considered a 'nation' entitled to both cultural safeguards and an equitable share of political power in an independent India. The metamorphosis of a minority community, defined by faith, into a nation may have been a matter of political expediency. But it was also a product of prolonged contestations and deliberate reconstructions of identity at multiple levels of Muslim discourse. For the discursive formulation to find reflection in political practice, a way had to be found to turn the Muslim claim to 'nationhood' into a credible demand for 'statehood'.

This was the task before the League's constitutional committee in the months preceding its Lahore session in March 1940. There were contradictory pressures from relatively unknown Muslims in both the majority and minority

[23]See Syed Abdul Latif, *A Federation of Cultural Zones for India*, Secunderabad, 1938. The publication was funded by Sir Haji Abdullah Haroon, a wealthy industrialist-cum-politician from Sind.

provinces. In a letter to Jinnah, Ahmed Bashir, the secretary of the Lahore based Majlis-i-Kabir Pakistan, reiterated his organization's 'unflinching faith in "separation" as the only solution of Hindu–Muslim problems'. A handful of urban Punjabi Muslims were planning a future without their co-religionists in the minority provinces. But they were 'fighting the battle single handed', Bashir complained, 'with no one to support nor even to encourage us'. Jinnah had ignored several of his missives. The Majlis was 'not ask[ing] for material help'. They only wanted Jinnah's 'moral help to the cause of Pakistan' which he could 'so easily, nicely and effectively afford' by putting 'a little more stress on the consolidation of Muslims in the North-West and North-East of India'. Ahmed Bashir was not being disingenuous in asking Jinnah: 'if you do not encourage us ... who else is going to do[sic]'.[24]

If such entreaties gave Jinnah a few awkward moments, pleas from Muslims in the minority provinces were no cause for comfort. To counter Latif's proposal for a common federation based on cultural zones, nine Muslims wrote to him supporting the Aligarh scheme. Muslims could avoid becoming 'a subject nation' only through a 'political partition' of India. As with the Aligarh professors, the nub of the proposed 'partition' was not the separation of the subcontinent's north-western and north-eastern extremities but the internal reconstitution of India. 'Pakistan' and Bengal were to underwrite the fate of an estimated forty-million-strong 'nation in minority' living in 'semi-independent' status within a drastically reconfigured 'Hindustan'.[25] Faced with these breathtaking notions of the possible, Jinnah avoided mentioning 'Pakistan' or 'partition' in the draft resolution presented to the All-India Muslim League at Lahore. Meaning different things to different people, the terms detracted from Jinnah's more immediate objective of elaborating a demand capable of generating support among a cross-section of Indian Muslims.

This required staying mum about the precise territorial boundaries of the 'Independent States' that were to embody the Muslim claim to 'nationhood'. Stated on 22 March 1940 on the sprawling green of Lahore's Minto Park, the crux of the League's demand was that all future constitutional negotiations had to proceed on the principle that Indian Muslims were a 'nation'. Tens of thousands,[26] including a large number of women, were present at this historic meeting held at only a short distance from some of the greatest Mughal monuments in undivided India. Amidst displays of poetic prowess, poor shadows all of the genius of a Ghalib or an Iqbal, this gathering of Indian

[24]Ahmed Bashir to Jinnah, 8 November 1939, QAP/12/File no. 1097.

[25]See Dr Syed Zafrul Hassan et.al to Jinnah, no date, QAP/File no. 135, pp. 12–13.

[26]Police reports put the figure at 25,000. (*SPPAI*, 30 March 1940, vol. lxii, no. 13, p. 166.) But the compiler of the All-India Muslim League's documents claims that over a hundred thousand were present. (See Pirzada [ed.], *Foundations of Pakistan*, ii, p. 326.)

Muslims had a perfect setting. Here the spiritual appeal of Data Ganj Baksh's shrine vies with the grandeur of the Lahore Fort and the austere but dignified lines of the Badshahi Masjid. With the exquisite red-stoned tomb of Jahangir and the much plainer one of his wife, Nur Jehan, in close proximity, this was to become the site for the mausoleum of Muhammad Iqbal, who had passed away in 1938. The visionary of a Muslim state in north-western India lies buried at the entrance of the Badshahi Masjid which together with Data Sahib beckons the faithful of the city. With Iqbal on the minds and lips of many who attended, it was at this geographical location that the All-India Muslim League advanced a demand of monumental consequences for India. The transformation of the Muslim nation to statehood was shrouded in subtle layers of silence. Without defining their geographical boundaries, a plurality of Muslim sovereignty was implied in the phrase 'Independent States'. There was no discussion of the future 'centre', Muslim or all-Indian. Yet the clear reference in paragraph four of the resolution to 'the constitution' protecting both sets of minorities gives an insight into Jinnah's line of thinking.[27]

If the Congress was ready to storm the British centre, there were Muslims in the Punjab toying with the notion of secession. Jinnah could see that power at any centre covering the whole of India would force Congress to deal with the regional demands of Punjabi Muslims. On the eve of the League's annual meeting, the atmosphere in Lahore was embittered by the Punjab government's crackdown on Mashriqi's Khaksar movement. Sikander Hayat Khan was the butt of widespread Muslim criticism.[28] Eager to make capital out of a popular cause, Jinnah had no intention of breaking with Sikander. Support from the Punjabi and Bengali premiers was crucial to the success of his strategy. It was significant that Fazlul Haq, the premier of Bengal, moved the resolution. Whatever the Congress's all-India pretensions, Muslims in the majority provinces were unwilling to sacrifice their 'identity and independence' for the sake of the ideal of a united Indian nation. This was stated by Shahnawaz Khan, the Nawab of Mamdot and the president of the provincial Muslim League formally linked with the all-India body. It was Mamdot who had financed the publication of *A Confederacy of India* by a Punjabi.[29] In his opinion, Muslims could 'never tolerate ... subjection to a community' with which they shared 'no common ground ... in religion, culture and civilization'. The 'Congress ... was not fighting for the

[27]See Pirzada (ed.), *Foundations of Pakistan*, ii, p. 341.
[28]For a detailed account of the Punjab government's confrontation with the Khaksars see, A.D. Mazhar (comp.), *Khaksar Tehrik aur Azad-i-Hind: Dastiwazaat*, Islamabad: NCHR, 1985, pp. 30–6, 61–108.
[29]He was among the few Muslim leaders who tried explaining the League's demand. In a document sent to Jinnah after the League's adoption of the Lahore resolution, Shahnawaz Khan defended a 'Pakistan' based on the Punjab minus the Ambala division and parts of the hill tracts.(See Shah Nawaz Khan, 'What is Pakistan', QAP/F/134.)

independence of India'. It only wanted 'the domination of the Congress and the Hindus after the departure of the British'.[30]

The conviction that independence from Britain would mean rule by upper-caste Hindus gave the resolution its cutting edge with Muslims. It also evoked one of the finest defences of 'Pakistan' by the scheduled caste leader B.R. Ambedkar.[31] Jinnah's 100-minute oration in English was heard with rapt attention by an audience which mostly had no knowledge of the language. Clad in a *sherwani*, the defender of the community noted that while 'brother Gandhi ha[d] three votes', he had 'only one'. A tour d'force, he proceeded to read out a letter written by Lala Lajpat Rai to C.R. Das fifteen years ago. It showed 'that you cannot get away from being a Hindu if you are a Hindu'. After studying the law and history of Islam for six months, Lajpat Rai had concluded that the religion of the Muslims was 'an effective bar' to their unity and co-operation with the Hindus. There were many fine Muslims, but 'c[ould] any Muslim leader override the Quran?'[32] Contesting Rai's reading of Islamic law and history, Jinnah conceded that while Hindus and Muslims might unite against the British, they could not 'rule Hindustan on British lines'. Applying the Westminster model of parliamentary democracy in Indian conditions meant perpetual minority status for Muslims and rule by the Congress, the pre-eminent party of the Hindu majority.[33]

In putting forward a claim to nationhood, Indian Muslims were decidedly revolting against minoritarianism, caricatured as 'religious communalism'. Proclaiming the Indian Muslims to be a 'nation', Jinnah confessed that the idea of being a minority had been around for so long that 'we have got used to it ... these settled notions sometimes are very difficult to remove'. But the time had come to unsettle the notion since the 'word "Nationalist" has now become the play of conjurers in politics'.[34] No less a conjurer than Lajpat Rai, Jinnah came away from the League's session with a mixed bag of tricks. The demand that all future constitutional arrangements be reconsidered 'de novo' because Indian Muslims were a 'nation' entitled to equal treatment with the Hindu 'nation' was non-negotiable. Once the independence of Muslim states in the northwest and the northeast had been conceded, Jinnah was prepared to

[30]Pirzada (ed.), *Foundations of Pakistan*, ii, p. 326–7. The view was shared by Dr Muhammad Alam, once a Congress stalwart, who 'from his experience in the Congress ... had come to realise that they wanted to establish a Hindu *raj* under British protection'. (*SPPAI*, 30 March 1940, vol. lxii, no. 13, p. 167.)

[31]Written in the 1940s, his is one of the most cogent and lucid defences of 'Pakistan' ever. (See B.R. Ambedkar, *Pakistan or Partition of India* (third edition), Bombay: Thacker & Co. Ltd, 1946, passim.)

[32]Jinnah's presidential address to the AIML in March 1940, in Pirzada (ed.), *Foundations of Pakistan*, ii., p. 335–6.

[33]Ibid.

[34]Ibid., p. 335.

consider making arrangements with Hindustan. The threat of secession had the advantage of placating Muslims, certainly of the Punjab, and getting repudiated by the Congress and the British. This offered Jinnah the chance to graft a long innings before securing a constitutional arrangement covering the interests of all Indian Muslims. But in giving territorial expression to the Muslim assertion of nationhood, Jinnah and a mainly minority-province-based All-India Muslim League had to make large concessions to the autonomy and sovereignty of the majority provinces, not a very tidy beginning to the search for statehood. If reconciling the contradictory interests of Muslims in majority and minority provinces had thwarted the All-India Muslim League's representative pretensions in the past, the sheer impracticability of squaring the claim of nationhood with the promise of statehood required something more than an artful conjuring trick.

The historiographical debate has focused more on the Muslim claim to 'nationhood' than on the ambiguities of the demand for 'statehood'. A product of the telos which presumes the orchestration of separate nationhood as an inevitable overture to exclusive statehood, it ignores the uncertainties which attended the Muslim League's movement for a 'Pakistan'. While the insistence on national status for Indian Muslims was absolute, the demand for a separate and sovereign state with no relationship to a Hindustan containing almost as many Muslims remained open to negotiation until the late summer of 1946. An analytical distinction between 'nation' and 'state' on the one hand, and between a partition of the provinces and India on the other, is necessary to grasp the contradictory dynamics underlying the demand for a 'Pakistan'.

Declaring Muslims a 'nation' was not incompatible with a federal or confederal state structure covering the whole of India. But for the federal idea to be acceptable, the logic of majoritarianism and minoritarianism had to be scrapped and the fact of contested sovereignty acknowledged. The confederal idea was more compatible with the Muslim claim for nationhood, leaving open the possibility of an all-India entity reconstituted on the basis of multiple levels of sovereignty. In keeping with the better part of India's history, the notion of shared sovereignty enunciated by Jinnah and the League seemed the best way of tackling the dilemma posed by the absence of any neat equation between Muslim identity and territory. With 'nations' straddling states, the boundaries between them had to be permeable and flexible, not impenetrable and absolute. This is why Jinnah and the League were to remain implacably opposed to a partition of the Punjab and Bengal along religious lines even while furthering the cause of a political division of India between 'Pakistan' and 'Hindustan'.

'PAKISTAN' IN THE NORTH-WESTERN REGION

A 'Pakistan', variously defined, was being mooted long before the All-India Muslim League's call for separate Muslim states in north-western and north-eastern India. The different connotations of the term led Jinnah to drop it altogether in formulating a Muslim demand. The Hindu press 'fathered the word upon us', he once complained. While its would-be Muslim constituents for the most part were unaware or uncertain as to what it was intended to accomplish, the opposition had pronounced 'Pakistan' a menace. If there was confusion in the Muslim ranks, a negative consensus among non-Muslims gave the League's demand such coherence as it came to possess. It was not the 'Pakistan' of Choudhary Rahmat Ali's imaginings but a variation of Muhammad Iqbal's Punjab-centred solution of the Indian Muslim problem which appeared to have an edge in the battle of ideas during the final drafting of the League's Lahore resolution. Iqbal's Muslim state was to consist of the Muslim-majority provinces in the northwest of India. This did not preclude a Muslim state in the northeast, as even Lajpat Rai had conceded in 1924 while proposing a partition of the Punjab along religious lines. The League's resolution similarly acknowledged the right of Bengali Muslims to have a sovereign state of their own in the northeast. Without denying Bengal's importance to the all-India arrangements, it was the Punjab which could tip the balance decisively between partition or a power-sharing arrangement covering the whole subcontinent.

Politics in the Punjab were doubly complicated by the determination of the Sikhs to secure a 20 per cent share of the spoils of power. Nudged on by the provincial Hindu Mahasabha, the erstwhile sovereigns of the Punjab since the early 1930s had been resisting Muslim domination of the province through their premier political party, the Akali Dal. By February 1940 the Dal was 'voic[ing] the alarm felt by the Sikhs at the *Pakistan* and other schemes'.[35] In early April the Shiromani Gurdwara Prabandhak Committee (SGPC) lost no time condemning the 'Pakistan scheme'. So did the Congress and the Ahrars, two parties that did not have Sikh interests foremost in their minds. But then the initial opposition to the League's 'Pakistan' did not follow strictly communitarian lines. Sikhs were the most vociferous and had the firm backing of Mahasabhites and Arya Samajists. Together this combination lent potency to anti-League sentiments among non-Muslims in the Punjab. Keeping its options open, the Akali Dal announced that it would 'not help Congress to establish any regime in which the Muslim League had a predominating influence'.[36] This did not make the Dal any more enamoured of the Unionist ministry which they accused of 'utilising public money to propagate the cause of Islam'.[37]

The Mahasabha–Congress–Sikh combination held a key to the future of the Punjab. Unless satisfied with their share of representation in a Muslim-

[35]*SPPAI*, 17 February 1940, vol. lxii, no. 7, p. 71.
[36]*SPPAI*, 28 September 1940, vol. lxii, no. 40, p. 557.
[37]*SPPAI*, 17 February 1940, vol. lxii, no. 7, p. 71.

dominated province, not to mention a separate state, there was no question of forcing non-Muslims into such an administrative unit. This was especially so given the precarious balance between separation and accommodation. A striking feature of the Punjab in the early war years was the increase in paramilitary formations. Daily displays of simulated warfare by the colonial state, the roaring of guns and the smell of ammunition smoke, created an impression on youthful minds and led to the spread of paramilitary organizations in the province.[38] Apart from Mashriqi's spade-wielding Khaksars who provoked a government crackdown, volunteer groups like the RSS, the Akal Fauj and the Muhammadi Fauj catered to specific religious communities. In a departure from other Muslim-led groupings, Mashriqi gave a prominent place to women in his organization. Sardar Akhtar Begum from Kanpur spoke before an audience of 12,000 in Rawalpindi in the presence of 400 uniformed Khaksars.[39] And in the Punjab itself, Baji Rashida Latif courted arrest in the Khaksar cause.[40] Hindus and Sikhs interpreted the stiff resistance of the Khaksars as a prelude to a general mobilization of Muslims. Reports from the districts indicated 'communal nervousness, particularly amongst urban Hindus'. The countryside was rife with 'rumours ... that Hindus and Sikhs [we]re arming'. There were 'numerous applications, mostly from Hindus, for gun licenses, and a sharp increase in the demand for ammunition'. Alarm at the war situation and distrust of paper money gave a fillip to Mashriqi's movement as well as recruitment to the Akal Fauj.[41] The Akali leader, Giani Kartar Singh, had allegedly 'evolved a scheme to organise the turbulent elements amongst the Sikh community' into a volunteer corps with a view to 'utilising it in the event of any large-scale disturbances' and, by 'intimidating other communities', eventually 'forcing them to abandon the *Pakistan* and any similar schemes that conflict with Sikh interests'.[42]

Threats of mass violence by Sikhs in turn fed Muslim fears. Even pro-Congress Muslims like Ghazi Abdul Rahman slammed the Akalis for their 'communal activities' and accused Tara Singh and the Maharaja of Patiala of 'cooking up a scheme to establish Sikh raj in the Punjab'. He complained bitterly about the Congress letting Akali speakers make 'anti-Muslim speeches' from its *pandal*.[43] The Ahrars were equally perturbed. With the Mahasabha

[38]Mirza, *Karavan-i-Ahrar*, iv, p. 4.

[39]*SPPAI*, 2 March 1940, vol. lxii, no. 9, p. 111.

[40]Khaksars presented the government's stern reaction as evidence of Islam in danger. There was fury over the arrest of a Khaksar woman. (*SPPAI*, 18 May 1940, vol. lxii, no. 19, p. 262.)

[41]*SPPAI*, 15 June 1940, vol. lxii, no. 23, p. 334.

[42]*SPPAI*, 23 November 1940, vol. lxii, no. 45, p. 683.

[43]He was speaking at a meeting of the Azad Khyal, or independent minded, Muslim Congress in Ludhiana. Sheikh Muhammad Abdullah who was present agreed that Tara Singh had 'no right to deliver communal speeches from the Congress platform'. (*SPPAI*, 28 September 1940, vol. lxii, no. 40, p. 559.)

'encouraging the *Akalis* to desert Congress altogether',[44] any Muslim party dreaming of power in undivided Punjab had to find a way of accommodating the Sikhs. However, both Leaguers and Ahrars considered this secondary to winning an adequate share of power in future all-India arrangements. Sikh hostility may have been a barrier to thinking creatively about power sharing in undivided Punjab. But it was no excuse for the lack of foresight shown by Muslim spokespersons with regard to the Sikhs.

Muslim conceptions of the Punjab's role in an independent India had avoided facing up to the fact of its non-Muslim minorities. Demanding sovereignty without specifying the rights of citizenship for those outside the pale of Islam was simply not credible politics unless cast in an all-India framework. The League's resolution explicitly mentioned reciprocal safeguards for both sets of minorities, Muslim and non-Muslim. But the overemphasis on the 'communal' nature of the demand stunted real debate on citizenship rights within sovereign territorial states. Instead the venom generated by the politics of religiously informed cultural identities hinted at the likely fate of minorities in post-independence subcontinental practice. After the League's 'Pakistan' resolution, clarifying the future of non-Muslims in the north-western and the north-eastern provinces became vitally important. But neither Jinnah nor anyone else in the Muslim League cared to explain what non-Muslims might gain from becoming citizens of a Muslim state.

A tactical omission, it proved to be a fatal defect. The more so since the enthusiasts of a loosely defined 'Pakistan' demand could make of it what they wished. Saluting the League's resolution, Zafar Ali Khan was delighted that 'from that day onwards the Muslims of the north-west and north-east zones had declared complete independence'.[45] Complementing this Punjabi view, a minority-province Leaguer 'asked Muslims to set up an Islamic empire between the walls of Delhi and the borders of Afghanistan and Iran.'[46] Under the circumstances, postponing an understanding with non-Muslims in the majority provinces until Muslims had been won over by the League and the British and the Congress conceded the principle of 'Pakistan' was dangerous. It left the propagandists and antagonists of 'Pakistan' free to vent their bigotry in increasingly shocking fashion. While the supporters concentrated on securing the sovereign gains of full independence, the opponents rejected the very idea of Muslim dominance in the north-western provinces. This was the flashpoint around which the politics of communitarian identities and contested sovereignties converged and exploded in the decisive decade of the 1940s. Taking much and adding something of their own to the narratives of

[44]Sikhs were worried about Congress overtures to the Muslim League spearheaded by Rajagopalachari, fearing it might secure 50 per cent representation. (*SPPAI*, 21 September 1940, vol. lxii, no. 37, p. 546.)

[45]*SPPAI*, 30 March 1940, vol. lxii, no. 13, p. 167.

[46]Ibid.

a religiously informed cultural identity, these dynamics are a clue to understanding the political context in which 'Pakistan' came to be nailed to the coffin of a united Punjab and Bengal.

Despite the virulent opposition it aroused among non-Muslims, the public airing of the League's demand was not intended to foreclose the prospect of an undivided Punjab. Interested primarily in mobilizing Muslim support for the League, Jinnah never lost sight of a negotiated arrangement covering the whole of India. The assumption was that once the principle of Muslim provinces being grouped to constitute independent states was accepted, there would be plenty of opportunity to reassure religious minorities in these provinces. It was this grand expectation coupled with alliances of convenience with supra-communitarian groupings like the Unionists in the Punjab and the Krishak Praja Party in Bengal which explains why the League high command did nothing to solicit non-Muslim support for 'Pakistan'. If caste Hindus appeared to be beyond persuasion, then tactical accommodations with the Sikhs and the scheduled castes could not be ruled out.

The Sikh attitude towards the Congress, as reflected by the Akali Dal, was at best an ambivalent one. There was little warmth of feeling between Master Tara Singh and the Mahatma who asked the Sikhs not to enlist in the non-cooperation movement as they were inadequately versed in the methods of non-violence.[47] Insulted by the remark, Tara Singh contemplated resigning from the Congress. His defiant posture against Gandhi was hailed by the Punjabi Hindu press, lending weight to Muslim suspicions of a Mahasabhite-backed Sikh conspiracy to undermine their position. Bhai Parmanand publicly 'expressed the hope' that Tara Singh would 'join the Hindu *Maha Sabha* in an agitation against the *Pakistan* scheme'.[48] Although he declined the Mahasabha offer, Tara Singh who was then also president of the SGPC made certain that there was no let up in the Sikh campaign against the League's 'Pakistan'. At an Akali meeting in Amritsar district, Udham Singh Nagoke formally accused the British for 'instigat[ing] Mr Jinnah to propound the *Pakistan* scheme in order to maintain their rule'.[49]

Yet the League's demand had failed to elicit an enthusiastic response outside a select circle of Muslims. It was Muslims averse to the idea of 'Pakistan' who sprang into action in the immediate aftermath of the League's session. In the

[47]One reason for the Akalis to distance themselves from the Congress was the large stake of the Sikhs in the recruitment drive under way following the outbreak of war. But they were equally wary of Congress working out a modus operandi with the League. Some like Ajit Singh, MLA, thought 'Sikhs should secede from Congress'. Others agreed with Giani Gurmukh Singh Musafir who 'urged Sikhs to join the Congress in large numbers to replace [Gandhi]'. (*SPPAI*, 28 September 1940, vol. lxii, no. 40, p. 558.)

[48]*SPPAI*, 5 October 1940, vol. lxii, no. 39, p. 577.

[49]*SPPAI*, 19 October 1940, vol. lxii, no. 40, p. 590.

Punjab, the Ahrars in conjunction with other pro-Congress Muslims vowed to defuse the 'Pakistan' bomb.[50] Meetings held to popularize the League's demand, never very large to begin with, were disrupted by Ahrar volunteers. The more voluble of the Ahrars tried queering Jinnah's pitch by questioning his representative credentials.[51] Posturing as outriders of an anti-imperialist Muslim front, the Ahrars poured scorn on the 'Pakistan' scheme. It was detrimental to the struggle for independence and would mean ruination for Muslims. The Muslim state demanded by the League was destined to be neither Islamic nor sovereign, but a 'Ghulamistan' or the abode of slaves.[52]

While sticking to his anti-Ahmadi rhetoric, even the Ahrar firebrand Ataullah Shah Bukhari now tempered his speeches with appeals for Hindu–Muslim unity. He was opposed to all 'communal' schemes, including 'Pakistan', and proposed setting up a volunteer corp so that 'Muslims would be seen guarding Hindu houses'. Bukhari offered his services to the Punjab premier to help preserve internal peace.[53] While berating Muslims for voting the Unionists into power, he was willing to co-operate with the government in its war effort.[54] The gesture was incompatible with efforts by other Ahrars to promote the Congress cause in the Punjab by launching a civil disobedience campaign. But if Bukhari was thinking of going on the government payroll, those dallying with the idea of an anti-imperialist struggle were prepared to exert their energies only if 'afforded financial support' by the Congress.[55] Demanding cash on the nail for services rendered damaged the credibility of the Ahrars, blunting the edge of their otherwise quite effective anti-League harangues. A deep-seated social conservatism was another potential handicap. Maulana Habibur Rahman, who was allegedly 'promised a sum of Rs 3000 for his services' by Subhas Chandra Bose,[56] attacked the government's education bill proposing co-education in the primary schools as 'anti-*Islamic*'.[57] Firm believers in mixing religion with politics, these were men promoting the radical Congress cause in the Punjab!

Where the Ahrars fumbled in their opposition to 'Pakistan', there were others ready to fill the breach, jointly and severally. Leading from the front in the campaign against 'Pakistan' at the time were men like Mian Iftikharuddin, Ataullah Jahanian, Maulana Daud Ghaznavi, Sayyid Habib, to name only a few, as well as those with pro-communist leanings like Daniel Latifi and Mazhar Ali Khan. This Punjabi contingent was not alone in its resolve. Khan

[50]See *SPPAI*, 9 March 1940, vol. lxii, no. 10, p. 127.
[51]See *SPPAI*, 27 April 1940, vol. lxii, no. 17, p. 237.
[52] Mirza, *Karavan-i-Ahrar*, iii, pp. 115–16.
[53]*SPPAI*, 6 July 1940, vol. lxii, no. 26, p. 382.
[54]*SPPAI*, 9 November 1940, vol. lxii, no. 43, p. 666.
[55]*SPPAI*, 17, August 1940, vol. lxii, no. 32, p. 472.
[56]*SPPAI*, 13, January 1940, vol. lxii, no. 2, p. 15.
[57]*SPPAI*, 27 August 1940, vol. lxii, no. 4, p. 41.

Abdul Qayum Khan, a member of the central assembly from the NWFP, declared that all 'true Muslims' in his home province would participate in the Congress's civil disobedience movement and 'help shatter the Pakistan scheme'.[58] A determined effort to combat the League's demand was made by the Azad Muslim Conference.[59] But the response to its call for an 'anti-Pakistan scheme' day was negligible in a province where horizons were shaped by more localized issues. Few were persuaded by Iftikharuddin's assertion that Congress's policy towards the minorities 'afforded [the Muslim] community every reasonable safeguard'.[60] Most workers and members of the Azad Muslim Conference agreed that 'the Muslim public was unlikely to be influenced if nationalist Muslims conducted propaganda against the Government from the Congress platform'.[61] Even the Kashmiri leader, Sheikh Muhammad Abdullah, concurred. At a meeting of the Azad Khyal Muslim Congress in Ludhiana, he 'condemned the Pakistan scheme' and regretted that it was 'the voice of the reactionary and not the nationalist Muslims to which the outside world paid more attention'. While 'blam[ing] caste Hindus for their illiberal treatment of Muslims, who had been second to none in offering sacrifices in the cause of liberty', Abdullah nonetheless hoped his co-religionists would join the Congress.[62] As the Ahrar historian wryly admits, 'the condition of Muslims in Congress politics was like that of the unenthusiastic child who had to be beaten constantly to make him go to school'.[63]

If Congress's chronic weaknesses in the Punjab were showing up at the wrong moment, there were alternative forms of resistance to the 'Pakistan' demand. By far the most significant was the Unionist premier's formal dissociation from the League's resolution. Sikander admitted drafting the resolution, but reported that its concluding passages calling for an 'agency centre' had been deleted. On 11 March 1941 he told the Punjab assembly that his was not a Muslim League but a purely Punjabi government. Speaking as an individual, he noted that there were many schemes which went under the name of 'Pakistan'. There was one ascribed to Jamaluddin al-Afghani. And for the one associated with Iqbal, there was another identified with Rahmat Ali. Even an Englishman had published a 'Pakistan' scheme and there was one attributed to the irrepressible Mahasabhite, Bhai Parmanand. Most of these had nothing in common with the League's scheme. It was not the Muslims but the Hindu and Sikh press which labelled the Lahore resolution 'Pakistan'. Now that it had stuck in popular consciousness, the League saw no reason to correct the misperception. An unshakeable believer in the continuation of the British connection, Sikander

[58]*SPPAI*, 20 April 1940, vol. lxii, no. 16, p. 219.
[59]Ibid., p. 222.
[60]*SPPAI*, 9 November 1940, vol. lxii, no. 43, p. 666.
[61]*SPPAI*, 7 December 1940, vol. lxii, no. 47, p. 731.
[62]*SPPAI*, 28 September 1940, vol. lxii, no. 40, p. 559.
[63]Mirza, *Karavan-i-Ahrar*, iv, p. 90.

pronounced that the only possible government in the Punjab was a Punjabi government and non-Punjabis had no business interfering in the matter.[64]

What Sikander Hayat Khan did not explain was whether he believed that a Punjabi government of the Unionist variety could survive the severance of the British connection. In explaining his position on 'Pakistan', the Punjab premier was seeking to dampen the effects of his concord with Jinnah and the Muslim League. Hindu-owned newspapers in the provincial capital had been demanding a clarification of Sikander's stance on the 'Pakistan' demand in the hope that he would 'embroil himself either with his non-Muslim supporters or with the Muslim League'.[65] Sikander opted to keep fences mended where it mattered most—among the agricultural combine that symbolized the Unionist alliance with the colonial state. Yet success in the formal arenas of politics could delay, not prevent, the spread of a nocuous kind of communitarian virus in the informal arenas debating the 'Pakistan' scheme.

Convinced that exigencies of war would persuade the British to 'make unlimited concessions to the Muslim community', Sikh leaders were equally paranoid about any Congress gestures towards the Muslim League.[66] They were not alone. Members of the League of Radical Congressmen were furious with M.N. Roy's overtures to the League and criticism of the Congress.[67] A gathering of 15,000 Arya Samajists in Lahore heard that if the Communal Award was 'proof of the Government's culpability' in undermining Indian nationalism, the 'Pakistan' scheme aimed at 'achiev[ing] a Muslim, conquest of India with British help'. Tara Singh, who was conspicuously present, 'warned ... that Muslims were smuggling rifles into the Punjab'. Fortunately, many had been seized by the government.[68]

Not all the demons let loose by the League's resolution in the Punjab fitted neatly into their communitarian packaging. Identity and sovereignty were intermeshing in intriguing ways, making the link between *qaum* and *sarkar* (government) a feature of localized realities rather than the singular 'nation' and 'state' envisaged by the narratives on inclusionary nationalism and exclusionary communitarianism. Location within the colonial system placed far more demands on the individual in relation to the community,

---

[64]*Punjab Legislative Assembly Debates*, 11 March 1941, pp. 348–62, cited in ibid., vol. i, p. 44 and Zahid Choudhury, *Pakistan ki Siyasi Tehrik. Muslim Punjab ka Siyasi Irtaqa (1849–1947)*, vol. v, Lahore: Adara Mutalliya-i-Tarikh, 1991, pp. 314–22. While Barkat Ali and Mamdot thought Sikander's ideas were in keeping with the spirit of the League's resolution, both the *Zamindar* and the *Inqilab* refrained from commenting on the speech.

[65]*SPPAI*, 6 April 1940, vol. lxii, no. 14, p. 190.

[66]*SPPAI*, 28 September 1940, vol. lxii, no. 40, p. 558.

[67]They threatened to form their own communist party unless he mended his ways. (*SPPAI*, 9 November 1940, vol. lxii, no. 43, p. 665.)

[68]*SPPAI*, 7 December 1940, vol. lxii, no. 47, p. 729.

real and imagined, than has been permitted by the simplistic renderings of post-colonial nationalist reconstructions. An individual's conception of space might be expansive or restrictive at the rhetorical level, but politics were influenced by the circumstances of personal geography. Consequently, many of the ambiguities inherent in the relationship between 'nation' and region were reproduced in the contested sovereignties struggling for state power.

The case of the Ahmadis is a good illustration of the point. As ever, antipathy towards them cut across the religiously defined communitarian divide. If Ahrars led the charge on behalf of the Muslims, Akalis and Aryas did so for Sikhs and Hindus. The Ahrar complaint that 'Ahmedis ha[d] undue influence over local officials' in Qadian was widely shared by the members of the other two communities.[69] Pandit Dhirat Ram ridiculed 'a claim of the Mirza Sahib to be an incarnation of Lord Krishna'. How events on the all-India scale were affecting politics in the localities was revealed at an Akali conference in Qadian where thousands learnt about 'the alleged scheme to establish an *Ahmadi* state within a radius of ten miles of Qadian'. Whatever the Muslim League's stated aim, Ahmadis were 'giving practical shape to it and ... forming an infant *Pakistan* in the Punjab'.[70] Fears of an Ahmadi '*Pakistan* in miniature in Qadian' would seem to challenge any privileging of the nexus between religious identity and sovereignty in late-colonial India. It could encourage a Hindu like Dhirat Ram to urge his Sikh brethren to 'intervene and prevent the extension of *Ahmadi* rule'. Whether Muslim, Hindu or Sikh, many Punjabis believed the government was encouraging a 'dangerous scheme of establishing an *Ahmadi* state'.[71]

What kind of a state the All-India Muslim League and Jinnah were proposing to establish was by no means clear. The common belief that it was the League which made relentless use of Islam to force the issue of 'Pakistan' is worth re-examining. An assessment of the initial reaction to the 'Pakistan' demand would be incomplete without expanding the focus from the Punjab to include the NWFP and Sind. This has the added merit of shedding further light on the curious coupling of religion and politics under the banner of Congress's inclusionary nationalism and the League's exclusionary communitarianism. At worst a picture of bigotry and at best an anti-imperial politics, both are worth dissecting in the two provinces of 'Pakistan' that were relatively less afflicted by communitarian tensions than the Punjab. If Ahrars combined social conservatism with a pro-Congress posture in the Punjab, they along with other Muslim organizations—including the Frontier Congress associated with the Khudai Khidmatgar leader Abdul Ghaffar Khan—have left even more curious traces in the historical annals of the NWFP and Sind.

[69]*SPPAI*, 9 Nomvember 1940, vol. lxii, no. 43, p. 666.
[70]*SPPAI*, 23 November 1940, vol. lxii, no. 45, p. 683.
[71]Ibid.

The Islamic Roots of 'Pakistan'?

With Muslims in a comfortable majority in the NWFP and Sind, accommodations with non-Muslims were in principle better here than in the Punjab. Although the NWFP remained under a Congress ministry for most of the 1940s, it was not exempt from the fury of the bearded men of Islam, almost none of whom supported the League's 'Pakistan'. And in Sind, where the Muslim League hung on to the ministry by hook or by crook, the economic power of Hindu commercial groups and the indebtedness of Muslims in both rural and urban areas gave the religious divide a potentially inflammatory dimension. Assessing the reaction in these two provinces to the prospect of a Muslim 'nation' attaining sovereign state power is at once instructive and sobering.

The one thing all Muslims shared was their inability to agree on the question of authority, whether spiritual or temporal. Displaying a fairly advanced stage of anti-imperialist consciousness, Pathans preferred their own metres and rhythms to those of the Congress or the League. They also kept their eyes firmly on landscapes closer to home than New Delhi. A healthy balance to be sure, it was never immune from the lure of more distant power. After entering politics in the early 1930s and establishing the Khudai Khidmatgar or Red Shirt movement, Abdul Ghaffar Khan aligned with the Congress. So did his brother Dr Khan Sahib. With support among the smaller and medium-scale landlords of the province, the Khan brothers became the bete noire of the pro-British bigger landlords or *khans*, many of whom later joined the Muslim League. Real economic and political differences notwithstanding, it was often personal factors which gave collective causes a menacing edge. Looking for his jugular but finding instead his Achilles' heel, Ghaffar Khan's opponents created an uproar over his son's marriage to a Parsi woman.[72] Jinnah might have felt some sympathy for the Frontier Gandhi when Jinnah's only daughter married a Parsi. But the Frontier was not Bombay.

It was adding to the sense of Pathan injury for Dr Khan Sahib's daughter, Maryam, to marry a Sikh flight lieutenant who had converted to Christianity. In an interesting insight into the intermeshing of the public and the private in the life of political leaders, the marriage infuriated many Pathans and elicited abuses more staggering than those heard in the alleyways of Punjab's gutter press.[73] It was seen to have 'destroyed the success which the Congress and M. Gandhi had achieved during the past twenty years'.[74] Ghaffar Khan distanced himself from his brother and niece, regretting the 'malicious propaganda'

---

[72]Both parties renounced their religion which 'annoyed orthodox Muslims'. (*Secret North-West Frontier Province Police Abstract of Intelligence*, Peshawar, 2 January 1940, vol. xxxvi, no. 1, NCHCR, Islamabad, pp. 2–3 (henceforth *SNPAI*,, followed by date, volume and page number/s.)

[73]See *SNPAI*, 9 June 1942, vol. xxxvii, no. 23, p. 64.

[74]Ibid., p. 66.

circulated against his family by government agents and emphasizing that the movement was 'a national one in which personalities find no place'.[75] But the incident tarnished the image of the Red Shirts and the Congress alike. Some Muslims contemplated severing all ties with the Congress, anticipating its impending demise. That the propaganda was effective is suggested by Dr Khan Sahib's public confession of helplessness and offer to retire from public life.[76]

Reactions to these two marriages in the Khan family, spread apart by roughly two and a half years, underline the socially conservative attitudes of the Pathans and allows for a more nuanced appreciation of their religious sentiments. Different from the *ashraf* classes in significant ways, they had stern notions of how to keep women in their place. There was open hostility when the Khaksar spokesperson, Sardar Begum Akhtar, appeared at a public rally without *purdah*. An Ahrar *maulvi* in Peshawar damned her to perdition for infringing local custom and charged the Khaksars of trying to silence their critics by inducting women.[77] This irritated Begum Akhtar into accusing the 'Congress [for] hir[ing] Maulvis to create dissensions among Muslims'. Her 'object in discarding purdah', she told the bemused Pathans, was 'to request them to unite to achieve the one-time glory of Islam'.[78] The most loquacious public speakers in the province wanted to achieve that end through *shariat* rule and, by implication, eliminate women's participation in politics, formal and informal.

Before the Muslim League secured a toehold in the province, the two purported allies of the Congress, the Ahrars and the Jamiat-ul-Ulema, were agitating for the implementation of the *shariat*. A common objective did not mean agreement on how to go about achieving it, either in form or in substance. Even mosques were disputed sites, with each group unwilling to let anyone other than its own number lead Friday and Id prayers.[79] In an ironic twist to the socialist platform of Bose's Forward Bloc, the president of its provincial wing, Abdul Rahim Popalzai, contended in Peshawar that 'Islam was in danger in a country where the Indian Penal Code was in force'.[80] As he explained to the Muslims, 'neither the holy Quran nor their religion was free

[75]*SNPAI*, 26 May 1942, vol. xxxvii, no. 21, p. 58.

[76]*SNPAI*, 19 May 1942, vol. xxxvii, no. 20, p. 54. The Provincial Congress Committee rejected the resignation. Shored up by the confidence reposed in him, Dr Khan Sahib slapped a Muslim Leaguer for saying that he was not a Muslim leader but 'a friend and leader of Hindus' who had now 'married his daughter to a Sikh'. He apologized for the outburst, insisting that 'the English not Muslims were his enemies'. (*SNPAI*, 23 February 1943, vol. xxxixi, no. 8, p. 18.)

[77]*SNPAI*, 27 February 1940, vol. xxxvi, no. 9, p. 65.

[78]*SNPAI*, 12 March 1940, vol. xxxvi, no. 11, p. 80.

[79]In Dera Ismail Khan, Congressmen and Ahrars considered Khaksars to be *kafirs* and refused to let one of them lead the Id prayers. (*SNPAI*, 23 January and 20 February 1940, vol. xxxvi, nos.4, 8, pp. 26, 59.)

[80]*SNPAI*, 9 April 1940, vol. xxxvi, no. 15, p. 105.

because they could only abide by those orders which did not infringe British law'. A supporter of the Faqir of Ipi whose operations in Waziristan kept the colonial authorities constantly on edge, Popalzai maintained that under the circumstances *jihad* was incumbent on Muslims.[81] Together with the penchant of the Congress's rainbow coalition to call their opponents *kafirs*, the Muslim League with its late start had plenty of catching up to do to establish its Islamic credentials on the basis of the 'Pakistan' demand.

As in the Punjab, Leaguers in the Frontier thought it 'shameful for Muslims to free their religion through a Hindu organisation such as the Congress'.[82] There was resentment that *zaildars*, *inamkhors* and *jagirdars*, in short all those 'employed by Government were called "toadies" by Congress while those ... given allowances by Hindus were called nationalists'.[83] It was not just the importance of Muslim identity which gave Islam such a prominent place in the political discourse of the Pathans. There was a darker underside which cannot be seen through the veil of 'communalism'. Assertions of Muslimness by Pathans were rooted in a regional culture whose tribal and patriarchal moorings could transform Islam into a vehicle for outright bigotry.

It was the personal attacks on Mohammed Ali Jinnah by the League's opponents which set the tone for the public debate on 'Pakistan'. At a Congress meeting in Bannu, the League's scheme was condemned and Jinnah described 'as a representative not of Muslims but of capitalists'. During 'National Week' speakers at various gatherings rejected 'Pakistan' 'as impracticable'.[84] Several people saw a British hand in the League's resolution.[85] This was firmly denied by the Muslim League. Its standard line was that after the experience with Congress ministries in the Hindu-majority provinces, Muslims could not depend on that body. According to Sardar Aurangzeb Khan, who later became the first League premier in the NWFP, Muslims only wanted to be able to rule in the six provinces where they were in a majority.[86] But if Muslim sovereignty in provinces where they were in a majority seemed reasonable enough, contestations over social and sacred space imbued the political dialogue with extra venom. In Bannu, at a Muslim League meeting it was heard that Muslims had been 'prevented from observing their religious rites' and 'frequently the flesh of pigs had been thrown in their mosques'. It was 'for these reasons that Muslims had proposed the scheme for partition'.[87]

Cultural justifications for Muslim-majority rule in the north-western provinces could easily descend into bigotry. Fazal Dad, the president of the

[81] *SNPAI*, 16 April 1940, vol. xxxvi, no. 16, p. 116.
[82] *SNPAI*, 2 January 1940, vol. xxxvi, no. 1, p. 5.
[83] *SNPAI*, 9 January 1940, vol. xxxvi, no. 2, p. 14.
[84] *SNPAI*, 9 April 1940, vol. xxxvi, no. 15, p. 103.
[85] *SNPAI*, 18 January 1940, vol. xxxvi, no. 16, p. 114.
[86] *SNPAI*, 23 April 1940, vol. xxxvi, no. 17, pp. 124–5.
[87] *SNPAI*, 7 May 1940, vol. xxxvi, no. 19, p. 146.

Dera Ismail Khan Muslim League, depicted 'Hindus as unclean atheists and nothing better than dogs'. It was 'quite impossible for Muslims to unite with people who believed in fire, snakes, cows and pipal trees'.[88] Muslims had to 'avoid becoming followers of Hindus like Jawaharlal Nehru and Mr Gandhi'.[89] The acclaimed Urdu orator Nawab Bahadur Yar Jang left his Deccan environs to join the All India Muslim League delegation that had been sent to court the Pathans. India's central assembly had 'a majority of Hindus' and was 'ruled from Wardha', the seat of the Congress high command. In a politically astute gesture, Jang 'alleged that Sikhs were more closely allied to Muslims than to Hindus'.[90]

Few Pathans rallied to the League until the first real organizational drive in early 1942.[91] The catalyst was provided by Aurangzeb Khan's efforts to form a League ministry, a goal which materialized only in 1943, long after the fortuitous resignation of the Congress ministry. In a shrewd tactic, Leaguers insisted that there was 'little difference' between them and the Red Shirts who should join together and press for 'Pakistan' which was the 'only practical way of achieving independence'.[92] Given the array of voices trying to explain the meaning of 'Pakistan', the Pathans had reason to be puzzled about its spatial geography. In September 1940 a meeting of the pro-League branch of the Jamiat-ul-Ulema in the province had heard that 'living in the Eastern part of Afghanistan [sic]', Pathans had 'no concern with India'. A resolution was passed calling for the 'formation of an independent Muslim State consisting of Eastern Afghanistan, Tribal territory, the Frontier Province, Kashmir, the Punjab, Sind, Baluchistan' which was 'to be placed under the Nizam of Hyderabad'.[93] This was why the League high command had to despatch speakers from other provinces to the Frontier, not necessarily to inject clarity into the minds of the Pathans. Zafar Ali Khan's son, Akhtar Ali, who came to boost the League, ran down Gandhi's policy of spinning his way to independence but believed that 'freedom lay in Hindu–Muslim unity'.[94] If this was not cause for confusion, Pir Said Shah told a League meeting in Kohat that if Gandhi 'accepted the principle of Pakistan, there could be no objection to Muslims forming a National Government with Hindus'.[95]

There were layers of meanings that could be attached to the League's demand.

[88]SNPAI, 4 June 1940, vol. xxxvi, no. 23, p. 177.

[89]Ibid.

[90]SNPAI, 11 March 1941, vol. xxxvii, no. 11, p. 35.

[91]For a detailed study of politics in the NWFP during the final decade of British rule, see Erland Jansson, India, Pakistan or Pakhtunistan: The Nationalist Movements in the North West Frontier Province, 1937–1947, Uppsala: ACTA Universitatis Upsaliensis, 1981.

[92]SNPAI, 6 January 1942, vol. xxxvii, no. 1, p. 3.

[93]SNPAI, 10 September 1940, vol. xxxvi, no. 37, pp. 277–8.

[94]SNPAI, 26 May 1942, vol. xxxvii, no. 21, p. 62.

[95]SNPAI, 25 August 1942, vol. xxxvii, no. 34, p. 95.

What helped conflate 'Pakistan' with a 'partition' based on separation from Hindu India were the more capricious utterances and practices of the League propagandists. A meeting of the organization 'voted that any Muslim having any intercourse with Congress was a "kafir".[96] Yet, alienating the minorities was not practicable politics once the first League ministry assumed office in the early summer of 1943. After talks with Giani Sher Singh, the League premier Aurangzeb Khan promised safeguards for the minorities. He had already inducted Sardar Ajit Singh into his cabinet.[97] This did not prevent Muslims and Sikhs in Haripur from feuding on the occasion of Guru Purab or birthday of Govind Singh. Two Sikhs were murdered in a *gurdwara* while another Sikh temple was burnt down. One Muslim died of injuries.[98] Irreparable damage to Muslim–Sikh relations was averted when one of those accused of the violence found his experience of Haripur jail mortifying enough to offer to reconstruct the demolished *gurdwara* at his own expense. This was seen to have 'created a good atmosphere'.[99]

So as in the Punjab and UP, communitarian relations in the Frontier had their own dynamics and ways of regaining a semblance of social balance. With communities sharing space at the local and regional levels, even the most jarring narratives of sovereignty had to ultimately resist making absolute assertions of a religiously informed cultural identity. But if the League's demand for 'Pakistan' helped sharpen inter-communitarian discord in the NWFP, the Islamic appeals of the Congress's allies in the Jamiat-ul-Ulema and the Ahrars did little to assuage non-Muslim fears about the implications of Muslim rule. Often treated as exclusive rather than mutually reinforcing, the conflicting strands in Muslim politics created the conditions that made it difficult for Hindus and Sikhs to divorce the politics of the League's demand from the religiously informed anti-imperialism of Congress's regional allies.

Jawaharlal Nehru who came to the Frontier at the end of May 1940, only to be flooded with requests for funds by Ahrar leaders, had cause for consternation. The paragon of non-religious nationalism might have been stunned by the propaganda conducted on the Congress's behalf in the NWFP. Exhortations 'to put into practice the teachings of the Quran' were common at Congress meetings. These could be overlooked when confined to urging audiences to 'fear God more than the police'.[100] It may also have been tactically correct to ignore outright calls by the Ahrars for 'an Islamic Government in India' based on the *shariat*.[101] This was because Muslims were being told that according to the *shariat* they ought to 'join Congress' since they could 'not

[96]*SNPAI*, 26 January 1943, vol. xxxvii, no. 4, p. 18.
[97]*SNPAI*, 25 May 1943, vol. xxxvii, no. 21, pp. 47–8.
[98]*SNPAI*, 4 January 1944, vol. xxxx, no. 1, p. 1.
[99]*SNPAI*, 11 January 1944, vol. xxxx, no. 2, p. 2.
[100]*SNPAI*, 6 August 1940, vol. xxxvi, no. 32, p. 245.
[101]*SNPAI*, 10 September 1940, vol. xxxvi, no. 37, p. 277.

remain under the rule of Kafirs'.[102] More complicated were the Jamiat-ul-Ulema's attempts at glorifying Islam and stressing the inferiority of European civilization. Claiming to be the 'religious and political representative body of Muslims', the Jamiat was proud of 'working side by side with Congress' while attacking Macaulay and the English language.[103]

For a secular nationalist, there were other more discomfiting tendencies in Pathan politics. At the forefront of the Congress's anti-recruitment drive, the Ahrar youth wing gave priority to eliminating the Ahmadis, 'a sect ... started by the English'. The Ahrar were 'civilised' unlike the *farangis* who 'danced naked and did not observe purdah'. It followed that the 'English ought to be removed from the world'.[104] Even if Congress could permit such excesses, it did not serve its cause in the Frontier to have Maulvi Abdul Qayum of Kanpur, then president of the All-India Majlis-i-Ahrar, assert that while Muslims had helped Hindus in UP during the freedom struggle of 1857, 'the Hindu majority there had indicated in a number of ways that Hindu control in India was their aim'.[105] As the champions of the red Islamic revolution, Mazhar Ali Azhar and his fellow Ahrar, Sahibzada Pir Fazlul Hassan, visited the NWFP and made their intentions plain against the green of the landscape. They 'condemn[ed] western education and culture' and the 'lack of the religious outlook in all parties, except the Ahrars'.[106] If this was the Frontier's brand of Congress's inclusionary nationalism, then its exclusiveness, even when justified by twisting Islamic idioms for anti-imperialist ends, cannot sustain the mythic separation of 'nationalism' and 'communalism'.

Sind furnishes corroborating evidence for this argument. Compared to the NWFP where they formed almost 95 per cent of the population, Muslims in Sind were just short of a three-quarter majority. As in the Punjab, Hindus dominated the commercial life of the province. Until the debate on the separation of Sind from Bombay occasioned bigoted narratives in the provincial press,[107] tensions along the lines of religious community were offset

---

[102]*SNPAI*, 24 September 1940, vol. xxxvi, no. 39, p. 284.

[103]*SNPAI*, 6 August 1940, vol. xxxvi, no. 32, p. 246.

[104]*SNPAI*, 18 March 1941, vol. xxxvii, no. 11, p. 39.

[105]*SNPAI*, 19 August 1941, vol. xxxvii, no. 33, p. 115.

[106]*SNPAI* 23 June 1942, vol. xxxvii, no. 25, p. 73.

[107]In 1933 there were forty-eight newspapers in Sind. The Karachi based *Al-Wahid*, edited by Shaikh Abdul Majid Sindhi, promoted the Muslim cause. Another leading Muslim paper, the *Sind Zamindar* from Sukkur, was owned by M.A. Khuhro and edited by Pir Ali Mohammad Rashidi. Among the more important newspapers with Hindu proprietors was the *Sansar Samachar* and *Qurbani* of Karachi and the *Sind Hindu* from Hyderabad. The bigoted and exclusionary communitarian narratives of the *Al-Wahid* and the *Sansar Samachar* dominated the discourse on identity and sovereignty in the Sindhi press. (*Annual Report on Indian and Anglo-Vernacular Newspapers Published in the Bombay Presidency for 1933*, Bombay, 1934, pp. 2–9.)

by a relationship of convenience between Muslim landed elements—*waderas* and *jagirdars*,—and Hindu commercial classes, known as *banias*. *Waderas*, *jagirdars* and the *banias* colluded in oppressing *haris*, the predominantly Muslim peasantry locked in bonds of labour servitude and debt.[108] With the separation of Sind and the holding of the first provincial elections under the 1935 Act, economic interests at different levels of politics gave new meanings to religiously informed cultural differences.

Even before the 'Pakistan' demand was articulated, the dispute over the Sukkur Manzilgah had been fabricated by provincial Leaguers to unsettle Allah Bakhsh Somroo's ministry which was dependent on support from the Congress and the Hindu Independent Party. Intended as a way station for Mughal troops on the move, the Manzilgah included a small mosque which had subsequently been abandoned. On a small island in the near distance was the temple of Saad Bela, sacred space for the large number of Hindus settled on the banks of the Indus at Sukkur.[109] The symbolic convergence of identity and sovereignty over a forgotten mosque provided ammunition for those seeking office at the provincial level. Making an issue out of a non-issue, the Sind Muslim League in early June 1939 formally reclaimed the mosque. Once its deadline of 1 October 1939 for the restoration of the mosque to Muslims had passed, the League started an agitation. The more moderate leadership of Abdullah Haroon, member of the central assembly, as well as Hashim Gazdar and G.M. Syed, was soon replaced by militant elements represented by Sheikh Abdul Majid Sindhi, a convert from Hinduism, and Pir Ghulam Mujaddid. Over a thousand League volunteers filled the colonial jails. With thousands more waiting in the wings, the government panicked. The mosque was handed over to the Muslims who offered prayers in the presence of the district collector.[110]

This exacerbated tensions in Sukkur district where Bhagat Kanwar Ram, a saint revered by both communities, had been murdered. Infuriated Hindus protested in large numbers outside the Manzilgah. In November, the Sind Hindu Provincial Conference, attended by local Congressmen and presided over by Dr Moonje, threatened retaliation in the Central Provinces if Muslims were not evacuated from the mosque. Once Ramazan was safely out of the

---

[108]For a contemporary account of the socio-economic complexion of Sindhi society, see Syed Ghulam Mustafa, *Towards Understanding the Muslims of Sind*, Karachi, 1944. Also see Zahid Choudhury, *Pakistan ki Siyasi Tehrik. Sind: Masla-i-Khud Mukhtari ka Aghaz*, vol. vi, Lahore: Adara Mutalliya-i-Tarikh, 1994, pp. 89–95.

[109]See Mirza, *Karavan-i-Ahrar*, iv, pp. 232–7 and Choudhury, *Pakistan ki Siyasi Tehrik. Sind*, vi, pp. 73–4.

[110]'Report A about the Communal Riots in Sukkur Towns and the Surrounding Villages' submitted to the Congress Working Committee by Abdul Qayum Khan, member of the central assembly from Chakwal in the NWFP, Peshawar, 18 January 1940, QAP File/965, p. 7.

way, the government regained control of the mosque after resorting to a *lathi* charge and tear gas. Ensuing eruptions left seventeen Muslims and forty Hindus dead in Sukkur town. Once the disturbances engulfed the countryside, local *maulvis* enraged villagers by recounting gory tales of how 'breasts of Muslim women had been cut off' by Hindus. Equipped with hatchets and clubs, Muslim villagers wreaked vengeance on their Hindu neighbours, setting fire to shops and houses. Four Hindu women were kidnapped and raped while a child died when the mother jumped to save herself.[111]

Abdul Qayum Khan who wrote the Congress enquiry committee report was in no doubt that Hindus had suffered more than Muslims. While touring the area for three days and interviewing witnesses, he realized that the Congress had no support among the Muslims. Even Muhammad Amin Khoso, the sole Muslim member of the Congress in the Sind assembly, maintained that the 'Congress and the Hindu Mahasabha in Sind [we]re interchangeable terms'. There was 'a general belief in Sind' that Congress members in the provincial assembly represented the Hindu trading and educated classes who consistently sabotaged legislation aimed at 'ameliorating the condition of Muslim masses', illiterate *haris* 'weighed down by poverty and debts'. Regrettably, 'the type of Congress leader ... who could act without any mental reservation [wa]s lacking in Sind' with the result that Muslims resented and distrusted the party. So long as 'the Congress [wa]s confined to Urban Hindus' and 'act[ed]' as a cheap edition of the Hindu Mahasabha', it did not have 'a very bright future' among the 'down trodden and ignorant Muslim peasantry in Sind'.[112]

Emulating the Frontier where Ghaffar Khan had taken up the cause of the rural poor, Hindus in Sind had somehow to 'shed their urban mantle' and 'undergo a complete change of heart'. Whatever the selfish and political motives of a handful of so-called leaders, 'the overwhelming majority of Muslims' who took part in the conflagration over the Manzilgah were 'actuated by genuine religious feelings in releasing as they thought the house of God from bondage'. Displaying his own sense of identity, Qayum Khan recommended returning the mosque to the Muslims. This would have no effect on Hindu worshippers at Saad Bela, especially if an entourage of *ulema* belonging to the Jamiat was despatched to the province to educate Muslims on how to live with their neighbours. He recommended posting more police in the area as Hindus were nervously buying guns which would only 'encourage Muslim desperados to break into ... [their] homes in villages for arms'.[113] There was an element of the prophetic in Qayum Khan's assessment. But the Congress in Sind could not discard its urban image. This gave the Sind League an opening, but only if it could overcome the sundry personal, class and sectarian divisions among Muslims in the province.

[111] Ibid., pp. 11–14.
[112] Ibid., pp. 15–17.
[113] Ibid., pp. 17–19.

Like its counterparts in the Punjab and the NWFP, the Sind League had to contend with better-organized rivals in the informal arenas, all claiming to be true representatives of Muslim interests. Among those looking to take advantage of the Sukkur Manzilgah to buttress their political standing was the pro-Congress Jamiat-ul-Ulema. At a meeting in Sukkur the Jamiat undertook to 'invite national-minded *Ulemas* of the Punjab and Sind for the purpose of preaching nationalism'. But the national unity it wanted to promote required the restoration of the Manzilgah mosque to the Muslims.[114] This was unacceptable to the supporters of the Hindu Sabha even though they concurred with the Jamiat's view that 'nationalism' meant supporting the Congress and opposing the 'communalism' of the Muslim League. Anyone uncertain of this reading of the political dynamics in the province had only to sample the *Qurbani's* vitriol against Jinnah. 'Jinnah [wa]s a communalist, a traitor and a man of degraded mentality'. His call for a day of deliverance after the resignation of the Congress ministries established the 'brutalism' of this 'brutish man' who deserved nothing short of 'damnation'.[115]

It was in an estranged communitarian atmosphere, interspersed with a spate of crude bomb explosions and murders of Hindus in different parts of the province,[116] that the League's scheme was first aired. Meetings held to promote the resolution drew a pathetic response. With the bulk of the Muslim population in the rural areas, only a few hundred in Karachi and Hyderabad learnt about the merits of 'Pakistan'. And in Sukkur, the scene of Hindu–Muslim tensions, a mere 150 joined the procession supporting the demand.[117] Only by seizing upon the Prophet's birthday celebrations did the League succeed in communicating its message to some 12,000 Muslims in Karachi.[118] In a province with a practically non-existent middle class, specifically League gatherings failed to enthuse the labouring classes. By contrast a meeting of the Majlis-i-Ahrar in Shikarpur was attended by a thousand people. Speakers appealed for Hindu–Muslim unity and 'condemned communalism' and the Muslim League while lauding the Congress's achievements.[119] Even while promoting communitarian peace, pro-Congress propagandists rarely failed to demand the introduction of *shariat* rule, a frightening prospect for non-

[114]*Secret Sind Police Abstract of Intelligence*, Karachi, 20 January 1940, vol. v, no. 3, NCHCR, Islamabad, p. 32 [henceforth *SSPAI*, followed by date, volume and page number/s).

[115]*SSPAI*, 27 January 1940, vol. v, no. 4, p. 41.

[116]In November 1940 Karachi was hit by four crude bombs, one at the Adam Bohri mosque, another near a tram terminus and the other two near a school and a theatre. (See *SSPAI*, 9, 23 and 30 November 1940, vol. v, nos 44–6, pp. 626, 651 and 669.)

[117]*SSPAI*, 20 April 1940, vol. v, no. 16, pp. 189–90.

[118]*SSPAI*, 27 April 1940, vol. v, no. 17, p. 208.

[119]*SSPAI*, 29 June 1940, vol. v, no. 26, p. 343.

Muslims already feeling terrorized by stray bombs and murders.[120] It was in February 1941 with the return of the Sukkur Manzilgah mosque to the Muslims, who undertook not to obstruct the playing of music by Hindus in the nearby temple, that the semblance of a truce was established in Sind.

Economic uncertainties caused by the war had been contributing to the erosion of social relations. With the vast majority of Muslims in debt to Hindu traders and moneylenders, it was no small matter that *banias* were refusing to accept paper money and hoarding silver and gold instead. Prices of raw materials fell and the *hundi* business came to a standstill due to the collapse of the market. G.M. Syed, one of the few Leaguers with a rural middle-class background, knew the predicament of Muslim debtors, whether *haris* or *waderas*. Though given to constant gyrations on the subject, from striking deals with the Congress to plotting an independent Sindhu Desh, Syed thought the 'salvation of Moslems lay in the Pakistan theory'. Demonstrating real antipathy towards *banias*, he characterized Hindus as Jews. If they did not stop 'creat[ing] dissensions amongst Moslems', Hashim Gazdar threatened, 'Hindus ... would be turned out of Sind like the Jews from Germany'.[121] Yusuf Haroon, the scion of the Memon commercial empire established by his father Abdullah Haroon and a Khaksar sympathizer, announced that 'if Hindus interfered in the Pakistan Scheme' which concerned only the Muslims and the British, they would 'meet the fate of Jews in Germany'.[122]

If there was a fascist tone in these utterances, Congress's Muslim supporters supplied the Islamic overtones. That a meeting of the Sind Jamiat-ul-Ulama in Pano Akil was attended by an estimated three thousand people should suffice to make the point. Dilating on his understanding of the nationalist outlook, the Ahrar leader Maulvi Abdul Karim Abdullah Chishti declared 'religion and politics as one, and indispensable ... [for] each other'. Husain Ahmad Madani in unison with the Islamic radical Obaidullah Sindhi 'described Mr M.A. Jinnah as a non-Muslim and asked the audience to keep away from his organisation'.[123] The Muslim League was attacked for 'insisting that religion and politics should be separate'. Speaking at the Jamiat meeting in Larkana, Madani exhorted his co-religionists to convert '40 crores of Hindus in India to Islam and thereby free them from eternal damnation'.[124]

It was the Ahrar and Jamiat combine, not the Leaguers, that most clearly spelled out the idea of a theocratic state in which the religious guardians

---

[120]A meeting of the Jamiat-ul-Ulema in Hyderabad not only endorsed *shariat* rule but demanded a ban on the teaching of music in schools, the enforcement of prohibition and an end to the fake *haj* at Luwari. (*SSPAI*, 19 October 1940, vol. v, no. 42, p. 583.)

[121]*SSPAI*, 6 July 1940, vol. v, no. 27, p. 351.

[122]*SSPAI*, 29 March 1941, vol. vi, no. 13, p. 144.

[123]*SSPAI*, 5 April 1941, vol. vi, no. 14, p. 156.

[124]*SSPAI*, 19 April 1941, vol. vi, no. 16, pp. 189–90.

were to enjoy supreme spiritual and temporal power. This was not the state as human organization in the Iqbalian conception which, far from quashing individual freedom, existed solely to ensure the realization of the spiritual in the temporal. Confusing these two very different strands of thinking on the Islamic state has been one of the persisting blind spots in post-colonial nationalist reconstructions. A careful distillation of the historical evidence on the internal contestations between the *ulema* and the professional as well as landlord politicians of the League makes plain that there was far more religion in the regional variants of 'nationalism' and the secular in 'communalism' than has been presumed.

Even those espousing the cause of the *haris* did so by invoking religion. Muhammad Amin Khoso, the disenchanted Congressman, told the Sind Provincial Hari Committee that with knaves like Allah Bakhsh and Khuhro as leaders, 'Islam, mosques and temples in Sind were in danger'.[125] Pir Ali Muhammad Rashidi, an advocate of 'Pakistan', said Muslims could not join with Hindus since 'freedom gained with the assistance of *kaffirs* was not worth having'. Considerable ambiguity surrounded the meanings attached to both 'Pakistan' and 'partition'. G.M. Syed thought that with 'the Pakistan Scheme the *whole country* [c]ould be converted into the house of God'.[126] This was not an endorsement of the Islamic state imagined by the *ulema*, but of a social order based on justice and equity. It was their failure to organize themselves politically which, according to Syed, had resulted in Sindhi Muslims alienating and mortgaging large chunks of agricultural land to the *banias*.[127] Stressing material factors and borrowing the Khaksars' pseudo-Nazi stance, Sindhi Leaguers were unlikely proponents of *shariat* rule—the stated aim of pro-Congress Ahrars and the Jamiat-ul-Ulema. 'Pakistan' for men like Syed, Yusuf Haroon and Gazdar was a means of escaping from the clutches of Hindu moneylenders.

In December 1941 a resolution of the Karachi city Muslim League alleged that during the past fifty years 'the *Banias* of Sind ha[d] expropriated nearly 40 per cent' of the land belonging to *zamindars* 'through opprobrious means'. Their opposition to the League's demand for a 'Pakistan' was a clever ruse 'aim[ed] at preserving their ill-gotten gains and keeping the Moslems in a state of somnolence'. Particularly alarming were the lengths to which Hindu *banias* were prepared to go to extend their sway over Sind. The Sind Encumbered Estates Act, then under consideration by the provincial assembly, sought to legalize the recovery of lapsed arrears of debt accumulated since 1892. Apprehensions of a massive appropriation of landed property by Hindu traders and moneylenders lent a sense of urgency to the Sind League's propagation

[125]Ibid., p. 191.
[126]*SSPAI*, 24 May 1941, vol. vi, no. 21, pp. 243–4 (my emphasis).
[127]*SSPAI*, 12 July, vol. vi, no. 28, p. 303.

of 'Pakistan'. The Quaid-i-Azam was 'begged ... to continue his ceaseless efforts till ... "Pakistan"had been attained'.[128] The presence of the Raja of Mahmudabad in Karachi scotched this attempt to make the League's scheme meaningful for Sindhi Muslims. According to this leading voice from UP, there was 'nothing in the [March 1940] resolution to create fear in the minds of the Hindus'.[129]

For Hindus the most troubling aspect of the 'Pakistan' demand was the prospect of Muslim sovereignty in a divided India. But as even the pro-League *Hayat* of Karachi argued, Hindu opposition to 'Pakistan' had nothing to do with 'the alleged division of India'. The real reason was the 'selfish and shrewd mentality' of Hindus who 'feared that if the Moslem scheme materialised, all other communities, who had for centuries been deprived of their natural rights by the Hindu Samaj, would agitate for *their* rights'.[130] There were Hindus in Sind who agreed. A cultural group of the town, Hindu People's Association in Karachi heard an address by P.V. Tahilramani, entitled 'Communal Unity in Sind Can be Established on Economic Justice'.[131] A Hindu woman, Guli Ram Sadarangani, wrote a novel in Sindhi called *Ittihad*, proposing intermarriages between the two communities as a way of forging a meaningful unity.[132] In an incisive, if ultimately flawed, piece in the *Karachi Daily*, Dr T.J. Lalvani thought true unity could be achieved only by setting up a new organization in which words 'such as Communalism, Hindus and Muslims' which 'divide[d] Indians' would be 'tabooed'. In his eagerness to do away with 'communalism', however, the learned doctor made light of the problem of cultural differences in a manner smacking of the Nehruvians yet betraying the spirit of an Ataturk. Indian unity required that 'all men ... [should] wear the same dress to avoid religious and communal distinctions'. Surnames would replace the use of first names while the organization working to achieve this miracle was to be called 'Akbar Ashram'.[133]

These may have been stray voices at the margins of Sindhi Hindu politics. But whatever their limitations in reckoning with cultural difference, they demonstrated a willingness to take cognizance of the socio-economic conditions in the province to try and bring about some sort of adjustment between the two main communities. In Sind efforts to promote both Hindu–Muslim unity and Congress–League understanding kept apace with the politics of cultural difference and socio-economic tensions to modulate relations between the two communities. Finding the terms of coexistence in Sind was not nearly as knotted an issue as in the Punjab, even as the nature of credit

[128]Ibid., p. 526.
[129]Ibid.
[130]*SSPAI*, 26 April 1941, vol. vi, no. 17, p. 207.
[131]*SSPAI*, 11 October 1941, vol. vi, no. 41, p. 421.
[132]Ibid., p. 424.
[133]*SSPAI*, 4 October 1941, vol. vi, no. 40, p. 414.

relations in the province gave a potentially explosive dimension to the politics of communitarian identity.

The religiously informed cultural identity of Sindhi Muslims in combination with the socio-economic resentment towards Hindu commercial groups could breed a style of politics conducive to the League's cause. But unlike the pro-Congress *ulema* for whom the implementation of the *shariat* was a primary concern, voices from League platforms most often spoke of the depredations of Hindu moneylenders. Even Abdullah Haroon, instead of raising the Islamic bogey, stressed on how 'Moslem civilization, Moslem culture and the Muslim language were in danger'.[134] Islam as religion was not Islam as Muslim culture. What made for the insistence on protecting Muslim culture in Sind was the prospect of national rule by a religious majority which although in a minority was the dominant economic force in the province. The prospect of Hindu dominance at the all-India level magnified the anxieties of Sindh's *waderas* and *pirs* who, much in the same way as the bulk of the labouring peasantry, were heavily in debt to the *banias*. It was convenient that the narratives of a Muslim Indian identity and sovereignty cohered so well with these fears.

The nexus between a Sindhi Muslim cultural identity and sovereignty found forceful expression in the League-owned *Al-Wahid* in a poem by Din Muhammad 'Wafai' entitled 'Id Ramazan':

In India the chains of slavery are around our necks,
What sort of *Id*? do you enquire from me—the *Id* of a lamenting Moslem?
With subdued voice and imprisoned heart,
What does the *Id* of a prisoner look like?
What is *Id*, and where does it exist?
Show me, where the *Id* of the Moslem exists?
In Palestine, in Syria or in Iraq,
I wish to see the *Id* of the Arabians,
Where is the Crown, the Throne, and where is the (king) himself?
Our eyes weep tears of blood over the *Id* of the Shah of Iran;
Long live the *Id* of Turkey,
And so be the *Id* of the natives of Khurasan.[135]

This invocation of Islamic universalism was not an instance of the politics of cultural identity striving for sovereign status outside the pale of India. It was nostalgia for a lost sovereignty in a genre popularized by Iqbal in the early 1930s. What was Id without freedom?

And what was freedom without a real share of sovereignty in an independent India? Congress's offer of non-intervention in the realm of religion made little

---

[134]*SSPAI*, 27 December 1941, vol. vi, no. 51, p. 525.
[135]*SSPAI*, 25 October 1941, vol. vi, no. 43, p. 442.

sense to Muslims groaning in debt in the land of the mystical visionary from Bhitshah. The spiritual and temporal needs of Sindhi Muslims, as indeed of their counterparts in other north-western regions, required a political arrangement capable of accommodating cultural differences. In the absence of any separation of the material and the spiritual realms in late-colonial Sind, the conflicting narratives of majoritarianism and minoritarianism hardly permitted a distinction between politics and religion. This was one reason why two and a half years after the passage of the League's resolution, there was no greater clarity of vision associated with 'Pakistan'. After Stafford Cripps had planted the 'local option' clause in the spring of 1942, Rajagopalachari offered a 'Pakistan' minus the non-Muslim-majority districts in eastern Punjab and western Bengal. The Quaid-i-Azam may have dismissed it as a 'shadow and a husk', or 'a maimed, mutilated and moth-eaten Pakistan', but a Sindhi Muslim Leaguer warmly saluted the Madras Congressman for accepting the 'Pakistan scheme' as it was 'the only course which could unite India'.[136]

A Gathering Storm, a Sobering Lull

During the remaining years of the war, the League's 'Pakistan' for varied reasons did come to enjoy support among pockets of Muslim opinion in India. But as ever the politics of cultural identity were neither united nor unanimous in articulating Muslim objectives. There were pitched battles for the leadership of the Muslim 'community'. Religion was deployed by all the campaigners. Periodic *fatwas* against Mohammed Ali Jinnah and the Muslim League point to a fierce struggle over Islam both as a religion and a way of life. A bevy of *ulema* objected to the League leadership's westernized outlook and disregard for Islamic values.[137] With antecedents dating back to the nineteenth century, western-educated Muslims were locked in grim competition with those reared in *madrasas* and religious seminaries, collaborators and bitter opponents of the British raj alike.

In 1857 the Barelvi *ulema* of *thana* Bhawan in Saharanpur district had decreed against a Muslim *jihad*. This drove a wedge between *thana* Bhawan and Deoband, though they had no serious disagreements on religion. Taking the lead in 1938 it was the Barelvis who ruled Jinnah a heretic. A *kafir* could not be 'Quaid-i-Azam'. Another *fatwa* ruled against Muslims forming

[136]*SSPAI*, 27 June 1942, vol. vii, no. 26, p. 217.

[137]On 21 March 1938 a questionnaire had been circulated on behalf of the Barelvi *ulema* of *thana* Bhawan. Claiming to represent the Ahl-i-Sunnat wa Jamaat, it solicited opinions on whether Jinnah and the Muslim League conformed to the *shariat* and if it was Islamic to call someone 'Quaid-i-Azam'. The response, not unpredictably, was that giving the title of 'Quaid-i-Azam' to someone who was not a true believer was against the *shariat*. (Mirza, *Karavan-i-Ahrar*, iii, p. 133.)

alliances with irreligious Muslims or *murtids* and *munqirs* even for the sake of political expediency. Both Jinnah and Iqbal were subjected to vituperative attacks by the Barelvis.[138] A more obnoxious pronouncement was that those supporting Jinnah ceased to be Muslims; their marriages were void and they had to re-enter the Islamic fold to avoid the bane of raising illegitimate children. As if this were not enough, the League's 'Pakistan' was roundly denounced as a *kufuri sultanate* or an infidel state. Leaguers tried countering this by arguing that Jinnah was a political and not a religious leader. Unconvinced, the Barelvis demanded declarations from Maulana Zafar Ali Khan, Nawab Ismail Khan and others that 'Mr Jinnah had no status other than of an infidel barrister'.[139]

Asking Zafar Ali Khan to expound on Jinnah's representative credentials, far less his religious status, was to beg the question. A *maulana* who had tested Congress's commitment to accommodating cultural differences at the Karachi session of 1931 could not feel at ease with a man more comfortable in Saville Row suits than in the Muslim *sherwani*. For the Punjab the distinction between the editor of the *Zamindar* and the barrister bearing the All-India Muslim League's emblem was of greater consequence than that between Azad and Jinnah. Two individuals reflecting different class backgrounds and cultural attitudes, Zafar Ali Khan and Jinnah are studies in contrast, laying bare the complex interactions between the individual Muslim and the community of Islam in India.

Zafar Ali and Jinnah reflect the distinction between Islam as culture and Islam as politics in assertions of Muslim identity in late-colonial Punjab. The former represented those in the Muslim League who opposed western civilization and saw 'Pakistan' as a means to establish *shariat* rule in the Muslim-majority provinces.[140] Whatever their ideological disagreements, most Punjabi Muslims who backed Jinnah and the League were from the disempowered urban middle classes, notwithstanding the entry of educated

[138]Ibid., pp. 136–40.
[139]Mirza, *Karavan-i-Ahrar*, iv, 143. Zafar Ali Khan gave poetic play to Muslim irritations with the founder of the Barelvis when he wrote:
Someone took away Turkey, another Iran
Someone took away the garment, another the collar
Only the name of Islam remained
That too, Hamid Raza Khan snatched away from us

... .
'We will erase the name of Islam in the world'
Oh man of God, why don't you say so clearly
His life is the kiss of death for the *millat*
Who is paying visitations to graves instead of the *kaaba*.
(Cited in ibid., p. 144.)
[140]*SPPAI*, 8 July 1944, vol. lxvi, no. 28, p. 376.

reforming landlords like Mumtaz Daultana. During the mid-1940s the Punjab Provincial League used the idioms of a Muslim identity in radically different ways than the *ulema*. Harbouring communists in its midst, it advocated social causes and tried parrying attacks from loyalist landlords and gabby religious propagandists of both the Congress and non-Congress varieties. A proponent of women's rights, the Punjab League—influenced by Daultana and communists like Sajjad Zahir, Abdullah Malik and Daniyal Latifi—couched its defence of Muslim rights in the language of Islamic socialism and equal citizenship. This ill-explored discourse needs to be rescued from the margins and studied in conjunction with that of its counterparts.

Not to be outshone by the League, pro-Congress Muslims gave their religious aspirations higher levels of expression, if not sophistication. The energetic projection by the Ahrars of a *hakumat-i-illahiya* or God's government is just one example of the multiple strands in Muslim thought and politics. Its idioms are worth assessing to gauge the significance of its rejection by the Punjab League. But if Muslims were divided into many more groupings than allowed by the League–Congress rubric, so too were the other two communities of the Punjab. It was around this time that the Hindu Mahasabha injected a strident tone to its chantings of popular nationalism. The Sikhs haphazardly continued their preparations for resisting any form of Islamic rule in the province. An analysis of these conflicting trends in Punjabi politics illuminates the darker ambivalences underlying the evolution of the League's 'Pakistan' demand in this north-western region.

Prostituting or Proselytizing Islam?

The League's propaganda and its nemesis in the form of the Ahrars, the Jamiat-ul-Ulema-i-Hind and the Barelvis, to say nothing of the Congress, the Mahasabha and the Sikhs, dissolves the dubious distinction between 'nationalism' and 'communalism' once and for all. Equally absolutist in their conceptions of communitarian rights, Muslim, Hindu and Sikh, these exchanges were marked by an inner diversity and some quite fascinating, if impracticable, configurations of identity and sovereignty. By failing to acquire precision, the 'Pakistan' slogan stirred Muslim and non-Muslim imaginings to multiple states of consciousness. But the wide gap between communitarian fictions and colonial facts invariably made itself felt whenever imagined identities were propelled to define their matching territorial space.

Contestations over sovereignty in the Punjab rarely conceded and usually claimed territory. Some twenty years after it was first proposed by Lajpat Rai as a solution to Muslim-majority rule in the Punjab, Muslims were no better prepared to countenance the partition of the province, and far less to discuss the geographical frontiers of a divided India. Jinnah ignored Barkat Ali's suggestion that a special League committee of geographers, historians, lawyers, economists, linguists, engineers, retired army officers, etc. should work out

the various aspects of the division of India into two states, includn.,
frontiers. As the Punjabi Leaguer Ashiq Hussain Batalvi recorded, 'For seve.
years we provided no map of the division of India, no formula, no blueprint;
seven years were spent sloganeering, speeches and statements and nothing
else.'[141]

All that changed after March 1940 was that 'Pakistan' became a familiar
name for an intangible congeries of imaginings. Most Muslims deemed it
consistent with an all-India arrangement; only a few rejected that prospect
altogether. In December 1942, Malik Firoz Khan Noon lent his name to a
proposal for the division of India into five parts and a federal centre limited
to defence, communications, foreign affairs and currency. In keeping with
Cripps' local option clause, each constituent unit had the right to opt out of
the union with a provision for its return at a later date.[142] This was not very
different from the Punjabi confederacy and Sikander's zonal scheme in its
view of the centre. What was agitating Punjabis most were the power-sharing
arrangements at the regional level and only, by extension, at the all-India
centre.

With many Muslims coming to subscribe in principle to 'Pakistan', however
defined, the Hindus stood firmly on an 'Akhand Bharat' or a united India. In
a province where the Mahasabhite mentality often found space in the Congress
carcass, the evocation of the martial spirit by some Punjabi Hindus caused
consternation among Muslims. As it is Sikhs under Tara Singh's direction
were angling for an 'Azad Punjab' or an independent province where they
might have a controlling hand. First floated by 'all sections of the Sikhs' at
the time of the second round table conference in London, it was the 'only
permanent solution to break the Muslim majority of the Punjab'. If an Azad
Punjab was conceded, Tara Singh predicted, 'Muslims would ... drop the idea
of *Pakistan*' and Sikhs would 'enjoy more privileges than at present'.[143]
Exclusively based on arguments about religious majorities and minorities,
these narratives of communitarian identity and notions of sovereignty
singularly lacked a careful spelling out of the rights of equal citizenship.

Attributing this to 'communalism' would be to overly simplify the issue.
The prospect of an independent India where numerical majorities would shape
the apportionment of power and patronage gave added importance to
communitarian rights. Drawing upon cultural differences, the expression of
these rights in the politics of Muslims, Hindus and Sikhs alike confounded
spirit and matter, the religious and the secular. Shades of bigotry informed all
versions of the narratives of communitarian identity and rights. But there was
also much in them which sheds light on the problem of equitable citizenship

[141]Cited in Mirza, *Karavan-i-Ahrar*, v, pp. 115–17.
[142]Ibid., v, p. 287.
[143]*SPPAI*, 4 March 1944, vol. lxvi, no. 10, p. 130.

rights in a region requiring an accommodation of cultural differences. To dismiss bigotry and cultural differences in the same breath as 'communalism' may serve the purposes of historical shorthand. It cannot explain why an inclusionary nationalism failed to excite the imaginings of so many in the Punjab.

The Muslim trickle to the League's 'Pakistan' is inexplicable without accounting for the activities of the Hindu Mahasabha and its paramilitary wing, the RSS. In late December 1943 between fifty thousand and sixty thousand people, including two thousand women, attended an All-India Hindu Mahasabha conference at Amritsar. Speakers harped on Hindu unity and organization, urged physical fitness and military training and affirmed violence in the cause of freedom. Muslims were attacked for oppressing Hindus in the Muslim-majority provinces; the British for pursuing divide and rule; Congress for appeasing Muslims, squandering money on the *khilafat* movement and eventually prompting the demand for a 'Pakistan'. It was apparent to observers that the 'extremely communal pan-Hindu aspect of the conference [wa]s not likely to make for any future compromise with Muslims' while 'other minorities ... c[ould] expect little consideration from the Hindu *Mahasabha*'.[144] Savarkar's slogan 'Hinduise politics and militarise Hinduism' by 'building a virile Hindu manhood' was a red rag to Muslims. The Bengal Hindu Mahasabha leader, Shyama Prasad Mukerjee, appealed for military training among Hindus and almost taunted Muslims by praising their exemplary unity. Qualifying his disagreements with the Mahatma, Mukerjee explained that he 'believed in violence not to attack or enslave other people, but to acquire one's own rights'.[145]

A conception of rights aimed at domination, not accommodation, gave an ominous tone to the Mahasabha's call for military training. An immediate reaction to the Mahasabha's conference, where the Azad Punjab scheme was denounced alongside 'Pakistan' as the work of 'traitors ... seeking political advancement', was the setting up of a new voluntary organization, the Sher-i-Punjab, by the Sikhs. Its establishment was attributed to the dissatisfaction of Sikh volunteers in the RSS who had been prohibited from greeting each other with 'Sat Sri Akal'.[146] Instead Akalis applauded the Maharaja of Patiala's decision to introduce Punjabi as a court language, but were utterly put off by his sister's marriage to a non-Sikh. Demonstrating the exclusivity inherent in communitarian narratives, the Akalis expressed indignation at the appointment of a Muslim prime minister in Kapurthala state. They may have been more justified in calling for the deletion of the controversial last chapter of *Satyarth Prakash*, a demand also voiced by Muslims.[147]

[144]*SPPAI*, 1 January 1944, vol. lxvi, no. 1, pp. 1–2.
[145]Ibid., pp. 3–5.
[146]*SPPAI*, 8 January 1944, vol. lxvi, no. 2, p. 42.
[147]*SPPAI*, 20 May 1944, vol. lxvi, no. 21, p. 292.

So Muslims were not alone in taking exception to encroachments on their sense of a religiously informed cultural identity. Despite ample provocation from the Mahasabhites, Muslims were slower to react on the organizational front. The protagonists of an *akhand* or united Hindustan believed its attainment was possible only if Hindus armed themselves with swords to demand their rights. There was no mention of the rights of non-Hindus. A troubling omission, given the Mahasabha's insistence that it was 'not a communal body but wanted independence for India'.[148] There was much furore over the Arya Samaj propaganda about Muslims abducting Hindu women and converting them to Islam.[149] Arya Samajists in Multan instructed Hindus to 'discard western education and culture' and join the Mahabir Dal.[150] An all-India Brahman conference at Amritsar denounced 'Pakistan'. The Hindu Succession Bill was condemned as an interference in religion and the Women's Property Act dismissed as defective. A thousand women attending the conference met on their own. Instead of focusing on their property rights, they demanded the abolition of the dowry system and deprecated European fashions.[151]

The League's opponents, as indeed some in its own midst, also adopted a distinctively anti-modernist stance. By far the most distinctive was the worldview furnished by the Ahrars, the pro-Congress reds seeking to discipline Muslims by creating God's government on earth! Ataullah Shah Bukhari was a leading proponent of this form of government. This ensured the idea widespread publicity, if not necessarily support. In an attempt to rustle up a mass following, Bukhari described the Muslim League as an 'irreligious' party. The Ahrars were portrayed as the *razakars* and the *mujahids* who, after the war was over, would establish peace 'by following the laws of the *Quran*', a necessary corrective to the 'irreligious mentality of Muslims'.[152] While there was no place for Ahmadis in the *hakumat-i-illahiya* of the Ahrar conception, other communities were to be 'governed according to the laws of God' as 'contained in their respective holy books'.[153] The *hakumat-i-illahiya*, a virtuous and moral order tailored to Ahrar tastes, was supposed to be a key to burying 'Pakistan' in the Punjab.[154] Mazhar Ali Azhar made 'plain that the *Ahrars* were against the vivisection of India' and alleged that 'prostitution and other vices were flourishing in the provinces' where 'according to Mr Jinnah, *Pakistan*

[148]*SPPAI*, 26 February 1944, vol. lxvi, no. 9, p. 124.

[149]*SPPAI*, 4 March 1944, vol. lxvi, no. 10, p. 130. Some 225 Hindu women were alleged to have been converted to Islam.

[150]*SPPAI*, 8 April 1944, vol. lxvi, no. 15, p. 204.

[151]*SPPAI*, 15 April 1944, vol. lxvi, no. 16, pp. 213–14.

[152]*SPPAI*, 15 January 1944, vol. lxvi, no. 3, p. 53.

[153]*SPPAI*, 29 January 1944, vol. lxvi, no. 5, p. 73.

[154]Among the notable personalities at an Ahrar gathering to popularise the *hakumat-i-illahiya* was Professor Humayun Kabir, a close confidant of Abul Kalam Azad. (*SPPAI*, 22 April 1944, vol. lxvi, no. 17, p. 232.)

had been established'. He 'doubted if any Muslim would wish to live in areas where such vices continued'.[155] Driving home the point, an Ahrar meeting described European civilization as an invitation to 'debauchery and moral degradation' and criticized both communists and capitalists. 'Religion could not be separated from politics' and 'schemes like *Pakistan*, *Azad Punjab* and *Akhand Hindustan* were useless unless all differences were settled and the law of God prevailed'.[156]

Facing stiff opposition from within the Muslim community, the Leaguers were treading on delicate ground, keenly aware of the charge of irreligiosity against them. So while minority fears were periodically addressed by some provincial Leaguers, most took an exclusively Muslim line. Attempts by Muslim Leaguers to reassure the minorities of their bona fides generally fell short of satisfying Hindu and Sikh expectations of equal citizenship rights. The reasons are not difficult to discern. Uncertain of what he might eventually get, Jinnah was reluctant to commit himself to specifics. His much-publicized intransigence flowed from efforts to strike a plausible balance between absolute demands and relational realities. Given the distinction between the all-India arrangements which concerned Jinnah the most and the regional requirements of the Punjab, it was not always easy to keep apart the absolute and relational aspects of any political strategy.

At a meeting of the Punjab Provincial Muslim Students' Federation at Lahore, Mumtaz Daultana explained that 'Pakistan' signalled the Muslim desire to have 'their own Government in one-fourth of India'. He saw 'no difficulty in evolving safeguards for minorities in *Pakistan* and *Hindustan*'. As far as he was concerned, 'Muslims were ready to satisfy any reasonable demands which the ... [Sikhs] put forward'. The League's opponents were trying to 'introduce tribalism into politics' by promoting '*Jat* and *Rajput* interests'. Islam taught equality and the League would foil 'all attempts to exploit the Muslim masses by feudalists, capitalists and imperialists'. Daultana asked Muslim youth to follow Jinnah's advice and take up industrial and commercial occupations. This would 'counteract the Hindu stranglehold on economic resources and production' and in time help initiate 'an elaborate scheme of State industrialization in Muslim areas'. Brimming with youthful idealism, Daultana proposed compulsory education for everyone, including women, who were promised rights of inheritance.[157]

In the spring of 1944 Jinnah came to the Punjab hoping to force the League's label on the Unionist ministry. During his visit he voiced his strong support for women's rights.[158] The League's endorsement of women's right

[155]*SPPAI*, 25 March 1944, vol. lxvi, no. 13, p. 183.
[156]*SPPAI*, 17 June 1944, vol. lxvi, no. 25, p. 342.
[157]*SPPAI*, 18 March 1944, vol. lxvi, no. 12, pp. 184–5.
[158]*SPPAI*, 1 April 1944, vol. lxvi, no. 14, p. 191.

to vote was an incentive for urban Muslim women to join its provincial women's wing. Unlike the Ahrar and the Jamiat-ul-Ulema-i-Islam, the provincial League, when not pursuing solely communitarian purposes, adopted a nominally accommodative attitude towards women. In addition to learning the Quran and needlework, women were encouraged to enroll in the League's National Guard to show that they were not 'lag[ging] behind men in working for *Pakistan*'.[159] Women at League meetings asserted their intention to 'seek emancipation on the line adopted in modern Turkey'.[160]

If the League aroused expectations among a section of Muslim women, religious minorities remained unconvinced that 'Pakistan' would not violate their citizenship rights. With the Mahasabha accusing League ministries of oppressing non-Muslims, there was no room for equivocation on the question of citizenship rights. Mindful of the can of worms such a debate might open within Muslim ranks, Jinnah declared that 'a constitution for *Pakistan* would not be framed until its territory had been acquired'. If this unsettled the Islamic ideologues in the League, Jinnah's crisp warning to communists to 'keep their hands off the Muslim League' was a disappointment for those envisaging an egalitarian and socialist future. But the master of ambiguity gave his seal of approval to the so-called 'progressive' wing of the provincial League by arguing that '*Pakistan* was a safeguard against the possibility of *Akhand Hindustan* being established by a settlement between the British white *bania* and the Hindu *bania*'.[161] This was all the communists needed to continue supporting the League in its attempts to overthrow the Unionist ministry. So despite Jinnah's failure to persuade Khizar Hayat Tiwana to accept the League's discipline, the well-publicized intervention gave some impetus to the provincial wing's propaganda against pro-Congress Hindu *banias* and pro-British Unionist landlords.[162] But it was apparent that for the duration of the war, there was no prospect of the League breaking the Unionist ministry. No perspicacity was needed to realize that Punjab's landlords would stick by the Unionists. It required political sagacity to anticipate their quandary once the British were on their way out. Jinnah's surprise upon learning that the 'Punjab was for the Punjabis' did not deter

[159]Ibid.

[160]*SPPAI*, 27 May 1944, vol. lxvi, no. 22, p. 302.

[161]*SPPAI*, 25 March 1944, vol. lxvi, no. 13, p. 185.

[162]Following Jinnah's departure for Jammu to recover from another setback in the Punjab, an ambitious scheme was prepared to extend the League's organization at an estimated cost of one lakh rupees. It included setting up a League office in Lahore and dividing the province into areas for propaganda and the opening of training camps. The use of mosques to propagate 'Pakistan' appears to have been first made in Lyallpur in an attempt to 'win the Muslim masses before coming to grips with the Unionist Party'. (*SPPAI*, 13 May, 20 June and 22 July, 1944, nos. 20, 24 and 30, pp. 277, 325, 411.)

him from 'prophesi[ng] that it would soon be the foundation of *Pakistan*'.[163]

His idea of citizenship rights in the Punjab, the cornerstone of 'Pakistan', merits attention. On his way to Jammu, Jinnah told an audience of four thousand in Gujranwala that the League had 'no intention of tyrannising over Hindus and Sikhs'. Instead 'all minorities would receive justice'. Throwing a bait to the Unionists, he maintained that the League was 'not hostile to *zamindars*'.[164] Jinnah rejected all caste and tribal distinctions among Muslims. While attacking non-Muslims for stubbornly opposing 'Pakistan', he also held out an olive branch. There was some space here for the Punjab League to manoeuvre itself into a position to negotiate with non-Muslims. Picking up from where Jinnah had left off, the recently dismissed Unionist minister Shaukat Hayat Khan at a meeting of the Punjab Muslim Students Federation (PMSF) in Rawalpindi 'assured non-Muslims of generous treatment under *Pakistan*'. But if 'Pakistan' was the product of Muslim fears of Hindu domination, non-Muslims needed more concrete evidence than Shaukat was able to provide.[165] Far from translating the League's ideal of minority safeguards in its own language, the PMSF went about goading 'Muslims to buy only from Muslim shopkeepers'.[166] The spectre of state-supported commercial boycotts by Muslims was too much for Punjabi Hindus to bear even if there were some Sikhs and members of the scheduled castes who saw advantage in the comeuppance of the hated *bania*s in a future 'Pakistan'.

Among the Akalis, Giani Kartar Singh was co-operating with Muslim ministers of the Unionist government and opposing the Congress. Nagoke wanted a Sikh alliance with the Congress. Unable to square these clashing positions, Tara Singh temporarily resigned from the Akali Dal to devote his life to religious causes. While Jinnah was exploring the possibility of forming a League government in the Punjab with Sikh support, the Akalis were divided in their responses. Looking to first strengthen his position within the Sikh community by spearheading the Gurdwaras Amendment Bill, Giani Kartar Singh was ready to do a deal with the League or the Unionists, depending on who offered the best terms. He himself was 'inclined to favour co-operation with the Muslim League' and press forward with the Azad Punjab scheme.[167] With majority support in the Akali Dal, Giani presented a window of opportunity for Leaguers in search of an understanding with the Sikhs. Even if Jinnah succeeded at a later stage, the Sikhs were prepared to strike a deal provided they were given two ministries instead of one in the Punjab, better representation at the centre and in other provinces as well as the preservation

[163]*SPPAI*, 8 April 1944, vol. lxvi, no. 15, p. 205.
[164]*SPPAI*, 13 May 1944, vol. lxvi, no. 20, p. 279.
[165]*SPPAI*, 24 June 1944, vol. lxvi, no. 26, pp. 351–2.
[166]*SPPAI*, 1 July 1944, vol. lxvi, no. 27, p. 363.
[167]*SPPAI*, 13 May 1944, vol. lxvi, no. 20, p. 278.

of the status quo on religious questions.[168] Other Sikh demands included cultural concessions on *jhatka* and Punjabi and enhanced representation in educational, legislative and governmental institutions. The Sikhs' willingness to compromise made the League's slippages on the question of citizenship rights the more unfortunate. Communist-minded Sikhs were eager to do a deal with the League.[169] Even Giani Kartar Singh virtually admitted that Sikhs had erred in opposing Jinnah's efforts to form a League ministry. Ready for a League coalition ministry in the Punjab, he thought it 'better for Sikhs not to approach Jinnah, but to let Jinnah approach the Sikhs'.[170] A proponent of Azad Punjab, he dismissed the call for a 'Khalistan' by some Sikhs as 'a poor substitute'. More significantly, Kartar Singh thought a 'settlement was possible if Jinnah would accept the right of self-determination as interpreted by the Communists'.[171]

Like the Sikhs, the scheduled castes in the Punjab were less concerned with the aptness of their anti-colonialism than with securing concrete concessions from the premier nationalist organization. With Ambedkar supporting 'Pakistan', the scheduled castes had no reason to oppose it if it guaranteed them gains vis-á-vis upper-caste Hindus. Diwan Kaljug Narain, an *achhut* from UP, attacked caste Hindus, asserting that the scheduled castes were 'not so much afraid of *Pakistan* as they were of *Hindustan* becoming *Achhutistan*'. After all, out of roughly thirty crore Hindus in India, some twenty crore were *achhuts*.[172]

So an alliance against Hindu commercial dominance in the Punjab cutting across communitarian lines remained on the horizon despite lapses in the League's discourse on citizenship rights. Since the League based the Muslim case on the right of self-determination, it could hardly deny the same to non-Muslims—a position implicit in Cripps' offer of 1942. In a mirror image of the Congress which wanted independence first and a settlement of communitarian rights afterwards, the Punjab League demanded acceptance of the principle of 'Pakistan' before indicating what it might concede to the non-Muslim minorities. That independence without accommodation of differences might precipitate a division of India had been brought out by the debate over the League's 'Pakistan' scheme. Rajagopalachari's offer to settle the Muslim problem by conceding a state shorn of western Bengal and eastern Punjab pushed self-determination to its logical conclusion. Here were signs

[168]*SPPAI*, 6 May 1944, vol. lxvi, no. 19, p. 252.

[169]At the District Kisan Conference in Ludhiana, Sohan Singh Josh 'allied himself with Mr Jinnah and the Muslim League'. But most Sikhs continued opposing 'Pakistan' despite reservations about the Azad Punjab scheme. (*SPPAI*, 1 April 1944, vol. lxvi, no. 14, pp. 190–1.)

[170]*SPPAI*, 10 June 1944, vol. lxvi, no. 24, pp. 324–5.

[171]*SPPAI*, 15 July 1944, vol. lxvi, no. 29, p. 398.

[172]*SPPAI*, 1 April 1944, vol. lxvi, no. 14, p. 191.

of what absolutist conceptions of rights might entail for centre and region alike. Preoccupied both by intra- and inter-communitarian rivalries, the leading men in the political arenas of the Punjab opted to remain unbending in the expectation of extracting beneficial results from an eventual compromise.

Some sort of a compromise was certainly anticipated. Few in the Punjab appeared to have accepted the notion of a 'Pakistan' wholly separate from India. Shaukat Hayat, who proudly proclaimed that the League's main objective was to 'promote Islam and to remove poverty', announced that 'if Muslims in non-*Pakistan* provinces were oppressed the whole of *Pakistan* would mobilize and seek redress'.[173] At the 1943 session of the All-India Muslim League, Jinnah had urged Muslims in the majority provinces not to forget the sacrifices of their co-religionists in the Hindu-majority provinces. In August 1944 he told an audience in Rawalpindi that he was working for the 'freedom of all communities' since '*Pakistan* could exist only in a free India'.[174] A similar remark was heard at a League meeting in Amritsar where 'Pakistan' was described by one speaker as 'meaning Islam in a free India'.[175]

Jinnah's talks with Gandhi initiated by Rajagopalachari's offer raised hopes of a League–Congress understanding. This was good news for communists seeking to exert their influence in the Punjab through the League and the Congress.[176] But it was bad for Akalis and Mahasabhites, fearful of being cast aside by the all-India parties. While communists took the opportunity presented by the Gandhi–Jinnah talks to try and cajole the Ahrars to support the Muslim League,[177] stolid Sikh opposition to Rajagopalachari's formula revived the Mahasabha's interest in forging a joint front with them in the Punjab. Tara

[173]*SPPAI*, 8 July 1944, vol. lxvi, no. 28, pp. 376–7.

[174]*SPPAI*, 5 August 1944, vol. lxvi, no. 32, p. 437.

[175]*SPPAI*, 12 August 1944, vol. lxvi, no. 33, p. 459.

[176]The Communist Party of India's acceptance of the Soviet Communist Party's line on the nationalities question had curious implications for Punjabi politics in the 1940s. Apart from supporting the demand for a 'Pakistan', the communists were among the first to call for Khalistan—long before Rajagopalachari's offer gave new direction to the politics of communitarian identities and ideas of sovereignty. While communist Sikhs tried winning over the Akalis, Muslim members joined the provincial League. Daniyal Latifi became office secretary of the Punjab Muslim League. Despite determined opposition from Mamdot and his cronies, Latifi and Abdullah Malik persuaded Mumtaz Daultana, the recently returned Oxbridge-educated landlord from Multan district, to give a socialistic flavour to the provincial League's manifesto. (See below.)

[177]The year 1944 saw the first signs of willingness on the part of some Ahrars to compromise with the Muslim League. In early July a private meeting of the All-India Ahrar Working Committee in Lahore decided to co-operate with the League 'only if ... [it] launched a civil disobedience movement in order to attain *Pakistan*'. (*SPPAI*, 8 July 1944, vol. lxvi, no. 28, p. 378.)

Singh was approached by the Mahasabhites and an All India Anti-Pakistan Board formed to which Sikhs were invited to join.[178] Suspicious of Hindu intentions, Tara Singh was quick to respond to the consequences of Rajagopalachari's acceptance of Muslim sovereignty in a state formed by the partition of the Punjab and Bengal. Disowning his own Azad Punjab scheme, he joined his co-religionists in wondrous imaginings of an independent Sikh state, 'Khalistan'. Giani Kartar Singh became an early supporter, an important conversion when it came to Akali politics. In the service of a politics of cultural identity, distinctions between prostituting and proselytizing religion were effaced by the Sikhs quite as much as by their Muslim counterparts.

Sikh Schemes for the Punjab

The Sikh response to the Madras Congressman's offer to Mohammed Ali Jinnah had important implications for Punjabi politics. Sikh *diwans* condemned it with a fury but hesitated supporting Tara Singh's scheme for an Azad Punjab, or 'the creation of a new province between the Jumna and Chenab rivers under the authority of the Central Government'.[179] This was a restatement of Lajpat Rai's idea of redefining provincial boundaries to deal with the logic of majorities and minorities. But it could also have been an invitation to a welter of localized assertions of autonomy. The point was not lost on the Sikhs. Many Sikhs at the *diwans* opposed a separate province since it 'might involve the risk of the *Pakistan* scheme being accepted'.[180] Noting the trends, the Central Akali Dal under Baba Kharak Singh, while preferring a 'Khalistan', decided that 'opposition to *Pakistan* was the best policy'.[181]

Tossing these cautionary words aside, Tara Singh along with Giani Kartar Singh continued to press the Central Akali Dal to endorse the scheme for a separate Sikh state. While confusing the League's demand with Rajagopalachari's offer, Tara Singh could see that any redrawing of the provincial boundaries of the Punjab would leave the Sikhs divided between 'Pakistan' and 'Hindustan'. Espousing the doctrine of self-reliance, he 'opposed the vivisection of India' and demanded independence on the grounds that the Punjab could 'not be controlled by any single community'. Other Sikhs argued that just as Muslims feared a Hindu majority, they too were 'afraid of a Muslim majority'. The odds were that the ' Punjab would become the battle field of India', much in the same way as Poland had in Europe. These were portentous words. Believing it to be their strongest card with the colonial rulers, Sikhs 'warned the British Government that the morale of Sikh soldiers would be affected if *Pakistan* were forced on the Sikhs'.[182]

[178]*SPPAI*, 19 August 1944, vol. lxvi, no. 34, p. 500.
[179]*SPPAI*, 5 August 1944, vol. lxvi, no. 32, p. 436.
[180]Ibid., p. 437.
[181]*SPPAI*, 26 August 1944, vol. lxvi, no. 35, p. 483.
[182]Ibid.

Since Hindus seemed more concerned with the rest of India than the Punjab, Tara Singh opposed forming an alliance with them and recommended approaching the British directly. He was afraid of Gandhi making concessions to Jinnah. In a throwback to his verbal militancy of the 1930s, Tara Singh advised the Sikhs to prepare themselves to struggle for their rights. If the Mahasabha and the Harijans chose to join them, so much the better.[183] Giani Kartar Singh drafted the scheme for a separate Sikh state if India was divided. It envisaged facilities for the transfer of people and property, with a boundary commission demarcating the borders. In an indication of their willingness to share sovereignty under certain conditions, the Sikhs 'reserv[ed] the right of deciding whether to join any Hindu Union or Muslim Union or to remain independent'. They were also to have safeguards like other minorities, including guaranteed representation in local bodies, government departments, legislatures and cabinets in the NWFP, Baluchistan and the part of the Punjab outside the Sikh state. Insisting on representation equal to and not less than the Hindus given their martial traditions, Sikhs wanted a continuation of their traditional share of the army as well as representation on various defence councils and commissions and an adequate share in educational services and charitable grants. Apart from political rights, Sikhs demanded assurances that the symbols of their religiously informed cultural identity, namely Punjabi in the Gurmukhi script, personal lands and religious endowments would be protected. These were the 'basic demands of the Sikhs in any future constitution of India' and a precondition for their co-operation in coalition ministries in the Punjab and the centre.[184]

Stated as the price for Sikh accommodation in an independent India, this was calculated to put pressure on Gandhi, Congress and the British. An agreement between Gandhi and Jinnah was expected to result in the Congress losing most of its Sikh support with the exception of a few communists. The Sikhs were more consistent in opposing than supporting causes. Instead of popularizing the 'Khalistan' idea, Tara Singh and Giani Kartar Singh used it mainly to threaten the Muslims to give up 'Pakistan' and the British to reject it out of hand. Ten thousand Sikhs in Jullundur heard Tara Singh demand 'joint rule in the Punjab'. Sikhs would 'neither rule over nor accept the domination of other communities over them'. Giani Kartar Singh was more to the point. If the British were 'unjust to the Sikhs', two lakh Sikh soldiers in the army would be asked to throw away their medals and protect their community, filling jails in the Punjab if necessary.[185] Akali meetings recalled the 'atrocities of Muslim kings' and condemned Gandhi's *charkha* as a poor substitute for the Sikh sword. Giani Kartar Singh 'compared Jinnah and Gandhi

[183]*SPPAI*, 2 September 1944, vol. lxvi, no. 36, p. 500.
[184]Ibid., p. 501.
[185]*SPPAI*, 16 September 1944, vol. lxvi, no. 38, p. 528.

to Hitler and Mussolini', alleging that they were 'bent upon usurping the rights and claims of Sikhs'.[186]

The failure of the Gandhi–Jinnah talks was greeted by Sikhs as a sign that India would not be partitioned. Uncertain about the future, however, they turned with greater alacrity to consolidating a community whose internal sectarian divisions could encumber any collective assertion of sovereignty. There were increasing displays of ritual sovereignty at Sikh gatherings and more emphasis on a distinctive cultural identity. Giani Kartar Singh delighted an Akali audience in Khanewal by riding an elephant in the company of ninety horsemen and two hundred Akalis bearing swords, some of them drawn. Also present was the redoubtable Tara Singh who said his community was fed up with Muslim rule in the Punjab. It was 'better for Sikhs to remain under British domination than under Hindu or Muslim rule'. If this was an unpromising note in an already dreary debate on citizenship rights, Tara Singh's assertion that Punjab 'belonged to the Sikhs' was deadly. Demanding a categorical assurance from the British against partition without the 'consent of the Sikhs' seemed more reasonable. Not a man to think through his public statements, the Akali leader proceeded to contradict his own absolutist view of Sikh communitarian rights by advising them to 'try and remove the idea of majority rule from the minds of persons of other communities'.[187]

For Muslims grappling with the certitude of Hindu-majority rule at the centre, this was a contradiction in terms. In the Punjab it was Muslim-majority rule that was being contested by Sikhs and Hindus in multifaceted ways. At the All-India Akali conference in Lahore, Tara Singh 'complained of Muslim communalism in the Punjab' and maintained that if it were not for the war the Sikhs would have been 'agitating against ... *Aurangzebi Raj*'.[188] This was insulting Khizar Hayat's heroic effort to withstand the monocled lawyer's harangue over the interpretation of the Jinnah–Sikander pact of 1937. The Jat Unionist minister from Rohtak district, Sir Chhotu Ram, might have contested such a conception of the Unionist government or at any rate defended some of its virtues.[189] His own Jat Sabha had members of all religious denominations. Pir Muhammad, the Muslim MLA from Gujrat, went so far as to say that he was 'a *Jat* first and a Muslim afterwards'. And with good reason. The Unionist government's agrarian legislation had benefited the Jats. Chhotu Ram was seeking to project a Jat identity cutting across religions. He claimed to have played a role in preventing

---

[186]*SPPAI*, 23 September 1944, vol. lxvi, no. 39, p. 541.

[187]*SPPAI*, 21 October 1944, vol. lxvi, no. 43, pp. 590–1.

[188]Ibid., p. 593.

[189]In early April 1944 the knighted Ram defended his Jat Sabha at a meeting in Lyallpur. Half a dozen Muslim members of the assembly were present at an occasion where only a hundred Muslims bothered to show up. The 'members of the *Sabha*', Chhotu Ram explained, belonged to 'different religions' and 'fully realised the sanctity of their religions'. (*SPPAI*, 15 April 1944, vol. lxvi, no. 16, p. 213.)

the sale of wives among the Jats and loosening the grip of the moneylender. At a time of intensely exclusionary assertions of identity, the Jat Sabha's membership was open to all religious communities who were expected to serve humanity equally.[190]

Sadly for the Punjab, this was not a style of politics that held any attraction for those left out of the network of colonial patronage. This in combination with religiously informed cultural identities produced an especially noxious brew of Punjabi discourse and politics based on assertions, not accommodation. In a baffling display of his capacity for self-contradiction, Tara Singh announced that if India was partitioned, 'the Sikhs would not object to being given 50 per cent representation in *Pakistan*'. He was right of course that Muslims were also 'asking for 50 per cent representation at the centre'. It required a surge of faith to claim half the total representation for a community which was a mere twelve per cent of the population. In his inimitable way the old campaigner had exposed the absurdity of a purely numbers game in contestations for sovereignty drawing upon a rich store of collective myths.[191]

Bringing the Sikhs under the Akali banner was easier said than done. With a plethora of sects, the Sikhs were not a homogeneous or homogenizing community progressing in a linear fashion to greater distinctiveness. In some ways, their sub-denominational politics had even more bewildering implications for territorial sovereignty than sectarian drifts in the Muslim community. Mazhabi Sikhs demanded a fully autonomous, if not sovereign, 'Mazhbistan', while the Ramgarhia Sikhs took strong exception to not being invited by Tara Singh to the All-Parties Sikh Conference. Claiming to be fifteen lakh in number, the Ramgarhias were opposed to both an Azad Punjab and a 'Khalistan' unless they were given a 50 per cent share in the rights and privileges of the state. They wanted Sikhs to have the right to self-determination, but only if it had the backing of all sections of the community, including not only the Ramgarhias but also the Sampurdas and Baradaris.[192] Add to this other sects like the Namasudra, the Nishan Sahib and Ahluwalia, and it becomes almost possible to sympathize with Tara Singh's predicament.

Hindus, Hindi and Hindustan

If the Sikhs had woes, Punjabi Hindus were no less precariously placed. But unlike the Sikhs, they had the consolation of an overall Hindu majority in India which was more than a match for Muslim-majority rule in the Punjab. However concerned about their future in an independent India, Punjabi Hindus had by no means abandoned their claims to the Punjab. What made their politics different from the politics of Muslims and Sikhs was the unofficial

[190]Ibid.
[191]*SPPAI*, 21 October 1944, vol. lxvi, no. 43, p. 593.
[192]*SPPAI*, 2 September 1944, vol. lxvi, no. 36, pp. 541–2.

relationship between the Mahasabha and the Congress. The equation of religious, regional and national rights coined long ago by Lajpat Rai continued to be salient to the politics of Punjabi Hindus, irrespective of their ideological leanings. There were stresses to be sure, but Hindus in the Punjab, whether to the left or the right, wanted to keep their lines of communication open with the Congress. The Hindu Mahasabha's charge that Congress was 'unrepresentative of Hindu opinion' was not a rejection of the nationalist organization. It was intended to force the Congress to conform to the Mahasabha's definition of a Hindu.[193] This was not too difficult given the constant overlap between the Congress and the Mahasabha in the Punjab. It was often the same individuals who voiced the Hindu, Hindi, Hindustan slogan. There was nothing unusual about Congressmen attacking the introduction of Urdu as the court language of Jaipur state from Mahasabha platforms.[194] But the two-way traffic could also give an interesting twist to Hindu political postures.

After the announcement of Rajagopalachari's formula, there was a frenzy of confused and confusing statements by Sikh leaders about what they would or would not accept and what they might or might not do. By contrast, a section of Punjabi Hindus were relatively more sanguine. Brij Lal, the secretary of the Punjab Hindu Vigilance Board, saw no reason for 'undue alarm'. Gandhi was all too 'conscious of the stiff opposition from Hindus in Bengal and the Punjab' and wisely believed that 'too much opposition from Hindus may have an adverse effect on those Muslims who might otherwise be against the partition of India'.[195] Not only did its members keep mum about the offer to the Muslim League, but actually thought 'Pakistan [wa]s unlikely to cause much harm to Hindus in the Punjab and the NWFP' as 'they already kn[e]w what Muslim rule [wa]s like in both provinces'.[196] This was contrary to the Mahasabha's official policy of blaming Rajagopalachari for the 'betrayal of Hindu rights'.[197]

What collapsed all ends of the Hindu political spectrum was the discovery that, all said and done, even the apex decision-making body of the all-India Mahasabha did not really oppose Rajagopalachari's conception of a 'Pakistan'. It was convinced that Gandhi would not take any steps 'detrimental to Hindu interests'. But opposing the Muslim League was concomitant with securing maximum benefits for Hindus in the Punjab and the larger north-western region. Keshab Chandra, a go-between for the all-India organization at the provincial level, told fellow partymen that 'these views should not be disclosed'.[198] This was the second instance within a span of twenty years that

[193]SPPAI, 20 May 1944, vol. lxvi, no. 21, p. 291.
[194]SPPAI, 1 July 1944, vol. lxvi, no. 27, p. 360.
[195]SPPAI, 2 September 1944, vol. lxvi, no. 36, p. 500.
[196]SPPAI, 16 September 1944, vol. lxvi, no. 38, p. 527.
[197]SPPAI, 14 October 1944, vol. lxvi, no. 42, p. 582.
[198]SPPAI, 21 October 1944, vol. lxvi, no. 43, p. 590.

Punjabi Hindus had shown a willingness to accept Muslim-majority rule at the price of separating the non-Muslim-majority districts in the eastern parts of the province. But it was still far from clear whether this stance of the Hindu Mahasabha actually conceded Muslims full rights to sovereignty in north-western and north-eastern India. Rajagopalachari envisaged an all-India centre over 'Pakistan', albeit restricted to fewer subjects than contemplated by the machine politicians of the Congress.

By tacitly accepting the principle of partitioned provinces, the Mahasabha was looking to weaken the Muslim position in the Punjab and Bengal. The Bengali Mahasabhite leader Dr Mukerjee had no doubt that 'Hindus of the Punjab and Bengal who were most affected by *Pakistan* ... would have to defeat it'. This required a sustained campaign against 'Pakistan' and any attempt by the Congress to pander to the Muslim League. Instead Hindus in the Punjab had to realize the 'dangers' of declining population proportions, a result of 'false census returns and conversion to Sikhism and Islam'. They had to fight the Unionists for dividing urban and rural Hindus, and reject communism and western civilization. India needed a strong central government and a constitution that protected the rights of minorities.[199] There was no room here for negotiating with the League's demand for 'Pakistan'.

Professor V.P. Despande, general secretary of the All-India Hindu Mahasabha, told a Provincial Hindu Students conference at Ludhiana that Congress had betrayed the Hindus. Charging Bhai Parmanand for wrecking the Hindu Sabha in the Punjab, he asked the students to grasp the nettle. Despande's view of the Hindu–Muslim issue highlights the problems in using cultural difference and bigotry interchangeably and placing them under overarching categories like 'communalism'. The learned professor attributed the 'communal problem' to the 'teachings of Islam'. He argued that the solution lay in 'making Muslims feel that they were the sons of *Hindustan* and not members of a foreign nation'. This proponent of a strong central government in an independent India thought Hindus had blundered by rejecting the federal provisions of the 1935 Act. Rectifying the damage required even greater central authority and the elimination of separate electorates and the Communal Award.[200] Bhai Parmanand's loss of stature among Punjabi Hindus was forcing major organizational changes in the provincial Mahasabha. The bete noire of the Muslims and now a fallen star in his own community, Parmanand confessed to the visiting Mahasabhite dignitary that 'internal dissensions were the cause of the weakness and inactivity of the Provincial Hindu *Sabha*'. Already convinced that the Punjab Sabha was 'in the hands of old and inactive leaders', Despande called for their constitutional removal by 'a widespread organisation of Hindu *Sabhas* ... which would enable the younger element to come to the top'. To

[199]*SPPAI*, 18 November 1944, vol. lxvi, no. 47, p. 639.
[200]Ibid., p. 643.

succeed against Muslims, Hindus had to form a common front with the Sikhs. Despande formed a 'poor opinion of Baba Kharak Singh' but was evidently charmed by Tara Singh whom he found to be 'sympathetic towards the Hindus'. Foretelling the end as beginning, Despande told a group of college students to unite 'to face the possibility of a civil war'.[201]

Few who heeded the call turned to the RSS in the Punjab. Routine drilling and the opening up of new branches by the provincial RSS was falling short of Nagpur's standards. This brought Apteji, the general secretary of the All-India RSS, to the Punjab. After witnessing the 'lack of enthusiasm displayed by local volunteers' in Lahore, he 'apprehended a collapse of the movement in the Punjab if no improvement was forthcoming'.[202] The head office in Nagpur promptly despatched Bachrajji, special organizer of the RSS in UP, to investigate the reasons for the 'deterioration of the *Sangh* in the Punjab'. He joined Apteji in Lahore to tell fifteen hundred volunteers that the *sangh*'s main purpose was to consolidate Hindus by 'reviving the spirit that had prevailed among ... [them] in ancient times'. RSS members had to be prepared, mentally and physically, to give their 'blood to keep the movement alive'. Underscoring the modernity of this evocation of ancient tradition, both Gandhi and Subhas Chandra Bose were held up as models worthy of emulation.[203] It is impossible to discern what this meant to the members of the RSS. They were under strict instructions to keep the activities of the *sangh* 'secret and ... strengthen the organisation ... to establish Hindu *Raj*'.[204]

Heralding Hindu raj without any agreement on its form and substance was fanciful play on the part of the RSS and the Mahasabha. Even if the scheduled castes could be ignored, there was no certainty of organizational unity or ideological consensus among Hindus. An annual meeting of the Balmiki Sabha resolved that while part of the Hindu religion, they 'must maintain a separate political entity as they had been neglected both by Hindus and Muslims'.[205] A group of *Balmikis* in Amritsar had asked Gandhi and the Congress to establish 'Ashwasthan' as 'a separate territory for the depressed classes if Pakistan came into being'. In the meantime, caste Hindus had 'to discard their prejudices about untouchability and ... allow members of the depressed classes to use Hindu drinking wells and ... enter Hindu temples'.[206] If these were the demands of a section of the scheduled castes, sixty Meo *chaudhuris* demanded the 'creation of a separate Mewat province', covering parts of Gurgaon, Delhi province and the princely states of Alwar and Bharatpur.[207]

[201] *SPPAI*, 25 November 1944, vol. lxvi, no. 48, pp. 659–60.
[202] *SPPAI*, 19 August 1944, vol. lxvi, no. 34, p. 469.
[203] *SPPAI*, 2 September 1944, vol. lxvi, no. 36, p. 503.
[204] *SPPAI*, 16 December 1944, vol. lxvi, no. 51, p. 693.
[205] *SPPAI*, 30 September 1944, vol. lxvi, no. 40, p. 557.
[206] *SPPAI*, 9 September 1944, vol. lxvi, no. 37, p. 515.
[207] *SPPAI*, 28 October 1944, vol. lxvi, no. 44, p. 610.

These are just a few examples of how identity and sovereignty were finding location in the discourse of citizenship rights at more localized levels. There were other more serious problems for the protagonists of a unified Hindu community. Instead of the RSS, many Hindus preferred their own volunteer organizations.[208] The Sanatan Dharm Sabha, bitter rivals of the Arya Samajists, supported the Mahabir Dal. In a mirror image of the Ahrars and segments of the Akali Dal, the Sanatan Dharm in Gujrat 'criticised western fashions, the cinema and tea drinking' in addition to calling for cow protection.[209] Another in Kangra demanded the compulsory teaching of Hindi in all the district schools. But it was the organizational meeting at Khanewal, Multan district, which gives the best insights into the Sanatan Dharm's understanding of the Hindi, Hindu, Hindustan axis. Pandit Jagan Nath declared that 'Sikhs were part of the Hindu nation'; they had been 'organised by Guru Gobind Singh as an army to protect Hinduism'. Hindus had 'always helped the Sikhs' and it was 'the acme of ingratitude' for them to now 'dissert [sic] the Hindus'. Other speakers believed Muslims and Sikhs could 'not harm Hindus' who had 'an overwhelming majority in India'.[210]

While agreeing with their rivals about the importance of a Hindu majority in India, the Arya Samajists had always been more imaginative in responding to western modernity. In an innovative solution to stop Muslims slaughtering cows, Bhim Sain Mantri of Lyallpur at an Arya Samaj meeting in Amritsar suggested putting 'the blood of a pig [i]n the mouth of all new born calves'.[211] Playing on Muslim prejudices for advantage was more compelling than the dire asceticism of the Sanatan Dharm. It was the latter's refusal to join the Arya-led protest against the Sind government's banning of the controversial fourteenth chapter of the *Satyarth Prakash* which highlights the ideological fissures among Punjabi Hindus.[212] Not all Hindus agreed with the extreme Arya position that the only retribution for the injury was to proscribe the Quran.[213] This diluted the Arya Samaj's campaign to restore the posthumously incorporated fourteenth chapter of Dayanand's magnum opus, ensuring continued fluidity in Hindu–Muslim relations in the Punjab.

Hindu differences, quite as much as those among Muslims and Sikhs, illustrate the problems in balancing the discourse and politics of communitarianism. Disturbing the seemingly well-settled dust of 'communalism', they point to the unformed possibilities of history in late-colonial India. The Punjab's three main communities had not ruled out negotiations. They had just trapped

---

[208]Like the Shakti Da in Rawalpindi and the Hindu Vir Sabha in Batala, Gurdaspur district.

[209]*SPPAI*, 8 July 1944, vol. lxvi, no. 28, p. 375.

[210]*SPPAI*, 21 October 1944, vol. lxvi, no. 43, p. 590.

[211]*SPPAI*, 26 August 1944, vol. lxvi, no. 35, p. 482.

[212]*SPPAI*, 25 November 1944, vol. lxvi, no. 48, p. 661.

[213]*SPPAI*, 2 December 1944, vol. lxvi, no. 49, p. 670.

themselves in a discourse of absolute rights when only relative solutions were possible, but which given the cut and thrust of their politics were becoming increasingly remote. This in large part explains the apparently uncompromising trajectory of Punjabi politics in the remaining years of the British raj in India.

Promises and Prospects: The League in the Punjab

With a provincial Muslim League fending off charges of irreligiosity and propagating an egalitarian future, Punjab during the mid-1940s provides rare glimpses into communitarian discourses of citizenship rights and contested sovereignties. Despite its growing reliance on mosques and religious idioms, the Punjab League was not the most persuasive harbinger of an Islamic order. It was more convincing as a potential vehicle for offsetting Congress domination at the centre and, by implication, Hindu commercial power in the Punjab. Overemphasizing the League's uses of religion obfuscates the ambiguities in the movement for a 'Pakistan', lending it a degree of coherence in articulating an ideology of nationalism that is belied by the evidence. What Islam meant to the propagandists of a Muslim state and the responses they evinced from audiences cutting across communitarian divisions requires careful historical enquiry.

With some of the best Urdu orators at their disposal, the Ahrars and the Jamiat-ul-Ulema-i-Hind had been kicking up a storm about Jinnah's lack of a religious disposition. But their listeners proved more savvy than they had reckoned. By the summer of 1944, Ahrar portrayals of the League leader as a godless, arrogant, self-opinionated, armchair politician was being viewed with 'mistrust' due to its 'blatantly obvious tactics'.[214] Maulanas Husain Ahmed Madani and Hafiz-ur-Rahman of Delhi came to the Punjab to energize the crusade. The duo took turns in wishing hellfire on Jinnah for 'having no beard, for not fasting during *Ramzan* and for frequenting clubs and cinemas instead of saying his prayers'.[215] Echoing their opinions, Mazhar Ali Azhar noted that Jinnah 'although a rich man, had never visited Mecca'.[216] Regardless of whether anyone was convinced, they succeeded in forcing Jinnah and the League to make more frequent uses of the Islamic idiom.

Taking to wearing the *sherwani* and a karakul cap, which came to acquire his name, Jinnah despite his anglicized Urdu did make a show of his Muslim cultural identity. Declaring his intention to take on the *ulema*, a breed for whom he had long harboured contempt, he had told the All-India Muslim League at Karachi in 1943 that the League and Muslim India had now become 'shock-proof, slogan-proof and stunt-proof'.[217] He was unfazed by men like Nawab Bahadur Yar Jang and Abdus Sattar Niazi who wanted to commit the all-India League to

[214]*SPPAI*, 8 July 1944, vol. lxvi, no. 28, pp. 373 and 377.
[215]*SPPAI*, 11 November 1944, vol. lxvi, no. 46, pp. 632–3.
[216]*SPPAI*, 1 July 1944, vol. lxvi, no. 27, p. 362.
[217]Pirzada (ed.), *Foundations of Pakistan*, ii, p. 449.

basing 'Pakistan' on Quranic principles.[218] As a lawyer, Jinnah might have foreseen the problems in establishing a state on a text which had only a few verses devoted to specifically legal questions. And as a politician and a constitutionalist he knew that there could be no accommodation of cultural differences which borrowed its rationale from the self-proclaimed guardians of Islam. Pragmatic to the core, he was not prepared to let the shock, slogan or stunt value of 'Pakistan' get shattered by ideological or sectarian divisions among Muslims. At his behest, the all-India League resisted demands to oust the Ahmadis from the Muslim community. By adopting the logic of inclusion, not exclusion, Jinnah gave breadth to the League's notion of citizenship rights, which some in his melange of regional associates seemed set on restricting to suit their own narrow purposes.

This created space for those hoping to win over some of the non-Muslims. Leaguers in Multan urged Sikhs to support 'Pakistan' and 'demand *Khalistan* for themselves'.[219] In Amritsar, Shaukat Hayat told Sikhs that Muslims wanted to give them 'similar rights to those claimed by the Muslims from the Hindus'. If Sikhs still insisted on separating from Muslims, they would have to submit a concrete proposal and could have 'their own government in any districts where they were in a majority'.[220] Significantly, these generous promises omitted mentioning the specifics of any future relationship between a 'Pakistan' and a 'Khalistan', or for that matter between them and 'Hindustan'.

Making vagueness the better part of virtue had the advantage of keeping options open for when the time came for serious negotiations. But the absence of any discernible policy vis-a-vis non-Muslims could boomerang badly for a League riven with ideological dissensions. For those ready to be accommodative towards the minorities, others more committed to an Islamic order muddied the waters with their emotive if ill-considered views on cultural differences. Zafar Ali Khan, who attributed the League's demand to Hindu oppression of Muslim minorities, declared that the 'Government ... [of] *Pakistan* ... [would] have no connection with any Central Government'.[221] Abdus Sattar Niazi, an even more committed Islamic ideologue from Mianwali district, damned Gandhi's one-nation idea and accused him of being 'a cheat' for refusing to admit that he was a Hindu leader. Jinnah at least admitted to being a Muslim

[218]See Jalal, *The Sole Spokesman*, pp. 95–6, 120.

[219]*SPPAI*, 21 October 1944, vol. lxvi, no. 43, p. 594.

[220]Ibid., p. 596. In his memoirs, Shaukat Hayat records his disappointment at Tara Singh's refusal to accept an offer 'on behalf of the Muslim League High Command' for a 25 per cent reservation of seats for Sikhs in the services, the teaching of Gurmukhi in schools, freedom to perform their religious ceremonies, including the carrying of a sword in public and the performance of *jhatka*. (See Shaukat Hayat Khan, *The Nation That Lost its Soul: Memoirs of Sirdar Shaukat Hayat Khan*, Lahore: Jang Publishers, 1995, p. 161.)

[221]*SPPAI*, 21 October 1944, vol. lxvi, no. 43, p. 595.

leader. Muslims needed their own state since 'in Islam politics could not be separated from religion'. Concurring whole-heartedly was no less a person than the Raja of Mahmudabad, a key financier of the All-India Muslim League, who announced that 'in *Pakistan* the law of the *Quran* would be enforced'.[222]

The publication of the Punjab Muslim League's manifesto on 31 October 1944 brought the disagreements within the provincial leadership on the future relationship between Islam and the state as well as between Muslims and non-Muslims to the fore. Authored by the communist ideologue Daniyal Latifi, it promised a Punjabi utopia to Muslims and non-Muslims under the League's rule. A programme for the uplift of the Muslims was to be implemented 'without interfering with the legitimate interests of any other community'. The manifesto pledged itself to extend civil liberties and ensure the freedom of the press. Industrial development was to be promoted with curbs on the private sector and the elimination of imperial preferences. Steps were to be taken towards improving the standard of living of the people as a whole with special safeguards to protect the interests of labour. The state was to play an anchor role in agricultural development through the provision of cheap credit and co-operative marketing at guaranteed prices. In an important concession to the landlords, the League undertook to broaden the scope of the Land Alienation Act. A number of promises were made to the agrarian sector, including the development of irrigation, roads and electrification and the redistribution of land. Urban areas were to have local self-government on a democratic basis with town planning, efficient sanitation and various civil amenities. There was to be universal adult franchise and all anomalies in the electoral system were to be removed.[223]

Tall claims matched by a puny organizational structure marred by personal as well as ideological rivalries were not the best insurance for the translation of the League's ideals into practice in the Punjab. The manifesto nevertheless serves as a worthy reminder of the intentions of a section of the provincial Muslim League which endorsed the document. In the rush to label the discourse 'national' or 'communal' a good deal of nuance has been lost. However unrealistic its claims, the Punjab League manifesto was a step in the direction of preventing a partition of the province. It did not require much intelligence to see that separating the non-Muslim-majority districts would be catastrophic for Punjabi Muslims. Stripped of its eastern districts, western Punjab would be enfeebled economically and politically. Muslims in eastern Punjab would be left with the choice of homelessness or a weakened future in a predominantly Hindu India. Given their contributions to the discourse of Muslim identity in

---

[222]Ibid., p. 596.

[223]Punjab Provincial Muslim League, *Manifesto of the Punjab Provincial Muslim League*, Lahore: Daniyal Latifi, 1944. Also cited in *SPPAI*, 18 November 1944, vol. lxvi, no. 47, p. 641.

India, this was a dismal prospect for Muslims in Amritsar, Jullundur, Ludhiana and Gurdaspur, to name only some of the places where the faithful had begun forking into a commercial realm dominated by Hindu entrepreneurs and men of finance.

Keeping a distinction between the politics of the western and the eastern districts helps to better map the winding path to the fateful moment of 1947. Sikhs in the western districts had to be placated if the province was to remain economically viable. This was why Shaukat Hayat had tried to convey the League high command's offer to Master Tara Singh through Sardar Makhbain Singh, who had also acted as an intermediary between Sikander Hayat and Sardar Baldev Singh which led to the Unionist–Sikh understanding.[224] Reflecting the spirit of compromise, a Muslim League meeting in Lyallpur advised Sikhs 'to throw in their lot with Muslims' since 'the two communities had a similar outlook on martial, economic and religious matters'.[225] By way of further assurance, the League vowed to replace the Unionists with 'a democratic form of Government'.[226]

There were other potentially encouraging signs on an otherwise darkening political horizon. Taking advantage of the Punjab League's new-found interest in civil liberties, communists stepped up their efforts to bring it closer to the Congress and the Akalis. A better bet for Indian independence than any Congress–Unionist understanding, this was akin to a game of snakes and ladders. Communists in the Punjab bore the brunt of the all-India party's official support for the League's demand for a 'Pakistan'. Their anti-imperialist sentiments were already suspect once the central command decided to co-operate in the war effort. On May Day in 1944, Punjabi communists condemned Subhas Chandra Bose as 'a traitor', lionized the Soviet red army and directed people 'not to be misled by enemy wireless propaganda'.[227] This was another error of judgement for which the communists paid heavily in the 1945-6 elections. Even while driving a nail into their own coffin, communists managed to give a different dimension to the discourse and politics of the Punjab. Apart from extending links with the Kirti and Kisan Sabhas, they had been infiltrating the ranks of not just the Muslim League but also the Congress and the Akalis.[228]

[224]Khan, *The Nation that Lost its Soul*, p. 161.

[225]*SPPAI*, 2 December 1944, vol. lxvi, no. 49, p. 682.

[226]There was a new note in the voice of Ghazanfar Ali Khan who objected to the stifling presence of police intelligence reporters at League meetings. This was a pure waste of public money. (Ibid., p. 672.) He had a point. But it missed the significance of intelligence gathering by the colonial state in disciplining and controlling a subject population.

[227]*SPPAI*, 13 May 1944, vol. lxvi, no. 20, p. 278.

[228]But the gap between communist ambitions and their limited support base continued to dog them in the Punjab. (See Bhagwan Josh, *Communist Movement in the Punjab, 1926–47*, Delhi: Anupama Publications, 1979.)

A League ministry, they were convinced, would prove to be 'a set-back to British Imperialism' as well as the Akalis, the bigger landlords and Chhotu Ram's Jat Sabha. By establishing contacts with the more approachable, if not necessarily like-minded, elements in the League, communists could pave the way for a Congress–League combination.[229] To their dismay, communists were 'rigidly excluded' from a Congress workers' meeting in Ludhiana. They were attacked for 'stabbing the Congress in the back' at the time of the Quit India movement in 1942.[230]

Though one of their number wrote the provincial League's manifesto, communists never came close to disturbing the power balance against the Punjab's rural moneybags. It was one thing to have Daultana's ear, quite another to gain a foothold in the provincial League. Mian Iftikharuddin's defection from the Congress in October 1945 proved more beneficial to the League than to the communists. The scion of a leading Arain family of Lahore was no match for Daultana's political gyrations. Following a brief graze with communists, the would-be maverick landlord began succumbing to the dictates of his own class interests in addition to flirting with bigoted elements within the Muslim community. Small wonder that the League was not a happy home for those fired by communist ideas.

Communists were also shunned by Sikhs. This was the price for supporting the League's 'Pakistan'. To placate them the communists on different occasions offered to accept the Sikh view of their religious identity and corresponding claims to a negotiable sovereignty. Before becoming the office secretary of the League, Daniyal Latifi defended an Azad Punjab on grounds of language and custom. Some of his co-party workers considered it as 'evidence of the patriotic urge of the Sikh masses for independence'.[231] In another bid, communists promised to help establish a separate Sikh state of 'Khalistan'.[232] But this only served to confuse matters, leaving communists in two minds about whether to promote a Sikh–Muslim government or an independent Sikh state.[233] The all-India communist leader Dr Adhikari tried clarifying matters in a pamphlet offering Sikhs a separate state, adequate representation at the centre and in 'Pakistan' or dividing the latter into two autonomous units, one dominated by them.[234] A plenitude of options only drew the ire of the Sikhs, themselves uncertain about which way to turn. Tara Singh drove a knife close to the communist jugular when he described them as 'unreliable' and 'opponents of Sikhism' who had 'to stop disrupting the Sikh community'.[235]

[229] SPPAI, 1 April 1944, vol. lxvi, no. 14, p. 193.
[230] SPPAI, 23 December 1944, vol. lxvi, no. 52, p. 699.
[231] SPPAI, 4 March 1944, vol. lxvi, no. 10, p. 133.
[232] SPPAI, 15 July 1944, vol. lxvi, no. 29, p. 398.
[233] SPPAI, 2 September 1944, vol. lxvi, no. 36, p. 504.
[234] SPPAI, 20 January 1945, vol. lxvii, no. 3, p. 5.
[235] SPPAI, 26 August 1944, vol. lxvi, no. 35, p. 501.

Coming under pressure, communist workers began growing beards to prove that they were 'as good Sikhs as the *Akalis*'.[236] But there was to be no reprieve. Akalis denounced them as 'immoral atheists attempting to pose as religious Sikhs'.[237]

Unable to deliver either Hindu or Sikh support, the communists were a liability and not an asset for the landed helmsmen of the Punjab League. By creating an illusion of their influence over Daultana, communists intensified power struggles between him and Mamdot. Even as the Muslim League reiterated its pledge to 'safeguard the rights of Hindus and Sikhs in *Pakistan*', class divisions within the Muslim community were undermining the manifesto's commitments to the labouring strata.[238] The communist objective in assisting its membership and organizational drive was to 'let the League perform the task of arousing the political consciousness of the Muslim masses', especially in the western districts, so that they could 'win them over more readily'.[239] To prevent this eventuality, Shaukat Hayat and his associates tried discrediting Daultana by accusing him of 'Communist sympathies'. But the blood of the landlord was thicker than the still waters of communist ideology in the Punjab. Daultana was re-elected general secretary of the Punjab League along with Mamdot as president.[240] However accommodating he may have been at the level of ideas, Daultana was first and foremost a representative of his own landed interests, unwilling to concede an inch to urban middle-class Muslims on the right or the left of the political spectrum. This made him acutely vulnerable both to landlords and religious ideologues who frankly loathed communists.[241]

A Punjab League winking to the left and staying put on the right had a hard enough time keeping a straight face, far less allaying non-Muslims fears on citizenship rights in a 'Pakistan'. It was in any case more concerned with enlarging its base among Muslims. With the bulk of the rural populace under the jackboot of pro-British landlords, there was no prospect in the Punjab of a broad-based Muslim mobilization for a 'Pakistan'. So even with help from young enthusiasts of the Punjab Muslim Students' Federation, the League soon abandoned its tactic of rousing the rural areas.[242] The 'summer school of politics', the name

[236]*SPPAI*, 9 December 1944, vol. lxvi, no. 50, p. 681.

[237]*SPPAI*, 16 December 1944, vol. lxvi, no. 51, p. 692.

[238]*SPPAI*, 20 January 1945, vol. lxvii, no. 3, p. 25.

[239]*SPPAI*, 17 March 1945, vol. lxvii, no. 10, p. 105.

[240]*SPPAI*, 26 May 1945, vol. lxvii, no. 19, p. 193.

[241]For the dovetailing of interest between pro-British landlords and religious ideologues, see Choudhury, *Pakistan ki Siyasi Tehrik. Muslim Punjab ka Siyasi Irtaqa*, v, chapter five.

[242]The PMSF's role in the League's propaganda campaign is documented by Mukhtar Zaman, *Student's Role in the Pakistan Movement*, Karachi: Quaid-i-Azam Academy, 1978.

given to the League's use of students for rural propaganda, instead of instituting learning became the playground of youth politics. By late 1944, furious at the shabby treatment of student workers by its district branches, the federation instructed its underlings not to render any assistance to the Punjab League.[243]

With even the students offended for the time being, the League had to find some way of keeping up the pretence of a movement. It could not but smile upon the Ahrars and Khaksars, the only two Muslim organizations in the Punjab which had shown some capacity for organization. But if Mashriqi's Khaksars could be accommodated, the Ahrars had to be bought and their price was non-negotiable. In November 1944 the Ahrars offered to support the League against the Unionists provided it 'denounce the *Mirzais* openly'.[244] In July, the All-India Muslim League at Jinnah's insistence had scuttled an attempt by Maulana Abdul Hamid Badayuni to debar Ahmadis from membership in the organization.[245] Despite Jinnah's firm stand on the matter, the League had started criticizing the Ahmadis in public by the turn of the new year. This alarmed the Ahmadis who decided to set up their own *nizamats*, literally governments, in Sialkot, Gujranwala, Gujrat, Shahpur, Multan, Ferozepur, Jullundur and Hoshiarpur.[246] Exclusion from the dominant narratives of communitarian identity entailed a corresponding loss of sovereignty over Punjab's assorted sub-denominational groupings. If not for the Quaid-i-Azam's clear understanding of the political and constitutional implications, the Ahmadis may well have been excommunicated from the Muslim community before the dawn of independence. No small victory for the Ahmadis, it was vital for a relatively balanced discourse of identity, sovereignty and citizenship during the twilight hours of the British raj in India.

The Ahrar onslaught against the Ahmadis was finding acceptance among a growing circle of Punjabi Muslims. A paid League worker said at an Ahrar meeting in Multan that there was 'no difference between *Pakistan* and *Hakumat-i-Illahia*'. At the same meeting Maulvi Fazlul Rahman told the residents of the city not to let the Ahmadis bury their dead in Muslim cemeteries.[247] Denial of social space preceded the formal excommunication of the Ahmadis by several decades. The Ahrars are the unchallenged pioneers of that variant of Muslim discourse and politics which, in dropping one sect of Islam, sets the precedent for excluding many more. Apart from fracturing the logic of inclusionary membership in the Muslim community, the slow but sure coming together of the Ahrars and Leaguers was a bad portent for citizenship rights. Under the learned guidance of Maulana Husain Ahmad Madani, the Ahl-i-Sunnat was

[243]*SPPAI*, 25 November 1944, vol. lxvi, no. 48, p. 663.
[244]*SPPAI*, 18 November 1944, vol. lxvi, no. 47, p. 643.
[245]Mirza, *Karavan-i-Ahrar*, vi, p. 289.
[246]*SPPAI*, 27 January 1945, vol. lxvii, no. 4, p. 37.
[247]*SPPAI*, 11 November 1944, vol. lxvi, no. 46, p. 632.

well as Ahmadis, and urging Sunnis to organize and propagate
rars were once again inciting Shia–Sunni tensions in Lucknow
1-i-Sahaba agitation. The arrogance of bigotry lies in claiming a
ound. At the annual Ahrar provincial conference in Ferozepur,
tern civilization were attacked in the same breath. But in the
next it was announced that the *Majlis-i-Ahrar* would assist the Muslim League
to attain *Pakistan* if Jinnah would give an assurance that Quranic laws would be
enforced'. Advertising their organizational achievements, they claimed to have
established 336 branches in a single year with the Ahrars in Gurdaspur and
Sialkot 'com[ing] out on top in performance in the urban areas'. A special vow
was taken to continue the Ahrar policy of 'unit[ing] all Muslims, except
Ahmediyas'.[249]

Jinnah, once bitten twice smart, was not ready to make the necessary
gestures to win over the Ahrars. Facing stolid opposition from pro-Unionist
officials in the districts, Punjabi Leaguers had to try roping in as many Muslims
as possible. So Mamdot told a gathering of ten thousand in Lyallpur that
'Pakistan' was the essence of the Ahrar's *hakumat-i-illahiya*, the Khaksar aim
of establishing Islamic supremacy and the Jamiat-ul-Ulema-i-Hind's goal of
an independent India.[250] After discussing the Ahrar scheme for a *hakumat-i-illahiya*, the Punjab Muslim League resolved that 'when *Pakistan* had been
achieved, the administration would be carried out according to the *Quran*'.[251]
Unable to organize a party, the Punjab League had no conception of what
government administration entailed. Flanking itself with Islamic idioms was
one way of parrying the litany of criticisms from all ends of the Muslim
spectrum. But this could also be an invitation to increasingly exclusionary
postures in relation to the non-Muslims. Ghulam Mustafa Shah Gilani may
have been delighted to see that the Ahrars, the Jamiat-ul-Ulema-i-Hind as
well as 'other political parties were slowly beginning to accept the *Pakistan*
scheme'. At the same time, Muslim women in Jhang were being told to stop
buying from Hindu shops and the men encouraged to picket them instead.[252]
This was also where Ahrars and Khaksars had joined hands with the Muslim
League's National Guards to work jointly for Muslim welfare.[253] Greater unity
among divided Muslims was requiring a more emphatic exclusion of non-
Muslims. Sunnis in Mianwali wanted only Muslim magistrates to hear cases
under the Muslim Divorce Act of 1939.[254] The demand for Sunni magistrates
to cases pertaining to Sunnis was not a long way from here.

[248]*SPPAI*, 24 March 1945, vol. lxvii, no. 11, p. 110.
[249]*SPPAI*, 14 April 1945, vol. lxvii, no. 14, p. 144.
[250]*Nawa-i-Waqt*, Lahore, 14 February 1945.
[251]*SPPAI*, 16 May 1945, vol. lxvii, no. 19, p. 195.
[252]Ibid.
[253]*SPPAI*, 23 June 1945, vol. lxvii, no. 23, p. 233.
[254]*SPPAI*, 10 March 1945, vol. lxvii, no. 9, p. 92.

Recognizing the pitfalls, Daultana directed Leaguers to make special efforts to explain their objectives to non-Muslims with whom they had to live in 'Pakistan'. Speeches were made stressing the idea of a 'Pakistan' in an independent India. Hindus were assured that the League was opposed not to them but to British imperialism. With a democratic system of government, 'Pakistan' would treat non-Muslims fairly and squarely.[255] Statements of the League's good intentions on future citizenship rights had to cope with the social and political dynamics among Punjabi Muslims. Whatever the view from Malabar Hill and the provincial capital, it was the internal politics of Muslims that were shaping attitudes on Islam, the Ahmadis and, by extension, the non-Muslims. Although privately willing to defer to the Ahrars on the Ahmadi issue, Punjabi Leaguers were unwilling to be dictated to by them. A meeting of the Lahore district Muslim League in Kasur, attended by Zafar Ali Khan and Shaukat Hayat, described the *hakumat-i-illahiya* as 'Ram Raj'.[256] A government of God could have meaning only under the auspices of the Punjab Muslim League. Yet no one had a clue how the League's 'Pakistan' was going to be run on Islamic principles. These were nagging questions left for future generations to work out. For now it was the immediate political struggle at hand which had to be won and victory secured at all costs. Tentative beginnings made in the direction of assuring non-Muslims of citizenship rights in a fully or partially sovereign Punjab were lost sight of in a frenzied race to hoist the League's flag in a province whose complex politics of communitarian identity were to inform and ultimately undermine constitutional arrangements covering the subcontinent as a whole.

Simla Sizzles and Election Fever

In the summer of 1945, Wavell's proposal for a conference in Simla raised political tempers nearer to boiling point. Educated circles hoped that a meeting of all-India stars like Gandhi, Jinnah and Azad with the British viceroy would create the cosmological conditions for ending the political stalemate. At a time when the League had no ministries in any province of British India with the exception of Sind, inviting Jinnah on an equal footing with the Congress leaders gave a much-needed fillip to his prestige.[257] Leaguers in the Punjab were pleased while the Akalis and communists seemed satisfied. Kept out of the deliberations, the Mahasabha was disgusted while the provincial Congress

[255]*Nawa-i-Waqt*, Lahore, 15 March 1945.
[256]*SPPAI*, 19 May 1945, vol. lxvii, no. 18, p. 189.
[257]Aurangzeb Khan's League ministry in the NWFP earned more notoriety for failing to redress wartime grievances than for promoting 'Pakistan'. On 12 March 1945 the Congress opposition succeeded in securing a no-confidence motion against Aurangzeb, paving the way for Dr Khan Sahib's second ministry. A fortnight later, the Bengal League ministry under Khwajah Nazimuddin also collapsed.

simply waited for the all-India organization's lead.[258] The collapse of the conference raised Jinnah's stature in Muslim politics. He had single-handedly wrecked the conference by insisting on the League's exclusive right to choose all the Muslim members of the viceroy's executive council.[259]

The aftermath of the Simla conference hardened political differences along communitarian lines with parties supporting the stands of their respective leaders. Ahrars, Khaksars and the Jamiat endorsed Congress's contention that the Muslim League was not the sole representative organization of Muslims. With the Momin Ansars, the Muslim Majlis and sections of the Shias doing the same, the League had to urgently make political capital of Jinnah's moment in Simla. Equating the League with the Indian Muslims required an energetic assault against pro-Congress Muslims. With general elections on the anvil, the League's propaganda became shrill and pugnacious. The Congress and its Muslim supporters were the main targets of attack. Maulana Abul Kalam Azad was pejoratively called 'Maulana Haw Haw' while Maulana Habibur Rahman was nicknamed 'Maulvi Hindu Niwas'.[260] This was mild in comparison to Husain Ahmad Madani's and Mazhar Ali Azhar's depiction of Jinnah as 'Kafir-i-Azam'. Azhar jeered at Leaguers with the couplet:

Left the fold of Islam for an infidel,
Is this the great leader or the great infidel?[261]

Setting new standards of decency in political discourse, the Ahrars published four pamphlets in Urdu from Lahore. Detailing the inconsistencies in the League's propaganda, these attacked Jinnah for marrying a Parsi woman and patronizing communists and Ahmadis.[262]

Accusing the Ahrars of being paid henchmen of the Congress was a favourite League repartee.[263] But keeping down all Muslim rivals at the same time was a trickier business. Signs of an Ahrar and Khaksar rapprochement were unnerving as was Zafar Ali Khan's revival of the Ittihad-i-Millat. Even with the induction of students and communists, Leaguers were uncertain of their electoral prospects in the land of the five rivers. Primary Leagues were hastily set up in key districts, including Amritsar, Gurdaspur, Gujranwala, Attock, Mianwali, Jullundur,

---

[258]SPPAI, 23 and 30 June 1945, vol. lxvii, nos.23, 24, pp. 231, 236.

[259]For Jinnah's tactics at Simla, see Jalal, The Sole Spokesman, pp. 129–32.

[260]SPPAI, 28 July 1945, vol. lxvii, no. 28, p. 261.

[261]Aik kafir ke wastee Islam ko chhora
Ye Quaid-i-Azam hey ke Kafir-i-Azam
(Cited in Choudhury, Pakistan ki Siyasi Tehrik: Muslim Punjab ka Siyasi Irtaqa, p. 381.)

[262]SPPAI, 22 September 1945, vol. lxvii, no. 35, pp. 317–18.

[263]The Karachi-based Dawn, founded by Jinnah, printed a scathing play in which Ahrars were portrayed as men who could be purchased for money and Mashriqi for a cup of tea. (Mirza, Karavan-i-Ahrar, vi, p. 294.)

Ludhiana and Ambala, and new offices opened in Jhang and Karnal.[264] A flood of defections from the Unionists and the Congress saved the Punjab League from organizational embarrassment. By September 1945, Mian Iftikharuddin was in the loop. Fifty thousand attended a jubilant League meeting in Lahore welcoming a leading member of the Arain *biraderi* into its fold.[265] Iftikharuddin's defection cemented the League's electoral alliance with communists in the Punjab. Another important recruit from the Congress was Abdul Qayum Khan of the NWFP—a much-needed relief for the Frontier League.[266] Firoz Khan Noon, a member of a leading Punjabi landed family, also resigned from the viceroy's executive council to bolster the League's electoral fortunes in his home province.

With *ulema* and *maulvis*, *pirs* and *sajjada nashins* beaming at the League, a confident Mumtaz Daultana instructed the district branches to 'maintain a high standard of behavior' and 'avoid at all costs any disturbances at meetings organised by other Muslim parties'.[267] Solemn appeals were made to Ahrars and Khaksars to join the League. Though some heeded the call on an individual basis,[268] the two organizations remained averse to playing second fiddle to the League. Fancying they had a chance in the tussle for leadership of Punjabi Muslims, Khaksars tried hijacking the 'Pakistan' demand by projecting their religious identity.[269] Carrying copies of the Quran instead of spades, wearing white handkerchiefs in the form of an Arab head-dress and saying their prayers five times a day was the Khaksar answer to the use of Islamic idioms by the League and the Ahrars.[270]

Although Shaukat Hayat tried luring Mashriqi by offering to make him 'the "general" of the Muslim League',[271] the Khaksar leader had his own ideas on how to secure the independence of India. Bitterly opposed to both Gandhi and Jinnah, he described the Khaksars as 'soldiers of God' who could not possibly combine with other Muslim political bodies.[272] Dismissing the Congress and the League as 'communal organisations', Mashriqi's spelled

[264]*SPPAI*, 13 October 1945, vol. lxvii, no. 38, p. 345.

[265]*SPPAI*, 20 October 1945, vol. lxvii, no. 39, p. 349.

[266]Qayum Khan lashed out at the Punjab Unionists but invited Dr Khan Sahib and Ghaffar Khan to 'discard Congress' which had 'forsaken its principles' and join the League, a party that was 'working to establish an Islamic rule' in the Muslim majority provinces. (*SNPAI*, 28 August 1945, vol. xxxxi, no. 35, p. 75.)

[267]*SPPAI*, 20 October 1945, vol. lxvii, no. 39, p. 351.

[268]Qazi Ahsan Ahmed Shujabadi, an Ahrar from Shahpur, 'declared his faith in Jinnah's leadership'. (*SPPAI*, 2 December 1944, vol. lxvi, no. 49, p. 672.) A Khaksar on the other hand argued that 'Pakistan' could not be obtained 'unless Muslims abided strictly by their religion' and praised Ilim Din, Rajpal's murderer. (*SPPAI*, 31 March 1945, vol. lxvii, no. 12, p. 122.)

[269]*SPPAI*, 17 June 1944, vol. lxvi, no. 25, p. 342.

[270]*SPPAI*, 4 November 1944, vol. lxvi, no. 45, p. 619.

[271]Ibid., p. 352.

[272]*SPPAI*, 11 August 1945, vol. lxvii, no. 30, p. 275.

out his solution to the Hindu–Muslim problem in a draft constitution for a free India. There was to be no division of the provinces. But in keeping with the local option clause of 1942, every province would have the right of secession and forming a totally independent unit, thus ensuring 'full Pakistan for all time'. A non-party civil servant was to be president of India and the position held alternately for a period of three years by a Hindu and a Muslim. There were to be Hindu and Muslim governors for the Hindu-majority and Muslim-majority provinces respectively. The president and provincial governors were to have veto powers, resembling 'kingly qualities', in addition to being 'elected rulers', while the representatives of the people were to be elected on the basis of joint electorates.[273]

Mashriqi's blueprint is intriguing for its detailed consideration of the fundamental rights of citizenship. There was to be Hindu–Muslim parity at the all-India centre with an additional 10 per cent seats for the scheduled castes. Declaring a war on hunger, he recommended basing the rupee on the wheat standard so that a one rupee coin would fetch sixteen seers of the grain everywhere in India. The goal was to raise the value of the rupee to thirty-two seers of wheat within fifteen years of attaining freedom. Though charged with 'indulging in day dreams',[274] the Khaksar's proposed utopia was a more explicit statement on the social welfare rights of citizenship than anything produced by the main contenders in the political game for power in an independent India. This conscientious attempt to accommodate cultural differences and outline the future course of equal citizenship from the margins was endorsed by men like Fazlul Haq, Humayun Kabir, Nalini Ranjan Sarkar and Tej Bahadur Sapru.[275]

Mashriqi's own followers were unimpressed. Seeing the larger battalions lining up for the final showdown, they started trickling towards the League, especially in the eastern districts of the province due to 'dissatisfaction' with the proposed constitution.[276] But on the INA issue, central to the Congress's electoral propaganda in the Punjab, Khaksars found themselves 'more in sympathy with the Congress'.[277] This was a ray of light for pro-Congress Muslims. To more effectively challenge the League's claim to represent all Muslims, Congress in the Punjab opted to contest only those Muslim seats for which an Ahrar or Khaksar candidate was not forthcoming. This saved an internally divided Punjab Congress from the disgrace of being snubbed by Muslim voters.

[273]Inayatullah Khan Mashriqi, *Constitution of Free India*, Lahore: Idara-i-Aliyyah, 1946. Also see QAP, File 1104, NAP, pp. 306–8 and Hussain, *Al-Mashriqi: The Disowned Genius*, pp. 204–9. Though published in 1946, Mashriqi was airing it publicly by the fall of 1945. (*SPPAI*, 22 September 1945, vol. lxvii, no. 35, p. 317.)
[274]*SPPAI*, 20 October 1945, vol. lxvii, no. 39, p. 350.
[275]Hussain, *Al-Mashriqi: The Disowned Genius*, p. 208.
[276]*SPPAI*, 10 November 1945, vol. lxvii, no. 42, p. 393.
[277]*SPPAI*, 3 November 1945, vol. lxvii, no. 41, p. 378.

The Punjab League may have had the most rudimentary organization, but with help from the press and publications market its propaganda was reaching out to a larger audience.[278] With the enlistment of *maulvis* and *pirs*, it could withstand the Ahrar momentum and the pseudo-military-cum-Islamic stunts of the Khaksars. Observers noted that the League's influence in the Punjab was 'steadily on the increase'. Its membership had swelled to five lakh and the provincial coffers were in credit to the tune of four hundred thousand rupees.[279] But this was not matched by greater consistency in the League's rhetoric which fluctuated widely between moderation and bigotry, cogency and gibberish, lending some curious overtones to its conception of an Islamic democracy with adequate safeguards for all communities.

Leading the moderates from the front but still 'harbour[ing] radical leanings', Iftikharuddin asked the people of Rohtak to vote Congress instead of Unionist if they were not prepared to support the League. Ignoring his new party's somewhat lukewarm response to the impending trial of three INA men for treason, he 'made a plea for Congress–Muslim League unity' before exhorting Muslims to vote for the League.[280] Learning how to cater to different audiences, Iftikharuddin in Gujrat threatened *sayapa*, a chant of damnation, outside homes whose inhabitants abstained from voting for the League.[281] And this was someone who not only stood out as the most effective speaker in the League but combined support for it with 'a flavouring of Communist doctrine'.[282] Firoz Khan Noon, for his part, professed to be uniting Unionists with the Muslim League. This did not make him better disposed to *zaildars* and *lambardars*, whom he described as 'Government dogs' who had 'sold themselves and their religion to Government'.[283] With such stellar language from the refined, it seems unfair to consider Pir Jamaat Ali Shah bigoted for stating that those 'disloyal to the Muslim League' would be 'regarded as ... non-Muslim' and refused 'buri[al]' in a Muslim graveyard'.[284]

A War of the Fatwas: Muslim versus Muslim

Browbeating Muslim opponents with more and more improbable uses of Islam did more to contaminate the atmosphere than any explicit attacks on

[278]In June 1944 the Muslim League purchased the *Pakistan*, a weekly journal of Lahore, and began exploring the possibilities of turning it into a daily newspaper. The result was the Urdu paper, *Nawa-i-Waqt*, started by Hameed Nizami and Hamid Mahmud. For a background to this venture, see Choudhury, *Pakistan ki Siyasi Tehrik: Muslim Punjab ka Siyasi Irtaqa*, pp. 368–74.

[279]SPPAI, 10 November 1945, vol. lxvii, no. 42, p. 592.

[280]SPPAI, 17 November 1945, vol. lxvii, no. 43, pp. 405 , 407.

[281]SPPAI, 24 November 1945, vol. lxvii, no. 44, p. 415.

[282]SPPAI, 8 December 1945, vol. lxvii, no. 46, p. 437.

[283]SPPAI, 10 November 1945, vol. lxvii, no. 42, p. 391.

[284]Ibid., p. 392.

non-Muslims. In October 1945, the League sponsored the formation of a new party, the Jamiat-ul-Ulema-i-Islam to counter the Jamiat-ul-Ulema-i-Hind and the Ahrars. The League's answer to pro-Congress *ulema* was structured, ironically enough, around the *ulema* of *thana* Bhawan, especially the followers of the reputed Islamic scholar Maulana Ashraf Ali Thanawi. They even managed to engineer a rift among the Deobandis. While Maulana Shabir Ahmad Usmani, a Deobandi, became president, Maulana Zafar Ahmad Thanawi, a Barelvi, was the moving spirit behind the organization.[285] With a segment of the *ulema* issuing periodic *fatwas* in their favour, Leaguers were better able to parry accusations of being *la-dini* or irreligious. A clash of the *ulema*, each with his own interpretation of Islam, was thoroughly confusing for ordinary Muslims. Making selective uses of Quranic and Hadith sources, pro-Congress *ulema* opposed joining the *murtids* and *munqirs* of the League while their counterparts warned Muslims against joining non-Muslim parties. In the ensuing war of the *fatwas*, the elections acquired the unenviable status of a *jihad* between Islam and *kufar*.[286]

When the exchange of low-lying sallies did not distract, there were substantive differences in League and non-League Muslim conceptions of the future. Roughing up pro-Congress Muslims like Azad and Madani, verbally or physically, did not prevent them from communicating their message. Nor did humouring Mashriqi deter him from expressing ideas that might have given the League a good run for its money were it not for the colonial state's clamp down on paramilitary formations like the Khaksars. There were others, no less vocal, ready to add their arguments against the Muslim League's 'Pakistan'. Of these, by far the most influential individual was Abul Ala Maudoodi who on 11 March 1941 had formed the Jamat-i-Islami in the district of Pathankot in eastern Punjab. Not a product of western education nor trained as a religious scholar—he was educated almost exclusively at home—Maudoodi was to make a name for himself in the world of Islamic scholarship far beyond the Muslim state he opposed in the 1940s.[287]

[285]See Mirza, *Karavan-i-Ahrar*, vi, pp. 290–2, 315–18.
[286]Ibid., pp. 324–73.
[287]Born in Aurangabad, Hyderabad Deccan, in 1902, Maudoodi became a journalist at the age of seventeen—a credit to his command of the Urdu language. In 1919, impressed by Abul Kalam Azad, he participated in the *khilafat* movement. Taken in by Gandhi's personality, he wrote a book on him which was seized by the police. By 1920 he was editing the pro-Congress paper *Taj* in Jubbulpore and subsequently worked for the Jamiat-ul-Ulema-i-Hind's paper *Al-Jamiat* in Delhi. He then left for Hyderabad to join his elder brother in running his journal, the *Tarjuman-ul-Quran*. An opponent of territorial nationalism, it acquired a following among Punjabi Muslims. It was a landlord admirer of the poet, Choudhury Niaz Ali Khan who, at the suggestion of another worthy admirer, Ghulam Ahmad Parvez, brought Maudoodi to Pathankot in 1938. He was to head the local Dar-ul-Islam, funded by Niaz Ali

In an article published in the pro-League paper *Nawa-i-Waqt* Maudoodi proposed a settlement of the Hindu–Muslim problem in an undivided India. There was no better solution for India, certainly for Muslims in the minority provinces who would be substantially weakened by the creation of a 'Pakistan'. He called for 'a state of federated nations', which would not be the sovereign domain of any single nation, but an entity organized on international principles of federation. The different nations constituting the federation would enjoy complete cultural autonomy in matters to do with religion and be equal partners in the running of the government. A federal centre would not have powers to intervene in the internal affairs of culturally sovereign nations. Each with its own national social system could discipline and punish members according to their personal laws.[288] This gave communities as sovereign nations, not the federation, power over marriage, divorce and inheritance with stern implications for women.[289] Maudoodi went to some lengths to stress that the laws of the sovereign nations would be on par with those of the federated state. A federal court was to decide conflicts between the different units. The nation most vigorous in the pursuit of its cultural ethos would be in a position to influence the laws of the federated state as a whole.[290] This was a scarcely veiled statement of intent by the founder of the Jamat to propagate his version of Islam throughout the length and breadth of India.

Before coming to the Punjab in 1938, Maudoodi writing in the *Tarjuman-ul-Quran* had criticized pro-Congress *ulema* for accepting a conception of Indian nationalism that denied any place to religious parties. Rubbishing them with the label *munafaqs*, he likened Muslims' joining the Congress to collective suicide. Unlike Iqbal's, Maudoodi's conception of the role of Islam in the state left no space for individuals to negotiate their own balance with the community. Submission to Allah, Maudoodi seems to have believed, meant obeying whoever could claim to be the authoritative interpreter of the divine will. Iqbal had recommended reposing that authority in an elected parliament. Maudoodi was himself a contender for that supreme position of authority. Turning cultural difference into an extreme form of bigotry, he execrated Jinnah and the Muslim League and practically excluded the majority of Muslims from his definition of the true community of Islam.[291] The Jamat-

---

Khan at the suggestion of Muhammad Iqbal to conduct research on Islam. This was the setting which turned Abul Ala Maudoodi into a formidable religious scholar. (Choudhury, *Pakistan ki Siyasi Tehrik: Muslim Punjab ka Siyasi Irtaqa*, pp. 324–8.)

[288]*Nawa-i-Waqt*, Lahore, 1 May 1945.

[289]For Maudoodi's view on the role of Muslim women, see his *Purdah and the Status of Women in Islam*, Al-Ashari (trs and ed.), Lahore: Islamic Publications Limited, in several editions from 1972 to 1986.

[290]*Nawa-i-Waqt*, Lahore, 1 May 1945.

[291]For a full exposition of Maudoodi's thoughts, see *Tehrik-i-Azad-i-Hind aur Musalman*, in two volumes. First published in 1946, it has had several reprints of a

i-Islami aimed at making true Muslims of the faithful in India as a whole, a task which made him a considered opponent of the League's 'Pakistan'.

Arguments against breaking up India to accommodate Muslim assertions of sovereignty were not new. What was different in the mid-1940s was the more urgent recognition by Muslims in the minority provinces that, short of some all-India arrangements, they would be left at the mercy of not a 75 per cent but a walloping 90 per cent Hindu majority. But the League's demand for a 'Pakistan' was geared to winning the principle of Muslim-majority rule in the north-western and north-eastern regions of India, and leaving the question of any all-India arrangements with 'Hindustan' open to negotiations. The insight was lost on pro-Congress *ulema*, the Ahrars, Khaksars and Maudoodi's Jamat. In Jinnah's eyes their opposition to the League at a critical moment in the history of Muslim India was nothing short of treachery. What he underestimated was that his own supporters in the majority provinces, the Punjab especially, rather than any 'quisilings' in non-League Muslim parties were better placed to undermine his capacity to haggle with the British and the Congress.[292]

Pro-Congress Muslims sustained their nuisance value, vociferating against Jinnah's 'Pakistan' while sharing some of his real aims. Maulana Mohamad Mian, the *nizam* of the Jamiat-ul-Ulema-i-Hind, wanted a single Indian centre with parity for Hindus and Muslims in the executive, legislative and judicial domains. The centre would not be able to intervene in any matter concerning the religious and political freedom of Muslims opposed by two-thirds of their representatives in the central assembly.[293] This was unacceptable to the machine politicians of the Congress looking forward to deploying the powers of the unified centre of the colonial state to realize their aims of an inclusionary Indian nationalism. But it made little sense to openly contradict its supporters. It was better to let pro-Congress Muslims express their disagreements with Jinnah and the League. An internally weakened Muslim community would be that much easier to square when the time came for serious negotiations with the British.

Congress's duplicity vis-a-vis so-called nationalist Muslims has received far less comment than Jinnah's and the League's towards their supporters in

---

revised version amended to suit the political circumstances of the Jamat-i-Islami in post-colonial Pakistan.

[292]Growing popular support for a vaguely defined 'Pakistan' was more a potential weakness than a measure of Jinnah's real strength vis-a-vis his followers in the Punjab. This key point escapes Ian Talbot in his otherwise useful study, *Provincial Politics and the Pakistan movement: The Growth of the Muslim League in North-west and North-east India 1937–47*, New York and Karachi: Oxford University Press, 1988. Also see his *Freedom's Cry: the Popular Dimension in the Pakistan Movement and Partition experience in North-west India*, Karachi: Oxford University Press, 1996.

[293]Mirza, *Karavan-i-Ahrar*, vi, p. 321.

the Hindu-majority provinces. There was something peculiar about a 'secular' nationalist party counting on the vocal support of anti-imperialist cultural relativists of the Ahrar and Husain Ahmad Madani cast to claim a Muslim following. A spate of pamphlets published by the Jamiat-ul-Ulema-i-Hind and the Ahrar delighted in exposing the League's lack of Islamic credentials, pointing to Jinnah's emphatic assertions about 'Pakistan' being a democracy in which Hindus and Sikhs would have an almost equal population.[294] Substantiation that pro-Congress Muslims did much to weaken the Muslim League's case on equal citizenship rights is the rejection by the Jamiat *ulema* and the Ahrar laity of any possible equation between a democratic and an Islamic government.

Throughout the run up to the 1945–6 elections and beyond, Punjabi Leaguers like Shaukat Hayat and Mumtaz Daultana, not to mention Iftikharuddin and a number of communists, tried reassuring Hindus and Sikhs that their citizenship rights would be protected in 'Pakistan'. They had considerable backing in the Punjab League and the Muslim press. With organizational help from communists, Leaguers attempted reaching out to Hindus and Sikhs in the districts, promising constitutional guarantees of their religious and cultural rights.[295] At a meeting of the district Muslim League of Sialkot, which began with recitations of the Quran, Daultana told Sikhs that in 'Pakistan' they would have a handsome share whereas in an Akhand Hindustan they would have a handful of representatives at the centre.[296] By contrast, the Ahrars ridiculed Sikh leaders for 'blowing hot and cold' by 'opposing India's partition' on the one hand and 'demanding a separate Sikh State on the other'.[297] This was a party which claimed it 'could not join the Muslim League because Jinnah's idea of *Pakistan* was bound to create hatred between Muslims and non-Muslims'.[298] Yet it felt no pangs of conscience spreading sectarian hatred among Muslims. While Bashiruddin Mahmud was excoriated for being 'a drunkard

[294]The Ahrar mouthpiece *Fazl* from Saharanpur published a pamphlet entitled *Muslim Leagui hazraat ke leya aik lamha fiqr*—a moment of worry for the Muslim Leaguers. Another Ahrar pamphlet was *Muslim League ki Mirziyat Nawazi*, the League's pandering to the Mirzais or the Ahmadis. The Jamiat's pamphlets included, *Aqliyat aur Aksiriyat ka Sawal*, the question of majority and minority; *Pura Hindustan hamara Pakistan hai*, the whole of India is our Pakistan; *Civil Marriage aur Muslim League*, civil marriage and the Muslim League; *Muslim League ki aath Muslim Siyasi Ghalitian*, the Muslim League's eight political mistakes; *Tehrik-i-Pakistan par aik nazar*, a look at the movement for Pakistan and *Shariat bill aur Muslim League*—the Shariat Bill and the Muslim League—which portrayed Jinnah as a self-seeking lawyer who had no respect for the tenets of Islam. (Mirza, *Karavan-i-Ahrar*, vi, p. 157.)

[295]*Nawa-i-Waqt*, Lahore, 2 January 1945.

[296]Ibid., 15 April 1945.

[297]*SPPAI*, 28 October 1944, vol. lxvi, no. 44, p. 609.

[298]*SPPAI*, 24 June 1944, vol. lxvi, no. 26, p. 352.

and a womaniser', Ahmadis were 'warned' that they would 'cease to exist' once the British quit India.[299] Mazhar Ali Azhar's threat to restart the *Madha-i-Sahaba* agitation against the Shias of Lucknow aimed at 'retard[ing] Muslim League propaganda by creating internal religious differences'.[300]

The adverse consequences of this policy were not confined to the Punjab. In the NWFP, individual *maulvis* as well as different Muslim parties had been making even more reckless uses of Islam. Shias were censured for wanting to celebrate Nauroz; Ahmadis denounced as *kafirs* by a Sunni organization called the Tablighul Islam while a local *maulvi* announced that 'Muslims would never prosper until they substituted the law of the Quran for British law'.[301] Hailing Dr Khan Sahib's Congress ministry as a step in the direction of *hakumat-i-illahiya*, Ahrars carrying 'well polished hatchets' and drawn swords demanded more emphatic evidence of *shariat* rule in the province. All talk of 'Pakistan' or 'Hindustan' was 'futile unless people followed the ways of God'. Posing as the true party of Muslim rights, the Ahrars urged Pathans to free themselves of non-Muslim domination.[302] The Frontier Jamiat-ul-Ulema-i-Hind also claimed to be 'the only representative Muslim body'. In its opinion, 'Hindus and Muslims belonged to one race' but it still wanted the Congress ministry to sanction a department of *qazis* to prove its Islamic credentials.[303]

The Khaksars, flaunting their Arab headgear and the Quran, proposed instituting *zakat*, the system of alms giving in Islam, as the solution to all economic ills. One of Mashriqi's followers in the Frontier condemned the parliamentary system of government and recommended relying on the rules of God and the Prophet in which there was 'no discrimination between races'.[304] Underscoring an amazing diversity of Muslim opinions in the NWFP were home-grown *maulvis*, lording it over congregations at local mosques, and showing just how incapable they were to agree on anything. While some Pathan worshippers were told that Jinnah was 'a true leader' of Muslims, others in neighbouring mosques heard that he was utterly 'devoid of Islamic principles'.[305] Pathans were obviously not persuaded by the Frontier Muslim Students' Federation's claim that *hakumat-i-illahiya* would be established in 'Pakistan' and the 'administration ... run under the Shariat law'.[306]

None of this can fully absolve Jinnah and his League for failing to amplify their stance on democracy and the rights of citizenship. Vicious attacks on Jinnah and the League leadership who were described as 'selfish, unscrupulous,

[299]*SPPAI*, 1 April and 10 November 1944, vol. lxvi, nos.14, 45, pp192, 619.

[300]*SPPAI*, 10 November 1945, vol. lxvii, no. 42, p. 392.

[301]*SPPAI*, 20 March and 3 April 1945, vol. xxxxi, nos.12 and 14, pp. 23, 28.

[302]*SPPAI*, 24 April 1945, vol. xxxxi, no. 17, p. 35.

[303]*SNPAI*, 8 May 1945, vol. xxxxi, no. 19, p. 40.

[304]Ibid., p. 41.

[305]*SNPAI*, 30 October 1945, vol. xxxxi, no. 44, p. 95.

[306]*SNPAI*, 19 June 1945, vol. xxxxi, no. 25, p. 56.

discourteous and cowardly' ought to have enraged and strengthened resolve. Equally objectionable were 'clever appeal[s]' to Sunnis, Congress and the Hindus as a community to launch a *jihad* against the Muslim League.[307] With material factors complicating religious concerns, it proved easier for the League to quietly fall prey to some of the better-prepared Islamic ideologues in its own midst.[308] But this does not efface the contradictions in the pro-Congress strain in Muslim politics which, in demanding equal citizenship rights in an independent India, denied its possibility in a Muslim state of 'Pakistan'.

Madani had a point when he faulted Jinnah's League for making political and religious mistakes throughout its history. In 1916 it was at Jinnah's prompting that the League had sacrificed the Muslim-majority provinces. Three decades later it was making the opposite error by abandoning three crore Muslims for the sake of the Muslim-majority provinces.[309] What was contributing to a result Jinnah wanted to avoid were the tactics of the very Muslims who most wanted to prevent a division of India. By forcing the Muslim League to go on the defensive on the question of Islam, they were making it increasingly difficult to sustain any sort of debate on equal citizenship rights which might pacify Sikhs and Hindus in the Punjab. After being manhandled by the League's goons, Madani abstained from attacking Jinnah's character but could not resist questioning his religious practices. He recalled how the lawyer-turned-leader of India's Muslims had consistently watered down *shariat* bills in the central assembly. During the debate on the Child Marriage Act, Jinnah had supported the right of educated Hindu and Muslim youth to contract a civil marriage. He dismissed the contention that this was contrary to the principles of Islam, noting that laws were constantly being passed which ran counter to the Quran. Even if the majority of Muslims disagreed with him, the soon-to-be Quaid-i-Azam had quipped, their opinion was not necessarily more correct than his.[310]

Intrepid in the face of his religious opponents, Jinnah's attitude is a reflection of the crisis of moral authority within the Muslim community. Hoping to lead it in some unison to the negotiating table, he was not ready to give quarter to

[307]*SPPAI*, 8 July 1944 and 8 December 1945, vols.lxvi, lxvii, nos.28 and 43, pp. 377, 437.

[308]Abdus Sattar Niazi is a good example of this genre. Making his way up from the ranks of the PMSF, he and journalist Mian Muhammad Shafi, popularly known by the pseudonym of 'meem sheen' from the Arabic letters   and ش, wrote *Pakistan Kya hae aur Kaise Banega*, (Lahore: 1945). While appropriating Iqbal's ideas on the individual as superman, Niazi and Shafi diverged from him in their emphasis on religious men, *mard-i-khuda*, who would command by personal example and active faith in Allah. (For a different and flawed interpretation of Iqbal's influence on Niazi's and Shafi's thinking, see Gilmartin, *Empire and Islam*, pp. 209–10.)

[309]Mirza, *Karavan-i-Ahrar*, vi, p. 373.

[310]Ibid.

who could live with Congress' contradictions but not with those of a ...tical party trying to extract maximum benefits for all Indian Muslims. So .hile there were no winners in the war of the *fatwas*, the posture of Congress's Muslim allies on Islam pushed the League into a blind corner in the majority provinces from where even the most enlightened discourse on equal citizenship rights could not win them a fair hearing with non-Muslims.

VOTING FOR RELIGION?: ELECTIONS AND THEIR AFTERMATH

The significance of the 1945–6 elections was not lost on the key players or the bystanders in the political arenas of British India. It is, however, debatable whether they fully grasped the momentous nature of the vote. Representative 'democracy' under colonial conditions flourished with authoritarian trappings and political denial. In the Punjab a mere 12.5 per cent of the population had the right to vote. Only 11 per cent of the Muslims qualified for the franchise.[311] Whatever the opinions of the rest, only a privileged few had the actual right of political choice. This does not diminish the role of the informal arenas of politics in the Punjab, especially the popular press and its networks of information and propaganda. There had been extensive debates in the press on the merits and demerits of an 'Akhand Hindustan', a 'Pakistan', an 'Azad Punjab' and 'Khalistan', to mention only the larger conceptions of territorial sovereignty in the province. A possible division of India with or without a partition of the Punjab had been in the realm of public discussion. Jinnah and the League were demanding the whole of the Punjab for 'Pakistan'—a prospect bitterly opposed by Hindus and Sikhs. Despite contradictory claims, no official clarification was given to enable Muslim voters to weigh the pros and cons of the League's 'Pakistan'. An ill-informed electorate was left to the tactics of a stream of propagandists for whom 'Pakistan' was either the panacea of all evils or a curse on all things good.

Jawaharlal Nehru, who visited the Punjab in early fall of 1945, categorically stated that 'federations were better than partitions'.[312] But he was no more able to instill substance into the electoral campaign than were the communists whom he damned as traitors.[313] Organizationally the Provincial Congress was in a shambles. By August 1945 the ban imposed in 1942 on the Congress had been lifted. But the age-old rivalry between Dr Gopi Chand Bhargava and Dr Satyapal, recently returned from serving in the British Indian army, 'prevent[ed] any effective propaganda by Congress'. Bhargava's energies were concentrated on Lahore where Congress workers displayed their Gandhian spirit by cleaning streets and drains in some *mohallas* in addition to opening

[311]Jalal, *The Sole Spokesman*, p. 149, fn.99.
[312]*SPPAI*, 1 September 1945, vol. lxvii, no. 32, p. 292.
[313]*SPPAI*, 7 July 1945, vol. lxvii, no. 25, p. 243.

charkha clubs and training centres. Satyapal focused on students, labour and women as a way to capturing the *mofussil*.[314] Attacked by his detractors for betraying the Quit India resolution, it was Satyapal's candidate, Kidar Nath Sehgal, whose victory in a by-election in Lahore marked the shift in Punjabi Hindu opinion in favour of the Congress. Even before the formal end of the war, 'the majority of Hindus in the Punjab fe[lt] that Congress ... to all intents and purposes' was 'a purely Hindu organisation' which would 'safeguard the rights and interests of the Hindu community'.[315] In Lahore they recorded their view by voting for Sehgal against the Hindu Mahasabha candidate, Beli Ram Kapur.[316]

Disgusted with the in-fighting among Congress workers in the province and looking to galvanize support, Nehru seized upon the INA issue. Paying rich tributes to Subhas Chandra Bose, he demanded 'sympathetic treatment' for the 'misguided patriots' of the Azad Hind Fauj, the rebel army which had fought against the British in South East Asia.[317] The vast majority of Bose's army was from the Punjab. There was much sympathy with the INA in urban Punjab cutting across communitarian lines.[318] In the rural areas it was strongest among families whose members had served in the INA. Harnessing these sentiments, Congress called a successful strike in Lahore on 5 November—the day a Hindu, Prem Kumar Sehgal, joined Shahnawaz Khan, a Muslim and Gurbaksh Dhillon, a Sikh at the Red Fort in Delhi to fight charges of treason brought against them by the colonial state. While the Muslim League and the PMSF restricted themselves to passing resolutions 'advocating lenient treatment to the INA', Congress took a leading part in the agitation.[319] In eastern Punjab, Congress's political graph rose sharply as a direct result of the INA issue. Colonial intelligence agents were mortified to record the 'extremely intemperate and unpleasant' speeches made from Congress platforms. One Congressman predicted 'a fresh Mutiny' if 'any INA prisoners were punished', while the opinion of the press was summed up in the comment that 'the light of freedom first lit in 1857 ha[d] been rekindled by the *Azad Hind Fauj*'.[320]

By late 1945 there was general confidence in Congress circles. Prisoners released from the Lahore fort 'indulged in severe criticisms of their treatment'

---

[314]*SPPAI*, 31 March and 7 April 1945, vol. lxvii, nos.12, 13, pp. 119, 135.

[315]*SPPAI*, 14 July 1945, vol. lxvii, no. 26, p. 249.

[316]*SPPAI*, 2 June 1945, vol. lxvii, no. 20, p. 201. Bhargava had to withdraw his candidate Virindra, giving Satyapal more weight in the provincial party.

[317]*SPPAI*, 1 September 1945, vol. lxvii, no. 32, p. 291.

[318]But even the INA issue was not immune to communitarian divisions. Muslim military families in Rawalpindi division, for instance, had little sympathy' for the INA and 'blame[d] the Sikhs' for 'maltreating Muslims and coercing them to join it'. (*SPPAI*, 17 November 1945, vol. lxvii, no. 43, p. 401.)

[319]Ibid.

[320]*SPPAI*, 10 and 17 November 1945, vol. lxvii, nos 42, 43, pp. 387–8, 401.

at the hands of some of their own compatriots. Government officials and loyalists were notified that their anti-Congress activities would be punished once Congress came to power.[321] Trawling for electoral support in the Punjab required more than a skilful use of anti-colonial symbols and promises of a glowing future. Here the Congress high command, which might have heeded M.N. Roy's prophetic words, had to appease a predominantly urban Hindu constituency. Excluded from power by the British-backed Unionist-agricultural combine, Hindus in commerce and credit, as well as in the press and publications market, were not prepared to compromise their religious, regional or national interests to let Congress make any meaningful concessions to the Muslim League.

So if the use of the INA aimed at rousing their anti-colonialism, the All India Congress Committee's declaration of 'a war against the Muslim League' was designed to satisfy the communitarian demands of Punjabi Hindus. It saw 'many Hindus' previously 'hesitating to join Congress' doing so with verve.[322] At least one MLA of the all-India party in the Punjab privately assured the Bengali Mahasabha leader, Mukerjee, that 'Congress had finally given up its policy of appeasing Muslims'. The provincial Hindu Mahasabha was 'disorganized owing to the defective leadership of Bhai Parmanand' and 'most Hindus in the Punjab were pro-Congress'. It made political sense for the Mahasabha to join the Congress, and possibly the Akalis, to 'smash the Muslim League'.[323] By early November 1945 Punjabi Hindus were 'solidly behind Congress'. This followed assurances by Gopi Chand Bhargava and Diwan Chaman Lal that they 'intend[ed] to oppose Hindu–Muslim parity at the centre and *Pakistan*'.[324] This made the chances of a negotiated settlement at the provincial level that much more difficult. Some Punjabi Hindu Congressmen were convinced that there would be a civil war in India after the departure of the British. One of their number in Multan 'assured his audience that the loss of life involved would be no greater than that which had occurred during the Bengal famine'. In any case, the 'chief casualties would be amongst the ranks of the Hindu Maha Sabha, the Muslim League and the Akali Party'.[325] With few Hindus willing to pay the price for supporting the Mahasabha, a transformation of the Congress in the Punjab was well under way. The remains of the Mahasabha in Rawalpindi tried inflaming Hindus by alleging that they had already had a foretaste of 'Pakistan' during the Bengal famine and the banning of the *Satyarth Prakash*.[326] But the Mahasabha was 'a spent force' in the Punjab. Seeing his days were numbered, Parmanand was understandably

[321]*SPPAI*, 29 September 1945, vol. lxvii, no. 36, p. 327.
[322]*SPPAI*, 6 October 1945, vol. lxvii, no. 37, p. 336.
[323]*SPPAI*, 25 August 1945, vol. lxvii, no. 31, p. 283.
[324]*SPPAI*, 3 November 1945, vol. lxvii, no. 41, p. 375.
[325]*SPPAI*, 22 December 1945, vol. lxvii, no. 48, p. 453.
[326]*SPPAI*, 20 October 1945, vol. lxvii, no. 39, p. 351.

'distressed at the turn events had taken'.[327] Failing to get elected to the central assembly, he was soon tossed into political oblivion. Congress made a grand sweep of the general seats.

With a spectacular victory, Congress was 'anxious' to strike a deal with the Akalis before the provincial election. This could seal its victory over the Muslim League in the Punjab and, by extension, at the all-India level. Playing the Ahrars and the Deobandi *ulema* of the Jamiat-ul-Hind against the Muslim League on the one hand and lending strategic support to Muslim Unionist candidates on the other, the Punjab Congress was hungry for success. Even if the League repeated its stunning performance of bagging all the Muslim seats in the central assembly, the electoral arithmetic did not ensure the formation of its ministry. The Akalis were resolute in rejecting 'Pakistan' and were willing to support Congress at the all-India level if this did 'not clash with Sikh religious interests'.[328] To outside observers, Congress and the Akalis appeared to be 'drawing closer together'.[329] But election activity, preceded by *gurdwara* elections, had sharpened rivalries between Akalis backing Nagoke and Giani Kartar Singh, who frankly preferred doing a deal with Muslims and the British.[330] The latter's supporters in the Akali party stonewalled a comprehensive understanding with the Congress.[331]

This kept alive hopes of the League coming to terms with the Akalis after the provincial assembly elections. Without denying the importance of the League winning all the Muslim seats to the central assembly, it was the contest for the Punjab ministry which mattered most. Barring individual communists, the Punjab League had no electoral understanding with any party. It conducted its election campaign solely on the 'Pakistan' demand. While the precise territorial jurisdictions of Muslim sovereignty had been left undefined, the party manifesto held attractions for the less well off classes who were disappointed that the end of the war had not brought down prices of essential commodities.[332] With the magic of 'Pakistan' left to popular imagination, there was a socio-economic vision in the League's propaganda, notwithstanding the rebarbative overtones of empty sloganeering in the name of Islam.

The Punjab League had ample funds at its disposal.[333] While the League

[327]*SPPAI*, 17 November 1945, vol. lxvii, no. 43, p. 404.
[328]Nehru had ruled out a Congress alliance with communists, Unionists and the Akalis. (*SPPAI*, 8 September 1945, vol. lxvii, no. 33, p. 297.)
[329]*SPPAI*,, 6 October 1945, vol. lxvii, no. 37, p. 335.
[330]*SPPAI*, 22 September 1945, vol. lxvii, no. 35, p. 316.
[331]*SPPAI*, 22 December 1945, vol. lxvii, no. 48, p. 453.
[332]*SPPAI*, 8 September 1945, vol. lxvii, no. 33, p. 297.
[333]The provincial League sanctioned Rs 90,000 to purchase thirty American cars equipped with loudspeakers. Subscriptions of Rs 170,000 had been promised, with Mamdot donating Rs 50,000. Daultana forked out Rs 40,000 and his kinsman, Allah Yar Daultana, gave Rs 25,000. (*SPPAI*, 22 September 1945, vol. lxvii, no. 35, p. 317.)

made free use of mosques and *idgahs*, its supporters showed sparks of commercial ingenuity by marketing not just souvenir flags of 'Pakistan' but also cigarette cases, tablecloths, cards and writing paper.[334] Marketing the national idea entailed a reapportioning of commercialized space which blurred the division between the public and the private. Jinnah's vocal opposition to *purdah* and his younger sister Fatima's appearance in public was a welcome relief for women confined to domestic chores and light-hearted social engagements. During the 1945–6 elections, there were exemplary displays of enthusiasm by Punjabi Muslim women. Some enrolled in the national guard while others formed League committees in different districts.

Greater participation by women in public affairs did not mean a better airing of their specifically gender concerns. The Muslim League took a stand against *purdah* and promised to restore women's rights of inheritance in the Punjab. But beyond this, the public narration of the national ideal did nothing to temper the patriarchal values of Punjabi Muslim society. When not overshadowed by the interests of the community or the 'nation', gender remained subservient to class and personalities. A section of women in Lahore were furious when Baji Rashida Latif, an erstwhile Khaksar, was not awarded a League ticket for one of the two reserved seats from the city. Begum Tassadaq Hussain and Begum Shah Nawaz, two otherwise-worthy champions of the League, were suspected of using their social and political connections to secure the tickets.[335] Male Leaguers were equally resentful of the triumph of privilege. There was much unhappiness over the distribution of party tickets in Lahore, Amritsar, Rawalpindi, Ludhiana, Gujranwala and Sialkot. Feeling excluded, 'representatives of the Muslim press' threatened to throw their weight behind the disaffections if their demands went unheeded.[336] They were justifiably afraid that the League, in angling to win, was perpetuating the disempowerment of the urban middle classes in a cheap imitation of the colonial rulers.

Signs of class-based jealousies were matched by regional biases. The PMSF 'resented the invasion of the province by a large number of students from Aligarh' and the 'attention shown to them'.[337] It had insisted on maintaining its independence from the League even while accepting financial remuneration for services rendered.[338] The decision to import one hundred Urdu-speaking students from Aligarh was a product of the linguistic myopia of elite Punjabi

---

Confirming the close links between the press and politics in the province, the *Nawa-i-Waqt, Ehsan, Zamindar* and the proprietor of Muslim Publishers in Lahore each promised Rs 50,000. (*Nawa-i-Waqt*, Lahore, 22 August 1945.)

[334]*SPPAI*, 1 September 1945, vol. lxvii, no. 32, p. 294.

[335]*SPPAI*, 1 December 1945, vol. lxvii, no. 45, p. 424.

[336]*SPPAI*, 8 December 1945, vol. lxvii, no. 46, p. 437.

[337]*SPPAI*, 15 December 1945, vol. lxvii, no. 47, p. 448.

[338]*SPPAI*, 13 October 1945, vol. lxvii, no. 38, p. 345.

Muslims. A costly venture, it was 'not ... an unqualified success owing to language and other difficulties'.[339] The students went unnoticed in many villages unless accompanied by Punjabi students. Steps were taken to ensure that the next batch from Aligarh consisted only of Punjabis.[340]

Class, regional, sub-denominational and personal differences, to say nothing of the ideological ones, all combined to make the 1946 provincial elections the most memorable in the history of Muslims in India. It is just that observers and scholars have thrust the complexity of these elections under the general banner of religion or, more likely, 'communalism'. Islam was undoubtedly much in play. But beyond the contradiction of an irreligious party demanding a Muslim state and most of the religious guardians rallying behind a nationalist party committed to a 'secular' vision, little is known of what the uses of religion conveyed to the voters of the Punjab. Religion was deployed by all parties. An indication of its inadequacies in drawing the voters was evident in the changed tactics of the Ahrars. Upon 'realising that they [we]re losing ground to the League', they had taken to provoking physical clashes with Leaguers. By involving the colonial police in the fracas, the Ahrars wanted 'to make it appear that their decline [wa]s due to official interference'.[341] The presence of Ahrar volunteers armed with axes and swords at political meetings led to frenzied activities in educational institutions where pro-League students were given training in fighting with swords and sticks.

With the Ahrars and the Leaguers arming themselves in anticipation of future clashes, Mashriqi sent 'secret instructions' to his subordinates to 'contact demobilised soldiers' and released personnel of the INA with a view to forming a 'reserve of trained men for future use'.[342] Though the Congress made the most of the INA issue, crediting itself for the release of Sehgal, Dhillon and Shahnawaz, all the political parties used it to advantage.[343] A provincial League committee under Ghazanfar Ali was formed to defend INA personnel while a special subcommittee was to look after the interests of ex-servicemen.[344] The Akalis were doing much the same—an indication that all the religious communities were preparing in earnest for a grand stand-off. Against such a jarring landscape, the religious hysteria generated by the League and its many

[339]SPPAI, 22 December 1945, vol. lxvii, no. 48, p. 454.

[340]SPPAI, 5 January 1946, vol. lxviii, no. 1, p. 3.

[341]SPPAI, 22 December 1945, vol. lxvii, no. 48, p. 455.

[342]SPPAI, 5 January 1946, vol. lxviii, no. 1, p. 4.

[343]Punjabi Muslims, and Leaguers in particular, 'nowhere participated in the extravagant welcome' given to the INA hero, Shahnawaz Khan. They 'strongly resented' his publicly stated 'readiness to worship [Subhas Chandra] Bose'. 'Cold shouldered by his co-religionists', Shahnawaz found few sympathizers in his home village. But his family failed to prevail upon him to sever connections with the Congress. (SPPAI, 19 January 1946, vol. lxviii, no. 3, pp. 21–2.)

[344]SPPAI, 13 and 27 October 1945, vol. lxvii, nos 38, 40, pp. 344, 362.

opponents had less to do with spiritual than material affairs. Directed more at Muslim opponents than non-Muslims, the call to Islam saw the faithful falling upon each other in murderous hate.

An Ahrar drew first blood, stabbing Mohammad Sadiq, a Muslim Leaguer of Ludhiana, who was immediately 'described as the first Pakistan martyr'.[345] This was no stray incident caused by a misguided individual. Mazhar Ali Azhar seemed to want Jinnah's skull. Ahrar workers concentrating on central Punjab and drawing 'Hindu rather than Muslim' audiences were instructed to tail Jinnah throughout his propaganda tour of the province.[346] Mashriqi, who was siding with Unionists, had the audacity to interrupt the League leader's speech at Islamia College. Turfed out by the organizers, he threatened to 'dog Jinnah's footsteps' in the province and 'interrupt any meetings' addressed by him. Since words could kill—in 1943 Jinnah had narrowly escaped getting assaulted by a Khaksar—an elaborate system of guards was put together to protect the Quaid-i-Azam for the remainder of his stay in the martial land.[347] His cavalcade was piloted by a motor cycle and accompanied by two cars carrying armed bodyguards. At a women's meeting, two young girls with drawn swords escorted Jinnah into the conference hall.[348]

Private security arrangements by political parties reflected a faltering confidence in the colonial state. Amidst temper and tension along inter- and intra-communitarian lines, the impression had been gaining ground that 'Government d[id] not exercise its authority'.[349] Many district officers thought they would be 'fortunate' if the elections were concluded without a 'serious riot'.[350] Incidents of violence involved members of the same religious community and castes. Leaguers wrangled with Ahrars and Unionists while pro-Congress Sikhs squabbled with their co-religionists in the Akali Dal. In Karnal there was a free-for-all between Jats and Gujars when the former jeered at their caste cohorts for voting in favour of a Gujar candidate.[351] By comparison, Hindus displayed more unity of purpose, heeding the Congress directives en masse to prepare for a final showdown with the Muslim League. But it is debatable whether this resolve on the part of the Hindus, no less divided than Muslims and Sikhs, can be attributed to religious sentiments alone. Quite as much as their counterparts, who in betting on the League and the Akalis were seeking to locate themselves strategically in the post-election scenario, Hindus expected a Congress victory to secure their interests in the Punjab once and for

---

[345]SPPAI, 26 January 1946, vol. lxviii, no. 4, p. 42.
[346]SPPAI, 19 January 1946, vol. lxviii, no. 3, p. 22.
[347]Ibid.
[348]SPPAI, 26 January 1946, vol. lxviii, no. 4, p. 42.
[349]SPPAI, 3 November 1945, vol. lxvii, no. 41, p. 373.
[350]SPPAI, 26 January 1946, vol. lxviii, no. 4, p. 39.
[351]SPPAI, 16 February 1946, vol. lxviii, no. 7, p. 81.

all. If in the process the RSS's hope of 'Hindus ... dominat[ing] the world' was realized, so much the better.[352]

For the time being, however, Hindus in the Punjab were heartened to learn that Congress leaders like Purushottamdas Tandon from UP 'viewed the prospect of a constitutional deadlock in India with equanimity'. He sanguinely told an audience in Amritsar that 'the loss of a few thousand lives' may well be 'necessary to prevent the partitioning of the country'. The Muslim League may have 'proved its claim to represent the Muslim masses', but with better organization the Congress could 'ignore the Muslims and other minorities and ... embark on a successful struggle with the British'.[353] A familiar Mahasabhite line, it coincided nicely with what many Punjabi Hindus thought was the best resolution of the communitarian question in an independent India. Whatever Nehru might have made of Tandon's opinion, Congress's pretence of wooing Muslims in the Punjab was turning out to be a disaster. There was an uproar among its remaining Punjabi Muslim supporters following Congress's electoral agreement with the Unionists. Some Muslim candidates were forced to withdraw in favour of the Unionists, leading the Muslim workers' board to boycott the elections.[354]

Signing its own death warrant among Muslim voters, the Congress left the anti-imperialist cause on the sturdy shoulders of the Ahrars and the Jamiat-ul-Hind *ulema* whose forked tongues had bitten into many raw nerves in Muslim Punjab. But 'castigat[ing] Jinnah and other League leaders for their religious shortcomings' no longer had a spellbinding effect.[355] So although Ataullah Shah Bukhari 'continued to be the busiest speaker', the Ahrars found the going tough. They accused Mazhar Ali Azhar of 'paying too much attention to Unionist interests' and 'too little ... to those of the Ahrars'.[356] His defeat in the elections confirmed their fears. Though they polled more votes than the League in a few cities where they had influence, the Ahrars were demolished in the elections. But there was an element of poetic justice in their enduring ability to test the League's patience in strongholds like Batala in Gurdaspur district. Fearing clashes, the district administration declined licenses for customary processions on Id-ul-Milad-ul Nabi, the birthday of the Prophet. While Leaguers honoured the decision, sixty-two Ahrars were arrested for taking out unauthorized processions.[357]

The rout of Congress's Muslim supporters in the Punjab should not detract from the impact they made at the level of political discourse. They had succeeded in putting the fear of God into the hearts and minds of the Leaguers

[352]Ibid., p. 86.
[353]SPPAI, 5 January 1946, vol. lxviii, no. 1, p. 2.
[354]Ibid., p. 1.
[355]Ibid., p. 4.
[356]SPPAI, 26 January 1946, vol. lxviii, no. 4, p. 42.
[357]SPPAI, 23 February 1946, vol. lxviii, no. 8, p. 93.

with their incessant harangues. Assisted by an impressive team largely comprising Barelvi *ulema* belonging to the freshly created Jamiat-ul-Ulema-i-Islam, Punjabi Leaguers tried surpassing their temporal calling by appropriating Islamic idioms. There was a marked 'tendency to combine a strong religious appeal with Muslim League propaganda'. Yet claims in the name of Islam did not entail any enlightening discourse on what this meant in concrete terms. 'Muslim audiences' were merely 'warned that if they fail[ed] to vote for the Muslim League' they would 'become *kafirs*'. The slogan 'Islam in danger' was a useful one; capturing Muslim fears of Hindu-majority rule, it was 'given more prominence than before'. Muslims were told that the elections were a crusade for 'Pakistan'.[358]

Two other slogans underlined the League's discursive uses of the Muslim category. 'If a Muslim, join the Muslim League' equated the religious category with a political party. 'What is the meaning of Pakistan? *La illah illa Allah!*' evoked any number of responses, from the imaginal to the mundane. For some it signified the League's commitment to basing 'Pakistan' on the Quran and the *sunnah*. It was, however, primarily used by the League to fend off charges that its politics were devoid of religion. *Maulvis* were paraded to show that 'religious leaders ... support[ed] the Muslim League demand for Pakistan'. At a conference of the Jamiat-ul-Ulema-i-Islam in Islamia College, speakers took turns in linking religion and politics before a resolution was passed exhorting Muslims 'in the name of Allah and the Prophet' to vote for the League.[359]

Though an open defiance of Section 171(c) of the Indian Penal Code, such uses of religion in the public domain did not invite administrative interventions. And this despite the fact that the Punjab government had delegated authority under this section of the law to all district and sub-divisional magistrates. *Maulvis* and *pirs* in the League's entourage deliberately 'contravene[d] the law', leaving local officials to ponder their moves. Maulvi Mohammad Ismail Ghaznavi showed his contempt for the law at Tarn Taran, Amritsar district, by asking his audience to 'repeat after him that in the name of *Khuda*, *Rasul* and *Islam*' they would vote for the League candidates. Pir Fazl Shah, patron of the shrine of Jalalpur Sharif in Jhelum, was a more ruthless taskmaster for unsuspecting rural Muslims. He told a gathering of Muslims in Gujrat to vote for the League or face ostracism from the community. They would be 'allowed no funeral prayers in addition to becoming *kafirs*'.[360] The Unionists in desperation employed eleven *maulvis* from Delhi to counteract the League's uses of religion.[361]

Not since the heyday of the *khilafat* movement had the *maulvis* and *maulanas* of Muslim India been in greater demand. The *pirs* of the Punjab with a few

---

[358]*SPPAI*, 26 January 1946, vol. lxviii, no. 4, p. 42.
[359]*SPPAI*, 2 February 1946, vol. lxviii, no. 5, p. 54.
[360]Ibid.
[361]Ibid., p. 55.

notable exceptions had also switched allegiance and, together with the *ulema*, were 'attempting to draw all religious leaders and teachers into the Muslim League itself'.[362] In combination with student greenhorns and more seasoned political speakers, the religious extravaganza rooting for the League did make an impression. 'So genuine was the fear of Divine displeasure they managed to inculcate' that in Rawalpindi division one gullible Muslim voter of Gujrat who had mistakenly voted for the Unionist candidate expiated his sin by feeding forty orphans. But not all Muslims were convinced. Many village officials—*lambardars* and *zaildars* alike—voted for the Unionists, even though they 'often advised all others they could influence to vote for the Muslim League'.[363] If these were the paid servants of the colonial state, 'leading Muslim families' also saw wisdom in 'keeping a foot in both the Muslim League and Unionist camps'. A hedging of bets was 'achieved by one member of the family joining the Muslim League, while a close relative remain[ed] a Unionist'. [364]

So although the League's electoral tactics reaped excellent results, the significance of its recourse to Islam cannot go unquestioned. Appeals to their *iman*—invoked in the signal phrase *La illah illa Allah*—had to be couched in a language accessible to an overwhelmingly illiterate Muslim rural audience. The induction of hellfire by *pirs* and *maulvis* for the greater cause of religion bore no resemblance to Islam's lofty principles—and even at their very best, only a fraction to Iqbal's translation of *tauhid* as 'equality, justice and freedom', the founding principles of any state in Islam. Using Islam for its purposes did not, in any case, win the League a blanket Muslim vote. Not every Muslim who voted in the Punjab voted for the League. The League's appropriation of Islam was less than complete. Imaginative and not-so-imaginative conflations of Muslim, League and Pakistan, even in a context of separate electorates, did not deter voters from opting for others in the fray.

With about a third of the total vote cast, the League secured seventy-five of the eighty-six seats reserved for the community in a 175–member assembly. If this was sweet revenge for Jinnah, there were disappointments in store for the provincial Leaguers. Electoral understandings with the Congress, Ahrars and Khaksars found the Unionists retaining a presence in the assembly, albeit at a considerably depreciated level. Yet its rump of twenty-one, together with Congress's fifty-one and twenty-one or so Akalis could keep the Muslim League out of office in the Punjab.[365] By the same token, the League as the largest single party in the provincial assembly, could try and win Sikh support and

[362]*SPPAI*, 9 February 1946, vol. lxviii, no. 6, p. 68.

[363]*SPPAI*, 16 February 1946, vol. lxviii, no. 7, p. 84.

[364]*SPPAI*, 17 November 1945, vol. lxvii, no. 43, p. 401.

[365]Rivalries between Gopi Chand Bhargava and Satyapal intensified after the Congress's electoral success. Azad had to rush to Lahore to work out a compromise. Bhim Sen Sachar of Satyapal's group was elected leader of the Congress's parliamentary party. (*SPPAI*, 2 March 1946, vol. lxviii, no. 9, p. 105.)

comfortably dominate the provincial ministry. Holding the balance in the assembly, the Akalis or Panthic Sikhs could play the role of healers or spoilers.

Appearing as a rainbow after a battering storm, Giani Kartar Singh told a Sikh *diwan* at Sargodha that 'Sikhs could expect better treatment in Pakistan than under Hindu domination'. But, as ever, they were undecided whether to form a coalition with the League or the Congress. Giani preferred going the League's way; Nagoke wanted a coalition with the Congress. No one could venture a guess which way the Sikhs might eventually turn. All that seemed clear was that the Akali leaders would 'try and extract the greatest possible personal gain out of the present advantageous position'.[366] The Muslim League had to seize the opportunity to lend credibility to its large promises to the Sikhs. Yet some Leaguers thought a coalition with the Congress would be more beneficial.[367] A crucial moment in the provincial League's history, it found the all-India high command in an uncompromising mood.

Ready to support a League ministry, the Akalis were not prepared to take responsibility for placing it in office. Efforts by Punjab Leaguers like Daultana to persuade Khizar to head a coalition ministry had nearly materialized. But Jinnah vetoed a proposal which might have altered the course of Punjab's history. With the League unable to satisfy the Sikhs, the British governor Bertrand James Glancy invited Khizar to form a coalition ministry with Congress and Akali support. Losing a battle after winning it was too much for Punjab's Leaguers to bear. There was widespread indignation. Urban Muslims were incensed by the League's exclusion, playing down their own sense of disappointment at seeing the landed elements cashing in on their 'Pakistan' propaganda. Students led the protests, condemning Khizar for his treachery and Glancy for yet again demonstrating the perfidy of Albion. Liaquat Ali Khan graced a meeting of 30,000 Muslims in Lahore and spoke of 'grave consequences' if 'a non-Muslim League Ministry was forced on the Punjab'.[368] Yet he was careful to reiterate the League's line that 'non-Muslims would be well treated in Pakistan'.[369]

Tens of thousands in Lahore chanted slogans 'Sardar Khizar Singh *murdabad*' and '*Qaum da chor Khizar murdabad*', wishing death upon the Unionist leader and calling him a thief of the Muslim 'nation'. There were mock funerals in Amritsar and the burning of Khizar's effigy in Ferozepur.[370] At the same time there were signs that not all Sikhs were pleased to see the

[366]*SPPAI*, 23 February 1946, vol. lxviii, no. 8, p. 96.

[367]Captain Abdur Rashid's conviction for his role in the INA gave Punjabi Muslims a cause to unite with Congress. The Punjab Students Congress and the PMSF jointly protested the sentence. (*SPPAI*, 23 February and 2 March 1946, vol. lxviii, nos 8, 9, pp. 98, 105.)

[368]*SPPAI*, 9 March 1946, vol. lxviii, no. 10, p. 123.

[369]Ibid., pp. 123, 127–8.

[370]*SPPAI*, 16 March 1946, vol. lxviii, no. 11, p. 136.

Akalis joining hands with Unionists and the Congress. Sikh and Muslim students came together in the provincial capital, ostensibly in support of the INA, but also to shout 'Akali–League Coalition *zindabad*' and 'Sikh–Muslim *itihad zindabad*'.[371] Within League circles there was debate on the best course forward. The decisions reached were 'far from unanimous' and even when accepted by the leadership were defied by the PMSF. Mamdot ruled out the option of launching a direct action; it could only prolong the tenure of the coalition ministry. Instead the provincial working committee called for an organizational drive to awaken the Muslim masses by 'ignor[ing] Hindus' and 'work[ing] for Muslim–Sikh unity'. At a meeting of League members of the assembly and district office bearers, Daultana and Iftikharuddin tried to stress the importance of Hindu–Muslim unity. They 'found few supporters'. Iftikharuddin thought Muslims should combine with Hindus but attack their leaders. This was summarily dismissed by Karamat Ali who maintained that 'all Hindus were the same and every one of them should be opposed'.[372] So even though the Punjab League agreed to carry on peaceful agitations against the coalition ministry, relations with Hindus, especially in Lahore, deteriorated to an alarming extent. Talukchand Mahroom, a Hindu poet who wrote in Urdu, bewailed the descent of darkness on his beloved homeland:

Punjab's honour stands tarnished
By its mutual infighting.[373]

With the prospect of a Muslim-Sikh or, better still, a League–Congress understanding actively engaging only a few minds, there seemed to be no saviour honourable enough to persuade Punjabis from striking at their own jugular. Blaming this on religious zeal, of whatever combination, can only satisfy those impatient with the Punjab and its history of short and intense warfare followed by protracted, if not necessarily easy, compromises.

---

[371]*SPPAI*, 9 March 1946, vol. lxviii, no. 10, p. 128.
[372]*SPPAI*, 16 March 1946, vol. lxviii, no. 11, p. 136.
[373]*Punjab ki abaroo pey phera*
Apas ki larayion ne pani.
(Abbas, *Urdu Mein Qaumi Shairi*, p. 205.)

Chapter 9

Lost Tracks to Unity:
Confrontation, Compromise and Civil War

Integral to any constitutional arrangement covering the whole of India, Punjab's destiny in the final months of colonial rule was no more predictable than in the past. Despite its share of communitarian bigotry, Bengal's chances of remaining united were better than those of the Punjab.[1] If political demands in the Punjab could be tempered and an element of reasonableness restored to the debate on the rights of religious communities, India might yet retain a loose unity based on a sharing of sovereignty between 'Hindustan' and 'Pakistan'. The elections of 1945–6, pitting Muslim against Muslim, and the politically significant aftermath of a Congress, Unionist and Akali coalition ministry had demonstrated the impossibility of exclusively Muslim rule in an undivided Punjab.

In allying with pro-British landlords and Akali Sikhs, Congress had issued a stern warning to the Muslim League. A 'Pakistan' based on undivided Punjab demanded an understanding with the Sikhs and the Congress. If they could overcome the shock of being stopped in their trails, Punjabi Leaguers might conceivably alter the balance between region and nation. But to do so without addressing the rights of religious minorities at the regional level was to court fate from the precipice, not the hilltop. The Punjab League's manifesto offering equal rights of citizenship to minority communities was an attempt at accommodating religiously informed cultural differences under Muslim-majority rule. Ideological dissensions within its own ranks did not bode well

---

[1] As late as April 1947 Jinnah expressed willingness to accept a united Bengal outside 'Pakistan'. 'What is the use of Bengal without Calcutta,' he told Mountbatten, 'they had better remain united and independent; I am sure that they would be on friendly terms with us.' (Cited in Jalal, *The Sole Spokesman*, p. 265.)

for the implementation of the promises. The denial of office was reason enough for provincial Leaguers to consider lending more substance to their strategy of wresting power in an undivided Punjab. Class and ideological divisions among Muslims, and not just political and cultural differences with non-Muslims, posed the more serious obstacle to addressing that vital question.

Efforts to work out a regional power-sharing arrangement have left hazier tracks than the well-charted path of confrontation. If the mood of the subjects-turning-citizens was unusually confrontational, it is arguable whether anyone considered a severance of ties between the eastern and western districts of the province a foregone conclusion. To many, this was inconceivable. More to the point, they were never consulted on the matter by any of the political parties fighting the elections. Punjabi reactions to the prospect of a drastic redefinition of provincial boundaries needs to be placed in its proper historical context and subjected to rigorous analysis. A product of competing sovereignties defined primarily in religious terms, entire communities as well as individuals were driven towards despair, desperation and destruction. Powerful emotions in epoch-making times were not new to the subcontinent. The coming apart of empires in its history had hardly ever been free of turmoil. The unprecedented and calamitous violence attending the end of British rule did not stem just from heightened communitarian sentiments. It was quite as much due to a slackening of will on the part of the colonial state. In the ensuing loosening of the reins of authority, subjects found their first taste of citizens' power. With members of the colonial service openly backing the Congress or the Muslim League, relations between state personnel and segments of society were becoming complicitous, giving the discourse and politics of the Punjab a darker tinge than previously witnessed in its history.

But there were murmurings at the margins hinting at possible alternatives to the politics of confrontation. Raising slogans for Sikh–Muslim unity soon after a bitter election campaign was not a small matter. The spectacle of Hindu, Sikh and Muslim students rallying together for their heroes in the INA was more than just youthful enthusiasm. A reconsideration of the evidence is useful in uncovering the lost tracks to a negotiated unity that might have prevented the painful division of a people sharing a regional culture based on a common language but splintered by class and religion.

THE MUSLIM GROUNDSWELL FOR 'PAKISTAN' AND THE CABINET MISSION

The denial of office to the Punjab Muslim League after a good electoral showing did much to strengthen support for a 'Pakistan'. Poets in Urdu and Punjabi alike had been voicing their aspirations for a Muslim homeland. Those using the regional vernacular were particularly successful in bridging the language barrier between urban and rural areas. The use of poetry at political meetings gave considerable fillip to the League's electoral performance which exceeded its own expectations. If the slogans were strident, poetry lent an emotive touch to popular appeals for a 'Pakistan'. As the Punjabi poet, Malik Abdul Qadir Khushtar Kunjahi, put it:

Listen O Muslims, the war of independence is underway
The nation that was chained is standing on its own feet
Licking other people's shoes, Khaksar and Ahrars don't know this nation
If you want real freedom, let your hearts believe in the Muslim League
Tell the government and the Congress, we want Pakistan.[2]

A popular poem by Ustad Daim Iqbal Daim of Gujrat exaggerated by simplifying the meaning of the League's electoral success:

Witness the Muslim League blooming in its glory
It will light the path to what is true and right
Clearing the darkness of Godlessness
It is bound to create Pakistan
Look at the faithful lining up to the Muslim League
Witness the Muslim League blooming in its glory.[3]

With the formation of a Unionist, Congress and Akali ministry, the League was a party in embattled gloom. Its efforts to attain power aborted, Leaguers found their Muslim foes in a more defiant and belligerent mood. Still looking to pitchfork the Khaksars onto the centrestage of Muslim politics, Mashriqi called for the establishment of an All-India Azad Muslim League. Committed

[2]Cited in Inamul Haq Javeid, *Pakistan in Punjabi Literature*, Islamabad: Maktaba-i-Fanoos, 1993, pp. 28–9.

سن لو سادہ مرادیا مسلمانوں اجکل جنگ آزادی دی ہو رہی اے
جیہڑی قوم نوں بمن دی جانچ نیں سی لوہ دی اپنے پیریں کھلو رہی اے
کنکوں بھنٹ کے جیہڑی گنڈ میل ہوئی کنڈے اپے لئی لوہ بو رہی اے
خاکساری احراری نہ قوم سمجھیں لبمدے تے غیر دیاں جوتیاں دھو رہی اے
جیکر کائل آزادی توں چاہو ندااں مسلم لیگ تیرا ایمان چاہیدا اے
اینوں بول حکومت تے کانگرس نوں ساڈا دکھ بنا چاہیدا اے

[3]Cited in ibid., p. 28.

کھڑیاں نیں گلزاراں مسلم لیگ دیاں
حق دا چانن لا کے جھڑنا
سکر اندھیرا مٹا کے جھڑنا
پاکستان بنا کے جھڑنا
دیکھو پاک قطاراں مسلم لیگ دیاں
کھڑیاں نیں گلزاراں مسلم لیگ دیاں۔

to Hindu–Muslim unity, the Khaksars swore to prevent a civil war. But given their dismal performance, few non-League Muslims responded to Mashriqi's invitation.[4] This did not deter the master of the spade-wielding brigade from continuing to try and hijack the 'Pakistan' demand. The Ahrars were equally eager to cash in on the League's frustrations. Claiming 90,000 Muslim votes in the provincial elections—the actual figure was closer to 35,000—they rejected the League as the sole representative voice of Muslims in the Punjab. Looking to reduce its membership in the assembly, the Ahrars reclaimed one of their bad pennies which had turned up on the League's side on the eve of the elections. After winning the elections, Mohammad Rafiq rejoined the Ahrars and had to be provided armed guards to prevent indignant Leaguers lynching him in the Ichara area of Lahore.[5] Fortified by their local triumph, the Ahrars joined the Azad Muslim Board constituted by the disgruntled Sindhi Leaguer G.M. Syed. This was potentially dangerous for Jinnah. The League had just gone out of office in Sind. But there were bigger upsets in the Punjab.

Manoeuvrings by non-League Muslims were matched by ideological and personal rivalries in the Punjab League. 'Religiously minded Muslim League leaders' were genuinely 'worried' about the left-leaning influences of Daultana and Iftikharuddin.[6] They included Abdus Sattar Niazi who, as one of the leaders of the PMSF, had helped draft the *Khilafat-i-Pakistan Scheme* which he published after the elections.[7] Intended to purge the Punjab League of communist influences, the pamphlet contained catchy quotes from Iqbal's thought and poetry—none of them acknowledged. Muslims needed an internal blueprint for revolutionary reform, not constitutional agreements with other communities. Damning the western model of the parliamentary system and reiterating the power of Islam, the document declared that the Muslim alone was a true human being. Non-Muslims had ample protection in Islam. They were, in any case, lesser beings who had to be converted to Islam.[8]

Muslim supremacy patterned on a bigoted conception of Islam may have had advocates in the PMSF. But short of persuading a landlord-dominated

[4]*SPPAI*, 2 March, 6 and 20 April and 4 May 1946, vol. lxviii, nos. 9, 14, 16, 18, pp. 109, 170, 197, 223.

[5]*SPPAI*, 16 March 1946, vol. lxviii, no. 11, p. 137.

[6]*SPPAI*, 23 March 1946, vol. lxvii, no. 12, p. 150.

[7]He was supported by Hameed Nizami, editor of the *Nawa-i-Waqt*, the journalist Mian Muhammad Shafi with whom he had authored the 172-page booklet *Pakistan kiya hae aur kaisa banega*, the Pir of Manki Sharif and a few others. Together they launched the Khilafat-i-Pakistan Party. 'Pakistan' as defined by them consisted of the entire north Indian Hindi-speaking belt, including Delhi, UP and Bihar. (See Mirza, *Karavan-i-Ahrar*, vii, pp. 262–4, 276–80, who argues that this movement was a conspiracy against the Muslim League and 'Pakistan'.)

[8]Punjab Muslim Student's Federation, *Khilafat-i-Pakistan Scheme*, published by Mohammad Abdus Sattar Niazi from the Himayat-i-Islam Press, Lahore (no date).

provincial League, such an agenda was unlikely to find acceptance beyond a circle of committed *khilafatists* of 'Pakistan'. If the Islam *pasands,* as the ideologues of religion came to be known, eliminated those they considered ungodly communists, the League could not realize its aim of exercising power over an undivided Punjab. In May 1946 at the provincial working committee's meeting, Iftikharuddin defeated a move by Raja Ghazanfar Ali Khan to expel communists from the League.[9] A resolution advising Muslims to buy only from Muslim shops carried only because the majority abstained from voting.[10] Those envisaging a Muslim sovereignty in undivided Punjab with equal rights of citizenship were dogged in their resistance to the religious ideologues. Iqbal's misappropriation by the champions of a thoroughly anti-modern critique of the west is worth noting. In the PMSF pamphlet, the invocation of *khudi* or the self was not a means to the *namod* or appearance of the dynamic individual. It was a device to outline the qualities of leadership needed to control the Muslim community. Giving only Muslims the right to vote, Niazi and his associates were proposing a government in which the *ijma-i-ummat* or democracy would be offset by the *itaat-i-amir* or dictatorship of a *mard-i-khuda,* a God-fearing leader with both temporal and spiritual authority. A sort of 'Pope and Caesar combined', the *amir-ul-momeenin* or ruler of the faithful, would command obedience and homage from the ruled.[11]

This was precisely the sort of autocratic leadership Iqbal had censured in his lectures on Islam. More disturbing from the point of view of undivided Punjab was the preoccupation with exclusively Muslim rights. Hindus and Sikhs were to have the status of *dhimmis* or protected religious minorities.[12] But the good faith of the offer was called into question by the explicit celebration of conversions to Islam. Hardly the most promising way of accommodating cultural differences, it debarred non-Muslims from participation in a Muslim government. A stark statement of Muslim exclusivity, the *Khilafat-i-Pakistan Scheme* had a closer family resemblance to Maudoodi's ideas than to Iqbal's modernist reconstructions of Islam.

Iqbal's poetry was susceptible to greater misinterpretation and misuse. But like his philosophy, it was also a source of inspiration for those who

[9]Hamid Nizami in an editorial called for the expulsion of communists from the League. The 'Pakistan' of the communists was not the 'Pakistan' of Muslims. By promoting self-determination, communists were encouraging Muslims to demand Baluchistan for Baluchis, Sind for the Sindhis and Pathanistan for the Pathans. (*Nawa-i-Waqt,* Lahore, 11 May 1946.)

[10]*SPPAI,* 25 May 1946, vol. lxviii, no. 20, p. 251.

[11]*Khilafat-i-Pakistan Scheme,* p. 27.

[12]For an exposition of the Islamic law on minorities, see Husain, *Administration of Justice During the Muslim Rule in India,* chapter eleven. He argues that in Islam, Muslim and non-Muslim are 'equal in the eyes of the law'. Denying non-Muslims the vote could hardly confirm their equal rights in a Muslim state.

shared his contempt for *mullahs* and their indiscriminate anti-western rhetoric.[13] In March 1946, Iftikharuddin furiously asserted that Leaguers were 'not communal-minded'; their 'national consciousness' reflected 'their urge for freedom.' Without winning Muslim confidence, the Congress could make 'no progress' towards independence. The former Congressman thought 'nationalist Muslims [we]re the greatest obstacle' in the way of Hindu–Muslim unity. What they were 'doing ... in opposing Pakistan, no Hindu ... c[ould] do'. By the same token, the Congress had to break its 'reactionary' coalition with the Unionists, traitors all to Islam and India, and 'march to the goal of freedom with the Sikh and the Muslim masses.'[14] This was anathema to the Islam *pasands* in the PMSF.

If Niazi and Iftikharuddin represented opposite ends of the spectrum, others borrowed elements of their thinking and added their own nuances. Unpacking Muslim assertions of a religiously informed identity and claims to sovereignty shatters the easy assumptions about cultural nationalism. Even in an atmosphere shot through with layers of communitarian bigotry and violence, it is possible to detect conciliatory signs in the discourse and politics of Muslims. If exclusivity marked most cultural assertions of a Punjabi Muslim identity, not all were bigoted. However nebulous, there was a notion of universal rights among a significant segment of Muslims. Haji Chiragh Din, a poet of Punjabi, tried reassuring his fellow Punjabis:

Everyone will have peace and freedom,
No one can prevent it from coming,
Fundamental rights will be granted
The whole country will rejoice
In a few days Quaid-i-Azam will make Pakistan,
O' brothers let's all try and free our country, so
that you may earn and eat here
God will help with His blessings.[15]

[13]See Khalifa Abdul Hakim, *Iqbal aur Mullah*, Lahore: Bazm-i-Iqbal (no date), passim.

[14]Mian Iftikharuddin, *Selected Speeches and Statements*, edited by Abdullah Malik, Lahore: Nigarishat, 1971, pp. 39–44.

[15]Cited in Javeid, *Pakistan in Punjabi Literature*, p. 31.

لے گی سب نوں امن آزادی۔ میں کر سکتی کے لباہ دی

حق حقوق ملن بنیادی۔ خوشیاں ملک منادے گا۔

کوئی دن پاکے قائداعظم

پاکستان منادے گا

سارے کوششش کرو بھر او۔ اپنا ملک آزاد کرو

ایتھوں کھٹو ایتھوں کھاؤ۔ اللہ برکت پاوے گا۔

If these dreams were to materialize, and non-Muslims persuaded of the wisdom of staying in rather than splitting, the Punjab League had to exploit potential cracks in the Hindu–Sikh alliance under the Congress–Akali rubric. An alliance of convenience did not dissuade Tara Singh from blasting the Congress as 'an entirely Hindu body' and urging Sikhs to resign from the party en masse.[16] But pro-Congress Sikhs were strongly opposed to a separate Sikh state, noting that it would be unviable since their community did not have a majority in any district.[17] Namdhari Sikhs were also in revolt against the Akalis. There were even rumblings among pro-Congress Hindus, dissatisfied with the boons of sharing power with pro-British Unionists. They wanted curbs on the powers of government officials, including the police, and effective control of the administration by provincial and district Congress committees.[18]

The fractured nature of most party organizations, together with variations in local circumstances, gave social dynamics in the Punjab a measure of autonomy from both provincial and central control. This found reflection in the activities of local units of paramilitary organizations like the RSS, the Muslim League National Guard (MLNG) and the Akal Fauj. Whatever their formal links with the main players in the provincial arena, the Congress, the Muslim League and the Akali Dal respectively, these volunteer organizations were responsible in large measure for the militarization of civic space in post-war Punjab.[19] Martial activities in public spaces saw civilians purchasing small arms and ammunition. Colonial laws prohibiting the procurement of arms without a license did nothing to stop the flow of weapons into civil society. Attempts at winning over demobilized soldiers of the INA and the British Indian army alike contributed, even if inadvertently, to just the sort of civil war conditions the British as well as provincial and all-India parties needed to avoid in order to arrive at a reasonably amicable resolution of the constitutional stalemate.

What made the Punjab unlike any other place in India was the triangular contest for a share of sovereignty between the protagonists of the Muslim, Hindu and Sikh communities. Stating maximum demands did not mean abandoning possibilities of accommodation. Seen in isolation from developments at the all-India level, and a sharp rise in conflicts along religious lines in the districts

[16]*SPPAI*, 16 March 1946, vol. lxviii, no. 11, p. 137.
[17]*SPPAI*, 30 March 1946, vol. lxviii, no. 13, p. 160.
[18]*SPPAI*, 23 March 1946, vol. lxviii, no. 12, pp. 147–8.
[19]An incident in Kartarpur, Jullundur district, reveals the mentality that was informing the subcontinent's politics of communitarian despair. After a fierce football game, Hindu and Muslim boys 'wrote on the ground the names of prophets and gods and then defiled them'. This poor display of sportsmanship was partly attributed to the increased activity of the RSS and the MLNG in the locality. If times had been ordinary, which they were not, 'this childish outburst would have been dealt with adequately by the parents of the boys'. Instead local leaders were drawn into a children's dispute and the matter blown out of proportion. (*SPPAI*, 28 July 1945, vol. lxvii, no. 28, p. 262.)

and localities, political currents in the provincial capital were marked more by flux which did not conform well with rigidly communitarian postures. Muslim Leaguers had not given up on the prospect of an agreement with the Congress or the Akalis. Nor had the Sikhs decided if they wanted 'Khalistan' or an accommodation with the League or the Congress. Before considering the reactions to the British cabinet mission in India, it is worth assessing how local flare-ups were moulding political attitudes in the Punjab. It was, after all, the interplay between these levels which would ultimately decide whether the province remained undivided, irrespective of the Muslim League securing 'Pakistan'.

Arming to Survive, Arming to Kill?

The formation of the coalition ministry found Lahore under Section 144. Public meetings were prohibited for three weeks as was the carrying of arms and gatherings of five or more persons. By contrast the order was enforced in Amritsar only after a scuffle left three people dead. The incident occurred when two water carts returning from Holi celebrations collided with a gateway erected by Muslims to receive a religious procession. Two Hindus perished in the fighting. When the procession arrived in the locality, the police resorted to a *lathi* charge to contain the outburst of public rage. This was followed by stray assaults in which one Sikh was killed. A mere ten miles away, in the small town of Jandiala Guru, angry Hindus sparked off troubles, leaving one Muslim dead and nine injured. Muslim toughs retaliated by looting shops. The district administration had to impose curfew after arresting those suspected of killing and looting.[20]

These incidents preceded the arrival of the cabinet mission. Congress leaders did not want communitarian disturbances for the duration of the British delegation's presence in India. There was considerable restiveness in Amritsar after one of the dead was identified as an RSS worker. His associates vowed to remain bare-headed until they had avenged the death. A squabble between a Muslim and a Hindu shopkeeper in Ambala led to another burst of violence. Social tensions in the two cities kept apace with increased activity by the RSS. There was a 'feeling of self-confidence' among the Hindus 'based on the conviction that they w[ould] be the future rulers of India'. Twelve Hindus, believed to be RSS members, attacked a Muslim with hockey sticks. In Rawalpindi, the RSS was heard 'den[ying] that the aims of the *Sangh* were the same as the aims of the Congress'. The *sangh's* sole purpose was 'to impose Hindu rule in India'. That it was not going to be all smooth sailing was indicated by a minor fracas at Sohna in Gurgaon district. Here the Rajput *biraderi* transcended the communitarian divide to attack local *mahajans*. The incident occurred when a Muslim Rajput boy hit a *mahajan* boy. This saw a number of *mahajans*, 'once more probably members of the RSS', breaking into the house of the Muslim Rajput boy and beating him up and his

[20]*SPPAI*, 23 March 1946, vol. lxviii, no. 12, p. 151.

father. Infuriated, Hindu and Muslim Rajputs 'invaded the Mahajan's *bazar*'.[21]

Local circumstance frequently overrode religiously informed cultural differences. The revival of the RSS in the Punjab has to be placed in context. In July 1944 a ban on government servants joining the RSS had 'resulted in the more timorous members dropping out' to the dismay of the organizers.[22] Showing tenacity, the RSS continued trying to recruit government officials.[23] But if membership figures are anything to go by, the *sangh* was unsuccessful in contesting the colonial state's injunction to its employees. With six hundred as the highest membership in Rawalpindi, the RSS had only a few hundred volunteers in cities like Peshawar, Sialkot and Sheikhupura. Jammu with 1500 training in the use of *lathis* and spears aced the RSS's record book of performance. The provincial organizer in the Punjab had to request Nagpur to transfer the organizational headquarters from Lahore to Jammu. It would 'he thought, tremendously strengthen the RSS organization in the Punjab'.[24] The RSS needed to keep a toehold in a province which could tilt the balance at both the regional and the national levels. In May 1945 RSS workers in Lahore were still trying to shift the headquarters to Jammu. Volunteers in Amritsar were told that the RSS was not 'disloyal to Government' and merely building up the physical strength of Hindus.[25] What helped sustain it, albeit marginally, was the general disquiet created by a constitutional impasse which was whipped up by the press with a mixture of disturbing reports of deteriorating communitarian relations in different parts of the province. Changes in the RSS's fortune were slow to come. By the spring of 1946 there were Hindus in Simla and elsewhere willing to heed the call of the *sangh pariwar*.[26]

This was part of a much larger trend associated with the arrival of a three-member British cabinet delegation to decide the terms of a settlement. Determined to establish the very Hindu raj which had seen Muslims turning every way except the 'nationalist' way, the RSS poured acid on communitarian wounds in the Punjab. But it was not alone in its efforts. Other volunteer organizations such as the Mahabir Dal and the Hindu Sewak Sabha also commanded the allegiance of some Hindus. There was 'deepening conviction' that 'a general communal struggle [would] follow ... the final pronouncement by the Cabinet Mission'. Urban Hindus were 'encouraged to collect *lathis* and other similar weapons.'[27] The RSS and the Mahabir Dal as well as individual Hindus were reportedly 'laying in stocks of *lathis* and similar weapons'.[28] The

[21]*SPPAI*, 13 April 1946, vol. lxviii, no. 15, pp. 182–4.
[22]*SPPAI*, 29 July 1944, vol. lxvi, no. 31, p. 428.
[23]*SPPAI*, 29 October 1944, vol. lxvi, no. 44, pp. 605–6.
[24]*SPPAI*, 31 March 1945, vol. lxvii, no. 12, p. 122.
[25]*SPPAI*, 19 May 1945, vol. lxvii, no. 18, p. 190.
[26]*SPPAI*, 20 April 1946, vol. lxviii, no. 16, p. 200.
[27]*SPPAI*, 27 April 1946, vol. lxviii, no. 17, p. 206.
[28]Ibid., p. 212.

RSS's physical training classes were being held more regularly with larger numbers attending in Lahore, Rawalpindi, Gurdaspur, Ambala and Sind.[29] Even organizations like the Arya Pratinidhi Sabha and the Anjuman-i-Himayat-i-Islam were getting affected by the acrimonious relationship among the communities.[30] District officers were 'practically unanimous in reporting a marked decline in the communal relations between Hindus and Muslims'. If they could have only broken out of the debilitating idioms of their discourse, colonial officials might have taken remedial measures to check 'a movement throughout all large towns to acquire arms and to enlist in communal volunteer corps'. Both the RSS and the MLNG were engaged in 'heavy buying of *lathis*, swords, hatchets and similar weapons.'[31]

The nexus between press and politics in the Punjab had never been more lethal. Mahasha Krishen, editor of the *Pratap*, addressed meetings of the RSS when he was not stage managing the war of vitriolics from his office premises. After violence in Jullundur left one Hindu dead, efforts to restore peace were 'hindered by the completely distorted reporting appearing in the *Pratap* and *Milap*'.[32] Key Muslims in the press were also actively supporting rival groups in the Punjab League. The Punjabi Muslim journalist Meem Sheen was an associate of Niazi as was Hameed Nizami, editor of the *Nawa-i-Waqt*, who backed Mamdot against Daultana and the communists.[33] Politics in the informal arenas were closely connected with the political outpourings of the popular press. Lurid details of violent outbursts in the localities, and outrageously partisan comment, were not conducive to compromises in conference rooms. But they were equally ominous indicators of the price of confrontation. The journalistic intelligentsia of the Punjab, along with pamphlet hackers, did much to spread the plague of armed volunteer organizations.

There was a profusion of them once some former INA members agreed to offer training. Examples included the Qaumi Khidmatgars, the Azad Hind Volunteer Corp and the Hindustan Scouts Association, not to mention the MLNG and the Akal Fauj. The RSS was by far the best organized. There was hectic activity between Lahore and Nagpur. In keeping with the all-India command's designs, defence committees set up in *mohallas* were instructed to 'combat Sikhs'. Volunteers in Lahore were told that if troubles broke out, they should 'commence stray assaults on Muslims without waiting for further instructions'.[34] With such

[29]Ibid., p. 215.
[30]Ibid., p. 206.
[31]*SPPAI*, 4 May 1946, vol. lxviii, no. 18, p. 219.
[32]*SPPAI*, 25 May 1946, vol. lxviii, no. 20, p. 253.
[33]Nizami is an example of an individual's role in constructing a communitarian discourse that some have described as the 'ideology of Pakistan'. Given the variations in the articulation of ideology, it seems more appropriate to describe it as the editorial policy of the *Nawa-i-Waqt*.
[34]*SPPAI*, 4 May 1946, vol. lxviii, no. 18, p. 225.

breadth of autonomy to local branches, the membership of the RSS grew by leaps and bounds.[35] Given the strict secrecy surrounding its affairs, it was apparent to colonial observers, better at recording than counteracting, that 'not all new developments' within the organization had fully 'come to light'.[36]

Intended as a trope for Muslim sovereignty, the League's plans for the national guard were more overt than covert. Alarmed by the growth of the RSS, the Punjab League's working committee appealed to Hindus and Sikhs not to join such a fascist organization. They were assured that the League was concerned about their welfare just as much as of Muslims.[37] Yet the most important item on the agenda of a meeting at Mamdot's villa in Lahore was how to convert 'both ex-INA personnel and demobilised soldiers of the regular army' into 'enthusiastic members of the Muslim League National Guards'. Two recent converts to the League, Firoz Khan Noon and Abdul Qayum Khan of the NWFP, publicly 'advocated that Muslims should arm for civil war' and 'prepare ... to fight the Hindus' if they resorted to violence. In Gujrat, Noon 'urged every Muslim boy to buy a sword and keep it with him'. Even Daultana was heard making intemperate speeches, but then thought it better to stress restraint on the grounds that if Muslims 'disturbed the peace they would only be harming the cause of Pakistan'.[38]

A civil war, Daultana knew only too well, was not in the interests of Punjabi Muslims. Lesser speakers more given to hyperbole were telling Muslims to take 'steps to protect their lives'. The prospect of acquiring swords brought a spate of fresh recruits to the MLNG in Gurgaon, Ludhiana, Jullundur, Simla and Gurdaspur.[39] Many more Muslims were arming themselves with *lathis* and swords than joining the League's national guard. Shaukat Hayat was unable to submit a report to the provincial working committee and merely 'excused himself for doing so little to date' on account of 'private troubles'.[40] He was replaced by Mian Khurshid Anwar as the provincial organizer. Mian Amiruddin, who became president of the League party in the Lahore Corporation, was entrusted to supply 500 *lathis* with iron ends.[41] Devoting 'considerable energy' to the effort, Anwar tried 'bring[ing] home' to League workers the 'danger spelt' by the RSS which he alleged was being 'financed by Congress'. Seeking to meet a quota of five lakh for the province, he addressed a women's meeting in Islamic

---

[35]In Simla, RSS membership had swollen to 3500; in Ludhiana district there were now eight instead of three centres with a total strength of 2200 volunteers. Elsewhere as well the RSS was doing well with its recruitment drive and opening up fresh branches. (*SPPAI*, 18 May 1946, vol. lxviii, no. 19, p. 244.)

[36]Ibid.

[37]*Nawa-i-Waqt*, Lahore, 25 April 1946.

[38]*SPPAI*, 4 May 1946, vol. lxviii, no. 18, p. 223.

[39]Ibid.

[40]*SPPAI*, 25 May and 1 June 1946, vol. lxviii, nos. 20, 21, pp. 251, 267.

[41]*SPPAI*, 18 May 1946, vol. lxviii, no. 19, p. 242.

college 'from behind the screen' and exhorted them to join the MLNG. In Lahore, Riffat Bashir, daughter of the late Leaguer Mian Bashir Ahmad was appointed *salar*, or commander of the women's national guard.[42]

Rising in defence of social space entailed bringing down the walls separating the public from the private. But arming for security could also lend itself to killing. There was a series of assaults and murders. In early May 1946, Multan had to be placed under curfew after a number of stray assaults and clashes which left two Muslims and three Hindus injured.[43] Enlistment into the RSS and the MLNG reflected popular fears gripping the districts. Hindus and Muslims were known to be stockpiling a strange array of weapons, some crueler than others. But no one from the special branch thought it feasible to carry out a police swoop. The police did nothing upon learning that 2789 tins of *sarson* or mustard oil had been purchased in Rohtak, 'allegedly for pouring on the enemy after first being heated'.[44]

Other than enforcing Section 144 in strategic locations like Lahore, the colonial state was suffering from a loss of nerve with crushing effects on its performance. Just when the coalition ministry needed to go into high action to stop the Punjab skidding into a whirlpool of hatred, nothing was done to stem the social rot in the lower echelons of the administration. There was widespread disaffection among low-paid government workers, some of whom issued strike notices.[45] Unrest among government employees reflected the more generalized unease in a war-worn society. Labour demands were coinciding with communitarian assertions of rights. But the potential for a discourse based on citizenship rights was limited in late-colonial Punjab. Congress mediation in labour strikes enhanced its prestige. It also made relations with the communists impossible.[46] The irony of Jawaharlal Nehru's ideas on nationality and citizenship lies in his strained relationship with communists. However deserving they may have been of this treatment, it showed how Nehruvian politics got the better of Nehruvian discourse. Hounded out by the Congress, the communists found a stack full of needles in the League's nest. After Iftikharuddin had stalled the expulsion of Abdullah Malik and Daniyal Latifi, the trio tried extending their influence in the League. They were given a slap in the face by the one-time communist Ataullah Shah Jahanian, which partly explains Daultana's waning support for his communist friends. More to the point, neither the Congress nor the League had any interest

[42]*SPPAI*, 1 June 1946, vol. lxviii, no. 21, p. 267.

[43]Ibid., p. 224.

[44]*SPPAI*, 18 May 1946, vol. lxviii, no. 19, p. 237.

[45]Ibid., p. 244.

[46]An example of this was the strike at Sutlej Textile Mill. (Ibid.) There were also labour shutdowns at Lyallpur Cotton Mills, the Okara Textile Mills and the Bata boot factory. Urdu calligraphers in the employ of Muslim papers also went on strike, proving yet again that a common faith did not always transcend class differences.

in organizing labour on the basis of class. So even with communists and socialists in their midst, there was no likelihood of organized labour taking on capital to the serious detriment of the colonial state.

More than the attitude of labour, the eclipse of colonial power was heralded in by the open display of political sentiments by members of the Royal Indian Air Force; they shouted anti-British and pro-Congress slogans while welcoming Azad and Patel to the Ambala cantonment. Some were heard 'making abusive and sarcastic remarks' about the cabinet mission.[47] In a province that was the sword arm of empire, this was no ordinary incident. Defiance of colonial authority was spreading far and wide. The INA hero Shahnawaz in an effusive rush of nationalist fervour claimed that members of Bose's army would 'take possession of the Treasuries, Tehsils, Police Stations and railway stations' after the departure of the British cabinet mission.[48]

To make matters worse, irregularities in the distribution of essential commodities in the districts were being blamed by the press on the religious affiliations of the officials. Non-Muslims constituted the majority of the personnel of the civil supplies department in Sialkot. An estimated 85 per cent of the population, Muslims resented being refused cloth for their turbans while there was no such restriction on Sikhs.[49] The material dimensions of politics—access to scarce commodities, better employment opportunities and claims on social space—were giving a sharper edge to communitarian ill-will. The governor of the Punjab regretted that his superiors in London had not fully grasped just how dramatically the provincial administration had declined in the past twenty-five years. In so far as government in the Punjab was able to function at all, it did so 'now mainly on oriental lines'.[50] Politicization along community lines nestled easily with administrative corruption. A politically correct, but weak-kneed, coalition ministry was proving to be the problem and not the solution. In Evan Jenkins' opinion, a League-dominated ministry enjoying Akali support was still feasible. But this required keeping calculations at the centre from muddling already muddled provincial equations.

All eyes were on the all-India leadership. Would they rise to the occasion or pursue the policy of drift to confrontation and civil war? The presence of the cabinet delegation gave salience to the question. Reactions to the cabinet mission plan of 16 May 1946 helped link the mood in the urban and rural localities of the Punjab with developments at the all-India level. Excluding the Akalis from

[47]Ibid., p. 237.

[48]Ibid., p. 238.

[49]Nawa-i-Waqt, Lahore, 12 April 1946.

[50]Abell's minutes on the governors' conference in Simla with the viceroy and officials of the government of India, 12 July 1946, in Nicholas Mansergh and Penderel Moon (eds), The Transfer of Power, 1942–7, vol. viii, London: Her Majesty's Stationery Office, 1979, p. 40 (henceforth TP, followed by volume and page number).

the tripartite discussions in Simla between the cabinet delegation and the Congress and League leadership may have seemed consistent with all-India imperatives. On the fault line of region and centre, the Sikhs could jeopardize a negotiated arrangement for the Punjab.

Sikhs, the All-India Federation and the League's 'Pakistan'

The mission's plan for a loose three-tiered federal arrangement covering the whole of India was potentially less detrimental to the Sikhs than some of their pet schemes. If offered safeguards by both the League and the Congress, they could yet end up holding the balance in the proposed all-India federation. Intended to dissuade Jinnah from pressing his maximum demands, the mission's formula conceded Muslim dominance in the majority provinces with about a third of the share of power at the all-India level. Full sovereignty was denied but something very near it was implicit in the provision to group the Muslim-majority provinces of the northwest and the northeast—the most important facet of the League's Lahore resolution. As Jinnah put it, this was the 'whole guts' of the issue.[51] An all-India arrangement would enable Muslims in the majority provinces to extend protection to co-religionists in other parts of India. The presence of non-Muslims in Muslim-majority groups was added assurance that there would be reciprocal arrangements for both sets of minorities as envisaged in the fourth paragraph of the 1940 resolution. So in principle the prospects of the League seeking an accommodation with the Sikhs in the Punjab were better than ever.

On 6 June 1946, the AIML accepted the mission's proposal. The provision allowing provinces to opt out of the Indian union after ten years was seen by many Muslims as a sufficient security for 'Pakistan'. Prominent Leaguers like Suhrawardy had been arguing that 'Pakistan' was not the last demand of the Muslims.[52] And there were those who believed Muslims had a right over the whole of India.[53] Reactions in pro-League papers were more mixed. A *Nawa-i-Waqt* editorial applauded the decision since it gave Muslims time to prepare for the attainment of 'Pakistan'.[54] But the *Inqilab* wondered whether the League had been wrong in demanding a sovereign 'Pakistan'.[55] Pro-Congress Muslims lashed out at Jinnah and the League for betraying the trust of the Muslims. The Ahrar paper *Azad* alleged that the League's endorsement of the mission's proposals proved that it had never been genuine about its proclaimed aim.[56]

[51] Cited in Jalal, *The Sole Spokesman*, p. 194.

[52] *Nawa-i-Waqt*, Lahore, 11 April 1946.

[53] Chaudhury Nazir Ahmad Khan, an advocate from Montgomery district, berated Iftikharuddin for saying that 'Pakistan' was the last demand of the Muslims. (Ibid., 24 April 1946.)

[54] Ibid., 8 June 1946.

[55] *Inqilab*, Lahore, 20 July 1946.

[56] Mirza, *Karavan-i-Ahrar*, vii, pp. 309–14.

These snipings from the usual quarters notwithstanding, Muslims in the Punjab were satisfied with the acceptance of the mission's plan. The tone of the Muslim press and statements at League meetings were 'more conciliatory ... towards the minorities, especially the Sikhs'.[57] If the Akalis could resist flying off the handle, there was every prospect of the League and the Congress making them 'flattering offers'.[58] Master Tara Singh along with Giani Kartar Singh and Nagoke denounced the proposals; they 'ignored' the Sikhs and 'left them at the mercy of the Muslims without any safeguards'.[59] A 'protest day' on 26 May advertised the unanimity of Sikh opinion. At a meeting in the Golden Temple, Isher Singh Majhail and Nagoke called for direct action against the British, charging them with a 'criminal breach of trust in not handing the Punjab back to the Sikhs'. Pleas were issued to the police and the army not to fire upon compatriots. Sabotaging the colonial state and arming the *panth* was necessary for the realization of Giani Kartar Singh's 'prophe[cy] that the Union Jack over Lahore Fort would soon be replaced by the Sikh flag'. But there were signs of nervousness as well. Congress was reminded of its 1929 pledge to the minorities.[60]

Seeing their moment, some Muslim Leaguers 'approached leading Sikh leaders privately' and offered them 'additional weightage'. While preferring this option, Sikhs were unconvinced that the League could give them weightage along with the Hindus.[61] Publicly, Sikh leaders were 'already on the war path'.[62] The Panthic Pratinidhi Board demanded rights commensurate with Muslims, reserving its decision on participation in the constituent assembly. Marshalling resources in men and money, Tara Singh asked Sikhs to boycott British goods and help raise a volunteer corp of 50,000 as well as funds to the tune of fifty lakh rupees.[63] But 'not even the alarm caused to the Sikh community' by the British proposals could heal divisions between the Giani and Nagoke groups or encourage Akalis to unite with other Sikh parties.[64]

If political fluidity in Punjabi communities could be maximized, there remained a thin glimmer of hope for a negotiated accommodation. The erstwhile sovereigns of the Punjab could not be given short shrift by the departing raj. Jenkins warned the viceroy that ignoring the Sikhs would 'seriously obstruct any agreed arrangement in the Punjab' which was 'vitally important to the League'. This was 'not a parochial point'. If Jinnah and Nehru offered safeguards to Sikhs, there was a possibility of peace. Sweetening the

[57]*SPPAI*, 15 June 1946, vol. lxviii, no. 23, p. 293.
[58]See Jenkins to Wavell, 4 July 1946, *TP*, viii, p. 7.
[59]*SPPAI*, 25 May 1946, vol. lxviii, no. 20, p. 250.
[60]*SPPAI*, 1 June 1946, vol. lxviii, no. 21, p. 266.
[61]Ibid., p. 265.
[62]*SPPAI*, 29 June 1946, vol. lxviii, no. 25, p. 319.
[63]Ibid., p. 322.
[64]*SPPAI*, 13 July 1946, vol. lxviii, no. 27, pp. 345–6.

package for the Sikhs would 'improve communal relations', make the League's position 'much easier' and permit communities to co-operate in the constituent assembly.[65] Sardar Baldev Singh handed Jenkins a proposal to amalgamate Sikh princely states into a single group.[66] Giani Kartar Singh admitted that Sikhs needed to focus on securing concrete safeguards in the Punjab-dominated Muslim-majority group. The problem was that the public announcements of Sikhs had been so excessive that they 'dare not counsel moderation' unless the British made 'a face-saving announcement'. Jenkins strongly favoured such a gesture since the Sikh position in the Punjab was 'temporarily of some all-India importance'.[67]

This was why at an earlier stage of his negotiations with the cabinet mission, 'Jinnah had been very anxious to come to terms with the Sikhs'. Giani Kartar Singh was advised by colonial officials, Penderel Moon and his associate Major Short, to 'make no move'. And this despite Jenkins' belief that Jinnah would 'offer substantial concessions if the Sikhs ... agree[d] to perpetual Muslim domination'.[68] Since the alternative was Hindu dominance, the Sikhs had a hard choice to make. Exploiting their dilemma, Jinnah had before the arrival of the cabinet mission acknowledged that the Sikhs were a separate nation, entitled to their own free state, provided they identified its precise geographical location.[69] On 28 March he proposed creating a separate state for Sikhs in east Punjab.[70] The all-India League's decision to forgo a sovereign 'Pakistan' gave its Punjabi lieutenants an opening into Akali circles where pro-Congress Sikhs were pitted against Giani Kartar Singh's group. Even as late as mid-July the Akali camp had not swung decisively in either the direction of the League or the Congress.[71]

Sober reflection on the cabinet mission dissolved into bitter acrimony after Nehru's rejection of the grouping scheme and a weak centre at a press

[65]Jenkins to Wavell, 3 July 1946, TP, viii, p. 2.

[66]Jenkins to Wavell, 4 July 1946, ibid., pp. 5–6.

[67]Ibid., pp. 8–9.

[68]Ibid., p. 8. The close involvement of these two British officers is recorded in Penderel Moon's Divide and Quit, London: Chatto & Windus, 1961.

[69]An obvious bluff on Jinnah's part, it startled the pro-League press. The Inqilab of 24 March 1946 was amazed that the Quaid-i-Azam had overlooked the fact that Sikhs did not form a majority in any district of the Punjab. If thirty-seven lakh Sikhs, a mere 13 per cent of the population, could make a historic claim to sovereignty, then seventy lakh Muslims in UP who formed 15 per cent of the population could do so as well by claiming that they had ruled India for six hundred years. Proving that a Punjabi Muslim can never cease being a Punjabi, Ataullah Shah Bukhari on behalf of the Ahrars reprimanded Jinnah for accepting the principle of a Sikh state. It merely confirmed him in the belief that 'Pakistan' was deadly for Indian Muslims. (Cited in Mirza Karavan-i-Ahrar, vii, pp. 50–2, 62.)

[70]Reuters Fortnightly Political Appraisal, #2914, 28 March 1946, L/I/1/665, IOL.

[71]See Jenkins to Wavell, 15 July 1946, TP, viii, p. 60.

conference on 11 July 1946. With the exception of the Akalis, it was 'fair' to say that 'neither the Hindus nor the Muslims of the Province ha[d] been spoiling for a fight' since the announcement of the mission's proposals.[72] This could change radically if either of the two all-India high commands 'dictate[d] such a policy'.[73] There was consternation in the Punjab that the 'more faults' all-India leaders could find in the mission's plan, 'the greater ... the likelihood that the nature of the actual proposals w[ould] be forgotten'.[74] And indeed, the Punjab Congress expressed dismay when the all-India high command came around to giving a hedged acceptance to the 16 May plan. Nehru's remarks proved the worst fears of Punjabi Leaguers. Solidly opposed to the grouping scheme, all-India Congress leaders now ventured forward as defenders of Muslims in the NWFP, Sind and Assam.

This gave a much-needed spurt to pro-Congress Muslims in the Jamiat-ul-Ulema-i-Hind, the Majlis-i-Ahrar, the Krishak Praja Party, the Momins and the All-India Shia Political Conference. Reflecting the growing anxieties of Muslims in Hindu-majority provinces, Husain Bhai Laljee, the president of the Shia Conference, had asked Jinnah if an estimated fifty million of the community he claimed to represent were to be 'sacrificed for the sake of Pakistan'.[75] Placing the figure at twenty-five million, Jinnah noted that the same number of Hindus would be citizens of 'Pakistan'.[76] But few pro-Congress Muslims were convinced by the notion of reciprocal safeguards and accused the League of misleading Muslims by accepting the mission's proposals. They preferred an all-India arrangement which gave Muslims parity at the centre, safeguards for minorities and maximum autonomy for the provinces. This was akin to Jinnah's own conception of the optimal arrangement for Muslims at the centre. It was the grouping scheme where the divergences between non-League and League Muslims were most pronounced. Sindhi Muslims like G.M. Syed and Pir Ali Mohammad Rashidi rejected grouping as a ploy to reduce Sind into a colony of Punjabi Muslims.[77] Pro-Congress Pathans had similar reservations. So did the Baluch Association which considered the Baluch an independent nation aspiring for self-government.[78]

Fissiparous tendencies within the Muslim community wilted the League's enthusiasm for the cabinet mission's proposals. Without guaranteed grouping, Jinnah was unwilling to risk participating in a constituent assembly where the League would be outvoted in the making of the constitution. Wavell's decision not to invite Jinnah and the League to form an interim government was a shock;

[72]*SPPAI*, 8 June 1946, vol. lxviii, no. 22, p. 282.
[73]*SPPAI*, 25 May 1946, vol. lxviii, no. 20, p. 247.
[74]*SPPAI*, 1 June 1946, vol. lxviii, no. 21, p. 263.
[75]*Reuters Fortnightly Political Appraisal*, 28 March 1946, #2914, L/I/1/665, IOL.
[76]Ibid., 4 April 1946, #3123.
[77]*Nawa-i-Waqt*, Lahore, 19 April and 7 June 1946.
[78]Ibid., 28 April 1946.

they had satisfied the main condition for office by accepting the May 16 plan as well as the proposals for a fourteen-member interim government.[79] The League's willingness to join the interim government had been 'welcomed in the Punjab'.[80] However, cantankerous exchanges on grouping and the controversy over the interim government saw Jinnah and the League reverting to the demand for a sovereign 'Pakistan'.

Even before the viceregal snub, Mamdot had told a press conference that without parity there was no question of the League joining the interim government. While it had accepted the mission's plan, 'the aim of the Muslim League wa[s] still ... an autonomous and sovereign Pakistan'.[81] Denied power at the centre, Punjabi Leaguers were less inclined to moderation. Daultana ordered Leaguers to steer clear of the Unionist-inspired movement to improve communitarian relations. Developments at the centre were pushing the provincial leadership to go on a war footing. In addition to the Islamia College campus, MLNGs were being trained in Iftikharuddin's palatial ancestral home in Baghbanpura and Nawabzada Rashid Ali Khan's equally spacious *haveli*. Women were training for civil defence and parading alongside men in uniform. Turning domestic space into forums for public posturing was facilitated by the decision to enroll all members of the PMSF into the national guard.[82]

None of this escaped the non-Muslims, alarmed at the lengths to which the British had gone to satisfy Jinnah's demands. Fears of a forced Muslim takeover of power in the Punjab were reinforced by the changing tactics of the Majlis-i-Ahrar and the Khaksars. Together with the Jamiat-ul-Ulema-i-Hind, they wanted a share of rights which, to many non-Muslims, seemed no different than the League's 'Muslim demand'.[83] The Jamiat in its Saharanpur resolution once again demanded complete freedom for Muslims in matters to do with their religion and culture. Although willing to accept a common centre restricted to a few specified subjects and adequate weightage for minorities in fully autonomous provinces, the *ulema* demanded parity between Muslims and Hindus at the all-India level. The resolution was endorsed by the Ahrars.[84] Congress's refusal to concede parity elicited strong rebuke from its Muslim supporters. Mazhar Ali

[79]For a detailed discussion of the cabinet mission plan and the negotiations surrounding it, see Jalal, *The Sole Spokesman*, chapter five.

[80]*SPPAI*, 29 June 1946, vol. lxviii, no. 25, p. 323.

[81]*SPPAI*, 22 June 1946, vol. lxviii, no. 24, p. 312.

[82]*SPPAI*, 13 July 1946, vol. lxviii, no. 27, p. 346.

[83]Ataullah Shah Bukhari thought it was naive to assume that the British or the Hindus were opposed to a division of India. It suited them perfectly but would destroy Indian Muslims. This was why a staunch Congressman like Rajagopalachari had supported 'Pakistan'. The Hindus press's opposition was similarly intended to strengthen Muslim resolve to secure 'Pakistan'. (Mirza, *Karavan-i-Ahrar*, vii, pp. 132–4.)

[84]Ibid., pp. 65–7.

Azhar 'deplored Congress opposition to Hindu-Muslim parity' after having 'admitted the justice' of the demand'.[85] Khaksars were condemning 'Jinnah's acceptance of an emasculated Pakistan'. Mashriqi was purportedly enlisting a two-crore-strong 'Pakistan Fauj' to seize 'Pakistan' from the British.[86] In what were further signs of a Muslim groundswell for some sort of a 'Pakistan', Maulana Daud Ghaznavi, president of the Punjab Congress and a member of the legislative assembly, defected to the Muslim League while Azhar resigned from the Majlis-i-Ahrar.[87]

These informal realignments in Muslim politics exacerbated non-Muslim insecurities. Sikhs were joining the RSS in Multan, Montgomery and Sargodha. In Chinoit, Congress workers equated their volunteer corps with the RSS.[88] Eager to cut the League's demands to size, the Congress high command kept its channels open with the Panthic Board and the Akalis. At Nehru's behest the Sikhs decided to contest elections to the constituent assembly, only to withdraw their papers at the last minute. The decision had the 'backing of practically all the community's leaders'.[89] This gave the Punjab Leaguers some breathing space. They had to try and 'get the Sikhs off the boil'. Mamdot confessed to the Punjab governor that 'he was in favour of safeguards for the Sikhs' in the north-western group of provinces since 'a League-Sikh rapprochement was the only solution here'.[90]

The decision of pro-Congress and Akali Sikhs to boycott the constituent assembly was welcomed in League circles. When in late July 1946 the AIML in Bombay withdrew its acceptance of the mission's plan, the Sikhs felt that the 'League ha[d] followed their lead'.[91] Determined to prevent them colluding with the League, the Congress high command pulled out all the stops in trying to appease the Sikhs. After hectic negotiations in Wardha, Sardar Baldev Singh was offered the defence portfolio in the interim government. Reasonably satisfied, the Panthic Pratinidhi Board agreed to participate in the constituent assembly following by-elections for the Sikh seats. Akalis were 'less obviously favourable' to the decision. But there was 'no doubt' that Wavell's approaches to the Congress had 'gone a long way towards securing their acquiescence in this decision'. Tara Singh and Giani Kartar Singh, however, made sure that the

[85]SPPAI, 29 June 1946, vol. lxviii, no. 25, p. 323.

[86]SPPAI, 27 July 1946, vol. lxviii, no. 29, p. 365 and also Mazhar (comp.), *Khaksar Tehrik aur Azad-i-Hind*, pp. 243-4.

[87]Ghaznavi was facing an enquiry for his alleged embezzlement of Congress funds during the elections. (*SPPAI*, 27 July 1946, vol. lxviii, no. 29, p. 362.) Mazhar's son, Kaiser Mustafa, had defied the party line and supported the Leaguer Mian Amiruddin for mayor of the Lahore Corporation. (*SPPAI*, 8 June 1946, vol. lxviii, no. 22, p. 282.)

[88]SPPAI, 22 June 1946, vol. lxviii, no. 24, p. 314.

[89]SPPAI, 20 July 1946, vol. lxviii, no. 28, p. 357.

[90]Wavell to Pethick Lawrence, 20 July 1946, *TP*, viii, p. 93.

[91]SPPAI, 27 July and 3 August 1946, vol. lxviii, nos 29, 30, pp. 361, 379.

decision left Sikhs the option of deserting the Congress and the path of constitutionalism if this suited them better.[92]

With the odds favouring a Congress–Sikh alliance, Leaguers had to contemplate how to react to the AIML call for 'direct action' on 16 August. Mindful of the risks to their regional position, the Punjab League's Working Committee decided not to defy the law and display 'no enmity towards Hindus'. There was of course nothing to stop *pirs* and *ulema* crying themselves hoarse with the slogan 'Islam in danger'.[93] It was Calcutta which fell to pieces on the League's 'direct action' day. In Lahore, Leaguers exercised restraint although meetings were held in mosques and Muslim businesses kept their shutters rolled down. Mamdot exaggerated his own achievement when he congratulated Punjabi Muslims for showing that they were 'more disciplined than those in Bengal'.[94]

The Punjab administration had reason to heave a sigh of relief. An extra-constitutional movement by the League could not be squashed in a province where the police was 70 per cent Muslim. To complicate matters, British civilians and army personnel thought the Muslim League had been treated badly and that Wavell ought to have invited Jinnah to form the government without the Congress. Jenkins thought proceeding with the constituent assembly minus the Muslim League would have 'more serious effects ... than the formation of a Congress Ministry at the Centre'.[95] The governor's views are significant in the light of Mamdot's contention that the League attached more importance to its share of power in the interim government than to issues that were to be settled in the constituent assembly.[96] Yet nothing could persuade Congress to accept parity with the League. Dismayed by 'Nehru's intemperate speeches', Britain's penultimate viceroy was shocked by the 'lack of generosity among the Congress leaders'. It left him feeling 'very doubtful about the future of a country ... guided by leaders with such a mentality'.[97]

Once the League rescinded its acceptance of the 16 May plan, Wavell felt obliged to invite the Congress to form an interim government. Taking advantage of Ramazan, enraged Leaguers gave speeches in mosques, attacking the British and swearing to lay down their lives for Islam. There were calls for a *jihad* against western imperialists and 'traitor Muslims' like Shafaat Ahmad Khan who was stabbed in Simla after he joined the interim government. Displays of the MLNG's muscle power in key urban areas found the RSS 'organising a group of Hindu *goondas* armed with knives and *lathis*'. Tension between the communities were aggravated by the 'reprehensible handling of news of the Calcutta riots'. Hindu papers were 'the principal offenders'. There was 'grave

[92]*SPPAI*, 17 August 1946, vol. lxviii, no. 32, pp. 397–400.
[93]*SPPAI*, 3 and 17 August 1946, vol. lxviii, nos. 30, 32, pp. 392, 401.
[94]*SPPAI*, 24 August 1946, vol. lxviii, no. 33, p. 412.
[95]Minutes of governors' conference, 8 August 1946, *TP*, viii, p. 206.
[96]*SPPAI*, 17 August 1946, vol. lxviii, no. 32, p. 401.
[97]Wavell to Caroe, 29 July, *TP*, viii, p. 239.

anxiety' in official circles at the 'electric' atmosphere in Lahore and other key urban centres. In Rawalpindi, an important recruiting ground for the army, the situation was 'definitely bad and full of danger'. Elsewhere too there were alarming rumours and reports 'alleging the collection of arms and acids' by Muslims and Hindus severally as well as through volunteer organizations. A sure sign of the sheer gravity of the situation in the Punjab, the more well-to-do were 'depositing their valuables in banks'.[98]

With the two main communities revving for civil war, the attitude of the Sikhs was critical for both the all-India parties. Congress scored a point by getting the Panthic Board to reverse its decision not to participate in the constituent assembly. But final victory had yet to be clinched. The new policy had 'not met with universal Sikh approval'. Many were 'perplexed and doubtful of the wisdom of a line of action, which ... must almost certainly bring about Sikh–Muslim conflict'. There were 'apprehensi[ons]' about a 'Congress game ... to use the Sikhs as shock troops against the Muslims'. It would have sufficed if the Sikh leaders had only agreed to participate in the constituent assembly. By biting on the cherry and joining the interim government, pro-Congress Sikhs were seen to have hurt the prospects of an amicable agreement with the League. Giani Kartar Singh and Tara Singh publicly opposed the Panthic Board's decision. They were backed by Baba Kharak Singh who had resisted doing a deal with the Congress. But this did not make them more amenable to talking peace with Muslims. In Gujranwala, Tara Singh, Giani Kartar Singh and Joginder Singh Man warned that 'if the Muslims created disturbances, they would be crushed by the Sikhs'.[99] At a meeting of the Panthic Board on 22 August, Giani proposed coming to terms with the League. Tara Singh opposed Baldev Singh holding the defence portfolio 'since Sikhs would end up shouldering responsibility for crushing a Muslim movement', if and when it took place. There was an uproar among pro-Congress Sikhs when the pre-eminent Akali leader accepted Jinnah's invitation to discuss the terms of an agreement. Yet the general belief was that though 'a belated move', Sikhs would 'benefit from a settlement with the Muslim League'.[100]

Sadly for the protagonists of united Punjab, the logic of a Muslim–Sikh agreement was coming to prevail just when the chances of its attainment were getting overwrought by a confluence of developments at the centre, the region and other parts of India. Denied power at the centre and province, Punjabi Leaguers detected 'a deep-laid plot between the British and the Congress'. Bitter, frightened and angry, a deadly compound, they had seen their world collapsing twice within a space of a few months. Their irritation was compounded by the jubilation among Punjabi Hindus. Proving to be

[98]*SPPAI*, 31 August 1946, vol. lxviii, no. 34, pp. 419–24.
[99]Ibid., no. 33, pp. 409–11.
[100]Ibid., no. 34, pp. 421–2.

'bad winners', they were doing everything possible 'to taunt and humiliate the Muslims'. There was irresponsible talk by Congress leaders of 'suppress[ing] the Muslims once and for all with British aid'. Much depended on the Sikhs. Despite an official alliance with the Congress, 'some influential Sikhs' were 'reluctant to break finally with the Muslims'. But the tone of their newspapers and spokespersons—'the most violent in the Punjab'—suggested that Sikhs would side with Hindus in the event of a major flare-up.[101]

This dismal political scenario assumed crisis proportions in a province where the government authority had 'never been at a lower ebb'. If Muslims thought Allahabad, Wardha or New Delhi were calling the shots in the Punjab, there was bound to be 'the most serious trouble'. British officials in the Indian Civil Service and the police were expected to 'stand firm' in an emergency only if it did not 'involve taking sides'. They would recoil from doing their duty, Jenkins apprised the viceroy, if 'His Majesty's Government promote[d], or acquiesce[d] in any systematic repression of our large Muslim population'. Suspicious of London drifting towards the Congress, the average British official in the province resented the prospect of doing HMG's 'dirty work'.[102] There could not be a grimmer statement on the political and administrative conditions in the Punjab. A social powder-keg that might be set alight via remote control, the province had been imploding since the elections of 1945-6. Glancy's grand gesture to parliamentary propriety and a delicate communitarian balance—a Unionist, Congress and Panthic Sikh coalition ministry—had done more for division than unity. Despite a succession of opportunities, the Muslim League was unable to take advantage of Sikh doubts about an alliance with the Congress. Obsessed with ousting the coalition ministry, Punjabi Leaguers neglected to build bridges with the Sikhs, far less satisfy their demands for political and cultural safeguards. The establishment of a committee to supervise 'direct action' signalled the beginnings of a Muslim League onslaught on the ministry. Preventing attacks on the ministry from ricochetting on relations with non-Muslims was difficult in a political atmosphere drenched in communitarian rancour and suspicion.

Anyone with an iota of sense could see the 'danger, ever present in the Punjab, of a competent riposte to League disorder from the turbulent Sikh minority'.[103] But there was no hard evidence of Sikhs gearing for a final showdown with the League. Quite as much as the other two communities, a common religiously informed cultural identity had never lent coherence to Sikh politics. Whether the attractions of controlling exceptionally well-funded *gurdwaras* or directing the Akali Dal and the Panthic Pratinidhi Board, the Sikh leadership was preoccupied with internal political disputes. This seems remarkable given the

[101]Jenkins' appreciation of the Punjab situation at the end of August 1946, *TP*, viii, pp. 371-2.

[102]Ibid., pp. 374-7.

[103]Intelligence Bureau (Home Department), 23 September 1946, ibid., p. 577.

preparations that were afoot to organize armed Hindu and Muslim militias. Akali *jathas* had existed since the 1930s but were formed on an ad hoc basis. None existed on 24 January 1947 when the besieged premier of the Punjab decided to ban the RSS and the MLNG, only to revoke the order within four days under pressure from the League.[104]

That it was well over six months before the Sikhs erupted to avenge their marginalization is critically important in evaluating the options open to Punjabis in the final few months of colonial rule. It was only in mid-February 1947 that Tara Singh finagled his way out of internal dissensions in Akali ranks to call for the revitalization of the Akal Fauj. By then the chances of a peaceful resolution of the provincial imbroglio had dipped further under the combined weight of Congress and League wranglings over the interim government and volatile reporting by the provincial press of killings by Muslims and Hindus in eastern Bengal and Bihar. Jumping from the sidelines onto centrestage, Sikhs seemed more theatrical than real. They added to social tensions in the localities a degree of violence that was beyond anything the actors at the all-India level or the region had imagined, far less needed.

Awaiting Peace, Affecting Strife—The Hindu–Muslim Tussle

During the second half of 1946 an uneasy armed truce prevailed in the Punjab which six months later, together with a crumbling administrative edifice, formed the historical backdrop to a social upheaval that turned the sword arm of India into its biggest killing field. The disjunction between flimsy organizational structures and offensive political rhetoric did more damage than anything the volunteer bodies could have mustered on their own. Religion did play a part as a marker of social distinction. But religion as identity owed little to religion as faith. Confusing the two, as a historiography operating in a binary mode is wont to do, has ended up essentializing religion and, worse still, blurring the myriad textures of localized social violence under the grand rubric of 'communalism'. Exposing the precarious balance between the individual and the community quite as often as the supposed triumph of the community over the individual, preparations for civil war and actual outbreaks of violence in the different localities of the Punjab need examining in their own light.

After a relatively quiescent month of Ramazan and an uneventful Id, individual Leaguers made rabble-rousing speeches, equating 'direct action' with *jihad*, and exhorting Muslims to wreck the interim government. In so far as there was a collective Muslim response, it consisted mainly of hoisting black flags on shops and houses. There was a distinct reluctance to submit to the rigours of training in the MLNG. Khurshid Anwar, the provincial organizer, was disappointed that the MLNGs were 'so small in number and so lacking in training'. He blamed this on the provincial League leaders, Mamdot in particular,

---

[104]Jenkins to Wavell, 28 January 1947, *TP*, ix, p. 570.

who had shown little real interest in the MLNG.[105] Fresh vows were taken to strengthen the MLNG so that the Muslim *jihad* would not be in vain. Many more Muslims were attending League meetings. The gender divide was no longer a bar to Muslim women organizing meetings and enlisting in the national guard. Many young women demonstrated that they could be just as adept with *lathis* and swords as with the provision of first aid. Yet neither the shifting balance between the private and the public, nor the growing numbers attending League meetings, was an adequate substitute for a co-ordinated organizational effort. There was a dire need for effective organization, especially in the rural areas. Appeals were issued to revive primary Leagues set up for the elections and equally hastily shut down.[106]

Although in political ferment, the organizationally more able Ahrars had no intention of offering the League a helping hand without exacting a hefty price. Staying aloof from the direct action movement, the Ahrars projected themselves as the 'spearhead of all nationalist Muslim bodies'. This involved raising a volunteer corp of fifty thousand uniformed men armed with hatchets and popularizing the *hakumat-i-illahiya* by leading an Islamic way of life.[107] There might have been an element of prophecy in Bukhari's assertion that 'when other Muslim organisations disappeared, the Ahrars would be triumphant'.[108] But brilliant oratory was no longer enough to enthuse Muslims into joining a party which had been routed in the elections by the Muslim League. In Jhang, the party president Maulana Mohammad Ali Jullunduri said that if Jinnah convinced Ahrars that 'Pakistan would really benefit them', they would 'join the League'. Mazhar Ali Azhar's resignation and mangling attacks on nationalist Muslims and the Congress hinted that some Ahrars were amenable to persuasion. At a 'predominantly Muslim League gathering', the former sage of the Ahrar 'criticised Mr Jinnah for retreating from his original Pakistan demand' for which he was 'prepared to lay down his life'. The speech was drowned by the audience crying 'come over to the League'. Unkind remarks were made about the one-time dictator of the Ahrars. Thoroughly affronted, Mazhar Ali swore never to join the League.[109]

Mashriqi, more thick skinned, was faring far worse. He had to leave a thinly attended meeting in Lahore before his frustration got the better of him. Attempts by Khaksars in Rawalpindi to stop inhabitants of neighbouring villages taking part in the League's direct action programme were 'completely ineffectual'. They were equally unsuccessful in raising an army to fight for 'Pakistan'.[110] If bland appropriations of the League's demand were eliciting a poor response,

[105]*SPPAI*, 7 and 14 September 1946, vol. lxviii, nos 35, 36, pp. 432–3, 442–3.

[106]*SPPAI*, 14 September 1946, vol. lxviii, no. 36, p. 442.

[107]*SPPAI*, 7 September 1946, vol. lxviii, no. 35, p. 433.

[108]*SPPAI*, 20 July 1946, vol. lxviii, no. 28, p. 359.

[109]*SPPAI*, 21 September 1946, vol. lxviii, no. 37, p. 453.

[110]*SPPAI*, 7, 14 and 21 September 1946, vol. lxviii, nos 35–7, pp. 433, 443, 453.

there were still fewer willing to listen to Unionist or pro-Congress Muslims preaching social harmony. In Amritsar, five thousand attended a League meeting while only a few hundred appeared at two meetings held on the same day to improve Hindu–Muslim relations. Saifuddin Kitchlew, looking to cock a snook at the League, might ridicule the 'Pakistan' demand but could do no more than 'regret ... the disruptive influence which both the Hindu and Muslim Press were exercising'.[111]

Empty words, spoken and written, had a magical appeal for Punjab's internally divided communities. But it was the relative differentials in organizational capacity which accentuated fears, lending potency to arming during a truce that could end in measured peace or unbridled war. Unlike the League's national guards, the Ahrar *razakars* or volunteers and a peripatetic Khaksar militia, the RSS represented a more determined organizational effort by Hindu commercial power in the Punjab to rise in self-defence. Muslim indignation over the formation of an interim government without the League saw Punjabi Hindus looking upon the RSS as the only organization capable of protecting their life and property. In more than one district 'the shopkeeper classes [we]re showing a particular interest in the Corps'.[112] RSS volunteers in Jhang and Chinoit districts were told to 'lay in a stock of acids'. A by-product of the ban on firearms as well as iron *panjas* or *guptis*, this was 'as anti-social as any advice could be'. Knives and bottles of acid were being purchased on behalf of all three communities.[113] Cutlery merchants of Wazirabad were doing 'very brisk trade in the export of daggers'. But the recovery of 318 knives by the police in Amritsar from two Hindus, and one Muslim and Sikh indicates that the procurement of arms was as yet an individual effort, even if frequently associated with volunteer organizations.[114] The habit of carrying a knife was responsible for many stray stabbings in the province in the months to come.

With the Sikhs napping, Hindus were the best organized. Muslims tended to act more in their individual capacity or in small batches than as members of an organized community. Multan was hit by violence when some Muslims running a bazaar announced that a *jihad* had already started. Reacting instantly, several Hindus quickly turned up with *lathis*. In an early instance of violence against women, both as victims and symbols of communitarian honour, one Muslim woman was stabbed in the stomach. She survived the injury. In Jullundur some Hindu Sewa Samiti members attacked Muslim youth for taking more than usual interest in some Hindu women on the occasion of a religious fair. Eleven were injured in the ensuing brawl.[115] Fears about the protection of domestic space, female honour and children led to the formation

---

[111]*SPPAI*, 21 September 1946, vol. lxviii, no. 37, p. 449.

[112]*SPPAI*, 7 September 1946, vol. lxviii, no. 35, p. 434.

[113]*SPPAI*, 14 September 1946, vol. lxviii, no. 36, pp. 439, 444.

[114]Ibid., p. 444.

[115]Ibid., p. 443.

of several *mohalla* defence committees by Hindus in Lahore. In one part of the city, the local enthusiasts staged a mock alarm which disclosed the extent to which private arming had taken place. The police beguiled the residents by sounding off a similar alarm on the next night and arrested eighteen Hindus for carrying arms. Also displaying signs of nervousness, Hindus in certain wards of Amritsar city 'arranged a system of pickets to keep watch during the night'.[116] In a significant development, the Hindu Mahasabha was threatening to rise from the ashes of electoral defeat. One thousand handbills appeared in Lahore on its behalf urging Hindus to prepare for self-defence.[117]

All communities welcomed Wavell's invitation to Jinnah to join the interim government. There was, however, only a partial easing of tensions. A major reason for this was the success of the League's 'Buy Muslim' campaign. Directed at Muslim women in particular, it was 'reaching an ever wider circle of hearers' who were 'reported to be increasingly convinced by the case put forward by their leaders'. As it was, Hindus and Muslims wanted a settlement at the centre only if 'the other party ma[de] all the concessions'. Even if the 'average Hindu' was 'more anxious' for some sort of a settlement, Hindu newspapers queered the pitch with 'their loud and repeated warnings to Pt. Nehru not to make any further concessions to the Muslim League'. This was in some contrast to Mamdot's indecision over direct action and view that 'a compromise with Congress might still be affected'.[118]

Left to their own devices, the *pirs, ulema* and *maulanas* of the League made what they liked of the *jihad* against *kafirs*. Ghulam Mustafa Shah Gilani told a meeting of two thousand Muslims in Jhelum to 'promise to die for Islam as their ancestors did in Babar's time and to follow the footsteps of [Imam] Hussain, who had shown how Islam was to be protected in times of danger'. When he asked for a show of hands from those 'prepared to follow Mr Jinnah in the next struggle ... almost the entire audience did so'.[119] Raja Ghazanfar Ali Khan, tipped to join the interim government, was 'one of the busiest speakers'; his main theme was 'to wage *Jehad* in the name of Islam'.[120] Given the virulence of its propaganda, the League's acceptance of office at the centre 'confused many' of its supporters. There was 'no lack of faith in the wisdom of [Jinnah's] move'. Expectations of a decrease in communitarian tensions were 'tempered by the feeling that there w[ould] be continual friction at Delhi'. Hindus strongly suspected that the League had entered office 'only to eject Congress'.[121]

Jinnah's shrewd manoeuvre to include Jogendra Nath Mandal, a scheduled caste from Bengal, among the League's nominees had 'driven this conviction

[116]Ibid., p. 444.
[117]*SPPAI*, 21 September 1946, vol. lxviii, no. 37, p. 452.
[118]*SPPAI*, 28 September 1946, vol. lxviii, no. 38, pp. 465, 468.
[119]Ibid., p. 469.
[120]*SPPAI*, 19 October 1946, vol. lxviii, no. 40, p. 485.
[121]Ibid.

home more than anything else'. If Hindus questioned his motives, Muslims were 'uncertain about Mr Jinnah's intentions'.[122] Some Punjabi Leaguers were puzzled to learn from Daultana that the Quaid-i-Azam wanted them to 'pay particular attention to supporting the interests of the Scheduled Castes'. Towards that end, joint League and scheduled caste meetings were held fairly consistently.[123] The anomaly of a Muslim *jihad* had never been more glaring. But what caused more consternation was Shaukat Hayat's assertion that Jinnah had abandoned direct action and joined the interim government due to the 'weaknesses of Punjab Muslims'.[124] Assurances that the League intended to co-operate with Congress in the interim government further bewildered its followers.

The League assumed office at the centre against a backdrop of class-based Muslim violence against Hindus in the Noakhali and Tippera districts of eastern Bengal.[125] This was followed by a major conflagration in Bihar where Muslims were the main victims. The disturbances in east Bengal left Punjabi Hindus 'doubt[ing] the wisdom of trusting Congress to protect the interest of their community'. Many more were turning to the RSS which was 'devoting more attention to the collection of knives and acid'.[126] Levelling charges and countercharges and publishing 'rumours based on one-sided and biased reports of events in distant places', Hindu and Muslim newspapers did much to aggravate the mutual distrust enveloping the province. Congress came in for 'severe criticism' as 'disgruntled and frightened Hindus' began exploring ways to resuscitate the Mahasabha.[127] Stunned by press reports of the carnage in east Bengal and Bihar, Muslims in Lahore were 'adopting an even more communal outlook'. Primary Leagues, where they existed, were instructed to ensure that 'Muslims d[id] not go singly and unprotected in non-Muslim areas'.[128] With tensions running at fever pitch, the different communities looked upon volunteer organizations as their 'first and most important line of defence or offence'. A growing number of Muslim men and women were joining the MLNG. Yet it was the RSS which made most of the situation in Bengal and Bihar. Threatening vengeance for Noakhali, its volunteers were

---

[122]*SPPAI*, 26 October 1946, vol. lxviii, no. 41, p. 501.

[123]*SPPAI*, 2 November 1946, vol. lxviii, no. 42, p. 516.

[124]*SPPAI*, 9 November 1946, vol. lxviii, no. 43, p. 526.

[125]See Sugata Bose, *Agrarian Bengali: Economy, Social Structure and Politics, 1919–1947*, Cambridge: Cambridge University Press, 1986, chapter six.

[126]*SPPAI*, 2 November 1946, vol. lxviii, no. 42, p. 513. Enquiries in Jhelum and Chakwal revealed that eighty more bottles of acid were sold by licensed dealers in January 1946 than in January 1945, 103 more in May 1946 than in the previous year and 155 more in August 1946 than in August 1945. (*SPPAI*, 7 December 1946, vol. lxviii, no. 47, p. 564.)

[127]*SPPAI*, 9 November 1946, vol. lxviii, no. 43, p. 523.

[128]Ibid., p. 526.

'spreading communal hatred in certain localities in Lahore' and stressing the need to strengthen the *sangh*. One thousand volunteers were receiving training in the provincial capital alone.[129]

The spread of violence to parts of UP and Delhi, 'heightened public apprehensions'. Even 'minor incidents [we]re rapidly inflamed by biased rumour and mutual suspicion'. Accusing the all-India party of not condemning Muslim aggression and cohabiting with League *goondas* in the interim government,[130] Punjabi Hindus were 'looking to other and more violent means of imposing their will'. There was rampant 'anti-Gandhi and anti-Nehru feeling'. The two all-India leaders had publicly expressed regret at the loss of Muslim lives in Bihar which many Hindus considered sweet revenge for Noakhali and Calcutta. The Hindu Sabha was being revived. Arya Samajists were delivering 'provocative speeches inciting Hindus to return blow for blow and to take revenge for atrocities committed on Hindus in Bengal.'[131]

Muslims were in an equally 'revengeful mood'. The Hindus press was charged with 'misconduct and attempts to inflame Muslims into violent retaliation'. Intelligence reporters thought there was 'some truth that peace ha[d] been kept in the Punjab only by Muslim good sense and toleration under severe provocation'.[132] While the killings in Bihar incensed Muslims throughout India, most reacted by assisting in the despatch of relief. The instinct for revenge ranged from social boycotts to preparations for more murderous ventures. In Jullundur, the MLNGs were seen picketing Hindu-owned cinemas during the Id celebrations and successfully persuading many Muslims to stay away. A joint League and *achhut* meeting of four thousand in the city deplored the happenings in Bihar.[133]

Significantly, there were no killings by Muslims or non-Muslims in any of the districts to avenge the deaths of co-religionists in Bengal and Bihar. Preoccupied with internal matters, the Sikhs also avoided getting embroiled. There was an increase in age-old disputes over cow slaughter, renewed battles over religious shrines as well as stray assaults. Students were especially restive. The PMSF was agitating to go to Bihar to observe a day in honour of the dead. Hindu students responded by commemorating Noakhali on the same day.[134] In Lahore four hundred women heard Begum Tassadaq Hussain give a 'lurid description of the Bihar tragedy'. It was Abdus Sattar Niazi who caused most offence with his remark that the 'blood of the Bihar Muslims had not been

[129]Ibid., p. 527.

[130]Three professors at the Sanatan Dharm College likened Ghazanfar Ali Khan to 'a Bhati gate bad character'—a reference to the mafiosi in one of the most vibrant parts of the inner city of Lahore. (*SPPAI*, 2 November 1946, vol. lxviii, no. 44, p. 517.)

[131]*SPPAI*, 16 November 1946, vol. Lxviii, no. 44, pp. 529, 531.

[132]Ibid., pp. 529, 532.

[133]Ibid., p. 532.

[134]*SPPAI*, 23 November 1946, vol. lxviii, no. 45, p. 539.

shed in vain' and 'immeasurably strengthened the cause of Pakistan'.[135] It was a near miracle that the League's call for Bihar day passed off without any violent outburst.

With a cross-section of Muslims angry about the Bihar massacre, the Punjab government on 19 November promulgated the Public Safety Ordinance (PSO). Newspaper bosses were forewarned against publishing 'any violent communal matter' or engaging in 'incitements to vengeance or disorder'.[136] MLNGs from the NWFP en route to Bihar were made to abandon their uniforms and arms before being allowed to proceed.[137] But nothing could deter the Ahrars, now 'even more dissatisfied with Congress', from raising funds in their remaining strongholds in eastern Punjab.[138] They collected a few hundred rupees while the League's relief funds swelled as the Ahrar *bete noire*, Bashiruddin Mahmud, contributed Rs 15,000 and Rs 5000 respectively for Bihar and Bengal.[139] The raising of funds by Muslims was less troubling than Mashriqi's plans to send twenty thousand volunteers to the strife-torn province; Khaksars were attending League meetings and assisting in the collection of funds.[140]

These rare signs of unanimity among Muslims found Punjabi Hindus responding warmly to Madho Rao Golwalkar, the chief organizer of the RSS, who was touring the province on the pretext of getting first-hand information of the situation on the ground. His real aim was to play on Hindu fears of Muslims avenging the Bihar killings in the Punjab. The arrival of ravished Hindu families from the tribal areas, the NWFP and Rawalpindi was grist to his mill. Aggression born of panic, as Golwalkar knew both from conviction and experience, could transform the fortunes of the *sangh*. Speaking in Hindi, the RSS leader derided the two-nation theory. Indians were one nation and India the 'sacred land of the Hindus' who had to 'acquire discipline in order to maintain their ancient culture and civilization'. Congress was blamed for the atrocities in Bengal and Hindus told to 'fight the Muslims without mercy' if they committed aggression in the Punjab. Behind closed doors, Golwalkar told a select group of *adhikaris* to teach volunteers how to use *lathis*, swords and spears. The RSS, he explained, was 'a Hindu military organisation' and could 'meet and crush Muslim aggressors'. But the 'utmost secrecy' was needed so that Muslims, the enemies of the *sangh*, could not gauge the organizational

[135]Ibid., p. 542.

[136]Ibid., p. 545. Enhanced security deposits were demanded from the *Pratap* and the *Eastern Times*. Warnings were issued to the Gurmukhi daily from Lahore, *Daler Khalsa*; *Saadat*, an Urdu weekly from Lyallpur; the *Zamindar*; the daily *Hindi Milap* of Lahore; the Ahrar paper *Azad*; and the Khaksar mouthpiece *Jarida Al-Islah*. (*SPPAI*, 30 November, 7 and 14 December 1946, vol. lxviii, nos 46–8, pp. 562, 564, 588.)

[137]*SPPAI*, 30 November 1946, vol. lxviii, no. 46, p. 551.

[138]Ibid.

[139]*SPPAI*, 7 December 1946, vol. lxviii, no. 47, p. 562.

[140]*SPPAI*, 16 and 23 November 1946, vol. lxviii, nos 44–5, pp. 532, 542.

strength of the RSS. After collecting nearly two lakh rupees, Golwalkar felt confident that the Punjab government would not be able to suppress the movement. Those in control were specifically instructed to avoid making themselves 'conspicuous' so that if 'any leader ... [was] arrested, another volunteer would immediately take his place'.[141]

Unaware of its clandestine activities, Muslims were disturbed by what they did learn about the RSS's strength during the tour of its chief organizer. Some 25,000 RSS volunteers paraded at various ceremonies presided over by Golwalkar. Nearly 40,00 passes were issued to Hindus and Sikhs attending the functions. Preparations were made with 'such secrecy' that large gatherings at Hoshiarpur, Jullundur and Lyallpur were held despite the ban on meetings under Section 144.[142] Once training activities were brought to an end by the PSO, the RSS displayed ingenuity in keeping close tabs on Muslims. Men armed with knives and equipped with bicycles were posted near all the local mosques to collect information regarding any incident of violence and swiftly reporting it to a central intelligence post.[143]

Incapable of such elaborate organization, far less intelligence network, Muslim Leaguers had reason to be worried. In Rawalpindi, Ghulam Mustafa Shah Gilani 'regretted that Hindu preparations for trouble had gone so far that every Hindu house was now a fortress containing weapons, petrol, powdered chilies and, in many instances, fire-arms'. The latter he alleged had been imported from the NWFP with the connivance of the coalition ministry headed by Dr Khan Sahib.[144] RSS activities were 'the subject of strong talk' at League meetings. Muslim papers demanded the banning of the organization.[145] The government did arrest a number of RSS volunteers. But pushing the RSS into the privacy of Hindu homes and temples was wholly in accord with its covert preparations for aggression.

Though Muharram passed off peacefully, the 'apparent calm seem[ed] little more than surface deep'. The 'gulf between Muslims and Hindus' was being made 'wider by the public pronouncements of leaders of both communities'.[146]

[141]SPPAI, 23 November 1946, vol. lxvii, no. 45, p. 544.

[142]Lahore with 7500 had the largest number of RSS volunteers. It was followed by Jullundur (5000), Amritsar (3500), Multan (2000), Hoshiarpur (2000), Lyallpur (2000), Sialkot (1500), Sheikhupura (1200), Jhelum (1000), Rawalpindi (800) and Montgomery (500). Ibid.

[143]SPPAI, 30 November 1946, vol. lxviii, no. 46, p. 562.

[144]Ibid., pp. 550–1. But the pro-Muslim League swing in the NWFP would suggest that if the ministry was indeed arming Punjabi Hindus, not an insubstantial amount was ending up in Muslim hands. Nehru faced an 'undisguisedly unfriendly reception' when he visited the Frontier in the fall of 1946. (SPPAI, 26 October 1946, vol. lxviii, no. 41, p. 501.)

[145]SPPAI, 7 December 1946, vol. lxviii, no. 47, p. 562.

[146]Ibid., p. 563.

On 6 December, HMG's clarification that grouping was the nub of the cabinet mission's proposals was acclaimed by the League and the Sikhs, but condemned by the Congress. There were now 'increasing doubts amongst persons of all communities and parties whether any solution of India's present difficulties [wa]s possible before civil war and chaos intervene[d]'. Many Hindus thought that 'the most likely outcome of the present impasse' was 'communal trouble on an even greater scale than any in the country so far'.[147] An Arya Samajist, Ram Gopal Shastri, was heard repeating the old allegation that the 'Quran preache[d] the murder of those who d[id] not accept it' and, consequently, should be 'done away with'.[148] Religiously informed cultural differences did seem to be interlocking with politics. Fears of violent reprisals inspired Hindus to make public displays of unity. The two provincial Congress ministers, Bhim Sen Sachar and Lehri Singh, attended the Arya Samaj's annual meeting in Lahore in which Badri Das, a prominent member of the RSS, played an active part.[149] In early November the death of Madan Mohan Malaviya had underlined the continuing 'swing over of Hindu political inclination from Congress to the Hindu Maha Sabha'. Nearly all those who lauded Malaviya's contributions to the nationalist cause were Congressmen.[150]

If Punjabi Hindus were at all the exception to the tenor of communitarian politics in the province, they did not disprove the norm. Talk of unity had not generated unity among the Muslims. Nor had the realization of the importance of organization welded Punjabi Muslims into a fortress of communitarian determination. An attempt to dislodge Mamdot and Daultana from the presidency and general secretaryship of the Punjab League by Shaukat Hayat at a conference of district workers in Lahore was narrowly averted. Few disagreed with him that the provincial League leaders had done nothing to oust the coalition ministry, the biggest obstacle to Muslim rule over the Punjab. Firoz Khan Noon gave a helping hand by arguing that the troubles in Bihar were entirely premeditated and carefully executed by Hindus in connivance with the Congress ministry and the Congress Socialist leader J.P. Narain.[151] Supporting the removal of the existing leadership of the League, Niazi called for a 'greater combination of religion and politics'. This was impossible under Mamdot's uninspiring leadership. There were demands for an agitation against the ministry and a tit for tat for the unhappy events in Bihar. Iftikharuddin

[147]*SPPAI*, 14 December 1946, vol. lxviii, no. 48, p. 569.

[148]The district magistrate of Lahore prohibited Shastri from making public utterances under Section 4 of the PSO. (Ibid., p. 570.)

[149]*SPPAI*, 7 December 1946, vol. lxviii, no. 47, p. 562.

[150]*SPPAI*, 23 November 1946, vol. lxviii, no. 45, p. 541.

[151]A *persona non grata* among Muslims, Narain was held responsible for stirring up anti-Muslim feelings in Bihar. His subsequent speeches made him 'even more unpopular' and he was 'not infrequently ... dubbed Muslim Enemy Number One'. (*SPPAI*, 4 January 1947, vol. lxix, no. 1, p. 4.)

intervened with his 'usual advocacy of tolerance and communal harmony until the matter was scotched by Sadiq Hussain Quereshi and Mamdot jointly asserting that 'retaliatory action was not Mr Jinnah's wish'. While the scions of the Hayat and Noon clans failed to prove that they would be better leaders than Mamdot and Daultana, the Punjab League was no closer to deciding what to do next.[152]

Waiting for something to turn up from somewhere was not atypical of Punjabi Leaguers. Nor were their internal schisms at a crucial moment in history. An all-pervasive sense of Muslimness did not make them any more capable of agreeing on the precise nexus between religiously informed cultural differences and the politics of communitarian identity. If this was true for Muslims belonging to the main Muslim party in India at the time, those in rival groupings made certain that the cultural identity of Muslims was not a seamless web or even cut out of the same political fabric. This was made plain by the leaders of the Jamiat-ul-Ulema-i-Hind who never desisted from 'making personal attacks on Mr Jinnah and praising themselves'.[153] On the occasion of Id, League and non-League Muslims said their prayers in different mosques. But by the turn of the new year, 'nationalist Muslim distress' was increasingly in evidence. The Ahrars resented being sidelined by the Congress. Together with the Jamiat-ul-Ulema-i-Hind they supported the grouping scheme and the right of provinces to opt out of the union after the drafting of the constitution. Unless Congress changed its stance on the grouping scheme, the Ahrars feared, 'nationalist Muslims w[ould] be forced to retire from politics'.[154] Yet they continued 'condemn[ing] ... the Muslim Leaguers as irreligious'.[155] Ataullah Shah Bukhari had not shifted an inch from considering 'Mr Jinnah as the single biggest obstacle in the way of India's freedom'.[156] When religiously informed cultural differences were so hotly contested from within, the politics of Muslims were scarcely capable of unifying the community in anything but a superficial and ephemeral manner.

The old and tired portrait of the Punjab in the grips of an all-pervasive communitarian fever, exclusively pitting Hindu against Muslim and Muslim against Sikh, is accurate only to a point. To fully ascertain the significance of religion or, more aptly, the politics of faith in the texturing of social violence, there can be no escaping the nuance that comes of detail. A tragedy, so long in the making, acquired an altogether different dimension once the British formally announced their intention to quit India. Investigating the responses of communities living at close quarters to a religiously informed separation conveys both the meaning and the pain that attended the dismemberment of the Punjab.

[152]SPPAI, 21 December 1946, vol. lxviii, no. 49, p. 586.
[153]SPPAI, 26 October 1946, vol. lxviii, no. 41, p. 506.
[154]SPPAI, 4 January 1947, vol. lxix, no. 1, p. 2.
[155]SPPAI, 9 November 1946, vol. lxviii, no. 43, p. 526.
[156]SPPAI, 21 December 1946, vol. lxviii, no. 49, p. 587.

ING AT CLOSE QUARTERS: THE PUNJAB PARTITIONED!

Not since its conquest and commodification in the late eighteenth and nineteenth centuries was space more at stake in the subcontinent than in the dying moments of the raj. The redesigning of the spatial landscape of India by the British, the Congress and the Muslim League provoked pitched battles for social space in the localities that were fought mainly, but not exclusively, along lines of religious community. Violence intensified communitarian feelings, but was rarely perpetrated by collectivities as a whole. Individuals, even when grouped in armed militias, could settle personal scores in the process of promoting and protecting members of their community. By keeping in view the balance between the individual and the community, far more penetrating insights can be gained into the human dimension of social violence than overarching categories like Muslim, Hindu and Sikh. It was precisely because collective imaginings had to be lived out individually even as they were shared jointly that the violence of 1947 assumed the tragic proportions that it did, scarring memories for generations to come. In emphasizing the individual as victim, historians and anthropologists have given insufficient attention to individuals as perpetrators. Barbarity attributed to entire communities effaces the role of individuals, giving greater legitimacy to the social violence that accompanied the partition of the Punjab than is warranted by the evidence.[157]

Questioning the homogeneous and consensual nature of collective motivations and actions does not entail invoking images of a disorderly rabble or denying the purposefulness of those perpetrating violence.[158] But it is worth considering why so many members of a community choose not to participate

[157]Both Veena Das and Gyanendra Pandey commit the fallacy of not deconstructing the 'community' in their accounts of partition violence. Consequently, they fail to pinpoint the pain of violence and dislocation experienced by both individuals and communities during the holocaust of 1947. (See Veena Das, *Critical Events: An Anthropological Perspective on Contemporary India*, Delhi: Oxford University Press, 1996, chapter three and Gyanendra Pandey, 'Prose of Otherness', in David Arnold and David Hardiman (eds), *Subaltern Studies VIII: Essays in Honour of Ranajit Guha*, Delhi: Oxford University Press, 1994.)

[158]Neither the 'rites of violence' nor a moral economy approach—influential in the field of European history—is helpful in explaining the mass social upheavals of 1947. (See Natalie Zemon Davis, 'The Rites of Violence: Religious Riots in Sixteenth-Century France', *Past and Present*, 39, May 1973, 51–91 and E.P. Thompson, 'The Moral Economy of the English Crowd in the Eighteenth Century', *Past and Present*, 50, February 1971, 76–126.) Suzanne Desan offers an insightful critique of both Davis and Thompson in her 'Crowds, Community and Ritual', in Lynn Hunt (ed.), *The New Cultural History*, Berkeley: University of California Press, 1989, 47–71. For similar reservations, see Stanley R. Tambiah, *Leveling Crowds: Ethnonationalist Conflicts and Collective Violence in South Asia*, Chicago: Chicago University Press, 1996, chapter eleven.

in violence against religiously demarcated rivals, often going against the grain of a supposed consensus by protecting the victims. The communitarian fog hovering over collective violence also dissipates the moment one considers how the arming of sections of the populace, followed by acts of aggression, can dramatically alter the balance of power between individuals and communities in localities constituting the focal point of the troubles.

The localized and personalized nature of the battles for social space in a province facing an impending division on the basis of religious enumeration shaped the frequency, intensity and thrust of the violence in the Punjab. Whatever the strides made by the RSS and the MLNG to militarize civilians in the districts, there were large segments of an unarmed society whose only implements of self-defence was the kitchenware in individual households. What the Second World War did for paramilitary organizations, the arming of the populace with *lathis*, knives, swords and acid did for the texturing of social violence, perpetrated as well as suffered. Without denying the communitarian dimension of the killings, it is important not to lose sight of the role played by human agency, jointly and severally. Nor can the possibility of personalized violence being passed off as 'communal', be discounted simply because of the presumed convenience of the term in both colonial and nationalist discourse.

For someone who lived through the social convulsions of 1947 with an ear to the ground, the Urdu short story writer Saadat Hasan Manto in 'Parhiya Kalima', or recite the *kalima*, gives a chilling account of a Hindu woman killing off her Hindu lover and acquiring a Muslim one on the condition that he help her dispense with the dead body. Taking advantage of the disturbed conditions and breaking the curfew, the new paramour threw the corpse in a garbage dump outside a mosque. That night the mosque was burned down by Hindus and the body was never found. After surviving a murderous assault by the woman, who moves on to a new lover, the Muslim ends up stabbing his replacement to death. This, as he explains in the story, had nothing whatsoever to do with 'Pakistan'. True, his victim was Hindu and he had also killed a few others in the past. But *la illah illa Allah*, he tells the Muslim policemen, this was at best a crime of passion and at worst an act of self-defence. What it could not be described as was 'communal violence'.[159]

Restoring perspective on the murderous hatred along lines of religious community requires probing the nexus between individual and collective identities, contested sovereignties and expectations of independent citizenship. Even as mounting violence saw religiously informed identities acquiring unprecedented significance, considerable ambivalence surrounded political attitudes within communities when it came to defining the territorial basis

---

[159]Saadat Hasan Manto, 'Parhiya Kalima', in *Manto Nama*, Lahore: Sang-e-Meel, 1990, pp. 259–67. For an English translation, see 'Nothing but the Truth', in Hamid Jalal, *Black Milk*, Lahore: Alkitab, 1956; reprinted Lahore: Sang-e-Meel, 1997.

of sovereignty and the rights of citizenship claimed on their behalf. If the leaders were at all able to lead, followers were not always willing to follow blindly. The vision of religiously defined communities banding together in absolute unison explodes in the face of harsh criticisms of the provincial and all-India leadership, as well as anger and horror at the bankruptcy and collapse of their political will. Punjabis may have been especially unwilling to make concessions to rival communities, but the vast majority were equally averse to a partition of the province on purely religious lines. The imposition of an all-India solution on the Punjab and the responses it generated in a society pulverized by colonial constructions is a tragic tale of woe. No one put it more poignantly than Talukchand Mahroom, the Punjabi Hindu poet of Urdu who in March 1947 bemoaned the destruction of a regional ethos of which he had once been proud:

Tearing the clothing off human superiority
This frenzied dance in the joy of nudity is destructive
You have shown such barbarity in your achievements
Reducing to dust the honour of humanity
From the high heavens the call will come night and day
Alas Punjab, pity on you and your culture![160]

'Alas Punjab!'—Waris Shah from the Grave[161]

Between Talukchand Mahroom's lament and Amrita Pritam's moving invocation to the author of the great Punjabi folk-tale *Heer-Ranjha* lies a considerable stretch of history waiting to be rescued from oblivion. It is to the credit of poets like Mahroom and Pritam and storytellers like Manto that individual pain at the moment of partition was not lost sight of in the

[160]*Admiyat ke libas-i-bartari ko phaar kar*
Shauq-i-Uryani mein ye raqs-i-janoon hey fitna gar
Too ne apni bartari ke dekhae wo hunur
Khak mein jin sey mili tauqir-i-insan sar basar
Asmanon sey sada aiye ghi ye sham-o-sehr
Heif ah Punjab, tuj pey aur teri tehzib pey.

آدمیت کے لباس برتری کو پھاڑ کر

شوقِ عریانی میں یہ رقصِ جنوں ہے فتنہ گر

تو نے اپنی برتت کے دکھائے وہ ہنر

خاک میں جن سے ملی توقیر انساں سر بسر

آسمانوں سے سدا آئے گی یہ شام و سحر

حیف اے پنجاب تجھ پر اور تیری تنذیب پر۔

(In Abbas, *Urdu Mein Qaumi Shairi*, pp. 205–6.)
[161]Adapted from Amrita Pritam's Punjabi poem 'Aaj Akhan Waris Shah Noon' (invocation to Waris Shah). See below.

recountings of a human tragedy attributed solely to religion. Escaping the exclusionary trapdoor of collective memories, Manto's characters resoundingly defy the straitjacketing of religious categories. Capable of being at the same time human and beastly, these were men and women for whom the politics of religious identity were not necessarily more important than personal relationships cutting across religious denominations. Celebrated in literary circles, Manto's social intuition has yet to inform historians searching for 'communal' trails to unknown ghosts in the killing plains of the Punjab.

Those witnessing the events realized that individuals, operating alone or in civilian militias, not communities as a whole posed a greater threat to peace in the Punjab. There was a danger of 'stranger elements' from disturbed areas avenging their losses.[162] Yet refugees fleeing strife-torn areas along the Rawalpindi–Hazara border or UP and Bihar were not the main hazard. What worried colonial officials most was the vastly expanded scale of activity by armed militias. Of these the RSS was the best organized with the MLNG in second place by virtue of the Sikhs temporarily defaulting. Imposition of the PSO had brought paramilitary activity to a virtual standstill. Both the RSS and the MLNG tried 'maintain[ing] their existing strength by holding many private meetings in houses and places of worship'.[163] Making domestic and sacred space the loci of public exertions further underlines the inseparability of spiritual and material concerns in the contest for dominance in the Punjab. It is no wonder that the violence which marked the failure to find a political accommodation of religiously informed cultural differences took such a heavy toll of not just property and the men defending it but also of countless women, children and the aged—those inhabitants of domestic space who had yet to find a voice in the predominantly male public sphere that was piloting the path to independent citizenship. It was amidst a drastic reordering of the balance between public and private that individuals acting in the name of religious communities turned the final lunge towards freedom into a bloodbath of cataclysmic proportions.

Wanting an end to the stalemate over the constituent assembly, moderate opinion in the Punjab had welcomed Congress's veiled acceptance of HMG's December 6 statement on grouping. The *Tribune* led the Punjabi Hindu attack against the AICC's decision. Sikhs also tended to see it as a 'betrayal' but were too absorbed in internal power struggles to give any firm indication of their future policy. Various schemes for dividing the Punjab were being discussed in Akali circles. With Jinnah and the League unwilling to accept Congress's apparent change of tune on the grouping scheme, the deadlock became deadlier. The League seemed intent on boycotting the process of constitution making. In an ill-judged decision, the Punjab ministry banned the MLNG and the RSS under

---

[162]*SPPAI*, 4 January 1947, vol. lxix, no. 1, p. 3.
[163]*SPPAI*, 11 January 1947, vol. lxix, no. 2, p. 17.

Section 16 of the Criminal Law (Amendment) Act. Popular reactions gave the first real indication of the strength of Muslim support for the League's bid to dislodge the ministry. Couched in the language of civil liberties, this was an effort by the Punjab League in which the converging of popular sentiments and Muslim politics was counterbalanced by debilitating organizational weaknesses. While the RSS succumbed to the order without a whimper, League leaders resisted police attempts at searching the premises of the MLNG and were arrested. For a party with a tradition of sitting it out of jails during civil disobedience movements, this signified a change of temperament.

Muslims were pleased to see their leaders finally willing to rough it out in colonial jails.[164] Leaguers delighted in defying the PSO, which led to more arrests, including fifteen members of the assembly. Muslim shopkeepers in the districts observed a *hartal;* processions were taken out despite the ban.[165] Stung by the League's charge that the move was an attack on the party, the ministry released the arrested leaders before withdrawing the ban within ninety-six hours. Encouraged by the government's lack of resolve, Leaguers now demanded retraction of the PSO. In the ensuing agitation the government rearrested the leaders and ignored the protestors. With the arrest of the leaders the agitational baton went into the hands of students and persons of no known political consequence. 'Women in some places' were 'playing a not inconsiderable part'. Although 'the response ... to the agitation by Muslims [wa]s by no means wholehearted', it 'create[d] a most troublesome situation' which demanded 'the very closest attention'.[166]

With the leaders in jail, the campaign became 'spontaneous and to a great extent haphazard'. Lahore was the nerve centre, but not a single district remained unscathed. Looking to spring back into action, the Khaksars offered a helping hand. Although rebuffed, they participated in the civil disobedience campaign in Lahore, Sialkot and Montgomery. But the stabbing of a Khaksar by a Muslim Leaguer in Rawalpindi showed that the blood of communities was not necessarily thicker than water. This was why Punjabi Hindus were 'more pleased than alarmed' by a struggle which would sooner exhaust the League than facilitate the formation of its government.[167] A gubernatorial communique to the viceroy summed up the more important fall-out of the agitation. Jenkins feared that 'the League ha[d] made it very difficult for themselves to form a Government' and 'greatly advanced the case for the partition of the Punjab'.[168]

[164]Those arrested included Mamdot, Daultana, Shaukat Hayat, Firoz Khan Noon and Begum Shah Nawaz.
[165]*SPPAI,* 26 January 1947, vol. lxix, no. 4, p. 39.
[166]*SPPAI,* 1 February 1947, vol. lxix, no. 5, pp. 47–9.
[167]*SPPAI,* 8 February 1947, vol. lxix, no. 6, pp. 57–60.
[168]Jenkins to Wavell, 3 February 1947, *TP,* ix, p. 610. For corroborating evidence on the sharpness of the non-Muslim response to the agitation, see Baldev Singh to Wavell, 6 February 1947, ibid., pp. 626–7.

The categorical refusal of non-Muslims to accept a League ministry or 'Pakistan' did not make the partition of the province any more acceptable to the vast majority of Punjabis. As even Jenkins admitted, it was 'possible that the League w[ould] in the end be more conciliatory to other communities'. He hit the bull's-eye consecutively on three points. First, in lamenting that the Muslim League 'as a party ... [was] very sadly lacking in brains and political sense'.[169] Second, in noting that while a compromise was the only solution, everything rested on an acceptable outcome of the controversies at the centre. And third, and most important, in recording that nobody in the Punjab League had grasped that they were 'wantonly throwing away [the] certainty of Muslim Leadership in a United Punjab for uncertain advantages of a partition which Sikhs w[ould] gradually now demand'.[170]

So it was perhaps just as well that most of the top leadership of the Punjab League had been tossed into jail. But leaving matters in the hands of intermediaries, more focused on localized and personalized battles over social space, could redound badly on the League's purposes at the provincial and the all-India levels. Without an organizational structure beyond the locality or the sub-locality where Leaguers were situated, the strength of popular Muslim reactions to the agitation and the potential for violence in defence of public or private spaces depended on the context of the flare-up. Individual acts of violence, both metaphoric and real, had deeper shades than those of the collectivities they represented. Nevertheless, they have informed the construction of shared memories to such an extent as to be forgotten in the 'communal' haze hovering over the violence of 1947. An inability to identify the perpetrators of violence does not make the individual any less constitutive, both as agent and victim, of the holocaust that accompanied Britain's dismantling of its raj. Historians may be less well equipped than creative writers to recreate the individual dimensions of the breakdown of social order. But this does not give them license to presume that violence in the cause of the community was devoid of individual direction and intent.

The League's agitation in the districts is a good testing ground for these observations. Official and non-official Muslims sympathized with the demonstrators. These consisted mainly of local politicians, their women kith and kin and a range of Muslims drawn from the lower social strata. Abuses hurled at Khizar Hayat Tiwana and vague cries of 'Pakistan' were the buzz-words of the agitation. There were a few deaths once the agitators took to disrupting passenger trains. A formal *hartal* on 10 February resulted in *tongawallas*, including non-Muslims, suffering the indignity of having their faces blackened for daring to work. Assertions of sovereignty were manifest in a short-lived hoisting of the League flag instead of the Union Jack over the Lahore

[169]Ibid.
[170]Jenkins to Pethick-Lawrence, 8 February 1947, ibid., p. 655.

High Court. The largest meeting was in Lahore where fifty thousand heard Mustafa Shah Gilani describe the agitation as an attempt to restore civil liberties. But few, least of all the students, had any doubt that the sole purpose was the overthrow of the ministry.[171] If not for the imposition of press censorship on news relating to the agitation, Leaguers might have created more mayhem than they did. The induction of *pirs* and *ulema* to persuade villagers that 'their religion [wa]s involved' bolstered the League's cause in the western districts. Fearful of their followers running amok, all-India leaders like Khwajah Nazimuddin and Ghazanfar Ali Khan condemned Muslims interfering with the running of trains and managed to put an end to this aspect of the agitation. They were less successful in inculcating discipline among Muslim crowds. The use of tear gas and *lathi* charge by the police led to a distinct hardening of attitudes among Muslim youth against government officials.[172]

This was the backdrop to Clement Attlee's statement of 20 February announcing Britain's decision to quit India no later than June 1948. Hints that power might be devolved to multiple centres excited Muslim ambitions in the majority provinces to Jinnah's and the League's chagrin. If the declaration of British intent to depart, come what may, raised the spectre of Muslim-majority provincialism beyond the pale of 'Pakistan', panic among non-Muslims posed the more immediate threat to the League's purposes. The League's agitation had seen the Panthic Board discussing a Hindu–Sikh province in districts where Muslims were in a minority. A subcommittee consisting of Baldev Singh and Tara Singh was authorised to draw up a proposal for submission to the minorities advisory committee of the constituent assembly.[173]

There were dim hopes that if push came to shove, 'Sikhs might see an opportunity of offering support' to a League ministry in exchange for solid constitutional guarantees.[174] A League ministry, abhorrent to non-Muslims, would be forced to come to an understanding with at least a section of Sikh members of the assembly. An unimaginative and bigoted provincial press, a revived Hindu Mahasabha and continued activities by paramilitary organizations allowed no room for cool reflection. This proved disastrous for the Sikhs. Sharing a common linguistic identity with Punjabi Hindus and Muslims, they could make no viable claim to any part of the Punjab on population proportions. Neither a partitioned Punjab nor a separate state presented an acceptable resolution of the Sikh dilemma. If anything, it smashed any hope of their religiously informed cultural identity cohering neatly with any claim to territorial sovereignty. All the major Sikh shrines—Panja Sahib in Hassanabdal, Nankana Sahib, Dera Sahib and the tomb of Maharaja Ranjit Singh—were in Muslim-majority districts. A partitioned Punjab would leave

---

[171]*SPPAI*, 15 February 1947, vol. lxix, no. 7, pp. 65–8.
[172]*SPPAI*, 22 February 1947, vol. lxix, no. 8, p. 86.
[173]*SPPAI*, 8 February 1947, vol. lxix, no. 6, p. 59.
[174]Pethick-Lawrence to Wavell, 31 January 1947, *TP*, xix, p. 584.

Sikhs straddling the frontiers of states dominated either by Muslims or Hindus.

Instead of trying to reconcile their sense of identity with claims of sovereignty and citizenship rights, Sikh leaders made gallantry the better part of valour. Tara Singh was working to revive the Akal Fauj.[175] So was Giani Kartar Singh, the League's best bet for settling matters with the Sikhs. Elected president of the Akali Dal after tortuous negotiations, Giani was expected to restrain himself 'from abandoning his connection with the Congress and aligning ... with the Muslim League'. Despite strong talk of Sikhs resisting 'Pakistan', these 'sentiments [we]re not universally held'. Many Sikhs still prefered to 'rely on their own strength and organisation'.[176] Some Muslims tried placating the Sikhs. In Amritsar, a letter of apology was sent to Tara Singh after Muslims blackened the faces of some Sikh *tongawallas*.[177]

More than tact was now needed to restore goodwill between Muslim and Sikh politicians. Leaguers and Congressmen had welcomed HMG's statement, recognizing that if the two major parties refused to 'buckle down and cooperate, civil war and chaos w[ould] inevitably result'.[178] At a meeting of the Shiromani Akali Dal in Lahore, Giani Kartar Singh summed up the Sikh response to the British statement. It gave them 'nothing'. It was 'high time' they 'consolidate[d] their position and ... ma[d]e a real and emphatic demand for their own homeland'. Tara Singh told audiences that the 'latest British decision was very likely to result in civil war'. The only honourable thing for Britain was to 'return the Punjab to the Sikhs, from whom they had received it on trust'.[179] Using the occasion of religious fairs and annual processions, Sikh leaders made 'hysterical appeals' against 'Pakistan' and swore to take the Punjab by force.[180]

There was no easing of tensions when on 26 February 1947 the Punjab League called off its agitation after coming to an agreement with the government. Under the terms, the ban on meetings was lifted but retained on processions. The PSO was to be replaced by a safety act enacted by the Punjab assembly at its next session; all prisoners except those standing trial for acts of violence were released. Leaguers considered this a 'major victory'. Muslim support had remained steadfast in the closing days of the campaign. Demonstrations on 24 February marking one month of the agitation had 'proved a trying day for the authorities' in many headquarter towns. Leading the Muslim charge was the city of Lahore. After a protest outside the district courts and the Punjab secretariat on the lower Mall, a large meeting was held in the day and a procession estimated at hundred thousand came out in the evening. In the Civil Lines area of Amritsar there was violence and one victim

[175]*SPPAI*, 22 February 1947, vol. lxix, no. 8, p. 85.
[176]*SPPAI*, 4 January 1947, vol. lxix, no. 1, pp. 3–4.
[177]*SPPAI*, 22 February 1947, vol. lxix, no. 8, p. 86.
[178]*SPPAI*, 1 March 1947, vol. lxix, no. 9 p. 91.
[179]Ibid., pp. 92–3.
[180]*SPPAI*, 8 March 1947, vol. lxix, no. 10, p. 103.

of police firing. People in Jullundur showed contempt for authority by greeting the police with brickbats, leaving thirty injured. The apocalypse of a populace rising in protest was everywhere in evidence. At a railway crossing in Ludhiana, a crowd holding up the Bombay Express dispersed only after hails of tear gas shells. Police in Ambala opened fire on a procession of four thousand but was 'pushed ... back'. Some eighteen rounds were fired, injuring six of whom one man and woman died later.[181]

Escalating violence led to the coalition ministry's understanding with the League but made its continuation in office impossible. Specially orchestrated victory celebrations on 2 March saw crowds outside Mochi Gate in the old city of Lahore reaching two hundred thousand, including five hundred uniformed members of the League's national guard. Care had been taken to ensure the presence of a representative of the scheduled castes and also of Mazhabi Sikhs.[182] Late at night the same day, the Punjab premier, a virtual hostage of Muslim League pressure, tendered his resignation. More a victim of circumstance than of conscience, Khizar's abject surrender signalled a general collapse of political will both at the provincial and the all-India levels. Instead of taking stock of the situation, Leaguers were more concerned about the modalities of forming a government than negotiating a power-sharing arrangement. Undiluted Muslim rule over a united Punjab was attainable neither by conquest nor consent. Congressmen lost no time recovering from their initial shock at the resignation to prevent the formation of a government by any single community. On 3 March a meeting organized by the Lahore District Congress Committee attracted an audience of one hundred thousand. The presence of Pratap Singh Kairon and Giani Kartar Singh suggested the cementing of the Sikh and Congress alliance. Of greater consequence was the emergence of a joint front of the Sikhs and the Mahasabha. Even before the outbreaks of violence on March 4, the Mahasabha was following 'a more militant and active policy' by organizing a Hindustan National Guard in both the rural and the urban areas. Wealthy Hindus were being approached for donations to equip regiments of the Akal Fauj which became allied to the RSS once Tara Singh 'in the national interest' declared that the 'two bodies must now be considered as one'.[183]

At 5.30 p.m. on 3 March 1947, the anti-Pakistan Council of Action consisting of Congress and Akali leaders held a meeting in Kapurthala House in Lahore and resolved to resist the League with all the forces they could muster. Tara Singh was elected to lead the campaign to bury 'Pakistan'. Later in the evening, Tara Singh, flanked by the ex-Congress minister Bhim Sen Sachar and other Akalis, brandished a sword outside the provincial assembly and pronounced that the Punjab would now have Sikh rule. Whoever wanted 'Pakistan' was

[181]*SPPAI*, 1 March 1947, vol. lxix, no. 9, pp. 91, 93.
[182]*SPPAI*, 8 March 1947, vol. lxix, no. 10, p. 104.
[183]Ibid., p. 103.

welcome to the *qabristan* or the graveyard. Tara Singh's speech in the grounds of Kapurthala House was even more rabid. Not a man to weigh his words and phrases in the best of times, the Akali leader was excited beyond measure when he declaimed: 'O Hindus and Sikhs! Be ready for self-destruction like the Japanese and the Nazis ... The Muslims snatched the kingdom from the Hindus, and the Sikhs grabbed it from the hands of the Muslims, and the Sikhs ruled over the Muslims with their might and the Sikhs shall even now rule over them'.[184]

'Go and finish off the Muslim League,' he shrieked, 'I have sounded the bugle.' No sooner had Tara Singh made his fateful speech that Sikh youth in Amritsar went on a murderous rampage against Muslims, shouting 'whoever wants Pakistan will get the graveyard'.[185] Reckless speech-making and newspaper headlines declaring a 'War Against Pakistan', 'pitchforked the Sikhs and Hindus into embarking on an even more dangerous experiment in lawlessness than the one recently concluded'.[186]

Once the powder magazine had been ignited, the province was set ablaze with hatred. Multan, Rawalpindi, Amritsar and Lahore were the worst affected. Though 'not prominent' in the earlier stages of the disturbances, Muslims soon came to 'notice for retaliating or starting trouble in rural areas'. In what was described as 'spontaneous' action, villages near Multan and Rawalpindi displayed a keen 'determination to give ... brutal expression' to 'communal hatred'. There were heavy casualties in Multan and considerable damage to property. On 6 March there was fighting and arson in Rawalpindi, enveloping its rural environs and extending to Campbellpur, Murree, Taxila and places like Attock in the proximity of the Hazara district of the NWFP. In Amritsar a twenty-four-hour curfew had to be imposed for two whole days. On the third day the curfew was lifted for a few hours; though 'chaos [wa]s ... prevented', communitarian feelings showed no signs of improving. Lahore also was placed under curfew after cases of stabbings, looting and arson on 'a widespread and formidable scale'.[187]

For all the talk of struggle and civil war, outbreaks of violence stunned Punjabis. Non-Muslims were the main victims as even Muslim Leaguers

[184]Gopal Das Khosla, *Stern Reckoning: A Survey of the Events Leading up to and Following the Partition of India*, reprint, Delhi: Oxford University Press, 1989, p. 100.
[185]Mirza, *Karavan-i-Ahrar*, viii, pp. 32–6. Also see Khosla, *Stern Reckoning*, pp. 99–100 which underlines the importance of social space in attacks on non-Muslims by bands of armed Muslims backed by the MLNG. While citing the work in the analysis below, it is worth noting that although Kholsa claims to have authored a historical narrative 'as near the truth as is possible', he has nothing to say about the killings of Muslims in eastern Punjab. His is a history in which Muslims were perpetrators; non-Muslims the victims.
[186]*SPPAI*, 8 March 1947, vol. lxix, no. 10, pp. 103, 105.
[187]Ibid., pp. 105–6.

admitted.[188] To keep up appearances, an all-parties peace committee was constituted which, among others, included Tara Singh and Giani Kartar Singh. Neither the Congress nor the Sikhs were 'genuinely desirous of seeing the communal situation improve until some permanent decision [wa]s reached regarding the future constitution of the Punjab'. In a statement on 8 March, Sikh and Hindu leaders, including three former ministers, announced that they would 'under no circumstance ... give the slightest assurance of support to the Muslim League' in forming a ministry since they were 'opposed to Pakistan in any shape or form'.[189]

If this was the overture, the All-India Congress Working Committee provided the finale on the same day by formally demanding the partition of the Punjab. Most Hindus and Sikhs predictably hailed the decision. Muslims created history by being unanimous in condemning the resolution which did more to 'widen ... the cleavage between the communities' than the violence itself. Neither Baldev Singh nor Nehru, who had rushed to the Punjab, attempted to reconcile the communities. Leaguers from outside the province concentrated wholly on Muslims. The agitation against the ministry and the impending division of the province had gone a 'long way to consolidate unity amongst Muslims'. By the same token, brutal attacks on Hindus and Sikhs by bands of Muslim roughs had 'brought the two minority communities very close together'. Joint meetings of Hindus and Sikhs were by now common. It was evident that the Mahasabha was leading the Congress high command from the front. Audiences at its meetings vastly outnumbered those at Congress gatherings.[190]

Past masters at shooting from the hip, Sikh leaders made the most of the annual Hola Mohalla fair at Anandpur Sahib in Hoshiarpur, making speeches of 'an extremely violent and exciting nature'. They detailed the terrible fate awaiting their co-religionists in a Muslim homeland: prohibitions on *jhatka* meat; Persianized Urdu, if not Persian, as the official language; and taxes heaped on Sikhs while Muslim peasants would be relieved of the burden. Canal irrigation had not been extended to the Doaba, where Sikhs held substantial landholdings, allegedly because a Muslim had been premier of the Punjab. Now that Tara Singh had given the lead, it was the duty of Sikhs to 'depend on their swords to attain their rights'. They had to 'stake their lives to prevent Pakistan' and 'establish Sikh rule in the Punjab'. Every Sikh family was asked to give at least one son to the *panth*. Alternatively, Sikhs wanted the British to restore them as sovereigns of the Punjab. Sikh pilgrims eagerly imbibed the rhetoric, an ominous development given the secret instructions issued to Akal regiments to expand their sphere of activities.[191] On 11 March,

---

[188]See Liaquat Ali Khan to Mountbatten, 15 April 1947, *TP*, x, p. 256 and Khosla, *Stern Reckoning*, pp. 104–16.

[189]Ibid., pp. 101–2.

[190]*SPPAI*, 15 March 1947, vol. lxix, no. 11, pp. 113–14.

[191]Ibid., pp. 114–15.

Tara Singh in Lahore refused to consider any understanding with the League unless the disturbances ceased. Although a member of the interim government, Baldev Singh agreed that there could be 'no compromise with a brute Muslim religious majority'. Co-operation with the League was possible only if it 'gave up its present theories'. He believed Sikhs should 'not try and come to a settlement with the local Muslims'; the matter was now of an all-India importance which 'Mr Jinnah would himself have to take up'.[192]

The Punjab League's council of action was 'much exercised by the situation'. It recognized that 'the recent bloodshed solve[d] none of the problems facing the Punjab'. As 'the two communities which count[ed] in provincial matters', Muslims had to come to terms with the Sikhs. They were 'disappointed' that this view was not shared by the Sikhs. Firoz Khan Noon intimated that the League would be willing to meet the Sikhs half way. As evidence of their bona fides, Leaguers offered Sikhs five of the positions in a coalition ministry of eleven. With Sikhs supporting a partition of the Punjab, Leaguers felt they could not make 'further overtures on a Provincial level'. Educated Muslims concurred that the Sikh leadership had 'no desire to come to a peaceful settlement'. They would think otherwise only if Tara Singh made known 'Sikh good intentions ... [with] a definite offer'. Meanwhile, Shaukat Hayat was asking district Leagues to prepare for the possibility of war.[193]

Congress's decision could not have had more devastating effects. Abandoning the unity of India and its secular creed, it was bidding for power at the centre in as exclusionary a vein as those ritually damned 'communalists'. Its Muslim supporters were dismayed. Nasrullah Khan, general secretary of the All-India Majlis-i-Ahrar, publicly condemned the decision. Another diehard anti-imperialist, Shorish Kashmiri, rued that the Congress had made the position of nationalist Muslims untenable. Ahrar opposition to the partition of the Punjab had 'crystallised' to such an extent that on being approached by Leaguers they agreed to 'work for Muslim solidarity by announcing their support for the setting up of Pakistan'. Khaksars also thought their position would be 'seriously endangered should the Punjab be divided'.[194] If not for his outrageous insolence, Mashriqi, an unlikely wizard of oz might have made a more definitive mark on the unfolding politics of Muslim identity. By late March 1947, many Khaksars were fed up of with the 'bankruptcy of Khaksar' policy and the 'ineptitude of Allama Mashriqi'. In Rawalpindi, where the Khaksar movement had been strong, Mashriqi was 'considered a mad man'. Not to let events sideline him so easily, Mashriqi invited all nationalist Muslim organizations except the Ahrars to a conference in Delhi in early April. These were pipe dreams with a direction. There were 'suspicions' that these 'preparations [we]re merely a "front"'and

[192]Ibid., p. 115.
[193]Ibid., pp. 115-16.
[194]Ibid., p. 116.

Mashriqi was 'inclining towards an understanding with the Muslim League'. It was plain to see that the Khaksars and the Ahrars were 'attempting to make a bargain with the Muslim League'.[195]

The Muslim League was in no mood for bargains with men who mattered little in the formal arenas of politics. By calling for a partition of the Punjab, and also Bengal, the Congress high command had sounded its own death-knell in Muslim politics in the two provinces. Maulana Azad has attributed the decision to Sardar Vallabhbhai Patel's 'irritation and injured vanity' at being vetoed by the League's finance minister in the interim government, Liaquat Ali Khan.[196] But Muslims who supported the Congress looked to Nehru—the incarnation of the secular nationalist—not Patel, a mouthpiece of the Mahasabha and the RSS. Whatever their disagreements with the Congress, anti-imperialist Muslims of both the Ahrar and Jamiat-ul-Hind variety, and individuals like Iftikharuddin and Saifuddin Kitchlew, had kept the nationalist tricolour afloat in the Punjab.[197] The breakaway of the Ahrars was accompanied by a telling discourse on Congress's dismal failure to accommodate Muslims under its political umbrella. Together with Kitchlew's last-ditch attempts to keep Muslims within the Congress's purview, the Ahrar reaction to its demand for a partition of the Punjab conveys the shock of 'nationalist' Muslims at the blatant letdown.

If there had been doubts about its inclusionary nationalism in the past, there were none whatsoever now. Within a week of the Congress's resolution, the Jamiat-ul-Ulema-i-Hind at Delhi denounced the proposal to partition the Punjab. On 23 March the working committee of the All-India Majlis-i-Ahrar presided over by Ataullah Shah Bukhari met in Lahore. After discussing the developments for twenty-six hours, the committee decided to sever links with the Congress pending the approval of the general council. Hindu and Sikh intrigues to deny Muslims their rightful share of power were deplored and Congress trashed for its volte face on the principles of a single nation by adopting the Mahasabha's demand for a partition of the Punjab.[198] Speakers were 'scathing' in their 'criticism of Congress'; it had finally 'shown its communal hoof' by 'disregard[ing] the sufferings of the Nationalist Muslims'. Apart from

---

[195]*SPPAI*, 29 March and 5 April 1947, vol. lxix, nos.13, 14, pp. 143, 158.

[196]Maulana Abul Kalam Azad, *India Wins Freedom: The Complete Version*, Madras: Orient Longman, 1988, p. 225. The first version was also published by the same press in 1959.

[197]Once Iftikharuddin jumped the fence, Kitchlew was one of the few remaining Muslims in the Congress. Symbolizing Congress's claims to represent Indians, irrespective of religious denomination, he was elected president of the provincial wing in May 1946. After surviving a no-confidence motion brought against him by the Satyapal group in February 1947, Kitchlew continued resisting Hindu political bigotry within the party. (See below.)

[198]Mirza, *Karavan-i-Ahrar*, viii, p. 152.

setting up a special subcommittee to outline plans to 'oppose Congress conduct against Muslims', the Ahrars asked all Muslim organisations to 'form a joint front for the emancipation of Muslims in India' to 'strongly oppose ... the partition of the Punjab'. They were prepared to fight to the last man if necessary. To that end, they wanted government to lift the ban on Muslims carrying swords. Harking back to their policy of wooing Muslims in Kashmir, the Ahrars condemned the repressive policy of the Dogra regime and demanded the unconditional release of Sheikh Abdullah. This was a hint that the Ahrars intended to concentrate wholly on the Punjab where Sikhs were preparing for civil war. Tara Singh's recent meeting with Sikh princely rulers was seen as part of the Mahasabha and the Congress drive to procure funds, if not arms and ammunition to fight the battle for the Punjab.[199]

With Bukhari still in command, a section of the Ahrars was in no rush to suspend all ties with the Congress. Until the outcome of negotiations in Delhi was known, the loquacious *maulana* preferred asserting the separate political identity of the Ahrars rather than merging with the Muslim League.[200] The offer to co-operate with Muslim organizations was too vague and ambiguous to command serious attention from the League. As it was, Maulana Habibur Rahman Ludhianvi's resignation from the all-India working committee was costing the Ahrars dearly in the Punjab. On 23 April 1947, the Ahrar paper *Azad* reprinted what Rahman had said sixteen years ago about the inwardness of the Congress's attitude towards Muslims. Contesting the pejorative label of 'communalism' reserved for Muslims who talked about the rights of their community, he had noted with dismay that even a Hindu who could kill someone for cooking beef was considered a 'nationalist' simply because he belonged to the 'majority'. Nothing underlined the perfidy of Congress's nationalism more than invitations to Muslims to join its ranks when it actually wanted them to stay out.[201] It was widely believed that 'Congress ha[d] brought pressure to bear on Ahrars', particularly in Bombay and UP, to defeat the resolution condemning the proposal to partition the Punjab at the general meeting of the party in Lahore. But even the spectacle of Bukhari leading two hundred *razakars* to the meeting could not save the Congress from elimination in Muslim Punjab. Ahrars in Sialkot and the Doaba were working informally in unison with the Muslim League while Shorish Kashmiri and other local leaders were preaching the creed of Muslim unity and agitating against the ban on swords.[202]

By the time the general council of the All-India Majlis-i-Ahrar convened in Lahore on 19 and 20 April 1947, the split in the body was complete. Most

[199]*SPPAI*, 29 March 1947, vol. lxix, no. 13, p. 143.
[200]*SPPAI*, 12 April 1947, vol. lxix, no. 15, p. 178.
[201]Cited in Mirza, *Karavan-i-Ahrar*, vi, pp. 213–14.
[202]*SPPAI*, 19 April 1947, vol. lxix, no. 16, p. 194.

Ahrars blamed Vallabhbhai Patel for Congress endorsing the Punjabi Hindu and Sikh conspiracy to deny the Muslim majority its right to rule the province.[203] According to Sheikh Hissamuddin, the Congress had not only been consistently duplicitous, it was now promoting bigotry in its quest for power at the all-India centre. It rejected the League's representative credentials and questioned Muslim support for 'Pakistan', pointing to the Ahrar and the Jamiat-ul-Ulema-i-Hind. But when the Ahrars and the Jamiat *ulema* went to the Congress to discuss an accommodation based on a single all-India centre, they were told that they were not representative of Muslims, the majority of whom supported the League, and so there was no question of conceding any demands. Congress's unjust attitude to Muslim demands, Hissamuddin alleged, was the nub of communitarian tensions. Now that it had become an instrument of the Mahasabha, the Ahrars had no choice but to join with other Muslim organizations to battle the forces of Hindu bigotry.[204]

Amidst such potent charges against the Congress, feeble attempts by two of its Ahrar henchmen from UP, Abdul Sattar of Delhi and Hakim Aftab Ahmad of Moradabad, to turn the pro-League tide came to naught. Bukhari in his response became 'so confused' that the meeting 'nearly ended in chaos'. But not before voting to break with the Congress and work with other Muslim parties for their liberation. The Muslim League's opinion of the meeting was that nothing had been decided and that the 'Ahrars were untrustworthy, wishing merely to bargain with the League'.[205] However reprehensible the manoeuvring of a defeated foe might have seemed to Leaguers, there was no denying the strength of the Ahrar opposition to the proposal to partition the province. They cannot be blamed for wanting to seize the initiative from the Muslim League in the process of organizing a campaign against the division of the Punjab.

There were others hoping to do the same, not least among whom was the Muslim president of the provincial Congress committee, Saifuddin Kitchlew. His was an uphill task, given the bigotry spawning the ranks of the party. He managed to prevent Congress buckling under pressure from Hindu donors and directing the relief funds for victims of violence to non-Muslims only. But he could not exploit divisions within the Punjab Congress to stop it from endorsing the all-India party's call for partition. A 'number of orthodox Congressmen of the eastern and, less frequently, the central Punjab' were openly expressing their 'displeasure' with the proposal. In Rawalpindi, Congressmen voiced 'strong criticism' of their leaders whom they 'accused of having become communalists' and passed resolutions 'expressing hostility to vivisection'.[206] At the same time the 'infiltration of communalism in the

---

[203]Mirza, *Karavan-i-Ahrar*, viii, pp. 172–3.
[204]Mirza, *Karavan-i-Ahrar*, vi, pp. 205–6.
[205]*SPPAI*, 26 April 1947, vol. lxix, no. 17, p. 206.
[206]*SPPAI*, 29 March 1947, vol. lxix, no. 13, p. 138.

Congress organisation [wa]s becoming more apparent' as was the 'inclination of its Hindu adherents to turn to the communal Mahasabha'.[207]

On 29 April, the Punjab Hindu Mahasabha attacked the governor for speaking out against a partition of the province since 'India belonged to the Hindus'.[208] Recording its agreement with this point of view, a poorly attended meeting of the Punjab Congress's working committee approved the proposal for a partition of the province. Its wording, however, indicated that the provincial Congress committee did 'not wholeheartedly support the partition idea'. It reaffirmed the desire for a united province while conceding the right of secession to any unit. This gave Kitchlew the opening he needed to 'appeal for a united Punjab'. Congress socialists like Abdul Ghani joined him in condemning the activities of the Anti-Pakistan Council of Action.[209]

Punjabi Muslims were united in opposing a partition of the province. The credit for this unprecedented unanimity of opinion, if not necessarily co-ordination of action, belongs solely to the Congress. 'Bitterly opposed to the suggestion', Leaguers viewed the arrival of Britain's last viceroy with trepidation.[210] But it was the draining away of Muslim support for the Congress in the Punjab which reflected the merging of Muslim religious and regional identities in most dramatic fashion. If Kitchlew was willing to defy the all-India high command's policy, there were many good-weather friends of the Congress ready to rise in defence of Muslim regional interests. The one-time Congressman, and now a mouthpiece of the Khaksars, Dr Muhammad Alam, pledged that he and his adopted party would sacrifice their lives in supporting Muslims in their drive against the partition of the Punjab and demand for homelands in northwest and northeast India.[211] Moreover, Maulana Hasrat Mohani, now a member of the constituent assembly from UP, came to Lahore 'urging the Punjab leaders to force Mr Jinnah to agree in no circumstance to any form of a truncated Pakistan'. Any 'compromise resulting in the partition of the Punjab' would result in 'the Muslim community taking matters into its hands'. Punjabi Muslims would do better following Suhrawardy's example in Bengal and keeping the province united. Joint electorates, the leader of the Jamiat-ul-Ulema-i-Hind explained, were 'no longer dangerous as Muslims [we]re politically conscious of their rights'.[212]

This was as sound a piece of advice as any emanating from a member of

[207] SPPAI, 10 May 1947, vol. lxix, no. 19, p. 231.

[208] SPPAI, 3 May 1947, vol. lxix, no. 18, p. 216.

[209] Ibid., pp. 231–2.

[210] SPPAI, 29 March 1947, vol. lxix, no. 13, p. 137.

[211] But it was Ishaq Zafar, the *salar-i-zabt* of the Punjab who disclosed that 'the aim of the Khaksar Movement was Islamic domination of the country' and 'the Allama intended to seize power from the outgoing British'. (*SPPAI*, 17 May 1947, vol. lxix, no. 20, p. 253.)

[212] SPPAI, 31 May 1947, vol. lxix, no. 22, p. 273.

the grand assembly of Muslim divines who had always supported the Congress. Demonstrating the strength of their regional identity, Punjabi Muslims dismissed the advice as 'suspect' given Mohani's past record of service to public causes. Ignoring Jinnah's exhortations, they preferred maximizing their regional gains, over and above the exclusive concerns of religious community. Bearing out the regional dimensions of his Punjabi Muslim identity, even an iconic collaborator like Khizar Hayat Khan agreed to support a coalition which included the League.[213] There could not have been a more drastic turnabout in the politics of Muslim identity in India than the one witnessed in the aftermath of the resolution to partition the Punjab and Bengal. Sensing their imminent exclusion from the larger chess game of power sharing, Muslims in majority and minority provinces reacted angrily to Congress's political opportunism.

Thick detail brings out the finer lines of interaction between religious and regional identities as they bore upon the battles for social space in the districts and localities of the Punjab. Being a member of a majority or a minority community in a particular district or locality was now a matter of life as well as property. Not only Muslims, but also Sikhs and Hindus, reacted to the impending division according to their social location in the political landscape of the province. Punjabi Hindus were the greatest enthusiasts of partition. It is worth recalling that the earliest proponent of partitioning the Punjab along the lines of religious community, Lajpat Rai, had no intention of conferring full sovereignty to Muslim homelands in northwest and northeast India. The same was true of Rajagopalachari's proposal in 1944 which had by and large been approved by the Hindu Mahasabha in the Punjab. There were nevertheless Congressmen in eastern Punjab who were far from reconciled to losing the western districts of the province, including Lahore. Sikhs resident in west Punjab also disliked the partition resolution.[214] A subcommittee of Panthic members of the assembly 'stoutly oppose[d] the partition proposal' which was supported by Sikhs of the 'capitalist and Akali persuasions' and rejected by those of the Congress nationalist ilk.[215] It has been easy to gloss over the reassertion of class and sub-regional interests in the face of fast moving events and horrific violence in the localities. Yet the Muslim and non-Muslim response to the partition proposal provides a useful vantage point in exploring the role of factors other than religion in the constitution of the partition holocaust.

Reflecting the close interconnection between religious identity and regional

[213]The president of the All-India Momin Conference, Zahiruddin, also decided to join the Muslim League in response to the Congress's demand for a partition. He was suspended by the organization and Abdul Qayum Ansari of Bihar elected as the new president. (*SPPAI*, 26 April 1947, vol. lxix, no. 17, p. 206.)

[214]*SPPAI*, 29 March 1947, vol. lxix, no. 13, p. 137.

[215]*SPPAI*, 19 April 1947, vol. lxix, no. 16, p. 190.

location, the Congress's call for a partition caused a 'scare in the Muslim minority settlements in the Eastern Punjab'.[216] There was panic among Muslims in Ambala division. Daultana was working on a plan for the migration of Muslims in Ambala to the western districts.[217] Mass-scale displacements were cause enough for anxiety. Daultana thought the 'only possibility' of a 'political alliance was now with Congress' since the 'two outstanding obstacles'—its claim to represent all communities and its commitment to the territorial unity of India— 'had now been retracted by high-ranking Congressites'. Shaukat Hayat and Daud Ghaznavi pooh-poohed the idea of Congress–League unity.[218] But their reaction betrayed some of Daultana's own doubts. In addition to thinking about evacuation plans, he was considering how the Muslim-majority districts of the west could come to the assistance of Muslims in central Punjab in the event of a civil war. Pathan labour in the Doaba was known to be engaged in the smuggling of arms.[219]

Preparing for civil war to prevent a partition may have made sense to the League leadership. But there were 'signs amongst the general Muslim public of dissatisfaction with the Punjab Muslim League High Command'. Proving Mohani's point that individuals in local communities would take matters into their own hands, the 'necessity to collect arms [wa]s felt by all'.[220] There were suspicions among the rank and file that League leaders were 'beginning to view [the] division of the Punjab with less abhorrence'. Jinnah's statement on 30 April 're-affirming the League stand against partition' failed to dispel 'rumours ... of dissension in the Punjab Muslim League High Command circles'.[221] Firoz Khan Noon published an article asserting Muslim determination not to surrender an inch of Punjabi territory.[222] After visiting the Punjab in May 1947, Liaquat Ali Khan felt that the 'available information' indicated the likelihood of 'a strong agitation to resist any effort aimed at partition'.[223]

Orchestrating a campaign against partition in the press was simpler than organizing one in the localities. Rising to the occasion, an all-India Muslim newspapers convention in Delhi undertook to counter the harm done by anti-Muslim propaganda in the non-Muslim press. Propaganda was to be 'directed to convincing the Sikhs that their interests would be served better by a united Punjab'.[224] But no one in the provincial League knew how to go about winning over the Sikhs. Unable to form a ministry, they wanted a dissolution of the

[216]Ibid., p. 141.
[217]*SPPAI*, 3 May 1947, vol. lxix, no. 18, p. 219.
[218]*SPPAI*, 12 April 1947, vol. lxix, no. 15, p. 177.
[219]*SPPAI*, 3 May 1947, vol. lxix, no. 18, p. 219.
[220]*SPPAI*, 12 April 1947, vol. lxix, no. 15, pp. 177.
[221]Ibid., p. 213.
[222]*SPPAI*, 10 May 1947, vol. lxix, no. 19, p. 235.
[223]*SPPAI*, 31 May 1947, vol. lxix, no. 22, p. 273.
[224]Ibid.

provincial assembly and fresh elections. Punjabi Leaguers were quite 'incapable of appreciating the effect of the recent communal fighting on the Hindu and Sikh communities'. There were 'distressing signs of irresponsibility'. While Daud Ghaznavi took the lead in spreading the word about the recovery of a huge supply of Patiala state rifles, Abdus Sattar Niazi asked Muslims to conceal their arms from the police which he accused of partiality. Even the relatively placid Mamdot was 'changing his tone' and blaming Hindus and Sikhs for the political stalemate and violence.[225]

Not one of the leaders had made the 'slightest effort to suggest a peaceful approach'. This woeful lack of statesmanship did not fail to 'stir ... the consciousness of people of intelligence' who realized that the policy of drift could only end in a bloodbath.[226] Unwilling to become cannon fodder for men they held in contempt, 'a growing number of people of all communities' were displaying 'increasing annoyance at the continued jingoism of their political leaders' and pinning their hopes on the outcome of talks between the new viceroy, Mountbatten, and the all-India leaders.[227] Increasing instances of violence matched by economic boycotts in different localities had made the 'average intelligent person ... anxious for peace'. But they realized that so long as the provincial leadership remained unchanged, there was 'no hope of return to normal times'. Sadly, this element was unlikely to 'ever achieve sufficient importance to dictate to the leaders' and 'signs of a civil war [we]re unmistakable'.[228]

The almost universal disdain for the quality of leadership in the Punjab, transcending the narrowing confines of religious communities, is replete with meaning. Political opinion in the province had exhausted its faith in the capacity of prominent men in the public domain to find an answer to a problem that was entirely of their own making. For those who followed the lead of a local or provincial politician, there were many more who preferred taking matters into their own hands in defence of life and property. Creating an amorphous configuration in what was now hotly contested space, groups of banded individuals were fighting battles for control in urban and rural localities that were as vital to them personally as they were to the purported interests of their respective communities. With entire districts being apportioned on the basis of religious affiliations recorded by census enumerators, gangs representing majorities fell upon minorities with a view to ejecting them through fear, terror and murderous means. Religion as faith, if it at all was the primary issue, had mostly profane manifestations. There was nothing holy about the ghastly developments that had begun rearing their head with greater frequency in the Punjab.

[225]SPPAI, 5 April 1947, vol. lxix, no. 14, p. 157.
[226]Ibid., p. 153.
[227]SPPAI, 12 April 1947, vol. lxix, no. 15, p. 171.
[228]SPPAI, 5 April 1947, vol. lxix, no. 14, p. 158.

The banding of individuals in localities to protect their home as well as their property owed something to the discourse and politics of communitarianism, Muslim, Hindu and Sikh. But it was so variously interpreted and deployed as to thoroughly implode the category of 'communal violence' within which each local incident has tended to be cast. To be sure, members of religious communities did join together in defence of their private sphere. But there was nothing to deter some of them from taking the cover of an impending division of the spatio-temporal landscape to advance their personal claims on public space. Outlandish territorial demands by community leaders were accompanied by strategies to appropriate the property of neighbours—the price of separating at close quarters could not have been crueller.

There had been a brief lull in localized violence after the initial outburst at the resignation of Khizar's coalition ministry. On 22 March the reported casualties were 516 dead and 945 seriously injured in the cities. The count was higher in the rural areas where battles for supremacy had been particularly savage, leaving 1547 dead and 161 seriously injured.[229] In Lahore, Amritsar, Ferozepur and Jullundur, police recovered knives, daggers and spear blades from passers-by. This is evidence yet again of undirected violence, even if incited by a directionless leadership with its empty promises and misplaced hopes. There were widespread complaints about the lack of assistance provided by the MLNG and the RSS.[230] The role of local toughs and rumours in sparking off violent outbreaks had been significant. In Multan and its rural environs, where tensions ran at the higher decibel points, the rounding up of 'bad characters' and the arrest of rumour-mongers helped to improve the situation. It should also be noted that there were individuals who resisted betraying neighbours simply on account of their religious affiliation. Mirza Mohammad Ibrahim, the pre-eminent leader of the railway workers, had the street power to tilt the balance decisively during disturbances in Lahore. He chose not to do so and instead 'worked fairly consistently for communal harmony and a cessation of rioting'. This reflected the 'genuine personal fears' of communists that 'they would lose their hold on Labour if they permitted their followers to take active part in the disturbances'. They had been able to sustain the support of labour 'only by the most slender of ties' and knew that 'communal rioting [wa]s a grave danger to their own solidarity'.[231]

[229]*SPPAI*, 22 March 1947, vol. lxix, no. 12, p. 131.

[230]The Mahasabha leader, Bhopatkar, expressed unhappiness with the RSS for failing to protect Hindus during the disturbances. This resulted in the RSS stepping up its activities in the different localities and districts. There was 'nervousness' among Muslims in Chamba where the RSS was appealing for the sympathy of Hindus. Muslims in Jhang were thoroughly alarmed. Here it was 'alleged that ... Hindu arms license holders [we]re handing their arms at night to Sangh members for guard purposes'. (*SPPAI*, 5 April 1947, vol. lxix, no. 14, p. 159.)

[231]*SPPAI*, 15 March 1947, vol. lxix, no. 11, p. 119.

If this was the attitude of the communists, ex-INA members were the other non-communitarian formation which tried to avoid becoming partisan. Wanting a semblance of harmony, they decided to remain neutral on 'Pakistan'. They were disgusted with Congress's failure to use its position in the interim government to wave through their long-standing demand for a sympathetic reconsideration of the INA case as a whole.[232] Earlier, many high-ranking INA officers in the Punjab had opposed formal association with the Congress since it would 'alienate Muslim ex-members of the INA' and, by 'damag[ing] their solidarity', destroy any chance of getting their demands accepted at the all-India level.[233] Released from any obligation to either of the two main parties, Hindu and Sikh members of the INA responded in their individual capacity to the 'boom in the demand for the[ir] service' as 'chaukidars and bodyguards'. The Lahore office was requested to supply five hundred men. But it was 'uncertain of the attitude to adopt' given the 'communalistic flavour' of the entreaties.[234] This left each individual member of the INA free to decide how to participate in preparations for a war of the communities.

With the provincial INA committee desperately short of funds, unemployed Muslims, Hindus and Sikhs could hardly be dissuaded from offering their services for remuneration. By April, the INA committee was finding it difficult to meet the increasing demand for bodyguards among former Hindu and Sikh INA members.[235] In Rawalpindi where Muslims were giving 'open expression' to their 'intense dislike' of non-Muslims, Hindus and Sikhs had lost faith in the law and order departments of the government and were hiring ex-servicemen, including former members of the INA.[236] Where employment of any sort was unavailable, former soldiers of the empire were not above resorting to criminal activities. Sixty INA men, mainly from Chakwal, had reportedly participated in looting and arson during the recent troubles. More and more Hindu members of the INA were joining voluntary organizations.[237]

The proportion of INA personnel to ex-servicemen in the Punjab was, of course, relatively small. But it underlines the growing association of former military personnel with groups of individuals as well as organizations preaching hatred and war. Shattering Bose's dream of a national army rising above the narrow concerns of religion, the INA was becoming stricken with bigotry and getting 'poorer every day'. There was 'a great deal of dissatisfaction amongst both officers and men'.[238] This found expression in a growing 'communal cleavage in the ranks of the Punjab branches of the INA'. Hindu and Sikh

[232]SPPAI, 18 January 1947, vol. lxix, no. 3, p. 26.
[233]Ibid.
[234]SPPAI, 29 March 1947, vol. lxix, no. 13, pp. 138–9.
[235]SPPAI, 12 April 1947, vol. lxix, no. 15, p. 172.
[236]SPPAI, 29 March 1947, vol. lxix, no. 13, p. 144.
[237]SPPAI, 12 April 1947, vol. lxix, no. 15, p. 172.
[238]SPPAI, 7 June 1947, vol. lxix, no. 23, p. 286.

members in Rawalpindi were 'openly disclaiming allegiance' with the organization, convinced that the former INA officer Colonel Tajammal Hussain, along with his father-in-law, had masterminded forced conversions in the Karor areas.[239] In the eastern Punjab district of Hoshiarpur, and in Lahore, Muslim members of the INA were joining the League and the MLNG, furious at the Congress high command's decision to partition the province and stung by Nehru's indifference to their demands to release convicted INA men like Captain Abdur Rashid.[240] By contrast, the League was actively recruiting former INA members to the higher ranks of the MLNG.[241]

So too were the Akalis. But like the other contenders they focused on all ex-servicemen and not just the INA. The story of ex-INA Sikh soldiers is meaningful only when seen in the context of the broader politics of the *panth*. Led by men given to frenzied moods and contradictory manoeuvres, the Sikh *panth* and the Hindu *sangh* were locked in symbolic counterpoint with the Muslim *millat* or *qaum*. Only by fleshing out the ambivalences, and even sheer contradictions, in their formal politics is it possible to assess the role played by Sikhs, individually and collectively, in the battles for social space that marked the conclusion of British rule in the subcontinent.

Much importance was attached to Master Tara Singh's visit to Calcutta to raise money from Marwari *seths* and arouse resentments of Bengali Hindus and Sikhs at their losses in the Punjab. He returned with half a lakh rupees from Hindu men of commerce and finance in Calcutta. The generosity of the Marwaris made Tara Singh an ardent proponent of 'a joint Bengal–Punjab front' to resist 'Pakistan'. Yet while promising 'ready Punjab support', he wanted Bengal to 'lead the way'.[242] Towards that end, Tara Singh was quite successful in allying Akali activities with those of the Mahasabha. Punjabi Hindus had been wooing Sikhs to participate in economic boycotts of Muslims which included the dismissal of their Muslim employees. This gave credence to the old Muslim League contention that 'the Hindus [we]re prepared to fight the Pakistan issue to the last Sikh'.[243]

What constituted a Sikh was, interestingly enough, still a relatively fluid question in the Punjab of the late 1940s. The colonial concession to Sikhs to carry a *kirpan* excited a medley of responses. Muslims were demanding the legalization of personal swords. 'Praying for a solution at the centre', Punjabi

---

[239]*SPPAI*, 19 April 1947, vol. lxix, no. 16, p. 190. In a last-ditch attempt, Muslim members of the INA, including some fervent Congressmen, tried forming 'a Left Consolidation' group to try and lure their former Sikh colleagues from the Akalis. When this failed, they had no option but to enter the League's fold. (*SPPAI*, 31 May 1947, vol. lxix, no. 22, p. 271.)

[240]*SPPAI*, 19 April 1947, vol. lxix, no. 16, p. 190.

[241]*SPPAI*, 12 July 1947, vol. lxix, no. 28, p. 369.

[242]*SPPAI*, 5 April 1947, vol. lxix, no. 14, p. 155.

[243]Ibid.

Hindus had sensibly decided to cast their lot with the Sikhs while actively supporting the RSS. The joint Hindu–Sikh relief fund was well subscribed to by men of commerce and finance in the Punjab.[244] Some Hindus thought their best self defence lay in converting to Sikhism. Within the Sikh community itself, there were droves seeking baptism to become members of the quasi-monastic Nihangs. The SGPC was distributing *kirpans*, which had also become longer. In the sensitively balanced district of Sialkot, 125 long *kirpans* were being issued to Sikhs on a weekly basis. The 'cult of unalloyed anti-Muslim hatred spread by Akali propagandists' in the localities 'le[ft] no reasonable doubt that the Sikh intention [wa]s one of anti-Muslim militancy'.[245] By late May 1947 the conversion of Sikhs to Nihangs had assumed 'alarming proportions'. It was obvious that there was 'no religious background to these conversions' which were 'purely a political move to arm non-Muslims'. Muslims were embittered by the government's failure to prevent these conversions. Apart from providing additional muscle power to the Akal Fauj, the Nihangs were often scooped up from a welter of no-gooders.[246]

With unemployment and inflation soaring in town and country, members of all communities were finding relief in armed militias. Sikhs blamed their lack of readiness on the heavy losses they had suffered at Muslim hands in north-western Punjab and the NWFP. This had bitten so deeply into their consciousness that there was 'no apparent wish now remaining to solve the communal problem without a partition', only 'a burning desire for retaliation in the event of further troubles'.[247] The 'bellicose propaganda' and 'preparations' of the Sikhs advertised their determination to fight for every inch of their patrimony. But there was no singular trend marking the choice of organizational affiliation of Sikhs. In Malwa, Sikh members of the INA were enlisting in the Akal Fauj. So too were those in Gujranwala, Lyallpur and Hoshiarpur. But in Simla they were contemplating joining the socialists, still keen to 'turn communal hatred into class war'.[248]

In so far as the Sikhs worked according to any organizational plan, there was considerable looseness in both control and co-ordination. Preparations of civil war were coloured by local realities. The 'unswerving determination' of the Akali leadership to assert Sikh sovereignty over the Punjab was 'greeted with enthusiastic response from amongst the lower ranks of the Akali hierarchy'. In Lyallpur, which Giani Kartar Singh had vowed to keep in Sikh hands, *kirpans* were being procured for the Akal Fauj. Sikhs in the rural neighbourhoods of Lyallpur city were 'arming themselves with spears and blacksmiths [we]re working feverishly producing all manner of arms'. A newly opened *kirpan* factory

[244]*SPPAI*, 12 April 1947, vol. lxix, no. 15, p. 174.
[245]*SPPAI*, 19 April 1947, vol. lxix, no. 16, p. 193.
[246]*SPPAI*, 24 May 1947, vol. lxix, no. 21, p. 263.
[247]*SPPAI*, 29 March 1947, vol. lxix, no. 13, p. 140.
[248]*SPPAI*, 3 May 1947, vol. lxix, no. 18, p. 214.

in Amritsar was churning out two hundred pieces a day and had already supplied five hundred to the Khalsa College. To facilitate greater dispersion of these symbols of Sikh identity, *kirpan* factories were started at Phagwara and Kot Kapura in Kapurthala and Faridkot states respectively.[249] Grief-stricken by the death of a former president of the SGPC, Babu Labh Singh, during an outbreak of violence in Jullundur, Sardar Darbara Singh Kalewal told his co-religionists to 'kill their Muslim antagonists' to avenge the death of their martyrs.[250] In his first report to London, Mountbatten acknowledged that of all the Punjabi communities the Sikhs were 'most businesslike and serious' in their preparations for civil war. Their plan was to seize the main irrigation centres in order to 'exercise physical control over the whole of the Punjab'.[251]

Preoccupied with matters in Delhi, the viceroy chose to monitor events in the Punjab via remote control. This made it easier to accommodate the Congress. The viceroy learnt from V.P. Menon that the Congress attached 'paramount importance' to the Sikhs. A 'very virile community', their support was vital for Punjabi Hindus who could 'not ... stand up to the Muslims, much less to a possible combination of Sikhs and Muslims'.[252] Convinced that a 'Pakistan' would have to entail the partition of the Punjab, Mountbatten summarily dismissed Liaquat Ali Khan's contention that Muslim violence against non-Muslims was due to extreme provocation by Hindu and Sikh leaders. As for Liaquat's plea that Muslims be permitted to carry swords, Mountbatten noted that two armed men were more likely to start a fight than one. It was of no concern to Mountbatten that by a curious logic of the colonial policy, a weapon which was 'an emblem of spirituality' for the Sikhs could in the 'hands of a Muslim ... become a menace to others'. He did not care to share the general view that 'the chief present danger to the Punjab c[a]me from the temper of the Sikhs'.[253] Describing Tara Singh and Giani Kartar Singh as 'two unkempt, jungly-looking old men' in one breath and 'scholarly old gentlemen' in the other, he 'pulled their leg' for coming to see him with the 'most enormous swords'.[254]

The ritual display of Sikh sovereignty might have been amusing for a representative of departing rulers. But the steel was closing in on Punjabi Muslims, foreclosing the possibility of the League securing Akali co-operation in restoring a semblance of peace.[255] As late as the third week of May 1947,

[249]*SPPAI*, 29 March and 5 April 1947, vol. lxix, nos.13, 14, pp. 144, 157.
[250]*SPPAI*, 29 March 1947, vol. lxix, no. 13, p. 141.
[251]Mountbatten's personal report no. 1, 2 April 1947, *TP*, x, p. 90.
[252]V.P. Menon to George Abell, 29 March 1947, ibid., p. 44.
[253]Liaquat Ali Khan to Mountbatten, 15 April 1947, pp. 257–58.
[254]Record of Mountbatten's interview with Tara Singh, Giani Kartar Singh and Baldev Singh, 18 April 1947, ibid., p. 323.
[255]Mamdot had formally invited Tara Singh to discuss co-operation. Before abandoning his peace-making mission, Mamdot appealed to Muslims in Jhelum and Gujrat not to attack their Hindu and Sikh neighbours since 'inter-communal goodwill

Punjabi Muslims were hoping against hope that the Sikhs would see sense in compromising with the League. Jinnah's meeting with the Maharaja of Patiala 'aroused some speculation' in Muslim League ranks which 'optimistically hope[d] that some compromise c[ould] still be reached between the League and Panthic leaders'.[256]

But nothing could steer Tara Singh away from the warpath. The method in the apparent madness of Sikh postures needs fleshing out. Tara Singh believed that supporting a partition of the Punjab would give 'Sikhs a very strong handle with which to bargain with Congress against the Muslim League' and its 'Pakistan' demand. Jinnah had already 'conceded the Sikh right to have their own homeland within Pakistan' and would agree to one outside the Muslim-dominated state if the demand for 'Khalistan' was articulated powerfully. Towards that end, he favoured Sikh migration from western Punjab, a position contrary to Congress's line that the continued presence of non-Muslims in 'Pakistan' would 'keep the good-will of the League on test'. But the Akali leader thought keeping Muslims in central and eastern districts as hostages was sufficient to guarantee 'the good behaviour of western Punjab Muslims towards their minorities'.[257]

Tara Singh had the backing of Giani Kartar Singh, a champion of Sikhs claiming Lyallpur, Sheikhupura and Montgomery for 'Khalistan'. Together these two men did much to confuse Sikhs, none of whom wanted to suffer displacement, however attracted they were to the evocation of Sikh sovereignty over the whole of the Punjab. Kartar Singh planned on defending Sikh religious places like the Panja Sahib Gurdwara in Hassanabdal with the help of hundred ex-military men. He was exhorting Sikhs of Majha and Malwa to avenge the wrongs done to their compatriots in the western districts.[258] But neither of the two Sikh leaders could quite explain how they proposed to reconcile their hopes with support for a partition plan which assumed that these places would be lost to the Sikhs. Whatever Tara Singh's and Giani Kartar Singh's illusions, Sikhs individually and collectively were afraid of finding themselves in a reconstituted province dominated by Hindu Jats. They looked upon Tara Singh's assurance of financial support from big non-Muslim industrialists with grave suspicion. Doubts about the wisdom of the master's plans were matched by difficulties in implementing his theory of a Sikh migration from western Punjab and the NWFP. Hindu and Sikh refugees from these areas were displaying signs of restiveness and wanted to return to their homes if afforded adequate protection.

---

was essential if Pakistan was to be realised'. (*SPPAI*, 22 March 1947, vol. lxix, no. 12, p. 130.)

[256]*SPPAI*, 24 May 1947, vol. lxix, no. 21, p. 261.

[257]*SPPAI*, 12 April 1947, vol. lxix, no. 15, pp. 174–5.

[258]In Gujrat, Giani Kartar Singh was advising Sikhs to migrate. Together with Sardar Swaran Singh he visited Kapurthala to arrange for the manufacture of *kirpans*. (Ibid., pp. 175–6.)

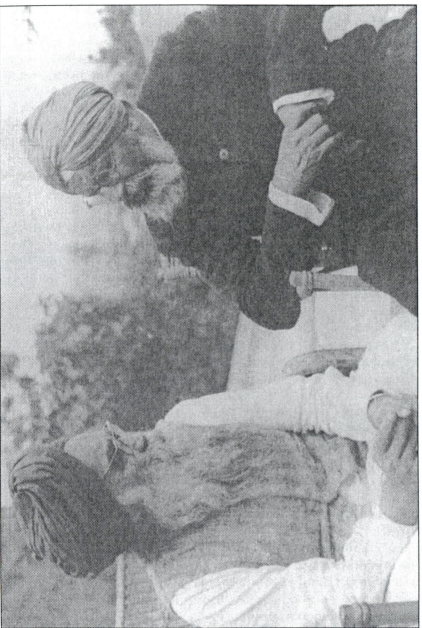

Tara Singh speaking to an Akali leader
Courtesy: Nehru Memorial Museum and Library

At the same time, Hindu and Sikh traders east of the Ravi were 'apprehensive of damaging competition' from their brethren in the west.[259]

Communitarian identities remained strained by subregional and class differences. The Congress's call for a partition of the Punjab had underscored the difficulties of reconciling religiously informed identities with imaginings of territorial sovereignty. The Sikhs were a prime example, though by no means the only ones. If Muslims in eastern Punjab were petrified at the prospect of their homes being parcelled out to the non-Muslim areas, Hindus in western and central Punjab were as averse to losing their properties to 'Pakistan' as the Sikh landed gentry. Sikhs with commercial and industrial interests wanted a partition, leading to the creation of a new province consisting of the Ambala and Jullundur divisions as well as Delhi. But Sikh landed interests, represented by Kartar Singh's group, wanted the territory between Chenab and Sutlej where they owned large estates. This was contrary to what Akali leaders in conjunction with nascent Sikh capitalist interests thought was in the best interests of the community. 'Perturbed over the recriminations and accusations levelled at them by refugees from the western Punjab', Tara Singh and Giani Kartar Singh had to instruct Akalis to join Congress leaders in persuading Sikh and Hindu refugees to return to their homes in northern and western Punjab. But in practice 'the Akalis secretly advocate[d] migration'.[260]

These political divergences between the Congress and the Akali did not augur well for the Sikh–Hindu front against 'Pakistan'. Sikhs had taken to demanding a partition of the Punjab on a property basis and refused to consider any proposal which made Amritsar the outer limit of the north-western boundary of the non-Muslim bloc. The demand of the landed Sikhs for the whole of the Punjab up to the eastern bank of the river Chenab 'appeare[d] fantastic to the average Hindu mind'. They were not about to support a proposition which would increase the number of Sikhs and reduce their strength in the non-Muslim area. With more and more Congress Hindus taking their cues from the Mahasabha, the way was being 'paved for a clear-cut political decision on the Punjab on the basis of religion'. But in keeping with subregional and class interests, there were considerable differences of opinion among Hindus and Sikhs about how to actually cut the provincial melon. The clash between Sikh landed and capitalist interests was reflected among Punjabi Hindus. In Ambala, Hindu Jats envisaged a new province extending from the western borders of the division and incorporating Delhi as well as western UP. Hindus in central Punjab wanted the inclusion of Lahore division in the non-Muslim province. In keeping with the old tendency of not knowing when to modify absolute demands, Punjabi Hindus and Sikhs wanted a partition but had no intention of parting with the choicest parts of

[259]Ibid.
[260]SPPAI, 19 April 1947, vol. lxix, no. 16, pp. 192–3.

the province. Their leaders might have seen that 'the demand for partition [wa]s much easier to make than to see realised'.[261]

On a visit that drew a shabby response in the Punjab, Acharya Kripalani, now president of the all-India Congress, stated his party's antipathy to mass migrations from western to eastern Punjab. He firmly believed that 'minorities in Pakistan w[ould] necessar[ily] be treated with circumspection to ensure reciprocal treatment for the Muslim communal minority in Hindustan'. Once sovereignty had been acquired, any 'repetition of the recent holocaust after the establishment of Pakistan would necessarily mean war' between the two states.[262] These assurances fell far short of the consolation offered by a circular issued by the Mahasabha leader, Vir Savarkar, supporting a 'truncated Pakistan' in northwest and northeast India on the presumption that it could be 'squeezed out of existence' and 'annexed by a Hindustan strongly centralized'.[263] This dovetailed nicely with what the Akali leaders really wanted, fortifying them in their determination to continue preparing alongside the Mahasabha and the RSS to fight Muslim pretenders to sovereignty in the Punjab with a vengeance. If 'Pakistan' was to be a temporary arrangement, then Sikhs had all the more reason to join Hindus in resisting Muslims poaching on their social space.

The alliance between the Akalis and the RSS was especially strong in Lyallpur where Hindus and Sikhs had raised two and a half lakh rupees.[264] Giani Kartar Singh had instructed Sikh villagers to move towards *jatabandi*, or collective defence. These were to be reinforced with mounted men and ex-military and INA personnel equipped with firearms. Special emphasis was being given to co-operation with Sikh states. What gave a more worrying dimension to Sikh and Hindu preparations to fight for their space in Lyallpur was the arrival of some two hundred Gurkhas to train the volunteers of the Hindu Scouts Volunteer Corps and the RSS. Lodged in the Sanatan Dharm *mandir*, the Gurkha visitors were being looked after by the local Hindu Mahasabha. Success of the enterprise is indicated by a request for another two hundred Gurkhas to be sent to the Mahasabha headquarters in Gorakhpur. The arming and training of non-Muslims in Lyallpur has to be seen in the context of Sikh readiness to fight for this as well as the Sheikhupura and Montgomery districts in central Punjab. If dissatisfied with the outcome of the all-India leaders conference in Delhi at the beginning of June, the Sikhs were likely to translate their threats into practice.[265]

[261] SPPAI, 10 May 1947, vol. lxix, no. 19, pp. 233–4.
[262] SPPAI, 24 May 1947, vol. lxix, no. 21, p. 261.
[263] SPPAI, 12 April 1947, vol. lxix, no. 15, p. 174.
[264] With a target of one crore, the Punjab Congress Committee had raised a mere five lakh—evidence of the party's rapidly evaporating presence in a province its larger interests were about to rent in twain. (SPPAI, 19 April. 1947, vol. lxix, no. 16, pp. 189–90.)
[265] SPPAI, 24 May 1947, vol. lxix, no. 21, pp. 261–2.

In the renewed outbursts of violence prior to the announcement of the 3 June partition plan, it was not Lyallpur but Amritsar and Lahore which bore most, though not all, of the brunt of the troubles. Amritsar was the 'central focus of Sikh preparations'.[266] Tension was rife in the city and the surrounding villages as a direct consequence of the sacking of Muslim labour by Hindu employers. Isolated incidents of violence had left thirty-three dead and eighty-eight injured when a bomb blast ripped the city, resulting in the arrest of six members of the RSS. Here the local RSS was co-operating with the Arya Vir Dal and the Sikhs.[267] Amritsar remained in the grip of high tension and violence for a month. On 16 April, the working committee of the Akali Dal met in Amritsar and resolved to enforce a comprehensive social boycott of Muslims throughout the Punjab. No Muslim menials were to be employed in villages; no Muslim doctors or lawyers engaged; no alms given to Muslim beggars; no land, houses or shops leased to Muslims; nothing purchased from Muslims; and no Muslim contracted as a labourer.[268]

To one close observer, the will to arm and collect funds, ostensibly for relief, but also to defend local communities had affected 'the mentality of the people like the bite of a mad dog'. Though extremely leery of the political stalemate, ordinary persons were 'cling[ing] to ... [their] community for survival'.[269] With social boycotts by all communities on the increase, tensions in Amritsar were replicated in other areas, not least in Lahore which was rocked by intermittent bomb explosions and incidents of arson. Reacting in the only way they could to Sikh provocations, Muslims on the instructions of local *maulvis* were asserting their claims on sacred spaces by offering prayers en masse in damaged mosques in Hindu-majority areas. Fears that 'the mosque may go in default to the other communities led to a dangerous quickening of interest by young Muslims'. They had to be 'pacified' by 'more responsible Leaguers', leaving many Muslims to suspect that the Khaksars and the Ahrars were promoting the new trend.[270] Reclaiming abandoned space was a main feature in the spreading graph of violence in the Punjab. The arrival of refugees from the NWFP, advertising the ghastly violence against non-Muslims there, caused extreme nervousness among Hindus and Sikhs in districts where they were in a minority. Migrations from Rawalpindi were on the increase to the joy of some local Muslims. Hindus were also leaving the Muslim princely state of Bahawalpur while those in Sialkot were heading for Jammu. Similarly, Muslims resident in Sikh princely states like Faridkot and Patiala were fleeing to the western districts.[271]

[266]*SPPAI*, 3 May 1947, vol. lxix, no. 18, p. 217.
[267]*SPPAI*, 26 April 1947, vol. lxix, no. 17, p. 209.
[268]Ibid., p. 204.
[269]*SPPAI*, 19 April 1947, vol. lxix, no. 16, p. 196.
[270]Ibid.
[271]*SPPAI*, 19 April 1947, vol. lxix, no. 16, p. 195.

The coming together of communities followed their victimization, not their agency in perpetrating violence. A close scrutiny of local manifestations of communitarian bonding reveal how old troubles between neighbours were reappearing in new forms. Outside the city centres, there was systematic burning of harvested wheat in Amritsar, Jullundur, Sialkot and Multan districts. The Odes, who tended to be armed and adept at stealing crops, were invited by local Leaguers in Ludhiana to join their ranks. This led to a clash between them and Sikhs in Karnal which sent ripples of fear along the Karnal–Ambala border. Migratory Pathan labour, known as *powindas*, created terror among Punjabi Hindus. They had participated in the recent troubles, killing a young Hindu boy in Muzaffargarh district. A police raid of four *powinda* camps in Sargodha district uncovered fifteen thousand yards of silk and cotton material, some of it charred, as well as other goods suspected to have been stolen from Amritsar and Lahore.[272]

The trend which gave a decisive fillip to the volume of violence in the Punjab was undoubtedly that of social boycott, especially the laying off of menial as well as semi-skilled and skilled labour along communitarian lines. Unemployed labourers in rural and urban areas were the most enthusiastic recruits to the MLNG, the RSS and Sikh Shahidi Jathas which had cast the Akal Fauj in the shade. The social and economic boycotts had hit the labouring classes the hardest and they 'openly expressed' their 'bitterness ... against the communal leaders to whom they ascribe[d] the miseries they [we]re suffering'.[273] In Amritsar, where there was wide-scale unemployment, the working classes were 'getting desperate and showing a marked tendency to take an active part in rioting' with the backing of voluntary organizations. A flustered Punjab League high command was wrestling to find ways of offering financial relief to Muslim labourers and their families in Amritsar.[274]

But whatever their concern for the plight of the sufferers of social and economic boycotts, all organizations were thoroughly distracted by the need to provide relief to victims of actual violence. By mid-May, the city of Lahore had been 'submerged completely' in an 'orgy of arson, stabbings, assaults and murders', a glaring replication of the pattern of violence in Amritsar during the preceding weeks. Yet 'not one of the political leaders ha[d] played a conspicuous part to call a halt to this senseless orgy of killing and damage to property'.[275] Until the results of the all-India leaders conference with Mountbatten became known, there was a general inclination to wait 'before abandoning restraint to the winds'.[276]

This was particularly true of Punjabi Hindus whose participation in 'a

[272]*SPPAI*, 26 April 1947, vol. lxix, no. 17, p. 207.
[273]*SPPAI*, 3 May 1947, vol. lxix, no. 18, p. 213.
[274]*SPPAI*, 17 May 1947, vol. lxix, no. 20, p. 252.
[275]Ibid., p. 253.
[276]*SPPAI*, 24 May 1947, vol. lxix, no. 21, p. 261.

communal war of attrition' was more indirect than direct. Relying on the 'belligerency of the Akalis and to a lesser extent the RSS', they were content with buttressing their own localities and extending financial assistance to the Hindu–Sikh front in the form of relief funds.[277] The RSS, however, was primarily interested in procuring firearms and bombs from army officers. The underground activities of the RSS in Lahore, which the Hindu Sabha was using as its strike force, came to the surface when its members were spotted 'committing arson and murder'.[278] Confirmation of the RSS's involvement in 'terrorist activities' left 'little doubt' that its activities had been 'organised and conducted' according to a carefully laid-down plan.[279] There was growing evidence of Hindus banking on 'extremist elements of the RSS'.[280]

The relative strengths of the RSS's covert operations compared to those of the MLNG and the Sikh Shahidi Jathas needs underlining. Broadcasting their intentions to cut the League down to size, the RSS engineered a spate of bomb explosions in Chinoit and Burewala in Multan district. In Jullundur city a police raid on a building bearing the notice 'Bachelors' Headquarters' disclosed several military bombs, acids, test tubes and laboratory material as well as a variety of daggers, bows and several arrows. Proof of RSS's impeccable planning was the discovery of three sixteen-inch maps of Jullundur representing Hindu and Muslim quarters as well as government buildings in different colours. Smaller scale maps, also found at the premises, identified those parts of the city where the two communities resided together with names of owners and tenants of houses. A two-page pamphlet entitled 'Lessons in Mine Engineering' capped the RSS's formula for clearing Jullundur city of the Muslim population. All eleven arrested by the police were students of the Doaba College. In combination with 'offensive actions of members of the Sangh in Lahore and Amritsar', these findings left 'no doubt that this militant branch of the Hindu community [wa]s engaged in planned subversive activities'.[281]

Despite differences in degrees of sophistication, Muslim Leaguers were displaying 'more preparatory organisation'. Vigilance committees were cropping up throughout the province, including the Lahore, Amritsar, Ambala, Jullundur and Ferozepur districts. Efforts were under way to strengthen links between the Muslim League and the MLNGs. Apart from organizing economic boycotts of non-Muslims in Jullundur, Jhang, Montgomery and Sialkot,[282]

[277]SPPAI, 17 May 1947, vol. lxix, no. 20, p. 250.
[278]SPPAI, 24 May 1947, vol. lxix, no. 21, p. 264.
[279]SPPAI, 31 May 1947, vol. lxix, no. 22, p. 269.
[280]Ibid., p. 271.
[281]SPPAI, 31 May 1947, vol. lxix, no. 22, p. 275.
[282]Separate Muslim marts were opened in Jullundur. Leaguers had opened up shops in Jhang while elsewhere residents were collecting money to assist Muslims in starting their own businesses. The Montgomery district League was securing licenses for cloth and sugar for Muslims in the more important towns. In Sialkot, Leaguers

Leaguers were busy recruiting Muslims to the national guard. In Lahore, the MLNGs were being posted at danger spots during the night and patrolling vulnerable areas in jeeps. The League's use of national guards was expected to grow more effective, enabling it to undertake 'plans of action, not dissimilar to those of the Hindu community'.[283]

The weeks leading up to the 3 June plan witnessed organized and semi-organized incendiarism, stabbings and bomb blasts in Lahore and Amritsar. In an indication of the speed with which social space was falling vacant in the province, an estimated seventy to eighty thousand people had fled Lahore and Amritsar because of the disturbances.[284] The general outlook was 'extremely gloomy' as the communities of the Punjab awaited, jointly and severally, the outcome of the viceroy's meetings with the all-India leaders. There was a sense of despondency among the middle- and lower-classes who were 'becoming extremely wary of the senseless reign of terror conducted by the political and communal parties'. It was 'very doubtful' that this strain of opinion could moderate 'the cry of the present Muslim League for domination' or, for that matter, deflect the call of the 'Akalis for resistance and retaliation'. Firoz Khan Noon had gone to Delhi to impress upon the League high command not to betray Punjabi Muslims by accepting the partition plan. But no one in the Punjab League knew how to sustain their claims over the entire province. The League and the MLNGs were working in great secrecy, though their activities had not been as 'obviously unlawful in Lahore City' as those of the RSS. Evidence of the League's alliance with local Ahrar leaders was the new tactic of securing pledges in mosques to resist a division of the province. While the Ahrars were 'wholeheartedly' backing the League, they were expected to break with it if Jinnah agreed to a redemarcation of the provincial boundaries.[285]

Whatever the official stance of the Akalis, there were even greater divisions among Sikhs over partitioning the Punjab. Baldev Singh, defence minister in the interim government, pleased Hindus and his own co-religionists no end with his statement in the *Tribune* carrying the banner headline 'The Punjab must be restored to the Sikhs'. Afraid that a partition of the province would give them only twelve districts out of the twenty-nine claimed for the non-Muslim bloc, the Sikhs were genuinely perturbed by the barrage of territorial demands, one more outlandish than the other. Although approached by Giani Kartar Singh, Mazhabi Sikhs preferred winning over the Nihangs by persuading them that the 'Akalis ha[d] never given them fair treatment'. Looking for stray pickings, the district League in Ferozepur promptly approached the Mazhabis

---

were opening general co-operative stores. (*SPPAI*, 10 May 1947, vol. lxix, no. 19, p. 236.)

[283]*SPPAI*, 24 May 1947, vol. lxix, no. 21, pp. 264–5.
[284]*SPPAI*, 31 May 1947, vol. lxix, no. 22, p. 277.
[285]Ibid., pp. 269, 273–4.

in the hope of their 'forming an opposition to the Akalis'. The All-India Sikh Students Federation dispelled all worries of a generational divide by producing a garbled circular proclaiming their opposition to both partition and joint electorates. Distrustful of Hindus and Muslims, these young Sikhs wanted a separate constituent assembly for a state consisting of south-eastern Punjab, the princely states of Patiala, Nabha, Jind, Faridkot and Kapurthala which would work out the modalities of a 'Sikh Confederacy'.[286] Quite unconnected with these demands, Sikhs by this time were battle ready in Moga, Malwa and the Doaba. The Majha, or central Punjab, was still unprepared even though Sikhs of Sirhali, Tarn Taran, the Beas and Narowal were 'thought to be armed'. So too were those near Qadian while Sikhs in Batala were lagging behind.[287]

Hindus may have been least confused and divided about a partition of the Punjab. But there were some still trying to air proposals for a united province. Diwan Chaman Lal proposed an undivided Punjab with joint electorates, equal representation for Muslims and non-Muslims in the cabinet as well as the services and the premiership on a rotating basis. Almost a carbon copy of the plan for a united Bengal, this was flatly rejected by the Congress and the Panthic Sikhs. Muslims had 'no faith' in the statement after seeing the Congress high command's hostility towards the agreement reached between Suhrawardy and Sarat Chandra Bose. Punjabi Hindus may have been using the subversive activities of the RSS as a cover, but they were equally incensed at the interim government's failure to quell Muslim violence. Nehru's visit to the Punjab ended in failure, forcing Kripalani to abandon his earlier ideas and urge Hindus and Sikhs to prepare for self-defence.[288] The Congress was at an end in the Punjab even as the booming market in daggers, spears, axes, acid and bombs highlighted the intention of loosely organized communities to take its call for a partition to whatever they considered to be the logical conclusion.

Punjabi bestiality against fellow Punjabis in the violence combing the province since early March had become the principal stumbling block for an agreement on power sharing. No less significant was the relative balance between centre and region in the final negotiations which produced the 3 June partition plan. The Punjab governor thought it was 'ludicrous' for 'so-called League leaders ... to take orders from Bombay from a person entirely ignorant of Punjab conditions'.[289] He was equally opposed to the Congress high command's meddling in the affairs of the province when they had no knowledge of the administrative difficulties involved in translating the proposal for a partition into practice. Carving up the province, Jenkins had been arguing all along would

[286]Ibid., pp. 273, 277.
[287]*SPPAI*, 24 May 1947, vol. lxix, no. 21, p. 262.
[288]*SPPAI*, 31 May 1947, vol. lxix, no. 22, p. 270. Many former Congressmen were 'apathetic and even hostile' to Nehru's visit and thought Patel ought to have come in his place. (*SPPAI*, 7 June 1947, vol. lxix, no. 23, p. 286.)
[289]Note by Jenkins, 20 March 1947, *TP*, ix, p. 997.

entail 'cut[ting] across a section of Punjabis homogeneous in speech and in many other ways, to create an artificial frontier for which geographically, economically, linguistically and socially there [wa]s no justification whatever'. By wielding the partitioner's axe to placate the Congress, the British would have 'reduced what might be a powerful country to two petty States incapable of real economic development' on account of being 'overloaded with overhead charges' and 'useful only as "buffers" between the rest of India and the outer world'. In sum, 'partition solve[d] no problem and d[id] not really make sense'.[290] This could dawn upon a foolish and irresponsible provincial leadership only if they were left alone by their respective high commands. Incapable of initiative and insensitive to the grievances of non-Muslims, the Punjab League leadership had, in conjunction with the larger imperatives of Jinnah and the Congress high command, 'already fooled away a kingdom'. A conception of India's future that required the picture at the centre to emerge before etching one for the Punjab, Jenkins warned, was completely 'topsy-turvy'. Neither a divided Punjab nor one in a state of civil war could possibly fit into the broader all-India arrangement. The 'right course', surely, was to 'determine the future of the units in a way acceptable to their inhabitants and then to sketch the all-India picture'.[291]

But it was arrangements at the centre, not the problem of individuals and communities inhabiting contested space in the regions, which enabled Mountbatten to dictate the terms of the all-India settlement. It was fortuitous that Nehru and Patel, despite their differences on other issues, agreed to accept a 'Pakistan' based on partitioning the two main Muslim-majority provinces. This was all the ammunition the viceroy needed to force Jinnah's acquiescence to the 3 June plan. But until the All-India Muslim League's council had given its endorsement to the plan, a nod of the head by the Quaid-i-Azam did not signify Muslim willingness to accept the partition of either the Punjab or Bengal.

The immediate reaction to the 3 June announcement in the Punjab may not have been 'dangerously averse'. But it was 'abundantly clear that none of the three communities [wa]s happy at the outcome'. The provision in the plan to consider 'other factors' in the demarcation of the final boundary was one way to push for changes in the notional division. Hindus were 'less critical' than the Sikhs who were 'hardening their antagonism' and pinning their hopes on the boundary commission which was to demarcate the frontiers of the two states. On the whole, Congressmen were satisfied with the scheme; Punjabi Hindus generally were 'not too despondent'. But there was 'consternation over the inclusion of Lahore in the Pakistan Zone'. Like the Sikhs, Punjabi Hindus intended to fight this issue before the boundary commission. Their ultimate hopes, however, rested on 'the collapse of Pakistan for economic or

[290]Enclosure to Jenkins to Wavell, 7 March 1947, ibid., p. 881.
[291]Note by Jenkins, 20 March 1947, ibid., p. 997.

other reasons'. Some expected the NWFP, still under a Congress ministry, to opt for Hindustan. This was a misreading of the situation in the frontier, but gives a measure of just how determined Punjabi Hindus were to be rid of 'Pakistan'.[292]

Sikh disappointment with the outcome of their demand for a partition was evident in their 'rising temper'. The Central Akali Dal asked Sikhs to continue struggling to keep Lahore, Lyallpur and Montgomery.[293] As Wavell had predicted, the central Punjab was going to be 'the battle ground for Pakistan'.[294] Despite Kartar Singh's threats to fight, Sikhs in Lyallpur were 'showing signs of demoralisation' while 'local Muslim morale [wa]s high'. There was nevertheless considerable material for a major combustion in Lyallpur and other districts in central Punjab with Sikhs likely to fall prey to bands of armed Muslims.[295] Sikh militancy had better chances of securing real gains in places where the demographic balance was more delicately poised, for instance in Gurdaspur district. Here Muslims had a slight overall majority but were outnumbered by non-Muslims in some tehsils. The local Singh Sabha had joined the Arya Samaj and the Sanatan Dharm Sabha of Pathankot to persuade the rulers of Jammu and Chamba states to ensure that the district was not given away to the League. With Nihangs dressed in yellow uniforms on the offensive, Sikhs were evidently gearing for revenge.[296]

This confounded an already 'more complex and diverse' reaction on the part of Punjabi Muslims to the partition scheme. Tara Singh's attitude 'caused considerable anxiety to the Muslims' who had 'very mixed feelings' about the 3 June announcement. Middle-class Muslims, who had suffered the most losses in business and income, hoped that the all-India agreement would 'stop political wrangling' and the incessant violence. 'Lower class' Muslims were 'openly in conflict with the plan' and a section of the Muslim League had expressed 'great resentment against Jinnah and his complacent attitude'. They were appalled at the way in which 'recent Muslim sacrifices had been forgotten' and felt Muslims in Amritsar and Jullundur could not be 'abandoned' in this abject manner. Leaguers from the eastern districts were preparing to oppose the partition decision at the all-India body's meeting in Delhi. Those Punjab Leaguers who 'accepted the principle of partition' wanted to somehow 'increase the boundary of Pakistan to the Sutlej'. They hoped that Sikhs would in the end 'come over and agree to unity'.[297]

This was an amazing stance on the part of a party that had failed miserably

[292]SPPAI, 7 June 1947, vol. lxix, no. 23, pp. 285–6.
[293]Ibid., p. 287.
[294]Wavell to Pethick-Lawrence, 12 March 1947, TP, ix, p. 926.
[295]SPPAI, 7 June 1947, vol. lxix, no. 23, p. 287.
[296]Ibid.
[297]Ibid., pp. 287–8.

in pacifying Sikhs who had been outraged at the beastliness of attacks by armed Muslim gangs in the NWFP and the Rawalpindi–Attock–Chakwal areas of the Punjab.[298] But perhaps there was, after all, a sense of the demographics of social space which prompted Leaguers to make a final attempt to win over the Sikhs. Firoz Khan Noon favoured approaching the Sikhs to join the 'Pakistan' constituent assembly or, alternatively, to demand the boundaries of the Punjab on the basis of language. In either case, Muslims and Sikhs would have a fair share of power in the province. If this was an attempt to create the conditions for a regional power-sharing arrangement, the pro-Khilafat-i-Islam Punjabi Leaguer Abdus Sattar Niazi signposted the indignation of Muslims at the machiavellian manoeuvres to exclude them from the all-India picture. The scheme was 'most detrimental to Muslim interests' and the proposed partition of the Punjab and Bengal just insidious. Muslims in the Hindu-majority provinces had been 'given no rights to raise their voices for their future security'. Niazi intended to not only oppose the 3 June plan at the All-India Muslim League's forthcoming meeting in Delhi but to 'press the demand for a corridor'.[299]

This received thunderous endorsement from the ace speaker of the Ahrar brigade. Ataullah Shah Bukhari attacked the Muslim League's 'wishful thinking in imagining that Muslims w[ould] obtain extra territory from the Boundary Commission'. He was 'bitterly antagonistic to[wards] the partition scheme', not least for being a resident of Amritsar with a string of political support in the eastern districts.[300] Punjabi Muslims ignored the All-India Majlis-i-Ahrar's decision in Delhi condemning the partition plan. Undeterred by the snub, the ideologically charged Ahrars did not give up even after they had reconciled themselves to the League's 'Pakistan'. Joining its bandwagon, they believed, entitled them to express concern at the exclusion of people with religious knowledge from the League's panel of members to the new constituent assembly. Despite decisive political setbacks, Ahrar leaders were 'confident' that they 'represent[ed] truly Islamic principles' and would 'eventually come

[298]For an abbreviated account of the violence, and reactions to it, see TP, ix, especially the organized attack on Murree by 'a party of Muslims in cars or lorries' which had mainly targeted the property of the well-known draper Kirpa Ram. The disfiguring of social space left several large buildings and at least three hotels charred. Yet in 'many villages ... Muslims were definitely protecting' non-Muslims. All civil officials present at the Punjab governor's meeting in Rawalpindi had discerned 'a certain amount of moderate Muslim opinion in favour of peace'. But individual notables of the city 'dared not co-operate with the authorities', as the Unionists might have done, believing that 'they must keep in with their party'. (Jenkins to Wavell, 9 March 1947, TP, ix, pp. 903–4). Where they seriously miscalculated was in 'discount[ing] the case for the minorities and the seriousness of the communal trouble'. (Ibid., p. 905.)

[299]SPPAI, 7 June 1947, vol. lxix, no. 23, pp. 288–9.

[300]Ibid., p. 289.

into their own again'.[301] Keeping their finger in the shrinking pie, they charged Jinnah with 'desert[ing] five crores of Muslims who live[d] in the Indian Union'.[302]

The attractiveness of this line for at least a section of Punjabi Muslims is worth spelling out, as are the ensuing confusions. Khaksars agreed with Mashriqi that 'a truncated Pakistan [wa]s a betrayal of the Muslims by Mr Jinnah'.[303] The Quaid was also censured by the leader of the Punjab Muslim Students Federation, Dr Zia-ul-Islam. Still 'committed to the unity of the Punjab', he thought the 'League High Command h[ad] proved politically inept'. In his opinion, the 16 May 1946 plan for a three-tier federal arrangement based on provincial grouping was 'better than the present one although it fell short of their demands'. The proposed division would 'strike at the roots of the administration and economic and political life of the Muslims'.[304] This was a theme that had been reiterated over and over again by a succession of Muslim League leaders, including Mohammed Ali Jinnah, in their meetings with Mountbatten. The Pathan Muslim Leaguer, Abdur Rab Nishtar, thought it was 'a crime to break up the economic unity of the Punjab and Bengal' simply because they included areas with non-Muslim majorities.[305]

These pleadings fell on deaf ears. If anything they reinforced Mountbatten's opinion that Jinnah and his followers were 'psychopaths' who had not done a day's work on the mechanics of establishing a separate Muslim state. The cold-blooded calculations emanating from the viceregal lodge at Delhi were quite in contrast to the gubernatorial observations from Lahore. There was 'a complete absence of enthusiasm for the partition plan' in the Punjab, 'nobody seem[ed] pleased and nobody ... want[ed] to get on with the job'. The political parties, however, for very different reasons were ready to 'acquiesce' to the plan. Muslim Leaguers thought it was 'a master-stroke by Jinnah' in the vain hope that he would ultimately 'get them all they want'. Congressmen considered the plan 'a master-stroke by Patel, who, having pushed the Muslims into a corner (or into two corners)' would 'destroy them before very long'. Patel's private views on the situation were 'menacing' to say the least. Muhammad Ibrahim Barq, the minister of education in Khizar's coalition government, had heard the Sardar saying that 'Hindustan would quickly make an end of its Muslim inhabitants if Pakistan did not behave'. Even if Barq can be dismissed as an unreliable witness, this was the 'attitude the Hindus hope[d] and the Muslims fear[ed] Patel w[ould]

[301] SPPAI, 5 July 1947, vol. lxix, no. 27, p. 356.

[302] SPPAI, 26 July 1947, vol. lxix, no. 30, p. 388.

[303] But many were hugely embarrassed by Mashriqi's instructions to his brigade in Delhi to adopt an aggressive attitude at the time of the AIML meeting. (SPPAI, 14 June 1947, vol. lxix, no. 24, p. 311.)

[304] Ibid., p. 313.

[305] See records of Mountbatten's interviews with Nishtar and Jinnah (21 and 26 April 1947), TP, x, pp. 349–51, 451–2.

Lord Mountbatten taking the salute before the transfer of power ceremonies. The
Quaid-i-Azam, Fatima Jinnah and Lady Edwina Mountbatten are also seen in the
photograph.
Courtesy: Information Division, Embassy of Pakistan, Washington, D.C.

take up'. As for the Sikhs, they trusted no one and were on red alert in districts
they considered vital. Until the boundary line had been announced, they 'refused
to go very far with partition'.[306]

The dilemma was real for members of all three communities, especially
minorities in districts allocated to one or the other of the two states under the
provisional boundary plan. Teasing out the contradictions in communitarian
aspirations unsettles the claims of nationalism in both its territorial and
religious variants. The only reason the Punjab Congress was satisfied with
the partition plan, it needs reiterating, was that it gave Jinnah the truncated
Pakistan he had rejected on two previous occasions. An attempt backed by
Bhim Sen Sachar was nevertheless made at a meeting of the Congress assembly
party on 23 June to keep the Punjab united. Prior to that Hindu reactions
came in diverse shapes and forms. Pleased at the division of Punjab, Bengal
and also Assam, they were unhappy that the provisional demarcation had

[306]Fortnightly report from Jenkins to Mountbatten, 15 June 1947, in *The Partition
of the Punjab: A Compilation of Official Documents*, i (second edition), Lahore: Sang-e-
Meel Publications, 1993, pp. 41–2.

not given them Lahore. Hindus in Gujranwala were despondent. But those in Amritsar thought that 'the cutting of the weak limb', namely the Muslim-majority areas, would leave the centre stronger than envisaged in the cabinet mission plan. Those further east had greater reason to rejoice. The Hindu Mahasabha dampened the satisfaction somewhat by formally condemning the partition plan and demanding Jhelum as the boundary line of eastern Punjab. As for Lahore, the Mahasabha thought its future should be decided not on numerical strength but on the contribution to education, commerce, industrial development, immovable property and revenue payments. It also wanted Hindu districts in Sind to be separated to create a new province.[307] Such demands fanned Muslim fears of ultimate Hindu intentions. If they had won acclaim in the western parts of the province, League leaders were facing criticism in the central and eastern districts. Muslims in Haryana and Amritsar openly charged the League of betrayal. Muslims in Malwa, where the youth were 'less tolerant' and 'inclined to indict the leaders', as well as the Doaba hoped that Muslim-majority pockets would be incorporated in Pakistan.[308]

Through a slow and tortured process, minorities living in districts designated for Hindustan or Pakistan did arrive at 'a certain fatalistic and grudging acceptance' of their predicament. But at the losing end of the numbers game, making the 'best of a bad bargain' was by no means easy. By the third week of June, with the exception of Haryana where 'purely local affairs' were of 'much more importance and reality to a politically extremely backward rural population', tensions were reported to have lessened in western and eastern Punjab. While most Hindus had accepted the provisional boundary line, their support for the 3 June plan was 'in a direct ratio to the position of each man's home in respect of Hindustan'. Those in the eastern districts were 'complacent' and those in the Haryana tract wanted amalgamation with the western districts of UP. The more cautious felt that the Sikhs might have to be weaned with the promise of the premiership of eastern Punjab. In the central districts, 'diehard Hindus combine[d] a malicious joy over the failure of Mr Jinnah to secure more than a truncated Pakistan with considerable criticism of Congress for having conceded even that much to the Muslim League'. They were nevertheless preparing to migrate and were transferring capital and material assets to safer places. That it was an excruciating experience is suggested by the return of Hindus who had fled Rawalpindi and Multan in the aftermath of the Muslim onslaught. Bhim Sen Sachar was still angling for a united Punjab even though he could not count on Khizar's support.[309] Other reactions to the partition proposal reflected subregional considerations more emphatically than purely communitarian ones. Muslims in the central districts and Jullundur division

---

[307]SPPAI, 14 June 1947, vol. lxix, no. 24, pp. 307, 309.

[308]Ibid., p. 307.

[309]SPPAI, 21 June 1947, vol. lxix, no. 25, pp. 326-7.

were distressed while those in western Punjab were 'selfishly jubilant'. In Ferozepur and Jullundur, the Muslim Students Federation and the MLNGs were 'indignant'. In Amritsar, the erstwhile editor of the *Siyasat*, Sayyid Habib, had started a movement for a united Punjab under an organization called the Anjuman-i-Wahadat. The 'Tipu regiment' was doing the same.[310] There were other such efforts, albeit to no avail.

It was Jinnah who prevailed at the All-India Muslim League meeting in Delhi. He had said in his radio broadcast on 3 June that the plan was less than satisfactory. The Muslim League only had to consider whether to accept it as 'a compromise or a settlement'. There was, significantly enough, no mention of the partition of the Punjab or Bengal.[311] At the meeting itself, Leaguers from eastern Punjab voicing their disapproval of the partition plan carried no weight. Nor did the spokespersons of Muslims in the minority provinces. While reserving its judgement on the partition of the provinces, the all-India League council voted four hundred in favour and eight against accepting the plan as a 'compromise'.[312] Leaving Muslims in the eastern districts to the tender mercies of their Hindu and Sikh neighbours, the provincial League council resolved to conduct a propaganda drive, proclaiming the achievement of 'Pakistan'. At the same time they hoped that by some miracle they would manage to 'drive a wedge between Congress and the Sikhs in the Punjab' before the boundary commission started its deliberations. 'Influential Muslims' were assigned the task of 'assur[ing] Sikh leaders and landowners' that the League was 'prepared to give them a practically autonomous homeland in Pakistan'.[313]

None of these assurances could convince the rank and file, far less the Sikhs. A meeting of the provincial council of action wanted the general council to explain its acceptance of the 3 June plan. Mamdot and Daultana were both afraid of 'unwelcome criticism and opposition' from delegates from eastern Punjab. Muslims in the Hindustan areas were 'demoralised' but on the whole 'resigned to their fate of living outside Pakistan'. The feeling was given forthright expression by the president of the Jullundur city Muslim League. Disheartened by the All-India Muslim League meeting in Delhi, where he was prevented from making a case, he pulled down the League flag from his home. The Khaksars considered the Pakistan the Muslim League had accepted as 'worthless'. For once the Ahrars agreed completely.[314] Behind the barricaded walls of his stronghold in Qadian, Bashiruddin Mahmud felt much the same. He had raised a fund of Rs 50,000 to establish a volunteer corp to protect the Ahmadis. Even

---

[310]*SPPAI*, 14 June 1947, vol. lxix, no. 24, p. 311.

[311]See text of Jinnah's broadcast of 3 June 1947 in Pirzada (ed.), *Foundations of Pakistan*, ii, pp. 563–5.

[312]For a surprisingly abbreviated account of the proceedings of the AIML council meeting in Delhi, 9–10 June 1947, see Ibid., pp. 565–8.

[313]*SPPAI*, 14 June 1947, vol. lxix, no. 24, pp. 310–11.

[314]*SPPAI*, 21 July 1947, vol. lxix, no. 25, pp. 328–30.

after the formal partition of the province, the Ahmadis were 'inclined to stick on at Qadian ... against heavy odds'. Determined to hold on to his local patrimony, Bashiruddin as late as September 1947 was advising his followers to evacuate the women and return to Qadian.[315] In another example of localized claims to territorial sovereignty, the Meos had been agitating for 'Meoistan' in Gurgaon district.[316] Asserting their authority with bravado, Meos had extracted a punitive tax of Rs 30,000 from Hindu *mahajans* in the form of relief funds.[317]

Punjabis, cutting across communitarian divisions, were jealously guarding their claims to social spaces, embodying both the material and the spiritual aspects of their individual and collective identities. The resistance to displacement was most pronounced among Sikhs and Muslims, neither of whom were 'showing any sign of being willing either to give up their present abode, or to submit lightly to any kind of domination by the other'. Sikhs were still refusing to consider any award by the boundary commission which gave Lyallpur, Montgomery, Gujranwala and Sheikhupura to a Muslim government. This kept the central districts on the boil. There were continuing incidents in Lahore and Amritsar which were spreading to Gujranwala and the rural areas of Amritsar, Gurdaspur and Hoshiarpur. With the Meos showing no signs of retracting their local claim to sovereignty, the situation in Gurgaon was 'extremely confused' with 'inter-village communal warfare of a very bitter nature'.[318]

The Muslim–Sikh stand-off in the central districts was accompanied by increasing support for the RSS among Punjabi Hindus. Officials were 'certain that the RSS [wa]s taking the lead in secret Hindu plans connected with the present disturbances'. Investigations showed that its members had been 'very much involved in many of the bomb cases' that had occurred in different parts of the province. This was hardly a revelation. RSS members had been making and using armed explosives with the help of demobilized soldiers for months. Grenades used in Lahore and Amritsar were 'fair imitations of the Military 36–M type' deployed by the British Indian army. In the Shakargarh sub-district of Gurdaspur, Hindus and the RSS were reported to be trying to raise an 'Agni Dal' which would specialize in explosives. Despite the mounting evidence against the RSS as 'an active militant body', the Punjab government felt unable to institute a ban on volunteer organizations. Although the MLNG was not nearly as conspicuous as the RSS, it was 'significant that 70 per cent of the new fires in Lahore ... occurred in non-Muslim houses'.[319]

Further investigations revealed that the MLNG's participation in disturbances

---

[315]*SPPAI*, 6 September 1947, vol. lxix, no. 37, p. 443. Also see Ahmadi memorandum and Bashiruddin Mahmud's letter to the chairman of the Punjab boundary commission in *The Partition of the Punjab*, i, pp. 428–70.

[316]*SPPAI*, 17 May 1947, vol. lxix, no. 20, p. 263.

[317]*SPPAI*, 19 April 1947, vol. lxix, no. 16, p. 194.

[318]*SPPAI*, 21 June 1947, vol. lxix, no. 25, pp. 325–6.

[319]Ibid., p. 330.

in Lahore was 'not on the scale of the RSS'. Indeed, the provincial capital was the 'focal point' of the activities of the *sangh*. With Punjabi Hindus unreconciled to the loss of Lahore, the RSS's high profile in the battles for social spaces in the wards and *mohallas* of the city made perfect sense.[320] Elsewhere too, influential members of the Mahasabha were 'directly inspiring the underground terrorist activities' of the RSS with the help of local Hindu roughnecks. Most of the relief and legal committees turned out to be 'nothing but a front behind which terrorist organisations ha[d] been built up'.[321] The RSS was also building its organization in Jammu and Kashmir in anticipation of a Muslim bid for power. Preferring to concentrate their energies on the princely state and areas whose fate was not yet sealed, most of the active workers of the RSS in time went underground or left Lahore altogether. After mid-July, the RSS was sending workers from 'outside to foment trouble' rather than banking on local efforts.[322] But isolated batches of RSS workers were continuing to operate in the city. In early August a 'large gang' of RSS workers apprehended in Lahore was 'found to be responsible for most of the worst bomb outrages'. Among the arms recovered were hand grenades, country-made bombs, revolvers, guns, sharp-edged weapons and steel helmets in huge quantities.[323]

With the League and its national guards less efficiently organized than the RSS, groups of Muslims carried out random attacks on non-Muslims. Banded individuals, referred to in colonial discourse as 'hooligan elements', were 'creating havoc with the tacit approval of the local Muslim League leaders'. These elements had adopted a 'scorched earth policy' in Lahore to force the non-Muslims to leave while in Amritsar the purpose was to cause as much damage to property as possible. Seeing his dreams crumbling in the Punjab, Jinnah had made one final attempt to give direction to local battles for social space at the coming apart of Britain's empire in India. He had instructed his provincial lieutenants to win the confidence of the minorities and establish peace at all costs. There were some 'grounds for the belief that the Punjab League High Command [wa]s serious in its expressed desire to stop the riots'.[324]

Jinnah's statement promising safeguards to minorities in mid-July 'caused satisfaction to the non-Muslims', now facing the implications of a partitioned province.[325] Such steps as were taken by the Punjab League to reassure non-Muslims aimed more at restoring peace in the Pakistan areas than preventing the partition of the province. After legislators from the eastern districts of the provincial assembly voted on 23 June to dissolve the administrative unity of the Punjab, the League seemed 'earnest in its apparent endeavour to recreate

[320]Ibid.

[321]*SPPAI*, 28 June 1947, vol. lxix, no. 26, p. 339.

[322]*SPPAI*, 12 and 19 July 1947, vol. lxix, nos. 28, 29, pp. 368, 376.

[323]*SPPAI*, 9 August 1947, vol. lxix, no. 32, p. 410.

[324]*SPPAI*, 21 June 1947, vol. lxix, no. 25, p. 342.

[325]Ibid., p. 376.

a sense of law and order' in Pakistan's territories. Assurances of fair treatment to minorities in western Punjab were looked upon with suspicion by Hindus, most of whom were planning to migrate. Yet those who migrated were also the first ones to reaffirm the bond of familiar social space by returning home. In one of those delicious ironies, Muslims in western Punjab who had 'suffered inconvenience on account of the absence of their *banias'* were seen to be capable of 'cherish[ing] them more if they ... [came] back'.[326] Even the most catastrophic breakdown in social relations could not erase the lingering economic ties between Hindus and Muslims. The problem lay at the leadership level where there was 'a childish elation on new found power' among the Muslim Leaguers. More troubling was the split in the Punjab League over the partition plan. It was seen to have weakened Mamdot and Daultana in the western districts where *zamindars* were supporting Firoz Khan Noon, fearful that the Punjab's future would be 'shaped by hands which [we]re not Punjabi'.[327] Muslim traders, for their part, were furious at the appointment of Syed Muratib Ali as the sole distributor of cotton cloth in western Punjab. The arbitrary nature of the 'choice' was widely 'attributed to capitalistic designs on the part of local League leaders' and their lack of 'interest ... in the common man'.[328]

No less ominous for the future were the ideological divisions within the Punjab League over nominations to the Pakistan constituent assembly. The selection of Iftikharuddin, Daultana and Begum Shah Nawaz, and the noticeable absence of religious leaders, had given rise to the feeling that 'Communists [we]re being afforded an opportunity to do as much damage to Islam as possible'. There was widespread belief that the constitution of the new state would be 'on modernised Islamic lines or framed after the Turkish constitution'.[329] This was unacceptable to a wide array of Islamic ideologues inside as well as outside the League. Abdus Sattar Niazi asserted that Muslims in the Punjab and the NWFP would 'never tolerate being governed by a system of law and order based on British law'. To avert 'serious trouble', it was imperative for the Pakistan constituent assembly to 'frame a constitution based on Islamic law'.[330] The *imam* of the Lohari Masjid in Lahore was consulting the *ulema* and *pirs* of the Punjab about 'drafting a constitution based on Shariat law' for presentation to the new constituent assembly.[331]

If these were the opinions of the League's supporters, its Muslim rivals had reason to exult. Political expediency had forced the Ahrars to reconcile themselves to Pakistan, it had not converted them to Jinnah's or the League's

[326]*SPPAI*, 28 June 1947, vol. lxix, no. 26, p. 339.
[327]Ibid., p. 341.
[328]*SPPAI*, 19 July 1947, vol. lxix, no. 29, pp. 375, 378.
[329]*SPPAI*, 5 July 1947, vol. lxix, no. 27, p. 355.
[330]*SPPAI*, 2 August 1947, vol. lxix, no. 31, p. 400.
[331]*SPPAI*, 19 July 1947, vol. lxix, no. 29, p. 378.

brand of Islamic modernism. These ideological contestations assumed myriad colours. Consider Mashriqi's effervescent imaginings, pronounced while dismantling the Khaksar organization and his paper *Al-Islah*. Posters signed by Al-Mashriqi, as he was known among his circle of admirers, were seen in Ludhiana condemning the partition decision. In Jullundur, Khaksars were under the impression that their organization wanted a Pakistan stretching from Delhi to Peshawar with Delhi as the capital . For a man who believed that sovereignty was a God-given right to Muslims, Mashriqi in his inimitable way underlined the dilemma of identity and territory in the closing moments of undivided India. To contemporaries, Mashriqi might appear to have joined the 'limbo of discarded politicians'. But there were Muslims who agreed with him that it was unthinkable for them to 'leave their holy places' under non-Muslim domination. It is of considerable significance that Mashriqi's list of sacred Muslim places included not only that ultimate symbol of temporal sovereignty, the Red Fort, but also the greatest monument to love, the Taj Mahal, and the leading Muslim educational institution, the Aligarh University. A poster 'advocating a crazy scheme' for a Muslim state consisting of the NWFP, the Punjab, Delhi, Ajmer, UP, Bihar, Bengal and Assam appeared in Ambala, advertising the Khaksar leader's conviction that any worthwhile sovereignty for Muslims in India had to make adequate allowance for both the spiritual and temporal dimensions of their identity.[332]

The strength of regional, class and ideological differences in a religiously defined community standing at the threshold of sovereign statehood was not restricted to the Muslims. Even in the moment of triumph, the Congress in the Punjab was racked by divisions of a subregional and class nature. There was growing opposition to the Congress leadership in certain Hindu quarters who charged it with having no definite policy. The election of Satyapal's arch- rival, Gopi Chand, as leader of the eastern Punjab Congress assembly party was unacceptable to the 'more prominent Congressmen of the Province' who were 'resentful of the domination exercised by Delhi in Punjab and Bengal politics'. The Jats of eastern Punjab were expected to be 'a real problem' since Gopi Chand was a non-agriculturist while the majority of Congressmen in eastern Punjab were agriculturists.[333] Hindu Jats of Haryana made no secret of their intention to keep non-Muslims of the western districts out of politics and services in eastern Punjab.[334] This was bad news for Hindu commercial groups in places like Lyallpur and Gujranwala who were preparing to move all their available assets to the non-Muslim-majority districts before they were vanquished by gangs of armed Muslims. There was 'an unusual rush on the banks to withdraw credit

---

[332]*SPPAI*, 5 July 1947, vol. lxix, no. 27, p. 356.
[333]Ibid., p. 353.
[334]*SPPAI*, 26 July 1947, vol. lxix, no. 30, p. 386.

in the Multan division'. But anticipating poor treatment at the hands of their own co-religionists, Hindus in Mianwali were veering towards staying and seeing what the future Muslim government had to offer.[335] The 'consensus of opinion' at a minorities convention in Rawalpindi was that 'non-Muslims should remain in the Pakistan areas and secure safeguards'. Matters got out of hand when it came to choosing representatives for the minorities protection board. Those not from Rawalpindi resented the domination of the board by residents of the city and the meeting ended in disruption. With the Akalis conspicuously absent, this Congress-inspired effort to get Hindus and Sikhs in northern and western Punjab to form a strong front to protect their interests collapsed.[336]

It was the Sikhs who were most deeply wounded by the implications of a partitioned Punjab. An estimated thirty-seven lakh of the population of the undivided province, the notional boundary line left some sixteen lakh in western Punjab. If the League's demands to the boundary commission were taken into consideration, the number of Sikhs in the 'Pakistan' areas rose to over twenty-five lakh. Sardar Harnam Singh, advocating the Sikh case before the boundary commission, had to argue that 'numbers ... [were] wholly irrelevant in the determination of a "homeland"'.[337] Facing the loss of their homes and properties, Sikhs had 'at last realised that their solidarity ha[d] been endangered by the demand for partition which they themselves inspired'. Their refusal to accept a boundary line short of the Chenab was bound to 'create a situation dangerous to the already unstable conditions'. Matters were only partially improved by the government decision to impose a ban on the carrying of weapons. This led to a decrease in the number of conversions to the Nihang cult proving the contention that these were 'merely a front to obtain arms'. But with ample supplies of arms and ammunition, the Sikhs were making more and more implausible demands. The latest Akali demand was for a sovereign Sikh state within the Indian union which would exclude Ambala but include the canal colonies. Clearly, the Akalis did not consider 'constitutionalism' to be the 'only means to enforce their demands'.[338] Overtures were continuing to be made to Sikh rulers of Faridkot, Patiala and Kapurthala to help establish a Punjab Sikh States Federation, and, failing that, to come to the assistance of the *panth*.[339]

If these were the tactics of the leaders, the Sikh populace at large was thoroughly bewildered by the barrage of contradictory instructions and schemes emanating from the leadership. There was 'a growing feeling, particularly amongst refugees, that the Akali political leaders had proved

[335]*SPPAI*, 5 July 1947, vol. lxix, no. 27, p. 357.
[336]*SPPAI*, 12 July 1947, vol. lxix, no. 28, p. 364.
[337]See *The Partition of the Punjab*, ii, pp. 121, 136.
[338]*SPPAI*, 28 June 1947, vol. lxix, no. 26, pp. 338, 341.
[339]*SPPAI*, 5 July 1947, vol. lxix, no. 27, p. 354.

themselves incompetent'.[340] Tara Singh was blamed for plunging the province into turmoil with his inflammatory speech on 3 March 1947. Some even advised him to consider Jinnah's assurances of a free Sikh state within Pakistan. This was the only way to prevent the separation of sacred places of worship such as Panja Sahib, Nankana Sahib, Dera Sahib and the tomb of Maharaja Ranjit Singh from the Darbar Sahib, a disaster for the religiously informed cultural identities of Sikhs.[341] The memorandum submitted to the boundary commission by Sikh members of the assembly made an impassioned plea for the incorporation of their sacred places in eastern Punjab. These included Sikh shrines in Lahore, a city which the community had referred to as the 'Guru's cradle' since time immemorial.[342]

Endorsing the arguments, the All-Parties Sikh Convention at New Delhi urged the Akali Dal to take steps against the 'unjust division of the Punjab'. The boundary commission would be 'raising a structure on sand if the demands of the Sikhs were not acceded'.[343] Basing their case on religious and economic arguments, the Sikhs believed they were entitled to an area described as the 'Shahidi Bar' consisting of tracts in Lyallpur, Sheikhupura and Gujranwala where they had substantial property and a number of important religious shrines. Weeks before the boundary commission award, Giani Kartar Singh was telling his co-religionists in south-western Punjab that there was 'a great hope' of getting not only Montgomery, Sheikhupura and Lyallpur but also Lahore. Despite this pious hope, it was apparent that the Sikh leadership was 'sinking in the estimation of the Sikh intelligentsia'. Men like Tara Singh and Giani Kartar Singh were accused of 'blundering' and 'land[ing] the Sikh community into a very unfortunate situation'.[344]

With Muslim Leaguers equally determined to resist any award by the boundary commission which gave them less than their demands, the final demarcation of the frontiers was expected to lead to 'destruction and devastation' on a greater scale than before. Secret instructions were said to have been issued to local Leagues in fifteen disputed districts to prepare for a struggle if the verdict was unfavourable. There was much agitation in provincial League circles about an alleged attempt by the boundary commission to place Sikh religious places in Hindustan.[345] This, as the Muslim League had made plain in its memorandum to the boundary commission, would result in Muslims demanding the whole of eastern Punjab by virtue of the many shrines and mosques dotting the landscape in non-Muslim-majority areas. Instead

[340]*SPPAI*, 28 June 1947, vol. lxix, no. 26, p. 339.
[341]*SPPAI*, 19 July 1947, vol. lxix, no. 29, p. 377.
[342]Sikh memorandum to the Punjab boundary commission, *The Partition of the Punjab*, i, pp. 382–3.
[343]*SPPAI*, 26 July 1947, vol. lxix, no. 30, p. 388.
[344]*SPPAI*, 2 August 1947, vol. lxix, no. 31, pp. 397–8.
[345]*SPPAI*, 5 and 12 July 1947, vol. lxix, nos. 27, 28, pp. 351, 378.

of demanding areas on the basis of religious sanctity, historical associations, sentimental attachment, proprietary interests, cultural considerations, educational facilities or any other similar factor, the League's case for Pakistan's borders rested on the population factor alone. If it was to be administratively viable rather than 'a nightmare tapestry of futurist design', Pakistan had to have a 'workable' and 'practicable' boundary, 'not ... a crazy line running backwards and forwards' in and out of villages in several districts. It followed that the commission had to take the tehsil as the basic administrative unit. Once the contiguous Muslim districts had been identified, tehsils containing a majority of Muslims should be appended to the Pakistan territories. By this logic the League demanded the incorporation of Gurdaspur, minus the non-Muslim-majority tehsil of Pathankot, as well as the Ajnala, Tarn Taran and Amritsar tehsils of Amritsar district and parts of Jullundur and Ferozepur districts.[346]

The League's claim to districts like Gurdaspur, fiercely contested by the Congress and the Sikhs, was strengthened by the Christian leader, Dewan Bahadur S.P. Singha of Batala, who 'declared unambiguously' that his community preferred to live in Pakistan. This was supported by the Central Christian Association which expressed confidence in Singha's leadership, making for an important local checkmate in the tehsil of Batala where Muslims on the basis of the 1941 census comprised 55.7 per cent of the population. With the addition of the Christians, a majority of 60.53 per cent in Batala could be seen as preferring Pakistan. It is well known that the disputed 1941 census itself was a site of intense contestations along lines of religiously informed cultural communities. But it was also a product of social manipulations of colonial categories. So it is hardly amazing that the statistical tabulations of the last decennial census were deployed in the narratives of negotiation.

The Ahmadi leader, Bashiruddin Mahmud, demanded Gurdaspur for Pakistan; it was the only way to perpetuate his local sovereignty in Qadian. He noted in the Ahmadi memorandum to the boundary commission that with the addition of the Christians, Muslims in Gurdaspur had an indisputable claim for inclusion in Pakistan.[347] Christians, according to the 1941 census, constituted 4.6 per cent of the population of Gurdaspur district. This meant that 55.6 per cent of the population of the district wanted incorporation into Pakistan, a considerable improvement over Jullundur district where the fact of a non-Muslim majority of 54.74 per cent had landed a substantial Muslim minority in Hindustan.[348]

The Christians did not require Bashiruddin to advocate their interests. In

---

[346]Muslim League's memorandum to the Punjab boundary commission, *The Partition of the Punjab*, i, pp. 283–4, 287–9.

[347]Ahmadi memorandum to the Punjab boundary commission, ibid., pp. 437–8.

[348]Ibid, p. 438.

Gurdaspur they were afraid that Hindus would not let them preach and were anxious about their religious centres in the district. They agreed with Singha that Pakistan with its Christian population of just under five lakh would be a safer place than Hindustan.[349] Of course not all Christians agreed.[350] Showing resolve, Singha dismissed opposition to his Pakistan Christian League, alleging that it was orchestrated by no more than a handful of left-leaning 'nationalist Christians' from six or eight families who represented no one but themselves. There was not a single Congressman worth his salt in the Punjab. All three Christian MLAs in the Punjab assembly had voted to stay in Pakistan. Only 60,955 out of five hundred thousand Punjabi Christians lived in eastern Punjab. Long associations with Muslims had considerably 'Muslimised' the Christians in 'culture and outlook'. They 'trust the Muslim more', pronounced Singha—the grandson of a Bihari with a Bengali grandmother, a Punjabi mother and a wife from UP. In their dress, poor economic status and religious beliefs, Christians in the Punjab were closer to the Muslims. The widespread practice of *chhut* or untouchability against Christians was 'a great sore in their hearts' and they had 'suffered a lot from social prejudices of non-Muslims'. Singha had seen villages where there were no Christian graveyards—an important leitmotif in the Punjabi Christian swing to Pakistan—and social sanctions against drawing water from certain wells. The 'Punjab mentality' and 'tradition' was 'quite different from that of the rest of the India'.[351]

As Bashiruddin had argued forcefully, no one could 'say that Christians d[id] not wish to go into Pakistan'.[352] The same arguments could be deployed with respect to the scheduled castes, albeit less effectively due to the Poona Pact.[353] The 1941 census listed seventeen categories of scheduled castes in the Punjab. Of these the vast majority lived in the eastern districts; all the scheduled caste members in the Punjab assembly had voted for Hindustan. Representations on their behalf were based on arguments of religious and cultural affinity with caste Hindus. The opposition was quick to note that the scheduled caste representatives in the Punjab assembly had received more votes from caste Hindus than from members of their own community. But

[349]*SPPAI*, 26 July 1947, vol. lxix, no. 30, p. 388.

[350]Banerji's arguments on behalf of the provincial Nationalist Christian Association to the boundary commission, *The Partition of the Punjab*, ii, pp. 191–8.

[351]Dewan Bahadur S.P. Singha's arguments on behalf of the Joint Christian Board to the boundary commission, ibid., pp. 224–5.

[352]Ahmadi memorandum to the boundary commission, *The Partition of the Punjab*, i, pp. 437–8.

[353]Salig Ram, who pleaded the case of the scheduled castes and the Mazhabi Sikhs before the boundary commission, argued that joint electorates was 'a wrong principle' and 'a wrong presumption' in a context where scheduled castes were treated worse than animals by caste Hindus. The 'authors of the Poona Pact just hushed up the voice coming from the opposite side'. (Salig Ram's arguments to the boundary commission, *The Partition of the Punjab*, ii, pp. 432–3.)

the scheduled castes of the Punjab and the Mazhabi Sikhs were trickier cards
for the Muslim League to play in claiming disputed districts and tehsils on
the basis of population proportions.

The Western Pakistan Scheduled Caste Federation under the presidentship
of Choudhry Sukh Lal had presented a memorandum to Mountbatten in July
alleging that 'Hindus c[ould] not possibly recognise the human status of the
Untouchables, so long as *Vedas and Shastras* [we]re sacred to them'. It was an
open secret that Hindus wanted to establish a *'Vedic Raj'* in the name of *Ram
Raj*. Under the circumstances, the victims of social untouchability would be no
more than *'Chandals'* under Hindu domination. By contrast, there was 'every
hope for the Untouchables in Pakistan'. Islam was based on the 'equality of
man' and there could be no denial of human status to anyone on the basis of
either colour or creed.[354] It was unimaginable for the *achhuts* to expect equal
rights of citizenship from caste Hindus who had 'no sympathy with them' and
did 'not even allow them to remain in the same *abadis*', draw water from the
same well, enter their kitchens or share places of worship. The same was true
for Mazhabi Sikhs who were untouchables in the eyes of other Sikh castes.
They had their own *gurdwaras*, if at all, received a different kind of *amrit* and
had 'nothing in common with the rest of the Sikhs'. In concrete social terms, as
opposed to census categories, an ordinary Sikh was much like a caste Hindu
while a Mazhabi Sikh was like a scheduled caste Hindu.[355]

It was impossible for the boundary commission to satisfy wildly clashing
claims to territories in the Punjab. This fuelled popular perceptions that the
boundary had been decided and that the commission was nothing more than
a 'camouflage'. The vigorous display of the determination of the Sikhs to
maintain their solidarity and sovereignty over sacred places saw a 'stiffening in
the Muslim attitude towards the minorities'.[356] Attacks on Muslims in Amritsar
by early August alarmed Sikhs and Hindus in western Punjab who feared
reprisals. Exhortations by Hindu and Sikh leaders to non-Muslim minorities
to remain in the districts to which they belonged and promises by Muslim League
leaders of 'protection and equal treatment' had 'failed to dispel the panic'. Those
who had escaped the Muslim *jihad* and returned were once 'again on the move'.
The Congress cut a sorry figure trying to plead the case of minorities in Pakistan.
Reactions to Gandhi's courtesy call on the Punjab after a visit to Kashmir said it
all. In Lalamusa along the Grand Trunk Road between Lahore and Rawalpindi,
the Mahatma was showered with posters 'asking him to retire from politics'.[357]

[354]Memorandum of the Scheduled Caste Organizations to Mountbatten, *The
Partition of the Punjab*, i, p. 145.

[355]Salig Ram's arguments to the boundary commission, *The Partition of the Punjab*,
ii, pp. 432–4.

[356]*SPPAI*, 2 August 1947, vol. lxix, no. 31, p. 400.

[357]*SPPAI*, 9 August 1947, vol. lxix, no. 32, p. 407. Gandhi's refusal to visit the
disturbed areas in the Punjab is entirely explicable.

The disregard of the human dimension in the political bargaining at the all-India level was coming home to haunt the national leadership with a vengeance. Shaukat Hayat has recalled his shock and horror at not just the violence against Muslims in Amritsar but also the painful discovery that Muslim men had abandoned their women and children for the safety of Lahore. Callousness was matched by cowardice in one village where Muslim men hid in the sugarcane fields while a band of Sikhs carried away young girls and set fire to a house where they had pushed all the old women and children. In one instance, a terrified young woman left her child on the roadside when told by the driver of a bus full of Muslims that there was space for only one person.[358] Collective memories of violence in social spaces, embodying some of the strongest identities of individuals and collectivities, have woven a dark shroud over the corpse of undivided Punjab. A scrupulous sifting of the threads, however, confirms the personalized and localized nature of the violence which accompanied the partition of the Punjab. Above all it brings out the horrific victimization of women, Muslim, Hindu and Sikh, by men battling to safeguard their communitarian interests.

Placing gender at the centre of the analysis of the violence, perpetrated as well as suffered in the Punjab, offers astonishing insights into the social attitudes which marked the birth of independent citizenship in South Asia. In April 1947 which saw Muslims in western Punjab massacring non-Muslims and raping and abducting women, one hundred Sikh girls were allegedly being held by their Muslim abductors with the object of forcibly converting them.[359] By August it was the turn of the Sikhs to give expression to their outrage. Naked Muslim girls are said to have been paraded outside Darbar Sahib in Amritsar.[360] This was not the only instance of the sacred turning profane in the process of taking the battle for sovereignty into different tehsils and districts. There are countless other examples of male inhumanity towards women in what have been presumed to be efforts to assert dominance over men of other communities. Some of the most telling ones can be found in the prose constructions of Manto, Krishan Chander, Rajinder Singh Bedi and many other writers and poets who experienced the tumult of 1947.[361]

---

[358] Khan, *The Nation that Lost its Soul*, pp. 184–6. Without revealing his own role, whether direct or indirect, in Muslim retaliations against non-Muslims in western Punjab, Shaukat Hayat only records that he has 'never forg[otten] the shrieks of the hapless creatures', old women and children, burnt alive by Sikhs in a village near the road to the river Beas.

[359] Minutes of Mountbatten's meeting with Sardar Patel, 25 April 1947, *TP*, x, p. 425.

[360] Khan, *The Nation That Lost its Soul*, p. 186.

[361] For a compilation containing the feelings of creative writers and poets about the gruesome events, see Mushirul Hasan (ed.), *India Partitioned: The Other Face of Freedom*, in two volumes, New Delhi: Roli Books, 1995–6.

The value of the available historical and literary evidence on the atrocities perpetrated in the name of religion lies in its exposing the human barbarity that attended the dawn of freedom. The wide publicity given to the 'horrors' perpetrated by Sikhs on Muslims in Amritsar by the arrival of refugees in ever larger numbers 'caused deep exacerbation' to Muslim feelings in Lahore. News of Muslim police constables in Amritsar being disarmed and the derailment of the Pakistan special in Ferozepur district greatly aggravated tensions.[362] There were attacks on non-Muslims as Muslims in western Punjab learnt of the sufferings of their co-religionists in the eastern districts. As the first Muslim signatory to the Punjab police abstracts admitted, the 'inauguration of Pakistan' which had been 'so eagerly awaited by the Muslims' brought them 'very little joy'. A 'grim shadow' had been cast by stories of how Muslims in eastern Punjab had been 'killed, maimed, despoiled, dishonoured and uprooted from their homes'. The arrival of refugees into western Punjab bearing 'scars of brutal assaults' and a willingness to talk had 'aroused sympathy and even anger'. The award of the Punjab boundary commission, whose announcement was postponed by Mountbatten to allow for the transfer of power ceremonies to proceed, predictably 'caused much disappointment'. The 'majority of Muslims were confident that the territory of West Punjab would be enlarged' and Muslim-majority tehsils in Gurdaspur, Amritsar, Jullundur, Hoshiarpur and Ferozepur districts would be 'added to Pakistan'. Sikhs were blamed for the abominations in eastern Punjab. But it was the British who were held responsible for 'engineer[ing] the Sikh rising which had resulted in the effusion of Muslim blood'. Some quarters were now convinced that the actual boundary line had been 'drawn long before by the British Government with a view to strengthening the Sikhs' and the boundary commission was established only to 'give the award a semblance of justice'.[363]

Muslim suspicions of British bad faith and the influx of refugees from eastern Punjab spelt the end for non-Muslims in the western districts. These refugees included men who had abandoned their mothers and sisters as well wives and children in Amritsar. Violence against non-Muslims spread from Lahore to the rest of the province. The beginning of the final phase of the violence in August 1947 saw clashing identities and contested sovereignties ripping apart the moral and the spatial landscape of the Punjab. Ahrars, Khaksars and disgruntled Leaguers tried stirring the refugees against the newly formed ministry. Ahrars were accused of 'show[ing] little concern over the happenings in the East Punjab' and 'passing ironical remarks about Pakistan' with a view to 'lowering the prestige of the Government'.[364] Khaksars were doing much the same. The premier, Mamdot, had to hide while his home

[362]*SPPAI*, 16 August 1947, vol. lxix, no. 33, p. 413.
[363]*SPPAI*, 23 August 1947, vol. lxix, no. 34, p. 419.
[364]*SPPAI*, 23 and 30 August 1947, vol. lxix, nos. 35, 36, pp. 423, 432.

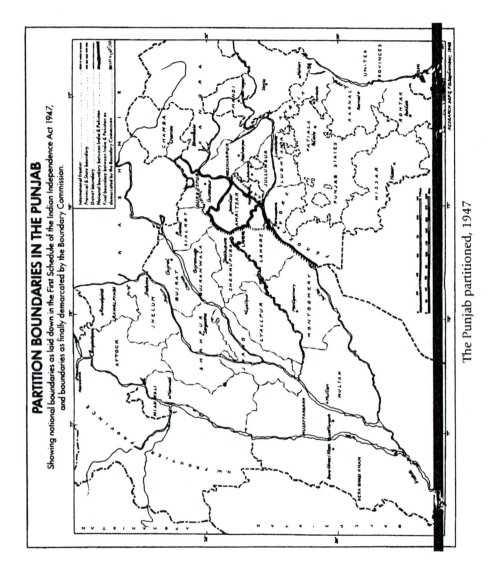

The Punjab partitioned, 1947

was surrounded by 'bands of aggressive and highly excited Muslims' from Amritsar, crying *Jan lene aye hain, Jan leke jaengey*—We have come to take life and will take it.[365] Significantly, while the people of Lahore wanted 'a quick return to normal conditions, the malevolent element from the East Punjab [we]re exploiting the discontent and advocat[ing] retaliation'.[366]

There were hopes yet of minimizing the social dislocations by offering allegiance to the new state. Chastened by the violence, the people of Rawalpindi received the news of Muslim deaths in east Punjab solemnly. Independence day was a colourless affair. Some Hindu refugees participated in the hoisting of the Pakistan flag, but Sikhs refrained. Congress non-cooperated while permitting individual members to participate if they so chose. In Chakwal and Jhelum districts, Sikh commissioned officers, active and pensioned, attended a march past and presented arms to the national flag. Non-Muslims in Jhelum made donations to Muslim refugees' funds and appealed to their co-religionists in eastern Punjab to put an end to the lawlessness. 'Sober-minded Muslims' were 'endeavouring to persuade non-Muslims to stay on in the West Punjab'. But non-Muslims had reason to panic. Several Hindu and Sikh railway workers had been killed. Non-Muslims who had courageously opted to remain in Pakistan saw their 'houses and shops burnt and looted'.[367] The general clearing of social spaces had begun in the localities and districts of the Punjab. Armed thugs, frequently assisted by the local MLNG, and even elements in the police and the army, carried out a systematic campaign of looting and burning.[368] The complicity of the district administration in many instances, to say nothing of the security forces, gave the Muslim bands their first joy of independent statehood.

Many non-Muslim police officers deserted, taking their firearms with them. With a League ministry finally in the saddle, the Muslims secured their demand to carry swords in public. The continued inflow of refugees from eastern Punjab with 'wild tales of atrocities' created a squall in Lahore, Gujranwala, Sialkot, Gujrat, Sargodha and Rawalpindi. There was acute tension in Mianwali, Campbellpur, Muzaffargarh, Multan and Sheikhupura. Some Congressmen and Hindus tried restoring cordial relations between the communities.[369] It was a herculean task given the evidence of the sheer brutality of the massacres in east Punjab. This was 'furnished by the arrival of dead bodies in trains and persons with wounds without discrimination of age or sex'. Enraged Muslims in Gujrat, Jhelum and Sheikhupura district as

---

[365]Ibid and Shaukat Hayat Khan, *The Nation that Lost its Soul*, p. 186.

[366]*SPPAI*, 23 August 1947, (signed by Anwar Ali, deputy inspector of police, CID, Punjab) vol. lxix, no. 34, p. 419.

[367] *SPPAI*, 23 August 1947, vol. lxix, no. 34, pp. 419–20.

[368]Khosla, *Stern Reckoning*, pp. 120–216.

[369] The information is from the second *SPPAI* also dated 23 August 1947 but signed by N. A. Rizvi, superintendent of police, CID, Punjab, vol. lxix, no. 35, p. 425.

well as the Kasur subdivision went on a rampage as did those in the northern districts of the province. The great migration had begun. Streams of Hindus and Sikhs abandoned their homes. The wealthier few made free use of the air services. For the vast majority, however, perilous roads and murderous railways offered the only opportunity for escape.[370]

High-sounding appeals by League leaders, including Jinnah, failed to alter realities on the ground. The statements were most often contradictory. After an announcement that shops deserted by Hindus and Sikhs could be sold, people were surprised to periodically hear that the evacuees should come back.[371] This was the Muslim strike at the heart of Hindu commercial dominance in the Punjab, and also Sind. Even before the new state had formulated its rules on evacuee property, the clearing of the localities and the appropriation of social space as property had acquired a momentum of its own. In western Punjab, members of the MLNG in consort with banded individuals in different localities made the most of the non-Muslim exodus. The grabbing of social space by armed thugs parading as protectors of Muslims hinted at the attitudes of a section of Pakistan's new citizens. Enjoying street power, vital for assertions of territorial sovereignty, these bands of Muslim men had found the El Dorado of their dreams. The nexus of citizenship in Pakistan and, by extension, India, as the Congress insisted Hindustan be known, was born of a bloody baptism that cannot be ascribed to religion as faith by any stretch of the imagination.

Muslim crimes against their Hindu and Sikh neighbours in western Punjab assumed appalling proportions which no amount of nationalist self-justification can wash away. So it is better to acknowledge the birth of independent statehood in not just its follies but also its depravities. This was not to be the ideal state of Islam of which the poet-philosopher of Punjabi Muslims had spoken in his reconstruction lectures. Far from providing any basis for the realization of the spiritual in each individual, far less the collectivity, in temporal activity, this was a state whose birth was stained by the material greed which the chaos of the British departure let loose in the Punjab. The Mahatma might have changed his mind and held ordered anarchy better than real anarchy.[372] But the real cause for grief was indubitably Jinnah's, the constitutionalist who had made a profession of defending the rights of minorities.

Muslims resident in west Punjab have pointed the finger at the refugee activists from the east for the attacks on their non-Muslim neighbours. There seems to be some truth in the accusation. In Lyallpur, Muslim refugees 'came to notice for the spirit of vengeance they had against non-Muslims'. But there was nothing strictly communitarian about their intentions, or of those who made common cause with them. There were 'instances of Muslims looting

[370]*SPPAI*, 30 August 1947, vol. lxix, no. 36, p. 431.
[371]*SPPAI*, 6 September 1947, vol. lxix, no. 37, p. 441.
[372]A reference to Gandhi's assertions after the failure of the Cripps' mission, calling on the British to leave India to God or anarchy.

shops owned by their own community'. If these were part of the general process of the clearing up of social space, there were some with more definite feelings about the separation. Malik Jamal Din of Rawalpindi thought Muslims should destroy the property of Hindus and Sikhs and begin building anew.[373] For the moment it was the destruction and despoliation of social space and the degradation of its inhabitants that seemed to be more pertinent.

The situation was much the same in India, the self-professed abode of secular nationalism and only too eager to confirm the legitimacy of its own ideals by dismissing the violence as religiously motivated. Yet Muslims in Delhi and other parts of India were attacked and their property seized not because they shunned the faith of their victimizers, however that might be construed, but because confiscating the material possessions of a religiously demarcated minority believed to have had a hand in the division of the country seemed like a just reward to the banded few perpetrating the violence. The predicament of vulnerable Muslim populations in the Indian capital and beyond had catalytic effects in western Punjab. Muslims here had congenital problems with the more militant Hindu strands in India's nationalist configuration. Most regarded Sardar Vallabhbhai Patel as the representative of this league. News from eastern Punjab coupled with horrific stories carried by refugees arriving in the new dominion from Delhi confirmed many in the belief that the Indian government was trying to flood Pakistan with refugees in order to place an unbearable burden on the incipient independent state. Few doubted that the 'extermination of the Muslims' had been 'planned with the knowledge and support of the top ranking leadership'. Attacks on Muslim villages and the abducting of women in Sialkot by Dogras from Jammu were countered by the banding together of armed Pathans from Mianwali and trans-border tribesmen. There were raids on villages in that district as well as neighbouring Campbellpur. In Sargodha, Muslim mobs looted Hindu houses in three villages, killing countless non-Muslims.[374]

Some of this was in retaliation against the Sikhs following a scorched earth policy prior to their evacuation. But the fury of Muslims asserting sovereignty knew no bounds. There were cases of conversion, both voluntary and involuntary, especially in Jhelum, Gujrat and Sargodha.[375] 'Well-to-do Hindus and Sikhs' who did 'not wish to part with their lands and other property changed their religion'.[376] Some five hundred conversions were reported to have taken place in Jhelum where non-Muslims constituted just over 10 per cent of the population. A major military recruiting district, it witnessed some of the more gruesome attacks on non-Muslims. Even an unsympathetic commentator like Khosla noted that it was 'not religious emotion or aggressive

[373]SPPAI, 6 September 1947, vol. lxix, no. 37, pp. 441–3.
[374]SPPAI, 13 September 1947, vol. lxix, no. 38, p. 451.
[375]SPPAI, 20 September 1947, vol. lxix, no. 39, p. 457.
[376]SPPAI, 13 September 1947, vol. lxix, no. 38, p. 451.

chauvinism ... but the prospect of personal gain' which prompted Muslim outrages against Hindus and Sikhs in Jhelum.[377] By late August a mere sixty members of the RSS remained in the district.[378] When it came to the crunch, volunteer corps formed during the previous years did less to protect the lives and property of co-religionists and more to shed innocent blood. Escaping to areas where numerical strength was on their side, the RSS quite as much as the MLNG preferred the offensive rather than the defensive path.

This weakened the capacity of religious minorities in western and eastern Punjab to resist encroachments on their social space. In Mianwali where bands of local and trans-border Pathans were pillaging non-Muslim villages, Hindus and Sikhs exchanged fire with the magistrate's party for thirty-six hours before giving up.[379] Underlining the strength of territorial identity, Hindu shopkeepers in Multan reopened for business once Muslims suspended the campaign of social boycott. Hindu evacuees from Montogomery wanted to return, provided they were given assurances by the government of Pakistan. Landed Sikhs in Lyallpur gave the impression that their migration was a temporary one, an attitude encouraged by their leaders' promise to forcibly regain control over the canal colony districts.[380] These illusions were shattered sooner rather than later. Assisted by the newly inherited administrative arms of the colonial state, bands of armed men were asserting their personalized authority in various localities and districts.

The organized nature of the clearing of social spaces would have been impossible without the collusion of the local police and, occasionally, also the military. In Gujranwala Muslims were procuring unlicensed rifles and revolvers under the watchful eye of the police. While bands of Muslims made away with cash and jewellery, attacking refugee caravans and evicting non-Muslims from key neighbourhoods, the better placed appropriated the richer plums in the districts. In Sialkot, for instance, prominent Muslims took possession of factories and buildings that belonged to migrating Hindus and Sikhs. A well-known pattern, it elicited an outcry from local Muslims. Three to four hundred people demonstrated in Pak Pattan against local Muslim League leaders whom they 'accused, along with some highly placed and influential persons of having grabbed valuable property'.[381] Agitators in Okara in Montgomery district charged the special magistrate, Mian Abdul Haq, with allotting valuable non-Muslim property at nominal prices to his friends and relatives. An organization was set up by refugees here to raise their voices against such blatant nepotism.[382] Individuals in Montgomery,

[377]Khosla, *Stern Reckoning*, p. 198.
[378]*SPPAI*, 23 August 1947, vol. lxix, no. 35, p. 423.
[379]*SPPAI*, 13 September 1947, vol. lxix, no. 38, p. 455.
[380]*SPPAI*, 27 September 1947, vol. lxix, no. 40, p. 468.
[381]*SPPAI*, 13 September 1947, vol. lxix, no. 38, pp. 452, 458.
[382]Ibid., p. 468.

pretending to be refugees, were obtaining land, shops and houses on a large scale.[383]

Amidst a general administrative and societal breakdown, it was the cynical and enterprising who made fortunes at the expense of their hapless victims. They were undoubtedly helped by the spirit of revenge among some of their fellow co-religionists. The arrival of train-loads of dead Muslim men, women and children embittered Muslim feelings in western Punjab, leading some to believe that 'vengeance was the only course open to them to stop these inhuman acts'. Non-Muslim evacuee trains and convoys were attacked in Lahore, Gujranwala, Jhelum, Rawalpindi, Campbellpur and Multan districts.[384] Rumours continued to circulate in Lahore of an impending invasion of Sikhs from east Punjab. These gained credence after several military parties from across the border raided Kasur and Sialkot district. Non-Muslim troops escorting Sikh evacuees in Sialkot left the imprint of their might by looting property and abducting several women.[385] In Shakargarh, Sikh *jathas* aided by non-Muslim troops attacked Muslim villages and had to be repulsed by the police. Pronouncements by Akali leaders vowing to return soon and reclaim the colony districts with the help of the armies of Sikh states were alarming to say the least.[386]

None of these fears and reactions can be seen as affording sufficient evidence of either communitarian or religious solidarity on the part of Muslims, Sikhs or Hindus. It was just that religious denominations had provided a fresh basis on which to settle claims of territorial sovereignty. The material benefits of the battles for social space in both parts of the Punjab accrued to individuals, not local communities. And there can certainly be no vindication of criminal actions in pursuit of *zar* and *zamin,* or wealth and property, which, together with *zan,* or women, were the three constitutive elements of material culture in the north-western areas constituting the territories of Pakistan. Even after the disorder and chaos had given way to 'some bright patches foreboding the return of peace', banded individuals were amassing wealth and property at other people's expense. There was no respect for commonality in religiously defined identities. In Campbellpur, Pathans from Mianwali and the NWFP, 'out for loot, more on criminal than communal lines', did not spare local Muslim residents.[387]

The numbers game had escalated into a looting spree in which respect for religious identifications was blurred by the more pressing enterprise of accumulating illicit property. But if the quest for *zar* and *zamin* had let to unpardonable offences against members of all three communities, the most

[383]*SPPAI,* 20 September 1947, vol. lxix, no. 39, p. 458.
[384]*SPPAI,* 27 September 1947, vol. lxix, no. 40, p. 467.
[385]Ibid., pp. 469–70.
[386]Ibid
[387]*SPPAI,* 20 September 1947, vol. lxix, no. 39, p. 461.

heinous crimes imaginable perpetrated against *zan* or women surely qualify for posthumous death penalties. The debasement of women in the Punjab assumed nightmarish proportions. Maulvi Maula Bakhsh, the *khatib* of the Juma Masjid in Rawalpindi told a congregation of three thousand Muslims that twenty five thousand Muslim girls had been abducted by Sikhs in eastern Punjab. Another *maulana* pointed to the atrocities of Dogra troops against Muslims in Poonch district who wanted accession to Pakistan.[388] The situation in Kashmir was 'a permanent menace to Muslims' and could be addressed only by coming to the armed assistance of helpless co-religionists against the Dogras who wanted to invade Pakistan and conquer western Punjab.[389]

Dogra raids on Sialkot and the abduction of Muslim women served to confirm the paranoia. The image of Kashmir as a powerless woman enslaved by Dogra rulers had never failed to excite Punjabi Muslims. Yet the decorum of wanting to rescue the symbol of a ravished woman meshed awkwardly with attitudes towards the living and the real. Banded Muslims in the different localities of western Punjab had been molesting non-Muslim women and adolescent girls, raping them in public and abducting many others ever since April 1947. There was nevertheless anguish upon hearing that a column of Muslim evacuees on its way to Pakistan had been mercilessly attacked by Sikh *jathas* in Ferozepur district. A number of young men were carried away and the 'women in the column stripped of their clothing'.[390] But if there were a few characters like Khushwant Singh's Jugga in the Sikh community, there were men of the Muslim community, as Manto has depicted in his classic story 'Khol Do', for whom Sirajuddin's daughter Sakina was first and foremost woman as prostitute, not ornament, irrespective of her religious identity as a Muslim.[391]

All said and done, the commonality of masculinity was thicker than the bond of religion. There were men in all three communities who delighted in their momentary sense of power over vulnerable women; such was the courage of these citizens of newly independent states. These lesser men might seek shelter in the scoundrel's ultimate refuge. Nothing in the discourses of the 'nation', however imagined, in late-colonial India, came even close to articulating a coherent notion of civic not to mention social and economic rights for women. The appearance of women on the public stage of nationalist politics has occasionally been cited as evidence of at least tentative progress in their quest for rights. But the rights which were debated most vigorously at

[388]In early September there were serious disturbances in Poonch state. Dogra troops were charged with extreme repression of Muslims in Poonch. Stories carried by Muslim refugees from Poonch to the NWFP and the Punjab elicited widespread sympathy for the plight of Kashmiri Muslims. (*SPPAI*, 6 September 1947, vol. lxix, no. 37, p. 441.)

[389]*SPPAI*, 13 September 1947, vol. lxix, no. 48, p. 452.

[390]*SPPAI*, 20 September 1947, vol. lxix, no. 39, p. 457.

[391]See Khushwant Singh, *Train to Pakistan*, New York: Grove Press, 1961 and Saadat Hasan Manto's 'Sakina', in *Black Milk*, pp. 43–6.

such gatherings were those of the communities-turned-nations. The individual, far less woman as individual, formed no part of a nationalist political agenda, whether of the League, the Akalis or the Congress. Gender eroded the barriers that religion had been forced to create. Whatever women may have achieved by aligning their interests with nationalist organizations of their communities, it was more as abstractions appended to the religious community seeking sovereign statehood than as substantive subjects constituting the nation.

Women's meagre achievements in defence of their own interests were writ large at the moment of the great human betrayal. There can be no disputing that women were among the main victims of violence perpetrated by bands of Muslim, Sikh and Hindu men. Their sufferings continue to resonate as they fracture the high-flown rhetoric of post-colonial states on equal rights of citizenship. Alas, the Punjab had betrayed its patriarchal bent more decisively than the affective affinities of religious community. In the memorable words of Amrita Pritam invoking the spirit of the author of the legendary *qisa* or folk-tale *Heer–Ranjha* while composing the ultimate epithet for undivided Punjab:

Today I call upon Waris Shah
To rise from the grave and speak
And plead with him to open another page in the book of love
One daughter of the Punjab had cried
And you were moved to write reams on her sorrow
Today thousands of crying daughters
Call upon you, O, Waris Shah
O you, the sympathizer of the broken hearted,
Arise and see your Punjab.
Today dead bodies are cramming the forests
And the Chenab is brimming with blood
Someone has mixed poison with the water of the five rivers
And that water has spread all over the land.[392]

[392]Amrita Pritam, 'Aaj Aakhan Waris Shah Noo' (my translation) cited without the final lines in Hanif Ramay, *Punjab ka Muqadammah*, Lahore: Jang Publishers, (fourth edition), 1988, pp. 25–6. For another English translation of the whole poem, see I. Serebryakov, *Punjabi Literature: A Brief Outline*, Lahore: Progressive Books, 1975, p. 107.

اج آکاں وارث شاہ نوں سے قبراں وچوں بول
تے اج کتابِ عشق دا کوئی اگلا ورقا کھول
اک روئی سی دھی پنجاب دی توں لکھ لکھ مارے وین
اج لکھاں دھیاں روندیاں تینوں وارث شاہ نوں کہن
اٹھ درد منداں دیا دردیا، تک اپنا پنجاب
اج بیلے لاشاں وچھیاں، لہو دی بھری چناب.

Chapter 10

Epilogue
An Unhealing Wound:
Paradoxes of Muslim Identity, Sovereignty and Citizenship

To our homeland came a high-spirited beggar
Came and with his mellifluous songs passed away
Deserted paths came alive with people
Desolate taverns saw their fortunes change
Only a few eyes could reach him
But his songs warmed the hearts of all
Now he has gone, that beggarly king
And the paths of our homeland are once again melancholy
A few recall his special graces
One or two insights remain with his dear ones
But his song lives in everyone's hearts
Thousands are enthralled by his melodies
Timeless are the virtues of his song
Its plenitude, its tremor, its pathos and music
The song's briskly shimmering blaze
Leaping and dissolving the winds of annihilation
As if unaware of the torch of dread
Like an evening gathering impervious to the coming of dawn.[1]

[1] Faiz Ahmad Faiz, 'Iqbal', in *Nuskha Haya-i-Wafa*, Lahore: Muktaba Karavan (no date), pp. 86–6.

آیا ہمارے دیس میں اک خوش نوا فقیر

آیا اور اپنی دُمن میں غزلخواں گزر گیا

سنسان راہیں خلق سے آباد ہو گئیں

ویران میکدوں کا نصیبہ سنور گیا

Born in the same city of Sialkot as the spiritual and ideational founder of Pakistan, this was how Faiz Ahmad Faiz commemorated Iqbal's poetic legacy to post-colonial South Asia. Yet in August 1947, Faiz in his famous poem 'Subah-i-Azadi' or freedom's dawn, made plain that 'this leprous daybreak, dawn night's fangs have mangled' was 'not that long-looked-for break of day' for which he and his friends had set out in quest of 'the star's last halting place', or even an 'anchorage for the ship of heartache'.[2] Nor could it be seen as the realization of Iqbal's ideal Islamic state or even his proposal for a Muslim state in north-western India. Where *tauhid* as equality, solidarity and freedom inspired manifold actions, none in the end could match the plenitude, tremor or lifting spirituality of Iqbal's poetry or sustain the premises of his idealistic philosophy. Sovereign space littered with profanities against fellow men and women, not to mention the aged and the young, was a shaky foundation on which to construct the sacred fortress of Muslims in South Asia.

If the Muslims left behind in India felt the loneliness of separation, those who sought the comforts of citizenship in a Muslim nation–state had to undergo excruciating pain, and much loss of life and property, to reach their adopted homeland. The gift of independence in 1947 came like a shroud of death for the vulnerable, weak and infirm. Events had not disproved Iqbal's assertion that donning the nation's apparel was to wear the shroud of religion. Women from the lower social classes were the primary victims of a horrific carnage in which Muslim, Hindu and Sikh men fell upon them as well as on

---

تہیں چند ہی نگا ہیں جو اس تک پہنچ سکیں

پر اس کا گیت سب کے دلوں میں اتر گیا

اب دور جا چکا ہے وہ شاہِ گدا نما

اور پھر سے اپنے دیس کی راہیں اداس ہیں

چند اک کو یاد ہے کوئی اس کی ادائے خاص

دو اک نگا ہیں چند عزیزوں کے پاس ہیں

پر اس کا گیت سب کے دلوں میں مقیم ہے

اور اس کی لے سے سینکڑوں لذت شناس ہیں

اس گیت کے تمام محاسن میں لازوال

اس کا فور اس کا خروش اس کا سوز و ساز

یہ گیت مثل شعلہ جوالہ تند و تیز

اس کی لپک سے باد و فنا کا چکر گداز

جیسے چراغِ وحشتِ سحر مرے بے خطر

یا شمعِ بزمِ صبح کی آمد سے بے خبر

[2]Victor Kiernan (tr.), *Poems by Faiz*, Lahore: Vanguard Book, 1971, pp. 123–5, also in ibid., pp. 116–17.

each other with staggering brutality and murderous hatred. As the poet of the east, never an ardent champion of women's rights, had warned:

Neither *purdah* nor education, whether new or old
Man alone is protector of woman
The nation not possessing this living reality
That nation's sun dulled all too soon.[3]

Stumbling fearfully across the newly demarcated frontiers of Pakistan and India, hundreds of thousands of hapless women who had yet to make an entry into the nationalist discourse were given their first taste of citizenship rights in the form of gang rapes, physical mutilation, abduction and death. Saadat Hasan Manto captured the psychological terror of partition and the serial brualization of women in a number of heartbreaking and chilling tales. He was roundly attacked for sensationalizing a human tragedy and then prosecuted by the custodians of public morality for writing 'obscene' and 'anti-state' stories about abducted women. Attitudes were not very different across the border.[4] The shattering experience of partition only hardened Muslim men, cutting across class divisions, in their opinion that a woman unprotected and exceeding the limits of the domestic sphere was the source of immorality, irreligiosity and social degradation.

The inequity rooted in this conception was to pervade the entire tenor of relations between state and society, not only in Pakistan but also in India. If women had been intrinsic to the rearticulation of social identities and the reapportioning of domestic space under colonial conditions, they were of key significance to the projects of the new nation–states of South Asia. Symbols of communitarian identity turned ornaments of national sovereignty, women's fate has been so interwoven with the discourse on citizenship rights underpinning the balance between state and civil society in the subcontinent as to stand out as a metaphor for the unfulfilled claims of Pakistani, Indian and, after 1971, Bangladeshi national narrations. The reconfiguration of state and civil society, public and private space, as well as the individual and the community, was sought to be based on silencing and erasing the suffering of those women which bespoke of the inhumanity that had greeted the arrival of independence in South Asia. These women from the lower social strata remained on the margins, if at all within sight, of a debate on citizenship rights which claimed to extend equality and dignity of life to individual members of the national community.

[3]Iqbal, 'Aurat ki Hafazat', or the protection of women, in *Zarb-i-Kaleem*, in *Kulliyat-i-Iqbal*, p. 88.

[4]See Das, *Critical Events*, chapter three; Urvashi Butalia, 'Community, State and Gender: On Women's Agency During Partition' and Ritu Menon and Kamla Bhasin, 'Recovery, Rupture, Resistance: Indian State and Abduction of Women during Partition', *EPW*, 24 April 1993, pp. 2–12.

The woman's question was salient in post-colonial debates on citizenship rights precisely because nationalist discourses, Muslim and Indian, had failed to address, far less resolve, this vital issue. Men who had written about women since the late nineteenth century had hardly ever thought of their gender counterparts as individuals with sensibilities of their own. Like their opposite number in Bengal, Muslim *ashraf* classes in northern India had merely sought to reform the women of their own families. The predicament of the vast majority of women from the lower classes was relevant only as a negative point of reference against which standards of respectability were to be established for women of the *ashraf* classes. Depraved and uncouth beyond redemption, these were women as prostitutes, not women as ornaments adorning male musings on *zan* or *aurat*.

If the discourse of the *ashraf* excluded the vast majority of women from their purview, Muslim divines like Husain Ahmad Madani had dropped women altogether while giving a philological meaning to the word *quam*.[5] While disagreeing with the *maulana's* exclusionary definition, Iqbal too had serious reservations about conceding too much ground to women. It was as domestic ornaments and mothers of children that he lauded them the most. However, the triumph of the poetic impulse in him did lead him to acknowledge:

She may not have written Plato's discourses
Yet it was her flame which broke Plato's spark.[6]

This is why it was all the more unfortunate that even when educated women tried making their presence felt in the public arena, they did so as symbols of their community rather than as representative of their gender. The fracturing of gender by class, more than anything else, had made certain that women from the subordinate social strata would find no place in the national question and, by implication, in the debate on equal citizenship rights.

The exclusion of the vast majority of women from the grand narratives of nationhood was reflected in the fate of religious minorities in post-independence South Asia in general and, in Pakistan, of the Ahmadi community in particular. While proclaiming the grant of equal citizenship rights, post-colonial nation-states could not shed the colonial logic which had done so much to confuse notions of public and private, the secular and the religious. India, professing an inclusionary nationalism, followed the colonial policy of privatizing religion.

---

[5]See Iqbal's essay on Islam and nationalism in response to a statement by Maulana Husain Ahmad Madani published in *Ehsan*, 9 March 1938 in Sherwani (ed.), *Speeches and Statements of Iqbal*, p. 257.

[6]*Mukalat-i-Aflatoon na likh saki lekin*
Isee kai shola saay toota sharar-i-Aflatoon.
(Iqbal, 'Aurat', in *Zarb-i-Kaleem*, in *Kulliyat-i-Iqbal*, p. 87.)

The religiously informed cultural identities of its Muslim citizens were to be assured by preserving the precepts of the Islamic *shariat* as defined by the *ulema*. By reducing the issue of religiously informed cultural differences to Muslim personal law codified under colonial auspices, the Indian state was laying the seeds of many future confusions. The creation of a truncated Pakistan was itself an advertisement of the problem of conferring equal citizenship rights on those excluded from the narratives of the Muslim nation. Religious divines had been demanding *shariat* rule in the area constituting Pakistan since the 1945–6 elections. If Congress was ready to tackle the issue of Muslim difference by restricting it to personal law, the Muslim Leaguers had to find some way of stealing the *ulema's* thunder on the Islamic front. Following India in taking its cues from the colonial state which had restricted the meaning of the *shariat* to personal laws, the managers of Pakistan tried establishing their Islamic bona fides by considering new social legislation on behalf of women dealing only with inheritance, marriage, divorce and the guardianship of children. Instead of establishing the basis for a civil society on the principles of equality, solidarity and freedom, Islamic Pakistan quite as much as secular India focused on the personal laws of religious communities, believing them to be a sufficient accommodation of cultural differences.

This required preserving a wholly false dichotomy between the public and the private sphere. Promising individual rights of citizenship, the post-colonial state sallied forth in defence of community-defined personal laws. Being an individual in public and a member of a religiously defined community in private has placed the citizens of both India and Pakistan in a serious quandary. In the case of women, the focus on their community-defined rights in marriage, property and divorce has distracted attention form their rights as public citizens. This has served to perpetuate the subjugation of women, particularly those belonging to the lower strata. The fate of religious minorities has been scarcely better. Concessions to their religiously informed cultural differences in the private sphere has not always assured equal opportunities in the public sphere. India could at least deploy its secular laws to maintain the appearance of accommodating its religious minorities, if not necessarily allowing space for the full expression of their sense of cultural difference. In Pakistan, the long-standing demand for the exclusion of the Ahmadis from the community of Islam was to utterly confound the nexus between community and nation with devastating consequences for not just the logic of equal rights of citizenship but also the very notion of Muslim identity.

DIVIDED COMMUNITY, UNITED NATION?

While failing to confer rights of citizenship on the weak and the vulnerable, the modern nation–states of post-colonial South Asia nevertheless managed to impose the rigours of citizenship on members of religious communities.

The individual's loyalty to the community of religion was now sought to be superceded by the citizen's unquestioning allegiance to the nation–state. But it was not easy for the partitioner to turn the poet into citizen by the mere stroke of the pen. The anguish of partition for the subcontinent's Muslims has been captured by poets and writers on both sides of the 1947 divide. Despair at the masterly deception that had turned the dream of independence into one of brutal separation pervades the literature written in the very Urdu language which many extremist Hindus hold responsible for stoking the fires of Muslim 'communalism' since the late nineteenth century. In his *Khoon ki Lakeer* or the line of blood, Sardar Jafri, one of India's leading leftist poets, rejected the newly demarcated boundary as an imperialist artifact:

Who is this cruel person who has with his burning pen
Cut a deep line of innocent blood across the motherland's breast
What happened? Suddenly all the instruments have changed their tune at this gathering.[7]

Across the border in Muslim Pakistan, Ahmad Riaz boldly repudiated the religious loyalty which had brought about the tragedy to reassure his friends in India:

The dawn of independence has come,
but still the paths of past and present are in darkness.
We are neither infidels nor Muslims.
Crushed by famine and hunger, we are the rejected ones.
Comrades, hold out your hands, even today we are together.
Who could ever divide the estate of literature?
Cities can be divided, the streets closed
but who can imprison intensity of feeling.[8]

Such warmth of feeling was to become rare as Muslims in India and Pakistan set about renegotiating their identity according to the dominant idioms of the two nation–states. With the Indian and the Pakistani states turning the binary opposites of secular nationalism and religious communalism into ideologies of legitimacy, the dilemma of a subcontinental Muslim identity was to become irresolvable. The imperatives of citizenship in mutually hostile nation-states meant that Muslims were no longer just a divided community but declared enemies of co-religionists beyond the nearest international check-point. Under such inauspicious circumstances even a Hali might have settled for the ashes than the politically injudicious task of breathing fire into the partitioned hearts and minds of Muslims with a rousing *Shikwa-i-Azadi*.

[7]My adaptation of Sardar Jafri cited in M. Yusuf Abbasi, *Pakistani Culture: A Profile*, Islamabad: National Institute of Historical and Cultural Research, 1992, p. 76.
　　[8]Ibid., pp. 77–8.

Far from being an indivisible property and a symbol of Muslim cultural identity, the Urdu language became an early and unrelieved victim of attack by the Hindu Mahasabha, the Jan Sangh and the RSS. They demanded a Hindi-only policy in the very region which had nurtured Urdu as its lingua-franca. The willingness of the Congress in UP to go along with these Hindu nationalist organizations dealt a grievous blow to the cultural pretensions of India's Urdu-speaking Muslim elite. The cruelest cut was the charge that by insisting on Urdu as their cultural heritage, now that the majority community had made the sacrifice of partition to settle the problem of difference once and for all, Muslims were furnishing evidence of their inveterate disloyalty to the Indian nation–state. Being born and raised in India, the Muslims learnt to their horror, was no longer sufficient evidence of their Indianness. Those whose faith in the secularism encoded in the Indian constitution made this a questionable proposition had only to be reminded of Sardar Vallabhbhai Patel's chilling exhortation to Muslims: 'I want to tell them frankly that mere declaration of loyalty to [the] Indian Union will not help them at this critical juncture. They must give proof of their declaration'.[9]

The taunt of disloyalty came from unexpected quarters. Abul Kalam Azad, the Muslim paragon of secular nationalism, reprimanded his co-religionists for vesting their trust in an undeserving leadership and party which had now tossed them to the winds. Nothing less than a complete change of heart was required to win the certificate of loyalty. But with Pakistan as a permanent albatross signifying their negative identity, switching from the Turkish *fez* to the *khadi* cap and innumerable other such gestures to India's composite culture and secular nationalism—for instance reluctantly giving up separate electorates and sullenly agreeing to let their children learn Hindi instead of Urdu—could not confirm the Muslim minority's positive affiliation with the nation–state. Even if segments of the elite saw political advantages in distancing themselves from the more controversial symbols of their religiously informed cultural identity, there were few such incentives for the mass of poor and illiterate Muslims. Confounding the dilemma of Muslim identity were the religious and political aspirations of that motley collection of *ulema* who, because they had chosen the Congress instead of the Muslim League, had somehow to be accommodated within the framework of a secular and democratic India. Having purchased tickets for the train purportedly taking India's Muslims to a secular nationalist destination, the *ulema's* ideological worldview could obstruct coherent communication between passengers in the first and third class compartments. Irritation with the never-ending journey of India's Muslims led to the menacing suggestion that the train would be better off on tracks leading straight across the sealed border.

[9] Cited in Moin Shakir, *Politics of Muslim Minorities: Some Perspectives*, Delhi: Ajanta Publications, 1980, p. 137.

THE MUSLIM 'ELSE' IN POST-COLONIAL SOUTH ASIA

Hali's *Shikwa-i-Hind* had come to haunt Indian Muslims with a vengeance. Under suspicion in India and unwelcome in Pakistan, their lot has been unenviable. Distortions of the historical evidence in both states have inculcated among the educated few an animosity towards the country for whose creation they are held responsible. That there is apparently so little love lost between upper- and middle-class Indian and Pakistani Muslims is hardly cause for surprise. The notion of the 'other' that permeates so much of post-colonial criticism is wholly inadequate in capturing the vexed nature of the relationship among Muslims of South Asia who became citizens of rival nation–states. Such a complex relationship marked by ambivalence rather than contradiction and mingling sameness with difference would seem to call for an alternative theory of the 'else'. The condition of 'elseness', as distinct from what we have repeatedly been told about 'otherness', is one that is separate from the self and yet a part of it, certainly tied to it in a paradox of ambivalences. It is characterized not so much by the opposites of attraction and revulsion but by the much more complicated attitude of suspicion. As citizens of rival, if not 'enemy' states, Indian and Pakistani Muslims have in a sense been living in a state of 'else(less)ness'—being without the presence of the else and yet mentally not apart from it. The emergence of Bangladesh as a sovereign nation–state represented the tragic transition from sameness to else(less)ness that has invariably left deeper psychological wounds than the contradictions defining otherness.

As in the late nineteenth century so in the mid-twentieth, the Muslims of the subcontinent were caught in the conundrum of turning the identity of language into the language of identity. The decision to make Urdu the state language of Pakistan harkened back to an overarching conception of Muslim identity which found few echoes in the regionally based cultural identities of its people. Reduced to being a subaltern language in its own regional setting, Urdu came to be regarded as an instrument of neo-imperialist domination. Bengalis in the eastern wing put up stout resistance against encroachment on their cultural autonomy. On 21 February 1952 students protesting the language policy were gunned down by the police. A common religious identity had never meant the denial of a separate cultural tradition. Proud of belonging to the same literary heritage as Rabindranath Tagore and Kazi Nazrul Islam, Bengali intellectuals deplored the official policy of deprecating their Islamic beliefs. There was 'no inherent contradiction in being a Bengali, a Muslim and a Pakistani—all at the same time'.[10] Bengalis were not alone in bearing the brunt of linguistic and cultural denial. In the Punjab, supposedly the political nerve centre of Pakistani imperialism, intellectuals working to

[10]Cited in Anisuzzaman, *Creativity, Reality and Identity*, Dhaka: International Centre for Bengal Studies, 1993, p. 104.

promote their regional language and culture were declared 'anti-state'. After the military coup of 1958, the state clamped down further on regional literary associations.[11] Bengali resentment found its fullest expression in the establishment of an independent state of Bangladesh. Shamsur Rahman conveyed the long-standing cultural alienation of Muslim Bengal in a poem written during the liberation struggle:

Freedom:
you are Tagore's ageless poetry,
his immortal songs.
Freedom:
you are Kazi Nazrul, wild-haired sage
trembling with the thrill of creation

Freedom:
you are that meeting at the martyr's monument
on the eternal twenty-first of February.[12]

The brief populist interlude in what remained of Pakistan came as something of a boon for regional language movements. Resistance themes in regional folklore were among the symbols of protest against the military regime of General Zia-ul-Haq. One Punjabi poet conveyed the growing disdain for the state's attempts to forge a singular national identity on the basis of an alien culture and language:

In vain you are looking for your identity in the imperial courts of Delhi?
Why do you ask deserts to provide you the shadows of pipal? You cannot find your own perfumes in others' gardens.[13]

If the Pakistani state's language policy generated more resentment than enthusiasm for Urdu as one of the dominant idioms of national identity, the response of a predominantly Muslim but regionally differentiated population to its ambiguous recourse to Islam proved utterly divisive. The emphasis on religion by its early managers was never intended as a commitment to the establishment of an Islamic state. At the helm of state power, the erstwhile Muslim 'communalists' were not about to pass the mantle of Pakistani 'nationalism' to the religious guardians. In fact the term 'communalism' practically disappeared from the discourse as 'nationalists' of all shades wrestled for political ascendancy.

The embattled politics of Pakistan's Islamic ideology scuttled any sort of consensus on national identity. Even as a military-bureaucratic state strained

---

[11]Fateh Mohammad Malik, *Punjabi Identity*, Lahore: Sang-e-Meel Publications, 1989, pp. 16–18.

[12]Cited in Anisuzzaman, *Creativity, Reality and Identity*, p. 115.

[13]Nirvan Noori cited in Mirza, *Resistance Themes in Punjabi Literature*, p. 201.

its nerves to keep the Islamicists at bay, it saw the advantages of formulating policies privileging the common religious bond of an otherwise culturally distinctive and economically disparate people. More successful in deluding itself than large segments of a society comfortably positioned to simultaneously live out multiple layers of identity, the inefficacy of the Pakistani state's Islamic card is a powerful indictment of the argument that the religious factor in 'Muslim consciousness' outweighs all other considerations. As electoral results consistently showed up the weak appeal of an exclusively Islamic ideology in politics, it was left to the military-bureaucratic state to embark on policies of Islamization in its search for legitimacy. Yet the most paradoxical legacy of Zia-ul-Haq, the self-proclaimed soldier of Islam, was the intensification of regional, linguistic and sectarian tensions. Attributable in large part to Zulfikar Ali Bhutto's controversial decision in 1974 to declare the Ahmadis a religious minority, the sectarian problem in Pakistan is nonetheless a direct legacy of the general's cultivation of the religious lobby. The subsequent burgeoning of *madrasas* and sectarian militias vowing to violently ostracize their rivals from the community of Islam, an unthinkable proposition prior to the exclusion of the Ahmadis, highlights the significance of the distinction between religion as social demarcator and religion as faith. It is this distinction that explains why despite all the Islamic rhetoric, whether of the state or various segments of society, the politics of identity in Muslim Pakistan continue to be structured around decidedly non-religious considerations.

If a state-supported Islam has been unable to impart any sense of commonality to the politics of identity in a predominantly Muslim country, its political utility for secular India's besieged Muslim minority appears even more uncertain. Apart from declaring the political uses of religion illegal, the Indian constitution by scrapping separate electorates removed the principal institutional barrier to the articulation of Muslim politics in other than 'communal' terms. Although there is scant evidence of Indian Muslims voting on the basis of religious considerations, the notion of minority 'communalism' remains enmeshed in Indian political discourse. This has given pro-Hindu as well as ostensibly secular parties the moral pretext to issue periodic condemnations of the narrow-mindedness of Muslims on the question of personal law and other matters to do with their religiously informed cultural identity. The tolerant secularist and the bigoted Hindu are really after the same pound of flesh—Muslims have to stop drawing upon the religious and cultural strands of their identity if they want complete integration into the secular and democratic framework of the Indian nation–state.

Discomfort with difference is a function of inclusionary nationalism and, its concomitant, equal citizenship which are among the defining features of modern nation–states. But despite ample evidence on the ground, the paradox of inclusonary nationalism ending up as a narrative construction of an exclusionary majoritarian identity has rarely commanded attention from votaries of the nation–state. In India matters are further complicated by the fact that the inclusionary idiom is expressed in an artificial binary opposition between secular nationalism and religious communalism.[14] To be secular and nationalist for a Muslim entails publicly disclaiming too close an association with the specific traits of the minority community, religious and cultural. Otherwise there is no escaping the pejorative label of 'communalism'. But the protagonists of Hindutva can get away with critiquing the state's pseudo-secularism while pitching their bid for the nationalist mantle.

Finding ways to accommodate a distinctive Muslim identity without launching a frontal assault on the contradictory official idioms of the Indian state can result in perilous logic. The inclusionary idiom flows from a singular conception of Indian nationalism whose ideological basis is a secularism with religion left out. But there is also the accompanying conception of a composite nationalism deriving its justification from India's pluralist religio-cultural tradition. The idea of a composite nationalism was in some ways an advance on the notion of India as a 'federation of faiths'. It entertains the possibility of the coexistence of religious communities without adequately addressing the problem of difference among them. Secular nationalism, on the other hand, avoids the problem of difference by projecting a singular narrative construction of Indian identity. Equating the pluralism implied in the 'composite' of nationalism with a 'secularism' devoid of religion leads to serious confusion of conceptual categories. This confusion which is expressed in varied ways in academic and political debates flows largely from an inability to retain an analytical distinction between Muslim identity and a Muslim 'communal' politics. A Muslim identity, however one might choose to package it, makes a claim on difference denied by the singular secular nationalist ideal. But in the absence of any neat equation between a Muslim identity and a Muslim 'communal' politics, beyond a handful of electoral constituencies where voting patterns might occasionally reveal such an overlap, there is no reason for a secular nationalist discourse to acknowledge, far less accommodate, difference.

So it is one thing to applaud the declining influence of religious obscurantism on the politics of the Muslim masses and quite another to see this as a triumph of the secular-modernist initiative recently launched by a voluble and variegated segment of the Indian Muslim elite. A socially and economically underprivileged and politically divided minority which is the target of bigotry and organized violence from a determined section of the majority community could do with some measure of electoral solidarity to

[14]Mushirul Hasan glosses over the close imbrications between nationalism and majoritarianism drawing on the religious distinction in his *Legacy of a Divided Nation: India's Muslims Since Independence*, Delhi: Oxford University Press, 1997.

force the agendas of the state. Dismissing this as 'communalism' of the sort which brought about the partition of the country, the new generation of the Indian Muslim elite in a leap of faith from an-all-too awkward reality firmly believe in the secular and democratic ideals of their state and polity. But forging a secular modernist Indian Muslim identity without dabbling in power politics may require more reason than faith. It is somewhat difficult to imagine how a Muslim elite who have maintained a studied aloofness from their regionally fragmented underprivileged co-religionists are going to mobilize support for a secular conception of identity 'outside the communitarian framework'. Blazing Azad's old trail 'to posit composite nationalism' against 'appeals based on religious solidarity' is a noble secular hope.[15] But it runs counter to the singular secular nationalist idiom in so far as it admits a problem of Muslim identity.

The Muslim quandary in post-independence India is an especially acute one. Needing the very political solidarity which the secular nationalist idiom damns as 'communalism' and the electoral scene renders impossible, the secular modernists can at best try and influence Muslim elite discourse. But as in the past that discourse has never been of a singular or homogeneous cast. Reforming Muslim personal law to fit a secular-modernist ideal, hung and drawn by tensions in the composite and secular conceptions of Indian nationalism without being quartered by the inescapable intervention of religious guardians, is a daunting task. The tragedy of the new breed of Muslim secular modernists in India quite as much as in Pakistan is their lack of facility in Islamic learning. Better trained in Marxist and Weberian paradigms than in the Quran, their pens are not necessarily more powerful than the sword. With no Sayyid Ahmed Khan, Syed Ameer Ali, Shibli or Azad, not to mention Muhammad Iqbal, waiting in the wings, the words of the insular and bigoted *fatwa*-giving bearded men will ricochet on any debate surrounding Muslim personal law. Indian Muslims with their multiple voices and splintered politics will undoubtedly continue to resist threats to their religiously informed cultural identity. Taking on a variety of forms, it will be a resistance so multifarious as to justify exploding 'communalism' and rescuing the problem of difference from essentialization as well as extinction.

Mazhab and Qaum: Khuda, Khudi and Khudikhtiyari

An exploration of the discourse and politics of Muslim identity over more than a century reveals the grave flaws in categorizing the multiple articulation of difference as 'religious communalism' or cultural nationalism. Muslim identity as difference has been riven with too many internal contradictions

---

[15]Mushirul Hasan, 'Minority Identity and its Discontents: Response and Representation', *EPW*, 19 February 1994, pp. 441–51.

to be capped by an all-encompassing 'communalism'. Historicizing and conceptualizing the related issues of Muslim difference and Muslim politics has suggested the inevitability of the one and the impossibility of the other. A common source of reference in the normative ideals of Islam does not warrant the essentialization of Muslimness implied by 'communalism'. But by the same token, ideological and political disagreements among Muslims does not nullify the case for unity in difference. What they indicate is that the problem of Muslim difference and identity in South Asia has been more complex and nuanced than conceded by the protagonists of the 'two-nation' theory or the practitioners of a historiography based on a binary opposition between secular nationalism and religious communalism. A partition of India along self-professedly religious lines has lent a teleological tendency to the processes of historical retrieval. Religion, neither adequately problematized nor carefully contextualized, has contributed to the perpetuation of a most awkward binary opposition between 'nationalism' and 'communalism' which in separating the temporal from the spiritual realms ends up blurring the distinction between religion as social demarcator and religion as faith.

The problem of difference in South Asia as a whole and of Muslim identity in particular cannot be addressed without forsaking the dichotomies between 'secular' and 'religious' as well as 'nationalism' and 'communalism'. Just as the first set of opposites can be found blending into the thought of a single individual, the second binary pair shares a common conception of majoritarianism and minoritarianism in the privileging of the religious distinction. The majoritarian premises of Indian and Pakistani 'nationalism' derive equally from the colonial project of religious enumeration. While Indian nationalism asserts its inclusionary idioms in the secular garb and Pakistani nationalism in an inclusionary religious mode, neither avoids the pernicious process of exclusion resulting from the implicit denial of difference. It is the singular and homogenizing agendas of both nation–states which have wittingly or unwittingly created the space for religious bigots seeking political power to target vulnerable minorities. To call bigotry 'communalism' is to implicate in the actions of the few the inaction of the many. So while there can be no denying the rampant bigotry of so-called Hindu majoritarian 'communalism' in India and religious 'fundamentalism' in Pakistan, their politics of oppositional identity construction need to be exposed to the full glare of analytical scrutiny. The self-defence of baited minorities produces its own venomous narratives and versions of bigotry. But dubbing the outrage of the Indian Muslim minority at the actions of the Hindutva brigade 'communalism' is to deny legitimacy to any strategy aimed at protecting or accommodating the problem of difference and identity. In much the same way, the regional counter-narratives of difference in Pakistan have to be seen as strategies of resistance seeking release from the fetters of an uncompromising discourse of Islamic identity rather than as a denial of Muslimness.

That the dominant idioms of states, and the ways in which these are reflected in elite discourse, so often fly in the face of the shifting structural contours of politics at the base is reason enough for abandoning some of their more questionable premises. Exploding 'communalism' to uncover the manifold and contradictory interests driving the politics of Muslim identity in South Asia might enable a better appreciation of difference as a lived cultural experience. Such an exercise will have to rescue the individual from the communitarian morass enveloping the idea of cultural difference. Only then can the individual self attain the full benefits of communitarian sovereignty and, in this way, realize the aspiration of independence in equal rights of citizenship.

A scholarly duty remains undone if religion is not retrieved from the debris of 'communalism'. The political thought of post-colonial South Asia, devoid of the spirit of religion, is of little help in the performance of this duty. In order to truly grasp the nuanced relationship between *mazhab* and *qaum*, religion and nation, one has to return to the poet-philosopher of Muslim India who affirmed the autonomy of *khudi* in absolute submission to *Khuda*. In the last year of his life, Muhammad Iqbal had severely castigated Maulana Husain Ahmed Madani–the pro-Congress leader of the Jamiat-i-Ulema-i-Hind—for asking Indian Muslims to embrace the vision of an inclusionary Indian nationalism in which they would have complete freedom with regard to their personal law and religious practices. Madani had maintained that the *millat* was something higher than the nation, likening the relationship to the cosmic one between heaven and earth. In Iqbal's opinion, the *maulana* had 'left no place for *millat* by preaching to the eight crore Muslims to lose their identity in the country, and therefore in the majority, and to make nation a heaven ... ignor[ing] the fact that Islam will thereby be reduced to the status of the earth'.[16]

He despaired that the religious leaders of Muslim India considered the Indian National Congress's ideal of territorial nationalism to be consistent with Islam: 'Strange indeed are the vicissitudes of time. Formerly, the half-Westernized educated Muslims were under the spell of Europe; now the curse has descended upon religious leaders'.[17] It was not that the Islamic worldview rejected love of one's homeland or *watan*. But modern nationalism was not merely about territorial attachments; it was 'a principle of human society', a 'political concept' based on the separation of religion and the state. It was this that clashed with Islam which 'for the first time, gave the message to mankind that religion was neither national and racial, nor individual and private, but purely human and that its purpose

---

[16]Iqbal's response to a statement by Maulana Husain Ahmad Madani published in *Ehsan*, 9 March 1938 and in Sherwani (ed.) *Speeches and Statements of Iqbal*, p. 256.
[17]Ibid., p. 252.

was to unite and organise mankind despite all its natural distinctions'.[18]

Without denying the modernist overtones in Iqbal's thought, this was not a conception of religion as a demarcator of difference. Rather it was the notion of religion as faith with the potential to erase national and racial differences in order to attain a universal human consciousness based on the multiplicity of existence in the unity of Divine creation.[19] The distinction between religion as difference and religion as faith is an important one, not least on account of the legitimation acquired by violent and murderous acts attributed to religious passions in late-colonial and post-colonial South Asia. It was nationalism, according to Iqbal, which gave rise to the 'relativity of religions', the notion that religions were territorially specific and unsuited to the temperament of other nations. It was nationalism, therefore, and not religion which by compartmentalizing people into different nations was the source of modern conflicts. The 'peculiar greatness' of the Prophet of Islam lay in destroying the 'invented distinctions and superiority complexes of the nations of the world', such as land, race or genealogy, without denying the fact of cultural differences or the manifold multiplicities of tribe, colour and languages which coexisted in the unity of the one and only God.[20]

In an early poem entitled 'Mazhab' (religion), Iqbal deployed the word 'nation' in the sense of *millat* or *qaum* to differentiate it from the idea of territorial nationalism which he saw as a weapon of European imperialism aimed at destroying the unity of Islam. *Millat* refers to religion, law and a programme while *quam* signifies a group of people unguided by a prophetic law and a religion. Iqbal interpreted *millat* as a religiously guided community of individuals while *qaum* could include both the guided and the unguided. A *quam* might have a *millat* or a particular way of life, but a *millat* of a *qaum* was inconceivable since the *millat* or *ummat* could encapsulate nations; they could never be merged in them.[21] As is evident in this poem first published in 1924 in the anthology *Bang-i-Dara*, Iqbal thought it a contradiction in terms for Indian Muslims to subscribe to a national polity by abandoning the principles of Islamic solidarity.[22]

---

[18]Ibid., pp. 252–5.

[19]W.C. Smith had tried arguing long ago that the distinction was important enough to justify dispensing with the very term religion. (W.C. Smith, *The Meaning and End of Religion: A New Approach to the Religious Traditions of Mankind*, New York: Macmillan, 1962, 1963.)

[20]Iqbal's response to Maulana Husain Ahmad Madani, Sherwani (ed.), *Speeches and Statements of Iqbal*, p. 262.

[21]Ibid., pp. 258–9.

[22]See Iqbal's presidential address to the AIML, Allahabad, December 1930, Pirzada (ed.), *Foundations of Pakistan*, ii, pp. 156–7.

Don't compare your nation with the nations of the west
Distinctive is the nation of the Prophet of Islam
Their solidarity depends on territorial nationality
Your solidarity rests on the strength of your religion
When faith slips away, where is the solidarity of the community?
And when the community is no more, neither is the nation.[23]

[23]Iqbal, 'Mazhab', *Bang-i-Dara* in *Kulliyat-i-Iqbal*, p. 202.

اپنی ملت پر قیاس اقوامِ مغرب سے نہ کر
خاص ہے ترکیب میں قومِ رسولِ ہاشمیؐ
ان کی جمعیت کا ہے ملک و نسب پر انحصار
قوتِ مذہب سے مستحکم ہے جمعیت تری
دامنِ دیں ہاتھ سے چھوٹا تو جمعیت کہاں
اور جمعیت ہوئی رخصت تو ملت بھی گئی!

Glossary

achhut	literally untouchable; term for Hindu outcaste
adhikari	functionary
ajlaf	the lower social orders among Muslims
allama	a learned man
amir-ul-momineen	leader of the faithful
anjuman	an association
arti	ritual worship of gods and goddesses with lamps
ashraf	(sing. *sharif*) respectable class
azad	free
badshahat	kingship
begar	forced labour
Balmiki	a group of Hindu outcastes
Bande Mataram	literally 'hail to the mother'; title of song by Bankim Chandra Chattopadhyay
bania	Hindu trader or moneylender
bhakti	devotion
Bharatvarsha	land of Bharata, legendary king of ancient India
charkha	spinning wheel
chaukidar	night watchman
chhut	social practice of untouchability
crore	one hundred lakh or ten million
Dar-ul-Aman	abode of peace
Dar-ul-Harb	abode of war
Dar-ul-Islam	abode of Islam
fatwa	opinion enunciated by the leader of a Muslim religious congregation

fitna	sedition
ghazi	Muslim warrior of the faith
goonda	hooligan
gurdwara	a Sikh temple
Hadith	traditions of the Prophet
haj	pilgrimage to Mecca
Hakimiyat	sovereignty of God
hakumat-i-illahiya	God's government
hari	sharecropper with no occupancy rights or landless labourer in Sind
hijrat	migration
hubb-i-watani	love of the homeland
hujras	cell or chamber of religious site where graves are located
imam	head of a mosque who leads Muslim prayer congregations
iman	faith
jagir	land grant
jhatka	slaughtering of animals by cutting off the head with one stroke as is customary among Hindus and Sikhs
jihad	striving for perfection; Muslim holy war
Kaaba	the holiest of Muslim religious places in Mecca
kafir	non-believer
khaddar	(from *khadi*) hand-spun and hand-woven cloth
khalifa	temporal and spiritual leader of Muslims
Khalsa	the pure; the Sikh community
khatma-i-nubaut	Muslim belief in the finality of the Prophethood of Muhammad
khilafat	institutionalized spiritual and temporal authority over the Muslim community
Khuda	God
Khudai Khidmatgar	literally 'the servants of God'; organization led by Abdul Ghaffar Khan in the NWFP
khudi	self
khudikhtiyari	self-determination
khutba	religious sermon
kisan	peasant or cultivator
lakh	one hundred thousand
lambardar	village headman
lathi	wooden stick
Marwari	a Hindu commercial caste
marsiya	poetic lament/dirge
maulana	title given to Muslim religious scholar
maulvi	title given to Muslim religious leader
mela chiraghan	festival of lights celebrated annually in Lahore to commemorate the birth of the Punjabi mystical poet Shah

	Hussain (1539–93/4), popularly known as Madho Lal Hussain
millat	religious community
miraj sharif	the Prophet Muhammad's heavenly ascent
mlechha	(sing. *mlechh*), derogatory term for foreigners/'non-Aryans'
mullah	term used for Muslim religious leader
mutafiqa fatwa	literally unanimous political opinion
naujawan	literally youth
pandit	title given to Hindu religious scholar
panth	Sikh brotherhood or community
pir	term used for spiritual guide
purna swaraj	complete independence
qaum	word loosely used for clan, community, sect or nation
qaumiyat	sense of community or nation
qazi	Muslim judge
Ramazan	Islamic month of fasting
ryot	peasant cultivator
sabha	an association
sahukar	moneylender
sangathan	organization
sangh	brotherhood or association
satyagraha	literally the way of truth; form of political agitation based on moral pressure pioneered by Gandhi
sharia/shariat	literally 'a clear path'; set of moral injunctions constituting Islamic law
Sheikh	title for Muslim spiritual leaders, it is also used more generally to designate respect
shuddhi	purification
swadeshi	of own country
swaraj	self rule
tabligh	religious preaching
tanzim	organization
tauhid	Islamic principle of the unity of all creation
ulema	(sing. *alim*) scholar of Islamic jurisprudence; a learned man
ummah/ummat	worldwide community of Muslims
wadera	big landlord in Sind
waqf	(pl.*awqaf*) property endowed and held in trust for the welfare of the Muslim community in Islamic law
watan	homeland
yavana	derogatory term for foreigners
zaildar	subdivisional officer in the Punjab
zakat	Muslim alms tax
zamindar	loosely used term for landholder, large or small

Select Bibliography

MANUSCRIPT PRIMARY SOURCES

India Office Library, London

Notes on the Native Press in the North Western Provinces for the years 1848, 1850 and 1851 *Selections from the Records of the Government, North Western Provinces*, vol. iii. 1855, V 23/118.

Note on Native Periodicals and Presses for the year, 1858 *Selections from the Records of Government, North Western Provinces*. V 23/120.

Report on Native Presses for the years 1862 and 1863 *Selections from Records of the Government, North Western Provinces*, V 23/121.

Report on the Native Presses for the year 1853 *Selections from the Records of Government, North Western Provinces*, 1868, V 23/126.

The Education of the Muhammadan Community in British India and their Employment in the Public Service Generally—Extract from the Proceedings of GOI, Home Department (Education) , Simla, 13 June 1873, *Selections from the Records of the Government of India, Home Department, no. cvv. Home Department serial no. 2. 1886.*

Selections from the Records of the Government, North Western Provinces, 1870.

Selections from Vernacular Newspapers Published in Punjab, North Western Provinces, Awadh and the Central Provinces, 1868–9,1871–4,1876–83,1885–7.

Selections from Native Newspapers Published in the Punjab, NWFP and Awadh, 1875, 1879, 1886.

Selections from Newspapers Published in the United Provinces, 1919.

Punjab Native Newspaper Reports. 1887, 1897, 1899, 1901, 1907.

Reuters Fortnightly Political Appraisal, L/l/1/665.

National Archives of Pakistan, Islamabad

Quaid-i-Azam Papers QAP/—microfilm and photostat copies of the 'Partition Papers'.
Syed Shamsul Hassan Collection/Press and Publications, vol. 1—part of the *All-India Muslim League Papers AIML/*—microfilm copies.
National Commission on Historical and Cultural Research, Islamabad.
Report by the Criminal Investigation Department on the Native Papers published in the Punjab for the year 1909.
Note on the Punjab Press, 1924.

Report on Newspapers and Periodicals in the Punjab, 1931, 1937

Secret Punjab Police Abstract of Intelligence, 1914, 1919–21, 1923–4, 1928–9, 1940–7.
Secret NWFP Police Abstract of Intelligence, 1940–4.
Secret Sind Police Abstract of Intelligence, 1940–2.

National Documentation Centre, Islamabad

Khilafat Movement in NWFP, Afghanistan and Bombay, Official Records of NWFP Tribal Cell.
'The Khilafat Movement in the North West Frontier Province', Officials Records of NWFP Tribal Cell.
The Ahmadiya Sect: Note on the Origin, Development and History of the Movement up to the Year 1938.

PRINTED PRIMARY SOURCES

Newspapers and Periodicals

Adabi Duniya, vol. vi, no. 19, March–April 1966, special issue on Kashmir,
Omar, Sabahuddin (comp.), *Intikhab Hamdard*. Lucknow, 1988.
Nawa-i-Waqt, Lahore, 1944–7.
Paigham. Calcutta, 1988.
Zamindar, Lahore, 1920s and 1930s.

Urdu

Afzal, Muhammad Rafiq (comp.). *Guftar-i-Iqbal*. Lahore: Research Society of Pakistan, 1969.
Al-Basar. *Ghaur Karne ki Batein*. Lucknow, April 1923, Urdu F. 496, IOL.
Ali, Imtiaz (comp.). *Mir, Ghalib, Dagh, Momin ki Mashoor 100 Ghazlain*. Lahore: Maktaba Imtiaz (no date).
Ali, Mohamed. *Bayan-i-Hurriyat*. Amritsar, 2 February 1922, Urdu D. 1365, IOL.
Allahabadi, Akbar. *Akbar Allahabadi ke Latife* (no date).
_____. *Kulliyat-i-Akbar*, ii. Delhi (no date).
Azad, Abul Kalam. *Masla-e-Khilafat wa Jazirat al-Arab* (1920), republished in *Intikhab-i-Khutbat-i-Khilafat*, compiled by Mahmud Elahi, 1988.

Baksh, Ali. *Hadiyat al-Haramain*, April 1874, published at Munshi Nawal Kishore's press at Lucknow, VT 530, IOL.

Faiz, Faiz Ahmad. *Nuskha Haya-i-Wafa*. Lahore: Muktaba Karavan (no date).

Ghafoor, Mian Mohammad Abdul (comp.). *Marika-i-Siyasat wa Khilafat yani Muqadama-i-Karachi—Mukammal Ruidad*. 2 February 1922, Urdu D.1371, IOL.

Ghalib, Mirza Asadullah Khan. *Nawa-i-Saroosh*. Compiled and annotated by Ghulam Rasul Mehr, Lahore: Sheikh Ghulam Ali and Sons Pvt. Ltd. Publishers (no date).

Hakim, Maulvi Abdul. *Mr Gandhi Musalmanon ke hargiz khairkhwah nahin*. August 1921, Urdu D. 1264, IOL.

Hali, Altaf Hussain. *Jawahar-i-Hali (Kulliyat-e-Hali ka Jama Intikhab)*. Lahore: Karavan Adab, 1989.

————. *Musaddas-i-Hali*, first published in 1879. Reprint, Lahore: Ferozesons (no date).

Hamid, Hafiz Abdul. *Azad Gao*. Jubbulpore, 21 July 1922, Urdu D. 1193, IOL.

Husain, Maulvi Saiyid Sajjad. *Ijaz-i-Daudi*. Delhi, 1912, VT 3788f, IOL.

Iblis ka Khutbah-i-Sadarat, first published in 1925 at the Aligarh Muslim University. This edition published by the Nizami press of Badiyaun in 1927.

Iqbal, Muhammad. *Kulliyat-i-Iqbal*. Karachi: Al Muslim Publishers, 1994.

Ismail, Haji Muhammad. *Pan-Islamism*. July 1907, Urdu D. 3929, IOL.

Lahori, Malik Lal Din Ahmed Qaisar. *Chand ghon se nikal aya*. 27 July 1920, Urdu D. 858, IOL.

Karim, Munshi Abdul. *Hindu Musalmanon ke Mazhabi Khiyalat Ka Numuna* (or unusual answers to conflictual writings). 1896, UT 1221, IOL.

Khan, Munshi Sirajuddin Ahmad (comp.). 'April Fool', articles published in the *Zamindar* on April 1 between 1904 and 1909, Karamabad, 1911, VT 3946a, IOL.

Manto, Saadat Hasan. *Manto Nama*. Lahore: Sang-e-Meel Publications, 1996.

Maudoodi, Abul Ala. *Tehrik-i-Azad-i-Hind aur Musalman*. Two vols. first published in 1945; reprint, Lahore: Islamic Publishers Ltd, 1979.

Mazhar, A.D. (comp.), *Khaksar Tehrik aur Azad-i-Hind: Dastiwazaat*. Islamabad: National Commission on Historical and Cultural Research, 1985.

Mirza, Hasan. *Jazabat-i-Qaumi or Gandhi ki Jai*. Lucknow, 1 May 1921, Urdu B. 648, IOL.

Mohi-ud-Din, Master. *Faryad-i-Muslim*. Amritsar, 16 November 1921, Urdu D. 1212, IOL.

Muhammad, Wali. *Gandhi ka Chark*. 1 July 1922, Urdu B. 649, IOL.

Nadvi, Maulana Abu Hasamat. *Khilafat-i-Islamia and Turks*. Delhi, 22 December 1920, Urdu D. 754, IOL.

Nadwi, Sayyid Sulayman. 'Khilafat aur Hindustan', in *Muqalat-e-Sulayman*. Compiled by Sayyid Sabahuddin Abdur Rahman (no date).

Nadwi, Sayyid Sulayman (comp.). *Kulliyat-i-Shibli*. Karachi, 1985.

Najibabad, Akbar Shah Khan. *Akhbar-i-Qaum*. Lahore, 3 March 1920, Urdu D. 997, IOL.

Nazir Ahmad, Deputy. *Mirat-ul-Arus*. Reprint, Lahore: Ferozesons (no date).

Niazi, Mohammad Abdus Sattar. *Khilafat-i-Pakistan Scheme*. Lahore: Himayat-i-Islam Press (no date).

Nizami, Khwajah Hasan. *Government aur Khilafat*. Delhi, 15 March 1920, Urdu D. 1197, IOL.

Piyam-i-Begum, Madras, 8 February 1922, Urdu D. 1232, IOL.

Qadari, Irtiza Hussain Hasani. *Tehrik-i-Imarat Sharia pai ak Tanqidi Nazar*. Etawah, 1921, Urdu F. 237, IOL.

Rahman, Sardar Abdul. *Sawal-o-Jawab Imamat wa Khilafat*. Amritsar: Wazir-i-Hind Press, 14 June 1922, Urdu B. 255, IOL,

Rahman, Shaikh Abdur. *Risala Safina-i-Najat*. 25 June 1921, Urdu D. 744, IOL.

Ramay, Hanif. *Punjab ka Muqadammah*. Lahore: Jang Publishers, 1988.

Sada-i-Begum, Madras, 8 February 1922, Urdu D. 1233, IOL.

Sada-i-Dukhtar, Madras, 12 March 1922, Urdu D. 1228, IOL.

Sahib (Muhammad), Khwaja Mohiyuddin. *Bahar-i-Charka*. Madras, 25 February 1922, Urdu D. 1227, IOL.

Sayyid, Mumtaz Husain. *Risala-i-Kafn-Posh Lidaran-i-Qaum*. Amroha, 8 July 1915, VT 3858k, IOL.

Shaikh, Ahmad Husain. *Baz Musalmanon ki Afsosnak Ghalat Fahmi*. 2 March 1897, Urdu B. 14a, IOL.

Sharar, Abdul Halim. *Urdu se Hinduon ke Ta'alluq* (the Relationship of Hindus with Urdu), lecture given at the Urdu Conference at Lucknow, 30 September 1916, VT 3890g, IOL.

Shradhanand, Shri Swami. *Hindu Muslim Itihad aur Congress ka aik Tarikhi Warq*. July 1924, Urdu D. 435, IOL.

Zahid, Maulana Abdul Hadi Muhammad. *Adalat Gawshala Parastan*. Jubbulpore, 29 July 1922, Urdu D. 1192, IOL.

Zulfikar, Ghulam Husain (comp.). *Intikhab-i-Kalam-o-Akbar*. Lahore, 1966.

English

Abdullah, Sheikh Mohammad. *Flames of the Chinar: An Autobiography*. New Delhi: Viking, 1993.

Ambedkar, B. R. *Pakistan or Partition of India*. Bombay: Thacker and Co. Ltd, 1946.
_____. *What Congress and Gandhi have done to the Untouchables*. First printed by Bombay: Thacker and Co. Ltd, 1945. Reprint, Lahore: Classic, 1977.

Annual Report on Indian and Anglo-Vernacular Newspapers Published in the Bombay Presidency for 1933. Bombay, 1934.

Aziz, K. K.(ed.). *The Indian Khilafat Movement 1915–1933: A Documentary Record*. Karachi: Pak Publishers, 1972.

Chaudhry, Nazir Ahmad (comp.). *Development of Urdu as Official Language in the Punjab (1849–1974)*. Lahore: Government of the Punjab, 1977.

Hunter, W. W. *The Indian Musalmans*. First published in 1871. Reprint, Delhi: Indological Book House, 1969.

Iftikharuddin, Mian. *Selected Speeches and Statements*. Edited by Abdullah Malik, Lahore: Nigarishat, 1971.

Iqbal, Afzal (ed.). *Select Writings and Speeches of Maulana Mohamed Ali* (first edition 1944). Lahore: Islamic Book Foundation, 1987.

Iqbal, Muhammad. *The Muslim Community—A Sociological Study.* Edited by Muzaffar Abbas. Lahore: Maktab-e-aliye, 1983.

————. *The Reconstruction of Religious Thought in Islam.* Lahore: Institute of Islamic Culture and Iqbal Academy, 1989.

————. *Shikwa and Jawab-i-Shikwa (Complaint and Answer: Iqbal's Dialogue with Allah).* Translated by Khushwant Singh, Delhi: Oxford University Press,1994.

————. *Speeches and Statements of Iqbal,* Latif Ahmed Sherwani (ed.). Lahore: Iqbal Academy, 1977.

Jalal, Hamid. *Black Milk.* Lahore: Alkhatib and Sang-e-Meel Publications, 1956 and 1996.

Kanda, K. C., *Masterpieces of Urdu Ghazal: From 17th to 20th Century.* New Delhi: Sterling Publishers Ltd, 1994.

Khan, Sirdar Shaukat Hayat. *The Nation that Lost its Soul: Memoirs of Sirdar Shaukat Hyat Khan.* Lahore: Jang Publishers, 1995.

Khosla, Gopal Das. *Stern Reckoning: A Survey of the Events Leading up to and Following the Partition of India.* Reprint, Delhi: Oxford University Press, 1989.

Kiernan, Victor G. (trs.). *Poems by Faiz.* Lahore: Vanguard Books, 1971.

————. (trs.), *Poems from Iqbal.* London: John Murray, 1955.

Kumar, Ravindra (ed.). *Selected Documents of Lala Lajpat Rai, 1906–1928.* vol. iii. New Delhi: Anmol Publications, 1992.

Latif, Syed Abdul. *A Federation of Cultural Zones for India.* Secunderabad,1938.

Malik, Hafeez (ed.). *Political Profile of Sir Sayyid Ahmad Khan: A Documentary Record.* Islamabad: Institute of Islamic History, Culture and Civilization, 1982.

Mansergh, N. and Penderel Moon (eds). *Constitutional Relations Between Britain and India: The Transfer of Power 1942–7.* Eleven vols. London: Her Majesty's Stationery Press, 1970–82.

Maudoodi, Abul Ala. *Purdah and the Status of Women in Islam.* Translated and edited by Al-Ashari. Lahore: Islamic Publications Limited, 1972.

Memorandum on the Disturbances in the Punjab, April 1919. First printed in 1920 by the Punjab Government Press, Lahore; reprint, Lahore: Sang-e-Meel Publications, 1997.

Minault, Gail (trs.). *Voices of Silence: English Translation of Hali's Majalis un-Nisa and Chup ki Dad.* Delhi: Chanakya Publications, 1986.

Mohammad, Shan (ed.). *Unpublished Letters of the Ali Brothers.* Delhi: Idarah-i-Adabiyat-i-Delhi, 1979.

————. (ed.) *Writing and Speeches of Sir Sayyid Ahmad Khan, 1817–1898.* Bombay: Nachiketa Publications, 1972.

Muhammad Iqbal, *Letters of Iqbal to Jinnah.* Lahore: Sheikh Muhammad Ashraf, 1943.

Nehru, Jawaharlal. *A Bunch of Old Letters* (Written mostly to Jawaharlal Nehru and some written by him). Oxford and Delhi: Oxford University Press, 1958.

_____. *The Discovery of India*. New York: the John Day Company, 1946.

Nicholson, Reynold A. (trans.). *Asrar-i-Khudi* (The Secrets of the Self). Muhammad Iqbal's Persian poem first published in 1920. Lahore, 1975.

'A Punjabi'. *Confederacy of India*. Lahore, 1939.

Punjab Muslim Students Federation. *Khilafat-i-Pakistan Scheme*, published by Mohammad Abdus Sattar Niazi from the Himayat-i-Islam Press. Lahore (no date).

Punjab Provincial Muslim League. *Manifesto of the Punjab Provincial Muslim League*. Lahore: Daniyal Latifi, 1944.

Pirzada, Syed Sharifuddin (ed.). *Foundations of Pakistan, All-India Muslim League Documents: 1906–1947*. Two vols. Karachi: National Publishing House, 1969–70.

Rahmat Ali, Choudhary. *Pakistan: The Fatherland of the Pak Nation*. Cambridge: Foister and Jagg, 1947.

Ray, Sibnarayan (ed.). *Selected Works of M. N. Roy*. vol. ii, 1923–27. New York and Delhi: Oxford University Press, 1988.

Rafat, Taufiq (trs.). *Bulleh Shah: A Selection*. Lahore: Vanguard Publications, 1982.

Singh, Khushwant. *Train to Pakistan*. New York: Grove Press, 1961.

Temple, Richard C. *The Legends of the Punjab*. First published in 1884. Two vols. Islamabad: Institute of Folk Heritage, 1981.

Thanawi, Ashraf Ali. *Perfecting Women: Maulana Ashraf Ali Thanawi's Bihishti Zevar*. Translated and edited by Barbara Metcalf. Berkeley: University of California Press, 1982.

The Partition of the Punjab: A Compilation of Official Documents. Four vols. Lahore: Sang-e-Meel Publications; 1993.

Zulfiqar, Ghulam Husain (ed.). *Select Documents on National Language*, vol. i, part 1 (Report 1882). Islamabad: National Language Authority, 1985.

Punjabi

Bhatti, Abdul Majid. *Kafian Bulleh Shah*. Islamabad: Lok Virsa, 1975.

SECONDARY SOURCES: BOOKS AND DISSERTATIONS

Urdu

Abbas, Muzaffar. *Urdu Main Qaumi Shairi*. Lahore: Maktabah-yi 'Aliyah, 1978.

Ahmad, Ejaz. *Mazloom Iqbal: Chand Yadeen, Chand Tasarat*. Karachi, 1985.

Ashraf, K. M. 'Ahiya-e-Islam kai Hami aur 1857 ka Inqilab' in Ahmad Salim (ed.). *1857: Adab, Siyasat aur Muashira*. Lahore: Nigarshat, 1991.

Batalvi, Ashiq Hussain. *Hamari Qaumi Jid-o-jehd: January 1939 saay December 1939 tak*. Lahore: Pakistan Times Press (no date).

_____. *Iqbal ke Akhiri Do Saal*. Lahore: Iqbal Academy, 1978.

Choudhury, Zahid. *Pakistan ki Siyasi Tehrik*. Ten vols. *Muslim Punjab ka Siyasi Irtaqa*, vol. v. *Sind: Masla-i-Khud Mukhtari ka Aghaz*, vol. vi. Lahore: Adara Mutalliya-i-Tarikh, 1994.

Fatmi, Ali Ahmad. 'Nazeer Akbarabadi ki Awami Shairi' in Qamar Rais (ed). *Urdu Mein Lok Adab*. New Delhi: Simant Parkashan, 1990.

Gami, Saleem Khan. *Iqbal aur Kashmir*. Lahore: Universal Books, 1985.

Hakim, Khalifa Abdul. *Iqbal aur Mullah*. Lahore: Bazm-i-Iqbal (no date).

————*Fiqr-i-Iqbal*, Lahore: Baym-i-Iqbal, 1988.

Haq, Inam-ul. *Muslim Bengal Adab*. Urdu translation from the Bengali *Muslim Bangla Sahitya*. Karachi: Government of Pakistan Press, 1957.

Iqbal, Javed. *Zinda Rawad*. Three vols. Lahore: Iqbal Academy, 1984.

Kabir, Fahmida. *Urdu Novel mein Aurat ka Tasawar: Nazir Ahmad saay Prem Chand tak*. New Delhi: Maktaba-i-Jamia Ltd., 1992.

Kashmiri, Shorish. *Syed Ataullah Shah Bukhari: Swanah wa Fikar* (third edition). Lahore: Mutbuat-i-Chitan, 1994.

Khurshid, Abdul Salam. *Sahafat: Pakistan wa Hind mein*. Lahore: Shaiq Press, 1963.

Majid, Sheikh Abdul. *Iqbal aur Ahmadiyat* (Critique of Dr Javed Iqbal's *Zinda Rawad*). Lahore: Choudhry Irshad Ahmad Wark, 1991.

Mirza, Janbaz. *Karavan-i-Ahrar*. Eight vols. Lahore: Maktabah-i-Tabsirah, 1975–83.

Quereshi, Badruddin. *Riwaj-i-Punjab* (Urdu translation of his *The Punjab Custom*). Lahore, 1912.

Shahjahanpuri, Payam (ed.). *Taqazah* (Urdu fortnightly). The Revolt of 1857 (annual number), Lahore, 1986.

Zulfiqar, Ghulam Hussain. *Maulana Zafar Ali Khan: Hiyat, Khidmat wa Asar*. Lahore: Sang-e-Meel Publishers, 1994.

Bengali

Sen, Sukumar. *Islami Bangla Sahitya*. Burdwan: Barddhaman Sahityasabha, 1951.

English

Abbasi, M. Yusuf. *Pakistani Culture: A Profile*. Islamabad: National Institute of Historical and Cultural Research, 1992.

Ahmad, Akbar S. *Millennium and Charisma Among Pathans: A Critical Essay in Social Anthropology*. London: Routledge, 1976.

Ahmad, Aziz. *Studies in Islamic Culture in the Indian Environment*. Oxford: Clarendon Press, 1964.

Ahmad, Qeyamuddin. *The Wahabi Movement in India*. Calcutta: Firma K.L. Mukhopadhyay, 1966.

Ahmed, Muhammad Basheer. *The Administration of Justice in Medieval India*. Aligarh: Historical Research Institute, 1941.

Ahmed, Rafiuddin. *The Bengal Muslims, 1871–1906: A Quest for Identity*. Delhi: Oxford University Press, 1981.

Ali, Parveen Shaukat. *The Political Philosophy of Iqbal* (second edition). Lahore: Publishers United, 1978.

Ali, Syed Ameer. *The Spirit of Islam: A History of the Evolution and Ideals of Islam with a Life of the Prophet*. First published in 1891, it has multiple editions. Lahore: Islamic Book Service, 1989.

Anderson, Benedict. *Imagined Communities: Reflections on the Origin and Spread of Nationalism*. London: Verso, 1991.

Anderson, Michael. 'Islamic Law and the Colonial Encounter in British India' in David Arnold and Peter Robb (eds), *Institutions and Ideologies: A SOAS South Asia Reader*. London: Curzon Press, 1993.

Anisuzzaman. *Creativity, Reality and Identity*. Dhaka: International Centre for Bengal Studies, 1993.

Ansari, Sarah. *Sufi Saints and State Power: The Pirs of Sind, 1843–1947*. Cambridge: Cambridge University Press and Lahore: Vanguard Publications, 1992.

Arnold, David and Peter Robb (eds). *Institutions and Ideologies: A SOAS South Asia Reader*. London, 1993.

Arnold, T. W. *The Caliphate*. New York: Barnes and Noble, 1965.

Azad, Abul Kalam. *India Wins Freedom: The Complete Version*. Madras: Orient Longman, 1988.

Barrier, N. Gerald (ed.). *The Census in British India: New Perspectives*. New Delhi: Manohar, 1991.

_____. *Banned: Controversial Literature and Political Control in British India, 1907–1947*. Columbia: University of Missouri Press, 1974.

Bayly, C. A. *Empire and Information: Intelligence Gathering and Social Communication in India 1780–1870*. Cambridge: Cambridge University Press, 1996.

Bhabha, Homi (ed.). *Nation and Narration*. London and New York: Routledge, 1991.

Biddulph, C. E. (ed.). *Afghan Poetry of the Seventeenth Century: Being Selections from the Poems of Khush Hal Khan Khatak*. Peshawar: Saeed Book Bank and Subscription Agency, 1983.

Bose, Sugata. *Agrarian Bengal: Economy, Social Structure and Politics, 1919–1947*. Cambridge: Cambridge University Press, 1986

Brown, Judith M. *Gandhi's Rise to Power: Indian Politics 1915–1922*. Cambridge: Cambridge University Press, 1972.

Bulliet, Richard W. *Islam: The View From the Edge*. New York: Columbia University Press, 1994.

Burckhardt, Titus. *Art of Islam: Language and Meaning*. London: Islamic Festival Trust Ltd, 1976.

Burke, S. M. and Salim al-Din Quraishi. *Bahadur Shah: The Last Mogul Emperor of India*. Lahore: Sang-e-Meel Publications, 1996.

Chatterjee, Partha. *The Nation and Its Fragments: Colonial and Postcolonial Histories*. Princeton/Delhi: Oxford University Press, 1993.

_____. *Nationalist Thought and the Colonial World: A Derivative Discourse?* London: Zed Press, 1986.

Cohn, Bernard. *Colonialism and its Forms of Knowledge: The British in India*. Princeton: Princeton University Press, 1996.

Corbin, Henry (trs). Philip Sherrard. *Temple and Contemplation*. London: KPI and Islamic Publications, 1986.

Das, Veena. *Critical Events: An Anthropological Perspective on Contemporary India*. Delhi: Oxford University Press, 1996.

Dasgupta, Uma. *Rise of an Indian Public: The Impact of Official Policy, 1870–1880.* Calcutta: Rddhi, 1977.

Davis, Emmett. *Press and Politics in British Western Punjab, 1836–1947.* Delhi: Academic Publications, 1983.

Derrett, J.D.M. *Religion, Law and State in India.* New York: Free Press,1968.

Desan, Suzanne. 'Crowds, Community and Ritual' in Lynn Hunt (ed.), *The New Cultural History.* Berkeley: University of California Press, 1989.

Devji, Faisal. 'Muslim Nationalism: Founding Identity in Colonial India', upublished doctoral dissertation, University of Chicago, 1993.

Douglas, Ian Henderson. *Abul Kalam Azad: An Intellectual and Religious Biography.* Edited by Gail Minault and Christian W.Troll. Delhi: Oxford University Press,1988.

Enayat, Hamid. *Modern Islamic Political Thought: The Response of the Shii and Sunni Muslims to the Twentieth Century.* London: Macmillan, 1982.

Fatehpuri Farman , *Pakistan Movement and Hindi–Urdu Conflict.* Lahore: Sang-e-Meel Publications, 1987.

Fisch, Jorg. *Cheap Lives and Dear Limbs: The British Transformation of the Bengal Criminal Law, 1769–1817.* Wiesbaden: Franz Steiner Verlag, 1983.

Fox, Richard G. *Lions of the Punjab: Culture in the Making.* Berkeley: University of California Press, 1985.

Freitag, Sandria B. *Collective Action and Community: Public Arenas and the Emergence of Communalism in North India.* Berkeley: University of California Press, 1989.

Gilmartin, David. 'Customary Law and *Shariat* in British Punjab', in Ewing, Katherine P. (ed.), *Shariat and Ambiguity in South Asian Islam.* Berkeley: University of California Press.

_____. *Empire and Islam: Punjab and the Making of Pakistan.* Berkeley: University of California Press, 1988.

Grewal, J. S. 'The *Qazi* in the *Pargana*' in J. S.Grewal (ed.), *Studies in Local and Regional History.* Amritsar: Guru Nanak University, 1974.

Haq, Mushir U. *Muslim Politics in Modern India, 1857–1947.* Lahore: Book Traders (no date).

Hardy, Peter. *The Muslims of British India.* Cambridge: Cambridge University Press, on p. 1, 1972.

Hasan, Mushirul. *Legacy of a Divided Nation: India's Muslims Since Independence.* Delhi: Oxford University Press, 1997

_____. (ed.). *India Partitioned: The Other Face of Freedom.* Two vols. New Delhi: Roli Books, 1995.

_____. *Islam and Indian Nationalism: Reflections on Abul Kalam Azad.* New Delhi: Manohar, 1992.

_____.(ed.).*Communal and Pan-Islamic Trends in Colonial India.* New Delhi: Manohar, 1985.

_____. *Mohamed Ali: Ideology and Politics.* New Delhi: Manohar, 1981.

_____. *Nationalism and Communal Politics in India, 1916–1928.* Delhi: Manohar, 1979.

Hasan, Zoya (ed.). *Forging Identities: Gender, Communities and the State in India.* Boulder: Westview Press, 1994.

Hassan, Riffat (ed.). *The Sword and the Sceptre: (a collection of writings on Iqbal, dealing mainly with his life and poetical work).* Lahore: Iqbal Academy, 1977.

Husain, Azim. *Fazl-i-Husain: A Political Biography.* Bombay: Longmans, Green & Co. Ltd, 1946.

Hussain, Syed Shabbir. *Al-Mashriqi: The Disowned Genius: The Story of a World Revolutionary Who Was Bogged Down in His Own Country, at Once Inspiring and Painful.* Lahore: Jang Publishers, 1991.

Iqbal, Afzal. *The Life and Times of Mohamed Ali: An Analysis of the Hopes, Fears and Aspirations of Muslim India From 1878 to 1931.* Lahore: Institute of Islamic Culture, 1979.

Islam, Mustafa Nurul. *Bengali Muslim Public Opinion as Reflected in the Bengali Press, 1901–1930.* Dacca: Bangla Academy, 1973.

Jalal, Ayesha. 'Exploding Communalism: the Politics of Muslim Identity in South Asia', in Sugata Bose and Ayesha Jalal (eds), *Nationalism, Democracy and Development: State and Politics in India.* Delhi: Oxford University Press, 1996.

————. *The Sole Spokesman: Jinnah, The Muslim League and the Demand for Pakistan.* Cambridge: Cambridge University Press, 1985.

Jan, Inamullah. 'Pukhtunwali in Historical Perspective', unpublished doctoral dissertation, Quaid-i-Azam University, Islamabad, 1979.

Jansson, Erland. *India, Pakistan or Pakhtunistan: The Nationalist Movements in the North West Frontier Province, 1937–1947.* Uppsala: ACTA Universitatis Upsaliensis 1981.

Javeid, Inamul Haq. *Pakistan in Punjabi Literature.* Islamabad: Maktaba-i-Fanoos, 1993.

Jones, Kenneth W. (ed.). *Religious Controversy in British India: Dialogues in South Asian Languages.* Albany: State University of New York Press, 1992.

Josh, Bhagwan. *Communist Movement in the Punjab, 1926–47,* Delhi: Anupama Publications, 1979.

Keddie, Nikki R. *An Islamic Response to Imperialism: Political and Religious Writings of Sayyid Jamal ad-Din 'al-Afghani'.* Berkeley: University of California Press, 1968 and 1983.

Khan, Nadar Ali. *A History of Urdu Journalism.* Delhi: Idarah-i-Adabiyat-i-Delhi, 1991.

Khurshid, Abd al-Salam. *Newsletters in the Orient, With Special Reference to the Indo-Pakistan subcontinent.* Assen: Van Gorcum, 1956.

King, Christopher R. *One Language Two Scripts: The Hindi Movement in Nineteenth Century North India.* Delhi: Oxford University Press, 1994.

Kozlowski, Gregory. *Muslim Endowments and Society in British India.* Cambridge: Cambridge University Press, 1985.

Krishna, Lajwanti Rama. *Panjabi Sufi Poets: A.D. 1460–1900.* First published by Oxford University Press in 1938. Reprint, Lahore: Panjabi Adabi Laihr, 1992.

Lelyveld, David. *Aligarh's First Generation: Muslim Solidarity in British India*. Princeton: Princeton University Press, 1977. Reprint, Lahore: Book Traders, 1991.

Malik, Fateh Mohammad. *Punjabi Identity*, Lahore: Sang-e-Meel Publications, 1989.

Malik, Hafeez. *Moslem Nationalism in India and Pakistan*. Washington, DC: Public Affairs Press, 1963.

Mani, Lata. 'Contentious Traditions: The Debate on Sati in Colonial India' in Kumkum Sangari and Sudesh Vaid (eds), *Recasting Women: Essays in Colonial History*. New Delhi: Kali for Women, 1989 and New Jersey: Rutgers University Press, 1990.

McClain, Ernest G. *Meditations Through the Quran: Tonal Images in an Oral Culture*. Maine: Nicholas Hays, Inc., 1981.

Metcalf, Barbara Daly. 'Reading and Writing about Muslim Women in British India' in Zoya Hasan (ed.), *Forging Identities: Gender, Communities and the State in India*. Boulder: Westview Press, 1994.

_____. *Islamic Revival in British India: Deoband, 1860–1900*. Princeton: Princeton University Press, 1982.

Minault, Gail. *Secluded Scholars: Women's Education and Muslim Social Reform in Colonial India*. Delhi: Oxford University Press, 1998.

_____. *The Khilafat Movement: Religious Symbolism and Political Mobilization in India*. New York: Columbia University Press, 1982.

Mirza, Shafqat Tanveer. *Resistance Themes in Punjabi Literature*. Lahore: Sang-e-Meel Publications, 1992.

Moon, Penderel. *Divide and Quit*. London: Chatto & Windus, 1961.

Murad, Mehr Afroz. *Intellectual Modernism of Shibli Nu'mani: An Exposition of his Religious and Political Ideas*. Lahore: Institute of Islamic Culture, 1976.

Mumtaz, Kamal Khan. *Architecture in Pakistan* (second edition). London: Butterworth Architecture, 1989.

Mustafa, Syed Ghulam. *Towards Understanding the Muslims of Sind*. Karachi, 1944.

Nanda, B. R. *Gandhi: Pan-Islamism, Imperialism and Nationalism*. Delhi: Oxford University Press, 1989.

Nandy, Ashis. *The Intimate Enemy: The Loss and Recovery of Self Under Colonialism*. Delhi: Oxford University Press, 1983.

Nasr, Seyyed Hossein. *Ideals and Realities of Islam*. Lahore: Suhail Academy, 1994.

_____. *Islamic Art and Spirituality*. Albany: State University of New York, 1987.

Nichols, Robert. 'Settling the Frontier Land, Law and Society in the Peshawar Valley, 1500–1900', unpublished doctoral dissertation, University of Pennsylvania, 1997.

Nicholson, Reynold A. *The Idea of Personality in Sufism*. Lahore: Sheikh Muhammad Ashraf, 1970.

Oberoi, Harjot. *The Construction of Religious Boundaries: Culture, Identity and Diversity in the Sikh Tradition*. Delhi: Oxford University Press, 1994.

Page, David. *The Prelude to Partition: The Indian Muslims and the Imperial System of Control 1920–1932*. Oxford and Delhi: Oxford University Press, 1982.

Pandey, Gyanendra. *The Construction of Communalism in Colonial North India*. Delhi: Oxford University Press, 1990.

_____. 'Prose of Otherness' in David Arnold and David Hardiman (eds), *Subaltern Studies VIII: Essays in Honour of Ranajit Guha*. Delhi: Oxford University Press, 1994.

Paras, Diwan. *Customary Law (of Punjab and Haryana)*. Chandigarh: Publication Bureau, Punjab University, 1978.

Qureshi, M. Naeem. *Mohamed Ali's Khilafat Delegation to Europe (February–October 1920)*. Karachi: Pakistan Historical Society, 1980.

Robinson, Francis. *Separatism Among Indian Muslims: The Politics of the United Provinces, 1860–1923*. Cambridge: Cambridge University Press, 1975.

Rogers, J.M. *Mughal Miniatures*. New York: Thames & Hudson, 1993.

Roseberry, III J. Royal. *Imperial Rule in Punjab: 1818–1881*. Lahore: Vanguard, 1988.

Roy, Asim. *The Islamic Syncretic Tradition in Bengal*. Princeton: Princeton University Press, 1983.

Russell, Ralph. *The Pursuit of Urdu Literature: A Select History*. Delhi: Oxford University Press, 1992.

_____. and Khurshidul Islam (eds). *Ghalib 1797–1869: Life and Letters*. Delhi: Oxford University Press, 1994.

Sadiq, Muhammad. *A History of Urdu Literature*. Delhi: Oxford University Press, 1984.

Schimmel, Annemarie. *Deciphering the Signs of God: A Phenomenological Approach to Islam*. Albany: State University of New York Press, 1994.

_____. *A Two-Colored Brocade: The Imagery of Persian Poetry*. Chapel Hill: The University of North Carolina Press, 1992.

_____. 'Sacred Geography in Islam' in Jamie Scott and Paul Simpson-Housley (eds). *Sacred Places and Profane Spaces: Essays in the Geographics of Judaism, Christianity, and Islam*. New York: Greenwood Press, 1991.

_____. *And Muhammad is His Messanger: The Veneration of the Prophet in Islamic Piety*. Lahore: Vanguard, 1987.

_____. *Calligraphy and Islamic Culture*. New York: New York University Press, 1984.

_____. *Islam in the Indian Subcontinent*. Leiden: E.J.Brill, 1980.

_____. *Gabriel's Wing: A Study Into the Religious Ideas of Sir Muhammad Iqbal*. Leiden: E.J. Brill, 1963.

Serebryakov, I. *Punjabi Literature: A Brief Outline*. Lahore: Progressive Books, 1975.

Shaikh, Farzana. *Community and Consensus in Islam: Muslim Representation in Colonial India, 1860–1947*. Cambridge: Cambridge University Press, 1989.

Shakir, Moin. *Politics of Muslim Minorities: Some Perspectives*. Delhi: Ajanta Publications, 1980.

Singha, Radhika. *A Despotism of the Law: Crime and Justice in Early Colonial India*. Delhi: Oxford University Press, 1998.

Smith, W.C. *The Meaning and End of Religion: A New Approach to the Religious Traditions of Mankind*. New York: Macmillan, 1962.

_____. *Modern Islam in India: A Social Analysis*. London: V. Gollancz Ltd, 1946.

Suleri, Sara. *The Rhetoric of English India*. Chicago: Chicago University Press, 1992.

Syed, Muhammad Aslam. *Muslim Response to the West: Muslim Historiography in India, 1857–1914.* Islamabad: National Institute of Historical and Cultural Research, 1988.

Syed, Najm Hosain. *Recurrent Patterns in Punjabi Poetry.* Lahore: Panjabi Adbi Markaz, 1986.

Talbot, Ian. *Freedom's Cry: The Popular Dimension in the Pakistan Movement and Partition Experience in North-west India.* Karachi: Oxford University Press, 1996.

————. *Provincial Politics and the Pakistan Movement: The Growth of the Muslim League in North-west and North-east India 1937–47.* New York and Karachi: Oxford University Press, 1988.

Tambiah, Stanley R. *Leveling Crowds: Ethnonationalist Conflicts and Collective Violence in South Asia.* Chicago: Chicago University Press, 1996.

Thapar, Romila. 'The Tyranny of Labels', Zakir Husain Memorial Lecture. Delhi: Zakir Husain College, 1996.

Tonyo, Muhammad Bachal. *Legacy of Bhitai Shah Abdul Latif.* Karachi: Muhammad Bachal Tonyo, 1992.

Zaman, Mukhtar. *Student's Role in the Pakistan Movement.* Karachi: Quaid-i-Azam Academy, 1978.

ARTICLES

Bose, Sugata. 'Nation, Reason and Religion: India's Independence in International Perspective'. *EPW,* 1–7, August 1998, 2090–7.

Butalia, Urvashi. 'Community, State and Gender: On Women's Agency during Partition'. *Economic and Political Weekly* (henceforth *EPW*), 24, April 1993, 12–24.

Chatterjee, Partha. 'Secularism and Toleration'. *EPW.* 9, July 1994, 1768–77.

Davis, Natalie Zemon. 'The Rites of Violence: Religious Riots in Sixteenth–Century France'. *Past and Present,* 39, May 1973, 51–91.

Hasan, Mushirul. 'Minority Identity and its Discontents: Response and Representation' *EPW,* 19, February 1994 , 441–51.

Menon, Ritu and Kamla Bhasin. 'Recovery, Rupture and Resistance: Indian State and Abduction of Women During Partition'. *EPW.* 24, April 1993, 2–12.

Qureshi, M. Naeem. 'The "Ulama" of British India and the Hijrat'. *Modern Asian Studies* (henceforth *MAS*). 1979, 13:1, 41–59.

Ray, Rajat K. 'Masses in Politics: the Non-cooperation Movement in Bengal 1920–1922'. *The Indian Economic and Social History Review* (henceforth *IESHR*), December 1974, 11:4, 343–410.

Robinson, Francis. 'Technology and Religious Change: Islam and the Impact of Print'. *MAS,* 1993, 27:1, 229–51.

Singha, Radhika. 'Making the domestic more domestic: Criminal law and the "head of the household", 1772–1843'. *IESHR,* 1996, 33:3, 309–345.

Thompson, E.P. 'The Moral Economy of the English Crowd in the Eighteenth Century'. *Past and Present*, 50, February 1971, 76–126.

Washbrook, David. 'Law, State and Agrarian Society in Colonial India' . *MAS*, 1981, 15:3, 649–721.

_____. 'Progress and Problems: South Asian Economic and Social History, c.1720–1860'. *MAS*, 1988, 22:1, 57–96.

Index

SOAS LIBRARY

पर कोशिश तो करनी होगी.
महज़ान से ही कुछ हेगा बदलेगा
इन अंधेरी गलियों पर बैठकर
बेढंग कविताओं लिखने से क्या कुछ
होगा?

दूसरे आज तक तुम्हें हिम्मत देने थे,
तुम्हारा आत्म विश्वास और उत्साह
बढ़ी तो बढ़ाने रहें हैं
लेकिन आज से तुम्हें ही वह काम करना
होगा
अकेले होकर भी तुम्हीं को अपनी पूरी
दुनिया बनना होगा
जैसे सूरज वहां भी और यहां भी अपना
का काम करता रहता है,
तुम्हें भी वहां का जोश यहां नई उमंग
का से जगाना होगा

वहां-यहां की खोज में अभी के पल
को न भूलना
वल अभी का ही तो पल है,
अगले पल वह भी पुराना हो जाएगा।

एक अलग तरह की शांती
एक अलग तरह का ठहराओ
कुछ देर अकेले बैठकर देखो
यह जिंदगी इतनी भी बुरी नहीं

जीने का कोई मकसद दिखाई नहीं देता
हमें खिलखिलाकर हंसने की कोई वजह
दिखाई नहीं देती
लेकिन भेड़ चाल चलती हो कर पहाड़ करने
से क्या होगा?
मगर कुछ मीनिंगफुल काम करने की हिम्मत
नहीं होती

दूसरों को देखकर डर लगता है
कितनी तेज़ी दौड़ रहे हैं सब के सब
हम कहीं पीछे तो नहीं रह जायेंगे?
यह सोचते सोचते वक्त निकल जाता है
जरूर पीछे दौड़ आयेगा

अंदर को कैसे उठाओं
वह हिम्मत कैसे जगाओं
खुद पर जो इतना विश्वास हुआ करता था
वह अकेली ही कैसे वापस लाओं

Printed in the United Kingdom
by Lightning Source UK Ltd.
103715UKS00001B/7-9